AMERICAN SAGA

"There is a grandeur and majesty in the irresistible onward march of a race created, as I believe, and elected to people and possess a continent. . . . Far from being without poetry, our whole country is one great poem. Sir, it is so, and if there be a man that can think of what is doing in all parts of this most blessed of all lands, to embellish and advance it, who can contemplate that living mass of intelligence, activity, and improvement as it rolls on, in its sure and steady progress to the uttermost extremities of the West . . . if there be a man, I say, that can witness all this passing under his very eyes, without feeling his heart beat high, and his imagination warmed and transported by it, be sure, Sir, that the raptures of song exist not for him!"

Speech of Hugh Swinton Legaré, of South Carolina, before the Civil War

AMERICAN

SAGA

―――――

THE HISTORY AND LITERATURE OF
THE AMERICAN DREAM OF A BETTER LIFE

―――――

MARJORIE BARSTOW

GREENBIE

―――――

GREENWOOD PRESS, PUBLISHERS
WESTPORT, CONNECTICUT

Originally published in 1939
by McGraw-Hill Book Company, Inc., New York

Reprinted from an original copy in the collections
of the Brooklyn Public Library

First Greenwood Reprinting 1970

Library of Congress Catalogue Card Number 70-109738

SBN 8371-4228-8

Printed in the United States of America

This is to acknowledge the kindness of Sydney Greenbie in introducing me to the whole of the romantic fur-trade background of our Far Western states. He generously let me trespass on his valuable preserve of materials for his own book *From Furs to Furrows* (now in press), even to the extent of lifting a fine character like Henry Sibley, the fur-trading father of Minnesota, bodily out of his book and putting him in mine. This, without in any way reproducing what he has used himself, makes him my collaborator in Chapters 14 to 21, if not the "onlie begetter" of the same. So, with many thanks, I herewith dedicate *American Saga*

TO SYDNEY GREENBIE

ACKNOWLEDGMENTS

I wish to acknowledge the kindness of the following publishers in permitting me to quote from material of which they control the copyrights.

D. Appleton-Century Company for quotations from Lyle Saxon, *Father Mississippi*, on pages 217 and 218.

Farrar & Rinehart and Stephen Vincent Benét for quotations from *John Brown's Body*, on pages 496 and 509.

Farrar & Rinehart, for quotations from DuBose Heyward, *Peter Ashley*, on pages 58, 59 and 60.

Alfred A. Knopf and Miss Willa Cather for quotations from Willa Cather, *Death Comes for the Archbishop*, on page 354.

Harper & Brothers for quotations from M. E. Ravage, *An American in the Making*, on pages 623, 624, and 632.

Houghton Mifflin Co. for quotations from Mary Antin, *The Promised Land*, on pages 633, 637, 638, and 640, and from Edward Bellamy, *Looking Backward*, on pages 609, 610, and 611.

The Macmillan Company for quotations from Hamlin Garland, *A Son of the Middle Border*, on page 596; from Vachel Lindsay, *Collected Poems*, pages 197, 199, and 255; and from John G. Neihardt, *The Song of Three Friends*, on pages 296 and 369.

Charles Scribner's Sons for quotations from Michael Pupin, *From Immigrant to Inventor*, page 630.

CONTENTS

AMERICA

Oh that my country were a little land,
    A little land all set about with sea,
Its life conformable to courses planned
    By men who lived long previous to me.
It would be easy then for bards to sing,
    Fitting their verses to the ancient tunes.
The plants we'd set for present blossoming
    Should draw their fragrance from a thousand Junes
That had shed summer on our ancient soil.
    But this our country, its enormous skies,
This great new start for man—these dreams, this toil—
    What poetry has patterns to its size?

All we can do is gather in our day
The stuff to make some future Homer's lay.

INTRODUCTION

 HESE states were settled by people with ideals. From the first gentlemen loafing on the shores of Virginia to the latest immigrant seeing the Goddess of Liberty emerge from the mists, the persons who have come here have been seeking a better life.

But while everyone desires a better life, no one knows exactly how to find it. The patterns of the better life were numerous in the old country. In America they have multiplied with every step westward. They have shone with new colors. They have taken new, sometimes bizarre, sometimes heroic forms. And now, our free land gone, our immigration officials standing guard by the sign "Keep Out!" ourselves somewhat disillusioned and disappointed, the true American still believes as firmly as ever that the better life for everybody is still to be worked out on this continent. If not here, God help the world!

And so it has seemed to me interesting to collect in one volume the records of our long struggle for better living, beginning with the first colonists at all the main centers on the Eastern coast, and continuing across the country to the Pacific, and down the line of history to the present. By better living I mean just what the average person coming to America meant

—better houses, land of his own, money in the bank, a little
fun, some leisure, ladies who were easy to look at, children
who might grow up to some education and a better chance,
safety in his home and possessions, and peace with his neighbor. Looking around among old books in the Library of Congress, among old newspapers, letters, oral traditions, and in the
popular literature that was really read and loved, I have tried
to find the words in which people expressed their notions about
these things, and the means by which they expected to find
them. Mainly I have found what I was looking for in three
places—in personal letters, or in contemporary travelers' reports of what seems particularly admirable or interesting in
someone else's way of life; in the contemporary discussions of
circumstances or dangers which led people either to seek new
homes or stand up where they were and fight for what they
wanted; and in the popular literature, the literature that was
really loved and widely read and remembered.

On the other hand there is a kind of material I have studiously avoided, though it seems to loom large in political and
literary history. In every age there is a large number of people
who talk and write a good deal. They seem to be persons of
importance. What they say gets printed. It is even kept, at
least in official places, like collections in college libraries or the
Congressional Record. But actually no one listens to what they
say. No one remembers it. And no one acts on it. It is what
one might call *official opinion*. It exists to satisfy a convention.

As an example of this sort of expression of ideals of living,
against what I have considered the real expression, I might cite
the Puritan Fathers. They were personages. Their literary
output was enormous. They gave intellectual dignity and a
certain austere beauty to New England life. Usually they get
a good deal of attention from scholars. But I doubt if they actually contributed one real idea to the average New Englander's
very definite conception of a good life. This was determined
by his occupation, which was seafaring. Careless people get
drowned at sea. So he was careful. Untidy people die of dis-

ease at sea. So he learned to be neat and clean. On the other hand, those who learn how to live on the sea have great security. They can go long distances. They can invest their money in profitable ventures. They can bring back all sorts of luxuries and adornments. They feel that they need not bow the head to anybody, nor envy anybody. What they want, they can go and get. By the time the New Englanders had been here for two generations, they were impressing everybody with their neat, secure, comfortable way of life, their keenness, industry, and thrift. These admiring descriptions of what they were doing and why they were doing it seem to me to be worth much more than expressions of theological opinion, even very beautiful ones, like some of Jonathan Edwards'.

So I have tried to strike under the official opinion, however excellent that might be, and try to tell what just ordinary people were trying to get out of life, and all the procedures and ideals they were developing in consequence. Many of the books I quote are now not easily available, but they were almost all of them well known and widely read in their day. But I have also drawn heavily on American literature which we all know, in a way, I hope, to shine up many an old familiar book, and make us want to look at it again.

As I strung these quotations together in a sequence which, because of the nature of our settlement of this country, was geographical and more or less chronological at the same time, I found that a wonderful thing was happening. They were telling our history, telling it in a new way, a way that seemed to me often dramatic and beautiful. This is not my doing. It is just in the record. Anyone can read it for himself. Though I have depended as far as possible on quotations, I had to put these together in a running narrative, with a little cement of fact or an occasional digest of opinion. Many of the phrases in this comment are lifted from contemporary popular records. In doing this I have avoided the formal histories and have depended almost entirely on the material I was using or on oral tradition. The greater part of our history is so recent that we

don't have to go back much beyond our own great-grandfathers to know all about it. For many reasons, some of which
appear in the book and some of which I leave the reader to
surmise through his own knowledge of local history or his own
family tradition, I have been able to draw on an immense
amount of oral tradition dealing with practically every section
of the country.

In choosing these quotations and weaving them together I
have followed two rules. One was that the quotation itself
should be good reading. I don't believe in digging up and reprinting any dull stuff. But this was very easy. The number of
people outside the literary profession in this country who have
written and talked extremely well about their own affairs is
amazing. The other rule I have made is that the quotation must
be so representative that I might have cited several others
which said the same thing.

Now that I have put this record together, I may say, since it
contains so many words that are not my own, that it seems to
me rather wonderful. I myself did not know what an amazing civilization I as an American am privileged to have a part
in, in this year of grace 1938. I hope other readers will feel
this way, too, that to them, as to me, this old patchwork quilt
made out of the words of the fathers will shine more than satin
or silk, and have about it even a new kind of social richness, a
something that seems to mark down the price of ermine on all
the counters of the world.

I

CONCEIVED

IN LIBERTY

1

TIDEWATER BARONIES

THEY must have looked like a second-rate road company all dressed up for minor parts in a play by Shakespeare. But they were the original founding fathers of our great republic, fifty-four "gentlemen," the first apostles of the American gospel of the better life for all, clinging to the marshy edge of the continent at Jamestown, Virginia, in the early fall of 1607. Many ideas of what constitutes the better life for all were to come sailing over the sea that now lay between them and all that they knew as civilization, but theirs was as simple as it was lovely. The better life as they had seen it in Europe was the life of a gentleman. But no one could be a gentleman without land. The seeds of honor, courtesy, and adoration of pure womanhood died when they fell on the rocky ledge of landless insecurity, where there was not even room to turn around in to make a bow or fight a duel. On the other hand, there was many a luckless fellow, goodhearted, with a notion of manners, a little education, swaggering about the inns of old England, sitting in the pit and looking at the plays of Will Shakespeare, who could be as good a gentleman as the next one if only he had a little farm of his own on which to practice these virtues.

So there they were, fifty-four gentlemen, stranded between
the woods and the sea, looking for their farms. Their doublets
and hose were torn to ribbons by the underbrush; their noses
were peeling with sunburn; their hands were blistered with
the first contact with the ax. But they were still gentlemen.
They swore their good round Shakespearean oaths, stood on
their honor, got drunk, so long as the liquor lasted, gambled
with each other for anything among their possessions which
had not yet disintegrated, and, when all else failed, fell to
brawling as handsomely as any company of Montagues and
Capulets, ill met in some alley of a Shakespearean town. And
all the while, as was afterward demonstrated by the social history of the Old Dominion, there must have been, under all
their absurdities, something more gentle and magnanimous
than their first chronicler gives them credit for. Somewhere,
struggling to life amidst their "very loose and profligate morals," was that idea of the gentleman which would take root
in Virginia and grow up like a sweet wild violet in the April
grass, making the first aristocrats of America also its first great
democrats.

2

Among these gentlemen, the fifty-four out of 104 first
would-be colonists of Virginia who were still alive at the end of
the summer, there was a person of different caliber—Captain
John Smith. Captain Smith had what it takes to set up a colony
in America, and springing out upon the shores, with a pen in
one hand and a stout cudgel in the other, he had become the
chronicler and work boss of the "gentlemen." By gentlemen,
he said, they apparently meant persons who did not want to
work for a living and had no training for any useful occupation. William Byrd later, following Smith's opinion, wrote:
"Happy was He and still happier was She who could get themselves transported, fondly expecting that their commonest
utensils, in that happy place, would be of massy silver." Smith,
writing home to the stockholders in England, said that he was

sending back the captain lest the gentleman should cut his throat. "When you send again, I entreat you rather send but thirty carpenters, husbandmen, gardeners, fishermen, blacksmiths, masons, diggers up of tree roots, well provided, than a thousand such as we have; for except we be able to lodge and feed them, the most will consume for want of necessaries before they can be made good for anything." After which, says Byrd coolly, they sent more laborers and fewer gentlemen, "who, however, took care not to kill themselves with work!" Early in the nineteenth century, John Kennedy, that genial novelist who wished to immortalize the whole Virginian tradition of life in literature before it was too late, was advised by a friend to begin with John Smith and his adventures between the Indians and gentlemen. Who but John Smith should be the hero of the American epic? But Kennedy could not see it. "It would not do," he said; "not a person but would pronounce it improbable, even beyond the bounds of the possible!"

One of these improbable circumstances has become the first great American legend, and tested, in its event, that sound heart of goodness and gentleness which seems to have been under the ragged coats of the good-for-nothing gentlemen. Smith at one time was captured by the Indians, and, after due ceremonies, they laid his head on a rock "ready with their clubs to beat out his brains." Whereupon the king's own daughter, "when no intreaty could prevail, got his head in her arms, and laid her own upon it to save him from death; whereat the Emperor was well contented that he should live, to make him hatchets, and her beads, bells, and copper." Perceiving how well the king loved this little daughter, Pocahontas, the Englishmen captured the young lady and held her as ransom, until the king returned seven Englishmen he had captured and with each "an unserviceable musket."

Meanwhile one of the gentlemen fell in love. The French had already set an example of the way in which one may settle such a state of mind in the wilderness. But not so the gentlemen. The adoration for pure womanhood beat sound and true

in their English hearts. A gentleman marries a woman and
makes her truly "his lady." If Pocahontas was not a lady, they
must make her one. So John Rolfe, the girl's lover, "and his
friends," set to work, and "with diligent care, taught her to
speak such English as might well be understood," and saw that
she was "well instructed in Christianity and was become very
formal and civil after our English manner." It cost John Rolfe
many heart burnings and prayers thus to lower his high English blood, and he tells about it all in a long and touching letter
to his friend, Sir Thomas Dale, saying that "my hearty and
best thoughts are and have been a long time so entangled and
enthralled in so intricate a labyrinth, that I am awearied to unwind myself thereout." But he protests that he is still man
enough to "strive with all my power of body and mind, in the
undertaking of so mighty a matter, no way led (so far as man's
weakness may permit) with the unbridled desire of carnal
affection."

It is a pathetic letter, because undoubtedly he might have
had the pretty Indian girl on a more direct and simple and, for
her, even more wholesome basis. But he really loved her, with
that strange, self-restraining, reverential devotion which the
English gentleman called love, and at any cost must lift her up
out of the simplicity of her savage affection to sit aloft on the
pedestal of genuine wifehood. All his friends seem to have been
equally tender and chivalrous, including shrewd John Smith
himself. So they combined forces to declare the Indian girl the
Lady Rebecca, and a true gentleman's real wife, and sent her
home with Rolfe to England to have her received and socially
established for them by the queen herself, John Rolfe still protesting that what he feels for this girl is not "hungry appetite,"
for, "I might satisfy this desire, though not without a seared
conscience, yet with Christians more pleasing to the eye, and
less fearful in the offense unlawfully committed. Nor am I in
so desperate an estate, that I regard not what becometh of me,
nor am I out of hope but one day to see my country nor so
void of friends nor mean in birth but there to obtain a match

to my great content: nor have I ignorantly passed over my hopes there, or regardlessly seek to lose the love of my friends, by taking this course. I know them all and have not rashly over-stepped any." All of this, English society, touched to the heart, chose to believe, for they declared that they had seen "many English ladies worse favored, proportioned, and be-haviored," and it "pleased both the King and Queen's Majesty honorably to esteem her, accompanied with that honorable Lady, the Lady De la Ware, and that honorable Lord, her husband, and divers other persons of good qualities, both pub-licly and at their masks and otherwise." In the midst of which, the young Indian girl soon died and never saw her own forests again.

3

Incompetent and absurd, the few gentlemen who survived, and others who followed, slowly hardened their muscles to the ax, inch by inch dug out fields and gardens from the marshy soil along the James River, and felt that generous heart which they seem to have brought along with their "profligacy" stir with a new idealism. How much better to be a gentleman this way than to do as some of their friends were doing in England, hanging around court circles, waiting for preferment, trying to devise ways and means of living on somebody else! Why, said John Smith, if you are descended so nobly, "pine with the vaunt of great kindred in penury, or to maintain a silly show of bravery toil out thy heart, soul, and time, basely, by shifts, tricks, cards, and dice? Or, by relating news of others' actions, shark here and there for a dinner or supper, deceive thy friends, by fair promises and dissimulations, in borrowing where thou never intendest to pay; offend the laws, surfeit with excess, burden thy Country, abuse thyself, dispair in want, and then couzen thine own brother and wish thy parents' death to have their estates, though thou seest what honors and rewards the world yet hath for them will seek them and worthily deserve them?"

As for us in Virginia, he says, we are going to be real gentlemen. He grants that two conditions are necessary for a gentleman's life—to have leisure and to know where his next meal is coming from. "But nature and liberty afford us that freely, which in England we want or it costeth us dearly. What pleasure can be more than, being tired with any occasion ashore, in planting vines, fruits or herbs, in contriving their own grounds, to the pleasure of their own minds, their fields, gardens, orchards, buildings, ships, and other works, to recreate themselves before their own doors in their own boats upon the sea, where man, woman, and child, with a small hook may take divers sort of excellent fish, at their pleasures. And is it not a pretty sport to pull up two pence, six pence, and twelve pence as fast as you can hale and bear a line? . . . If a man work but three days in seven he can get more than he can spend unless he will be excessive. Now that carpenter, mason, gardener, tailor, smith, sailor, forgers or what other, may they not make this a pretty recreation, though they fish but an hour in a day to take more than they can eat in a week! . . . And what sport doth yield a more pleasing content, and less hurt and charge, than angling with a hook, and crossing from isle to isle, over the silent streams of a calm sea?"

And so, what between wood chopping and fishing, between laying out the house grounds and the meadows, and floating from isle to isle in homemade boats, the early Virginian gentlemen ultimately laid out the land along the James River in big farms which grew tobacco as a cash crop but which supplied most family needs through the combined efforts of the family, dependent relatives, some indentured white servants working out a term in the hope of earning land of their own, and later some black slaves purchased from the West Indies. Their struggling desire that, even in the wilderness, there should be more to life than grubbing, some leisure even if not much wealth, some comeliness in the domestic layout and graciousness in the relation of persons, found its first expression in domestic architecture and in manners.

All during the colonial period the plantation life was tied to the tidal rivers, developing first along the James River and, then, as shoreland there began to give out, along the Rappahannock and the Potomac. Every plantation had its own dock, where the tobacco was loaded on a ship for England, at first on English-owned vessels but, after a generation or two, almost exclusively on Yankee vessels—the New Englanders having absorbed this along with all other carrying trade. With the tobacco went a long shopping list and a list of errands for the family, which the captain was to perform in England, letters for friends, verbal messages, delicate matters to be inquired into. He was everything for the family from purchasing agent to private detective and Cupid's go-between. A few months later the ship came sailing up the river. On the dock it unloaded mahogany furniture, books, draperies for the windows, satin slippers for the young ladies, and swords for the gentlemen. Then the captain came to dinner and further unloaded the personal items of his cargo, news, London gossip, letters, newspapers, everything that he knew about fashions and what was what in the smart world. Occasionally one of the young people of the family went along with the tobacco, to get some education and see the great world. Since the family, providing for most of its grosser needs at home, did not need any large portion of its cash crop for actual subsistence, it was mainly used for the wherewithal to live like ladies and gentlemen. Virginians followed the changing fashions of the smart world at home, but unconsciously idealized them, selecting them in accordance with their own notions of the beautiful and the fit, making them more romantic and chivalrous.

4

There were no cities in tidewater Virginia, and no roads. The nearest thing to a city was the pretty little village of Williamsburg where the House of Burgesses met and where all the higher education there was in tidewater was to be got at the College of William and Mary which was founded in 1693.

But at the falls of the tidal rivers gradually grew up stations from which goods that had come up from the sea by boat were transferred to mules and pack horses and sometimes to wagons to be carried up into the mountains to the few straggling white settlers who had moved on from tidewater or been thrust out as bad characters, and to the Indians who gave furs in exchange for the various white man's goods. Sugar and molasses and rum from the West Indies were principal items in this exchange. The station at the head of the James River became the city of Richmond. That at the head of the Rappahannock, the city of Fredericksburg. At the end of the seventeenth century the Indian trade at the falls of the James was in the hands of a self-made country merchant, William Byrd, who became the father of William Byrd, the Second, whom tradition delights to honor as the first great gentleman of Virginia. Of comparatively humble origin, and engaged in an occupation not included in the narrow circuit of the gentleman's ideal, William Byrd, Senior, had demonstrated that what made a real gentleman even in Virginia was ability, intelligence, and hard work —putting under the fair superstructure of gracious living the foundation of solid cash. He died an honored figure in the affairs of the colony, master of the great mansion of Westover and of spreading plantation acres on the James. When Virginia points with pride to the head and fountain of aristocracy, it quite properly points to Westover.

His son, William Byrd, the Second, has left one of the most charming records of colonial America. Educated for years in England, he undoubtedly became as polished a gentleman as Europe could produce. But his writings show that he had another education, that singular education of the frontier and of the Indian trade, which had a way of giving the educated man who engaged in it a sophistication, a detachment, an imperturbability of observation, beyond the power of the drawing room to emulate. These writings, left in manuscript at Westover, were records of his various trips in connection with frontier activities. Based on notes taken by him while traveling on horseback and camping, they had apparently been polished with an eye to future publication; for William Byrd was a natural-born writer and loved to tone and tune a good sentence. One of these is the *History of the Dividing Line between Virginia and North Carolina.* He rode through the woods and mountains, laying out the boundary line between the two provinces, and recording his experiences as he went. It is a narrative sweet with the breath of the woods, full of clever little pen sketches of the white squatters in the mountains and the ways of the Indians. "It is by no means a loss of reputation among the Indians," he observes, "for damsels who are single to have intrigues with the men. . . . But after these women have once appropriated their charms by marriage, they are thenceforward faithful to their vows, and will hardly ever be tempted by an agreeable gallant, or provoked by a brutal, or even a fumbling, husband to go astray." With what a twinkle he slips in that phrase about fumbling!

His narrative of the *Journey to the Garden of Eden* is also full of the forest, but in his *Journey to the Mines,* he stops at country estates along the way and gives amusing pictures of his various social predicaments. At one time he was kept by rain at an estate where there was only one precious bottle of wine to see them all through bad weather. His hostess was a widow, and he felt that the situation was one which would "try her patience and my good breeding." But he manfully set himself to find a subject of conversation, "which a dull married man could introduce that would bring the widow to the use of her tongue." He finally lighted on the subject of symptoms, ailments, and medicines, which started the lady off in high style but soon bored him. At this juncture he discovered in the house a copy of *The Beggar's Opera.* So he assembled the household after dinner, and with some graceful preliminary remarks about the production of the play in London, he read it aloud to them. This took them through a rainy spell in the country very nicely.

At another time he found a lady pining for her husband

who was away on a short journey and gravely told her that it was good for husbands and wives "to fast from one another" that they might "come together with a better stomach," which, he adds, "was strange doctrine to this fond female, who fancies that people should love with as little reason after marriage as before."

In these writings he does not fail to pay his respects in passing to the besetting sins of Virginia—the objection to honest work, the pretense of birth and breeding, and a too adolescent attitude to sex. Of one woman he remarks that she was "just enough of a fine lady to run into debt and be of no signification in her household." That great pother about Indian intermarriage which had been the occasion of such high and chivalrous drama in the early colony when John Rolfe lifted Lady Rebecca, née Pocahontas, to his side as lady and wife, seems to him a little absurd. He thinks that a lot of trouble would have been saved and the Virginian stock improved if most of the first settlers had married Indian girls, who were, he said, all things considered, no greater heathen than the first white men. As for tinting our fair English complexion, "If a Moor may be washed white in three generations, surely an Indian might have been blanched white in two." When he was considerably past youth, he wrote a letter to a friend in London on the subject of the generally immature attitudes to sex in various romantic persons he saw around him, and congratulated himself on outgrowing this foolish state of mind. But lest his friend should indulge at this point in a "sardinian smile," he added, "I have the pleasure to tell you very feelingly that my fancy was more vigorous formerly, but *not my constitution*."

William Byrd had a daughter who was sent abroad for a season in London, and so impressed the court with her loveliness that King George I congratulated himself on possessing a province which produced such "beautiful birds." But when Charles Mordaunt, Earl of Peterborough, began to pay court to her, her father, doubtless for reasons sufficient for such a wise and worldly gentleman, hastily removed his beautiful bird to the wholesome groves of Virginia. Whereupon, according to tradition, she pined away, faithful to the last to her high-born lover, and died a spinster at the age of twenty-seven. Apparently her father thought that this tale of Evelyn's faithfulness to the lordling across the seas was not romantic, but only silly and undignified. To his friend, the Earl of Orrery, he wrote that the only reasons why Evelyn should remain "an antique virgin" were that either "our young fellows are not smart eno' for her, or she seems too smart for them."

But legend prefers the other story. A hundred and fifty years later, young collegians from William and Mary, staying as guests at Westover, were looking for a glimpse of Evelyn's unhappy ghost and listening at night for her restless step upon the stair.

As for William Byrd himself, he is said to have died as debonairly as he lived. On his deathbed he heard that a friend of his, a rich old Scotchman named Patrick Coutts, was dying. So he dispatched a courier to his friend, saying, "Don't be in a hurry. Wait for me." To which Patrick Coutts sent the reply, "When Patrick Coutts makes up his mind to die, he will wait for no mon."

5

In William Byrd the Virginia ideal of the gentleman came of age. The amiable weaklings of the early picture have disappeared. The hard-drinking, hard-riding, dueling young dare-devil of the later tradition, with his bigoted but courtly old father, the colonel, are yet to come. There were two generations, at least, when the record of Virginia was the record of truly great gentlemen. The soft fiber but generous heart of the first gentlemen had been developed by a century and a half of semifrontier life into such granite character as that of Washington, "clean as a rain-washed rock." The shallow, easygoing radicalism, implicit from the first in the gentlemen's mild revolt against their cavalier kin in England, had widened and deepened into a theory of democracy, substantial and coherent enough to serve as the foundation of a great republic—in the Bill of Rights and the Declaration of Independence.

Yet it is touching to see how important all the Virginia ideals of gentlemanly behavior and use of leisure remained to men of such genuine grandeur of character as Washington or of such mental reach as Jefferson. George Washington had compiled *Rules of Civility and Decent Behavior* among his boyish school exercises, and, amidst the pressure of desperate events, he sometimes applied them with unexpected grace, as when he wrote to Phyllis Wheatley, the young Negro poet in Boston, who sent him her verses: "If you should ever come to Cambridge, Miss Phyllis, or near headquarters, I shall be happy to see a person so favored by the muses, and to whom Nature has been so beneficent in her dispensations. I am with great respect, your humble servant, George Washington," which from a Southern slaveowner to a Negress, and from the middle-aged general of the American armies to a young woman who writes poetry, is very sweet. As for Jefferson, his notion of youthful happiness was "dancing with Belinda at the Raleigh"—the old tavern in Williamsburg, now so handsomely rejuvenated with the money of Mr. Rockefeller. To the end of his life he lived, thought, and wrote amidst a racket of hospitality and social gaiety.

The best feature of all this hospitality, from first to last, was the talk. The favorite hours for it were the long afternoons, after the late noon dinner, when the ladies retired and the men sat around the mahogany table, smoking and drinking, while the sun sank low behind the trees, the ladies napped, and the hum of the plantation activities sank to a drowsy murmur. Washington referred to the mellow interchange of those hours when he wrote to Mr. Fitzhugh of Fredericksburg, "I have put my legs oftener under your mahogany at Chatham than anywhere else in the world, and have enjoyed your good dinners, good wine, and good company more than any other."

Later the British and the French both marveled at the excellent writing of the first American state papers, mainly penned by Virginians, and the high quality of both thought and eloquence, the just political and philosophical insight, of the first group of Virginian statesmen. It was no chance product. They had worked on it for a hundred years or more, hour after hour, with their legs under the mahogany, and wit meeting wit and judgment sharpening itself against judgment, across the polished board.

6

After the death of the great Revolutionary generation of Virginian statesmen, which included three of the four first American presidents, literary and intellectual leadership in the South passed from Virginia to Charleston. This was mainly because the Virginians were too busy moving west. Even at the time of the Revolution, aspiring gentlemen had lifted up their eyes to the blue mountain border of Virginia. Jefferson and Monroe had both developed estates at Charlottesville, and Washington's wealth was in western lands. Already the great American plan of despoiling the land and leaving it was beginning to drain tidewater of its most enterprising people. So when these old plantations reappear in the record, in the early thirties, they seem to literary gentlemen, in hustling centers of western migration at Richmond or Baltimore, to be only "jovial memorials" of an elder day, ruins "of antiquity fast crumbling into oblivion for want of some competent adventurer to throw around these venerable relics the richer and more attractive hues of romance." So a group of jolly writers, with their roots in the old plantation country but residences in Richmond or Baltimore, undertook to contrast with the "elegance of life" in the thirties and its "comfortable insipidity" the ways of old Virginia and the "raciness of her insulated caste of manners." The most interesting of these were John P. Kennedy, William Carruthers, and later John Esten Cooke. They are usually credited with initiating the plantation school of literature, which, taken up by prolific popular writers like

Mrs. Southworth and Laura Jean Libbey and by the theater, has gone on developing ever since, frequently at the hands of people who never saw a plantation and would not know a tobacco leaf from a burdock.

Though in histories of American literature Kennedy's *Swallow Barn* is usually credited as the book which established the literary mold of Virginian character, the nineteenth century version of a gentleman from these parts was already well set in tradition. It was the prototype of a kind of character which was to become the hero of the typical American "western." One good early western, written by Owen Wister, was entitled *The Virginian*. The grandfather of Owen Wister's Virginian, with manners all set for the great open spaces, appears in Cooper's novel, *The Spy*, in the persons of Trooper Lawton and his daredevil riders not used to authority. An English soldier thinks he has killed one of them. "He would not fall if you killed him," muttered another. "I have known these Virginians to sit their horses with two or three balls in them, aye, even after they were dead."

Trooper Lawton encounters a clergyman of the Episcopal Church who is afraid of being scalped by the "natives." "Scalped," echoed Lawton, "if it's to Dunwoodie's squadron of Virginia light dragoons that you allude, it may be well to inform you that they generally take a piece of the skull with the skin."

While the Virginian gentleman as daredevil was riding away into the West, on the old tidewater estates "visiting, junketing, and merrymaking were followed as the chief business of life." This is reported in a novel entitled *The Valley of the Shenandoah* by George Tucker, written in 1824, a fast disintegrating copy of which is to be found in the Rare Book Room of the Library of Congress. It tells the story of a tidewater family which followed the movement west into the valley of the Shenandoah. It begins with a rather charming report of a trip, with stops at the old tidewater estates. Of one family he writes, "It scarcely ever happened in the summer or winter,

that two or three families, commonly their relatives or sometimes others, were not domesticated with them and pursuing
the arts of leisure. . . . A boat equipped with an awning, oars,
and sails was always ready for the accommodation of those who
either wished to cross the river or go on a fishing expedition or
sail or row up and down the river on a party of pleasure. Besides, as further provision against ennui, there were also backgammon, shuttlecock, chess and cards, an old-fashioned harp-
sichord, a flute, a violin, and two or three bookcases of books
which were exclusively those which had been of greatest
celebrity when Colonel Barton was a young man. With all
these means of getting rid of time, it yet seemed to pass on
heavily, in the intervals between breakfast and dinner and
dinner and supper; but at these times, it must be confessed,
there were few sorry hearts or sad faces. Mrs. Barton's loud
and good humored laughs, the Colonel's lively jests and urbane
suavity of manner, and their excellent fare made every one
cheerful and happy."

But in Tucker's story, the tidewater estate is only the
backdrop of Virginia facing west. It remained for Kennedy to
make a whole book about the old plantation and embalm it
permanently in American literature, in *Swallow Barn*. He
wished, he said, to write of old Virginia before it was too late,
to record "the mellow, bland, and sunny luxuriance of her old
time society—its good fellowship, its hearty and constitutional
companionableness, the thriftless gaiety of its people, their
dogged but amiable invincibility of opinion, and that overflowing hospitality which knows no ebb."

Swallow Barn, as described by Kennedy, "is an aristocratical old edifice which sits like a brooding hen on the southern
bank of the James River." It is a one-story building with a
hipped roof that resembles a boat turned upside down, pierced
with very small bedroom windows which look in on beds
"large enough to hold a platoon." This roof is inhabited "by
some pragmatical pigeons strutting and bragging at each other
from morn till night." The farm is full of sleepy brooks,

crossed by bridges of rough logs, and running into swamps and little lakes where squadrons of ducks, "against all nautical propriety, turn up their sterns to the skies." There is also a woodland spring, where four or five Negro women spread out the family linen, and keep up a war with an army of bow-legged black urchins who insist on jumping on the clothes. From cabins in the bushes here and there, one hears the "plaintive moan" of the spinning wheels.

The master of this plantation is one, says Kennedy, "in whom the solitary elevation of a country gentleman begets some magnificent notions." "He thinks lightly of the mercantile interest and undervalues the large cities generally." The mistress is a "fruitful vessel who makes her annual contribution" to the family. The father is "somewhat restive under these multiplying blessings." The book goes on to describe the doings of these blessings of all ages, each one attended by an appropriate horde of small black images of Adam, with chickens and ducks flying squawking before them, dogs, colts, and mules bringing up the rear, and mammy with a stick and mother with a medicine bottle after them all.

This was in the thirties. Already literary tradition was ready to write finis to the drama of the Virginian gentleman. Tidewater Virginia, said Carruthers, has "lived a generous life, but spendthrift and wasteful, and has come to evil days." He saw but one hope. In the west, beyond the mountains, a newer and more vigorous life was rising that would "sweep away the melancholy vestiges of a former and more chivalrous and generous age."

But the finis was never really written. A quarter of a century later the last great Virginian gentleman walked out of his beautiful home overlooking the Potomac and the capital city of Washington, and, knowing sadly what he was doing, led the great cavalier tradition of the South to heroic suicide, in a war whose ghastly folly will always be lost, in legend and in story, in the glamour of its utter gallantry. But standing on the heights overlooking Arlington Cemetery the memory of

Robert E. Lee now plays host to all the dead whom the nation delights to honor, to everything that is heroic and great and has perished nobly in the service of the American faith. They lie all around the portals of his home, still and peaceful under the trees of his own estate, and, to all the great dead of the American nation who come home here to rest, the hospitality of a Virginian home is still boundless.

But the Virginian gentleman is no less our elected host to the living. The capital city of Washington though made out of a piece of Maryland, stands on the edge of the tidewater country, and has incorporated into its life the colonial settlements of Alexandria and Georgetown. It was a sure instinct which elected just this spot as the social center of the national life, dispensing from the white portals of the President's house, which is just a larger and more elaborate Southern home, the hospitality of the nation to the world. More and more it seems that the end of our great rush and hurry of national life, of the drawn battles between capital and labor, the piling up of fortunes, the organization of the machinery and materials of existence will be to give back into the hands of every citizen just what the first gentlemen of Virginia were looking for as the basis of the better life for all—leisure, with a sure knowledge of where the next meal is coming from. They found it for a while. Perhaps we shall all find it, and in the golden grace of some far future day, when we all have time to be gracious, we may think we did well to set the capital city in the tidewater country; and to let Thomas Jefferson make to the first great declaration of our inalienable right to life and liberty, the truly Virginian addition, "and *the pursuit of happiness.*"

2

ALL BEACH WITHOUT A BACKGROUND

WHEN the little band of English exiles in Holland, who were to become our Pilgrim Fathers, petitioned King James to allow them to move to northern Virginia, meaning apparently the coast of Maine, "to enjoy liberty of conscience and to endeavor the advancement of His Majesty's dominions and the enlargement of the gospel by all due means," His Majesty said that it was "a good and honest notion." But, he asked, "What profits might arise in the parts intended?"

"Fishing," said the Pilgrim Fathers.

To which he replied, "So God have my soul, 'tis an honest trade. 'Twas the Apostles' own calling."

And so it happens that to this day a golden codfish adorns the State House of the great commonwealth of Massachusetts, as a symbol of Christian humility and the accumulation of capital through reverent use of the bounty of the Lord. Long ago the first Christians had graved the fish on the walls of their catacombs, as a kind of hieroglyphic for the name of their Lord, partly because he was a fisherman, but chiefly because the first letters of the words Jesus Christ, the Son of God, Our Saviour, when written in Greek spelled the Greek word for fish, *ichthus*. The transplanted Christians, who in-

tended to set up a new city of God in the wilderness, made the
fish the emblem of their commonwealth with even better reason, for this humble vertebrate had become, in a thousand
ways, not only the symbol of their security, but the nurse and
mother of their virtues and reminder of their most heroic
living.

When the Pilgrims turned westward to America, necessity
and conscience were only making them first in a business venture that a lot of people were thinking of. For the Christian
significance of the fish had put a great strain on European
waters. Christians had at first eaten fish on Fridays and other
fast days. But with the development of religion, and the increasing number of saints to be honored, and of sins to do
penance for, it began to seem to good beefeaters in Europe
that every other day was a fish day. This pious attack on the
fish had largely driven them from European waters, and put a
premium on the enterprise of those who would follow them
in their flight. The common opinion was that the fish had all
gone to America.

Ever since Columbus discovered America, and—according
to at least one piece of apparently authentic written evidence
—for two centuries before his discovery, Basque fishermen had been quietly slipping over to the banks of Newfoundland and bringing back fish, keeping the source of their
marine wealth a trade secret. At the time when the Pilgrims
began to look westward the Newfoundland fisheries were the
best paying adventure in the New World, and already it was
whispered along European water fronts that the long, rocky,
and broken coast stretching away southward might prove a
new El Dorado. One of the earliest pieces of verse inspired
by the American scene in 1625 tells how

> The costly cod doth march with his rich train
> With which the seaman fraught his merry ship;
> With which the merchant doth much riches get:
> With which plantations richly may subsist,
> And pay their merchants debt and interest.

In the marketplace in Leyden the Pilgrims may have heard that the French, whose fishermen from Saint-Malo had already preempted the Grand Banks, were taking to the southward stretching shore, for apparently when they turned to the New World, they were aiming for the mouth of the Penobscot, where the French had made the first actual settlement of white men in New England, at Castine, in 1613. As soon as they could, after settling at Plymouth, they sent some of their scanty number up the long wild coast to take Castine. When the French objected and said that they were there first, the Pilgrims sent up Miles Standish, no less, to drive off the French and reinstate the Pilgrims. They could not spare enough men to make good their claim over such an immense stretch of wood and water, but they hung on to it, and Maine was a part of Massachusetts till after the Revolution, on the strength of the old grant to the Plymouth Company.

Following the Pilgrims there was an extraordinary mobilization of men and money for the fishing grounds of the New World. The great and godly group that came to Massachusetts Bay in 1628, to set up a theocracy presided over by a learned ministry, had a number of aristocrats among them and apparently intended at first that the foundation of the new Puritan commonwealth should be landed estates, worked by tenants or hired labor, as in Virginia. But they were accompanied by flying squadrons that had no intention of letting the "righteous and godly ministers" grab all the fish. A group of Dorset fishing interests transferred themselves across the ocean *in toto*, and became Dorchester. Another company settled fishermen at what is now Scituate. Fishermen from Cornwall and the Channel Islands moved over and took the pile of sea-washed rocks that became Marblehead. And one enterprising company with a vision that saw even further settled Salem with the purpose of establishing trade with the West Indies. It is amazing how many people crossed in those little boats in one generation. In 1628 when the Massachusetts Bay Colony was founded, there were 2,000 people in New England. Thirteen years later there were 16,000, more than all other English settlers in America combined.

From the first, the shores buzzed with maritime activity. The little bands that perched here and there on these sandy spits and tumbled rocks usually lived on fish and clams and lobsters for nearly a year till they could raise crops. They fertilized their fields with fish, the fragrance whereof rose rank to heaven, a little too much flavoring the sweet air. They used fish oil for lamps, congratulating themselves that here everyone could have oil for lamps, which were in the Old World a luxury of the rich. "Their boats ordinarily take more than they are able to haul to land, and for want of boats and men they are constrained to let many go after they have taken them; and yet sometimes they fill two boats at a time with them." The lack of boats they promptly undertook to remedy. The first boat built in America, "The Blessing of the Bay," was launched in 1631. Thereafter shipbuilding went on rapidly, the New Englanders developing a small stout fishing boat that became an article of commerce in London and was built for European fishing interests. Finally so many shipwrights and men skilled in maritime trades moved over that the English master shipbuilders petitioned the Lords of Trade to forbid shipbuilding in New England, because all the good workmen were going thither.

These maritime folk were often thorns in the flesh of the Puritan theocracy. "Our ancestors came not for religion," said an old Marblehead fisherman. "Their main end was to catch fish." "It is a matter of saddest complaint that there should be no more serious piety in the sea-faring tribe," said Cotton Mather. Yet there is a report of a "pious and Christianlike passage," from which "all that love and use fasting and prayer" may "take notice that it is prevailable by sea as by land." This ship was manned by a company of "religious, honest, and kind seamen." "We constantly served God morning and evening by reading and expounding a chapter, singing, and prayer. . . . Besides the shipmaster and his company

used every night to set their eight and twelve o'clock watches
with singing a psalm, and prayer that was not read out of a
book." There is no record that this pious example was followed
by any other ship.

Many of the fishing folk that alighted like gulls on the
outlying sand piles and heaps of rocks were Quakers. They
would not support the Puritan ministry, nor obey laws they
did not approve of. The Massachusetts Bay Colony whipped
them and cut their ears and finally banished them on pain of
death. But it did no good. They retired to the outer rim of
New England and fished for whales. They took Nantucket
and Martha's Vineyard and kept them, and their pestilent doctrines spread up Cape Cod.

So while the Puritan commonwealth was trying to form
itself into neat little villages around a white-spired church,
with a council of godly elders overseeing and ruling all, with
farm lands reaching cozily into woodlots and creeping up the
river valleys, there was always this wild belt of people—people
with a strange independence and security, able to live like sea
birds where nobody else could live, safe in the craft of their
hands, ready at any moment to spread their wings and fly
away from neighbors and church courts and the interference
of magistrates, and, as the years went on, going farther and
farther afield and coming back to feed a steady stream of gold
into those Puritan villages, to set mills working by the streams,
to buy the product of farm and forge. The godly minister
might rule the conscience, but that wild devil of a captain
riding the gale like a witch held the purse. The sea and the
activities of the sea were the source of that ferment in New
England which made the colonial period one long series of
fights and persecutions and migrations of people out of settled
towns to wilder places. There was, as Emerson said of later
New England, always a "living mind agitating the mass and
afflicting the conservative class with some odious novelty or
other."

2

These early followers of the apostles' calling brought with them some new and odd notions about the better life for all. In practically all societies everywhere, and certainly in every society they could have known in Europe, it was generally accepted that the good life was impossible for two kinds of people—those who engaged in manual labor and those who engaged in trade.

A few religious sects, like the Catholic brotherhoods, had tried to transcend this objection by making manual labor a religious discipline. But so far as I have been able to discover, no one had ever had the temerity to suggest that shopkeeping, selling things right over the counter, might be similarly sanctified. But the New Englanders from the first not only flew straight in the face of this prejudice, all sails set and a spanking wind behind them, they drove over it with a fervency, a kind of transcendental perception of new values, that made shipwreck of every snobbery. The two foundations of a good life, they said, were manual labor and trade. They said it with poetry and religion. They lived it henceforth with imagination.

The almost mystical faith in and enjoyment of manual labor, and of all the contrivances which the hand may shape out of matter, has survived through all the changes of New England life. The Pilgrim governor Winslow announced a new dispensation with regard to honest work in a broadside against the kind of persons that had settled in Virginia and their gentlemanly illusions. He warned newcomers that the fountains of Plymouth did not "stream forth wine or beer," and that the woods and rivers were not "like butcher's shops or fishmonger's stalls." There were some things they didn't want in New England, and among them were "a proud heart, a dainty poise, a beggar's purse, and an idle hand." To use the hands, to use them cleverly, with originality, was a universal panacea—a protection against Satan, a relief from boredom, a remedy for pain, a partner of quiet meditation.

"Idleness is the most heinous sin that can be committed in Nantucket," writes Crèvecoeur in 1782, and what he says was remarked of most of these seafaring towns. "Either to transact business or to converse with their friends, they always have a piece of cedar in their hands, and while they are talking will, as it were instinctively, employ themselves in converting it into something useful, either in making bungs or spoyls for their oil casks or other useful articles."

When Edward Bok met that old Brahmin of the Boston Brahmins, Oliver Wendell Holmes, and asked him to tell him the secret of a happy life, Holmes took him into his carpenter's shop. The best secret, he said, was always to have an avocation which you could pursue with your hands. "We must," said Emerson, "have a basis for our higher accomplishments, our delicate entertainments of poetry and philosophy, in the work of our hands. We must have an antagonism in the tough world for all our spiritual faculties, or they will not be born. Manual labor is the study of the external world. The advantages of riches remain with him who produces them, not with the heir."

This religious respect for manual labor has left its mark on our American speech. It was the New Englanders who made the word "handy" an epithet of honor; rescued a word fast falling into low company in the old country and set it circulating warm with pleasure in the home and its needs—the word "chores." What chores meant to the New Englander is told by one of the last voices of the New England seafaring race, in the chapter entitled "Chores and Their By-products" in *The Goodly Heritage*, by Mary Ellen Chase. It is the story of her upbringing in the Maine seacoast village of Blue Hill where the old seafaring life has lingered longest and is still remembered by middle-aged people today. "Chores," she says, are "little odd miscellaneous pieces of business which must be performed if the wheels of family life were to turn freely. . . . They were sharply distinguished from jobs of all kinds. One was paid for a job, but never for a chore." The New Englander settled many an emotional conflict, decided many a knotty problem of just or prudent behavior, while going about his chores. Emerson even suggested the doing of chores as an assistance to seclusion and reflection for the would-be scholar.

Along with this respect for manual labor went a great pride in seeming to do things with as little drudgery as possible, and this brings us to another New England word of early origin and wide and worthy use—the word "faculty." "Faculty," said Harriet Beecher Stowe, "was the Yankee equivalent of *savoir faire* and the opposite of shiftlessness." "To her who has faculty nothing shall be impossible. She shall scrub floors, wash, wring, bake, brew, yet her hands shall be small and white. She shall have no perceptible income, yet always be handsomely dressed; she shall not have a servant in her house and with a dairy to manage, hired man to feed, a boarder or two to care for, unheard of pickling and preserving to do—and yet commonly you see her every afternoon, sitting in the shady parlor, behind the lilacs, cool and easy, hemming muslin cap-strings or reading the last new books." In *The Minister's Wooing*, Katy, as a young lady of faculty, is described as one who could harness "a chaise or row a boat, saddle or ride any horse, cut out any garment, make any cake, wine, or jelly, and never derange that trim, well-kept air of ladyhood that set jauntily upon her." One of the traditions of frontier literature, later, was the Yankee girl in the West who set the German and Scandinavian girls to dreaming restlessly of a new dispensation for young womanhood. Hamlin Garland tells the story of the *Creamery Man*, the young fellow driving a milk wagon who undertakes to educate a German girl up to the standard of his other sweetheart, the Yankee damsel. "The Dutchmen had big fine brick houses, but their women were mostly homely and went around bare-footed and bare-legged, with ugly blue dresses hanging frayed and greasy round their lank ribs and big joints." He teaches his sweetheart, the German Nina, to go about her business like the Yankee girl. "She was kneading cake dough, and she looked the loveliest thing he had ever seen. Her sleeves were rolled up. Her neat brown dress was covered with a big apron, and her collar was open a little at the throat, for it was warm in the kitchen."

This neat, trim, and shipshape way of getting through anything reached its fullest development in all kinds of mental and social "handiness." Mrs. Stowe tells about a young man who was the hero of his neighborhood because he had the kind of ability which the New Englander holds the highest—"the ability to do everything without trying, to know everything without learning, and to make more use of one's ignorance than other people do of their knowledge."

This paragon knew "the geography of everybody's cider barrel and apple bin." He knew all about "arithmetic and history and catching squirrels and planting corn." He made "poetry and hoe-handles with equal celerity. . . . He wound yarn and took out grease spots for the old ladies and made knick-knacks and nosegays for the young ones. He caught trout on Saturday and discussed doctrines on Sunday with equal adroitness and effect." This last was undoubtedly the result of being brought up with a sea captain at one elbow and a godly and righteous minister at the other!

3

But it was in their glorification of shopkeeping that the New England capacity for transcending the aristocratical landowning snobbery enjoyed its most gaudy triumphs and anticipated the whole social and industrial development of later times. The first settlers had come to fish, and at the same time to glorify God and enjoy Him forever, but within two generations they had combined their metaphysical interest in the intentions of the Lord and their handiness in using boats in the most remarkable passion for retail selling ever known among any people.

Something in the New Englander's attitude to the distribution of goods makes all other commercial people look woodenheaded. It was founded in a kind of observation which fills the pages of Thoreau and Emerson, but, at least in that particular homely, yet poetic, form, is rare in other literature. Moving about, setting things to rights, actively using his hands, the New Englander constantly observed that the great trouble with the world is that things are not in the right place. By simple locomotion you can turn a deficit into an asset, and turn misfortune into a gift from the gods. Take ice, for example. There is altogether too much of it in winter. It destroys vegetation, keeps you busy hurling cordwood into fireplaces, and if you are not careful will altogether freeze you out of the joy of the living. But move the ice to the tropics. Carry it over into summer, and just one little piece of your winter misfortunes becomes a heavenly balm, preserving food, soothing the brow of fever, and clinking sweet music within the Calcutta Englishman's whisky peg. One of the great Yankee culture heroes, Frederick Tudor of Boston, reasoned in just this style. Moving ice out of winter into summer became a religion with him. He wasted hundreds of thousands of dollars—his own money and his friends'—before he found how to do it; but he set an ice wagon on the August streets of every sweltering American town and made "blocks of Yankee coldness" the blessing of the tropics. Thoreau delighted to see the Irishmen cut ice for Tudor in Walden Pond. "Thus it appears," he says, "that the sweltering inhabitants of Charleston and New Orleans, of Madras and Bombay and Calcutta, drink at my well." He has been reading the philosophy of India. "I lay down the book and go to my well for water, and lo! there I meet the servant of the Brahmin . . . and our buckets grate together in the same well. The pure Walden water is mingled with the sacred water of the Ganges. With favoring winds it is wafted past the site of the fabulous islands of the Atlantis and the Hesperides, makes the periplus of Hanno, and floating by Ternate and Tidore and the mouth of the Persian gulf, melts in the tropic gales of the Indian seas, and is landed in ports of which Alexander only heard the name."

Within two generations after they had started fishing off the rocky outposts of New England, the Yankee art of ped-

dling was well under way. In another two generations it began
to be the astonishment of the world. It did not reach its height
till the nineteenth century when, in the most beautiful ships
that ever skipped the waves, ships so lovely that poets and artists
have exhausted themselves trying to find words and pigments
for them, the New Englanders were swinging around the
world—carrying their department stores on wings into every
harbor that had a dock, and when there was no dock, anchor-
ing out in the sea, and happily chinking coins and wrapping
up parcels on their own decks. They began with the West Indies, and were soon usefully moving rum and molasses and
dried fish back and forth between them and Boston, feeding
the black slaves with Boston fish, and sweetening Boston pancakes with West Indian molasses. They stopped en route and
annexed all the plantations along the Southern tidal rivers,
taking the young ladies' shopping lists and only too ready to
find them slippers for their pretty feet and just the combs they
would want for their hair the next time they passed along by
London. To be sure all captains were not paragons as shoppers.
William Byrd, doubtless exasperated by the flurry of shopping
among his young ladies, said that they were "most of them
arrant sea-calves, and the tritons that swim under are just as
wise as these that sail upon it. The most they can be taught to
do is, sometimes, to deliver a letter, and, if they have superior
parts, they may be instructed perhaps to call for an answer.
One may as well tutor a monkey to speak or a Frenchwoman
to hold her tongue as to bring a skipper to higher flights of
reason." All of which merely shows that William Byrd, clever
as he was, did not understand them. Delivering a letter was
just something you asked the darky boy to do. It was not part
of that shining fabric of new values New England was weaving round the seas.

When the skipper arrived home again, it was with a number of bright ideas about those things that people made for
themselves on farms. Barrel staves now, and ax handles—he
could think of lots of people who needed them. And butter—

foolishly lavishes in a few days of intoxication the fruits of half a year's labor. On the contrary all was peace here, and a general decency prevailed throughout. The reason I believe is that almost everybody here is married, for they get wives very young, and the pleasure of returning to their families absorbs every desire. The motives that lead them to sea are very different from those of most other seafaring men; it is neither idleness nor profligacy that sends them to that element, it is a settled plan of life, a well-founded hope of earning a livelihood; it is because their soil is bad that they are early initiated into this profession, and were they to stay at home, what could they do?"

Crèvecoeur reports something else which, with the movement of the American westward, began to be widely noted early in the nineteenth century. This was the generally superior development of the Yankee women, as a result of being left in sole charge of affairs for two-thirds of the time—their spirit, affability, cooperation among themselves, self-assurance, and wide reading. This feminine life, free for long periods from the shackles of masculine supervision, and perhaps the greater shackles of living up to masculine ideals and being pure womanhood on a pedestal, as in the South, was to blossom in a whole series of American institutions—foreign missionary societies, temperance societies, abolition societies, societies for the rights of women, societies for the improvement of the poor, societies for the amelioration of prisons. It was to create college education for women, to open wage-earning careers to women, to lead to votes for women. Its greatest value was felt later in the West. Despite the tenderness for women and children which frontier life engendered, the tragedy of settlement was that forlorn generation of prairie wives, bedraggled, unwell, lonely, submerged in unwashed dishes and crying children, never able to get far enough ahead to put up clean curtains at the windows, even if they had saved butter-and-egg money enough to buy them. Among these poor souls the Yankee woman, young wife or school-

teacher, mother, or even grandmother, appeared again and
again like an angel of deliverance. She was so competent in
turning off work and "managing," so authoritative in asking
her men for what she wanted and expecting to get it, and
above all—and here the testimony of the grateful male, glad-
dened at last by something easy on the eye, is practically
universal—she always looked so nice. She not only rallied the
women. She rallied the men, too; and many a goodhearted but
ignorant man from other sections of the country gave his wife
little lectures on how to manage like the Yankee woman and
took lessons from her on the way to treat a wife.

For despite a certain shrillness of sex antagonism that later
crept into women's movements, the general self-assertiveness
of the Yankee girl and woman was by no means antagonistic to
her menfolk or obnoxious to them. Husbands who come home
only now and then to wives they are reasonably fond of are
pretty indulgent creatures. On the whole, these wives, in their
spick-and-span houses, turning out apple pies and baked beans
and fish chowder for a man who had lived on hardtack and
salt beef, warming the bed so cozily with a warming pan and
turning back the patchwork quilts and hand-woven snowy
linen—these trim, sharp-tongued, stirring women were pretty
wonderful institutions in the eyes of returned husbands and
lovers, and they knew it. Husbands who were so much away
and had so many other things on their minds had comparatively few of those notions about what was or was not a
woman's province which the homekeeping Southerner, always
about the place, had to develop in self-defense. When told of
some unseemly and unwomanly thing his smart wife had been
doing, his normal tendency was to listen somewhat inatten-
tively and say, "Sure, let her do it. Whatever she says goes."
Crèvecoeur says that their employments while their husbands
are away ripen their judgments "and justly entitle them to
rank superior to that of other wives." "The men at their return,
weary with the fatigues at sea, full of confidence and love,
cheerfully give their consent to every transaction that has hap-

pened during their absence, and all is joy and peace. 'Wife, thou hast done well,' is the general approbation they receive, for their application and industry." He adds, being himself a Frenchman, that the only wives that can equal them, in competence and honor with their husbands, are wives of fur traders in Montreal, who also are away from home for long periods.

Later, it was the custom, in Maine seafaring towns, for the wives and children to go along with the husband on his trading voyages; and this opened a whole field of feminine and family adventure which is only now getting into literature in the reports of the daughters and granddaughters. *Mary Peters*, by Mary Ellen Chase, tells the tale of one such woman, following closely the experiences of her own grandmother; but one may hear the same story from the lips of other women on the Maine coast, among them Joanna Colcord, who in the summer of 1936 very charmingly told, in the Portland *Press-Herald*, the story of her childhood swinging round the world on a trading vessel. The Searsport high school and other seacoast schools were quite used to mapping out lessons for sea captains' children, to be done while the boat bobbed around in the harbor at Hong Kong, and sending their examinations after them to all the ports of the world, to be administered under the watchful eye of mother.

4

The last of the great trading ventures of the New England coast was the China and India trade. Cut off by the British, after the Revolution, from their old ports in the West Indies and Europe, the New Englanders, after a discouraged pause, suddenly reached out and took the Orient as their portion. Ships from Salem developed the route around the Cape of Good Hope to India and China. Ships from Boston struck out a path of their own, around the stormy Cape Horn, up to the Northwest coast and across to China. A great generation of shipbuilders developed the old tubby boat into a new

thing altogether, with clean rakish lines and enormous clouds
of canvas—those clipper ships of the early nineteenth century, with names as lovely as their lines—"The Flying
Cloud," "The Star of the Waves," "The Sea-Witch." It is
the most beautiful, the most spectacular story in the annals of
the sea, and it is still outside the record of literature. Hawthorne, descendant of East India captains, dallied with it but
never felt equal to writing it, beyond a few charming references in the preface to *The Scarlet Letter*, describing the
Salem Customs House in the last stages of its decay. The only
man who might have done it was his friend and neighbor, Herman Melville, but he exhausted himself on the other great
epic of New England seamanship, the whaling industry, in
Moby Dick. It lives on only in family tradition, in the unpublished letters of the firm of Sturgis, genial communications from Canton and the Sandwich Islands, in the Harvard Library, from which we drew freely in the first real
attempt to get any part of this tale on paper in *Gold of Ophir*.
It is written large in the family memorials of the old East India families in the Essex Museum at Salem, and in the furnishings and private papers of mansion after mansion on the Atlantic coast. One family document recently published, originating
in Philadelphia, Nora Waln's *The House of Exile*, aroused
great interest. Louisa Alcott referred to the Oriental trade in
passing, gilding most of her aristocrats with the gold of the Far
East, including the grandfather of the inimitable Laurie and
the family of the Eight Cousins. But mainly it is there, still unwritten, in a thousand homes and a thousand aging memories,
and in junk shops and historical societies all up and down the
Atlantic coast.

Only two really memorable records remain of that great
period—*Moby Dick* and Dana's *Two Years Before the
Mast*. Richard Henry Dana was a Harvard student who in
1834, being in poor health, shipped as a common seaman on
one of the more humble vessels which made the trip around
Cape Horn to California for hides. A notable piece of honest

reporting, it gives the complete, day-by-day story of a sailing ship and all its homely housekeeping. Though his ship was far from being one of the greatest clippers, one cannot easily forget his description of even such birds of the ocean as this, as they appeared just before they were to vanish from men's sight forever.

"One night, when we were in the tropics, I went out to the end of the flying jib-boom upon some duty and, having finished it, turned around and lay over the boom for a long time, admiring the beauty of the sight before me. Being so far out from the deck, I could look at the ship as at a separate vessel, and there rose up from the water, supported only by a small black hull, a pyramid of canvas, spreading out far beyond the hull, and towering almost, as it seemed in the indistinct night air, to the clouds. The sea was as still as an inland lake. The light trade wind was gently and steadily breathing from astern. The dark blue sky was studded with tropical stars, and there was no sound but the rippling of the water under the stern, and the sails were spread far and wide—the two lower studding sails stretching on each side far beyond the deck; the topmast studding sails like wings to the topsails, the topgallant studding sails spreading out fearlessly above them; still higher the two royal studding sails, looking like two kites flying from the same string, and highest of all the little skysail, the apex of the pyramid, seeming actually to touch the stars and to be out of reach of the human hand. So quiet, too, was the sea, and so steady the breeze that if these sails had been sculptured marble, they could not have been more motionless. Not a ripple upon the surface of the canvas; not even a quivering of the extreme edges of the sail—so perfectly were they distended by the breeze. I was so lost in the sight that I forgot the presence of the man who had come out with me until he said (for he, too, rough old man o' war's man as he was, had been gazing at the show) half to himself, still looking at the marble sails, 'How quietly they do their work.' "

"A whaleship," said Herman Melville, "was my Yale Col-

lege, and my Harvard." Fishing smack, whaler, merchant
schooner, tea clipper—they had been an incomparable school
for a section of the American people, a section whose influence
was to spread to the outermost limits of the American domain
and be potent long after the last sail was furled. By this means
the whole idea of manual work, of industry, of manufacturing,
and of trade had been lifted up out of the mud into which a
landowning idea of aristocracy had trampled it from the beginning of civilization, and had been given wings. Manual
labor, manufacturing, retail buying and selling—they could
never be to the American again the despised grubby things
they had been to all people hitherto. The old idea had burst
like a chrysalis, and unfurled white pinions, and lifting itself
into the light of the sky, had demonstrated that in any useful
work whatsoever there may be a winged soul.

3

GODLESS GOTHAM

ARLY in the nineteenth century, a Moravian missionary, writing about the history of New York, said that the name Manhattan given by the Delaware Indians to the island in the bay was originally "Manna hattanik" and meant "the place where we all got drunk." If Manhattan did not mean this to the Indians, it probably did mean it to the Moravians. To persons leading a godly, righteous, and sober life in their own burgs, it seemed to be a real consolation to think that there was one city in America where people had no morals at all, a city, as Edgar Allan Poe quaintly said, "full of *legitimate* liveliness—the life of money-making and the life of pleasure."

On the long Atlantic coast, settled from Maine to Georgia by people with ideals, this one island remained, from first to last, impervious to all glimmerings of the higher life. New York was just the four corners, an inn and a place of entertainment, for Northerners going south and Southerners going north, for Easterners going west and Westerners going east, for Europeans coming into the country and Americans of any origin going out. Within less than a dozen years of its founding, New Englanders and Virginians were using it as a halfway house when they went visiting each other, which caused De

Vries, that most engaging gentleman among the first five patroons, to say a little word in the ears of the Dutch West India
Company. The English, he said, always build a beautiful
church as soon as they settle anywhere, and around this church
they group their houses and places of entertainment. If we
want to look like somebody in the eyes of our visitors, we must
build a nice church—saying which, De Vries himself put down
a contribution for it and saw to its building. So even religion
was established in this great city as an amiable social gesture in
the direction of visitors who might want some place to go on
Sunday.

On this gay and crowded little raft of land in the sea, there
never seemed to be room for that pack of notions which you
had brought from the home town, and which suddenly began
to feel very heavy as you saw how the rest were light-footing it
up and down the island. So you dropped it off on the hither
side and ferried across without it, in your best clothes and with
your best foot forward, feeling suddenly rather happy and
easy and free without your customary virtues. If you persisted
and brought your ideals into New York, the testimony from
earliest times to the present is that you lost them there anyway.

It is amazing how early the character of this wicked city
asserts itself in the record. Even when it was a small Dutch fur-
trading village, only a fort and a few houses on the tip of the
island, it is reported that it was very cosmopolitan and that
eighteen languages could be heard in its streets. From the first
it was an asylum for people who suffered from the "narrow-
mindedness" of their home towns. One of these was Anne
Hutchinson, that scandal of early New England, who undertook to talk back to the godly ministers and even set up a kind
of religious salon in her house, "to which resorted sundry of
Boston and other towns about to the number of fifty, sixty, or
eighty at once; where, after she had repeated the sermon, she
would make comment upon it, vent her mischievous opinions
as she pleased, and wreathed the Scriptures to her own purposes." Driven out of New England, Mistress Hutchinson

came to Manhattan. It was not that the Manhattanites welcomed her exactly. They just didn't mind her, and there she lived and said what she pleased without molestation until she was scalped by the Indians.

This is an example of the way in which New York has always added to its population.

2

This town on the island was from the first sharply distinguished from the rest of what came to be known as "York state." York state was a province of New England. Outside of the line of Dutch patroonships reaching up the Hudson River to Albany and constituting a special landed aristocracy with the center of their life on the island, the state was mainly settled by Yankees and was the great highway of New England going west. On the frontier people from New York state were always spoken of as Yankees, though persons with geographical discrimination would, of course, say "York state Yankees," just as they said, "Connecticut Yankees" or Vermont Yankees."

Though New England annexed the state, it never annexed the city. Culturally that remained unique—becoming from its busy, cosmopolitan beginning under the Dutch flag a magnificent city-state, like Venice or Tyre and Sidon, wielding the power of money over land and sea. Because of its position at the crossroads, it was able to act as the arbiter for all the conflicting culture patterns of America, to pick out in manners and fashion and current opinion something that would serve as the greatest common denominator for all. From being the overnight inn of the nation it developed naturally into being its fashion show and emporium, its center of news and publishing, its financial exchange, and its theater. It was very rich, for everyone who went through dropped some money here. It was tolerant, partly out of self-interest and necessity, as landlords usually are, but partly because into its bright and frivolous fabric there was woven from the beginning one single thread of

pure gold—the idea, then new and startling in the world, that
no one must be bothered in the possession of an opinion or a
social custom provided he held it peaceably.

That this was more than just a constitutional indifference
to the conflicting claims of virtue was demonstrated very early.
When it was noised about that every idea and custom was welcome in Manhattan, all those persons who found difficulty
squaring their notions of the good life with those of other
groups on the continent came thither. In 1647 the island presented a pleasing picture of Huguenots, Lutherans, Presbyterians, Moravians, and Anabaptists, all living sociably together.
Then along came Peter Stuyvesant, newly appointed by the
company to be governor of the place, and like the other executives of this ill-advised commercial outfit, he was a fussy and
tactless soul. Reviving a dormant rule that the religion of the
town should be that of the Dutch Reformed Church, he applied
it against a resident of Flushing who was holding Quaker meetings in his home, sentencing him either to pay a fine or to be
flogged and banished. Whereupon the officers of the town
refused to carry out the decree. A letter signed by a number
of prominent citizens said that the love of law, peace, and liberty was the true glory of Holland, and that they desired not
to offend one of Christ's little ones under whatsoever name he
appeared. "Should any of these people come in love amongst
us, we cannot in conscience lay hands upon them." Upon receiving this, Peter Stuyvesant cashiered and fined the sheriff of
Flushing, imprisoned the town clerk, and imposed various fines
on the signers of the document. But when word reached his
betters in Amsterdam of his performances, they sent him a hot
rebuke. The Chamber informed him that "the consciences of
men ought to be free and unshackled, so long as they continue
moderate, inoffensive, and not hostile to government," and reminded him that toleration in old Amsterdam had brought the
oppressed and persecuted of all countries to that city as an
asylum. In this respect, they said, they expected New Amsterdam to follow the example of the old.

3

In a world full of bigots, the policy of always giving the devil his due, consistently maintained, may fall little short of heroism. And so it was in New Amsterdam. The stoutest and most highhearted of all the colonies in really standing by a principle, its early history has been obscured by persistent seriocomic misrepresentation. Partly this was the fault of Diedrich Knickerbocker, otherwise Washington Irving, an agreeable person who started the Manhattan kind of writing which is still continued in the pages of the *New Yorker*. He wrote an amusing history of the early colony which would have been funnier if he had known more of what he was talking about. Against his nonsense the facts of the case stand out with a special poignancy.

These facts are recorded by David Frederick De Vries, one of the first five patroons, and, as he says, the chief of them, in a book translated and published by the New York Historical Society in 1857. De Vries, with four other men, including Van Rensselaer, was invited in 1630 by the Dutch West India Company to take large grants of land in this New World and to settle colonists under their personal rule. The West India Company was a group of commercial speculators who, after Hendrick Hudson's discovery of the island and the river, had got from the government of the New Netherlands the exclusive right to settle this country. They had begun, in 1623, by transporting thirty families of Walloons, Protestant refugees from Belgium, distributing them in groups of three or four families, on Manhattan, on Long Island, and at Fort Orange, now Albany, to trade in furs for the company. Other fur traders had followed, and a good many people had just come into the territory and stayed there, including Yankees seeping in from New England. In charge of this conglomerate was a governor appointed by the company and a garrison of Dutch soldiers.

Finding the need of a more systematic settlement of the territory, the company now proposed to establish a landed aristocracy, and offered huge grants of land to a few men who would establish agricultural colonies, working for them and ruled by them as their tenants. De Vries, who had been a super-cargo on ships trading with the East Indies, a gentleman, as he tells us, with 200 years of honorable ancestry behind him, was offered one of these grants, and arrived with colonists for Staten Island. Looking with disdain on the soldiers and good-for-nothing hangers-on about the fort, he said that what this country needed was certainly some honest agriculture, and he went to work with a will, seeing his meadows cleared, import-ing cattle, establishing his tenants in homesteads, proud and happy in his proprietorship. Then one day his people were scalped by the Indians, and his fields laid waste. De Vries dis-covered that some of the soldiers caught in misdemeanors had blamed their own faults on the Indians, that Governor Kieft had then punished the Indians, and the Indians in turn had fallen on the first white-man's settlement in their way and de-stroyed it.

De Vries was outraged—not only because of the loss of his colony and destruction of all his work. He felt his honor as a white man deeply wounded. These Indians, he said, were "poor simple souls." For a Dutch soldier to pass his own mis-demeanors off on an Indian and have the Indian executed was like a grown-up coward blaming a child for his own crimes and making the child take the punishment. He did not blame the Indians for retaliating, and so he told the governor and the soldiers. He went further. He saw some of the old chiefs him-self and tried to discover where the trouble was. He found that the settlers had established the most amiable relations with the Indians, and that the Indians on their part had been peaceable and generous. The mutual traffic was satisfactory to everyone. But the chiefs said that the soldiers would sell the young In-dians liquor, which immediately made them "act crazy." Then the minute an Indian was found doing anything inconsiderate, he was strung up before the populace and often his whole fam-ily murdered. All the settlers felt outraged, partly by the cruelty and injustice to their humble friends, partly because they feared retaliation. The old chiefs on their part were very much worried.

With touching simplicity and kindliness De Vries tells of his various encounters with the poor Indians. One day as he was walking through the woods, a drunken Indian met him and struck him on the arm, "which is with them a token of friendship. He said I was a good chief, that when he came to my house I let him have milk and everything for nothing, that he had just come from this house, where they had sold him brandy in which they had put half water, that he could scoop up the water himself from the river and had no need of buying it, that they had also stolen his beaver coat, and that he wanted to go home and get his bow and arrows and would kill some of the villainous Swannekans (Dutchmen) who had stolen his goods. I told him that he must not do so. I then proceeded to the house of Herr Vander Worst and told the soldiers and some others who were there that they must not treat the Indians in this manner."

Soon an Indian chief came to him in distress. A drunken Indian had shot a Dutchman. What should he do about it? He talked to De Vries earnestly, saying the trouble was with the sale of liquor. Couldn't De Vries stop it? De Vries went to the governor, William Kieft.

Kieft strutted and swore and said he was going to settle these Indians once and for all. He was going to send his soldiers out and shoot the whole gang of them that very night.

De Vries said, "You cannot do this."

"Who is stopping me?" said Kieft.

"I am the chief of the patroons, and head of the council of twelve men who represent the colony."

"But I," said Kieft, in effect, "have the soldiers."

De Vries saw that he was caught. There was no way of rallying the scattered farmers against a garrison of soldiers. He perceived that Kieft "had, with his co-murderers, determined to commit the murder, deeming it a Roman deed."

His heart anguished with pity, pity for the poor Indians whom he looked on kindly as children, pity for the white settlers, shame for his disgraced white man's blood, De Vries did not leave the governor's house that night but went and sat in the kitchen waiting with every nerve on edge, hoping against hope that the governor's threat to kill all the Indians was only bluster. And then he reports the murder in words that even at this distance of time seem to fall, one by one, like acid on the consciousness. "This business was begun between the twenty-fifth and the twenty-sixth of February in the year 1643. . . . About midnight I heard a great shrieking and ran to the ramparts of the fort. I looked over to Pavonia, and I saw nothing but firing and heard the shrieks of the Indians murdered in their sleep."

An Indian and his squaw burst in on him in terror, seeking safety in the fort. They said the Indians from Fort Orange had surprised and murdered their people.

De Vries said, "My poor people, there is no safety here. Those murderers were not Indians but *white men.*"

He took the Indians to the door, and finding no sentry there sped them away swiftly into the woods.

"When it was day, the soldiers returned to the fort, having massacred and murdered eighty Indians, and considering they had done a deed of Roman valor in murdering so many in their sleep, where infants were torn from their mother's breasts and hacked to pieces in the presence of the parents, and the pieces thrown into the fire and in the water, and other sucklings were bound to small boards and then cut and stuck and pierced and miserably massacred in a manner to move a heart of stone. Some were thrown into the river and when the fathers and mothers endeavored to save them, the soldiers would not let them come on land but made both parents and children drown, children from five to six years of age and also some old and decrepit persons. Many fled from the scene and, concealing themselves in the neighboring sedge, and when it was morning came out to beg a piece of bread and to be permitted to warm themselves, but they were murdered in cold blood and tossed into the water. Some came by our lands in the country with their hands, some with their legs cut off, and some holding their entrails in their arms, and others had such horrible cuts and gashes that worse than they were could never happen. And these poor simple souls, and also many of our own people, did not know any better than that they had been attacked by a party of Indians—the Maquas. After this exploit the soldiers were rewarded for their services, and Director Kieft thanked them by taking them by the hand and congratulating them."

The Indians retaliated, and, in the horrors that followed, poor Anne Hutchinson and her family lost their lives. The Indians fell upon a De Vries colony that had escaped the former scalping expedition, and burnt the farms, cattle, corn, tobacco, and the house, though De Vries adds, with a bitter, oblique glance at the Dutch soldiers, "we have never heard that they permitted women and children to be killed." During this attack on Vriesland, "the Indian whom I had aided to escape from the fort came and told the other Indians that I was a good chief, that I had helped him out of the fort, and that the killing of the Indians took place contrary to my wishes—hearing this they all cried together to my people that they would not shoot them."

The old Indian chiefs, as distressed as De Vries himself by this turn of affairs, invited him to a parley in the woods, and their best orator made him an elaborate speech, laying down one pointed stick after another on the ground, to emphasize each successive point in his discourse. Among other things he said that when "we (the Dutch) left our people behind with the goods to trade until the ships should came back, they had preserved these people like the apple of their eye; yea, they had given them their daughters to sleep with, by whom they had begotten children, and there roved many an Indian who was begotten by the Swannekins, but now our own people had become so villainous as to kill their own blood."

His houses in ashes, his fields in which he had taken such

pride one far-reaching, blackened ruin, De Vries stepped on a ship that came into the harbor and sailed away, but before he left he walked over to say good-by to Governor Kieft. "I told him that this murder which he had committed was so much innocent blood, and that it would yet be avenged upon him, and thus I left him." To a Virginian gentleman he said: "I tried to make a plantation, but it was destroyed through the stupidity of the governor, and I am going home."

Home he went and published this narrative in Holland, and so passed out of the American picture. It is interesting to speculate what would have been the history of the Dutch settlements in America if the commercial company had followed the plainest common sense and had made this chief of the patroons, established by his natural ability and authority as the chosen leader of the settlers—this gallant, just, and tenderhearted gentleman—their governor in the New World, and instead of hired soldiers had allowed him to organize the settlers for their own defense.

4

De Vries left behind some persons as outspoken as himself. Good old Dominie Bogardus thundered every Sunday from the pulpit of the Dutch Reformed Church against "the murders, covetousness, and other gross excesses of the governor." The governor retaliated by spreading the word that Bogardus was a drunkard, which caused the dominie to collect affidavits from his friends to the effect that he was a sober man and the governor was a liar. What between the report of De Vries at home and the fury of the people in Manhattan, Kieft was at last got on a ship and sent home to be tried in Holland, the stout Bogardus and one Cornelis Melyn going with him on the ship as his accusers. With him he also took the papers of the colony and 400,000 guilders of probably ill-gotten gold. But that vengeance which De Vries had foretold was waiting for him. The ship was wrecked on a shoal in the Bristol channel, broke into pieces, and drifted all night, Kieft clinging to it in agony and crying for forgiveness until the waters washed him away to his death. Poor Bogardus was also drowned, but Cornelis Melyn, who reports this wreck, escaped and carried his scorching tale home to Amsterdam. To him is credited a downright account of the governors of New Amsterdam published in Holland in 1649 in the form of a dialogue between a Portuguese soldier, a student from Sweden, a Spanish barber, a French merchant, a Neopolitan, a poor English nobleman, and a high Dutch gentleman, and entitled *Broad Advice on the West Indies*. All these persons are represented as being utterly astounded by the character of the governors sent to Manhattan, including the new one, Peter Stuyvesant. "How does the company know where to look for all these rascals? I believe they must have magazines full of them." The dialogue closes with a general agreement among them all that the future city of New York has a "godless, indecent, wicked, and profligate government, which is too well known to all the world, and which must be redressed."

Meanwhile Peter Stuyvesant had arrived in New Amsterdam, and was, as the honest burghers were not afraid to say, "stirring up hell" in his own style. Not content with continuing the brawls with the Indians, he raised the question of religious toleration. But on this subject the company, aroused by the reports of those who had gone home, sharply brought the club down on his head. By this time the English were beginning to take a hand in the troubles of their Dutch neighbors. A convention of delegates from New Amsterdam and the Long Island towns was called and a "Humble Remonstrance" was drawn up in which the hand is the hand of the Dutchman but the voice is that of the Englishman. " 'Tis contrary to the first and genuine principles of every well regulated government that one or more men should arrogate to themselves the exclusive power to dispose at will of the life and property of any individual." As a people, "not conquered or subjugated, but settled here on a mutual covenant and contract entered into with the Lords Patroons, with the consent of the natives," the convention protested against the enactment of laws without their consent. To which Peter Stuyvesant replied, "We derive our authority from God and the Company, not from a few ignorant subjects, and we alone can call the inhabitants together."

The inhabitants said nothing, but the rule of the Dutch Company was doomed from that day. In 1664 a fleet of English ships sailed into the harbor, apparently understanding full well that the inhabitants were disaffected and only too ready to join forces with the English towns under a more reasonable home government. Peter Stuyvesant, who was a brave man even if he was a fool, sprang on his silver-nailed wooden leg to his old rusty cannon and called on the inhabitants to defend themselves. He called in vain. Not a Dutchman lifted his hand. He might derive his power from God and the Company, but the day was gone when he could call the inhabitants together.

Thus was struck the first real blow for liberty in the New World. New York was tolerant and easygoing and indifferent to the Sabbath. It loved money, fine clothes, and a good dinner, and had no inhibitions about alcohol; but it had fought the cleanest, manliest fight in all our early history for principle and for honor. Above the silence of this smokeless, bloodless battle one might have heard, far down the century ahead, the opening gun of the American Revolution.

4

CACIQUES
OF THE RICE COUNTRY

S A Paradise for gentlemen, Virginia was very charming. But it was only an amateur experiment. After two generations in which the ideal of the gentleman had been growing as sweetly in the tidewater country as a crocus in the March snows, it was now proposed to set down the highest, most philosophical ideal of the gentleman's life in the American wilderness, and to nourish it henceforth on special privilege, like an orchid in a greenhouse. Charles II, coming back to the throne of his fathers in England, now wished to match the pestilent Puritan commonwealth which the Roundheads had established on Massachusetts Bay with a Cavalier commonwealth, planned, like the Roundhead one, with forethought and philosophy and ready to fight the Puritans henceforth for any advantage there was to be got in America, by land or sea. So, in 1663 with a courtly gesture, he gave to Lord Clarendon and seven of his other friends whatever remained of the southern coast of America with all the wilderness beyond, and any and all territory claimed by Spaniards which an Englishman could lay hold of by sword or guile.

The plan for this new commonwealth of gentlemen was drawn up by no less a person than the philosopher Locke, then the private secretary of Lord Ashley. The scheme included an hereditary nobility of two orders, landgraves and caciques, whose dignity was to be supported by large landholdings. These estates were to be made inseparable from the titles and privileges of the orders. In other words, you couldn't sell your land to somebody else, to be cut up into house lots or defaced by a factory, and still be a cacique. You had to keep it, intact and handsome, planted to that vegetable produce which could alone nourish a gentleman and worked by slaves. It was a trial to the founders of this philosophical society that at first the holders of lands found pigs and cattle easier to raise than anything else. There was something not quite elegant about a bacon aristocracy. It smelled little better than the codfish aristocracy of Boston.

There was another trouble, too. Charleston, the capital of this new princedom, crowded on a narrow triangle of sand between two rivers and the sea, was a handy port for all purposes. It required all the wits of Boston to keep the trade of the West Indies from straying thither, and no matter how the gentlemen might be enticed and wooed by grants of swamp along the tidal rivers, there would pour into the port a rabble who knew that the quickest way to get rich in the new country was to head for the woods and trade with the Indians. They taught the gentlemen bad habits. They soon reconstructed the pattern of Carolina not to a gentleman's liking. There were still two orders of this society, but, as someone said, it consisted of the nobility and the mobility.

The mobility, consisting of ex-pirates, adventurers from all the southern seas, old Indian traders, and bad characters generally, began to draw forest products from a thousand miles of wilderness. In 1707 ninety-seven ships left the port laden with pitch, tar, beaver, bear, and deer skins, sarsaparilla, turmeric, snakeroot, and other herbs. Down the streets on that little wedge of land between the Ashley and Cooper rivers careered the jangling bells announcing the passing of a string of twenty or thirty horses, driven by Indians or half-wild traders from the woods, and bearing packs of roots, herbs, and skins which had been collecting for months in the Indian villages. As the little ships loaded them uproariously, and the sailors swaggered and drank, and Spanish gold jingled to the jangling of the bells, it took real self-control to remain a Southern gentleman preoccupied with vegetation and the land, sure that trade was the business of vulgarians and that the direct touch of any coined metal would soil your white hands.

2

Nevertheless, the developing aristocracy of Charleston acquired a social culture both polished and beautiful. This aristocracy consisted of English and Huguenot families and some families who emigrated from the West Indies. Bringing in armies of black slaves, they fell on the swamps along the rivers, and lifted the muck into blooming fields and gardens. This achievement of the black men, with due credit to them for it, is narrated in a poem entitled *The Hireling and the Slave*, by William Grayson, in 1856, which contains so many good lines that it ought to be rescued from its grave in the Library of Congress and set to shine anew among the jewels of American literature.

> Swept by the ax, the forests pass away,
> The dense swamp opens to the light of day.
> The deep morass of reeds and fetid mud,
> Now dry, now covered by the rising flood,
> In squares arranged, by lines of banks and drain,
> Smile with rich harvest of the golden grain
> That wrought from ooze by Nature's curious art
> To pearly whiteness, cheers the Negro's heart,
> Smokes on the master's board in goodly show
> A mimic pyramid of seeming snow.

Besides the rice, which was the principal staple of the country, Grayson reminds us that there were other products. There was sugar, without whose help "no bridal cake delights." There was cotton.

In broader limits, to the loftier maize,
The silklike cotton all its wealth displays.
Through forked leaves, in endless rows unfold
Gay blossoms tinged with purple dyes and gold.
To suns autumnal bursting pods disclose
Their fleeces spotless as descending snows.
These, a rich freight, a thousand ships receive,
A thousand looms, with fairy fingers weave,
And hireling multitudes in other lands
Are blessed with raiment from the Negro's hands.

But it is on the blessing of tobacco that he waxes most eloquent. This, flowing out from the low-country estate,

Cheers the lone scholar at his midnight work,
Subdues alike the Russian and the Turk,
The saint beguiles, the heart of toil revives,
Ennui itself of half its gloom deprives,

And with strange magic, and mysterious charm
Hunger can stay and bores and duns disarm!

On these estates were built comfortable houses of the coun-
try-manor type, with their outlying blocks of slave quarters
and endless stables for fine horses, and along the river front
were little boats, fitted with awnings, where gay ladies and
gentlemen could float at ease or embark for picnic parties on
some other waterside estate.

As more and more of the swamplands were reclaimed by
the Negroes, the plantation life, white and black, spread out.
"As for the plantation," says DuBose Heyward, whose description of Charleston and the low country before the Civil
War in his novel *Peter Ashley*, sums up the testimony of many
records of and of many travelers, with more succinct literary
expressiveness, "it had been generations since a slave had been
sold from the Wake fields, the natural procreation which took
place in the Negro yard having been accompanied by an equal
increase in the successive families in the big house. Land was
cheap. It had been the custom in the plantation country, as the

boys attained manhood and returned from college, to extend
the domain and present a certain number of families to each
son. So as time passed, and the process was repeated, the Negroes became as indigenous to the locality as the masters themselves."

Against so large a background of black people, and it must
be added of mulattoes carrying in their veins the best blood of
gentlemen, was maintained, as the cherished flower of this society, the pampered and exclusive grace of the Charleston lady.
Northern tradition, based apparently on the reports of New
Englanders who went south as governesses to the Charleston
estates, represents her as a spoiled darling indeed. In Mrs. Sarah
Hale's story of *Norwood*, in 1827, which purports to contrast
life North and South, the matron is the prototype of St. Clair's
wife in *Uncle Tom's Cabin*—sickly, fretful, continually tyran-
nizing over a husband too good for her. The Charleston tradition is that their ladies were the loveliest in the world. After
being displayed as fair opening buds in the annual St. Cecilia's
ball, they lived a life of elegant seclusion, it being said that a
true Charleston lady should be heard of by the public only
twice in her life, once when she was married and once when
she was buried. DuBose Heyward sums the matter up, in
rather modern terms, in *Peter Ashley*: " 'Generations ago the
Charleston matron was established as the most gracious and accomplished hostess on the globe. But there is something more,
something requiring infinite finesse, something that we ourselves have imposed upon them, and that must require a special
and very subtle talent. We demand that they satisfy the hunger of our bodies and still remain divine; that they conceive
our children and continue immaculate. That, in short, they
shall consort with us and exhibit no signs of contamination.
We have created a deity of our womanhood and we can for-
give it anything short of disillusioning us.'

" 'And for many of us,' Peter commented bitterly, 'the
brothel or the Negro yard is the preparatory school.' "

Presided over by fair deities before whom breathed a per-

petual smoke of masculine reverence, the old plantation society
had a great charm, combining the utmost sophistication of
wealth and social habit with a kind of country simplicity. And
here again, Heyward sums up the oral tradition when he calls
off a long roll of Carolina names, Huguenot and English,
"names that meant long evenings on broad moon-drenched
front steps, the warmth of friends, and above in the shadowed
depths of the piazza, the older people, rocking, talking, faintly
swaying white forms in the blue darkness, glowing cigar ends,
roses and tobacco smoke blowing by in alternate waves, then
mingling poignant and bitter sweet." Singing under the high
stars—*Juanita*, *The Spanish Cavalier*, *Nellie Gray*, *In the
Gloaming*. Then with boys in their saddles, *Auld Lang Syne*.

"Then full-bodied, resonant, sustained, swelling suddenly
up and possessing the night, the voice of the swamp, the voice
that those who are bred within its sound never hear until they
go away, and then listen for always in their dreams until they
return."

Thus, he says, was South Carolina society made. "Axes had
rung in primeval forests, plantations had grown and spread,
life had provided itself with necessities, then clothed itself in
individual and appropriate beauty. There had been a time for
work and time for play. There had been a spaciousness about
the days, room for youth to ride untrammelled under the high
St. John sky, to love in privacy, to beget, to know the unre-
strained laughter of children. And at the last, time for a man to
grow old gently, and, still loved, to pass into the graveyard on
the land that his feet had always trod. And down the years, like
a wand passed from hand to hand of runners in the race, the
tradition of gentleness, hospitality, loyalty to one's own."

3

This charming plantation life alternated with life in the
city or visits to the resorts of the North, to Newport or Sara-
toga Springs. In Northern eyes these Southerners, flashing by
in their shining equipages, the ladies a veritable flower garden

of millinery, lace, and ribbons, with their soft Southern speech and frank manners, "balmy as a May morning," the gentlemen riding their sleek horses and springing at a lady's slightest gesture to wait on her, were an amazing spectacle. And of course they had, in more severe societies, their occasional detractors. The *Salmagundi Papers* report on October 15, 1807, that the ladies from the South are appearing with the annual produce of a rice plantation in their clothing or with hogheads of tobacco on their heads, or a bale of cotton trailing at their heels. Gentlemen from the South are drinking, gambling, and sporting generally. One poor fellow lost his equipage, having been reported to have eaten the horses and "drank the Negroes." Thus there began to be fixed in Northern literature the image of the "immaculate South Carolina gentleman, proud, obstinate, cultured, violent, generous," and his "resolute consideration for his slaves who happen also to be his children."

When they did not go north, they came down in the summer to their town houses in Charleston, "going down to the Salt," they called it. Their presence added to the natural liveliness of the town. There is in the old records none of that languor which now seems to hang over the ancient mansions, with their still mossy gardens, that atmosphere which, as someone has said, combines the "stench of the water front with the dry perfume of aristocracy." Charleston on the make was as active as Boston. Great wealth was piling up, not always by strictly vegetable means, and was spent in England and Europe for all the gauds of life—fine carriages, fine furniture, pictures, books, wines. Fine horses were bred, as in Virginia, and horse racing and gambling on the races were favorite sports. There were fencing schools and dancing schools. There were clubs, salons, newspapers. In many respects the early social life at Charleston resembled the life of some of the present Oriental colonies of white men, in such a city as Shanghai, a gay, showy, idle existence, carried as the froth and sparkle on the dark tides of an alien life. But what was imported of eighteenth century taste and splendor was shaped by the spirit of the place—the warm climate, the southern seas, the vast subsidiary foundation of black slaves, the high-spirited, blade-flashing, down-with-the-rabble attitude of lords and ladies maintaining their place against the desperadoes, the adventurers, the inpouring and outpouring of people looking for their place in the sun, which pressed them on the east and south from the ocean and on the west from the frontier. The natural contacts of the city were with the West Indies, the mixed Spanish and Indian settlements of the Caribbean, with slave societies long established, and with the proud and caste-bound Spaniards in Florida. Access to the rich western hinterland was easy. There was every temptation to exploitation, every opportunity for accumulation, a spirit of hazard and adventure.

During the eighteenth century, which was the heroic period of the colony, there was some picturesque battling with the pirates of the Caribbean and with the Spaniards in Florida or the Indians stirred up by the Spaniards. This dashing age is depicted in *The Yemassee*, one of the most famous of the novels by Simms—the Yemassees being a tribe of Indians who held the country from Port Royal to the Savannah River, and who were armed and incited against the English by the Spaniards. It is a story on the order of those by Cooper, many of the scenes being in Indian villages and representing the stoic opposition of the truly noble red man, but there is also the coming of mysterious characters by sea, the intrigues of the Spanish, the easy, masterful bearing of cavalier gentlemen, the faithful slave. This adventure of Governor Craven against the Indians took place in 1712–1715.

Another famous adventure was the exploit of William Rhett in clearing the port of Charleston from pirates. He seems to have done his work much more honestly than William Kidd, who had been dispatched from New York to get rid of the pirates but who turned pirate himself and became the hero of innumerable legends along the Atlantic coast. Poe credits William Kidd with burying some of his famous treasure on Sullivan's Island, in the harbor of Charleston, and wrote his notable story of *The Gold Bug* about it. Apparently William Rhett, the doughty and really successful fighter of pirates, was one of the inspirations for the character of Rhett Butler in Margaret Mitchell's *Gone with the Wind*. Nicholson wrote the Lords Justices in England that Rhett was a "proud, haughty, insolent fellow." "Old Rhett is dead," he announced. "Please send us some one to take his place." Rhett Butler in Mrs. Mitchell's story is one of the most complete developments in fiction of the typical Charleston gentleman—a buccaneer, but something also of a genuine man, under the varnish of Southern behavior which time and tradition had sweetened with social sirup raised in Virginia. His type is lightly sketched in many of the Simms novels. It grins at us debonairly from the local record.

4

Among these dashing gentry of Charleston there arrived in 1732 a cacique of rather different ideals, but in person as grand a cavalier as the best of them—General James Oglethorpe, the founder of Georgia. A gallant young man, he lived to be a very grand old one, and, having founded the last of the American colonies, lived to welcome John Adams as minister to the Court of St. James's and died at the age of ninety-seven. In his nineties he was still shining in London society. "I have a new admirer," wrote Hannah More, "and we flirt prodigiously. It is the famous General Oglethorpe, perhaps the most remarkable man of his time. He was foster brother to the Pretender and is much above ninety years old, the finest figure of a man you ever saw. He perfectly realizes all my ideas of Nestor. His reading in literature is great, his knowledge of the world extensive, and his faculties as bright as ever. He was the intimate friend of . . . all the wits of his time. He is perhaps the oldest man of his generation living. I went to see him the other day and he would have entertained me by repeating passages from Sir Eldred. He is quite a *preux chevalier* and full of the old gallantry."

This charming gentleman, still in the flush of early manhood, brought to Charleston a beautiful idea. He would form a state between the colony and the Spaniards—a brave, sober, and dedicated commonwealth, in which every man should be both a farmer and a soldier; and to this colony he would bring worthy persons who had been thrown into prison for debt in Great Britain and also various distressed Protestant groups from the Continent. In this colony there should be, he said, "no Negroes, no rum, no land jobbers, and no Catholics." "As many Negroes, so many enemies to us and friends to the Spaniards." As many Catholics, ditto. The inhabitants were to be "industrious men with wives, and Germans such as go to Pennsylvania." The standard of the soldiery was to be set by a company of Scotch Highlanders, such men as later told him, with regard to the Spaniards, "We are here resolved to die hard and will not lose one inch of ground by fighting." The intellectual and spiritual standards of the colony should be kept up by the schoolmasters and the best Protestant pastors of the time.

Charleston, not yet completely committed to large slave-owning and looking enviously at the settlements of New England and Pennsylvania which throve on dissenting Protestantism and free labor, was not inhospitable to the idea. The South Carolinians welcomed a bodyguard between them and the Spaniards. As for the rest of the scheme, they were philanthropically ready to help. So the colony of Georgia was established to the south of Charleston, as its free white foster child and armor-bearer. Charleston received the first 130 settlers, entertained them hospitably and sent them on their way, and ever afterwards looked after them when necessary. They on their side did the military part of their work nobly, effectively pushing back the Spaniards at the battle of Bloody Marsh in 1742, and, as long as Oglethorpe was with the settlement, maintaining just and friendly relations with the Indians.

The most glorious hopes were entertained for the new settlement. What those pious nobodies in New England and Pennsylvania were accomplishing in a hit-or-miss way was now to be done handsomely, philanthropically, in high-gentleman's style. In England the poet Thomson celebrated the idea in sonorous blank verse.

> Lo, swarming northward, on rejoicing suns,
> Gay colonies extend, the calm retreat
> Of undeserved distress; the better home
> Of those whom Bigots chase from foreign lands;
> Not built on Rapine, Servitude, and Woe,
> And in their turn some petty tyrant's prey,
> But bound by social freedom, firm they rise
> Such as of late an Oglethorpe has formed
> And crowding round the charmed Savannah Seas.

The new province consisted of land between the Altamaha River and the Savannah River, "stretching westward to the South Seas," and was described by Robert Montgomery as: "The most amiable country of the universe; that nature has not blessed the world with any part which can be preferable to it; that Paradise with all her virgin beauty may be modestly supposed at most but equal to its excellence. It lies in the same latitude with Palestine herself, that promised land, which was pointed out as God's own choice to bless the labors of a favorite people."

This land was to be called the Margravate of Azilia, and was to be a land of silk and wine and olive oil, emulating the Mediterranean countries, making it unnecessary for Britain to purchase these articles from foreigners and Catholics. "We shall certainly succeed in silk and wine," said Oglethorpe, "in case the planters are supported by the Public. This colony bridles the Spaniards in America and covers the frontiers."

To assure such decency and order and virtue as made New England and Pennsylvania so prosperous, Oglethorpe imported John and Charles Wesley, who here started one of the first Sunday schools of the world. The Wesleys were followed by George Whitefield, the great evangelist. Unfortunately Whitefield brought an idea of far-reaching consequences, for he suggested that slavery was not such a bad institution. It was probably an arrangement ordained by God to

Christianize and civilize the poor African heathen. The many philanthropic but capitalistically minded gentlemen who were trying to build up large estates in eastern Georgia seized upon this idea. They were finding free labor hard to attract and stubborn to manage, too inclined to press westward and set up on its own among the "old red hills of Georgia," or, when it was more shiftless, to steal away to the pine barrens and become ancestors of the Georgia crackers. Somehow, despite all inducements, despite Oglethorpe's charming personality, wise leadership, and wide acquaintance among philanthropic and liberal groups, large bands of self-disciplined, pious, thrifty artisans, such as had come to the religious and moral colonies of the North, did not arrive in Georgia. They seemed to smell large landowners, aristocrats, and Negro slavery afar off, and headed instead of the port of Philadelphia or Boston.

So the planters along the eastern coast of Georgia yielded to what they deemed necessity. When Oglethorpe's charter expired in 1752, and the colony reverted to the crown, they removed the ban against Negro slavery. One of these planters was Jonathan Bryan from South Carolina whose estate of Brewton Hill in Georgia became the largest rice plantation in America. Genuinely convinced that he would be able to help the poor Africans by making them slaves, he was bitterly disappointed that the exigencies of a large plantation did not permit this, and very sore in his conscience. His letter to a friend on the subject is tragic in its implications: "But, dear Sir, what concerns me more than all is the unhappy conditions of our Negroes, who are kept in worse than Egyptian bondage. The clothes we wear, the food we eat, and all the superfluities we possess are the produce of their labors, and what do they receive in return? Nothing equivalent. On the contrary, we keep from them the key of knowledge, so that their bodies and souls perish together in our service."

With the introduction of Negroes the large estates prospered and the Negro population increased so fast that in 1773 there were 15,000 Negroes to 18,000 white men. Of the original groups of white laborers and rehabilitated debtors who were to form a snug middle class, as in the colonies of the North, a few had developed large plantations; many had taken refuge among the pines and were barely existing; and a saving minority remained self-respecting citizens, not rich but not poor, giving to the state always a leaven of democracy. The plantation life itself was but an extension of that of South Carolina, and the aristocracy was drawn largely from that colony, with a few wealthy additions from England. Some of these wealthy persons had been friends of Oglethorpe and annoyed him by the luxury with which they set themselves up in his new city of Savannah. "People who come at their own charge live in a manner too expensive which will make sumptuary laws necessary for the province." Oglethorpe did his best, but circumstances and the climate were against him. Finally he departed for England, leaving to his colony the beautiful city of Savannah, which he had laid out, and the pathetic memory of a great idea.

The plan for the city of Savannah had been brought by Oglethorpe to Charleston in his strong box, and to this day all its squares and streets conform to his design. Four miles outside of Savannah is the old cemetery of Bonaventure, where six generations of the famous dead of Georgia sleep under "live-oak trees so thick that they make a perpetual dimness." Coming out of this soft Southern city so squarely and symmetrically laid out upon its bluffs, walking here over the thick beds of green moss swept from above by the streamers of ashen gray moss, it seems that something very sad and precious is buried here. Charleston and the low country have been blamed as the most determined proponents of slavery, and Georgia was ravaged from end to end with fire and sword in the bitterest retribution of the Civil War. But here, in this old cemetery, under these weeping Spanish mosses, in this soft mourning darkness, where are buried some of Charleston's proudest names, the recording angel still remembers how nobly some of them once tried to do otherwise.

5

During the Revolution South Carolina and Georgia carried the war on dashingly, both against the British and against the innumerable Tories within their bounds. When the war broke out the South Carolinians sent down a body of men to reinforce Savannah and put it in a state of defense and carried off Negro slaves from all plantations in the way of attack to keep them safe for their owners. Savannah fell into the hands of the British in 1778 and Charleston in 1780, but the fight was carried on with romantic gallantry by Francis Marion, a South Carolinian of Huguenot ancestry, who harried the British and the Tories from the swamps. Of Marion's Band, William Cullen Bryant wrote:

> Well knows the fair and friendly moon
> The band that Marion leads,
> The glittering of their rifles,
> The scampering of their steeds
> Across the moonlight plain.
> 'Tis life to feel the night wind
> That lifts the tossing mane—
> A moment in the British camp,
>   A moment and away,
> Back to the pathless forest
>   Before the break of day.

Of Marion, Simms wrote: "With a force constantly fluctuating and feeble—half-naked men feeding on unsalted pottage—forced to fight the enemy by day and look after their little families concealed in swamps or thickets by night—he still continued to keep alive and bright the sacred fires of his country's liberties at moments when they seemed to have no other champion. . . . The language of song and story has been employed to do them honor, and our children are taught, in lessons they love, to lisp the deeds and patriotism of his band. Marion—Marion's Brigade and Marion's Band—have passed into household words which the young utter with an enthusiasm much more confiding than that which they yield to the wondrous performances of Greece and Ilium. They recall when spoken a long and delightful series of brilliant exploits, wild adventures by day and night, in swamp and in thicket, strange and sudden maneuvers, and a generous, unwavering ardor that never found any peril too hazardous or any suffering too unendurable. The theme, thus invested, seems to have escaped the ordinary bounds of history. It is no longer within the province of the historian. It has passed into the hands of the poet, and seems to scorn the appeal to authentic chronicles. . . . His history is a people's history, written in their hearts rather than in their books—which their books could not write, which would lose all its golden glow if subjected to the cold details of the phlegmatic chronicles."

When the treaty of peace with England was signed, the Tories moved out of Charleston into the ships which stood waiting in a semicircle in the harbor, ready to take them off. They carried away with them 5,333 slaves, the bells and books of St. Michael's Church, thousands of dollars in gold, pictures, mahogany, books, and jewels owned by the wealthiest families, and 3,794 irreconcilable aristocrats. So Charleston stood, purged of her most concentrated essence of gentility, as Hayne, the South Carolina poet, wrote:

Pallid, yet proud, half sad, yet joyous hearted,
As one who hears far off the roll of thunder clouds departed,
And on whose brow war had left furrows hot and gory,
Yet she stood, with calm, exultant smile, her dark eyes flushed with
    glory.

6

After the Revolution, the plantation aristocracy built itself anew. In his novel *The Sword and the Distaff* Simms gives a picture of the disorganized and impoverished plantation of post-Revolutionary times. But unlike tidewater Virginia, from which leadership was being drained to the west, and which fell into gentle decay, the South Carolina low country was all ready for a new birth of prosperity and pride. With the development of the West, the value of the port grew, receiving immigrants and sending them west, receiving products and sending them out, taking a toll of money each way, as New York City was doing in the North. And with the invention of the cotton gin, cotton planting became an enormous industry in itself.

So Charleston became the political and intellectual, as well as the social and financial leader of the South, polishing a kind of opinion which more and more the Southerner everywhere was inclined to flourish like a sword. Against the increasing literary activity of the North a lively group of writers set about it to put South Carolina on the map. The head and front of these was the genial, bushy-bearded, broad-browed scribe of Irish ancestry, William Gilmore Simms. Surrounded by polished poets and journalists he kept up a lively literary life, with its hangout, at times, in Russell's Book Store, Russell publishing at least the minor and local works of the authors. Between publishing some seventy books Simms wrote helpful and manly advice to young authors, among them Poe, corresponded with distinguished persons in the North, and was admired by visitors to Charleston, but he was never admitted into the closed inner circle of Charleston society even after he had married one of the plantation daughters for his second wife. With a taste for history as broad and as dashing as Scott's and an interest in low life as omnivorous and observant as that of Dickens, he poured out novel after novel about his native state. The whole series is even now a somewhat gaudy but most amazingly vital and impressive panorama of Carolina social history, from early colonial times down to the Civil War. His *History of South Carolina*, many times revised, is still used in the South Carolina schools.

In all this flash and heat of intellectual life in Charleston certain social philosophies began to take dramatic form. One was the idea that Charleston was destined to realize at last the life of the Greek democracy, the free and liberal life of persons relieved by slavery from the burden of manual labor. Another was that Charleston was solving the problem never solved by any free society, of genuine social security for those who worked with their hands. Any criticism of slavery from the North or from Europe was met by some telling remarks on the subject of the factory system and "hireling" labor. Remarks about the successive financial panics in the cities of the North, the breadlines, the strikes, reports on child labor and the miserable destitution in the slums were pitched flaming by the Charlestonians into the growing fury of national discussion about slavery. "You are going to talk about slave labor," said they. "All right, you low-down, mealy-mouthed hypocrites, let's talk about it. Let's talk about the seamen and their wages and their food and their bunks on the glorious Yankee clippers. Let's talk about children and women who are slaves in the fine New England factories. Let's talk about men and women and children in New York City who are slaves of the financial manipulators. Let's talk about the Western farmer who is the slave of the man who holds his mortgage. When we are short of money do we close down our cotton plantations, and throw our slaves out to starve? No, we feed them. We feed them so long as we have bread for ourselves. When they are old and sick and can't work, do we pitch them into a slum and forget them? No, the lady of the house herself goes down among them with food and medicine, like a ministering angel. Have our slaves any mortgages on their huts? Are they afraid of losing their jobs with us? And why is our system better? Because we know those who work for us as human beings. They are black, but we think they are human. That is more than you think of your workmen and the poor fools who put their money into your banks and lose it."

This sort of thing flashed out of Charleston, on tongues and pens. One of the best examples of it is Grayson's poem *The Hireling and the Slave*, already quoted.

Documented with a whole series of quotations from current sources on conditions of workingmen in factories and on

life in the slums of the North and of Europe, the poet contrasts the miserable condition of the free "hireling" with the
secure and happy life of the slave on the plantation.

Grayson admits at the outset that the lot of the toiling
masses is hard in any case, but holds that this is inevitable so
long as so many of them remain at a rudimentary stage of human development. We have yet to discover a "shorthand
method to enrich mankind."

> How small the choice, from cradle to the grave
> Between the lot of hireling and of slave!

But he says that the Southern masters are at least aware of
the problem and are trying to meet it humanely, which is more
than can be said of some masters of hired labor. As for the
Negro,

> Guarded from want, from beggary secure,
> He never feels what hireling crowds endure,
> Nor knows, like them, in helpless want to crave
> For wife and child the comforts of the slave!

He says the worker of the North is "free but in name, the
slave of endless toil." No matter how good he is, he never
knows when a financial panic or a change of fashion will
throw him out of a job.

> Vain is his skill in each familiar task.
> Capricious fashion shifts her Protean mask.
> His ancient craft gives work and bread no more,
> And want and death sit scowling by the door.

He describes the factories

> Where hireling millions toil in doubt and fear
> For food and clothing all the weary year,
> Content and grateful if their master give
> The boon they humbly crave—to work and live.

He tells of coal mines and of the wan child laborer

> . . . compelled in mines to slave
> Through narrow seams of coal, a living grave.

He compares this with the state of the slave, in his nice little house on the plantation, with his garden, his dogs, his church on Sundays, his Negro sociables, his music and his Bible.

> Secure they toil, uncursed their peaceful life
> With freedom's hungry broils and wasteful strife.
> No want to goad, no faction to deplore,
> The slave escapes the perils of the poor.

He says that if any white angel should appear in light above the dark millions of toilers in industries, of the destitute in the slums, and hold out to them a promise of what the slave has,

> How freely would the hungry listeners give
> A life-long labor thus to live!

It was specious. It was brilliant. It was Fascism springing full armed into the fray, eighty years ahead of time!

7

Now, looking back across the years, all one can say of the Charleston pattern of life was that it was lovely—for the few. This gentleman was a social buccaneer. He did not deny it. He was proud of it. It was inevitable, he thought, that the few should live on the many, but they ought to do it handsomely, without hypocrisy, and without apology, and make it as comfortable for the many meanwhile as they decently could. To all other prosperous persons, drawing their living comfortably from below, he said, "I know what I am, and I know what it means, even to the poor fellow I stand on. So I at least live by code. But you, you whining hypocrite—don't snivel to me about virtue!" And in this spirit Charleston threw the gauntlet in the face of the North and called on the South to follow her in 1860. And now the old portraits on the walls of Charleston mansions seem still to look down with a sardonic smile on all financial pride and social pomp and power, as if they would say, "When your day comes, can you go down as handsomely?"

Probably Grayson was right. If the plantation lords had to go, the industrial lords and financial lords would someday follow after them. And fortunate indeed will they be, if they can leave so many flowers of romance as Charleston has left, such a beguiling screen of legend and story, to hide the gaunt reality of their unregretted graves.

5

THE REGION OF BROTHERLY LOVE

HERE is a fellow who roams at large through late seventeenth and early eighteenth century literature in Europe. He is the decayed grandson of the gay gentlemen of Shakespeare's plays—the poor relation of the caciques of Charleston. He wears gold lace and silk hose, but lacks a warm coat and clean linen. He drinks largely at social routs and at taverns, but seldom enjoys a square meal, because his women are too fine for housewifery and his ill-paid servants and tradesmen cheat him. He owns a good deal of land, but lacks ready cash and is deep in debt. He can barely read, and knows only enough about writing to put his name to an IOU. He has no arts and crafts except swordsmanship, and in any crisis his one idea is to fight. This person has fine manners of a sort, considers himself wellborn on the strength of a real or fictitious ancestry that did not work for a living, distributes titles of honor largely among his friends, and puts a lot of them after his own name, but he seldom does a real kindness. At best he is absurd, at worst, vicious.

By 1680 a generation of warfare in Europe had created a deep-seated implacable hatred for this man, and a determination on the part of a great many people to be just as different

75

from him as possible. In Germany he and his kind, mainly followers of the big landowners and Catholic noblemen, had warred for thirty years on the rising class of artisans, tradesmen, professional men, and small freeholders, who had saved a little money and bought their own land from the larger estates. These people, though mostly of plebeian origin, had begun to take advantage of several new techniques which the so-called nobility were still inclined to neglect. The invention of printing had made books readily accessible, and many of these poorer people had not only learned to read but were going very far in making books a means of distributing information and creating a new sense of values. Finding that all the sacred wisdom of the Christian revelation was in one great book which printing put in the hands of everybody, they had decided to depend on that book, and say good-by to the great organized church which had hitherto represented their only means of attaining to the higher life. In other words, they were Protestants.

With the spread of reading there was a spread of general knowledge—improved tools, better housekeeping, better agriculture, knowledge of places to trade and means of turning a little profit. And so most of these people were quietly setting against the large landowners a new kind of wealth. It consisted in stores of saved coin—in other words, *capital*. In recent years, social philosophy has set labor over against capital as if they were antagonistic orders of society. But modern civilization began when the laborer became a little capitalist. Saved materials of their own to be used as capital first lifted the laborers out of serfdom and out of military and political oppression. And late in the seventeenth century, when people were getting so tired of the feudal gentleman, some common folks knew that, swagger as he might, man must eat, and in their pockets, not his, was the wherewithal to buy food.

Still the gentleman had for ages held the sword, and the organized political power, and for nearly a century he had been making the reading, working, saving, trading citizens of

Europe thoroughly miserable. In Germany the Protestants had been pretty well beaten out—their farms laid waste, their villages in ruins. But silently, stubbornly they were still organized in little underground groups, and the sympathy of liberal and less unfortunate persons in other countries, especially in Holland and England, was with them. In England, the Puritans, representing the new class, had broken the neck of feudalism when they lifted the head off Charles I. During the days of the Puritan Commonwealth, Cromwell had kept the ragtag style of feudal gentleman in wholesome subjection, but after the return of Charles II to the throne in 1660, he was back again, swaggering in every inn. A good many of the Lowland Scots had meanwhile moved over to northern Ireland, and were daring any sprig of feudalism to keep *them* under.

Early in the struggle a certain type of artisan and small capitalist—those concerned with the crafts and profits of the sea—had settled New England. They had brought their books, and their tools, and their little stores of money, and their determination to run life in their own way. Thus they had escaped a lot of trouble, and their prosperous example heartened sufferers at home to do likewise. So now, on a larger and an international scale, the skilled-labor-small-capitalist-intelligentsia complex of people determined to set up another state in the new world, and that state was Pennsylvania. It was also New Jersey, Delaware, most of Maryland, and as much of New York State as had not been annexed by New England or was not ruled by the great city. Pennsylvania was the last of the great settlements—the most numerous and powerful of them all. Here in this lovely middle region of the Atlantic coast, bounded on the north by the Hudson, and on the south by the Potomac, the American nation really began—began not as a colony of one country or another, but as a deliberate complex of oppressed peoples of all nations, an asylum for the world, a new nation conceived in liberty and dedicated to the proposition not only that men are created equal, but that they may live in peace together if they want to.

This new state was founded to prove that the utmost of personal liberty for each is quite consistent with the utmost liberty on the part of the other fellow. Into the quiet towns of Pennsylvania, into the beautiful cultivated green countryside, they wrote large one motto: Peace on earth and good will to men. To this day the funny little groups speaking a kind of German gibberish, the queer people coming to market in their quaint bonnets—the Mennonites, the Amish—stand as a living proof that you may differ from your neighbor in every respect —speak a different language, wear a different kind of coat, and worship a different God in a different church—and yet, if he has good will, and you have good will, you may all live happily together, and the fabric of common life be the richer for your difference. In this they set the pattern of the great complex of many peoples which was to become the United States of America.

2

William Penn, the founder of Pennsylvania, was a sunny-hearted English gentleman who belonged to the executive classes in England, and had the genius of those classes for compromise. His mother was a Dutchwoman. Always in close touch with Holland, Penn had also inherited opinions about America set in circulation, if not by the great Dutch patroon De Vries, at least by Dutchmen of his generous and liberal colonial outlook. William Penn's father was a compromiser before him, but not, like William, a noble one. He had been an admiral in Cromwell's navy, but only lukewarm, and had so furthered the cause of Charles that when that merry monarch returned to the throne, he took Admiral Penn into high favor and showed his good will, like the grand gentleman he was, by borrowing from him some £18,000. Young William Penn, growing up between Cromwell and Charles II, looked around for more congenial society, and discovered the Society of Friends.

The Society of Friends wanted to outlaw war, and to stop

all persecution of opinion. Let every man think just what he pleased and behave as he pleased in all intimate and minor details, provided he did not interfere with his neighbors. Since the ex-feudal gentleman was the main nuisance of the time, let us, said the Friends, be just as different from this fellow as possible. He gives everybody fancy titles. We will call no man by any title except "friend," and then we will try to act like a friend. He bows and scrapes and addresses even his wife in public by the formal pronoun *you*. We will speak simply and intimately to all men, as we do in our own households, and use the heartfelt pronouns *thy* and *thee*. For English, in those days, had two pronouns, one for private and affectionate address, and one for formal use, as French and German still have. The plural form has conquered in English, and is now used as the simple second person. But in those days the Friends thought this business of speaking of yourself and your friends in the plural was ridiculous. It was part of the gentleman's inflated notion of life—to be swelling up like that and pretending he was not a person but a whole company. All this has so completely passed out of our life that we have forgotten that it was once important.

Continuing the process of being different from the feudal gentleman, the Friends would wear no gold lace and fine feathers, but their clothes would be warm, dignified, well made, and comfortable, and their linen would be white. They would drink no toasts, but their food would be good and all friends welcome to their excellent board. They would have comfortable, well-furnished houses, plenty of heat, plenty of water, but would degrade no man in servitude or slavery to provide them. They did not care about vast landholdings or a great show of wealth, but they wanted the security of a little saved cash and the peace of owing no debts. They would not fight, but they would work. For idle and silly amusements, they would substitute reading and study and a sober interest in arts. For exhausting social routs, balls, dances, card parties they would substitute entertainment at home and in the family circle, and membership in clubs and associations devoted to learning or the arts or cooperation in social effort. We need no books or documents to tell us that this was what the Friends wanted out of life, for they wrote all their tastes and ideals into the city of Philadelphia, and there one may still read them, in the secure, seemly, cultured life of the city.

The Friends were by no means alone in their opinions. Various groups were coming to the same general conclusions. This was the beginning of what we call bourgeois civilization, and differed in practically every respect from the feudal civilization preceding it. For their eminently sensible opinions the Friends spent much of their time in prison and some of the rest of the time sitting in the stocks. With them to prison went young William Penn. This distressed his worldly old father. It was not quite a fashionable proceeding for a young man who had entrée to the court of Charles II. But Penn stuck to the Friends, and his father continued to show that he, a least, had a proper appreciation of a king's friendship by lending His Majesty more money. Gradually William Penn became the acknowledged leader of the English Friends, and proceeded in statesmanlike style to lay plans for removing all men who wanted peace with liberty from the neighborhood of the feudal gentleman and his idleness, pretenses, brawls, and schemes for robbing the industrious.

As an agent for the English Friends, Penn began to purchase land in what is now New Jersey, and so came into control of much of that territory. But the more he learned about New Jersey the more he realized that the finest stretch of the Atlantic coast was still unappropriated to the southward—the lovely, rolling, wooded land, broken up in the east by rivers and inlets from the sea, rising into valleys and mountains as you went westward. A rich land, a genial flowering land, neither too warm nor too cold, and abundantly watered with rain from Heaven and streams from the mountains. When he came up the Delaware River and saw those low green shores shimmering in the misty sunshine, and the bland waters widening to the sea, he said, "What a noble place for serving God!"

Here and there between the Hudson and the Potomac this wilderness had been made an asylum. The policy of tolerance enunciated by the Dutch in New Amsterdam had been continued among the outlying suburbs of New York, and Germans, Swedes, and Dutch were seeping into northern New Jersey, and living in peace together. A colony of Swedes on the Delaware River, forming the nucleus of what is now the little state of Delaware, had set up a neat, thrifty, friendly life and a policy of getting along amiably with the Indians. They welcomed Penn on his visits and would be glad to cooperate with him. Southward along the Potomac River, the valiant little colony of Maryland, under the liberal leadership of Lord Baltimore, had established an asylum for Catholics, and then opened this sanctuary to persecuted English Puritans who were not wanted in Virginia, and had passed an edict of general religious toleration in 1649, the first of its kind in the New World.

Penn, observing these amiable settlements, and seeing how much good farmland rolled away, still unoccupied, knew that he had found a place for people he had been worrying about for ten years. For in 1671 he had gone on a missionary tour through the distressed areas of Europe, seeking out worn and beaten little bands of Protestants, victims of the Thirty Years' War, preaching cooperation with men of good will of all nations, and offering them the friendship of others in like case. Now he could offer them more than good words.

His chance came with the death of his father. The old admiral's estate showed a large debt owing him from the king, which His Majesty, being a true feudal gentleman, could not pay. So Penn suggested that, instead, the king give him all this unoccupied land in America. With the beautiful generosity of his kind, Charles II gave Penn not only the unappropriated land but the territories which he had already given to Lord Baltimore, including most of Maryland and all of Delaware, which was in Lord Baltimore's grant. This later led to much troublesome litigation between the Penn and Baltimore families.

The boundary was finally fixed years afterward by two English surveyors, Mason and Dixon, who drew between the two estates a line which was destined to become of great historic importance as the boundary between slavery and free labor. By this the Baltimore interests got much the worst of the bargain. Maryland barely retained her entity, and Delaware cut loose and became a little province on her own. New Jersey, also, of which Penn had bought large sections, was later separately organized as a province. But the whole region remained culturally one, warmed by the sun of loving kindness from Philadelphia and imitating the Philadelphia patterns of life, even to the building of houses in long low blocks with *stoeps*, and feeling new lifeblood pumped into its veins by the vigorous heart of life in that great city.

3

Having obtained his woods, Penn immediately planned his city—the city of Brotherly Love—and built into its outward form all his notions of a good life, laying it out in rectangles, with streets intersecting at angles of ninety degrees. This plan, so often imitated since in new cities and new sections of old cities, was then an innovation. But Penn loved a straight line and a well-proportioned space. They were outward and visible signs of order and good government. Most of the streets were, for that time, generously wide, but between the wider streets ran narrower ones on which the houses of the poorer people might front. The theory of this was that the richer man, having the poorer man's troubles right under his nose, might be disposed to help him—that propinquity would break down class distinctions, and bring people together as neighbors; and that self-interest alone would make the richer man unwilling that a house so near him should degenerate into a slum. This plan has been followed in the capital city of Washington, where the alleys, largely inhabited by Negroes, run between wide and fashionable thoroughfares. This somewhat dubious arrangement has not prevented a great degeneration of life in the alleys, but it has the merit of distributing the slums and making them the concern of everybody. But William Penn expected to have no slums in his city. There would be only a seemly variation of wealth among men who all lived comfortably above the poverty line, and in neighborly communion.

These streets of Philadelphia were planted with shade trees, which had also their symbolical meaning for Penn. They stood for rest and tranquillity, for sober retirement, and meditative perambulation. "It is the still, the quiet, the religious life which must be exalted over all," he wrote. "The humble, meek, merciful, just, poor and devout souls and everywhere of one religion; and when Death has taken off the mask, they will know one another, though the divers liveries they wear here make them strangers." . . . "Oh how sweet is the quiet of these parts," he wrote, "freed from the anxious and troublesome solicitations, hurries, and perplexities of woeful Europe." More than a century after its founding, a European visitor found in Philadelphia just what Penn had tried to build into it. "What a comfortable place is this city of Penn. How is Philadelphia adorned with neatness and with peace. How do her in-dwellers linger about her good things, and strangers delight in her rectangles!"

This rectangular town between the rivers, with its tree-shaded avenues, was for nearly a century so unusual that people constantly mentioned it, as they might the Pyramids or the Hanging Gardens of Babylon. And if there is any student of Latin now in Penn's great city who wants to hear how/very much like some ancient wonder of the world, in some far-off classical age of gold, his metropolis may sound, let him read Thomas Makin's "Description of Pennsylvania," published in 1729.

> Pulchra duos inter sita stat Philadelphia rivos;
> Inter quos duo sunt millia longa viae.
> Delawar his major, Sculkil minor ille vocatur;

Indis et Suevis notus uterque diu.
Hic plateas mensor spatiis delineat aequis,
Et domui recto est ordine juncta domus.

This was Englished by Robert Proud thus, though without
adequately translating the most characteristic line of all: *Et
domui recto ordine juncta domus.*

Fair Philadelphia next is rising seen
Between two rivers placed, two miles between;
The Delaware and Sculkil, new to fame,
Both beauteous streams, yet of a modern name.
The city formed upon a beauteous plan,
Has many houses built, though late began;
Rectangular the streets, direct and fair;
And rectilinear all the ranges are.

The patterns of social life to be established in his territory
Penn described in a style as mellow as a ripe apple. Few states
have had such beautiful documents. "Government," he writes,
"seems to me a part of religion itself, a thing sacred in its institution and its end. Government is as capable of kindness, goodness, and charity, as a more private society." Government is
free to the people under it, "whatever its name, where the laws
rule and the people are a party to those laws." But he reminds
his colonists that no laws can be better than the men who administer them. "Though good laws do well, good men do better." As for himself, as proprietor, he promises his people that
they shall have laws of their own making, and live "a free, and
if you will a sober and industrious people." He himself will
comply with "whatever free men can reasonably desire for the
improvement of their own happiness."

To the Indians he announced that the new colonists "desire
to enjoy this country with your love and consent that we may
live together as neighbors and friends; else what would the
great God do to us who hath made us not to . . . destroy one
another, but to live soberly and kindly together in the world.
Now I would have you well observe that I am very sensible

of the unkindness and injustice that hath been too much exercised toward you by the people of these parts of the world, who have sought . . . to make great advantages by you rather than to be an example of justice and goodness unto you, which I hear hath been a matter of trouble to you, and caused you great grudgings and animosities, sometimes the shedding of blood that hath made the great God angry. I am not like them nor the people I send."

So Penn made a treaty with the Indians, in that famous pipe-smoking ceremony under the great elm which Benjamin West has painted and which remained the proudest tradition of Philadelphia.

4

Penn meanwhile had been busy gathering up the humble, meek, poor, just, and devout souls who are everywhere of one religion and transporting them to his woods. German, Swiss, Dutch, Welsh, Dunkers and Dumplers, Amish, Mennonites— all were welcome in Pennsylvania, and as fast as new sects developed among the troubled people of Europe a home was found for them in the New World. They might dress as they pleased, talk as they pleased, worship as they pleased, and teach their own children as they pleased. All that was asked was that they be willing to dwell together in peace in a land where no one would be hindered in "any conscientious practice."

So the poor, the meek, the humble, and the just came flocking. Penn had thousands of Germans sheltered in tents outside of London, and transporting them to Pennsylvania gave them a chance to start there again "with nothing but their bare hands." He sent over a "ship-load of first cousins" from Wales who settled the towns of Paoli and Radnor and gave the Welsh name to Bryn Mawr, and furnished the nation with one of its most picturesque characters—mad Anthony Wayne. Several notable Americans are of the mixed German-Welsh strain— among them William Dean Howells, and Lizette Woodworth Reese, the poet. Penn's friend, Pastorius, a lawyer of Frankfort,

Germany, bought a large tract of land and transported some intelligent Germans to Germantown, near Philadelphia, among them a number of weavers. Over his first home in the New World Pastorius put an inscription: "A small house, but friendly to the good. Depart, ye profane," "which," he says, "when Penn saw, he burst out laughing, but told me to go on building."

As in all times of social disorder, the greatest difficulty in Europe was that those who could and would work had not the opportunity. Artisans' skill and professional learning were going to waste. Small farmers in Germany, who, having little land, had learned to make the most of it by introducing those intensive methods of farming not so necessary on the large estates, had been ruthlessly robbed of their acres. All this artisan and agricultural skill Penn gathered in.

And now, for the first time, the land was authoritatively possessed, as the New Englanders possessed the sea. No more clinging to the riverbanks. These people made roads, and then they made wagons to run on the roads. In the heyday of its development the Yankee clipper was fittingly matched by the Conestoga wagons of these German farmers which ended their days far from Pennsylvania—the "Carriers of Empire." The Pennsylvania farmers first made the settlement of the West possible by showing people how really to live away from the water fronts, and how to use the good earth without despoiling it.

As the woods of Pennsylvania burst into green pastures full of fat cattle, neatly fenced and trimmed woodlots, great barns bulging with hay and grain, kitchen gardens raising more kinds of vegetables than anyone ever heard of; as people saw the blue-eyed and flaxen-haired German girls bouncing to market on their white-hooded market wagons, and rumors of cheeses and butter of their making ran up and down the coast, all the other colonies began to compete for these remarkable people. Lord Baltimore, feeling his colony to be a rather anemic affair against this lusty new baby to the north, promptly offered them lands. They moved in and built the city of Frederick—still one of the most quaintly charming of their creations—with its blocks of houses in all the pastel colors—blue, pink, yellow, orchid—strung ribbon-like along the streets, and the general air of thrift and good order, of things built a long time ago and kept in excellent repair ever since. They filled up western Maryland and laid a solid foundation for Baltimore.

Later George Washington, planning to settle the country that is now Ohio, wrote to a friend in Philadelphia asking him how the country of Penn obtained these Dutch people. Apparently thinking they were Hollanders, he wished to know how he should go about it to advertise in Rotterdam and other Dutch ports his willingness to make good terms for them in Ohio.

The Germans and their farms and settlements long continued to be one of the sights of the New World. Kipling speaks of the land "back of Philadelphia among the German towns, Lancaster way. Little houses and bursting big barns, fat cattle, fat women, and all as peaceful as Heaven might be if they farmed there." People laughed at their quaint English. When the round-faced girl answered the door and said, "Oh, did you bell? It didn't make," how was one to know that she meant, "Did you ring? It made no sound." As they spread westward, always marching in a solid phalanx of families, carrying a schoolmaster and a pastor and their musical instruments, their fame spread with them. An early observer reports: "They study to be quiet and mind their own business, speak a most amusing mixture of English and German, keep the Yankees out of their borders as well as they may . . . always build a bakehouse just before the door; eat sausages, sauerkraut, and biscuits; rejoice in baked meats and sweetmeats; and make fortunes in every part of the Union by the exercise of their gift for sugar baking and their skill in confectionery. . . . They supply the Philadelphia market with the richest produce of the farm, erect huge signposts before their little inns, exhibiting most egregious portraits of Lafayette and Solomon, larger than life;

and certainly are, with all their oddities, the staff and pride of their beautiful state."

Doctor Benjamin Rush of Philadelphia, in 1787, went through the German farming district and described its methods as an example to all other Americans. What particularly charmed him about the very high state of well-being and financial security was that it was attained, as in New England, with almost no hired labor, through the joint and happy labors of the various members of the family, which seemed to him a very good argument against birth control. "Upon the birth of a son, they exult in the gift of a ploughman or a waggoner. Upon the birth of a daughter, they rejoice in the addition of another milkmaid or spinster to the family. Happy state of human society. What blessings can civilization confer that can atone for the extinction of the ancient, patriarchal pleasure of raising up a numerous and healthy family of children to labor for their parents, for themselves and for their country and finally to partake of the knowledge and the happiness thus annexed to existence. The joy of parents in the birth of a child is the echo of creating goodness."

5

The skilled labor which Penn had brought to his country made some very practical contributions to the better life. One of these was the Philadelphia water supply. No city had been so well provided with water since the Romans turned the mountain streams loose in Rome to bring pure drinking water and to carry away sewage. Strangers laughed to see housewives and housemaids out early in the morning, scrubbing down the white front steps, and thriftily dumping the scrub water on the little square beds where petunias glistened. But there was admiration and envy in the laugh.

Another contribution was food. The market in Philadelphia was one of the wonders of the age, with its vegetables and dairy products. Up to this time the American idea of garden produce was that of the English who, says a wag, have three vegetables—cabbage, cabbage, and more cabbage. But the Germans introduced the lady in the kitchen to cucumbers, peas, beans, carrots, chives, and greens. All visitors made haste to go to market. They liked to buy brown crocks of butter from the rosy-cheeked German girls, and pumpernickel bread and different cheeses.

A third contribution was heat. Till then heat had been furnished by open fireplaces which ate up wood, burned your face, and froze your back. The Germans, however, brought stoves to Pennsylvania, and what this meant is lyrically described by Doctor Benjamin Rush. No more feeding and stoking the fire every minute. The wood in great green chunks burned for hours, and when the stove was closed might last all night. You didn't have to run back a dozen times during a single task to warm your frozen fingers. Stoves furnished much more heat and used much less wood. On the farms the men relieved from the endless drawing of wood had time to tinker with their houses, mend their farm machinery, and put up shelves in the pantry for the wife. Some people, however, retained a sentimental attachment for the open fire. These Benjamin Franklin satisfied, in helpful Yankee fashion, with the Franklin stove, which could be closed up and burn like any stove or, opened up, cheerfully blaze like a fireplace.

6

The Quakers and the Germans by no means confined their contributions to the good life to material comfort. Quaint little centers of the higher life and learning were also springing up all over Pennsylvania. There was the little monastic community of Ephrata near Lancaster, where white-robed brothers and sisters lived as Protestant monks and nuns, and cultivated prayer, science, and music. One traveler tells of the singing there—of the "small, sweet, shrill voices of women" which thrilled him to his very soul, and of the "pale faces and white garments" of the brothers and sisters which made them look like spirits. Several of the brothers were well-known characters

in the intellectual circles of Philadelphia. Brother Jabetz of
Ephrata later translated the Declaration of Independence into
seven languages. He was a scientist, and used to walk eighty
miles into Philadelphia to attend the meetings of the Philosophical Society founded by Benjamin Franklin.

One of the sweetest centers of the higher life was that of
the Moravians at Bethlehem. For Penn's great example later
drew to his land one of the most charming characters of the
next century, Count Zinzendorf, a German nobleman, born
in Dresden, who, in the next generation, dedicated high position and wealth to finding out and rehabilitating the various
groups of religious and social liberals who had been driven into
cruel poverty in the long struggle between Catholicism and
Protestantism, between aristocracy and democracy, between
the vested interests of large landowners and the rising indus-
trialism of Europe. On his own lands he gave a new start to the
ancient church of the Waldenses, whose persistence and long
persecution is one of the melancholy romances of Protestantism, and built a village as a home for the wandering followers
of John Huss from Moravia. Finally he had a large group of
people convinced and rehabilitated, with a communal discipline developed in a simple, practical way as a means of living
together on his estates, but founded not in monastic but in
family ideals. And now he was ready to send his Moravians
forth to other lands to make asylums for other Christian
radicals.

The obvious place to turn to was Penn's colony. So hither
he came in 1741 and settled the town of Bethlehem, which he
named for the birthplace of Christ, and in which, in the first
solitary log cabin of the settlement, he kept vigil through the
frosts of a Christmas night. In the Moravian community he
founded there, goods and services were in common; the young
men were provided with wives by casting lots among the
eligible maidens; and the girls received a higher education
than was yet available elsewhere. The old Moravian seminary
for girls at Bethlehem still carries on, and has some claims to

being the first women's college of America. These Moravians were a pleasant and cheerful body of people, and they cultivated literature and music and made an attractive center which intellectual and liberal people of all sorts liked to visit. Benjamin Franklin describes them in his *Autobiography*.

The influence of the Moravians on liberal and intellectual men outside their fold had, in one case, a far-reaching consequence. In 1736, a few years before Count Zinzendorf's own visit to Bethlehem, John Wesley came to the philanthropic colony which General Oglethorpe had recently founded in Georgia. On the boat he met some Moravians, and gained from them, as he tells us, a conception of possible warmth and depth of Christian feeling till then unknown to him. The memory of the transfigured faces of these brethren stayed with him. Later, in London, he met Peter Boehler who had been ordained by Count Zinzendorf to carry his message to North Carolina, and he was again convinced that, in comparison with these people, he lacked the "faith by which alone we are saved." Pondering on the release and gladness these Moravians had found, "about a quarter of nine, on May 24, 1738," while attending a religious meeting in London, "I felt my heart strangely warmed. I did trust in Christ, Christ alone, for salvation, and an assurance was given me that He had taken away my sins, even mine, and saved me from the law of sin and death." The conviction which thus flashed upon "one of the most powerful and active intellects in England," says Lecky, "is the source of English Methodism," and, one might add, of its greater American branch, which was to become the typical church of the frontier and one of its greatest civilizing agencies.

The founding of ideal communities in Pennsylvania continued into the nineteenth century. One of the later successful communities was that of George Rapp, in Butler County, Pennsylvania, founded in 1805. After a most prosperous start in a community called Harmony, it was so annoyed by unsympathetic neighbors that it removed in 1814 to a tract of 30,000 acres in the then wilderness of Indiana. While the Rap-

from the Nantucket Quakers, he was the quintessence of the Yankee, salted and toughened by the brine of the sea, without even a glimmering of the metaphysical poetry of the Puritans. Coming to Philadelphia as a lad, with the most valid of Yankee intentions—that of bettering himself—he sauntered into the town chewing on a roll of bread, followed some quiet, well-dressed people into a Quaker meetinghouse and went to sleep there, and so began the greatest intellectual and civic career of colonial America. He lived the best part of the century in the town of his choice, and left it sprouting with institutions of his sowing—the Philadelphia Library, the fire companies, the Philosophical Society, the University of Pennsylvania, and the *Saturday Evening Post*. Its social life and civic striving he immortalized along with himself in his *Autobiography*, the one great literary production of colonial America.

The remarkable personality of Franklin was achieved by putting a smooth Pennsylvania varnish on a Massachusetts base. Adopting the unworldly manners of the Friends, he made them the instrument of the most consummate worldliness. "I learned," he said, "the impropriety of presenting one's self as the proposer of any useful project, that might be supposed to raise one's reputation in the smallest degree above that of one's neighbors, when one has need of their assistance to accomplish this project. I therefore put myself as much as possible out of sight and stated it as a scheme of a number of friends. . . . In this way my affair went more smoothly, and I ever after practiced it on such occasions, and from my frequent successes can heartily recommend it."

Similarly in conversation he learned, "to forbear all direct contradiction to the sentiments of others, and all positive assertion of my own." As a young tradesman he established his credit by bettering the grave appearance of the Quaker brethren. "I took care not only to be in reality industrious and frugal, but to avoid all appearances to the contrary. I dressed plainly. I was seen at no places of idle diversion. I never went out fishing or shooting. A book, indeed, sometimes debauched me from my work, but that was seldom, snug, and gave no scandal, and, to show that I was not above my business, I sometimes brought home the paper I purchased at the stores through the streets on a wheelbarrow. Thus being esteemed an industrious, thriving young man, and paying duly for what I bought, the merchants who imported stationery solicited my custom; others proposed supplying me with books, and I went on swimmingly." Covering thus the Yankee wisdom of the serpent with the Quaker plumage of the dove, he acquired a skill in getting just what he wanted, in any circumstances, which few men before or since have equaled, and which he later made of the greatest public service.

His own quaint personality as a young tradesman distilling wisdom, Yankee fashion, from humble practical employments, Franklin dramatized under the name of Poor Richard. Poor Richard's conclusions about life he sprinkled in bits of printing through the dates in the almanac which he published. Many of these sayings have passed into common speech: God helps them that help themselves; A stitch in time saves nine; Early to bed and early to rise makes a man healthy, wealthy, and wise; Many a little makes a mickle; Experience keeps a dear school, but fools will learn in no other. They have the very accent of folk wisdom, as if they should be as old and nameless in origin as the mother tongue itself.

He loved to devise schemes for self-improvement, turning his Yankee inventiveness loose in the Pennsylvania realm of pure virtue. So he made a plan for practicing thirteen moral virtues, a different one each week, and checking up his progress in them each day, keeping grades for himself in a class book, like a teacher. His choice of virtues is as interesting as his mechanics of moral progress. They are: temperance, silence, order, resolution, frugality, industry, sincerity, justice, moderation, cleanliness, tranquillity, chastity, humility. It is a long list and William Penn would have approved it. But imagine a cavalier trying to shop at this counter for the furnishings of a gentleman! Where are honor, courtesy, mag-

nanimity? Where are those virtues which Charleston passed
like a wand down the generations—gentleness, hospitality,
loyalty to one's own?

It is said that when the great-great-granddaughter of Benjamin Franklin applied for admission to one of the women's
patriotic societies on the strength of her ancestry, she was refused because the "ancestor in question was not a gentleman."
Whatever the good ladies may have meant by that, it is undoubtedly true that, in the conventional sense, Benjamin
Franklin neither was nor wished to be a gentleman. Born to
the virtues and wisdom of the artisan and small tradesman
class, the ever-widening experience of one of the greatest
minds of his century never showed him the slightest reason
for departing from them. The more he saw of kings' courts,
fine gentlemen and fine ladies, the more easily and serenely,
with his tongue in his cheek and a twinkle in his eye, he settled
back into the life pattern of Poor Richard. And when he appeared in Europe, with his grave deportment, his bland, non-
committal speech, his plain dress, his social success in salons
and drawing rooms was almost incredible. Hostesses competed
for his presence in their parties; the great belles of high life
turned down their lovers for the sake of sitting next to the old
man and holding his hand; pretty girls kissed him; great scien-
tists consulted him; literary men acclaimed both his speech and
his writings; and Edmund Burke, observing with amusement
how he twisted interlocutors in the House of Commons around
his fingers, remarked that he made them all look like school-
boys.

Why then should be put himself out to be more than an
honest tradesman's son? And so he records suavely: "My
father having among his instructions to me when a boy, frequently repeated a proverb of Solomon, 'Seest thou a man
diligent in his calling, he shall stand before kings, he shall not
stand before mean men,' I from thence considered industry
as a means of obtaining wealth and distinction, which encouraged me, though I did not think that I should ever literally

stand before kings, which however has since happened; for I have stood before five, and even had the honor of sitting down with one, the King of Denmark, to dinner."

9

This prosperous paradise of people who didn't want to be gentlemen was bounded north and south by two of the American orders of professional gentry—the great manor families of New York and the tidewater gentlemen of Virginia and the Maryland eastern shore. The only other gentlemen by profession in America were the caciques of Charleston. Any gentleman's blood that came to New England was quietly absorbed into the rich and ruddy stream of self-respecting working-people's life. But as Philadelphia grew rich, there was a considerable migration thither of rank and money. Aristocrats settled here and there in New Jersey, making a continuous line of "polite society" between New York and Philadelphia. Some settled in Delaware and Maryland.

Valiant little Maryland had a hard time making up its mind whether it wanted to be a social colony of Philadelphia or of Virginia. It ended by conceding one city to the pattern of Philadelphia and the other to Virginia. Annapolis, the capital, was a charming replica of Williamsburg. There, in the bare, bright blue light of the sea, stood square mansions of red brick, with square open rooms, white carved woodwork, and fine stairways. Set high on little eminences wherever possible, with gardens sloping away from them, they had the openness and visible dignity, the social showmanship of the South. But Baltimore, with a solid base of German industry and money under it, acting as a center for westward expansion, was built like Philadelphia in blocks of identical houses, with *stoeps* in front and gardens in enclosures behind; and it cultivated industry and intellect while Annapolis cultivated politics and manners.

From north and south, and from Europe, culture converged on Philadelphia, and from the ever-expanding back blocks came in richer and richer streams the wherewithal to make it flourish. The city grew fashionable despite the Quakers. The witty, the clever, and the modish would come there and be happy in their own way. As the city which was opening the West, mixing all creeds and peoples, it was the most truly American. When the first rumbles of discontent with Great Britain began to draw the colonies together, it was natural both from its midway position and its predominant importance that it should become the administrative center for the Revolution.

Washington's sense of style, and that of his two favorite young aides, Alexander Hamilton and the Marquis de Lafayette, gave to Philadelphia for almost a generation a social pattern of dignity and hospitality, of suitable and adequate appearance which, superimposed upon the Quaker base, set the standard of the new republic. And the Declaration of Independence, the sittings of the Continental Congress, and the position of the city as the first capital, covered the roads between New York and Philadelphia, and between Philadelphia and Virginia, with a fine network of legend and story. Here bourgeois civilization blossomed out in chivalry and adventure and put on all the panoply of state, and the hero of peaceful political assemblies has his exploits as dashingly recorded as the hero of arms. Hence many legends and one spirited ballad tell of the desperate ride of Caesar Rodney, one of the Delaware delegates to the Continental Congress, whose arrival broke the tie in his state delegation and caused its vote to be cast in favor of the Declaration of Independence.

> Ho, saddle the black, I've but half a day
> And Congress sits eighty miles away,
> But I'll be in time, if God gives me grace,
> To shake my fist in King George's face,
> It is five and the beams of the western sun
> Tinge the spires of Wilmington gold and dun;
> Six and the dust of the Chester street
> Flies like a cloud from his courser's feet;

It is seven; the horse-boat, broad of beam,
At the Schuylkill ferry crawls over the stream,
And at seven fifteen by the Rittenhouse clock
He flings his rein to the tavern jock.

The Congress is met, the debate's begun,
And liberty lags for the vote of one,
When into the hall not a moment late
Walks Caesar Rodney, the delegate.

Not a moment late, and that half day's ride
Forwards the world with a mighty stride
For the act was passed ere the midnight stroke
O'er the Quaker City its echoes woke.
At Tyranny's feet was the gauntlet flung;
We are free. All the bells through the colonies rung,
And the sons of the free may recall with pride
The day of Delegate Rodney's ride.

—ELBRIDGE STREETER BROOKS

An immense number of social records survives from the Revolution in Philadelphia. They reflect a gay, polished, youthfully clever and exuberant life—smart speech, graceful manners, decorative dress, gracious and comfortable domestic procedures. Here during the Revolution Philip Freneau wrote pretty and elegant verse. Here Thomas Paine, imported from England by Benjamin Franklin, published his vigorous and powerful pamphlet *Common Sense*. Here dozens of bright journalists wielded clever pens in defense of the colonies, and dozens of young ladies wrote sprightly verses and letters.

One of these young ladies was Anne Boudinot, whose father was president of the Continental Congress. Another was the half sister of young Lawrence whose dying words, "Don't give up the ship," rudely sewn on blue bunting as the banner of Perry's flagship, now hang in state in the great hall in Annapolis. His half sister Elizabeth wrote of this young hero:

My brave, brave Jim's a sailor Jack
Upon the treacherous sea,

> A sailor who loves poetry,
> All taught to him by me.

Elizabeth, who called herself Madame Scriblerus, wrote some verses for her friend, Peggy Chew, who was invited to supper in the city and, when she got there, found that her hostess had to recall the invitation.

> Just in from the country, with nothing to wear,
> At Bingham's to-night I am bidden repair.
> My one silken pelisse is all in a tangle,
> And I know I have lost my Parisian bangle;
> Not a whiff of hair-powder to light up my head.
> Methinks 'twould be better to get into bed.
> My slippers the parrot has quite eaten up.
> Oh, why am I bidden to come in and sup?
> Now, Rebecca, do try to make that child stop its wailing,
> At the thought of the company, my courage is failing
> There's a chair going past, and a coach with a clatter.
> If I go as I am, pray what does it matter?
> Here, give me some Rose-bloom, to ease up my face,
> And a patch on my chin would give it a grace
> My new brilliant necklace, my white turkey wrapping—
>
> A word from the Bingham's—you say a postponement?
> An illness—alas, tis a hurried atonement,
> With nothing to wear, and nothing to eat,
> Come blow out the candles, and gaze on the street!

During the long and anxious period when the British held Philadelphia and New York, and Washington's army shuttled back and forth between the two cities, the young people of the whole district incorrigibly enjoyed themselves. A vivid record of balls, parties, escapades, and romances of all sorts clings about the old Revolutionary mansions between the Hudson and the Delaware. To the eye of the young, the Revolutionary soldiers on the highways were romantic figures. "As I walked on the road leading from Princeton to Trenton, alone, for I ever loved solitary rambles," wrote William Dunlop, American painter and playwright, "ascending a hill suddenly appeared a group of cavaliers, mounting and gaining the summit in my front. The clear autumnal sky behind them equally relieved the dark uniforms, the buff lacings, and the glittering appendages. All were gallantly mounted. All were tall and graceful, but one towered above the rest, and I doubted not an instant that I saw the beloved hero. I lifted my hat as I saw that his eye was turned to me, and instantly every hat was raised, and every eye fixed on me.

"They passed on, and I turned and gazed as at a passing vision. I had seen him. All through my life, used to the pride and pomp and circumstance of glorious war, to the gay and gallant Englishman, the tartaned Scot, and the embroidered German of every military grade, I still think that old blue and buff of Washington and his aides, their cocked hats worn sidelong, with the union cockade, the whole equipment as seen at that moment was the most martial thing I ever saw."

10

During the Revolution the English-German-Swedish-Welsh-Scotch-Irish mixture of this brotherly middle region was further improved by some contributions from France. The most famous of the French exponents of the better life for all was a stocky one-eyed Frenchman from Bordeaux named Stephen Girard, who ran his little ship "L'Aimable Louise" past the British blockade of Delaware Bay in May, 1776, and sold his vessel and settled down to keep shop on Water Street. He was then twenty-six, and loaded with debts to Bordeaux merchants who had financed his first unsuccessful voyage. Like most of the creators of the excellent life of Pennsylvania, his whole theory of living was formed by suffering. In struggling to unwind himself from the ropes of debt, he developed business techniques which made him one of the two richest men in America—the German-American merchant of New York, Astor, being the other. From trading with the West Indies he expanded his operations around the world till he became one of the greatest of the China and East India traders, sending his ships out to all the ports of the Orient. But never again, in all his vast business operations, did he undertake anything on credit. Every single one of his many investments was made out of cash in hand, with every possible loss discounted ahead of time.

In struggling to get out of debt, he turned his keen realistic mind to every means of creating wealth. He studied agriculture and later established an experimental farm. He bought great tracts of anthracite coal land in northeastern Pennsylvania, foreseeing the great development of the use of coal as wood became less plentiful. A man of intense feelings and passionate resentments, he turned his continual flame of anger at these creditors in Bordeaux into new study and thought about wealth and the way in which it could be wrung from the earth and the desires and needs of men. Stephen Simpson, his first and not always flattering biographer, says of the knowledge he thus squeezed out of want and humiliation: "No man, perhaps, ever possessed so great and perfect a genius for trade and commerce as Stephen Girard." He speaks of "that sound penetration, and various knowledge of the products of the countries and the state of the markets; the seasons and climates of various nations, which constitute what may be termed, the mental chart of the intelligent, talented, and liberal merchant; combined with a constant observation of the political and domestic situation of countries, and their international relations, as they tend to influence their pacific or belligerent attitude towards one another."

His keen and independent mind, struggling with all the disadvantages of a not very attractive physical presence, of poverty, of comparatively slight education, and of being a foreigner, he nourished almost exclusively on the radical literature on which those who were tired of the feudal gentleman were feeding themselves in France preparatory to systematically taking off the heads of those gentlemen at the guillotine two decades later. Of his simple library of 150 books, half were books by Voltaire. Later he named his ships after the radical philosophers of France, launching "The Voltaire," in 1796, "The Rousseau" in 1801, "The Montesquieu" in 1806.

While the poor young man was fiercely working his way out of debt, he married a lovely girl, named Mary Lum. After eight years of happiness, the poor lady's mind became affected, and she quickly lapsed into hopeless insanity. "I do truly pity the frightful state I imagine you to be in," wrote his brother Jean to Stephen, "above all knowing the regard and love you bear your wife," adding, "I should presume that the grief which this lovely woman has always shown to me at having no children is the cause of her misfortune, to which it is necessary to be resigned as to the will of God."

Living out his life in a house that was "childless and worse than wifeless," the intense and passionate Frenchman, with his clear realistic mind, did a great deal of fierce thinking about human suffering and about the stupidity of people who ought to alleviate it. Turning this way and that in his suffering and finding no help outside himself, he came to despise doctors and priests and preachers with equal energy. So out of the independent and eccentric businessman was forged the independent and eccentric philanthropist.

When yellow fever broke out in Philadelphia in 1793, this independence rose to heights of heroism which have been celebrated ever since in the annals of the city. Fiercely protesting that the deaths and suffering were greatly increased by the panic of doctors, and the inhumanity of those who fled from the sick, he undertook to nurse the sufferers himself and stay well in the process. To one of the excited refugees from the city in Princeton, Girard wrote: "Believe me when I say that by leading a regular life it is quite possible to live here in good health." Assisted by Peter Helm, a German who volunteered to do all that he did, Girard put the sick in the old mansion once occupied by Alexander Hamilton. And for sixty days he performed both day and night the tasks of receiving, nursing, and caring for the sick. Into houses whence all the family had fled, he would go and himself carry out the sick in his own arms. In

the absence of nurses, he performed the lowliest personal services for the patients, comforted them in their last hours, and
himself wrapped them in shrouds and carried them out to the
burial. To his Marseilles correspondent he wrote: "A malig-
nant fever which has prevailed here for the last month, added
to the ignorance of the doctors and the fright of our people,
has carried off more than 4,000 of our friends. . . . The few
inhabitants who have the courage to remain have established a
hospital at a short distance from the city for the reception of
the unfortunate victims. I am an active director of this hospital,
and my duties . . . give me a great deal to do."

Stephen Girard wound up this work by making a careful,
businesslike report on the hospital and on conditions in the
poorer sections of the city and suggestions for opening and
cleansing houses shut up during the plague. The mayor summoned the citizens of Philadelphia and surrounding towns to
hear the report, and to appoint a committee to prepare a statement expressive of the "cordial, grateful, and fraternal thanks
of the citizens." Thus did Stephen Girard, the somber, one-
eyed Frenchman, step into the limelight in the city of good
will and there he stayed till he died, full of riches, years, and
honors.

At the outbreak of the War of 1812, when the United States
treasury was practically bankrupt, and the response of the
public to the loan which the government tried to raise was
very disappointing, Girard called on John Jacob Astor to join
with him in taking over the whole of the unsubscribed portion
of the loan. For this Girard subscribed practically his whole
fortune, but his bank, the Girard Bank of Philadelphia, subsequently marketed part of it among small investors. Thus was
the federal government enabled to fight the war.

During the whole period between the French Revolution
and the overthrow of Napoleon in 1815, Girard drew to Philadelphia many French *émigrés*, entertaining them at his home,
giving them advice on business activities and investments in the
new world, and helping to settle them in New Jersey, Pennsyl-

vania and Delaware. One of these was Joseph Bonaparte, Napoleon's brother, King of Naples and later King of Spain, whom as Comte de Survilliers, he established at Bordentown, New Jersey. One of the *émigrés* of this time was Pierre Samuel du Pont de Nemours, French political economist and statesman, the friend of Jefferson, who became the founder of the du Pont family in this country. During the old regime he had been something of a liberal and had made wise suggestions for reforming the French monarchy. But during the Revolution he allied himself more and more with the conservatives, and, barely escaping the guillotine, established at Wilmington, Delaware, one of the great dynasties of "economic royalists."

Though Stephen Girard's great wealth and influence was helping to settle the region of good will with some late blooming sprigs of the old feudal gentry from France, he himself remained as plain a protestor against show and idleness as any Quaker in the land. He lived severely; he dressed plainly; and he worked continuously and furiously—work being his one anodyne for lifelong pain and regret. Because he had no home and children, he thought continually of educating young people. And when he died it was found that most of his fortune had been left to found a home and school for the orphan children of Philadelphia which continues to this day as Girard College. His will provided that "the orphans admitted to this college shall be fed plain but wholesome food, clothed with plain but decent apparel (no distinctive dress ever to be worn) and lodged in a plain but safe manner. Due regard shall be paid to their health, and to this end their persons and clothes shall be kept clean, and they shall have suitable and rational exercise and recreation. . . . I would have them taught facts and things, rather than words or signs. And especially I desire that, by every proper means, a pure attachment to our republican institutions and to the sacred rights of conscience as guaranteed by our happy institutions shall be formed and fostered in the minds of the scholars. . . . To enjoin and require that no ecclesiastic, missionary, or minister of any sect whatsoever shall ever hold or exercise any station or duty whatever in the said college, nor shall any such person ever be admitted for any purpose, or as a visitor, within the premises appropriated for the purposes of said college. . . . My desire is that the instructors and teachers in the college shall take pains to instil into the minds of the scholars the *purest principles of morality*, so that, on their entrance into active life, they may, from inclination and habit, evince benevolence towards their fellow citizens, and a love of truth, sobriety, and industry, adopting at the same time such religious tenets as their matured reason may enable them to prefer."

Along with this bequest went a number of bequests for improving conditions to which he had always objected in Philadelphia. One of these bequests was to enable the citizens "to pull down and remove all wooden buildings, as well as those made . . . of other combustible materials . . . that are erected within the limits of the city of Philadelphia and also to prohibit the erection of such buildings within the said city's limits at any future time." He also left money to hire policemen "really suited to the purpose" and to improve the looks of the city and diminish the burden of taxation "now most oppressive especially on those who are least able to bear it."

This will, which enabled him to say his last words on a number of subjects, was contested by members of the Girard family, to whom he had been very generous in his lifetime, and this contest was supported by the outraged sentiment of many churches. Finally it even came before the Supreme Court of the United States. Because of the wealth involved and the personality of Girard, the greatest legal talent was massed on both sides, and the speeches in this case have become legal and even literary classics. Webster argued for three days for the breaking of the will in what he termed a "defense of Christianity against the inroads of paganism and infidelity." Of the speech by Horace Binney in behalf of the will, Mr. Justice Strong of the Supreme Court said: "The remembrance of it lingers around the courtroom until this day. It is in print and has ever been the wonder and the admiration of the legal profession in this country, and almost equally of the profession in Great Britain. It lifted the law of charities out of the depths of obscurity and confusion that covered it before, and while the fullness of its research and the strength of its reasoning were masterly, it was clothed with a precision and beauty of language never surpassed." The Supreme Court decided that the will should stand, since "there is nothing in the devise establishing the College, or in the regulations and restrictions contained therein, which are inconsistent with the Christian religion or are opposed to any known policy of the state of Pennsylvania."

Though, in the course of this great battle, Girard's name was pretty well blackened by the churches, who looked on the exclusion of clergy from the school as an insult to them, the great Frenchman was probably innocent of any real intent to offend. He thought he was simply fulfilling the original ideal of Pennsylvania. His friend William Duane, speaking before the Pennsylvania House of Representatives in 1842, said: "Mr. Girard in speaking of his will always had the most beneficent view—he thought that it would regenerate Pennsylvania and the states around it." Girard believed that his educational ideas would realize in Pennsylvania the success of that "holy experiment" which William Penn came to establish in the New World. But true to the original objections of the founders of Pennsylvania, he said that he did not want to enrich any of his own family with his wealth. "No man," he said, "shall be a gentleman on my money!"

A strange, intense, tragic man. Life was hard on him. His passionate reaction to injustice was intensified by a bleak realism of mind, which interposed no illusions between him and pain. But few men ever won greater triumph out of misfortune, or felt a profounder gratitude to the country whose blessed institutions enabled him to do so. The dominant man of Philadelphia in her greatest days of glory, when she was the gateway to the opening West, the mistress of the China seas, center of learning and culture, wealthiest town on the Atlantic seaboard, he poured back his wealth in gratitude into the good soil which had enabled even him, stricken as he was, to grow and bear so rich a burden of his stormy-colored blooms and bitter-sweet, nourishing fruit.

6

CHIEFS OF
THE MOUNTAIN BORDER

DOWN the mountain border from Pennsylvania into Georgia, between those lovely flowering slopes of rhododendron, azalea, and laurel, the Scotch-Irish chieftains come riding into the American story, early in the eighteenth century. Chieftains one must call them, for that was a race in which every man was chief, and his stout conviction that he himself was king and army, judge and executioner, teacher and priest, for himself and in his own right, was to have a potent effect in shaping the American democracy.

The immense importance of the Scotch-Irish migration during the later colonial period, beginning in the early decades of the eighteenth century and continuing through the Revolution and into the next century, has often been overlooked in the popular histories because they did not happen to form one colony. Instead they took the western half of two colonies—Pennsylvania and Virginia—and most of a third, North Carolina, and then reached down and put a backbone into the weak but well-intentioned settlement of Georgia. And while no one was looking, they dipped over the mountains during the Revolution, and turned up immediately afterward, having peopled and organized two new states, Kentucky and Tennessee. Incidentally they provided the country with its two greatest presidents between Washington and Lincoln—Andrew Jackson, and, by a stretch of the epic Scotch-Irish imagination, Jefferson—gave the institution of slavery its brains and leadership in the person of John C. Calhoun, the frontier its favorite hero in Kit Carson, and the South its toughest fighting strength during the Civil War, and its best generalship, after Lee, in Stonewall Jackson and Joseph E. Johnston, and the North its match for them in Grant. After all this, there was still executive capacity left in the race to survive into the present century and make President Woodrow Wilson. An incomparable people when they happened to fight on the right side, but able to bring more logic, pertinacity, and moral idealism to the wrong side of a matter than any people that ever were.

Like all the more potent groups of early American immigrants, the Scotch-Irish were, when they arrived on these shores, a highly selected group, with a definite pattern of the good life. Properly speaking, they were neither Scotch nor Irish—that is, they were not Celts. They were mainly descendants of Scandinavian freebooters, Saxon adventurers, and others of a strongly Nordic type, who had settled on the western coast of Scotland and spread eastward into the lowlands. When James I took possession of northern Ireland and opened it for settlement to the Scotch and English colonists, they moved thither, but after a century found themselves at loggerheads with the British government because of unjust tariffs on their woolen industries. In vain they reminded the crown that they had "saved Ireland for the British." They got no redress, and burning with indignation, they began to set sail for America, and to pour in by clans and regiments through the port of Philadelphia. The number of these immigrants has been estimated to have been as high as 200,000. In any case, they were probably the largest single group of colonial immigrants outside the English of New England. Their preponderant influence on the frontier was a matter of numbers as well as of personality.

Finding lands preempted to the eastward, the Scotch-Irish pressed on to the mountain borders of Pennsylvania, and then southward through the valleys. On their way they dropped off preachers, teachers, and capitalists, all along the line. The preachers were, of course, Presbyterian. At a time when New England Calvinism was fading into Congregationalism and soon to be watered down into Unitarianism, the Scotch-Irish brought in some of the original vintage, and poured it, among other places, into the veins of Princeton University.

Princeton had been founded by Aaron Burr, son-in-law of Jonathan Edwards, and father of the polished gentleman who later killed Alexander Hamilton. Burr had moved seventy boys under his tutelage in Newark, New Jersey, down into the wilderness to keep them away from "promiscuous converse with the world, the theater of dissipation and folly." So Princeton developed, as someone said, as a town "more remarkable for its college than its learning." But Calvinism in these parts was an alien plant, far from home, crowded by the more fashionable New Jersey Episcopalians and by Quakers in Philadelphia, and by all manner of odd German sects. Looking around for something that seemed to them even remotely godly amidst such a collection of heathenish doctrines and practices, the Scotch-Irish found the slender sprig of Presbyterian learning at Princeton and began to nurse, prune, and water it.

As for their capitalists, like all harassed people, forced to live among aliens and buy their way out of trouble, they had some among them who knew the great value of saved cash. As it happened, the mountain borders to which they turned were rich in minerals. The little rills of capital they began to turn into them ultimately swelled into a mighty flood and became the great iron and coal industry, and they themselves were the backbone and lifeblood of a roaring industrial city that grew up in the west, at the head of the Ohio River, and became Pittsburgh. By the time they reached the borders of Virginia, they began to take to themselves the true Scotchmen who were coming in by way of Richmond. Since Virginian tobacco had been carried mainly to the Scotch port of Glasgow, it was natural that Scotchmen should come back with the ships. Many of them had settled in Richmond, and made there a prosperous, highly literate block of people, clannish as ants and proud as Lucifer. One of these families reared Edgar Allan Poe as an adopted son. These commercial Scotch were different in looks and type, and even in racial origin from the Scotch-Irish, but they had a certain amount of Scottish tradition in common. Less numerous than the Scotch-Irish, and not like them lordly and all-conquering in personality, they merged with them and became to all intents and purposes one people. When the Scotch-Irish got farther south, in the Carolinas, they encountered the Irish who were coming in by the way of Charleston, and similarly annexed them. All along the coast, from New Jersey to Florida, these good Calvinists also picked up, as mates for their own beaux and damsels, large numbers of French Calvinists called Huguenots.

The Scotch-Irish way of annexing kindred spirits, on the basis of Calvinism or Scotch or Irish origin, is illustrated in their habit of claiming Jefferson as one of them. Jefferson grew up on the Scotch-Irish frontier, went to school to a Scotchman, and was undoubtedly shaped by the social outlook of his neighborhood. Though the Jeffersons were said to have migrated from Wales to Virginia, the Scotch-Irish never forgot that, on his mother's side, through the Randolphs, Thomas was related to the great Scotch family of the Murrays. Of this family Jefferson said, "They trace their pedigrees far back in England and Scotland, to which let each person ascribe what faith and merit he chooses." So the Scotch-Irish regarded Jefferson as their president, and carried Jeffersonian democracy westward, till they found in Andrew Jackson a leader of the truly authentic breed.

From all of which it may be seen that the American Scotch-Irishman, when he reached his full bloom on some plantation in the bluegrass region of Kentucky or the flowering valleys of North Carolina, was considerably more than an Ulster Irishman. His personality was expanded by the American frontier and softened by the Southern sunshine, and probably he had had a French grandmother.

2

The pattern of the good life which the Scotch-Irish brought to this country and imposed as perhaps the leading idea of the Western frontier may be described as a theory of personality. In their wanderings and their battles they had arrived at the conclusions the Greeks had apparently arrived at long ago when, as a small body of newcomers, they had to make a place for themselves on the edge of the Orient. Being few they had to make one Greek worth twenty-five Orientals. So the Scotch-Irishman seems to have determined that just one of him should be worth a whole battalion of anybody else. It was a fierce determination. It went hissing down the baby's throat with his mother's milk. Andrew Jackson set his five-year-old foster son on a horse. When the horse ran away, Jackson proudly reported that the child clung to him for half a mile, and "never even hollered." Jackson's mother, bringing up her boy just before the American Revolution, told him never to go to law for redress of slander and personal grievance or ask anybody's assistance in his troubles. "Andy, settle them things yourself." Certain maxims circulated among the Scotch-Irish and were repeated to the children on all occasions: Let every tub stand on its own bottom; Fear God and take your own part; Right is Right, and Wrong is Wrong, and Right Wrong is *Nobody*.

Puritans as they were, their less godly members were also adept in the cavalier dissipations and never let any sprig of feudalism put anything over on them. This person the Scotch-Irishman would deal with by coolly beating him at his own vices. He would outswear him, outride him, outshoot him, outdrink him, and then win all his money away from him at cards. The amount of whisky some of them could drink was equaled only by their reputation for holding it, but they were in the main a temperate people, lean and hard, despising corpulency and all that was soft and luxurious.

Their preoccupations were love and war. Some said they fought just for love of it—"They would rather fight than eat." But this was not really so. The more primitive of them had inherited from the wild Scottish and Irish frontiers, and perhaps even from barbaric Scandinavia, the idea of the blood feud, and brought it to America where it still persists among their less cultured descendants in the mountain country. Their wilder spirits were too quick on the trigger and helped to keep the duel alive in the South long after it should have died. But the more advanced and cultivated among them were never ones to volunteer for war just for the glory of it. In many ways they were shrewd and canny and ready to keep out of trouble and save their own skins. Except where their particular system of principles was touched, they were generous, easygoing, and peaceable to a fault. But they were people whose emotions had been simplified by racial experience to a small number of intense loves and hates. They loved God, honor, country, and glorious woman. They hated cheats, liars, poltroons, scandalmongers, and people who lived on somebody else. They fought for honor, personal freedom, for justice to the underdog, for hatred of liars and cheats, and for love. And when they fought, they made history. Jackson, meeting Dickinson in a duel, felt the bullet strike him and thought that he was killed, but he coolly cocked his pistol and shot. He walked away victorious, his opponent dead, a ball in his own breast, and his boot full of blood. When they cried, "The ball is in your breast, Sir," he replied, "I'd have hit him if it was in my brain!"

But Jackson's fights were for the honor of the woman he loved. "God! Do you speak her sacred name?" he cried, when Sevier made a sidelong reference to Rachel in the course of a political squabble. Though Sevier was governor of Tennessee and Jackson was justice of the Supreme Court of the state, he held up all public business while he hounded, tormented, and publicly shamed Sevier out of the state and to the frontier where, despite the Tennessee law against dueling, they could fight it out man to man. Later during his presidency, when his young friend Peggy Eaton, the "gorgeous hussy," was gossiped about among the wives of his official family, he forced the resignation of the whole cabinet.

This Scotch-Irish attitude to women set the standard for the frontier. Prizing a woman less as a housekeeper and a mother than as a companion and a sweetheart, the Scotch-Irishman set a high value on what we should call "sex appeal." He liked a lady who "makes your blood race, Sir," but he required her to be able to fence with all comers, keeping herself inviolably at her own disposal. For such a lady his sword was always out. He pooh-poohed merely conventional appearances against her, judged her with a swift appraising eye, and, when sure that she was what he called "straight," was ready to hang to the nearest tree the first person who opened his mouth against her. Personal love was to him the one valid reason for marriage, and personal love of the most intense and romantic variety he could and did keep till death. This idea of personal love as the basis for marriage was not so common then as now. Even such advanced people as the Moravians looked askance at it, and thought that parents should arrange for the marriage of their children or even choose wives for them by casting lots among suitable maidens, thus letting God decide the issue. But personal love was one of those things that the Scotch-Irishman referred to as "sacred." Against it even parents had no claim. This idea persists to the point of absurdity in the Kentucky and Tennessee mountains, where the marriage of a nine-year-old girl was justified by her mother, who said, "If they love each other, they ought to marry." Spreading westward, making among these dramatic people the poetry and story of the frontier, the Scotch-Irish ideal had a potent effect in shaping the American idea of "romance" in marriage, and the validity of divorce where romance has failed.

The Scotch-Irish belief in the sacredness and potency of

personality was reflected in certain traits of looks and bearing which were assiduously cultivated among them. "No other people," said one observer, "have so much presence." Presence was not only born in them and enhanced by standards of mutual selection in marriage, it was artificially developed as one of the elements of their very simple but effective personal culture. The presence of the Scotch-Irishman depended on two things—his high, erect bearing and his flashing eye. Tradition was that mothers laced their children up to boards to make them stand and walk like that. The pictures of Andrew Jackson show the characteristic bearing. It is more than an erect posture. It has a curious tension of will in it, a straightness of spirit stretching the body higher than the bones and ligaments will go.

As for the eye, there are many traditions about the Scotch-Irish glance. An early observer of these people in the western part of Scotland comments that they have "blue eyes but much brighter than the English." Actually light in color, sometimes a pale gray, the typical Scotch-Irish eye was not remarkable in physical configuration. Its power was the concentration of will and emotion it conveyed. One constantly hears of their "blazing glance," the "steely piercing look," the "look that strikes men cold." Andrew Jackson was called by the Indians "Hawk Eye," and many attempts were made to describe his most effective use of his eye in quelling disorder or compelling obedience. Calhoun's eyes were similarly described. When he leaped to his feet in the Senate, it was said that his pale quivering face and burning eyes forced immediate silence. Harriet Martineau, describing Calhoun, as "that cast-iron man who looks as if he had never been born and never could be extinguished," speaks of "his splendid eye." She also mentions the "stern brow," and the "inflexible mouth." "It is one of the most remarkable heads in the country." "His moments of softness in his family," she says, "are as touching as tears on the face of a soldier." When these intense and dramatic people, including the parents of Andrew Jackson and of Calhoun, began to spread southward along the mountain borders, a new chapter in colonial history began. They were princes of the common man, aristocrats of the masses. Their belief in personality led to the most absolute democracy. Man just as man, without learning, without property, without opportunity, had in himself all potentialities. Alone he could fight an army. Ignorant he could at any age learn anything he had to know. And to this absolute democracy they brought a leadership which had all the glamor of chivalry and the bearing of kings. Coming to America with a grudge against the British crown, they were always potential leaders of rebellion. From the first their backs were to the seacoast and their faces to the west.

3

When the Scotch-Irish began to come down from Pennsylvania through the Shenandoah Valley, both western Virginia and the mountains of North Carolina between the tidewater baronies and the rice country of the Charleston caciques were already a refuge for Englishmen who had been crowded out of the larger acreages and were not friendly to government by aristocrats of the lowlands and lace-rimmed officials from overseas. The great legend of the Virginia frontier was Bacon's Rebellion. In 1676 Nathaniel Bacon, who was kin to the great Francis Bacon, had applied to Governor Berkeley for a commission to protect himself and his neighbors from the Indians. Not receiving the commission, he "in some elated and passionate expressions swore that, commission or no commission, the next man or woman he heard of who was killed by the Indians, he would go out against them, though but twenty should adventure the service with him." "Now it so unhappily fell out that the next person the Indians did kill was one of his own family. Whereupon, having got together some seventy or ninety persons, good housekeepers, well armed," Bacon cleaned up the Indians and embarked on a long struggle with the governor for the legalization of these proceedings.

The struggle went on and became a full-fledged rebellion,

"the people of Virginia" joining Bacon in accusing the governor not only of criminal ignorance of frontier necessities, but of "unjust taxes to enrich his own favorites," of disgracing magistracies by advancing scandalous and ignorant persons, of assuming monopoly of the beaver trade, and of emboldening the Indians against His Majesty's subjects. When at one time the governor besieged Bacon in a stockade, Bacon made a sally and captured the wives of his opponents, and had each one of his men advance to battle with the wife of one of the enemy marching before him. "The poor gentlewomen," we are informed, "were mightily astonished at this project." The enemy thought it "no less wonderful that their innocent and harmless wives should thus be entered as the white guard to the devil," for "this action was a method in warfare they were not well acquainted with." So, says the chronicler, "these ladies' white aprons were a greater force to protect him than his very inadequate earthworks," and whatever the cause, the "enemy kept their swords in their scabbards." This mighty quarrel was ended only by the death of Bacon, who was forthwith celebrated in a variety of classical epitaphs of which this may be taken as a sample:

> Death, why so cruel? What! No other way
> To manifest thy spleen, but thus to slay
> Our hopes of safety, liberty, our all,
> Which through thy tyranny with him must fall.

But, like John Brown, his soul went marching on, and when the Scotch-Irish began to come down the great valley, they were only too happy to fall in behind it.

North Carolina, meanwhile, had become a refuge for independent Englishmen and small groups of other self-respecting people—Huguenots near the Trent River and Swiss at New Bern—who wished not large lands but safe freeholds, and felt secure under the shadow of the hills. Early in the eighteenth century William Byrd, riding through the mountains, laying the dividing line between Virginia and North Carolina, was a little chagrined to find how many people did not want to live in Virginia. "Some borderers, too, had a great mind to know where the line would come out, being for the most part apprehensive lest their lands be taken into Virginia. In that case they must have submitted to some kind of order and government whereas in North Carolina everyone does what he pleases. . . . The men, for their part, just like the Indians, impose all the work on the poor women. They make their wives rise out of their beds early in the morning, at the same time that they lie and snore till the sun has risen one-third of his course and dispelled the unwholesome damps. Then after stretching and yawning for half an hour, they light their pipes and under a protection of a cloud of smoke venture out into the open air, though if it happens to be never so little cold they quickly return shivering to the chimney corner. When the weather is mild, they stand leaning with their arms on the corn-field fence, and gravely consider whether they had best take a small heat at the hoe, but generally find reason to put it off till another time. Thus they loiter their lives away like Solomon's sluggard with their arms across, and at the end of the year scarcely have bread to eat. To speak the truth, it is a thorough-going aversion to labor that makes people file off to North Carolina where plenty and warm sun confirm them in their disposition to laziness for their whole lives."

But he adds, "This much, however, may be said for the inhabitants of Edenton; that not a soul has the least taint of superstition or hypocrisy, acting very frankly and above board in all their excesses. Provisions here are extremely cheap and extremely good, so that people may live plentifully at trifling expense. Nothing is dear but law, physic, and strong drink, and the last they get with so much difficulty that they are never guilty of the sin of letting it sour on their hands."

Though it was included in the grant of Carolina to the founders, this northern section had never been interesting to the tidewater and low-country type of gentleman. Of one beautiful section, Byrd remarked that it would be a valuable tract of land in any country but North Carolina, where "for want of navigation and commerce the best estate affords little more than a coarse subsistence." For their part the first settlers or squatters in this country were anxious to keep out the big landowners, and favored grants of no more than 640 acres. This was enough for the Scotch-Irishmen, and by 1730 they had settled on the Eno, Ham, and Catawba rivers, in Bladen, Cumberland, Robeson, Richmond, Scotland, Harnett, and other counties, not gathering in villages but settling separately on large farms, mainly worked by themselves and their kinfolk, but helped out by some Negro slaves.

Hitherto the North Carolinians had got along nicely without either education or religion. The only exceptions to the habit of man to adore his Maker known to William Byrd were, he says, "the Hottentots on the Cape of Good Hope and the people of North Carolina." Back in Pennsylvania where the Scotch-Irish had started their Southern march, Presbyterian synods and Quaker and German groups began to hear of this heathenish condition, and preachers and teachers followed fast behind the galloping hoofs of the new border chiefs. Presbyterian ministers set up churches; Count Zinzendorf sent a group of Moravians; and Quakers stole in gravely, one by one. As for learning, the Scotch-Irish imported that from Princeton. "Princeton College had more to do with educating North Carolina than all other forces combined."

So civilization took root in the mountains of North Carolina. This increase in population and enterprise was recognized by cutting it off from South Carolina in 1752 and making it a separate province. Life became comfortable and picturesque on these North Carolina farms, anticipating some of the quality of Kentucky and Tennessee, simpler than in tidewater Virginia, but more dashing and dramatic. Among the border gentry were the various MacDowells, handsome men and magnetic, great hunters, and breeders of thoroughbred horses. There was also the numerous clan of Johnstons. Of the old

Johnston House at Edenton it has been said that "Not even Drayton Hall on the Ashley, near Charleston, nor splendid Hampton near Baltimore nor Livingston Manor on the Hudson nor Rosewell on the York speaks more gloriously of home refinement in the olden time, nor looks down more eloquently on the shining waters."

"Most of the plantations naturally have a very noble and beautiful prospect," wrote John Brickell, who practiced medicine in Edenton in 1737 and published a *Natural History of North Carolina*. From the farmhouses, one may, he says, "see large and spacious rivers and creeks abounding with variety of fish and fowl, as also pleasant and delightful savannas or meadows with their green liveries, interwoven with various kinds of beautiful and most glorious colors and fragrant odors in the several seasons, and fenced in with pleasant groves of the fine tulip tree, laurel, and bays, equalizing the oak for bigness and growth." It is, he says, "a sweet, moderate, and healthful climate to live in all manner of plenty . . . there being few housekeepers but what live decently and give away more provisions to guests that come to see them than they expend among their own families."

While they were thus settling the back country, building houses on "noble eminences" and planting the flower gardens which make fragrant the traditions of the state, the North Carolinians had to get rid of pirates on their coast. One of these persons who appeared with the pretext of selling slaves to the new plantations is celebrated in a ditty which may be found in *Ballads of Courageous Carolinians*, published at Raleigh in 1914.

BLACKBEARD, THE PIRATE

> He had thirteen loving spouses
> To share his earthly joys.
> He had several hundred daughters
> And ninety little boys.

And when within the nursery
　　These brats began to cry,
He'd start out on a voyage
　　In a ship he didn't buy.

He raised his sable standard
　　Beside the Spanish main,
Then scuttled twenty galleons
　　And started North again.
In bleak New England's waters
　　He rode before the gale
And for the coast of Africa
　　Put forth his dreaded sail.

Along the sands of Guinea
　　He went in search of gold,
And came off with some natives
　　Stored snugly in the hold.
When he was home again, he said
　　He'd sell his human goods
To planters in the Albemarle
　　In Carolina's woods.

But the North Carolinians were not impressed with his offering and instead,

High on a mast his head they kept
　　A warning sad and dire,
While all his little children wept
　　To lose their noble sire,
And all his winsome widows, too,
　　With grief would nearly choke,
When thinking of their lover true
　　Who died at Ocracoke.

4

Meanwhile the planters liked less and less the officers whom
the king was sending over to rule them. Disaffection was
spreading in all the colonies, but here in the mountains they
dealt with their problems in simple and highhanded ways. So

the mountain planters banded together in an association called "the Regulators" for self-protection against the "wrongs of public officers." The idea originated in the peaceful head of a Quaker preacher named Hermann Husbands, but in the hands of Scotch-Irishmen with rifles it was soon headed on a very un-Quakerlike course. As the Regulators grew in numbers and menacing organization, Governor Tryon formed an army in the eastern part of the state and marched out to subdue them. On May 16, 1771, this army of 1,100 men met the Regulators at Alamance in the county of Orange, and routed them in a fierce and bloody fight. Thereupon groups of the Regulators led by John Robertson moved over the mountains and joined with a few settlers there to set up a state of their own called the Watauga Settlement, and in 1772 established there a "Tribunal of Notables" to govern them.

This little state in the woods went along through the Revolution, and in 1783, at the end of the war, when North Carolina ceded her western lands to Congress, announced that as for them, they were ceded to nobody. They were the completely independent state of Franklin, and so they continued until they were ultimately tied into the Union as Tennessee.

The mountain border had been seething and sizzling ever since the Battle of Alamance, and when news of the Battle of Lexington reached them, they leaped to full, free, and unconditional independence. In a tumultuous meeting at Mecklenburg, on May 20, 1775, it was voted that "We, the citizens of Mecklenburg, do hereby dissolve the political bands which have connected us with the mother country, and absolve ourselves from all allegiance to the British Crown, abjuring all political connection with a nation that has wantonly trampled on our rights and liberties and inhumanly shed the innocent blood of Americans at Lexington."

And so, we are told,

> The hero shout flew on the breeze,
> Rushed from the mountains to the seas,

Till all the land uprose,
Their faces to their foes,
Shook off the thralldom they so long had borne,
And swore the oath that Mecklenburg had sworn.

On the principle that it takes the devil to fight the devil, the British organized a company of Scotchmen, including some Scotch Tories from the mountains, to fight these Scotch-Irish rebels, and the Revolutionary War was henceforth carried on in these parts with all the individual prowess of a Scotch ballad. Paul Hamilton Hayne, the South Carolina poet, thus celebrates Macdonald's raid.

In a thrice we were mounted. Macdonald's tall form
Seated firm in his saddle, his face like a storm,
When the clouds of Ben Lomond hang heavy and stark,
And the red veins of lightning pulse through the dark.
His left hand on his sword belt, his right lifted high.
With a prick from the spurred heel, a touch from the knee,
His lithe Arab was off like an eagle awing.
Hah, Death to the red-coats, and down with the King!

In the battle of King's Mountain the North Carolinians gave heart to the Revolutionary cause at a time when heart was desperately needed. And in the long retreat of the North Carolinians before Cornwallis across the mountains, under the leadership of Colonel Campbell of Virginia, they helped to end the war.

5

The Revolution over, North Carolina prepared to cultivate the graces of home. So at least it was announced at the time, in some verses by young Governor Burke to a young lady.

No more shall dread apprehension affright
Our soldiers by day, and assassins by night;
Secure, bright, and cheerful our days shall now prove
And our nights know no tumults but transports of love.

To make home delightful henceforth be our care,
With delicate ease the feast to prepare,
To converse with variety, freedom, and ease,
And, with elegant novelty, always to please.

When mothers, to rear the young heroes to fame
And infuse the true spark of the future bright flame,
To deck the young virgins with graces refined,
And embellish with sense and good humor the mind.

Something like this must have been the ideal of various homes set up by officers of the Revolution in North Carolina. There was, for example, the home of General Lenvier in the "Happy Valley," twenty miles from the source of the Yadkin River. Like most of the places in this lovely climate it was overgrown with flowers. Years after when it was but a ghost of itself, it was reported that "The old sun-dial still stood in the middle of the garden, surrounded by sweet fringed pinks and camomile. Dark old spruces still stand. Tulips, jonquils, crocuses, hyacinths, snow-drops still come up."

The old Williams House at Panther Creek was described in 1860 as resembling some of the splendid old baronial possessions in England. "The forest of oak, pine, cedar, and chestnut formed a complete circle, leaving an open space of about ten acres in the midst of which stood the mansion, a neat and antiquated looking building which was commenced before the Revolution and finished after its close—almost entirely hid fom view by wide-branched oaks, which flung their gnarled arms over a thick carpet of the most delicious greensward. On our left as we approached the mansion from the large gate of the outside enclosure is a meadow of tall waving grass, and on the right is a lovely flower garden environed by a beautiful juniper hedge."

The life of these old plantations is preserved in reminiscences of Major Hinton's place, where Johnson, the uncle of the Andrew Johnson who afterward became president of the United States, was employed to superintend the weaving women. One is told of "lavender scented linen and spotless napery, gardens full of roses, jonquils, hyacinths, crepe myrtles, syringa, lilacs, snow balls, sweet betsies, honey-suckles, and lavender, and herbs of tansy, rue, thyme, sage, mint." One is told of Major Hinton's slaves Blind Jim, totally sightless, who always saddled the riding horses and brought them to the door, Old Mingo and Mammy Kizzy, fresh from Africa, "Mammy Kizzy having been a princess in the dark continent and proved it by always wearing bouquets of fresh flowers in the holes in her ears." Mammy Kizzy was an expert dairymaid. There was also Jeffrey, who traded a horse belonging to his master for some green peas reputed to be of remarkable quality. When the peas were planted and proved to be up to specifications, Jeffrey was forgiven, and the peas were always afterward called "Jeffrey's peas." There was the old cook, who was sometimes drunk, but was tolerated because she knew so well how to prepare her master's spring dinner, which consisted of "boiled chicken, a bag pudding, and a bunch of lettuce leaves and mint, tied with a shalote and dipped in dressing."

Settling down in this mild flowery climate, under the shadow of the hills, the fierce democrats from the northernmost frontiers of Europe found some little peace and luck at last. Those who did made plantation life as lovely and poetic as it has ever been, employing slaves mainly as house servants and as individual field hands, not seriously degrading the idea of white labor, surrounded with comfort and noble mountain beauty but separated by circumstance from the opportunity for great wealth or servile exploitation. Much of the state remained of necessity poor and undeveloped, and many of the Scotch-Irish settlers were lost in the mountains and remained a primitive people, while others of an equally primitive type pressed on to the west. But the more prosperous Scotch-Irish section had its own peculiar charm, being as some said, the land "of the stiff backbone and the warm heart."

But mainly the border chiefs were a restless folk. Tennessee beckoned over the mountains, and Kentucky and Missouri beyond, and the illimitable West. For a generation after the Revolutionary War North Carolina, which seemed itself so sparsely settled, fed into the West a notable stream of pioneers. Completely without book learning, some of them were wise in the skills of the forest and in force of personality and native intelligence—such men as Daniel Boone and Davy Crockett, who became legendary heroes of the frontier, the focus of widespread myth and story. While North Carolina cannot claim Jackson and Calhoun, since they were born over the line in South Carolina, they, too, were sons of the Scotch-Irish border. With some education and opportunity they carried to the highest stage of public affairs the same atmosphere of the heroic, keeping through all the mudslinging of politics and the belittlement of journalistic report the bearing and speech of men born to make destiny and have only epics and sagas written about them.

7

GIVE ME LIBERTY,
OR GIVE ME DEATH

OME time between the year 1750 and the year 1760,
the United States of America was born. European
observers saw only a few British colonies, scattered up
and down the seacoast of a ragged and savage continent,
whose raw militia were helping the mother country to drive
out the French from the Mississippi Valley. But young men,
crude young riflemen, perched in trees and coolly picking off
the French and Indians that charged the helpless redcoats
below, lifted up their eyes, and wherever the smoke of battle
cleared away over the endless dark tide of forests beyond,
they saw—sudden and clear—a vision. A vision not of colonies, but a vast nation, an "asylum for the world," stretching
free, proud, and triumphant on and on to the "western ocean."
When they returned to their country villages, they talked
about it. Bold, high, clear the tide of conversation ran down
the coast, from mouth to mouth of young men.

There are several evidences of this conversation, but one is
particularly touching because it is directly addressed to us who
have inherited what they only dreamed of. Nathaniel Ames
in New England, publishing an *Almanac* in 1758, confides the
talk of the young men of his day to the hurrying year. "The

curious have observed that the progress of human literature like the sun is from east to west; that it has travelled through Asia and Europe and now is arrived at the eastern shore of America. . . . So the arts and sciences will change the face of nature in their tour from hence over the Appalachian mountains to the western ocean; and as they march through the vast desert, the residence of wild beasts will be broken up and the obscene howl cease for ever; instead of which the stones and trees will dance together in the music of Orpheus; the rocks will disclose their hidden gems; and the inestimable treasures of gold and silver be broken up. Huge mountains of iron ore are already discovered; and vast stores are reserved for future generations."

Then, speaking as if with a prescience of the railroad, steel, automobile, and electrical industries to come in the Middle West, he said: "This metal, more useful than gold and silver, will employ millions of hands, and not only to form the martial sword and peaceful share alternately, but an infinity of utensils improved in the exercise of art and handicraft among men. . . . Shall not then those vast quarries that team with mechanic stores—those for structure be piled into great cities, and those for sculpture into statues to perpetuate the honor of renowned heroes; even those who now save their country? Oh ye unborn inhabitants of America! Should this page escape its destined conflagration at the year's end, and these alphabetical letters remain legible—when your eyes behold the sun after he has rolled the seasons round for two or three centuries more, you will know that, in *Anno Domini 1758, we dreamed of your times.*"

The dream was shaping itself in the minds of a dozen able youths, in each according to his temperament. Young John Adams returning from a party in which, as he says, everyone talked politics, in the year 1755, sat down and wrote his musings on the subject to a friend, "if we remove the turbulent Gallics," he says, we Americans must inevitably spread westward, and "ultimately set up on our own." If we do not, we shall simply swallow the old country and make her an appendage to us. "In another century we shall have mastery of the sea, and be more numerous than England herself. . . . Not all the force of Europe will be able to subdue us." Years later he confessed that he always knew that the conflict with Great Britain was coming in his lifetime, and that it had been the shadow across his youth and early manhood, making all other beginnings tentative, throwing across his struggles to get started as a lawyer, across his marriage and the birth of his children, that ominous word "Until—" Washington, Jefferson, and hundreds of lesser but able boys must have felt the same way. It seems to have been a common opinion among the young men. The new nation must be made in their lifetime, and they were the ones that must toil and suffer and think through the making of it. To young John Adams it was not a pleasing prospect. He married a delightful girl. He had hopes of rising to a reasonable competency and honor in his profession. He preferred to be left in peace. Later this was always the burden of Washington's and Jefferson's words. They had beautiful homes. They prospered. They were happy in their families. Oh, to stay where they were!

For it was commonly said that the American colonies before the Revolutionary War were the happiest places in the world. There were no poor. There were only frontier people, living ruggedly and hopefully, expecting to be better off next year. Franklin visiting England was shocked beyond measure by conditions in the British Isles. Compared with European poor, he said, "every Indian is a gentleman." Visitors to America commented unceasingly on the fine dress; the use of tea and coffee among even the people of the farthest frontiers, not as a luxury as in Europe, but as a daily sociability and comfort; the universal use of carpets on the floors, so that even the poorest home had a cozy look. It was constantly noted that any workman "who has the use of his hands," could get land, set himself up as a proprietor, and in a few years not only support a growing family from the land but have a cash surplus which the "activity of their commerce" immediately converted into a thousand articles of use and luxury from all over the world. This was to raise a whole people to the level of landed aristocracy in Europe. Amidst such general well-being, the able and ambitious got much more. Almost any young man of gifts—such men as Adams and Jefferson and Washington and Franklin—by reasonable application could rise to wealth and honor and to the enjoyment of what French visitors during the American Revolution were amazed to see was really a "liberal and cultivated society."

2

Both the prosperity of America and the new sense of nationality had developed with the tremendous push inland of the German and Scotch-Irish migrations, supplemented by the expanding Yankee commerce. Taking the mountain valleys, which for the most part ran north and south, the newcomers distributed themselves longitudinally across the whole back of the existing provinces, making highways on which men from all the provinces went up and down, and little nests among the mountains where the sons and daughters of diverse comers married and made farms and towns. Even in New England, the tendency of the long Connecticut Valley was to take the New Englanders from their individualistic little seaport towns, separating them from their maritime preoccupations and mixing and mingling them to make a new people allied in type to the border farmers to the south.

Where the New England frontier ended, at the Hudson River, the German frontier began. After the peace of Utrecht in 1711 Protestant German bands, of the same type as those coming into Pennsylvania, had been granted land along the length of the Mohawk Valley—long called "the German Flats" —and spreading southward united with their German brethren coming up from Pennsylvania through the mountain valleys. Southward of the Germans, the Scotch-Irish took up the mountain border and continued to Georgia. This appearance

of a group here and a group there among the mountains gave
great fright to the French hunters and trappers in the Mississippi Valley beyond. When here and there a bronzed, bold face
began to look over the mountains and down into the Mississippi Valley, fright became panic.

One of these affrighting visages was that of young George
Washington. In 1748 a group of Virginians and Britons had
incorporated the Ohio Land Company and had been given
200,000 acres west of the Allegheny Mountains. One of these
incorporators was Lawrence Washington, elder brother of
George Washington; and young George got his first training
by going out with the surveying party to examine the new
territory. Soon the plans for settlement buzzing in Virginia
came to the ears of the French on the Great Lakes. They immediately sent a party down the Allegheny and Ohio rivers
to plant lead plates in the ground with inscriptions announcing that this was the property of the King of France. In the
angle between the Allegheny and Monongahela rivers at what
is now Pittsburgh, they then raised a French fort to challenge
the right of Americans to go farther. A mission to demand the
abandonment of this fort was the beginning of Washington's
public career.

The outcome of this excitement all along the mountain
line was the last French and Indian War, which ran along
parallel with the Seven Years' War in Europe, and ended with
the surrender by France of her right to all territory westward
of the colonies as far as the Mississippi River. In this war, the
British thought they were consolidating an empire, but the
colonists knew they were beginning a nation. They were
fighting for their right to spread westward now, together, as
one people and fill up the fertile valley. At first, they had
been a little timorous, and when the French unloosed the full
fury of Indian warfare on the western frontiers, they had
looked to Great Britain to protect them. Braddock, says
Franklin ironically, "was met with requests from the governors of Virginia, Maryland, and Pennsylvania that he would

post his troops on the frontiers so as to afford some protection to the inhabitants; but he continued his hasty march through all the country, not thinking him safe till he arrived at Philadelphia where the inhabitants could protect him. This whole transaction gave us Americans the first suspicion that our exalted ideas of the prowess of British regulars had not been well founded." Young Washington, seeing the horror of Indian war on the frontier, wrote: "The supplicating tears of the women and the moving petitions of the men melt me into such deadly sorrow that I solemnly declare that, if I know my own mind, I could offer myself a willing sacrifice to the butchering enemy, provided that would contribute to the people's ease." In the deadly sorrow of the eager young officer on the frontiers was tempered that cool steel blade of leadership which a quarter of a century later he held over the heads of the British in America.

So the colonists fought it out, made safe their frontiers as best they could behind their own rifles, and at Lake George in the north turned back the French with New Englanders under provincial leaders. And when the war was over, they made ready to saddle the old horse and move on to the West. The land was theirs. The line of advance was hallowed with the blood of their own slain.

Then the blow fell. Down the mountain frontier, just along the edge of the existing settlements, the British drew a line and announced that all land and territories lying to the "westward of the sources of the rivers which fall into the sea from the west and northwest are reserved under the sovereignty, protection, and dominance of the king." This line was called the Proclamation Line. The idea of the British government seems to have been that the area of settlement should not grow faster than it could be effectively controlled. But Americans looked shrewdly past these noble imperial objectives and said, "Pooh! They only want to keep it all for a parcel of fur traders." So they kept on walking westward across the Proclamation Line, and wondered where King George and all the pacifiers of the wilderness who were going to stop them were keeping themselves.

The British government then decided that the colonies, being obviously so rich, should help to pay for the late war. The Americans thought this was some more humbug. What it really meant was that a few commercial people were jealous of them and were trying to stifle their industries. Franklin, analyzing the *Causes of American Discontent*, says that the various taxes and impositions which the British now proceeded to lay "reflected how lightly the interest of all America had been estimated here when the interests of a few inhabitants of Great Britain happened to have the smallest competition with it. . . . Not only the interests of a particular body of merchants but the interests of any small body of British tradesmen or artificers has been found, they say, to outweigh that of all the King's subjects in the colonies. . . . It is of no importance to the common welfare of the empire whether a subject of the King's obtains his living by making hats on this or that side of the water. Yet the hatters of England have prevailed to obtain an act in their own favor restraining that manufacture in America. . . . In the same manner have a few nail makers and a still smaller body of steel makers (perhaps there are not a half dozen of these in England) prevailed totally to forbid by an act of Parliament the erection of slitting mills or steel furnaces in America."

3

The proposal that prosperous son should now help to pay off the mortgage on the old homestead was received with derision on the American side of the water. Peter St. John of Norwalk amused his friends with a rhymed report of the high British councils.

> These subtle arch-combiners
>   Addressed the British court;
> All three were undersigners
>   Of this obscure report—

There is a pleasant landscape
    That lieth far away
Beyond the wide Atlantic
    In North Amerikay.

There is a wealthy people
    Who sojourn in that land,
Their churches all with steeples
    Most delicately stand;
Their houses like the gilly
    Are painted red and gay;
They flourish like the lily
    In North Amerikay.

Their land with milk and honey
    Continually doth flow.
The want of food and money
    They seldom ever know;
They heap up golden treasure;
    They have no debts to pay;
They spend their time in pleasure
    In North Amerikay.

On turkeys, fowls, and fishes
    Most frequently they dine.
With gold and silver dishes
    Their tables always shine.
They crown their feasts with butter;
    They eat and rise to play;
In silks their ladies flutter
    In North Amerikay.

Peter St. John then goes on to say how the British Ministry decided that these rich people could very easily spare "The tenth of all their current" for the old folks at home. But this idea, he says, does not suit us here in "North Amerikay."

To what you have commanded
    We never will consent,
Although your troops are landed
    Upon our continent.

> We'll take our swords and muskets
> And march in dread array,
> And drive the British red-coats
> From North Amerikay.

This was very bright, but most of the American back talk to the British was bright. There is no more amusing literature in the history of statecraft than the early American pamphleteering.

The first suggestion of taxes brought some plain words from rich son to poor old extravagant mother. Of the national debt, James Otis said: "The colonists never occasioned its increase, nor ever reaped the sweet fruits of involving the finest country in the world in the sad calamity of an overgrown mortgage to state and stock jobbers." As for taxes, we must respectfully decline. We have no notion of paying for a lot of bribes, sinecures, and pensions for the further demoralization of old England!

As for the British protecting the colonists, the colonists all knew that they were protecting the British. If this foolish king still had an empire in America, it was because he still had some intelligent people here to look after the property. In 1767 Benjamin Franklin, in his examination before the House of Commons, said: "Numerous as are the people in the several provinces [meaning the thirteen original American colonies, as distinguished from the new provinces set up since 1763 at Quebec and in East and West Florida], they cost you nothing in forts, citadels, garrisons, or armies to keep them in subjection. They were governed by this country at the expense only of a little pen, ink, and paper." Later in a pamphlet addressed to His Majesty's Commissioners, Samuel Adams said: "If your excellencies mean by this to apply for offices in the department of our finance, I am to assure you that it will be necessary to procure very ample recommendations. For as the English have not yet pursued measures to discharge their own debt and raise the credit and value of their own paper circulation, but, on the contrary, are in a fair way to increase the one, and absolutely to destroy the other, you will instantly perceive that financiers from that nation would present themselves with the most awkward grace imaginable."

The literary brilliance with which the Americans were conducting their battle struck Europe with surprise. They were outthinking the best philosophers! They were outtalking the best literary men! Where did these Americans get their remarkable capacity for general ideas?

Several explanations were offered. John Quincy Adams, speaking for the New Englanders, said later that it was due to the training of the churches. The perpetual theological dispute had accustomed everyone to relate the smallest matter of personal conduct to vast cosmic propositions. And so he says, ideas developed on higher levels of thought were transferred to what might seem to others a mere pecuniary imposition. But general ideas also seemed to grow wild in Philadelphia, where Benjamin Franklin picked them up in youth and distributed them much improved in middle age among simple artisans and small tradesfolk. And they bloomed like magnolia trees on the Southern estates, fertilized by what appears to have been a fresh and vigorous reading of British law and discussion of the British constitution among gentlemen seeking guidance for a ruling class in a wild world.

Francis Hopkinson, of Philadelphia, writing during the Revolution, credits the brilliance of the Americans in this dispute to the training of the frontier. Saying that the whole trouble with the Americans is that the "best of kings" can't convince them that two and two make five, he compares American and British brains as follows: In Great Britain, he says, "a manufacturer [meaning a skilled workman] has been brought up to make pinheads; he has been at this business for forty years and of course makes pinheads with great dexterity; but he cannot make a whole pin for his life. He thinks it is the perfection of human nature to make pinheads. He leaves other matters to inferior abilities. It is enough for him that he believes in the Athanasian Creed, reverences the splendor of the court, and makes pinheads. This he conceives to be the sum total of religion, politics, and trade. . . . It is not so in America. The lowest tradesman there is not without some degree of general knowledge. They turn their hands to everything; their situation obliges them to do so. A farmer there cannot run to an artist upon every trifling occasion. He must make and mend and contrive for himself. This I observed in my travels throughout that country. In many towns and in every city they have public libraries. Not a tradesman but will find time to read. He acquires knowledge imperceptibly. He is amused with voyages and travels and becomes acquainted with the geography, customs, and commerce of other countries. He reads political disquisitions and learns the great outlines of his rights as a man and a citizen. He dips a little into philosophy, and knows that the apparent motion of the sun is occasioned by the real motion of the earth. In a word, he is sure that *notwithstanding the determination of the king, lords, and commons to the contrary, two and two can never make five.*"

Enjoying the applause which they were getting, even in Great Britain, the Americans kept right on with their tart comments on His Majesty's government. The sum total of it all was that Great Britain didn't have herself to thank that she still had her colonies; that she had better let them alone now, for she was going straight to ruin herself and they didn't propose to go with her. If she would let them alone, they would look after themselves, guard their own frontiers, send any Frenchman or Spaniard that turned up packing, and on the basis only of a sentimental loyalty to the crown, call themselves a British Empire and keep their beautiful land open for all other Englishmen who wanted to live sensibly and keep out of trouble as they did. Thus between 1760 and 1775 they formulated the philosophy that still keeps Canada, Australia, New Zealand, and all the rest of our great strapping half brothers peaceably under mother's roof.

Some of the best British sentiment approved of this attitude—Burke and Chatham among the men of brains and the intelligent core of the artisan, professional, and commercial classes. But the king and his ministers were so little inclined to see reason that the Americans soon withdrew their offer about the crown. Said Samuel Adams: "We have a due sense of the kind offer you make us to grant us a share in your sovereign, but really, gentlemen, we have not the least inclination to accept it. He may suit you extremely well, but he is not to our taste."

As for the alternative, Adams said, "We are not so romantically fond of fighting, neither have we such a regard for the city of London as to commence a crusade for the possession of that happy land. But still—" Benjamin Franklin had long since driven the nail home by publishing in England a series of *Rules for Reducing a Great Empire to a Small One.* As for the average man, he settled it all more simply. A British officer reported that when he tried to talk to a Yankee about "duty to king and country," the Yankee merely replied, "Damn your king and country!"

4

But the British Ministry went ahead and laid a stamp tax. Every legal and public document must have a stamp purchased from the agent of the British government. John Adams reported rather soberly the happenings of the first day after this wise law was put into operation in Boston. It is morning, and from a tree hangs an effigy of the new stamp collector. Around it crowds are gathered. No one dares to take it down. The people keep it there all day. Then they put it on a bier and carry it through town in a funereal procession. They carry it to the projected stamp office which they level to the ground in a few minutes. Then they take it to Fort Hill and burn it in a great public bonfire. Meanwhile houses of other British officials are invaded and rifled. Next day the stamp collector resigns. Of all this John Adams disapproved. But he said that there was the greatest difficulty in restraining the people. Six or eight persons were caught and condemned for the outrages and sent to prison. But keys were got away from the jailers and the rioters let out. No one dared to send them back to jail.

The British government then entreated the provincial Assembly to use its influence with the people. The Assembly replied politely that the stamps were brought to the province without the direction of the government of the province, and they couldn't interest themselves in the matter!

The British government then tried a tax on tea. A group of Bostonians took the load of tea and dumped it into the bay. As news of these performances flashed southward, some New Yorkers clapped their hands, while others looked sober; the Quakers in Philadelphia were quiet and noncommittal, but many of them not too disapproving; and Virginia burst into a loud cheer. Nobody else found it necessary to behave like that. They just let the tea alone till it got moldy.

British redcoats were then quartered on the Bostonians. There was something very irritating to the colonials in a red coat. It was a symbol of all that stupidity of the French and Indian Wars when the redcoats of the regulars had served everywhere as targets for the enemy in the woods. A Boston preacher with Tory leanings used to tease the people by pointing out the British soldier, "There," he said, "stand all your wrongs red-dressed!" On the whole, one's sympathies are with the soldiers. There are many descriptions of the New England crowds, and they must have been hard to bear. The worst thing was the old women. A British prisoner of war later gives some idea of what these gentry in red had to put up with. Once when two or three old women were looking them over, one of the soldiers said, "So, you have come to see the British lion!" "British lion, humph," said one old lady, "I declare you look just like lambs." Another time they heard that there was a young lord among the soldiers. An old woman came up and peered at them, "Well, now, which one of you is a lord?" Thereupon the soldiers dragged up the young lord, and one of them stood forth and proclaimed his titles like a herald—Lord of So and So, etc., etc. "You don't say!" cried the old lady. "Well, if that is a lord, the only lord I ever want to see is the Lord Jehovah!"

The Virginians were exercising their wits a little more aristocratically but just as brightly. They had found a spokesman in the young Scotch-Irishman Patrick Henry. One passage of Henry's famous speech on the stamp tax in the House of Burgesses has come down to us. "Caesar," he cried, "had his Brutus; Charles First his Cromwell." "Treason," cried the Speaker. "Treason, treason," echoed some of the conservative members. Henry looked around at them with a grin and coolly completed his sentence, "and George the Third may profit by their example. If that be treason, make the most of it." His friend Jefferson was standing in the door listening. "He appeared to me," he said, "to speak as Homer wrote." They loved words, all these people. They were writing their own epic as they ran, and amidst all the noise and tumult were never too busy to polish up a phrase.

While the fireworks exploded verbally in Virginia, the Bostonians kept on running their heads into trouble. Ultimately the inevitable happened. The exasperated soldiers fired into the crowd. Instantly the eloquence flamed up in Virginia. "The war is actually begun. The next gale that sweeps from the north will bring to our ears the clash of resounding arms. Our brethren are already in the field. Why stand we here idle? What is it that gentlemen wish? What would they have? Is life so dear or is peace so sweet, as to be purchased at the price of chains and slavery? Forbid it, Almighty God! I know not what course others may take; but, as for me, give me liberty, or give me death!"

5

The rest is history. On the whole it was but half a war. There was only one really decisive engagement in it, and that was the defeat of Burgoyne, when the British tried the only strategy that could have given them a strangle hold by coming down from Canada by Lake Champlain, hoping to possess the

Hudson and cut New England off from the other colonies. There the Americans, fighting on their own ground in their own way, made a cleanup. The mountain border of New England along Lake Champlain had been at that time a subject of dispute between New York and New Hampshire, both of the provinces claiming it. This dispute the inhabitants under the leadership of Ethan Allen settled to their own satisfaction by simply setting up as a separate commonwealth, which they called Vermont. Vermont was not in the American Confederacy. It made no contributions to the American army. But it made it very unpleasant for British soldiers to pass by, and in the Battle of Bennington, the Green Mountain boys well fortified by gingerbread which their womenfolk sent in to feed and comfort them, broke the back of Burgoyne's proposed invasion of New York via the Hudson.

Burgoyne's expedition is described in a book by one of his officers, Thomas Anbury, entitled, *Travels through the Interior Parts of North America*. Anbury was a nice fellow, kindly, civilized, chivalrous by all British standards. He looked upon himself as a deliverer coming to "restore peace to a deluded people."

As the army traveled southward from Canada through the interior parts of North America, Anbury's hopefulness gradually evaporated. "A great disadvantage which we experience . . . and which the Americans avoid is that we have to transport all our provisions with us, whereas they have magazines stored with great abundance every thirty or forty miles where in case of any disaster attends their army the loss of their provisions is easily recruited. But if any such event should happen to us, we should be obliged to make a stand at some strong point till provisions could be sent from Canada. . . . Added to this the Americans are by much our superiors in woodfighting, being habituated to woods from their infancy. Our success in any engagement must greatly rest on the bayonet."

The Americans had no notion of meeting the British bayonet if they could help it. Instead they used the rifle. In a land that gushed with foaming brooks, they had all water so well covered with unseen riflemen in trees that no British soldier could get a drink! This was one of the worst privations in the march. The soldiers would scoop up muddy water made by their own bootholes in the wet ground, with the sound of roaring waterfalls in their ears. There were times when this deadly rifle fire from unseen sources instantly laying low one who stepped out of the main ranks gave them the blue horrors. They used to amuse themselves by hoisting up a cap above their breastworks on a stick to see if they could catch the enemy rifles napping. They never could. Instantly there would be two or three shots, and just as many holes right through the cap.

During the night, in a few hours, the Americans would lay so many obstructions across their march that it took the British most of the next day to clear them out. But with incredible speed they would themselves throw up strong stockades. They never stopped anywhere, even for a night, without this protection. And all the while, Anbury says, they seemed to go on the principle that the contest for a single life was equal to an army's victory. In the end the whole British army surrendered, and the Americans added the crowning touch. A Tory had made a derisive song about them entitled *Yankee-Doodle*. As the British surrendered, the American bands struck up *Yankee-Doodle* and played it happily as the British prisoners were marched across New England. They even enticed away the British band, hired it themselves, and had it playing the obnoxious song!

This was the kind of fighting the Americans were prepared to do all along the line, should they be actually driven back on their own semisavage resources. Down in the mountains of North Carolina they wore out the invading British in the same way, and Marion, operating from the swamps of South Carolina, made the life of Tories a burden. But Washington, planning always if defeated to fall back on his own Ohio lands and fight it out from the mountains in frontier style, took the ungrateful task of staying out in the open and leading Howe a dance up and down between New York and Philadelphia, with a final successful dash into Virginia where Cornwallis surrendered. There he was at a perpetual disadvantage, whipping inexperienced men into line according to the notions of European fighting, and never sure from one day to the next how much of an army he would have. The soldiers would enlist awhile, go home and look after their families, and come back and fight some more. The skillful provisioning of the country districts was impossible where commercial speculators and Tories constantly intervened. Even so, giving the enemy, as it were, the choice of weapons, fighting it out in a European style as a soldier and a gentleman, his stature in the eyes of Europe as well as of his countrymen constantly grew. Chastellux, coming with the auxiliary French army in 1780, says of Washington: "The continent of North America from Boston to Charleston is a great volume which presents his eulogium. . . . Brave without temerity, laborious without ambition, generous without prodigality, noble without pride, virtuous without severity. . . . This is the seventh year that he has commanded the army, and that he has obeyed the Congress; more need not be said, especially in America where they know how to appreciate all the merit contained in this simple fact. . . . It will be said of him that at the end of a long civil war, he had nothing with which he could reproach himself. If anything can be more marvelous than such a character, it is the unanimity of public suffrages in his favor. Soldier, magistrate, people, all love and admire him; all speak of him in terms of affection."

Because of Washington's constant complaints of the inadequacy of his army, it is the habit of the debunking historian of today to underestimate that force of loyalty and courage, and determination that he always had behind him among the great mass of plain citizens. There were rascals. There were speculators. There were Tories. But the testimony with regard to the people is unanimous and conclusive. Thomas Anbury, going through New England as a prisoner of war after Burgoyne's defeat, reports: "Every town is raising two or three companies for Washington's army. The wants and miseries of the inhabitants in general are inconceivable, even to the conveniences of life, yet you would be surprised with what cheerfulness they bend to them to obtain that idol, Independency. In many poor habitations, they have parted with one of their blankets where they had only two, to supply their soldiers, and although the interior part of these states have not been the seat of war, yet the distresses of the inhabitants are equally as great as if they had.

"If the other provinces enter as heartily into the cause of rebellion, I am afraid we shall find it a difficult task to subdue them; for, exclusive of all the various modes of furnishing men and supplies, it is in these provinces become, in some measure, a religious cause in which the people being enthusiasts, their clergy artfully increase the warlike spirit among their flock. . . . In all religious contests men will fight to desperation. . . . We find an unexampled bravery that no danger can disconcert, and a firm constancy that no force can withstand."

But this was in the country towns of New England. Washington found in Philadelphia and the rich coast towns "idleness, dissipation and extravagance, speculation, peculation, and an insatiable thirst for riches, party disputes and personal quarrels." But apart from this class, the Marquis de Chastellux says that he went up and down through the new states and never saw more than two or three men over twenty who had not fought in the Revolution, and who would not go back and fight again and keep on fighting as long as necessary. Claude Blanchard, commissary of the French auxiliary army in 1780, reporting on the limitations of the training and equipment among the Americans says, generously: "Such are the inconveniences, but they vanish when we remember that, notwithstanding all obstacles, the power of England has been baffled in America by the love of country and of liberty which has hitherto animated the Anglo-Americans, that many English

generals have been successively defeated there, that Burgoyne
has shamefully passed under the yoke, and that there, more
than anywhere else, Voltaire's verses have had their effect: 'Injustice had finally produced Independence.' "

He adds that in this war Congress and the ordinary require-
ments and character of armies are beside the point. It is Washington and the plain man fighting together. "Our military and
naval generals arrived. They had an interview with General
Washington from which they returned enchanted. An easy
and noble bearing, extensive and correct views, the art of making himself beloved, these are what all who saw him observed
in him. It is his merit that has defended the liberty of America,
and if she enjoys it one day, it is to him alone that she will be
indebted for it."

6

All the while the brains of this new people were trying to
think out law for the coming nation. It began in the Continental Congress. It is easy to laugh at these poor gentlemen. They
laughed at themselves. But as John Adams said, when he was
one of them: "When fifty or sixty men have a constitution to
form for a great empire, at the same time that they have a
country of 1,500 miles to fortify, millions to arm and train, a
naval power to begin, an extensive commerce to regulate, numerous tribes of Indians to negotiate with, a standing army of
27,000 men to raise, pay, victual, and officer, I shall pity those
fifty or sixty men." But he adds: "The fidgets, the whims, the
caprices, the vanity, the superstition, the irritability of some of
us is enough to . . ." and again: "We have not men fit for
the times. We are deficient in genius, in education, in travel, in
fortune, in everything. I feel unutterable anxiety. God grant
us wisdom and fortitude. Should the opposition be suppressed,
should the country submit, what infamy and ruin. God forbid.
Death in any form is less terrible." He did not forget, Washington never forgot, that as leaders of a rebellion they were

guilty of high treason against Great Britain. If they should fail, all would be brought as "malefactors to the block."

Though the governmental machinery of the confederacy was inadequate, though the Continental Congress was confused and, as Adams said had "the fidgets," their political problem was somewhat like the military problem of Washington. The apparent activity, the setting up a government in European style, the carrying on of the usual functions of government, was only a screen for more important activity backstage. While keeping the British generals busy and the European world interested in helping them, their real business was to make good their hold on the land across the mountains and open the road to it. The general game of politics they seemed often to bungle. Their own game they played well enough. At no cost must they permit the Frenchmen to return in their rear, even at the moment when they were bowing and smiling and receiving his gifts at the front door. On this subject Washington wrote a long and careful letter to Congress. The gist of it was that the French know too much about America. If France should come back, "possessed of New Orleans on our right, Canada on our left, and seconded by numerous tribes of Indians in our rear, from one extremity to the other . . . which she knows so well how to conciliate, she would . . . have it in her power to give law to these states. . . . I am heartily disposed to entertain the most favorable sentiments to our new ally, and to cherish them in others to a reasonable degree. But it is a maxim founded on the universal experience of mankind, that no nation is to be trusted further than it is bound by interest."

As for the French assistance in the war, they had another way of rewarding that. The prospect of this reward is foreshadowed in a remark made by one of the French officers with Washington. Observing with interest the various small dishes, glasses, and decorative gadgets used by Americans in serving even a simple meal, he says that here in America there is a market among all the people for the kind of thing that in Europe sells only to a small upper class. After the war, he says, it is we who must furnish the Americans their elegancies. The first mass market of the world for the luxuries of life! This was something for France to contemplate. The Americans were quite satisfied to turn French attention in that direction. Rewarding a faithful ally, they would be at the same time in position to bargain with Great Britain for commercial advantage.

Meanwhile, the Americans made good their hold on the back blocks in some effective military perambulations. At a time when all hands were apparently needed to meet the British on the coast, General Sullivan was sent into central New York state to clean out the Indian Confederacy which blocked the New England road across New York state to the West. Beyond that rather dull, level country of which the Germans had taken possession lay the beautiful Indian land, long silvery lakes like the fingers of a gigantic hand lying placid between rolling hills cut by deep gorges. Here the Iroquois Confederacy had a rudimentary civilization, including gardens of beans and corn and squash from which they sold vegetables to the British armies. Since frontier Americans always hoped that if they could not beat out the English, they would at least starve them out, these succotash fields were most obnoxious. So down between these gracious sunny hills went Sullivan and his army warring on the beans and the squash, burning Indian houses, putting even these stern braves to the rout. It was true frontier fighting, savage on both sides. In an old diary which survives, it is recorded that Sullivan's soldiers had boots made of the skin of the Indians! So the poetic land of middle New York state, which Cooper has described in his *Leatherstocking Tales*, was open for the march of Yankee-Doodle westward.

Meanwhile the British had enlarged the province of Quebec to include the French towns on the Great Lakes, and in Indiana and Illinois. With Detroit as a center, they were stirring up the Indians against the Pennsylvania frontier and against the white settlers now pouring over the mountains into

Kentucky. So the government of Virginia dispatched a bold young man of twenty-five, George Rogers Clark, to go through the French country and annex the French villages. Launching a few frontiersmen on flatboats down the Ohio River, Clark started off, with Sir Henry Hamilton, the British commander at Detroit, hot behind him. Clark wintered at Kaskaskia in Illinois, and Hamilton at Vincennes in Indiana. In the dead of winter, while Hamilton was peacefully waiting for spring to begin the battle, Clark led his men across the frozen marshes of southern Illinois and captured him and his forces, and so set up an amateurish stars and stripes which he had improvised from such cloth as he could find to wave over the whole Mississippi Valley.

All these skirmishes in the backyard the Continental Congress was attending to while carrying on a real war in public. Meanwhile, with the same rude skill, the various states having claims to Western land were slowly inducing each other to pool their possessions and plan a means of advancing westward as one nation. This effort flowered in the great Northwest Ordinance of 1787 passed after the Constitutional Convention had been called and the poor old Continental Congress was about to go out of business forever. A great constructive scheme of government for the West, including a bill of rights, and the plan of apprenticeship for statehood which has been followed ever since, it was a worthy forerunner of the Constitution and showed with what political originality the American mind could think when it was working in its own field of frontier experience and frontier necessity.

7

They were met again in that smug gray city, under the shadow of the Liberty Bell, to devise a constitution for these states. Thirty years had passed since the sentiment of nationality had first thrilled the breasts of young men in the French and Indian Wars. Those who had been young then, like Washington and John Adams, were growing gray. Those who had been middle aged, like Benjamin Franklin, had grown old. And in these thirty years, "We, the People," had doubled in size. There had been about 1,600,000 people in the colonies that first dreamed of nationhood. There were now nearly four million. Even since the surrender of Cornwallis, the nation had swelled and grown strong. Kentucky, Tennessee, and Ohio were already clamoring at the back door for the right to come in and be a nation, too. The overseas commerce of the United States had reached out and encircled the world. Already there were American factors side by side with the British in Canton, and fleet-winged boats from Salem, Providence, New York, and Philadelphia were racing past the British East Indiamen, homeward bound with tea.

Two great forces were pressing these states together and making them one—their maritime commerce and their frontier. When one goes abroad, one wants to do it with the sense of a single great nation behind one, not thirteen little provinces that may go flying off in all directions away from each other before one can circle the world and come home again. As for the frontier, in the long mountain valleys and on Wilderness Road people of all states meet and mingle. They go west as one people and need one people behind them. "Two voices are there, one is of the mountains, one is of the sea." These two voices speak sometimes together, sometimes in choral antiphony, in the checks and balances of our Constitution.

It was a mighty responsibility these gentlemen had undertaken. Benjamin Franklin thought it would be becoming if they would at least open their sessions with prayer. Some of the shallower minds thought it amusing to see the genial old Epicurean, the sage wise in the flavors of the fleshpots of the world, the deist who never let a religious dogma stop his great mind from moving in any direction it pleased, the humorous citizen who could not be dragged to church because, as he said, he had so many other employments for his leisure—some people thought it amusing to hear Ben, of all people, propose prayers. There was indeed his usual shrewd worldly wisdom in the suggestion. By uniting them for a moment in a common solemnity, he hoped to lift the discussion to some ground of unity where they could not be divided by "little partial local interests." But there was much more. Someone had to go on record in recognition of the great and dreadful responsibility which they were all taking, and the unfitness of the best of us to draw up an instrument of government for a people forever.

So, rising in his place, the grand old man, heavy with the burden of his years and his multitudinous services to the people, said gravely: "In the situation of this assembly, groping as it were in the dark to find political truth, and scarce able to distinguish it when presented to us, how has it happened, Sir, that we have hitherto not once thought of applying to the Father of Lights to illumine our understandings. . . . I have lived, Sir, a long time, and the longer I live the more convincing proofs I see of this truth that God governs the affairs of men. And if a sparrow cannot fall to the ground without His notice, it is probable than an empire cannot rise without His aid." Afterward on a copy of these remarks, Franklin wrote in his own hand, "Convention, all except three or four, thought prayer unnecessary!"

Even without prayer, they made a noble fabric. Though one of the younger members among the Virginians, James Madison, did much of the writing and shaping, the government of the United States as it was projected then and established during the early presidential administrations was the work of five men thinking together with remarkable unanimity, despite apparent disagreement. They were John Adams, representing scholarly and maritime New England, Alexander Hamilton, of West Indian planter ancestry and commercial training, representing New York business and trade, especially the East India trade, Benjamin Franklin, representing Pennsylvania and the middle colonies, and Washington and Jefferson representing the South and the new West. What was remarkable among them was what Chastellux thought the supreme virtue of Washington—they were whole men. There was health and balance in all their faculties. They were personally honorable and self-devoted to the point of heroism. Each had the capacity for practical success in his own life. They were shrewd. They were articulate. They could act and talk with equal facility. Representing no fixed point of view, not formally religious, not committed to specific categories of thought, they had each and all of them imaginative vision, some ultimate philosophy of good and right for all men, some grand sense of destiny. One and all they were healthy, attractive, lovable and interesting men—patterns of bearing and behavior to their day.

It is true that they differed greatly in style and in minor social ideals. John Adams was a little duller than the others. Hamilton was elegant in dress; Jefferson plain and careless. Hamilton quarreled with Jefferson, then with Adams. They had their differences. But they lived and worked and argued and fought with each other on a plane that sets them high and clean above most politics before and after. And they ended their days as grandly as they lived—Hamilton prematurely, dashingly, but chivalrously, falling by Burr's bullet without shooting his own; the others in peace and honor and ripe years. The appropriate end of this bright epic of the American Revolution is the renewed friendship and correspondence in old age of John Adams and Thomas Jefferson. Separated for a while by a difference of political opinion, they later wrote to each other and expressed their lifelong respect for each other's honor and intelligence; and then began a long, ripe, mellow interchange of letters about everything, about life and manners, about science and books. And when they died, they died on the same day—the fiftieth anniversary of the Declaration of Independence! Plutarch has nothing finer.

II

HALF SLAVE AND HALF FREE

8

BLUEGRASS
AND CANEBRAKE

ALL that long June day, the seventh of June, 1770, Daniel Boone had been climbing—up, up through the undergrowth, crisp with new leaves, over those creeks and up those hills whose cussedness the pioneers later celebrated in such names as "Hell for Sartin," "Upper Devil," "Lower Devil," "No Worse Creek," "Cut Shin Creek." Just at sunset he reached the top of the mountain and looked westward. And there lay—Kentucky.

He had no fine words in which to tell what he felt then, but he remembered it and later when a literary young schoolmaster named Filson came out into the wilderness, he told him about it, and Filson wrote it out in what he thought appropriate language, and published it in 1784 with an affidavit from Daniel Boone, Levi Todd, and James Harrod, dated May 12, 1784, to the effect that they knew what was in the book and it was correct. This is what Boone saw, in the style of Filson: "I had gained the summit of a commanding ridge, and looking around with astonishing delight, beheld the ample plains and beauteous tracts below. On the one hand I surveyed the famous Ohio, rolling in silent dignity and marking the western boundary with inconceivable grandeur. At a vast distance I beheld moun-

tains lift their venerable brows and penetrate the clouds. All
things were still. I kindled a fire near a fountain of sweet water
and feasted on a loin of the buck which a few hours before I
had killed. The shades of night now overspread the earth. . . .
I laid me down to sleep and woke not until the sun had chased
away the night."

In 1784 when Filson published this charming little book,
entitled *Kentucke,* 30,000 souls had already followed Daniel
Boone into the West. "Thus," says Filson, "we behold Kentucke, lately an howling wilderness, the habitation of savages
and wild beasts, become a fruitful field . . . where agriculture,
industry, laws, arts, and sciences flourish, where afflicted humanity raises her drooping head, where springs a harvest for
the poor; where conscience ceases to be a slave; and laws are
no more than security for happiness; where nature makes
reparation for having created man, and government so long
prostituted to the most criminal purposes establishes itself as an
asylum in the wilderness for the distressed of mankind."

So Filson wrote the first great piece of advertising literature for the West, and back in the towns of Pennsylvania, and
in Wilmington, Delaware, it was èagerly read and several
times reprinted. All alight with the wonders of this virgin
world, eager to see what lay north of the Ohio, Filson crossed
the river one morning, and set forth with surveying instruments
into the woods. He never returned. No trail was ever found to
show where or how he left the earth that seemed to him so
beautiful. But it is pleasant to record that the Filson Club in
Kentucky still keeps alive his memory by publishing, from
time to time, brochures about the history and traditions of that
Arcadian state.

2

Daniel Boone, who had come originally from Pennsylvania
to the Yadkin valley in North Carolina, had been a wagoner and
blacksmith for 100 North Carolina frontiersmen in Braddock's
army. Though he was not the first actually to explore or to

settle in Kentucky, something there was in the personality of this bold, simple, honest woodsman which caught the imagination and made him the hero of the frontier for fifty years. Several people had been to Kentucky before him, and at least one of them, the John Harrod who made the affidavit for Filson's book, beat Boone back to Kentucky with settlers. Harrod had already settled Harrodsburg when Boone arrived in 1774 with settlers for Boonesborough. Shortly afterward, in March 1775, a company was formed by Judge Henderson of Virginia to buy Indian lands in this new-found paradise. For 12,000 pounds in goods, the Indians ceded him half of the present state of Kentucky and part of Tennessee—all of which land was already claimed, partly explored and surveyed, and generally administered as the western part of Virginia.

In the spring of 1775 Judge Henderson himself went to see how the Boonesborough settlers were getting along. They had strange tales to tell him. Felix Walker, who had come with Boone's party, said that, on entering the plain, "we were permitted to view a very interesting and romantic sight. A number of buffaloes, of all sizes, supposed to be between two and three hundred, made off from the lick in every direction, some running, some walking, others loping slowly and carelessly with young calves skipping and bounding through the plain. Such a sight some of us never saw before and perhaps never may again."

Of his own observations and adventures Henderson kept a diary, written in that fresh, flavorsome English which so many early Americans knew how to write. One of his first acts was to save a beautiful big tree from destruction and to establish its ample circuit of shade as the first church and public assembly of the colony. "This tree," he says, "is placed on a beautiful plain, surrounded by a turf of fine white clover forming a green to its very stock, to which there is scarcely anything to be likened. Its trunk is four feet through, so symmetrical as to form the most beautiful tree that can be imagined. Between one and two hundred people may commodiously seat themselves under its branches. . . . This divine tree . . . we came in time to redeem from destruction. Not owing to its beauty—that was unnoticed; the leaves were not yet out and the lazy could find no pleasure in basking under it. . . . I believe 'twas the dread of cutting this tree that made my way easy in endeavoring to obtain the lot for the purpose of building this fort."

Having obtained the lot, Henderson decreed that "this same tree is to be our church, state-house, council chamber," and so forth. "By Sunday sennight" he expected "to perform divine service for the first time in a public manner, and that to a set of scoundrels who scarcely believe in God or fear the devil, if we were to judge from most of their looks, words, and manners."

Under this tree, on May 24, 1775, the first rustic parliament met and established institutions and public law. The plan, says Henderson, "was simple and plain. 'Twas nothing novel in essence; a thousand years ago it was in use and found by every year's experience to be unexceptionable. We were in four distinct settlements. Members and delegates from every place bound themselves by writing to obey and carry into execution such laws as should be made from time to time by representatives of the majority of the proprietors present in the country."

The first problem of government was to stop the waste in the meat industry. Some of the hunters could not shoot well and would merely cripple the game. "Others of wicked and wanton disposition would kill three or four or half a dozen buffalo and not take a half horseload of them all." The question of controlling the food supply was a serious one, in a world where all food ran wild on four legs, "many complaining that they were too poor to hire hunters; others loved it much better than work; and some who knew little of the matter, but conceity, from having a hunting shirt, tomahawk, and gun, thought it an insult to offer another to hunt for him, especially as pay was to be made." And so, "for want of a little obligatory law" the game was being driven away. The ideal would have been to put the hunting into the hands of a picked body of skillful men and have them, under rigorous restriction, provide food for everybody. But since this was not possible, "strictest inquiry was made into every hunter's conduct." Censure, said Henderson, was the only available weapon, but "I am convinced that it saved the lives of many buffalo, elk, and deer."

Henderson, meanwhile, set up a land office at Boonesborough, and the rustic parliament proceeded to organize courts and militia, to provide for writs of attachment, to prohibit profane swearing, protect the game, and preserve the breed of horses. On September 25, Judge Henderson sent a written application to the Continental Congress asking it to admit Transylvania, as they called their settlement, as the fourteenth colony. But through the general political uncertainty of the time, Judge Henderson's enterprise collapsed, and he lost the title to his lands. He was recompensed by being given 200,000 acres in what is now Tennessee and proceeded to open a land office on the site of the city of Nashville, in 1778.

Regardless of land titles, Kentucky filled up. In 1776 Boone returned with more settlers, including his wife and daughters, and set up real housekeeping.

All within is neat. Brightly shines the puncheon floor,
For Rebecca has been trained in useful household lore,
And the simple table piled with nature's gifts was spread
With bear-steak and wild lettuce and venison for bread.
The wild plum and the paw-paw and the grape crowned the board,
And freedom, love, and health beyond the miser's hoard.

Life was simple and crude, but had a gala holiday atmosphere, as if they were all off on a camping or hunting party. In 1784 Filson reported that the 30,000 souls of Kentucky were in general "polite, humane, hospitable, and very complaisant. Being collected from different parts of the country, they have a diversity of manners, customs, and religion." Already they had started a little college for their children, with a library bestowed by the Reverend John Todd of Virginia, and Presbyterians and Anabaptists were seeing that they did not grow up utter heathen. By 1795 Lexington was inhabited by "refined and educated persons," and had twenty-four retail stores, where, among other things, one might purchase nankeens, dimities, bertha laces, Paisley shawls, and French slippers with high heels. The town was maintaining a silversmith and a dancing school, and offered a market for "china and queensware, wine and toddy glasses." These Kentuckians enjoyed themselves from the first. Their favorite social events were weddings, for the more weddings the more citizens. These weddings, we are told, were commonly celebrated in the daytime, and "were scenes of carousal and of mirth and merriment of no very chastened character."

Doctor Drake, who thus described the weddings, was himself of a more sober character. When Jefferson was inaugurated in 1801, he says that he—then a student of medicine—sitting in his chamber in a small white farmhouse, "drank in cold water thirteen toasts in celebration of the triumphant event."

In the states back home a roaring activity was going on. Providing 30,000 people with the luxuries of life kept everybody busy, and more were trekking westward all the time. Audubon says: "The Virginians thronged toward the Ohio. An ax, a couple of horses, and a heavy rifle were all that was necessary." More patrician adventurers went with their own hunters, who would have fire and venison ready and camp pitched when, flanked by their Negroes, they rode up at nightfall. In their wagons they carried bedding and changes of clothes, and behind them came their cattle, which the Negroes turned out into the forest at nightfall, with light bells at their necks to announce their whereabouts.

The great point of entry was Wilderness Road. At the spot where the road from Pennsylvania had joined the road from North Carolina, Boone had branched off to the west, finding the easiest trail over the Cumberland Gap. Between 1780 and 1800 this trail widened into the famous Wilderness

Road, and began to take on the appearance of a highway with men all along the line laying logs across it, and covering them with dirt, thus making the famous corduroy or washboard road, over which wagon wheels careered in a steady, even bounce. Meanwhile the road from Philadelphia to Pittsburgh was becoming the first great through freight line in America. The wagons of the Pennsylvania Dutch farmers—those wagons which, assembled by Benjamin Franklin in Braddock's campaign, had proved themselves unique and priceless among things that run on wheels—these wagons were going through, first by hundreds, then by thousands, hauling everything known to civilization from Philadelphia to Pittsburgh, there to be loaded on flatboats and floated hundreds of miles to settlers down the river. These wagons, rolling along, behind regiments of vast, strong, German-fed horses, their lower parts painted blue, their upper parts red, and vast white tops domed over all, were a symbol of Uncle Sam on the march. When they returned, they were laden with ginseng for China, the Americans having a monopoly on this weed which seemed to grow nowhere else outside the Orient, and was the sacred cure-all for Chinese aches and pains. Dispatched from Philadelphia to China by Stephen Girard, this ginseng would come rolling back two years later as a great van of tea and silk for the ladies of Kentucky.

All along these roads, taverns sprang up and grew, in the next two or three decades, from one-room log houses to white-pillared mansions. They had quaint names—Fried Meat Tavern, Indian Queen, Sheaf of Wheat. Many of them were run by the Pennsylvania Dutch, and their tables were set with scrapple and apple butter and rich sugared cakes and wonderful cheeses. These innkeepers had a passion for rhymed communications to their guests, usually provided by a passing schoolmaster, such as: "Our food is good, our prices just; but gentle Sirs, we cannot trust." Schoolmasters were variously useful in these inns. One communication still preserved, reads:

"Gentlemen who are learning to spell are requested to use *last week's* New Letter."

3

While Transylvania was making good its place in the forest, Tennessee emerged as the state of Franklin. On August 23, 1784, the followers of John Robertson and his Notables, disdaining to be ceded to Congress as just the western lands of North Carolina, met at Jonesborough and elected John Sevier as governor. Though Sevier had a Huguenot name, he was a hero of the Scotch-Irish, and represented all that they appreciated—being handsome, gallant, and highhanded. For a few years he ruled his little state to the satisfaction of its citizens, and even tried to reconcile it to North Carolina. But in 1788 Governor Johnston of North Carolina issued a warrant for his arrest on the charge of high treason. "His dramatic escape from the one-roomed log-courthouse at Jonesborough, his rapid flight over the mountains on his fleet-footed race-mare, bought for his flight by his staunch friend, Doctor James Crosby"— all this, retold in gossip, started Tennessee off with history of the high ballad style.

Not long after this public life in Tennessee was enlivened by another event in the ballad style which thirty years later was still making American social history. A Virginian named Robards of a border clan had married a charming young woman of another clan, the Donelsons. She was a fetching girl with round dark eyes, and round sweet face, and a full-bosomed round figure, sporting that warm, natural, female enticement which the gentlemen of the clans liked to see a woman adding to the gaiety of nations, and whose security in the chaste display of the same was to be defended by sword and pistol. But Rachel's husband was apparently a mean-spirited cuss, and became violently jealous of her. Jealousy is legitimate among some tribes, in a similar stage of development. Among the Latins, a jealous husband was always right. But not so among these people. Even Robards' mother defended Rachel.

She was a good girl and a good wife, and as for men looking at her, what do you expect your wife to be—a hag?

Word of Rachel's troubles with her husband reached her family—the Donelsons, who appealed to their young friend, the rising lawyer, Andrew Jackson, to bring her home to them. Off dashed Andrew, and back with Rachel to her home and waiting kin. Whereupon Robards appealed to the Virginia legislature to pass a law enabling him to get a divorce in Kentucky—which, if it was anything, was still part of Virginia—on the ground that his wife had "eloped" with Andrew Jackson. There was consternation among the Donelsons, for a woman's honor was as sacred as her right to be seductive. On the border wives did not just carelessly "elope." Instantly, not waiting for time to sully the fair name of the lady, Andrew Jackson married Rachel. Apparently he and she and the Donelsons all thought the law was a divorce. But it proved that it was only a law enabling Robards to get a divorce, which he obtained two years later, and then only on the grounds that Rachel was living in sin with Andrew Jackson. Instantly they celebrated the union with another marriage ceremony. Andrew Jackson said before God and his friends and the community as a whole, this pure and noble lady was his wife, and anyone who took her sacred name into his mouth . . . and for thirty years he made good those words with pistol in hand, even to dragging Sevier out to the frontier beyond the borders of Tennessee either to eat his words or die right there and be damned to him.

This was the fatal scandal which followed Rachel to Washington and secretly preyed upon her all her gentle and kindly life. It was not that she cared for herself. It was that she did not want to be a dishonor to him. As for him, no man ever wore a woman's love more proudly, and few had greater power to force public obeisance to the lady he loved than came in the end to this rude democrat of the woods. A little old woman smoking a pipe—so she seemed to others. As for him, she was queen of the White House and the nation, and they had better bow, for his foot was on their necks.

4

While the gentry were thus making history, the plain man was not without his drama. Just as the plain man of Kentucky has his semimythical hero in Daniel Boone, so the plain man of Tennessee has his in Davy Crockett. Crockett later came to Washington with Andrew Jackson as Congressman and captured the imagination of the smart journalists who poured out book after book purporting to be written by himself, most of them apocryphal; and he was the starting point of a myth which spread by word of mouth over the whole frontier. But one book, the *Autobiography*, published in 1834, bears evidence of originating with David himself. Davy, remarking that it was strange that a fellow that "can't scarcely read and write" should be one of the most popular authors in America, certified that in this one case the book really was his, "every sentence and sentiment," though he did allow someone to correct the spelling and the grammar. Probably it is his own. No one can doubt it who compares its style with Filson's translation of Daniel Boone's story or even the style of such a keen listener and accomplished literary man as Cooper. Here is the new American speech, perfected by illiterate men in stories around the campfire, or around a good keg of whisky—fresh, flexible, picturesque, with merits quite beyond grammar.

Since Davy is the frontiersman really talking for himself, it is worth while to let him tell his experiences at some length. David was the son of an immigrant from Ireland who married an American woman, and settled, more or less, in Pennsylvania. Like many of the families at the entrance to Wilderness Road, the Crocketts kept inching along, getting deeper and deeper into the forest, settling in a clearing, planting a crop, seeing the crop fail, hearing of better land over the next hill, moving on, working for some other settler, trying to save money, not saving it, moving on. Davy, growing up, went forward in the same way, trying to find land, hiring himself out to pay off his father's debts, always able to live by hunting, now and then collecting a few skins and trading them off for cash, looking for a girl of his own, always poor, always hopeful.

Once when he was working for a Quaker, to earn some clothes, the Quaker's niece arrived from North Carolina and introduced him to all the agonies of "hot love." "Though I have heard people talk about hard loving, yet I reckon no poor devil in this world was ever cursed with such hard love as mine has always been, when it came on me. . . . I thought if all the hills about there were pure chink, and all belonged to me, I would give them if I could just talk to her as I wanted to; but I was afraid to begin, for when I would think of saying anything to her, my heart would begin to flutter like a duck in a puddle; and if I tried to outdo it and speak, it would get right smack up in my throat and choke me like a cold potato. It bore on my mind in this way till I concluded I must die if I didn't broach the subject; and so I determined to begin and hang on a-trying to speak till my heart would get out of my throat, one way or tother. So one day at it I went, and after several trials I could say a little. I told her how well I loved her; that she was the darling object of my soul and body; and I must have her, or else I should pine down to nothing and just die away with consumption. I found my talk not disagreeable to her; but she was an honest girl and didn't want to deceive nobody. She told me she was engaged to her cousin, the son of the old Quaker. This news was worse to me than war, pestilence, or famine; but still I knowed that I could not help myself. I saw quick enough that my cake was dough, and tried to cool off as fast as possible; but I had hardly safety pipes enough, as my love was so hot as mighty nigh to burst my boilers."

However, he discovered another girl, and soon "got to love her as bad as I had the Quaker's niece. . . . We fixed the time to be married, and I thought that if that day come, I should be the happiest man in the created world, or in the moon or anywhere else." Inspired by love to industry, he earned the wherewithal for a capital rifle, won a shooting match (the match consisting in shooting at an ox, the winner to have the beef) and sold his beef for five whole dollars wherewith to be married. So he started off "with a light heart, my five dollars jingling in my pocket, thinking all the time that there were few greater men in the world than myself." Arriving in this "flow of good humor" at the home of the girl's uncle, he learned that his bride was to be married to another man next day!

"This was as sudden to me as a clap of thunder on a bright sunshiny day. It was the capstone of all the afflictions I had ever met with, and it seemed to me that it was more than any human creature could endure. It struck me perfectly speechless for some time, and made me feel so weak that I thought I should sink down." Her sister tried to comfort him, following him out to the gate and urging him to go and argue with his recalcitrant bride. "But I found I could go no further. My heart was bruised and my spirits broken down; so I bid her farewell, and turned my miserable and lonesome steps back again homeward, concluding that I was born only for hardships, misery, and disappointment. I now began to think that it was entirely forgotten to make my mate; that I was born odd and should always remain so, and nobody would have me."

After which it is pleasant to add that Crockett found not only one good wife, but two. Having lived happily with one till her death, he then made overtures to a widow lady near by who had a "snug little farm." Time and marriage had tamed his hot heart, for this time, when he began to pay his respects to her, "I was as sly about it as a fox when he is going to rob a hen roost." "I thought I could treat her children with so much friendship as to make her a good stepmother to mine. . . . We soon bargained and got married, and then went ahead. In considerable peace we raised our first crop of children, and then had a second crop together."

These numerous children he supported by hunting, becoming a fabulous bear hunter, but experimenting with whatever else the frontier offered, and from time to time moving on to a better place. Years afterward, when he had become a famous character, and there was a hungry public appetite for more and more stories about him, a reporter undertook to find his cabin in the woods. The reporter's picture is probably applicable to most of the more respectable forest homes.

"It was in appearance rude and uninviting, situated in a small field of eight or ten acres, which had been cleared in the wild woods; no yard surrounded it and it seemed to have been lately settled. In the passage of the house were seated two men, in their shirt sleeves, cleaning rifles. I strained my eyes as I rode up to see if I could identify the great bear-hunter; but before I could decide, my horse had stopped at the bars, and there walked out, in plain homespun attire, with a black fur cap on, a finely proportioned man, about six feet high, aged, from appearance, about forty-five. His countenance was frank and manly and a smile played over it as he approached me. He brought with him a rifle and from his right shoulder hung a bag made of coonskin, to which, by means of a sheath, was appended a huge hunter's knife."

With a cordial invitation to enter the house, Crockett said: " 'You see, we are mighty rough here. I am afraid you will think it hard times, but we have to do the best we can. I started poor and have been rooting hog ever since, but damn apologies, I hate 'em. What I live on always I think a friend can stand for a day or two' . . ." and with that he offered the stranger the hospitality of his home.

The home showed what even in the wilderness a good wife can do for a man who, for his part, tries to be a good provider. "His cabin within was neat and clean, and bore about it many marks of comfort. The many trophies of wild animals spread over his house and yard—his dogs in appearance war-worn veterans lying about sunning themselves—all told truly that I was in the house of the celebrated hunter. His wife was rather grave and quiet, but attentive and kind to strangers; his daughters were diffident and retiring, perhaps too much so, but uncommonly beautiful. . . . There are no schools near them, yet they converse well. . . . The colonel has no slaves. His daughters attend to the dairy and the kitchen while he performs the more laborious duties of his farm."

5

After their long, spirited, and turbulent apprenticeships, Transylvania and Franklin finally came into the Union—Transylvania as the present state of Kentucky in 1792, Franklin as Tennessee in 1796. Kentucky was by this time a thriving place; the canebrakes were everywhere yielding to fenced fields and pastures, and the beautiful bluegrass was running like green mist over the rolling hills. Already there were Kentuckians of wealth and substance, breeding their blooded horses, clinking their mint juleps against the frosted glass. Tennessee, still raw, was rapidly taking on the new way of life. The eastern mountains were filling with frontier farmers—the backwash of the migrations, primitive folk, content to live on in primitive ways, keeping to this day the habits and life of the first frontiersmen. But central Tennessee was being fenced and gardened and built up. There persons like Jackson were putting more money than they could afford into high-bred horses to enter in the races, and were acquiring more and more slaves. Slaves were to the new settlers something between a necessity and a nuisance. The Kentucky legislature had made a gesture toward abolition of slavery, but it had been voted down. In general, slaves were kindly treated. At a time when he was loaded with debt, and greatly in need of ready cash, Andrew Jackson paid $1,800 to reunite some of his slaves as a family, noting the expenditure in his accounts with the remark "Purpose—humanity." While central Tennessee around Nashville was beginning to develop as another bluegrass region, the western part of the state which was later to join the cotton kingdom was still the Indian frontier.

With the Indians on the frontier, the British fur traders in the Northwest, and the port to which they must float their goods, New Orleans, in the hands of the Spanish, the new states were peculiarly exposed to those dangers against which Washington warned his people in his Farewell Address. As was pointed out by Sydney Greenbie in an article entitled "Washington Never Meant That," in the *Christian Science Monitor*, Magazine Section, February 19,1936, Washington, in begging his people to keep clear of entangling alliances, was thinking not of treaties which the Union might make as a whole with foreign governments, but of alliances by the separate states with neighboring great powers which might draw them away from the Union. The Union, he tells them, is their bulwark and protection. In that is their hope and their liberty; let no interests of factions draw them asunder.

At the time when the Great Chief took this touching farewell of his people, there was reason enough for worry. The people beyond the mountains were exposed on all sides. In particular the Spaniards were wooing them. When Daniel Boone, through failure to register his title to his lands, lost all property in the state of which he was, in popular tradition, the finder and founder, the Spaniards offered him and his friends lands across the Mississippi, and thither he went. Similarly large groups of Americans were moving into the Southwest. Who could say when the pull of these Americans would draw the new states of the valley after them?

The difficulty about the Spaniards was partly obviated by the Louisiana Purchase in 1803, which bought for the Americans most of the land into which their settlers had seeped, together with the glamorous city of New Orleans, which had already become the outlet for all that the Ohio Valley had to export. But new trouble appeared in the form of a persistent wooing of the Americans of the valley by Great Britain. When the War of 1812 threatened, a British officer issued these orders to the inhabitants of Kentucky: "Either range yourselves under the flag of your forefathers or observe strict neutrality. If you comply, whatever provisions you send down will be paid for in dollars and the safety of the persons bringing it as well as the free navigation of the Mississippi will be guaranteed to you."

This sort of thing made Andrew Jackson see red. To the end of his days he waxed furious when he spoke of the British in the Mississippi Valley in the years between 1803 and 1812. He said that they did not accept the Louisiana Purchase as valid, declaring in the Treaty of Ghent: "We do not admit Bonaparte's construction of the law of nations; we cannot accept it in relation to any subject matter before us." He claimed that they intended to make an exception of the city of New Orleans and the whole Mississippi Valley in the treaty which ended the war, and it was only the capture of New Orleans by his men from Kentucky and Tennessee that made them change their minds, showing them that they couldn't possess the valley—the people wouldn't let them. "All that cunning of English diplomacy," he said proudly, "was torn to pieces and soaked in blood by the never-missing rifles of my Tennessee and Kentucky pioneers, and that ended it." William Cobbett, the British Liberal, substantiated Jackson's statement, saying: "The Battle of New Orleans broke the heart of European despotism. The man who won it did in that one act more for the good and honor of the human race than ever was done by any other man."

So the War of 1812 as fought by Kentucky and Tennessee became a holy crusade, a second American Revolution. In it Kentucky and Tennessee felt that, alone and unaided, they saved the whole transmontane region for the Republic. They had no illusions out there. Every time an Indian or a Spaniard stirred, they smelled the blood of an Englishman, and battle flamed in Old Hickory's eyes. The first difficulty was with the Creeks in Alabama, brave Indians, led by a chief named Weatherford who wasn't the less brave for three-quarters of white blood, one-quarter being of Jackson's own Scotch variety. "French urbanity, Spanish deceit, Scotch thrift, and Creek savagery saw him far," but not so far that he did not have to yield before Kentucky and Tennessee on the warpath. The surrender of Weatherford, as reported by Jackson's young aid, John Reid, had that high quality that always marked the great chief's encounters with men of his own stamp.

" 'I am come,' " said Weatherford to Jackson, " 'to give myself up. I can oppose you no longer. I have done you much injury. I should have done you more . . . but my warriors are killed . . . I am in your power. . . . Dispose of me as you will.'

" 'You are not,' " said the general, " 'in my power. . . . I had ordered you brought to me in chains. . . . But you have come of your own accord. . . . You see my camp; you see my army; you know my object. . . . I would gladly save you and your nation, but you do not even ask to be saved. If you can contend against me in battle, go and head your warriors.'

" 'Ah,' " said Weatherford, " 'well may such language be addressed to me now. . . . There was a time when I could have answered you. . . . I could animate my warriors to battle; but I cannot animate the dead. . . . General Jackson, I have nothing to request for myself. . . . But I beg you to send for the women and children of the warparty, who have been driven into the woods without an ear of corn. . . . They never did any harm. But kill me, if the white people want it done.' "

Whereupon General Jackson poured him a cup of brandy, said kindly that of course he would look after the women and children, and as for himself, good-by and good luck.

The Creeks disposed of, and Alabama open to the advance of cotton, Tennessee and Kentucky turned their eyes to New Orleans. Jackson was not without his troubles with his wild riflemen. Davy Crockett, who was one of them, reports that he told them they were the damnedest volunteers he'd ever seen. First they'd volunteer to come with him, and then just as he needed them most, they'd volunteer to go home again. But plunging hither and thither on horseback, he had them lined up. "He's tough," they said admiringly—"tough as hickory."

So Old Hickory he became and they followed him for the glory of the phrase.

When Jackson appeared in New Orleans there was consternation in social circles. A lady prepared a feast for the general in "that style of cookery for which Creoles are renowned. 'Ah, Mr. Smith, you asked me to receive a great General. I make your house *comme il faut* and prepare a splendid *déjeuner* . . . and all . . . for an old Kaintuck flatboatman!' " But there was one socially correct person who had a better eye to the social potentialities from Kaintuck. This was Edward Livingston, of the famous New York family, grandson of one of the men who had financed Captain Kidd's pirate-hunting expedition on which Kidd himself turned pirate. Edward Livingston was now the attorney for Jean Lafitte, the pirate of Barataria Bay. Livingston had Emerson's notion that the hero is always the aristocrat of the drawing room. With his eye on the tall, straight, thin figure and high bearing, he thought that the only thing the matter with this particular Kaintuck flatboatman was his clothes. This he promptly remedied. "I ushered General Jackson into the drawing room . . . in the full dress uniform of his rank . . . a blue frock coat, white waistcoat, and close fitting breeches. . . . 'Madame and Messieurs, I have the honor to present Major General Jackson of the United States army.' I had to confess that the new uniform made another man of him. He had two sets of manners, one for headquarters, the other for the drawing room."

Livingston then proceeded to bring all his sophistication to bear on the problem of making the honest Kaintuck flatboatman accept the pirate as an ally. Lafitte, approached by the British to aid them to take the city, seeing the opportunity to earn a pardon from the United States government for his past offenses had offered his services in his own inimitable style. "This point of Louisiana which I occupy is of great importance in the present situation. I offer myself to defend it. . . . I am the lost sheep who desires to return to the flock. . . . In case, Monsieur le Gouverneur, that your reply shall not be favorable to my ardent wishes, I declare to you that I leave immediately so not to be held to have cooperated with an invasion. . . . This cannot fail to take place, and puts me entirely at the judgment of my conscience."

But Jackson would have none of the Lafittes. Pirates were pirates in the country he came from. Free Americans could get along, he said, without the aid of such "hellish banditti." Even Livingston, with his New York polish and his subtle appreciation of heroes, could not move him. The Lafittes then sent Jackson a present of some claret. Jackson drank the claret and said they were hellish banditti just the same. The suave little buccaneer now took matters into his own hands. He went and called on General Jackson. Jackson never could withstand a man who approached him in his own high fashion. What they said to each other is not known. It is a loss less to history than to literature. Lafitte and Jackson both conversed in the grand style. It would take more than a Shakespeare to imagine anything as good as what they probably said. But the end was inevitable. "Mr. Lafitte solicited for himself and all the Baratarians the honor of serving under our banners, that they might have the opportunity of proving that if they had infringed the revenue laws, yet none were more ready than they to defend the country. . . . Persuaded that the assistance of these men could not fail of being very useful, the general accepted their efforts."

At two o'clock one afternoon Jackson heard that the British forces had landed. "By Heaven," he said, "they shall not sleep upon our soil." And they didn't. Through twilight and the long night Kentucky and Tennessee charged furiously, with Mississippi beside them, and a lot of gay gentlemen from Louisiana, out for *la gloire* and *la guerre*. These gallants were a little disappointed when Jackson thrust spades into their hands and made them dig for their lives, throwing up entrenchments. They weren't used to these Northern barbarians who conducted warfare with a woodsman's ax in one hand, a spade in the other, and a rifle between their teeth.

So New Orleans was saved, and with it, as Jackson and the West believed, both the eastern Mississippi Valley and the whole of the Louisiana Purchase. One more sally, and Kentucky and Tennessee rested in their career of conquest. The Indians were stirring down in Florida. Every time an Indian or a Spaniard began to move on the frontiers, Jackson looked for the Englishman. There was not an Englishman this time, but worse. He was Alexander Arbuthnot, one of Jackson's own Scotch breed, who seems to have been a disinterested friend of the Seminole Indians, a white-haired old Indian trader. This "noted Scotch villain," as Jackson called him, was forthwith captured, and it was proved that papers calling on the British governor at Nassau for troops, arms, and ammunition with which to fight the Americans were in his handwriting. Whereupon Jackson immediately had him hanged. There is no use following up the story. It was as usual, hard on the Indians. Jackson and the good men of Kentucky knew that as long as anyone but the Americans had Florida, the British would be stirring up the Indians, and they would have to dash down there and shoot everybody. So ultimately it was arranged to keep Kentucky, Tennessee, and the British all at home by purchasing Florida and opening it to American settlers. Jackson, with his wife and a brigade of Tennesseans, went down there as "momentary" governor of the territory.

6

Having saved the Mississippi Valley for the nation, the next thing for Kentucky and Tennessee to do was to send Andrew Jackson to the White House to save the nation from the money-changers. Loaded with debt, afraid of losing his equity in all he possessed, the average farmer had a great fear of the Eastern capitalist and all the abracadabra of credit, mortgages, and inflation. Money he thought ought not to be a kind of algebra. After all, money stood for wealth, and wealth was real things, things you could use—food, land, houses. In this kind of wealth the Western farmer was growing richer and richer.

He wanted to make sure that he did not lose it by some kind of hocus-pocus just as Daniel Boone had lost his lands to the speculators.

So to the White House Andrew Jackson went, and he made a great president—so great that some think he was the second founder of our democracy. The theory of his democracy was simple. It was that all matters of economics and government can be reduced to plain propositions and put in terms which any man of normal native intelligence, either educated or uneducated, can understand, and anything in government or economics that can't be put into those simple terms, and meet the test of the real judgment of the simplest honest fellow, probably has something shady about it. This was the basis of his long fight over money and the United States Bank. He was determined to make money simple. Coin instead of paper, and real things instead of coin—butter, eggs, wheat. This Western belief in real things as wealth was satirized by a humorist who wrote of admission prices at a Western theater: "Box tickets, two pair of chickens and a dozen eggs; pit, three pounds of butter and a cabbage head; gallery, any quantity of peas and potatoes."

Similarly, Jackson was determined to support the real settlers against the land speculators. With land speculation Jackson had had plenty of experience. Most of his friends and associates, most of the early promoters of Kentucky and Tennessee —Sevier, Robertson, Henderson—had been involved in it, and the leadership of his own world was rank with scandals. Only his invincible personal honesty had kept him from being as blackly tarred as the rest. Generous and believing, and except where his own set of principles was touched, easygoing, he had again and again joined with friends or lent his name and influence to some proceeding which had been handsomely presented to him in fine phrases—only to find, when he got involved in it, that it smelled of one of those things to which he gave ugly and plain names. His withdrawal then was instant and open and at any cost to himself. Of Burr, with whom he had been induced to associate, he had said, to a friend: "I don't believe Burr meditates treason. But if he does I will see him hanged as cheerfully as I would see you hanged in a like case." And so he went forth to face the bankers and the cultivated East with the simple new formula of Western democracy. "If you are honest, you can speak plain. And if you speak plain, the plain man will understand you, and the first thing we talk plainly about is money."

Another thing he intended to call by plain names was this fancy talk in the South about states' rights, and all Calhoun's subtleties about powers delegated by the states to the confederation of states, which could be taken back every time a state wished it. In 1832 the state of South Carolina made its first attempt to test its position by declaring the new tariff null and void. Some people, tired of South Carolina's perpetual threats to leave the Union, were inclined to say, "All right, go." But Jackson snorted, "Secession! States' rights! I call it treason," and dispatched two battleships and some federal troops down there forthwith. Years later, when slavery had become the burning issue, and the South was threatening to call a meeting at Nashville to discuss secession, Daniel Webster dared them to meet at Nashville and vote secession over *the bones of Andrew Jackson.*

The appearance of this simple heroic force of the border in politics asserted a new principle in democracy—that there was a great common denominator of intelligence and moral goodness in men regardless of culture and opportunity. The business of culture was not to lead the plain man, not to think for him, but only to interpret and translate for him, and let him do the thinking and acting.

Of the kind of plain man the West was setting up, Davy Crockett became the sample. And Davy's self-education in politics is typical of the hordes from over the mountains that now swooped down on Washington.

The education began when he settled on an outpost of Wilderness Road. "We remained here some two or three years without any law at all; and so many bad characters began to flock in upon us that we found it necessary to set up a sort of temporary government of our own. . . . We met and appointed magistrates and constables to keep order. But we didn't fix any law for them [the magistrates] tho; for we supposed that they would know law enough whoever they might be, and so we left it to themselves to fix the laws." Crockett found himself one of these magistrates.

Being a magistrate was the beginning of his book education. He could barely read and could not write legibly, but as a magistrate he wanted to write out warrants and keep records. So he sat down betimes to practice penmanship, and soon got so he could read his own handwriting. As for knowledge of law: "My judgments were never appealed from, and if they had been they would have stuck like wax, as I gave my decisions on the principles of common justice and honesty between man and man, and relied on natural born sense and not law learning to guide me, for I had never read a law book in all my life."

Gradually the country filled up. Crockett, having been a magistrate, was invited to come out for the legislature. Now, he learned, he was to tell the people something about the government, "and an eternal sight of other things that I knowed nothing more about than I did about Latin and law and such things as that." But he soon learned that, when asked his opinion about something he had never heard of before, there was a simple way out. "I kept dark, going on the identical plan that I now find is called non-committal."

"A public document I had never seen, nor did I know that there were such things." Of the procedure of legislatures he was completely ignorant. He had never heard any political terms nor any general question of public policy discussed, even local public policy. But the people of this new country believed in him and now he must go to the Tennessee legislature. At this point he got a teacher in an unexpected quarter. The opposing candidate had come in, all primed with education and knowledge, "knowing my ignorance as well as I did my-self. . . . The truth is he thought my being a candidate was a mere matter of sport and didn't think for a moment he was in danger from an ignorant backwoodsman." But the back-woodsman said to himself: "This fellow knows what it is all about if I don't. So here is where I listen to him myself, and keep all the rest of them from hearing a word he says."

So at political meetings he would give his opponent a chance to speak first and would listen carefully to everything he said, trying to understand it and to make up his own mind. Then instead of answering him, he would get up and tell amus-ing stories and lead the people off to get drinks. Finally he had to go to a big state rally, where he was slated to speak and scared to death about it. "As good luck would have it, these big candidates spoke nearly all day, and when they quit, the people were worn out with fatigue, which afforded me a good excuse for not discussing the government. But I listened mighty close to them and was learning fast about political mat-ters."

Crockett was elected. But his troubles were not over. When he met Colonel Polk, then a member of Congress from Ten-nessee, Polk said to him, "Well, Colonel, I suppose we shall have a radical change of the judiciary at the next session of the legislature." "Very likely, sir," said Crockett, and instantly moved out of Polk's way, "for I was afraid somebody would ask me what the judiciary was, and if I knowed, I wish I may be shot."

From the legislature he went to Congress, educating himself all along the way, with the help of his opponents. Politics al-ways remained as simple to him as it did to Will Rogers. Once when he was a candidate for Congress, his opponent, speaking for the tariff, pointed out that cotton was bringing twenty-five dollars a hundred. As soon as Crockett heard this: "I might as well have sung psalms over a dead horse as to try to make the people believe otherwise; for they knowed their cotton had been raised sure enough, and if the colonel hadn't done it, they didn't know what had."

Knowing that you couldn't beat the price of cotton, Crockett was forthwith resigned to not going to Congress, though actually he lost by only two votes. His opponent went on "and served out his term, and at the end of it cotton was down to six or eight dollars a hundred; and I concluded I would try him once more and see how it would go with cotton at the common price."

Whereupon Crockett went back to Congress!

At the Jacksons in the van and the Crocketts in the rear of the new democracy, the polite and the elegant of the East might sneer. But everywhere, in the highest strongholds of the old culture, were persons who observed the new leaders with the same thoughtful eye that Livingston had cast on Jackson's tall figure, finding it potentially distinguished in the drawing room. Something there was in these men from the West that made culture look common, and elegance vulgar. And up in Boston, in the very stronghold of the intellectuals and of established capitalism, a quiet voice was raised which steadily, for thirty years to come, interpreted the new American aristocracy to the world. "These rough riders—" said Emerson, "these legislators in shirt sleeves—let them drive as they may; and the disposition of territories and public lands, the necessity of balancing and keeping at bay the snarling majorities of German, Irish, and of native millions, will bestow promptness, address, and reason at last on our buffalo hunter, and authority and majesty of manners. The instinct of the people is right. Men expect from good Whigs put in office by the respectability of the country much less skill to deal with Mexico, Spain, or Britain than from some strong transgressor, like Jefferson, like Jackson, who first conquers his own government and then uses the same genius to conquer the foreigner. . . . There is always room for the man of force, and he makes room for many."

Culture at its highest point knows only what these rude

democrats instinctively believe, said Emerson. "The secret of culture is to learn that a few great points . . . are alone to be regarded—the escape from all false ties; courage to be what we are, and love of what is simple and beautiful; independence and cheerful relation, these are essentials—these and the wisdom to serve—to add something to the well being of mankind."

7

While Kentucky and Tennessee were thus blowing through the Eastern world of capital, politics, and culture on the heroic winds of the West, the whole bluegrass region was ceasing to be the West and becoming the South. "Rank and fashion from tidewater Virginia" rolled in. Gentlemen with money bought out the claims of the pioneers. The strongest among the early settlers who were able to hold on to their lands took the polish of the Old South. Yet something of the original charm of this new world remained. The strong Scotch, Irish, and Huguenot base retained a dash and simplicity, a chivalry and exuberance of character. Thomas Flint, an early observer, reports: "There is a distinct and striking moral physiognomy to this people—an enthusiasm, a vivacity and ardor of character, courage, frankness, generosity that has developed with the peculiar circumstances under which they have been placed." Audubon, a young Frenchman, speaking English oddly because he had learned it from a Quaker, coming to Louisville, Kentucky, and in those days often without funds, wrote gratefully that among these Scotch and Huguenot people, the "matrons acted like mothers toward my wife, the daughters proved agreeable associates, and the husbands and sons were friends and companions to me. If I absented myself on business or otherwise for any length of time, my wife was removed to the hospitable abode of some friends in the neighborhood until my return, and then I was several times obliged to spend a week or more with these good people before they could be prevailed upon to let us return to our residence."

Kentucky remained Arcadia to Audubon, and so he

painted it in words and in pigments in his great epic of the wild woods—*The Birds of North America*. Who will forget his account of the Kentucky barbecue, mellow as an old painting, rich as the traditions of country festivals in southern France? It was the Fourth of July, he says. "Every open spot forming a plantation was smiling in the luxuriance of summer harvest. The farmer seemed to stand in admiration of the spectacle; the trees of his orchards lowered their branches as if anxious to restore to their mother earth the fruit with which they were laden; the flocks leisurely ruminated as they lay on their grassy beds." In this idyllic world, he says, the "free, single-hearted Kentuckian, bold, erect, and proud of his Virginian descent," prepared to celebrate Fourth of July. It is a veritable *fête champêtre*—"wagons laden with melons, peaches, plums, pears, flagons of every beverage; . . . hale and rosy elders, . . . blooming children, and, plunging joyously among them, youths and maidens on horses, handsome as disguised divinities."

The Kentuckians of that early day not only cultivated fine looks, but they wished if possible to preserve them for posterity. So portrait painting flourished among the prosperous farmers of the bluegrass region—a quaint early school of art, some of whose masters have since been of great interest to collectors —among them Jouett, Price, Grimes, Frazer, and Morgan Hunt. Some of their portraits are reproduced in a brochure published by the Filson Club of Kentucky entitled *Old Masters of the Blue Grass*. There one sees the striking moral physiognomy of this released and happy people, in the first generation of their rustic prosperity, translated into the flesh and clad in the early nineteenth century costume. Round-faced, round-eyed, strong, contented, full-bodied, looking out at you with fresh, candid good nature and the sweet repose of a matchless physical well-being, there is one after another of the notables of Kentucky, presidents of banks, chief justices, statesmen, together with their wives and daughters. There are also some of the quaint native characters, preserved because the people wanted them remembered. The painting of Simon Kenton, pioneer, won applause in a Philadelphia exposition. The quaintest of these is King Solomon painted by Sam W. Price— round-faced, round-eyed, serene as the rest. King Solomon was an idle drunken fellow, a local ne'er-do-well, till the time came when his neighbors were dying of cholera. Then King Solomon rose up, laid aside his bottle, and going with reverent dignity from house to house in trouble, offered to lay out the dead, and to dig their graves and bury them. The grateful neighbors insisted that he should be immortalized for them by their local portrait painter. King Solomon refused, but was finally persuaded by an offer of unlimited grog and cigars so long as he would consent to sit.

But over this Arcadian landscape a shadow was falling. It did not seem a shadow to all of them. Some congratulated themselves that it was the development of rank and fashion. In 1847 Doctor Daniel Drake, remembering his childhood in Kentucky, wrote a bitter indictment of the progressive dispossession of the free white owners and settlers of this beautiful land to make way for slaves. "In a single walk I passed over foundations, decayed logs and dust of twelve cabins on the broad hearths of which I used to warm myself in winter. . . . Weeds and briars were growing around the door, and an unutterable feeling of awe and melancholy came over me as I trod upon the sill on which I used to sit with my little sisters and brothers and be pushed aside by my dear mother as she went in and out on her quiet willing duties. . . . In a slave state, new investments are continually made in land and negroes, and hence the soil is constantly passing from the many to the few. Slaves take the place of freemen, negro quarters replace the habitations of happy families; he who had a stirring and laborious father rules over augmented plantations as a lord, and the hired man with his axe or sickle is replaced by the overseer with his thong."

Once more the Kentuckians took up the march. The poor and unlucky began to move because there was no place for them in a world growing black, and so they seeped northward into Illinois and Indiana and Ohio. But there were border chieftains—all glory to them!—who at great inconvenience to themselves moved for freedom and conscience' sake. When I was a very young woman, I met a distinguished old mulatto gentleman who was conducting a school for Negroes in the South. He had been brought to Ohio from Kentucky just before the war with a family who treated him pleasantly, had him eat at the table with them and gave him a good education. He did some services about the place, but never with the implication that he was a servant, and shared in all family festivals, such as birthdays and Christmas. Not till he was a middle-aged man did the truth about this family dawn on him. Then he suddenly understood that he was the son of the head of the family, and these boys and girls were his half brothers and sisters. With quiet self-sacrifice, the family had freed their other slaves, and brought him north, and the wife had joined with her husband in making such reparation and acknowledgment as they could in affection and education and sharing of the family life. But he took another surname, and after he knew the relationship he kept the secret as carefully as they. "I still hear from one of them occasionally," he said. "Since I came myself to the South and began to understand all that was involved in what they did, I have come to honor them more and more. But I have never presumed to let them know that I realize the relationship, and that I appreciate them very much."

9

THE BEAUTIFUL RIVER OHIO

HE talk on the banks of the Hudson, that spring of
1783 when the Revolutionary War ended, was all of
the river Ohio. "The Beautiful River," the Indians
called it, and looking down on the deep, cold waters of the
Hudson, between these shaggy mountainsides, the imagination of soldiers wove a dream of another river, in a warmer
and kindlier land. Ohio—it was a word often on the lips of
Washington. Here in his headquarters at Newburgh and West
Point during some of the darkest days of the war, he used to
talk to his officers about it, on somber afternoons of inaction
when they sat around Washington's board after the late dinner,
sipping wine and cracking endless hickory nuts, and munch-
ing the crisp, spicy, sour apples which Dutch farmers would
bring down to them from farms up Middletown way. However they might be defeated here, he would tell them, there
was still Ohio. And he would enlarge on the promise of the
rich forest land there, and the potentialities of the Mississippi
Valley. Let the British drive them out here, and they would
all migrate, with a safe headquarters and capital for the government somewhere in the Alleghenies. It was a dream. But it
consoled and heartened them all.

One of the officers who listened most eagerly to these accounts of Ohio was General Rufus Putnam, the builder of the fortifications at West Point, cousin of Israel Putnam, the rough old hero of the New England frontier. Washington did not like Israel, being irritated by what seemed to him a slovenly democracy in his way of drinking with his soldiers and letting them talk back to him, and by his disposition to disobey orders from general headquarters. But Rufus stood better with the Chief. He was, said Washington, the "best engineer officer" in America at the time. In two years, under his direction, West Point, says the Marquis de Chastellux, "a desert almost inaccessible . . . has been covered with fortresses and artillery by a people who six years before had scarcely seen a cannon."

Here in this wild and warlike abode, as De Chastellux calls it, "where one seems transported to the bottom of Thrace and the dominion of the god Mars," the heart of the Revolution beat with a peculiar fervor. Here they had guarded the most important point in America, the entrance to that great gorge which provided a highway from Canada and which, if captured, could cut in two the colonies. It was here, as De Chastellux says, that Benedict Arnold, "a horse dealer transformed into a general or rather become a hero, always intrepid, always victorious, but always purchasing victory at the price of his blood; here that extraordinary man, at once the honor and opprobrium of his country, actually sold and expected to deliver this palladium of American liberty to England." The French nobleman, riding up the mountain road to meet Washington for the first time, felt that in this wild landscape, where "so many extraordinary circumstances are brought together in the physical and moral order," he was riding straight into some old heroic tale. But what he found, he said, were some "pretty women and an excellent dish of tea!" He also found officers "with a becoming and military carriage, who unite much politeness to a great deal of capacity. . . . The headquarters presents an appearance neither of want nor inexperience. Truly these people have nothing barbarous in their discipline!"

During the lengthening spring days of 1783, when the shad-blow was white in the woods on the dark heights above them, and "Dutchmen's breeches" twinkled on every gray ledge, what these officers were talking about was Ohio. They were conscious that they were ending one great story, and they thought it should be but the beginning of another. Devotion to each other, devotion to Washington—something must be done to keep alive the high feeling which had given them their country, which had sustained them through so many common perils. So in May, 1783, the officers under Putnam met at Newburgh and formed the hereditary Society of the Cincinnati, naming themselves after the great Roman general who had gone from his victories straight back to his farm. Their farms, they hoped, would be in Ohio. In this society they and their sons might keep alive the memory of the hardships and glories of the Revolution forever.

Following the organization of the Cincinnati, the men under Putnam, with the approval of their officers, met and presented a petition to Washington. They wanted him to take the lead in organizing a soldiers' state in Ohio, where any soldier of the Revolution might obtain lands in return for the depreciated paper with which he was being paid off by the Continental Congress. Washington received the plan with sympathy, and hesitated only because he was involved in a larger scheme for opening the Ohio country. He was afraid that if settlers went out there without a trade route from the east arranged for them ahead of time, they would have to float their goods down the Ohio to New Orleans, and so would be tempted to annex themselves to the Spanish in that city.

Puzzling over the problem of tying up the proposed settlement with the East, Washington did not act on Putnam's plan immediately. But eight months after he surrendered his commission as general of the American armies, in the comely, white-pillared room in Annapolis which has the record of the surrender inscribed on its walls, Washington himself made a horseback tour of Ohio, looking it all over and considering. Following this, the Continental Congress made arrangements for a land survey of the district to which each state was entitled to nominate one member. Massachusetts nominated Putnam, but subsequently sent General Benjamin Tupper in his place. One difficulty about Putnam was that he lived in Rutland, Vermont, and Vermont was not yet a part of the United States. It was operating as an independent commonwealth pending the claim that the land along Lake Champlain which men from New Hampshire had taken, was really part of New York State. But Putnam was still in the picture. When Tupper came back from Ohio, he went to visit the enterprising frontier engineer in Vermont. There, before the blazing hickory fire in the dignified, square house in Rutland, over apples and cider, Tupper and Putnam laid plans for really putting through this idea of a soldier's state.

On the first of March, 1786, they called a meeting of their military friends at the Bunch of Grapes Tavern in Boston, and formed a land company called The Ohio Associates, to be financed out of the worthless paper with which Congress had paid them. Good land for bad paper was their plea. It was as a result of their appeal to Congress that the Northwest Ordinance was passed in 1787, anticipating the Constitution as the first great American instrument of government, and providing an organic basis for the states of Ohio, Indiana, Illinois, Michigan, and Wisconsin. In this new region slavery was forbidden, and religious tolerance was established. "No person demeaning himself in a peaceable and orderly manner shall ever be molested on account of his mode of worship or religious sentiments in the said territories"—which, considering how many strange religions were to be fostered here, and to survive to this day, was a provision of more than usual importance. Above all, the necessity for schools was written into the organic law of the territory. "Religion, morality, and knowledge being necessary to good government and the happiness of mankind, schools and the means of education shall forever be encouraged."

Along with these provisions there was established that system of apprenticeship for statehood which has been followed ever since. Having thus written into the law of the territory the best liberal opinion of the day, Congress opened the land to the soldiers. A section of which Chillicothe became the center was reserved for Virginia and her heroes. New Jersey took the district around Cincinnati. Connecticut, ceding a claim she had to this Western country, kept the strip of territory of which Cleveland is the center, called The Western Reserve. Then General Putnam with a group of Vermonters built a boat which he called "The Mayflower," and sailing through the Ohio gateway into the Northwest in May, 1788, started, with a grand gesture, the Revolutionary migration. The town which he and his pilgrims founded was Marietta, the first permanent settlement in the state of Ohio.

An interesting account in verse of the first Ohio Pilgrim Fathers, too long to quote here, may be found in Elizabeth Peck's *American Frontier*, published in 1937.

2

It was a lonely, somber, and at first almost impenetrable world—this Land of Promise for the soldier. The vast inland seas stretching a thousand miles through the forests to the north were still inaccessible. Only the Ohio River was securely American, with Kentucky spreading safely along the other side and a way out to civilization through the Cumberland Gap. If you put your goods on the river and floated the other way, you came out into strange regions where not even English was spoken—Spanish, French. In the woods to the northward and westward and along the lakes were little French towns—Detroit, Vincennes, Kaskaskia, Prairie du Chien, the Sault Sainte Marie.

Yet it was a lovely land. Under the leaf mold the soil was deep and rich and blessedly without stones. Spring came early with a mist of blossoms through the woods, white and pink, feathering the trees; autumn lasted long, not brief, splendid, high colored as in New England, but mistily rusty and dimly gold, lingering dreamily through days and days which invited you to build just another shed for the stock, and spade just another garden against next spring, and cut just a little more wood before winter should really set in. But when winter came, "Snow, snow, snow—above us, around us and under our feet to the depth of some half-dozen inches. In large feathery flakes it floats downward through the still air, and it also muffles our footsteps as we tramp through the pathless and desolate woods. . . . Slowly and heavily without game or a single adventure we are compelled to trudge along, and when we come in sight of the pleasant village, not a penny we care for anything else in the world but a roaring fire and a warm supper."

During the lifetime of the first settlers Ohio was hemmed in rather closely by the Indian frontier. The Indian tradition of the Great Lakes regions was not without its romance for the more thoughtful Yankees. Transmitted to New England, and returning in the verses of the favorite New England poet, it was to become the heritage of every American schoolboy. The grandchildren of those who fought back the Indians in Ohio with Revolutionary muskets, the children of those who defeated Tecumseh at Tippecanoe in Indiana, were to be declaiming on Friday afternoons in schoolrooms in the West,

> Forth upon the Gitchie Gumee,
> On the shining Big Sea Water,
> With his fishing line of cedar,
> Of the twisted bark of cedar,
> Forth to catch the sturgeon Nahma,
> Mishe-Nahma, King of Fishes,
> In his birch canoe exulting
> All alone went Hiawatha.

Potent, too, in its effect on the Yankee imagination was the great French tradition of the Great Lakes. Seeping back into

New England the romance of the French in the Great Lake country and up and down the Mississippi, merging in Longfellow's imagination with the traditions of the Maine coast, became the lovely little story of Evangeline. The tradition, living on, always renewed by the New Englanders of the Northwest, touched the mind of a student at Harvard, and became the magnificent work of Parkman. Parkman was to tell how Champlain coming to Lake Ontario and hearing of miles and miles, leagues on leagues of sea beyond, had seen "the Pacific, Japan, China, the Spice Islands, and India stretching in flattering vista before his fancy, and had entered with eagerness upon the chase of this illusion." "In these ancient wilds to whose ever verdant antiquity the pyramids are young, and Nineveh a mushroom of yesterday; where the sage wanderer of the Odyssey, could he have urged his pilgrimage so far, would have surveyed the same grand and stern monotony, the same dark sweep of melancholy woods—here while New England was a solitude, and the settlers of Virginia scarcely dared venture inland beyond the sound of cannon shot, Champlain was planting on shores and islands the emblems of his faith."

In a world oppressively new and barren it comforted the imagination to reach back to the older civilization which had been here before—to Champlain and to the Jesuit fathers who followed him. The curiosity of the more cultivated reached out with interest to the little French towns here, to Detroit on Lake Michigan, to Vincennes in Indiana and Kaskaskia in Illinois, and Green Bay, Wisconsin. "There are few spots in our country which may lay more undisputed claim to antiquity than these early French settlements in the western valley," wrote E. F., an amusing Yankee who a generation later went from French village to French village in Illinois and wrote a book about them which Harpers published. It delighted E. F. to think that "yon aged church tower has thrown its venerable shadow alike over the Indian corn dances, the rude cotillion of the French village, the Spanish fandango, the

Virginia reel, and the Yankee frolic." He is particularly pleased when he finds old people still wearing the original costume of these parts—a capote, which was a coat with a cap attached to the shoulders and hanging back like a cape; a blue handkerchief bound around the head, a long queue sticking out behind; and on their feet moccasins instead of shoes. He enjoyed the dances where old and young, bond and free, united, and reported that, while slaves were held wherever the federal government had not specifically forced their release, he never saw a "fleshier, happier looking set of mortals than the blacks of these old villages."

On the southern shores of the Great Lakes the British had taken the French fur posts and were keeping some of them garrisoned with soldiers, especially Detroit. Though the transmontane territory south of the lakes was supposed to be ceded to the Americans at the end of the Revolution, actually the British fur traders did not expect the states to hold together or to be able effectively to occupy the Mississippi Valley. So they thought they might as well stay there and go on trading, and at the same time keep the Indians stirring. This state of affairs was settled when Washington dispatched another Revolutionary hero, "Mad Anthony Wayne," to that territory. He went like a whirlwind through the land, defeated the Indians at the Battle of Fallen Timbers in 1794, forced the British to evacuate Detroit, and made a treaty with the Indians at Greenville on August 3, 1795, in which they accepted the American occupation of Ohio and agreed to move westward. This gave the settlers peace for about a dozen years.

Meanwhile there grew up in Ohio an Indian boy named Tecumseh who, touched with a few white man's ideas, began to dream Hiawatha's dream of uniting all the Indians south and north in a confederation to resist the further advance of the whites. This confederacy was to be dedicated to sober and industrious living, communal possession of wealth, and democratic procedure, and inspired to high ideals by Tecumseh's brother, "The Prophet." But unfortunately Tecumseh had

British advisers, and, in the growing tension in the Mississippi Valley previous to the War of 1812 it was felt that these Indian plans were but a cloak under which the British were preventing the Americans from occupying the valley. In 1809 Tecumseh was defeated by Americans under William Henry Harrison near the Indian headquarters called "The Prophet's Town," by the Tippecanoe River, in Indiana. When the War of 1812 broke out, Tecumseh joined the British forces and was made a brigadier general. He and the British were again defeated by Harrison in the battle of the Thames, and with Tecumseh dead upon the field died the abortive reachings of the Indians for a state of their own. As usual, the more intellectual Yankees looked with rueful sympathy upon the Indian, but were later able to compensate for all the difficult and ugly facts in such blandly romantic poetry as "Hiawatha." The story of Tecumseh was written down by Benjamin Drake and published in Cincinnati in 1841.

3

Because of the hostile hinterland, settlers had to stay together, in close communities, for protection. This solid way of settling, in little communities dominated by New England village tradition, gave a special character to Ohio, as contrasted with the spreading backwoods settlements of the states across the river. It also facilitated the development of those educational standards which were provided for in the Ordinance. The Congregationalists of New England, the Quakers of Pennsylvania, and the Scotch-Irish Presbyterians of New Jersey and the whole southern border all had their emissaries out there, ready to turn the first timber of the falling forest into school desk and pulpit. Of these the Yankees were so numerous, vocal, and sharply distinguished in all their ways that they easily dominated the others, and along the border Ohio was referred to with amusement as "Yankee-land."

The peculiarities of this Yankee-land are referred to in one of Stephen Foster's early nonsense songs.

They had Ohio Yankees of Western Reserve
Who live upon cheese, ginger cake, and preserve.
Abolition's their watchword, their rod, and their staff,
And they'll fight for a sixpence an hour and half.

But apparently no inconvenient Puritanism prevented the Yankees from having a good time, for we are told that the young people went to balls three times running in one week. And Marietta had its own picturesque traditions. There were the Blennerhasset family, living in feudal splendor on an island in the river. They fitted up the expedition for Aaron Burr—fifteen large bateaux, built on the Muskingum River, laden with cornmeal, bacon, pork, flour, and whisky, and setting out to do God knows what. The mystery that hangs over this polished grandson of the great Yankee saint and mystic, Jonathan Edwards, clings to the island and the Blennerhassets, and to "Mrs. Blennerhasset, dashing along forest paths in her riding dress of scarlet broadcloth, accompanied by a favorite black servant." From Blennerhasset Burr embarked on some strange plan of conquest in the Mississippi River, dreaming apparently of an American Empire in the Southwest, of which some said he hoped to be Emperor Aaron the First. But he was arrested under a charge of treason against the United States and the home of the Blennerhassets was destroyed by the Ohio militia. Reading the records over carefully, even the plain and downright testimony of Andrew Jackson, one is still puzzled to know the rights and wrongs of the matter.

Meanwhile, the Yankees were effecting a much more sober conquest of the French and Spanish hinterland. Bringing to the wilderness their great faith in the creation of value by moving things about, they were helpfully peddling things from town to town along the rivers. In *Grandmother's Hundred Years*, it is reported that grandfather took bacon down the river and exchanged it for molasses at plantations, and then exchanged molasses for sugar. This sugar was shipped in hogsheads up to the mouth of the Hocking River, and thence hauled in wagons sixteen miles. It came wrapped in purple paper which, soaked in water, produced a dye for the young ladies' gloves. The cash returns of the voyage grandfather brought back in Mexican silver packed in ax-head boxes in a small horsehair trunk. This profit amounted to about $2,000. Taking this, he went to Pittsburgh and invested in machinery and household furnishings which he then proceeded to carry through the Northwest. Here were the old tricks of the Yankee seamen, safely transferred to land and to river boats.

Along with their peddling, the Yankees brought their religious disputatiousness. Peter Cartwright, the great circuit-riding preacher of Kentucky and Tennessee, whose *Autobiography* is one of the most delightful of Western documents, was frightened when he had to go over into Ohio. He had heard that these Yankees were dreadfully learned, that they couldn't bear loud preaching, and that they were just waiting to make a monkey of the poor backwoods preacher. But Bishop Asbury said, "Go, my son. It will make a man of you," and Peter, ignorant, but able and manly, admits that it did. "These Yankees," he said, "were generally educated, and had every kind of ism—Deism, Universalism, Unitarianism." They were good for him, he says, "waked me up on all sides." As usual, it was the old Yankee ladies that did the waking. These bright old persons, celebrated long before by English prisoners of war in New England, were by this time a tradition. Of one of them Cartwright says: "She was a thin-faced, loquacious Yankee, glib on the tongue, and you may depend on it, I had a hard time to keep up with her, but I found it a good school, for it set me reading the Bible." As for the Congregational preachers, having with the help of the smart old women taken the measure of the rude young backwoods preacher, they proceeded, to his amazement, to open their churches to him. A charming story, this little episode of Cartwright among the Yankees, and a credit to both him and them!

Meanwhile the Yankees were taking their own characteristic attitude to the slavery across the river. At the time of the

settling of Ohio, almost the only Americans officially opposed
to slavery were the Quakers and some of the German sects of
Pennsylvania. New England, as a whole, had not put its mind
on the subject. Next to Pennsylvania, the state in which there
was the strongest objection to slavery was Virginia. Washington, Jefferson, and George Mason had all disliked it intensely and had been instrumental in writing the provision
against it into the Northwest Ordinance. Across the river in
Kentucky there was active and vocal opposition to pushing
slavery westward. The Yankees, coming into Ohio, having no
experience with slavery and no particular opinion about it,
were not long in making up their minds on the subject.
Wrong, of course it was wrong! But that wasn't the worst
thing about it! Imagine having to chase these shiftless black
people about their tasks all day long! They'd rather a thousand
times do things themselves! The result of this attitude was soon
evident. The Scotchman, John Mellish, going down the Ohio
in 1811, makes one of the first of those invidious comparisons
between the two sides of the river which were to become ever
more frequent as the century drew to its climax. "We had
found by this time that the settlers on the Ohio side were by
far in the most comfortable circumstances, and we never failed
to make an application for lodgings or victuals on that side.
On the Virginia side, we had of late made frequent attempts,
but were always unsuccessful. On stopping there, we generally found a negro, who could give us no answer, or a poor-
looking object in the shape of a woman, who, 'moping and
melancholy,' would say 'We have no way.' I never saw the bad
effects of slavery more visible than in this contrast. On the
Virginia side they seemed generally to trust to the exertions
of the negroes, and we found them, as might be expected,
'miserable and wretched and poor and almost naked.' On the
Ohio side they trusted to the blessing of God and their own
exertions and 'God helps them that help themselves,' as Poor
Richard says, in his almanac. We found them increasing in
wealth, population, and domestic comfort; and we resolved

hereafter to apply on the right bank only for accommodation."

4

The general independence and intellectual vitality of the Yankees in Ohio showed during the early nineteenth century in a good deal of fresh, frank, mystical religious thinking. Quaint characters and bold speculations on social and moral questions came in by two trails—from Vermont and points east across New York State, and from Pennsylvania. Potent in shaping religious and social speculation, both at home in New England, and here in Ohio, was the great Swedish scientist of the eighteenth century, Emanuel Swedenborg. He had himself been the intellectual prototype of the Yankee, for beginning as a scientist with great curiosity and independence of thought and observation, he had also had a strong mechanical bent, and was the author of several mechanical improvements and inventions. After a useful and practical career in his earlier years, be became in his older years a mystic, and wrote out his visions of the heavens and hells of existence in a gorgeous, pictorial style. When the independent, inquisitive, mechanical Yankees turned to religious speculation they tended to become visionaries of the same type as the independent, inquisitive, mechanical Swedenborg.

And so it happens that the folk hero of Ohio, corresponding, in tradition, to Daniel Boone in Kentucky and Davy Crockett in Tennessee, was a self-elected Swedenborgian missionary, called Johnny Appleseed. Johnny Appleseed is typical of the forces which Ohio brought to bear upon the Western frontiersmen who were pouring through the Cumberland Gap into Kentucky and Tennessee, but seeping northward also. He was not an indigenous hero, compact of their own virtues, magnified in story and tradition. He was a stranger and an alien, queer, disturbing. He pointed the way to new values, displacing rifle and bearskin with hoe and blossoming apple tree, offering, instead of the rude humorous yarns of the frontier, strange Swedenborgian visions,

> I have seen priestesses of life go by
> Gliding in samite through the incense sea—
> Innocent children marching with them there,
> Singing in flowered robes, "The earth is free,"
> While on the fair, deep-carved unfinished towers
> Sentinels watch in armor, night and day—
> Guarding the brazier fires of hope and dream—
> Wild was their peace and dawn-bright their array
> And, scattering dreams and glory,
> Prophets' boats sailed in from far-away,
> And angels' boats sailed in
> From Chaos seas and many a stormy day.

These words which Vachel Lindsay puts in the mouth of Johnny Appleseed are only typical Swedenborgian visions set to rhyme and meter.

The story of Johnny Appleseed was told in an article in *Harper's Monthly Magazine*, November, 1871, based on oral tradition, and has been several times retold from that source since. Johnny Appleseed's real name was Jonathan Chapman. He first appeared at Licking Creek, Ohio, a slender dark-eyed young man in buckskin and coonskin cap, leading a pack horse which carried bags full of apple seeds, obtained from cider mills in Pennsylvania. He seems to have been a Yankee from Massachusetts, a person of some education, ready to spread the doctrines of Swedenborg as he led his horse along the forest paths. To him the apple tree had some mystical signification. Gracious in fruit, beautiful in blossom, it was the symbol of love—love of God for His created world, love and kindness between man and man. But he also possessed the usual Yankee capacity for combining mystical imagination with shrewd usefulness. The settlers out here would need orchards, and it takes a long time to grow a tree. He might as well start now and have trees ready for them. So he cleared a patch in the forest, built a brush fence around it, planted his seeds in neat rows, and started a nursery of young apple trees. His first trees he distributed to settlers, usually adding to his gift of an orchard an offer to read to them from the Bible, or from some Swedenborgian book. Since reading matter was scarce in the settlements, interested eyes would occasionally be cast on one of Johnny Appleseed's books; whereupon he would generously tear out a few pages and leave them. He couldn't give away the whole book, for somebody else might want to read, too. Out there even print had to be made to go a long way.

In 1806 Johnny Appleseed had expanded his operations. Down the Ohio he went, with two boats lashed together, bearing apple seed. Stopping here and there, wherever he found settlers, he started a little nursery. From the Ohio he branched off into the Muskingam, and thence up the White Woman Creek, and into the Mohican, and into the Black Fork. Later with his seeds in leather bags on his back, he tramped the trail from Fort Duquesne to Detroit by way of Fort Sandusky, starting nurseries all along the line. Thus for more than half a century Johnny Appleseed went just ahead of the oncoming farms with his little nurseries from which they could get trees, through Ohio, into Indiana, to Fort Wayne. A hundred thousand square miles of the Northwest he thus provided with orchards.

As time went on, Johnny seemed to the settlers to become queerer and queerer. A spiritual forerunner of Thoreau, he was always trying to find ways of simplifying the burden of property. Clothes, now—hard to keep in order, hard even to keep hitched together in this continuous tramping and moving about—why do we bother with all this complicated armor of cloth and leather? So his clothes became simpler and simpler, till at last he was going about in nothing but a coffee sack with holes in it through which he could thrust his head and arms. So with transportation. From the horse he advanced to the boat, which did not need to be fed. The boat he abandoned for his own legs and his own back, which couldn't float away from him downstream.

To the settlers the charmed life he bore through the wilderness was no less wonderful. Themselves accustomed never to go into the woods without a rifle, it was amazing to see Johnny Appleseed surviving without shooting game, just on nuts and berries; and more amazing that neither Indians nor wild animals ever bothered him. He seemed to be friends with all creatures. During the War of 1812, flitting her and there through the wilderness, he "became a dismounted Paul Revere, of Ohio, arousing the people and warning them to flee to the blockhouses. Day and night he traveled delivering his message, preserved to this day in family archives. 'The spirit of the Lord is upon me, and He hath anointed me to blow the trumpet in His wilderness; for behold, the tribes of the heathen are round about your doors, and a devouring flame followeth after Him.'"

So he slipped back and forth for half a century through the forests, a strange man, thinking strange thoughts, speaking a strange tongue, but kindly and harmless. One night in Indiana he rested on a cottage doorstep, accepted bread and milk from the housewife, and read the Beatitudes to her, and went to sleep forever on her hearthstone under a quilt she threw over him.

> Oh mesa and throne mountains that I found!
> Oh strange and shaking thoughts that touched me there,
> Ere I beheld the bright returning wings
> That came to spoil my secret, silent lair!

5

Just as Kentucky and Tennessee celebrated their coming of age by sending a president to the White House, so Ohio had its hero of the West and made him president, too. This hero was William Henry Harrison, a man more interesting for all he represented than for his own personality. Harrison had not only defeated the Indians of the Northwest in the crucial battle near Tippecanoe Creek, but he had made it possible for settlers really to take possession of the lands now that the Indians were driven back. The land law sponsored by Harrison, and signed by the president of the United States on May 10, 1800, as McMaster says, "did more for the good of his country than his great victory over the Prophet at Tippecanoe or his defeat of Tecumseh at the battle of the Thames." Harrison made it possible for settlers to acquire freeholds out of the public domains on a down payment of ten cents an acre, and to pay for them out of the proceeds of their crops. There was much criticism of this arrangement later, especially when settlers evaded their debts to the government or made a failure of their contract. But it enabled careful and thrifty men to get a foothold with very little capital. As the lands of Kentucky and Tennessee fell into the hands of large landowners advancing with slaves, this seemed a great boon, and the grateful frontiersmen later rolled Harrison into the presidency behind a miniature log cabin set on wheels, the troops of his adorers marching along, dispensing hard cider to all and sundry and calling for him and his running mate in the yell "Tippecanoe and Tyler too."

The irony of it is that this plain and unassuming gentleman was not a backwoodsman at all, but a scion of the stock which in America stood for aristocracy pure and undefiled. Social imagination on this side of the water could go no higher than tidewater Virginia. Not only were the Harrisons a tidewater family, but William Henry Harrison's father had been a signer of the Declaration. In the Northwest, however, the Harrisons were heroes of the common man and had to wear his regalia, as plainly as royal purple. Years later William Henry Harrison's grandson Benjamin, later president of the United States, came as a guest to my grandfather's house in northern Indiana on a political campaign. My grandfather, who had known the family in Ohio, gave a luncheon in his home, to which local dignitaries were invited, after which Harrison spoke to the people from my grandfather's porch. How vexed the old doctor was when his guest carefully removed the frock coat and white stock in which he had appeared at luncheon and proceeded to open his collar and roll up his sleeves and otherwise make himself look like a plain dirt farmer. My grandfather fumed and said he thought it was "high time we stop wishing on the Harrison family the tricks of cheap democrats." Down in Virginia the highest title to elegance that can be imagined is that of a president of the United States born of a tidewater family whose grandfather had also been president of the United States and whose great-grandfather had signed the Declaration of Independence. There was only one family with such a record, and look what happened to them! Such is American social history!

6

Probably the greatest single contribution of Ohio to the American idea of the better life for all was the development of free school education for everybody. At the time when Ohio was settled the only section of America in which there was anything like general literacy was New England; but even there free common schools, publicly supported and available for every child, had not yet developed. Education was variously provided in the towns and by the churches, and was supplemented by the high degree of literacy among Yankee women who felt it their personal responsibility to teach their own and sometimes other children. The Yankee mother as schoolteacher is one of our unique heroines. She taught her children, as they swung around the world on sailing ships. She organized classes and taught them as they traveled into the prairies in covered wagons. The most remote Yankee settlement could generally boast one educated mother who gathered her own brood and often their friends for instruction in reading and writing.

With such feminine ingenuity in doing something about education the New Englanders had got along and had a greater degree of education than their actual public arrangements for schooling apparently offered. Other groups which had similar informal provisions for education were the Quakers and the more literate of the Scotch-Irish of Pennsylvania, the education in this case being in the hands not so much of the women as of the preachers. Among the Pennsylvania German groups, schoolmasters were also generally supported. But they taught in German, and had an ingrown, isolated sort of culture neither influencing nor influenced by their neighbors. When all these groups combined in Ohio, they had one great common denominator of culture: They all thought that all children should learn to read and write and were ready to unite in making this possible. Their common idea was favored by the provision in the Ordinance for the establishment and support of schools.

With the pouring of the Germans into Ohio, and the coming from abroad of considerable groups of Swiss, a problem which was then agitating the educated mind became crucial. How were these states to keep one universal language? If they kept English—the most obvious language and the one on which most of the immigrants were willing to agree—how, in isolated settlements spread over great areas, were they to keep it from degenerating into a series of barbarous dialects? There was a good deal of discussion of this question, the upshot of which all over the country was an enthusiasm for spelling books and dictionaries. The publication of Noah Webster's great dictionary, then the most advanced and useful dictionary of English on either side of the water, was one result. The other was the immense popularity of spelling. A community of Yankees talking with a twang and converting all vowel ends into y, of Quakers playing havoc with the second person, of Scotch-Irish varying from broad Scotch to purest Irish brogue, and of Germans mixing vowels and consonants, in a jumble of their own, found a knowledge of the actual spelling of a word indispensable to communication with each other. So in every village spelling bees flourished and were attended by young and old; and the spelling book was the basic textbook of all education. The printed word was a standard on which they could all fall back. So Ohio, emerging from the backwoods preoccupations of the first generation, had the

most avid appetite for print. As early as 1826 Cincinnati publishers were printing 61,000 almanacs, 55,000 spelling books,
30,000 primers, 3,000 copies of the *Bible News*, 50,000 table
arithmetics, 3,000 copies of the *American Preceptor*, 3,000 of
the *American Reader*, 3,000 of an introduction to the *English
Reader*, 3,000 of Kirkham's grammar, and 14,000 Testaments.

There then arose in Ohio a remarkable personage who
successfully guided this groping after the true English word
to a new common culture, so simple, and so really charming,
that it set the standard for popular education all through the
West and spread its genial influence eastward over thousands
of the little public schoolhouses. This personage was the
author of the famous *McGuffey Readers*. William Henry Mc-
Guffey, professor of languages at Miami University, was a
Scotchman from Pennsylvania, a typical specimen of his breed,
with keen snapping eyes, reddish-gray hair, a "portentous
nose," and a smile which made him look like a "genial mon-
ster." McGuffey cast his keen and humorous eye on the only
primer available—the *New England Primer* imported by the
Yankees, and the literature for babes he found there was this:

> There is a dreadful fiery Hell
> Where wicked ones must always dwell,
> When wicked children mocking said,
> To an old man, "Go up, Bald Head,"
> God was displeased with them and sent
> Two bears which them in pieces rent.

And then he looked out on the sweet, mellow Ohio landscape,
and saw the children, brown and noisy, coming in from the
woods, with their hands full of flowers and berries, and perhaps a dozen frogs, bugs, and fish they had joyously been
collecting, and he apparently thought: "Is this stuff about
Hell the right literature for children? Must we abuse them
and scold them and make them feel that childhood is a wicked
thing, and this lovely earth just a vale of tears? Let us put
Ohio and childhood as we know it into the children's own

lesson books. Let them feel that their simple country life is beautiful and romantic. Turn their thought upward from their own happy preoccupations to the wonders of nature and the mystery of God." So he proposed to substitute for the verses about Hell and the wicked children something like this, which is lifted from one of his readers:

> Oh, for boyhood's time of June,
> Crowding hours in one brief noon,
> When all things I heard or saw
> Me, their master, waited for.
> I was rich in flowers and trees
> Humming birds and honey bees.
> For my sport the squirrel played,
> Plied the spotted mole his spade;
> For my taste the blackberry cone
> Purpled over hedge and stone;
> Laughed the brook for my delight,
> Through the day and through the night,
> Whispering at the garden wall,
> Talked with me from fall to fall.

Let them think of God and of death and the destiny of man, but why not like this:

> Life, we've been long together.
> 'Tis hard to part when friends are dear.
> Perhaps 'twill cause a sigh or tear.
> Then steal away. Give little warning.
> Choose thine own time. Say not good-night,
> But in some brighter clime
> Bid me good-morrow.

So in 1833 from the busy presses of Cincinnati issued a little book, which, though not much in itself, was world shaking in its cultural implications and consequences. It was entitled *McGuffey's Eclectic Pictorial Primer*, and inaugurated that great series of readers which, undergoing constant changes and improvements through the century, became the true alma mater of American democracy. Thousands of grateful testimonies from famous men now living speak the gratitude of America to the good schoolmaster. One of his most devoted pupils is Henry Ford, who has reverently collected all memorials of McGuffey, and whose unique character and personality and cultural ideals are, as he says himself, the creation of the McGuffey Readers. They were his college curriculum, and he doesn't think Americans need a better one.

The word *eclectic*, chosen by McGuffey to characterize his readers, he explained himself. It was borrowed from the followers of Pestalozzi, who aimed "at embodying all the valuable principles of previous systems without adhering slavishly to the dictates of any master or the views of any party." In his reference to Pestalozzi, and in his choice of material from Maria Edgeworth, Lindley Murray, Mrs. Barbauld, etc., McGuffey thus openly declared his adherence to the new school of education which in those days was to the orthodox system what the so-called "progressive education" is to the regular school system of today. But he also announced his intention to proceed in complete independence—to give the children of Ohio words for the highest experiences of their own simple rural life in a new country, not to impose English classics on them, but to lead them gradually out from Ohio into the general American scene, and thence by easy stages into the literature of England and Europe and all the great world beyond. When he began, little American literature was available. He borrowed what he could from the progressive English writers for children and, it is believed, wrote some of the primer and early grade material himself. But as fast as interesting American literature was available and the children advanced into the higher readers, he served them an attractive menu selected from Cooper, Irving, Bryant, Longfellow, and others. In the fourth reader he introduced them to English literature, choosing carefully with a view to the American child's interests and understanding. His aim, he said, was to steer a middle course between the "idolatrous homage to the

classics" and the tendency of Americans to be interested only
in the practical—between a proper emphasis on virtue and
good citizenship, on the one hand, and pleasure and beauty, on
the other. So he mixed together some simple lessons in ethics,
some material about the wonderful natural world, some homely
humor, some passing philosophical observations, some classical literature, some well-chosen literature not classical, designed to express the romantic charm of their own simple
rural life, like the famous "Old Oaken Bucket," and some
solemn thoughts about God and immortality. His ethics were
those of the best Scotch household tradition, but entirely
agreeable to Yankees, Quakers, and Germans. He hated a lie.
Truth in word, honesty in action, were to him the foundations of all virtue. He counseled benevolence and tender-
heartedness, obedience to parents and to all constituted authority, and an attempt to understand the other fellow.
Through his books he scattered a variety of observations
which, to the intelligent backwoods child, were as windows
opened suddenly into new worlds of thought and opinion.
"Asceticism," he held, "is mischievous both in philosophy and
religion. . . . Operatic music (meaningless in great measure)
is inferior to the masses and the hymns. . . . The young
enjoy life, the old existence. . . . Painful duties lead to pleas-
urable consequences." Here and there he gave the student
advice about the way to read and to study. "Read," he said,
"not to learn, but to *think*. . . . The class is a joint stock company; the stock is attention and common sympathy. . . .
Add, in reading, to the dry light of science the gay coloring
of fancy and imagination." And all the while, mindful of the
problem of Ohio and of many other American communities
—the problem of establishing an agreeable, expressive, and
generally intelligible spoken word—he made all his selections
with a view to "reading aloud with sense, and clearness, and
appreciation."

How well McGuffey performed his mission is shown in
the chorus of love and gratitude which has gone up in our

own time from readers of the old books now grown historic. "It remained for McGuffey," said one of his admirers, "born in the midst of the struggling poor of the new country . . . to compile with understanding a series of readers. . . . The McGuffey readers comprised a course of instruction which successfully conducted its way between the rugged and sometimes violent abolitionist of the North, and the Cavalier slaveholder of the South, between Protestant and Catholic, between the ever-increasing immigrant and the native born, between the radical sectarian and the liberal Jeffersonian. . . . This new mind of the West, eager to be commonized, found agreement in the sturdy, consistent moral and social principles taught by the *McGuffey Readers*."

7

With its learning and habit of life thus drawn from Pennsylvania and New England, and its hero and first contribution to the presidency from tidewater Virginia, and its earliest population largely drawn from the Revolutionary soldiers of all the old states, Ohio attained to statehood as the first legitimate offspring of the Federal union. Vermont, Kentucky, and Tennessee had preceded her, but they had been born out of wedlock, as it were, and had got themselves legitimatized only after they had brought themselves up to strapping manhood. But Ohio had been planned for, baptized in the blood of the Revolution, provided with an inheritance of public lands, put to school to New England and the Scotch, taught to farm by the Pennsylvania Dutch, and so arrived at maturity a well-bred, well-educated, capable, and industrious young state, ready to be the schoolmistress of the West.

ing ghostly curtains of gray Spanish moss, amidst fruits and flowers, and finally lost himself in a maze of waterways and islands and could not even find the Mississippi again. When he finally discovered the place where it spilled the mud of twenty states into the blue waters of the Gulf of Mexico he found that he was still on the eastern side of this incredible continent.

"No other river," says Mark Twain, "has so vast a drainage basin. It draws its water supply from twenty-eight states and territories, from Delaware on the eastern seaboard and from all the country between that and Idaho on the Pacific slope—a spread of forty-five degrees of longitude. The Mississippi receives and carries to the Gulf water from fifty-four subordinate rivers that are navigable by steamboats, and from some hundreds that are navigable by flats and keels. The area of its drainage basin is as great as the combined areas of England, Wales, Scotland, France, Spain, Portugal, Germany, Austria, Italy, and Turkey, and almost all of this wide region is fertile. The Mississippi Valley proper is exceptionally so."

No wonder that when a visiting European said boastfully "How little you Americans know of the world! Know you not that there are rivers in Europe so large that this Mississippi is a rill figuratively speaking?" a Creole gentleman promptly flung his glove into the liar's face, saying "Sir, I will never allow the Mississippi to be disparaged in my presence by an arrogant pretender to knowledge." "Whereupon," says Lyle Saxon, "a duel was fought, and the Chevalier Tomasi was wounded (it is hoped) mortally."

2

The town at the mouth of the river which the Americans had acquired with the Louisiana Purchase in 1803 was quite a social responsibility for a respectable, homespun, and slightly puritanical young nation to undertake. The history of New Orleans had been gaudy from the first. Most of the original citizens had been lured hither by the advertisements of John Law, a great French speculator of Scotch birth, who started a

real estate boom in the Mississippi Valley in the early eighteenth century. In Law's publicity New Orleans was to be a
dream city beneath palms by tropical seas, where fruit drops
into your mouth and men live surrounded by beautiful bronze
women, waited on by naked Nubian slaves, and supported by
unlimited incomes from gold and silver mines and vast vine-
yards and orchards. One of his placards showed an Indian giving a white man lumps of gold in exchange for a knife.

Eagerly whole boatloads of people from France, Germany,
Switzerland, and Scotland set sail, bringing their household
goods and sometimes even their court finery. What they found
was a "wild and desolate place, full of ruffians and naked savages," and always about to be washed away by floods. New
Orleans, says La Harpe, is "situated in flat and swampy ground
fit only for growing rice; the river water filters through and
crayfish abound, so that tobacco and vegetables are hard to
raise. There are frequent fogs and the land being very thickly
wooded and covered with canebrakes, the air is fever-laden
and an infinity of mosquitoes causes further inconvenience in
summer."

Here such deluded metropolitans as could survive the first
fevers and get their hands hardened to the ax-built houses of
cypress logs. The spaces between the logs were daubed with a
mixture of mud and Spanish moss, and the house was whitewashed inside and out, and surrounded by orange trees and a
tall fence also whitewashed. The floor of one such house, we
are told, was covered with furs lying so close together than no
boards could be seen. But the wife had not forgotten Paris in
the wilderness and "was dressed in the fashion of the French
court."

Since Germans, at this time, were popular colonists in
America, and every settlement was anxious to get them, advertisements had been spread about among the dispossessed
classes upon which William Penn had drawn for colonists, telling them that in the Mississippi country they would be able to
draw silver from the earth, and that the kindly Indians would

receive them with open arms. "Savages will make healing herbs known to us, infallible ones for the fruits of love." Accordingly Germans had poured into New Orleans and had been moved up the river some twenty miles above the city. There stretching for forty miles on both sides of the river was the "German coast"—neat white houses in endless rows, inhabited by rosy flaxen-haired people, whom the sun seemed never able to brown, only freckling their noses and making the skin peel off their stout red arms in flakes. At the mouth of the Arkansas there was a Swiss settlement, similarly lured thither.

In 1734 the Ursuline nuns arrived and established their famous school, gathering in the little daughters of French fur traders from up the river, and sending them back to their Indian mothers, with demure gentle manners and the notions of a lady. One of these nuns was the spirited Sister Madeline, whose gay letters from the convent were published in 1728. "And as for us, do not be scandalized, my dear father," she writes, "we are taking a Moor to serve us as is the fashion of the country; and we are also taking a very pretty little cat that wanted to join the community, supposing apparently that in Louisiana, as in France, there are rats and mice."

As for the other ladies who had preceded the sisters to the city, Madeline writes: "The women here are extremely ignorant as to means of securing their salvation, but they are very expert in the art of displaying their beauty. . . . Most of them reduce themselves and their family to the hard lot of living at home on nothing but sagaminty and flaunt abroad in robes of velvet, damask, ornamented with costly ribbons." In 1734 the nuns took possession of their convent, in a procession of forty respectable ladies bearing lighted tapers, twenty young girls dressed in white, and twelve young girls dressed as angels. The young lady representing St. Ursula wore a costly robe and mantle and a crown glittering with diamonds and pearls and in her hand she bore a heart pierced with an arrow.

The school thus established was an institution in the city long after the Americans came. As Saxon says, "It must have

seemed strange to them, particularly to that one old sister who
lived through it all to shake hands with Jackson in 1815, that
no government in the community was steadfast except that of
St. Ursula, nothing lasting in life except the mission of wives
and sisters." Here, during the early nineteenth century, the
flowers of Southern womanhood learned English, French,
sewing, music, and the art of entering a room gracefully.

In 1763, by the Treaty of Utrecht which ended the last
French and Indian war, the city passed into the hands of the
Spanish. On March 21, 1788, "the crowded French wooden
city burned down and a stately Spanish city rose in its place—
a city of brick and plaster, with arches of heavy masonry and
roofs of tile." But the light French touch reappeared, and the
slender ladies continued to import their clothes from Paris, and
wear them with a Parisian air. The day when the city was
turned over to the Americans, and the American flag was
slowly raised to float above the palms, was to the old families a
day of mourning. The only Americans they knew were the
flatboatmen who came down the river with loads of grain and
hogs and tobacco. Rome in the hands of the barbarians could
have felt no worse.

3

Indeed the tall Kentuckians and men from Ohio, striding
along in their blue jeans, must have looked to the bright eyes of
the New Orleans ladies very much as the savages from Great
Britain or the forests of Gaul looked to the Roman dames.
What size, and what a whiteness! The children sometimes, like
angels—men, too, often formed like statues of gods. But how
rude, how uncouth! Did they never shave or bathe? How they
spouted tobacco juice! And their clothes—*mon Dieu!* Clothes
were indeed the main difficulty, and it was not long before
there was a little sartorial shaping up of Americans exposed to
the smart influence of this Parisian city.

His produce sold and his money safe in his pocket, the
American was ready to see a little of "life" and New Orleans

made haste to show it to him. The place was full of lounging
gentlemen whose business it was to win away the products of
prairie industry at cards. The gambling hells of New Orleans
grew to be fabulous—curtains of vermilion brocade, crystal
sconces, carpets, brass inlaid furniture. There were bullfights
and theaters and displays of all sorts of oddities in shows which
must have been a kind of cross between a Barnum and Bailey's
circus and a Major Bowes amateur hour, displaying everything
from wild animals and foreign acrobats to the latest musical
talent out of the backwoods or off the plantations. Of course
there were also a great many ladies no better than they should
be—so many that respectable wives and daughters were kept
in strict seclusion, and if they ventured out must go clothed in
simple dresses, and move along quietly, under escort and chap-
eronage usually of trusted blacks, keeping their eyes and
tongues to themselves. There were few things in which old
families of New Orleans took more pride than in the chaste seclusion of their ladies, and few things that were less interesting
to visitors from elsewhere—either from abroad or from the
American towns to the North. One gathers that even among
the gay young blades of the Creole families such virtue was
more admirable than attractive.

The romance which the "flowers of Southern womanhood" were prevented from giving to the city, except to the
favored few within the family circle, was abundantly provided
by other ladies of New Orleans. These were the young quadroons of free colored families from the West Indies, carefully brought up by mulatto mothers to be the mistresses of
white men. These girls were also decorous, but they were allowed to be visibly lovely, and each was carefully chaperoned
by her mother until she could attach a protector, a young white
man who set her up in a little house "beyond the ramparts," as
the unacknowledged wife of his youth. Tradition credited the
quadroon girl with utter faithfulness to the one white man,
and when her lover left her to marry the secluded daughter of
one of the "families," it was generally believed that she would

refuse to marry a young man of her own color or to "form any other connection" with a white man. Refined, gentle, pathetic, they were said to live out their lives in secret widowhood, the memory of their brief bright day of love smoldering like a fire sinking slowly to ash in the depths of their somber dark eyes.

The quadroon girls, like other ladies of society, had their coming-out parties. These were the so-called quadroon balls, to which young white men were invited, no young man of color being allowed to cross the threshold. There, in their beautiful dresses, the girls danced and coquetted, while their dark-skinned mothers in turbans, stiff with virtue, sat around the room against the walls, each keeping a stern eye on her damsel, checking and guiding her as carefully as any other woman who wishes a daughter to make a good match. The young Duke of Saxe-Weimar-Eisenach, who visited New Orleans in 1825, says: "Like many others, I find the quadroon balls more amusing than those of a more decorous nature." He reports that one of the troubles of New Orleans hostesses was that the young men would leave their parties and the society of pure womanhood to be wall flowers ("make tapestry" as the Duke says) while they went off to dance with the quadroons. He speaks of their "subtle and amusing coquetry, lovely countenances, full dark liquid eyes, sylph-like figures, beautifully rounded limbs, exquisite garb, and ease of manner."

Tragic the quadroon mistress was, but at least she had her day. One's sympathies are all with the gentle good girl of the "best families" behind the red damask curtains of the great house, and the patient and uninquiring wifehood she would inherit when the dance should be over and all the music be stilled.

The quadroon mistress was something to make stories of all up and down the river, but there was much to make stories about here—fearful and fantastic. There were tales about the voodoo dances. One morning, it was said, the cook rattling her pans would be singing a Creole song to the end of which she would tack a few words—just those flourishes the Negroes were always adding to songs, improvising as they went. But this flourish would be different from others. It would be a voodoo message. The Negro passing along the street would hear it, and start singing and add the same flourish. Another Negro would take it up, and so from mouth to mouth all over the city would go the message. Secretly, at midnight, they would steal forth, gathering in dreadful crowds on the edge of a dismal swamp. There would be gyrating dances, fainting spells, hysterics, strange and awful moans. "The tumultuous orgy would continue until the savage participants, entirely deprived of reason, fell to the ground from sheer lassitude, and were carried panting and gyrating into the open air." Whispers of voodooism ran from mouth to mouth, gripping the heart with a horrible fear. If Negroes could gather thus secretly, what would prevent them from falling on the city in the night and murdering everyone in his bed?

Bland, misty, smiling amidst the mild waters, soaked in a kind of solution of water and sunshine, the city was thus very beautiful and, to the homespun person from up river, very dreadful. Even the perpetual summer was something to fear, and the water which ran so clean and sparkling off the Kentucky hills was here a concentrated poison. For drainage in the city was difficult, the water being only a foot underground, and in consequence there were at first dreadful epidemics of yellow fever and bubonic plague. When you had told the folks back in Ohio and Kentucky about the quadroon mistress and the voodooed servants, you could tell also of victims of yellow fever—eyes prominent, glistening yellow, staring, face discolored with orange color and dusky red.

A dreadful city, but lovely, a city of pestilence and gaiety, of love and death—a city where they understood the art of good living as in few places in the world. There was delicate and beautiful dress, perfect cooking, soft and gracious manners. There they thought that, in the face of crime and fever, man's business was to be happy. There it was believed nothing could be so bad in this world, either physical or moral, that it could not be met with a shrug and an amiable gesture and a courage not the less invincible because it was so soft and so very polite. And lying so low and so hot, always about to be dissolved and to float away, it was, to eyes off the prairies, picturesquely beautiful. There were old Negroes with striped turbans. There were nuns. There was a brown boy with a basket of roses on his head. There was a coffeehouse with hot black coffee in little cups and cakes flavored with honey. There was the fish market and the flower market. And walking along the street, you could catch a glimpse through the iron gate of a courtyard where bamboos were growing and palms waved in the sunlight. There was a fountain in the courtyard and a tall white statue. There were goldfish in the fountain. A breakfast table was set there, out in the open air, and above it the wistaria were in flower. That is the kind of backyard some people had in New Orleans. And men went back to the clearing in the forest, to the log cabin or the still featureless frame house with a wistful vision in their hearts. That was the way some people managed to live!

4

After New Orleans became part of the United States, many Americans with money who believed that the end of life was to be happy and to do things beautifully, made haste to come thither. So northward along the river on both sides, in Mississippi and Louisiana, there developed that beautiful belt of plantation homes, whose pillared white houses, set back beyond pastures nibbled by sheep to lawnlike greenness, have still a charm that neither castle nor château can overpass.

"Outside the plantation house the world is saturate with moonlight. The trees of the long avenue are fountains, dripping streamers of Spanish moss into the dark pools formed by their shadows. Down the walk from the white-pillared house comes a man leading a small boy by the hand. Slowly they pass through the pale night—figures in a dream. . . . They pass through moonlight into shadow, back into moonlight again.

"Winter time on the plantation. Frosty nights and sunny days, crisp and cool. Wood smoke rises from the cabin chimneys and upon the wide hearths are blazing fires of pine knots. At twilight the smell of sizzling bacon. The fields are brown, and brown men toil in the furrows, 'gettin' ready for spring.' The sugar cane has all been cut and carried to the sugar house. Grinding time is over, and the sugar in barrels and hogsheads has been carried down aboard the steamboats and shipped away down the river.

"The pecan trees are bare of leaves, and the branches make a curious pattern against the sky; but the live-oaks are as green as ever, and palms and Spanish daggers in the garden seem doubly green against bare tree trunks. The banana trees will survive the winter unless there is an unusually heavy frost; their large leaves are ragged, though, and flap in the wind. Red winter roses are blooming in the flower garden. Inside the plantation house the children are cracking pecans for pralines that Aunt Rhody promised to make for us."

So after the Battle of New Orleans Louisiana, which had been admitted to the Union in 1812, settled down to being the garden and sugar factory at the mouth of the river. New Orleans, receiving the products of the barbarians of the North, and, taking its toll of all, got richer and richer. And the plantation gold coasts reached up through Louisiana to Natchez, Mississippi, which was at one time said to be the richest city in the world. Its lovely old houses still stand and its inhabitants, in all the glamour of the bland, sweet, inconsequential life of the "new rich" of the South, live again in the pages of Stark Young's *So Red the Rose*.

5

Up in the North where advanced schools were beginning to get started, they used to read Vergil. Some people living along the river thought Vergil's famous words about going down to

Hell surely applied to New Orleans. The descent was easy, but oh, the problem of getting back! To row against the swirling muddy currents was a task for Hercules. To go overland was almost as bad, for there were swamps and thickets all the way which even a Southern horse found it hard to get through. But down they went and back they came—back mainly over the old Natchez Trace, the road between Natchez and Nashville.

This difficulty was solved when, in 1811 Nicholas Roosevelt, the great-great-uncle of Theodore Roosevelt, launched the first steamboat on the river. All along the way the settlers crowded the shore, eager to be on the death. They thought it was idiotic enough for him to set out in this contraption, belching smoke and wood sparks, pounding with steam, sure to burst pretty soon or go up in fire. But when it was heard that he also had his wife on board, there was consternation in their chivalrous hearts. Along the river a man might do all sorts of fool things, but he drew the line on dragging a lady into them. But Nicholas Roosevelt and Mrs. Roosevelt went right along. Here and there they stopped at towns and took the more reckless of the municipal dignitaries for a ride *upstream*. Thus was started the most gaudy of all American commercial enterprises, steamboating on the Mississippi River.

In a few years time there was measured, not by clocks, but by the passing of the steamboats. The cry "steamboat around the bend" was the signal for all work to stop, and everyone from grandfather to mammy to rush to the shore. There, for a brief half hour, at your own door was everything gorgeous and amazing in the world. The latest styles from Paris paraded the decks. The fruits of the tropics, bananas, oranges, were thrown off on the melting snows. You knew what was happening "up North" before the New Orleans café knew it. You heard about the latest lynching in the South before the magnate in New York had opened his newspaper. There wasn't anything you couldn't send on a steamboat and nothing it wouldn't dump into your yard.

It wasn't what the steamboat carried that was its greatest revelation. It was its own gorgeous and magnificent self. This traveling palace was, says Mark Twain, a "sumptuous glass temple, with showy red and gold window curtains, bright fanciful cuspidors, and a tidy white-aproned, black texas-tender to bring up tarts and ices and coffee during midwatch, day and night." There was a clean and dainty drawing room, gilded saloon, and an oil picture on every stateroom door. It glittered with no end of prism-fringed chandeliers, and the "bartender had been barbered and upholstered at an incredible cost." More exciting even to an American boy was the vast array of machinery. "The fires were fiercely glaring from a long row of furnaces and over them were eight huge boilers." This, as he says, was "unutterable pomp."

Here, as a daily object lesson, you had instruction in the niceties of living. You learned that table linen might be changed every single meal, and no napkin put in a napkin ring, but just thrown carelessly on the table; that you didn't merely wash your hands in the old tin basin before meals, but delicately dipped the tips of your fingers into water in glass bowls after dinner; that a meal could not be negotiated on the tip of one knife, but required whole lines and battalions of silverware laid out on each side of the plate; that there were many drinks besides whisky, and that beautiful ladies might even sip these decoctions, and still be ladies afterward; that the hired girl or black mammy could look as smart as the mistress, in trim uniforms and white aprons; that there were ideals of personal cleanliness undreamed of as yet in American philosophy, and not among idlers and sissies either, for the captain and officers not only appeared in a clean white suit every day, but it was rumored that they put on absolutely clean underwear every day, right down to the skin.

In less fortunate sections of the world, magnificence like this was shut away behind thick mansion doors, guarded by ranks of servants. You couldn't really see it and touch it. You could only look from a distance and wonder and surmise. But

here it was yours. You could have it all for the price of a
ticket. You could live in it and sleep in it and eat in it, and loll
on the deck and see the continent go by, just as large as any
lord. When you came back from a trip—and poor and unfortunate indeed was he or she who did not go on a trip sometime
—you felt socially cleansed and uplifted, and if you did not
surreptitiously straighten out the silver by the plates at dinner,
and speak sharply to Johnnie about his manners for a day or
two thereafter, you were an insensible lout indeed. With such
an example the Western towns flashed into such dressiness and
stylishness, such trimness and neatness in household appointments, such ideas of what one must have to be comfortable
and how one must behave to enjoy one's belongings, as amazed
and confounded Eastern visitors. Where did they get their
ideas of sumptuous appointments for bathrooms, of trim housemaids, of long and elaborate dinners served letter perfect to the
last detail of etiquette. Where?

> Listen to the whistle
> Of the steam-boat going by.

The steamboats made life not only gorgeous, but fantastic
and dangerous. Every now and then a steamboat blew up.
"There are always companies of gamblers on these boats who,
being awake and dressed during the hours of darkness, are
able to seize the boats on the first alarm of an accident in the
night, and are apt to leave the passengers behind." There were
great steamboat races, on which everybody bet, while the con-
tending boats churned furiously against the current, gleaming
with lights all the night long, belching forth sparks and red
rolling smoke. "In the West," said Monsieur B. Dureau, a
Frenchman who wrote a book about *Les États Unis en* 1850,
"Americans frequently give balls on the steamboats, and they
celebrate many of their marriages there. The line from Cincinnati to Louisville is renowned for its nuptial chambers. The
Americans frequently make voyages on the steamboats to pass
the honeymoon at a pressure of six or eight atmospheres. They

love the noise and smoke, and the hissing of steam makes music in their ears."

The most desperate characters traveled on these boats, sometimes looking very flashy, with diamond stickpins and patent-leather boots. In a book entitled *Gambling Unmasked*, published in 1830, there is a description of Rock in the Cave, a cave beside the river about one hundred miles below Louisville, where criminals assembled to play games of chance, to perfect their disguises, to turn out counterfeit money. Here they brought the spoils of piracy and the bodies of people they had murdered. And here sometimes they ended their wretched lives with suicide or mutual murder.

A special form of the steamboat was the "showboat." "The Chapman company," says Joseph Jefferson, "had fitted up a steamboat and converted it into a floating theatre." This huge dramatic barge would go along, making one-night stands in the water just off the river towns, and everybody, white and black, gentle or simple, would hasten to buy tickets. The white people sat downstairs in the pit, and the Negroes in the gallery. The plays were usually rich red melodrama. But why go on? We know all about it, for most of us have seen *Show-Boat*, and one song at least from that appropriately tuneful memorial to a great American institution bids fair to go forever as a folksong—*Ole Man River*.

All sorts of lesser barges, rafts, keelboats, were in the show business on the Mississippi. Joseph Jefferson tells about going down the rivers with a stock company whose principal item of entertainment was *The Lady of Lyons*. They started on the Cumberland River. "The whole of the trip was to me delightful. It was in that rich and mellow season when the foliage seems to change from day to day. The river was full of ducks, which I could sometimes shoot from the deck of the flatboat; great flocks of wild pigeons filled the air for days together, so that I could supply our table well with game." When they came to the Ohio, they hoisted one of their stage drops for a sail. "A hickory pole was cut from the shore, and a drop scene, with a wood painted on one side and a palace on the other, was unfurled to the breeze." People on other steamers and on shores, gathered in crowds as they went by. Whereupon they would dress up in some gaudy costume and get out their old broadswords and fight a combat on deck. He adds that they had some "very riotous rude audiences."

6

Flatboats, keels, rafts, dugouts, steamboats, all moving along from town to town, state to state, climate to climate, are the best means in the world of transporting stories. And because everything seemed to swell up and begin to be strong and violent when it reached the Mississippi River, the frontier habit of hanging mythical tales about a real person, such as Daniel Boone or Davy Crockett, and telling lies for fun, began to give birth on the river boats to Gargantuan legends. The favorite hero of these legends was Mike Fink, a kind of understudy for Paul Bunyan, originally a "mountain man" in Missouri. He was the hero of the boatman, vast, strong, unconquerable. He could eat more, drink more, fight more, and love more than any other man. He was said to have red hair, and every red-haired youngster along the river was chalked up to his credit by the boatmen. He was the hero of 10,000 fights, but died in one of them —Why? Because he was fool enough to fight a pal over a woman!

Another legendary character was Annie Christmas, forerunner of Calamity Jane and all the other Lady Wildcats of the West. Lady Buffalo would have been a better term, for Annie, like Mike, was physically prodigious. In some of the legends Annie ran a saloon on board her boat. There wasn't any man drunk or sober that she couldn't lift up by the seat of his breeches and throw overboard. She could lift a barrel of whisky off the floor and set it on the counter of her bar. All sorts of things happened to Annie, in these tales. Among other things she committed suicide for love!

The lore of the river, however, was not without its own

rude ethics. The basic virtue of the river had been established before the Americans arrived by the *voyageurs* of the fur trade. Tradition represents these as happy-go-lucky fellows, swinging along in their canoes, and charming the birds off the boughs with their songs. But there was a sterner side to the business. The man who went far into the Indian country, conducted satisfactory bargains with them, and then, with his hair still on his head, brought back his fur against all hazards, and rendered a satisfactory financial accounting to the company that had staked him with supplies—this man had to be a person of some moral fiber and mental agility. The fur trade was built on the supreme virtue of reliability. What a man was expected to do, he was to do—despite desert and famine, despite treachery and murder, despite hell and damnation. Where he said he would be, he was to be. What he was to protect—if only a dried piece of buffalo hide—he was to protect. And he was to use his wits about it, too. If half the fur-trading party was murdered, the rest were to get the goods home. If they lost their leaders, they were to settle on other leaders and go on.

This tradition of character was later carried over into the whole enterprise of the rivers. Men who were trusted with goods to take down to New Orleans on the flatboats might and did commit all the sins of the Decalogue. But they must be faithful. Mark Twain pays his tribute to the rivermen, those brutes "half alligator and half horse," who succeeded to the virtues of the fur traders, "heavy fighters, elephantinely jolly, foul-witted, profane, prodigal of their money, fond of barbaric finery, prodigious braggarts; yet in the main, honest, trustworthy, faithful to promises and duty and often picturesquely magnanimous." In the *Pike County Ballads*, John Hay describes Jim Bludsoe of the steamer "Prairie Bell" in the same terms.

> He weren't no saint, and them engineers
> Is all pretty much alike.

> One wife in Natchez under the hill
> And another one here in the Pike.
> A keerless man in his talk was Jim
> And an awkward hand in a row,
> But he never flunked, and he never lied—
> I reckon he never knew how.

And when Jim had died for those he was trusted with, this is his epitaph:

> He seen his duty, a dead sure thing
> And went for it thar and then,
> And Christ ain't agoing to be too hard
> On a man that died for men.

7

For a river like this there was no precedent in the books of any European language. Europe had no river civilizations. All river civilizations before this were old and far away—the civilizations of the Nile, of China. Here was a new thing, coming back to the world after 2,000 years in which men had dwelt snugly, in areas cut off from each other by hills, and when they had gone boating had done it, in a lonely fashion, on the sea. A new river civilization, the only civilization among men which appears to be immortal, as witness the persistence of civilized life along the Nile and the Ganges and the rivers of China, bound therefore, it might be, to go on, when Europe is wilderness again and bats hang from the skyscrapers of New York!

It was fortunate, therefore, that there arose one American writer who got his education from the river. Mark Twain was born on the river at Hannibal, Missouri, and all his best writing is about it. After one has looked at all the vast array of documents of this region, the efforts of even such a great historian as Parkman, and the reports of travelers, one looks into Mark Twain's books and finds that he has said it all and said it better. He even lifts the best quotations from Parkman and sprinkles them into *Life on the Mississippi,* and the necessary facts from the encyclopedias and sets them down, crisp and crackling with his own interpretation.

Mark Twain got his preparatory or high school education as a printer on a country newspaper, and then matriculated for college on the river, where he was a steamboat pilot for several years. All that college means to anyone, this meant to him. College means intellectual discipline, the training of the mind. He found that out when day after day he stood with the captain trying in vain to memorize all the bends and turns, the shoals and sand bars of the river, and then discovered that the river had changed its course overnight, and he had to learn them again. "When I learn the river," he said, "will it stay learned, or will it go fooling around?" Finally he gave up. "I just haven't brains enough to be a pilot," he said. But the old captain answered, "You quit that. When I undertake to larn a man the river, I larn him. I either larn him or I kill him." And right then he knew what real learning was.

College also widens one's intellectual outlook, makes one aware of other civilizations, larger possibilities of living. The river did this for Mark Twain. Embarked upon it, "I had a sense of being bound for mysterious lands and distant climes I have never felt in so uplifting a degree since." College teaches you to use your mother tongue effectively. He listened humbly when he heard the boatmen yelling, "Vast heaving, vast heaving, I tell you. Where you going with that barrel? Forard with it, fore I make you swallow it, you dash-dash-dash-dashed *split between a tired mud-turtle and a crippled hearse horse!*" He wished he could talk like that. Finally one values college for the contacts one makes there, the friends who last through life. Mark Twain said later that everyone he ever met anywhere in the world he had known already on the river!

Life on the Mississippi is his basic textbook on the subject, but the river runs large and free through several other stories, through *Tom Sawyer* and *Pudd'nhead Wilson*, and in his greatest book Mark Twain photographed it complete—in *Huckleberry Finn*. Huck Finn, the little poor white boy, is all of frontier America floating down it, seeing all the pretensions of gentility, all the dignity of learning and tradition, humbly and shrewdly, from below. He respects the morals and customs of civilized life, but when they tell him he will go to hell because he is helping Jim, the Negro, to escape from the woman who is his lawful owner, he guesses he'll have to go to hell. The widow tells him Bible stories—about Moses in the bulrushes. "I was in a considerable sweat to find out all about him; but by and by she let it out that Moses had been dead a considerable long time. So then I didn't care no more about him, because I don't take no stock in dead people." Tom Sawyer tries to tell him about the great and splendid history of other lands, "I reckon he believed in the Arabs and the elephants, but I think different. It had all the marks of a Sunday School."

Little Huck Finn, and not the Gargantuan boatman, is the ultimate hero of the river, a bit of scrap out of the junk pile of humanity, set afloat on this great water, drifting along, under the sun and the stars, in and out of every kind of social situation, held fast as little by the bad as by the good, slipping out of every danger, free as the water itself, just going along and, after the kickings and cuffings, the chains and starvation, which his kind have endured through all the centuries, now "thinking about things, and feeling rested and rather comfortable and satisfied."

11

GO HEAVE THAT COTTON

ALONG with granite, ice, and salted fish, New England exported education to the South. So Mrs. Nathanael Greene, widow of the Revolutionary general, had as a guest on her plantation a young graduate of the class of 1792 at Yale, who was looking around for a position as a tutor. Being a well-brought-up New England boy, taught to do chores and make himself useful to a kind hostess, young Eli Whitney occupied himself with making various little contrivances for the house and farm. One day some of Mrs. Greene's friends were discussing the growing of cotton. The soil, they said, was excellently suited to it, but it could never be made a profitable crop unless some better way of clearing the seeds from the fiber could be found. Eli listened with interest, examined the cotton himself, and began to figure and experiment. In a few weeks he had constructed a little machine which could clean fifty pounds of lint in a day.

This was the original cotton gin, which, elaborated and developed, worked one of the greatest social changes of modern times. It provided the world with such luxury in the way of unlimited cheap clean clothing, sheets, and draperies, as it could never have known otherwise. It built one of the greatest sources of work and wealth in modern society, and incidentally it brought the social conflicts innate in the United States from the beginning to their tragic crisis in the Civil War.

Until the invention of the cotton gin little cotton was raised in the Southern states. In 1778 William Bartram, speaking of the fertile islands along the Carolina and Georgia coasts—the so-called sea islands—said: "It may be a subject worthy of some inquiry why these fine islands are so thinly inhabited. . . . The soil . . . appears to be particularly favorable to the culture of indigo and cotton. . . . The cotton is planted by the poorer class of people, just enough for their family consumption." Up to the real conquest and annexation of the cotton belt by Andrew Jackson and his Kentucky and Tennessee wild men, the development of the cotton plantation was rather tentative. Bounded by the aristocratic rice plantations of South Carolina and Georgia on the east, and the aristocratic sugar plantations of Louisiana on the west, the future cotton country was mainly one gaudy center of intrigue and barbaric adventure. Here the French had had plantations but had abandoned them—the ruins of their houses still visible amidst a new growth of jungle; their orange trees bearing fruit that nobody bothered to pick. Here and there along the sluggish rivers, Indian traders, many of them old Scotchmen, lived happily in stockaded feudal state, with Indian wives, Indian relatives, and dogs and tamed wolves. A few Spaniards had set up here and there, but not many.

In 1778 William Bartram, on a botanical expedition to these wilds, found the city of Mobile. "It had been near a mile in length, though now chiefly in ruins, many houses vacant and mouldering to earth; yet there are a few good buildings, inhabited by French gentlemen, English, Scotch, Irish, and emigrants from the northern British colonies." Wandering amidst "high forests and rich swamps, midst canes and cypress trees of astonishing magnitude," he found frequent ruins of French plantations. At Pensacola he saw "several hundred habitations; the governor's palace is a large stone building ornamented by a tower, built by the Spaniards. The town is defended by a large stockade fortress."

But it was the Indian towns which interested him most. The Indians of this district, under half-breed chiefs, and with the help of the Indian traders, lived in rather civilized communities. "The great or public square," says Bartram, "generally stands alone, in the center or highest part of the town; it consists of foursquare or cubical buildings, or houses of one story, uniform and of the same dimensions, so situated as to form an exact tetragon, encompassing an area of half an acre of ground, more or less, according to the strength or largeness of the town. . . . The pillars and walls of the houses of the square are decorated with various paintings and sculptures which I suppose to be hieroglyphic, and as an historic legendary of political and sacerdotal affairs; but they are extremely picturesque."

Before the country could be opened for general settlement it was necessary to dispossess these Indians and to establish title to the country. Part of Alabama was claimed by Spain and was not securely in the hands of the United States until after 1819. Northern Alabama and most of the state of Mississippi were claimed by Georgia, and were granted to four land companies who were to negotiate with the Indians. The whole became something of a scandal—the so-called Yazoo land frauds—and the Indians were in the end rudely and somewhat unjustly dispossessed, being forced to migrate to lands beyond the Mississippi. Henry Clay of Kentucky made himself their advocate in the Senate, seeking to gain for them the right of appeal to the Supreme Court against the state of Georgia, and to have them provided with land, stock, and implements if they would voluntarily emigrate beyond the Mississippi. The great scene in Congress when Henry Clay spoke for the Indians is described by Harriet Martineau. "As many as could crowd into the gallery leaned over the balustrade, and the lower circle was thronged with ladies and gentlemen, in the centre of whom stood a group of Cherokee chiefs, listening immoveably. I

never saw so deep a moral impression produced by a speech.
. . . I saw tears of which I am sure he [Clay] was wholly unconscious falling on his papers as he vividly described the woes
and injuries of the aborigines. I saw Webster draw his hand
across his eyes; I saw every one vividly moved except the vice-
president, who yawned somewhat ostentatiously, and the
Georgia Senator who was busy brewing his storm."

Having gained the right of appealing to the Supreme
Court, the Cherokee chiefs were cheered by the Court's decree, in 1832, that Georgia had no right over them and could
not force them to move. President Jackson, however, supported Georgia and refused to carry out the Supreme Court's
order. Not unkindly in his personal attitude to the Indians,
he was convinced that they would remain only tools in the
hands of British traders or of chiefs largely of British or Scotch
blood. But he tried to facilitate their removal, to the West,
which was finally accomplished in 1838. Like the struggle with
Tecumseh in the North, it is a tragic story, and leaves the Muse
of History something of a headache.

2

Meanwhile the settlers pressed in, buying off the Indians,
pushing them back, making themselves safe. In 1816 Mississippi
became a state, and, in 1819, Alabama. Across the rich low
land of the South from the feudal strongholds of aristocracy in
South Carolina and eastern Georgia to the princely gardens of
privilege in Louisiana came the advancing line of cotton plantations. They dipped down amidst the few remaining dons of
Florida; they took up whole areas of North and South Carolina; they took part of Tennessee. They reached over the river
and struck root in the lowlands of Arkansas, and began to
spread in great snowy fields into still Spanish Texas.

Imbibing aristocracy from the air, the new-rich of the cotton world were actually a very mixed crew. There were sons
of Erin with the flannel in their mouths, like Gerald O'Hara,
and some Scotch who had been Indian traders. There were ex-

pirates. There were bold mountain chieftains. There were commercial gentlemen who had made money in trade and trusted to the dews of the Southern night to wash it clean. There were sober gentlemen of the New England community in Charleston, long established there, persons of weight and authority, and carrying as much of the social sanctity of the place as the gentlemen of Huguenot or cavalier origin.

A presentable Yankee, Scotchman, Irishman, or other outlander would make haste to sanctify himself by marrying some fair daughter of the Southland, acquiring with her a family tree and a large cousinage. This self-made character of the cotton gentry is glorified in the career of O'Hara in *Gone With the Wind*. It is confessed with disarming candor in the memoirs of a fair lady of the South, Mary Norcutt Bryan, whose true story really betters the career of Scarlett. Writing her story for her grandchildren after the war, she tells them with pride that her father earned his plantation, and wants them to remember that a "self-made man is the noblest work of God."

Mary Norcutt was sent to school in Washington, where she "attended President Buchanan's levees, admired Miss Lane's graciousness, took walks to the Capitol, and heard great speeches, went to art galleries, and, best of all, had an informal soiree every month at the school to which our sweethearts always managed to come." Becoming a young lady, "I was so happy, the world was so beautiful, every one was so kind, that I smiled all the time. Life held nothing but roses and sunshine for me, and with the most indulgent and intelligent mother in the world, I had nothing to desire. . . . I enjoyed my winter at home immensely. I went to parties, took sails on the river, danced the dear old dances, the Virginia reel, lancers, cotillion, and waltzed in a dignified way, played consequences, stage coach . . . and at home backgammon with Mother. Then the summer at the Virginia spas. . . . Oh, how I did ride horseback and drive in those days. . . . Then in October we went to New York and stayed at the St. Nicholas. I had several months before become engaged to your father. We met many spring acquaintances in New York and had a royal good time. I had lovely clothes and what dreams of beauty my dresses were, and how unconscious I was of any personal charm if I possessed any, except to be happy all day long!"

From New York she went on a visit to friends in Mobile, which she found charming, with wide shady streets, and bay glimmering in the sunshine, "the sweet old home, and the dear people." Her friend Edith Whitfield lived on a plantation containing 900 slaves, who, Mary reported, were "all polite and happy." "Edith had a lovely house with everything in it that heart could desire, a ballroom, the white pillars reaching to the ceiling, broad verandas, a sweet place in which to while away the sultry hours, a lake in front surrounded by evergreens on which swam swans and ducks." The perennial joyousness of Mary's young existence was temporarily dashed when she went to see the slave market at New Orleans. But she reassured herself by looking around on the contented and pleasant faces of slaves in her own family and among her friends.

After a joyous round of visiting how charming it was to return, in the fall, to the old home! "At the open gate a broadly smiling dusky group stands with welcome depicted on every face. Hearty handshakes of real affection are exchanged, while the children are being hugged, caressed, laughed over and extolled for their grace and beauty. The master and mistress pass under the trees whose long shadows rest upon the soft green grass between streams of sunshine. The old piazza, gilded with brightness, smiles a welcome home."

When the war broke out, Mary fled to the mountains with her mother. The house that had been built for her marriage she left behind, with a backward look at "a year's provisions in the smoke house, and in the pantry all sorts of jellies, pickles, catsups, and cordials." She established her mother in a log cabin and made her mother's room very neat. "The white table was covered with snow white dimity, the four window panes had muslin curtains, her wrapper and slippers were near, and on a stand by the bed her well worn Bible and hymnal." And then this spoiled daughter of privilege remembered that she was the daughter of a self-made man, and what he did she could do. And this is what she did: "I made a good deal of money of which I was very proud. I had several suits of brown woolen goods for gentlemen's wear made on my own loom. I had a present of a number of bolts of yellow homespun from the Rockfish factory, which I exchanged to great advantage. I made neckties and other fancy things and sold them and often had several thousand dollars of Confederate money in my purse. I cut up a Marshall sash, and made money out of that. I had a shoe last and made my little daughter many pairs of shoes out of goat-skins bound with ribbon."

3

Though the leaven of aristocracy spreading from Charleston and New Orleans was, as these things go in America, of unexceptional antiquity and purest quality, much of the planter society was of mushroom growth and had all the faults of sudden wealth. And much of the cotton-planting South was never really touched by the civilization of the few lovely Southern cities, but remained incredibly savage. Wealthy planters had not one but half a dozen or even a dozen plantations, only one of which had a "great house" and harbored a lovely daughter. The others were managed by overseers, and often by one of the members of the family, a man living there alone, with a Negro mistress. There being in the South almost no roads, no industries, and no free schools—once you were out of the charmed circle of the great plantations in the neighborhood of the cities, you were in a wilderness indeed.

Fanny Kemble, the English actress, the niece of Mrs. Siddons, married a member of the Butler family of South Carolina, whose surname Mrs. Mitchell borrowed for her hero Rhett Butler, and moved South to two of his plantations in Georgia. Her *Journal of Residence on a Georgian Plantation*, in 1838–1839, was published in England during the Civil War.

"A sadder book the human hand never wrote," said the *Atlantic Monthly*. And sad it is. Compared with the unrelieved blackness of this day-by-day record, *Uncle Tom's Cabin* is painted in violet and rose. "My house," says Fanny, "consists of three small rooms, and three still smaller which would more appropriately be designated as closets, a wooden recess by way of a pantry, and a kitchen detached from the dwelling, a mere wooden outhouse, with no floor but the bare earth, and for furniture a congregation of filthy negroes who lounge in and out of it like hungry hounds, at all hours of the day and night, picking up such scraps of food as they can find about, which they discuss, sitting on their hams. . . . Such being our abode, I think you will allow that there is little danger of my being dazzled by the luxurious splendors of a Southern slave residence."

However, she set herself to master the aristocratic life of these parts, and to get acquainted with Darien society, "its aristocracies and democracies, its little grandeurs and smaller pettinesses, its circles higher and lower, its social jealousies, fine invisible lines of demarcation, imperceptible shades of different respectability, and delicate distinctions of genteel, genteeler, genteelest. . . . One of my visits this morning was to a certain Miss —— whose rather grandiloquent name and very striking style of beauty exceedingly well became the daughter of an ex-governor of Georgia. As for the residence of this princess, it was like all the planters' residences that I have seen, and such as a well-to-do English farmer would certainly not inhabit. Occasional marks of former elegance or splendor survive sometimes in the size of the rooms, sometimes in a little carved woodwork about the mantelpieces or wainscottings of these rooms, but all things have a Castle Rackrent air of neglect, a dreary careless untidiness, with which the dirty barefooted negro servants are in excellent keeping."

Challenged with regard to some of her statements by people who had visited the charming plantations along the Mississippi or had been handsomely entertained in Charleston, Fanny

Kemble wrote in the *London Times:* "The inhabitants of Baltimore, Richmond, Charleston, Savannah, and New Orleans, whose estates lie like suburban retreats of our city magnates in the near neighborhood of their respective cities are not the people I refer to. . . . There commerce, the arts, and travel humanize the slave-holder of the great city into some relation with the spirit of his own time and country. But these men are but a most inconsiderable portion of the slave-holding population of the South—a nation, for such they should be spoken of, of men whose organization and temperament is that of southern Europeans, living under the influence of a climate at once enervating and exciting; scattered over trackless wildernesses of dried sand and pestilential swamp, entrenched within their own boundaries, surrounded by creatures absolutely subject to their despotic will, delivered over by hard necessity to the lowest excitements of drinking and gambling and debauchery for sole recreation; independent of all opinion; ignorant of all progress; isolated from all society—it is impossible to conceive a more savage existence within the pale of any modern civilization."

Again, making an exception of Maryland, Virginia, and Kentucky as generally charming and civilized states, she says that we must remember that there is slavery also in the interior of Tennessee and Alabama, and that this, "like the cotton fields and rice swamps of the great muddy rivers of Louisiana, and the Georgia pine barrens and the woody wastes of North Carolina" is a very different kind of countryside. "These, especially the islands, are like so many fortresses, approachable only at the owner's will." In the "dismal swampy rice grounds of the Savannah or the sugar-brakes of the Mississippi or the up-country cotton lands of the Ocamulgee the master and over-seer are as much alone and irresponsible in their dominion over their black cattle as Robinson Crusoe was over his small family of animals on his desert habitation."

She admits, however, that "the Southerners are infinitely better bred men, according to English notions, than the men of the northern states. The habit of command gives them a certain self-possession, the enjoyment of leisure a certain ease. Their temperament is impulsive and enthusiastic and their manners have the grace and spirit which seldom belong to the deportment of a northern people. But upon a more familiar acquaintance the vices of the social system to which they belong will be found to have infected them with their own peculiar taint, and haughty overbearing irritability, effeminate indolence, reckless extravagance, and an aroma of profligacy and cruelty which is the immediate result of their irresponsible power over their dependents are some of the less pleasing traits which acquaintanceship develops in a southern character."

4

The savage wilderness which surrounded the little islands of grace and culture in the plantation country was naturally a tempting theme for romantic writers. Several of them regaled large bodies of readers with such descriptions as that by Carl Postl, the Austrian writer of American romances whose works, published under the name of Charles Sealsfield, were widely read in America, and remain strikingly vivid to this day. Longfellow greatly admired Sealsfield and spoke particularly of his description of the cypress swamps in Sealsfield's collection entitled *Louisiana Sketches*. "The cypress swamp extended four or five miles along the shores of the creek. It was a deep lake of black mud, covered over and disguised by a deceitful bright green veil of creeping plants and mosses which had spread themselves in rank luxuriance over its whole surface, and over the branches and trunks of the trees that were scattered about it. . . . Thousands, tens of thousands, of birds and reptiles, alligators, enormous bullfrogs, night owls, chinjas, herons, whose dwellings were in the mud of the swamp or on its leafy roof, now lifted up their voices, bellowing, hooting, shrieking, and groaning. Issuing from the obscene retreats in which they had hitherto lain hidden, the alligators raised their hideous snouts out of the green coating of the swamps, gnashing their teeth and straining toward us, while the owls and other birds circled round our heads, flapping and striking us with their wings as they passed. We drew out knives and endeavored to defend our heads and eyes; but all was in vain against the multitude of enemies that surrounded us, and the unequal combat could not possibly have lasted long, when suddenly a shot was fired, followed by another."

The plight of the runaway slave, hiding in these swamps for days, was another tempting subject for the romancers. Audubon, lost in the canebrakes, uncovered there a slave who looked like a panting and frightened animal. When Audubon reassured the black man and persuaded him to give him refuge for the night, "all of a sudden he emitted a loud shriek, not unlike that of an owl, which so surprised me that I instantly levelled my gun. 'No harm, master. I only give notice to my wife and children that I am coming.' A tremulous answer of the same nature gently echoed through the tree tops. The runaway's lips separated with an expression of gentleness and delight, when his beautiful set of ivory teeth seemed to smile through the dusk of evening that was settling around us. 'Master,' said he, 'my wife, though black, is as beautiful to me as the President's wife is to him. She is my queen, and I look on our young ones as so many princes:—but you shall see them all, for here they are, thank God.'

"There in the midst of the cane-brakes, I found a regular camp. A small fire was lighted, and on its embers lay broiling some large slices of venison. A lad nine or ten years old was blowing the ashes from some fine sweet potatoes. Various articles of household furniture were carefully disposed around, and a large pallet of bear and deer skins seemed to be the resting place of the whole family. The wife raised not her eyes to mine, and the little ones, three in number, retired into a corner, like so many discomforted raccoons, but the Runaway, bold and apparently happy, spoke to them such cheering words, that at once one and all seemed to regard me as one sent by Providence to relieve them all from their troubles. My clothes were hung up by them to dry, and the negro asked if he might clean and grease my gun, which I permitted him to do, while the wife threw a large piece of deer's flesh to my dog, which the children were already carressing."

The savage wilderness, which was never far from the plantations in any one of the cotton states, covered the greater part of the territory in the two latest states to be carved out of the cotton kingdom, Arkansas, which was admitted in 1836 as a partner to Michigan, and Florida which came in in 1846 as a partner to Iowa. Substantial planters were moving up the river valleys in Arkansas, and were able to get together a constitutional convention in 1836 at Little Rock. But the Cherokee Indians had been settled to the west of them, and amidst the gorges and hills, the deserts, the great open spaces, it was pretty hard to get the mellow old-time plantation started, with its flower gardens, its shaded verandas, its charming ladies tinkling at pianos. In a popular romance of the time this Southwestern frontier is described in a lavish combination of all that spelled "South" to the Northern reader as a "land of fevers, alligators, niggers, and cotton bales; where the sun shines with force sufficient to melt the diamond, and the word ice is expunged from the dictionary, for its definition cannot be comprehended by the natives; where to refuse grog before breakfast would degrade you below the brute creation; and where a good dinner is looked upon as an angel's visit and voted a miracle; where the evergreen and the majestic magnolia tree, with its superb flower unknown to northern climes and its fragrance unsurpassed, calls forth the admiration of every beholder; and the dark moss hangs in festoons from the forest trees like the dreary shade of a funereal pall; where bears the size of young jackasses are fondled in lieu of pet dogs, and knives the length of a barber's pole usurp the place of tooth-picks."

As for Florida, the greater part of this lovely peninsula remained the haunt of birds, Indians, and runaway slaves. To Audubon, as to the philosophic traveler Bartram, it seemed a wild Paradise, where "the blossoms of the jassamines ever pleasing

lay steeped in dew, the humming bee was collecting her winter's store from the snowy flowers of the native orange; and
the little warblers frisked along the twigs of the smilax." He
enjoyed the company of the friendly "live oakers," companies
of wood choppers who came down from other states to earn
some wages cutting the great trees; found entertainment on an
occasional plantation; and was entranced by the birds. "Rose
colored curlews stalked gracefully beneath the many coves;
purple herons rose at almost every step we took; and each cactus supported the nest of a white ibis. The air was darkened by
whistling wings."

Lovely as the land was it had always resisted settlement.
One of the early settlements had been that tragic colony of
Huguenots which Simms celebrated in his novel *The Lily and
the Totem*. Of them it had been said: "The ground doth yield
victuals sufficient if they would have taken pains to get the
same, but they, being soldiers, desired to live by the sweat of
other men's brows." The Spanish, trying also to live by the
sweat of other men's brows, did not succeed much better. Sidney Lanier, in his charming book on Florida, says that "the history of Florida for three hundred years is but a bowl of blood.
. . . The Spaniards had this magnificent country for two hundred and fifty years, and nearly the entire results of their
labors are the beggarly settlements at Saint Augustine and Pensacola, even these mostly consisting of soldiers and office-hold-
ers." Much of the difficulty was the bravery and tenacity of the
Seminole Indians, who would not be dispossessed. The United
States decreed that they were to be removed to the West in
1836, but they took to the swamps and maintained there a
refuge not only for themselves but for fugitive Negro slaves.
Through the whole administration of Van Buren a considerable portion of the Federal army was busy searching out their
lairs one by one. Yet there were sufficient planters in Florida to
put in a plea for a constitution in 1845, and this the federal government, dominated by Southerners, made haste to grant them,
for some state holding slaves must keep pace with Iowa. So the

two states came in together, and were hailed as "stars to the union which will insure a democratic Senate for the support of the measures of the new administration." That this was a perfect balance of South against North may be seen by the fact that in the next census Florida had 87,445 inhabitants and Iowa 192,214!

5

During the early years of the nineteenth century the rapid development of the cotton industry gave the South an illusion of great hope and prosperity. Slavery which had been a languishing and dying institution was now again profitable, and as it became profitable it became increasingly moral and to be fostered at any cost by social philosophy. Even good old Virginia and Kentucky, true homes of democracy, and of sweet, kindly, and honest living, were reluctantly tied into the plantation economy as breeders of slaves for the Southern market.

From the first this new cotton aristocracy was looking for an ideal of government more suitable to its economic structure than the political democracy of the North. In John C. Calhoun of South Carolina the plantation gentry found both philosopher and spokesman for their caste. Calhoun attacked the question fairly by disapproving *in toto* of the form of government then established in the United States, and elaborating instead the ideal of the corporate state, which he called "concurrent democracy." The idea of the state as a living body, in which each class corresponds to a bodily organ, is an old one in European thinking and was elaborated by medieval political philosophers from whom Italy and Germany have since borrowed it. Calhoun found his immediate patterns for it, as he tells us, in the Confederacy of the Iroquois in central New York, and in the government of medieval Poland. His idea of the way in which it might be applied to the American continent he elaborated in a book entitled *Disquisition on Government*.

The true state, the state suitable in particular to gentlemen who are cotton planters, was, according to Calhoun, a corporate state in which the interests of the different orders or classes are adjusted by compromise under the direction of the head or brain of the community. "The government of the concurrent majority where the organism is perfect, excludes the possibility of oppression by giving each interest or portion or order— where there are established classes—the means of protecting itself against all measures calculated to advance the peculiar interests of others at its expense. Its effect then is to cause the different interests, portions, or orders—as the case may be —to desist from attempting to adopt any measures only as would promote the prosperity of all, as the only means to prevent the suspension of the action of the government, and thereby to avoid the anarchy, the greatest of all evils."

Grandiose and high minded, Calhoun's *Disquisition on Government*, with whose main ideas he favored the Senate off and on for thirty years, really reads very well. The only trouble with it is that modern life is fluid, and American life in those days was particularly so. The established classes would not stay established even among planters—not with mortgages and bankruptcy always over their heads. And so the next thing to establishing a corporate state was, in the language of the modern attempts of the same sort, to "freeze" it—to be sure that the class or order or portion you had settled on as your hand of labor should not mistake itself for a foot and run away, or, finding Jove nodding sometime, even begin to act like the head.

Withal Calhoun was a grand personage. As Daniel Webster his great opponent said in pronouncing his funeral oration in Congress, he was a man of such high integrity, such intense personal honor and self-devotion, that whatever we may think of his opinions they must "go down to posterity under the sanction of a great name."

Thus established, the idea of the Southern state went on developing in ways which have a strangely familiar sound to our ears today. Meeting the Northern criticisms of slavery with references to the slums and strikes, and workingmen's troubles of the North, Southern theorists said the United States must choose between socialism or a state in which all labor is in a condition similar to that of Southern slaves—guaranteed the minimum of subsistence, through rain or shine, but ruled by the upper classes. "Otherwise there must be a combination of the greater number of the weak and the foolish to take by physical force enough of the acquisitions of the smaller number of the active and the sensible to minister to their wants. Or in the second place the only remaining alternative must be adopted and some system devised by which it shall become to the interest of the latter voluntarily to supply the necessities of the former. The result of the first is socialism; the consequence of the second is slavery."

With their children going to college and money for the family tucked away everywhere snugly in banks, the Northerners listened with angry amazement to the suggestion of the Southern senators that they would all have to be enslaved to a few owners of large wealth in order to be happy! At first the idea was amusing, but as it continued to be reiterated, Daniel Webster himself rose in the Senate to protest. In his great Seventh of March speech in 1850 he said in solemn warning that ideas emanating from the South "exasperate, alienate, and produce a most mischievous effect on the public mind at the North. Sir, I would not notice things of this sort emanating from an obscure quarter, but one thing has occurred in this debate which struck me forcibly. An honorable member from Louisiana addressed us the other day on this subject. I suppose that there is not a more amiable and worthy gentleman in this chamber, nor a gentleman who would be more slow to give offense to anybody, but that he did not mean by his remarks to give offense. But what did he say? Why, Sir, he took pains to run a contrast between the slaves of the South and the laboring people of the North, giving the preference in all points of condition of comfort and happiness to the slaves of the South. The honorable member doubtless did not suppose that he gave any offense or did an injustice. He was merely expressing his opinion. But does he know how remarks of that sort will be received by the laboring people of the North? Why, who are the laboring people of the North? They are the North. They are the people who cultivate their own farms with their own hands, freeholders, educated men, independent men. Let me say, Sir, that five-sixths of the whole property of the North is in the hands of the laborers of the North. They cultivate their farms. They educate their children. They provide the means of independence. If they are not freeholders, they earn wages; these wages accumulate, are turned into capital, into new freeholds and small capitalists are created. This is the case, and such the course of things among the industrious and frugal. And what can these people think, when so respectable and worthy a gentleman as the member from Louisiana undertakes to prove that the absolute ignorance and abject slavery of the South is more in keeping with the high purposes and destiny of immortal rational human beings than the educated, the independent, the free laborers of the North?"

Meanwhile, the plantation gentry went on, through the inevitable cycle of ideas which recent European history has again made familiar to us. Having discovered the corporate state, and setting this idea up as the only way of saving the country from socialism, they now entered upon the question of race. So the Southern magazines published at Richmond and Charleston inquired into the real origin of folks South and North, and found that the North was peopled mainly by descendants of Saxon serfs—slaves, in other words—white slaves; but the South had been peopled by the Normans, chivalrous, bold, brave, military men—in fact, knights.

Having discovered that their ancestors were Norman knights, it was proper to wish that such might rule them again. So, in May, 1856, there was a call in *The Southern Literary Messenger* for a dictator, such a man as Alexander Hamilton, planter's son of the West Indies, or Andrew Jackson—God rest his soul, poor simple democrat! "They made administration popular in the only way in which it can be made popular by making it conform to the national temper—the temper of a bold, enterprising, impatient, proud, warlike, conquering race, fevering for action, impatient of delays, looking to material results and fearless of consequences, and full of the pride of nationality, and love of individual and national glory."

Anything so high and holy as a corporate state, peopled by descendants of the "noblest of the knightly race" "full of pride of nationality," can be maintained only by constant attention to purity. In the years before the war, the South became enamored of purity, so much so that, as Abraham Lincoln sarcastically suggested, it was only a question of time when they would begin to find that Roman Catholics, Irish, etc., etc., were not "pure."

> Oh, Rose of Purity born,
> Be Purity's guerdon forever
> On the brow of youth be worn,
> Or the bosom of virtue adorn,
> Forever, forever!

So sang the Southern poet, and that was pretty enough. It was not so pretty when they began to specify. Northern women, it seemed, were impure. They want to substitute "brutal lust" for "love and protection." They delivered "lectures on free love and spiritualism." In fact all the North was impure, and its private life "stained by every extreme known in the annals of lust and crime. . . . Not a breeze is blown from the Northern hills but bears upon its wings taints of crime and vice, to reek and stink, stink and reek, upon our Southern plains." Altogether, "The Cavaliers, Jacobites, and Huguenots who settled the South naturally hate, condemn, and despise the northern Puritans who settled the North; the former are master races; the latter a slave-race, descendants of Saxon serfs."

Reading this kind of thing, the North remarked dryly, in the person of Lowell's Mr. Biglow:

Them that rule us, them slave-traders,
    Haint they cut a thunderin swarth
(Helped by Yankee renegaders)
    Through the vartu of the North!

6

This voice of a great mushroom industry had of course little to do with the genuine folk ideals below the Mason and Dixon line. It remains the permanent heritage of American culture that in several different centers in the South—men and women had staked their lives on the faith that life might be happy and beautiful. And in their idea of beauty they included great kindness—kindness limited in its scope to family and friends and dependents, but gracious in manner, patient in self-sacrificing devotion, and capable, in a crisis, of the finest chivalry. To this great Southern ideal, each center made its characteristic contribution—Virginia its free and generous thinking; Charleston and Savannah their eighteenth century polish in social life; Kentucky and the mountain border their romance of character and aptitude for the fine ballad gesture; New Orleans its Parisian sense of measure and fitness, and metropolitan bonhomie. Where else in the world have people over so wide an area been so sincerely convinced that beautiful behavior matters—beauty of manner and beauty of feeling? Fragrant and lovely, as a water lily unstained by the mud out of which it grew and by which it was, perforce, nourished, there was always this loveliness of life in the South. Only a very small fraction of the sugar and rice and cotton that went out through the ports of New Orleans and Savannah and Charleston was ever touched by the perfume of this ideal. Only one in thousands of black slaves ever felt the ministering touch of the lady in the great house, but that one did. As Harriet Beecher Stowe says, of the Southern mistress, "Many of them, surrounded by circumstances over which they can have no control, perplexed by domestic cares, of which women in free states can have very little conception, loaded down by duties and responsibilities which wear upon the very springs of life, still go on bravely and patiently from day to day, doing all they can to alleviate what they cannot prevent, and, so far as the sphere of their own immediate power extends, rescuing those who are dependent upon them from the evils of the system."

And those thus rescued amply repaid master and mistress in loyalty and in their own species of beautiful behavior. As one considers the omnipresence in the South of the ideal of lovely living, rooted in kindness, and its independent origin in several centers, one wonders whether the unifying force in it might not have been the rich imagination of the enslaved race itself. All ideals were transmitted through mammy and the house servants. It was they who brought up the little white child to the standards of his caste. It was they who furnished the admiring audience for fine behavior and the sullen disapproval of the reverse. To them the master's family were actors on a handsome stage. They looked on them with the eye of a theatrical director, putting them in childhood through their parts, reserving even in age the right of judgment. These lovely people were their handiwork, and into the making of their fine life went the suppressed dreams of the race. The mistress is one of the heroines of Southern tradition, but mammy is the other. And which was responsible for which? Did the mistress make mammy what she was, or did mammy make the mistress?

Amidst all the pretentiousness of the new cotton South, there were many, especially men from the older Southern sections like Virginia, who as Whittier says of Randolph of Roanoke,

> . . . never stooped
> His proud and manly feeling
> To poor excuses of the wrong
> Or meanness of concealing.

Once when a Northerner had tried to speak placating words about slavery in Congress, Randolph had said, "Sir, I

envy neither the heart nor the head of that man from the
North who can speak in defense of slavery."

It was the limitation of these men that their patriotism
never went beyond the narrow boundaries of their own immediate state or group, and when trouble came, right or wrong,
they stood with their own. But like Randolph, like Calhoun,
they maintained their own integrity of opinion and feeling.
Of Randolph Whittier wrote:

> Too honest or too proud to feign
>   A love he never cherished
> Beyond Virginia's borderline
>   His patriotism perished.
> While others hailed in distant skies
>   Our eagle's dusky pinion,
> He only saw the mountain bird
>   Stoop o'er the old Dominion.
>
> He held his slaves, yet kept the while
>   His reverence for the Human.
> In the dark vassals of his will
>   He saw but Man and Woman.
> No hunter of God's outraged poor
>   His Roanoke valley entered;
> No trader in the souls of men
>   Across his threshold ventured.

And of all these men of the South, one may say with Whittier

> Shut out from him the bitter word
>   And serpent hiss of scorning
> Nor let the storms of yesterday
>   Disturb his quiet morning.
> Breathe over him forgetfulness
>   Of all save deeds of kindness,
> And save to smiles of grateful eyes
>   Press down his lids in blindness.

12

SWEETWATER OCEANS

OR nearly a quarter of a century after the settling of Ohio, the remainder of the Northwest Territory was Indian land, presided over most of the time by General William Henry Harrison, with his headquarters at the old French town of Vincennes on the Wabash. This Indian territory was not completely a savage land. For more than a hundred years it had been one of the dominions of that great wilderness civilization of France, reaching up the Mississippi Valley from New Orleans, and westward along the Great Lakes from Montreal and Quebec. The northern seat of this civilization had been the Mission of Sainte Marie du Sault, three leagues below the mouth of Lake Superior. There in 1671, on a beautiful day in June, there had been a great ceremony in which the French intendant "caused the cross to be planted there and the King's standard to be raised with all the pomp that he could devise." Thereafter, mainly in spots which were already natural gathering places for the Indians, little French towns had grown up. These towns consisted mainly of a mission church, with outlying workshops, priests' dwellings, perhaps a hostel for strangers or people in trouble, sometimes farms and gardens; and a fort, with such dwellings as the soldiers and officers required. Houses and fort were at first rudely and strongly built of logs. Later the low-eaved houses were made rather smartly of planks fitted in patterns. Here and there the church was of stone, long since overgrown with ivy. Around the houses were orchards and gardens, the gardens small and neatly fenced, as in a European town. It is not reported that anyone ever paved the streets. Grass-grown in summer, muddy in spring, they served well enough for light moccasined feet or men coming in on horseback.

These villages were centers of the fur trade. From them Frenchmen made long voyages out into the wilderness for furs, on to Montreal or Quebec for supplies. Most of the early fur traders attached to themselves Indian girls. The priests, if possible, would follow up these affairs and nurse them into marriages, looking after and instructing the women while their men were away, baptizing their children and bringing them up in the church, and sending Jean or Jacques back to his Indian mistress whenever he came to them in a repentant mood and ready to confess his sins. When the fur trader prospered, the children were sent to Montreal or New Orleans to a convent school to be educated. So, as time went on, considerable decency of life developed; and there were families of girls of mixed Indian and French parentage, handsome, accomplished, well to do, for whose hands there was considerable rivalry among the young bucks of the fur trade. In type these French people were much like the French Canadians of today. Some virtues were as inherent in the fur trade as the virtues of New Englanders were in seafaring—handiness and a certain kind of neatness, reliability, honesty, and a matter-of-fact sort of courage in meeting hair-raising difficulties. With the cash proceeds of their furs, supplemented by the garden and the orchard and the hunt, people lived in great comfort in these old villages—so much comfort, in fact, that they never seem to have thought of other possibilities—neither tilling the land on a large scale, nor building up a timber industry, nor even showing great excitement about the lumps of copper which they occasionally fished out of the clear waters along the shores of Lake Superior.

There were several clusters of these French towns, each cluster the nucleus of one of the states—a considerable group of them in what is now Wisconsin; a group around Detroit, in what is now Michigan; several on the Wabash in Indiana; and a group on the Mississippi in Illinois, in the neighborhood of Saint Louis, which was the Spanish fur mart. The principal center on the Wabash was Vincennes; the two principal towns in Illinois within the Saint Louis range were Cahokia and Kaskaskia. A full record of the pre-American life of this region is in *The Jesuit Relations*, those long, interesting letters which the Jesuit priests were required to send home yearly from America. During the Revolution young George Rogers Clark had gone through these towns and annexed them to the United States, and his own record of his gallant progress was published in 1927 under the title *The Capture of Old Vincennes, The Original Narratives of George Rogers Clark and of His Opponent Governor Henry Hamilton*. The story has been retold as a fiction in *Alice of Old Vincennes* by Maurice Thompson, which gives an attractive and probably a truthful picture of life in these towns.

Around these French villages swayed an ever-changing horde of Indians, coming and going, off on the warpath and back to camp awhile, mostly friendly enough, but unstable, suspicious, easily inflamed by rum and not able to control their own rascals. Harrison, as American administrator operating from the French town of Vincennes, tried to deal with the Indians as they were accustomed to be dealt with, and at the same time to persuade them to settle down, or move up closer together and leave a little room for some white settlers. Slowly, tactfully, Harrison bought sections of land from them. He watched suspiciously while they went up and down to the town of Malden on the extreme western tip of Lake Ontario to which the British moved their center for the fur trade after evacuating Detroit. He saw Tecumseh move in next door to him and build up an Indian capital at the Prophet's Town below the mouth of Tippecanoe Creek, above the present site of Lafayette. For several years, while Tecumseh organized the Indians, Harrison carried on diplomatic relations with the chief, visiting and receiving him in state. All the while, into lands which Harrison had obtained and opened to settlement, the backwoodsmen from across the Ohio River, driven out of Kentucky by slavery, crept up the streams, settling here and there, tending to be just where the French and the Indians already were, in rich or open land, or perched on something that was not still swamp. A strange melee of people! Ohio looking westward thought they needed schools and ought to be educated. Physicians knew they needed medicine, and made some adventurous long swings around, in, and through the backwoods settlements, and, clattering by their sides, came the horseback-riding preachers of the Methodist Church, the circuit riders.

The original culture hero of this frontier was the French priest. Unlike the Latin democracies, the early American settlers, however Protestant, Puritan, or Presbyterian they might be, seem to have had little anticlerical prejudice. They liked and admired the good fathers and looked on them with reverence. All stories and traditions deal tenderly with them, as good and gentle and most unselfish men whose black-robed figures consecrate a land otherwise bare of culture.

To the men of the Northwest Father Marquette was a peculiarly touching figure, dying at thirty-eight, alone in the woods, in a shed built of saplings, alone except for his two boatmen who carried him in and laid him by a freshly lighted fire. Dying, he confessed them with his last breath, and so sank to rest while they held the crucifix before him. The town of Marquette in Michigan perpetuates his name, and so also do the Marquette monument and Marquette building in Chicago. The feeling of the Northwest about this heroic young priest was expressed in 1887 when the state of Wisconsin presented a statue of him to the Hall of Fame in Washington. Demo-

crats and religious liberals as the early settlers were, they were
happy to receive from the French father the blessing, if not
of the church, at least of ancient and poetic tradition.

Of the monastery on one of the Indian mounds near
Cahokia Micah P. Flint, an early Western poet, wrote:

> Here, midst a boundless waste
> Of rank and gaudy flowers, and o'er the bones
> Of unknown races of the ages past,
> They dwelt. Themselves knew not the deep, dark thoughts
> Of their associates. . . .
> Man's heart is made of iron, or 'twould burst
> 'Midst the endurances of woes like these.
> I saw the sun behind the western woods
> Go down upon their shorn and cowled heads.
> No vesper hymn consoled their troubled thoughts.
> Far o'er the plain the wolf's lugubrious howl,
> The cricket's chirp, and the nocturnal cry
> Of hooting owls, was their sad evening song.

2

After the War of 1812 there was a sudden rush of settlers,
reinforced by many people from the Eastern seaboard, entering the West by way of the Cumberland Gap. In 1805 the
Detroit region had been cut away from Indiana and organized
as Michigan Territory. In 1809 Illinois was cut off and separately organized. By 1816 it was decided that Indiana had
enough people to make a state. These people were practically
all in the valley of the Wabash and along its eastern tributary
the White River, where the French already were. Northern
Indiana remained an empty grove, swamp, and flower garden,
for more than a decade afterward, and for the most part was
left to the Indians.

It was a trial to the federal government that the people
from the South and East would not settle one state at a time,
but spread all over the map, a settler here, and a settler there,
preempting what seemed to be the most likely land. So while

they were trying to get Indiana governed and provided with schools, the increasing steamboat traffic on the rivers and the busy stir of life at Saint Louis, across the river from the Illinois French towns, were bringing people into that region, too. There was a legislature at Kaskaskia from 1812 on, trying to govern these people, and a capable young chief justice of Kentucky, Ninian Edwards, had been sent over by President Madison to administer the territory. He brought with him his wife's sister, Mary Todd, who married Abraham Lincoln.

Though Illinois was accepted as a state in 1818, for nearly two decades afterward it was comparatively empty territory. In 1832 William Cullen Bryant, writing home from Illinois, found only scattered settlers on a "wide unfenced prairie stretching away on every side until it met the horizon. Flocks of turtle doves rose from our path scared at our approach; quails and rabbits were seen running before us; the prairie squirrel, a little striped animal of the marmot kind crossed the road; we started plovers by the dozen, and now and then a prairie hen which flew off heavily into the grassy wilderness." He met militia companies—the men "unkempt and unshaved wearing shirts of dark calico and sometimes calico capotes." One of them had as a captain a raw youth in whose quaint and pleasant talk Bryant was much interested. His name was Abraham Lincoln.

Everybody he met in Illinois, says Bryant, came from Kentucky except a man named Shurtliff from Massachusetts and a Quaker named Wilson from Pennsylvania. On the wide prairie, he was put up for the night by "a scarlet-faced Virginian and his tall prim-looking wife, who gave us a rasher of bacon, a radish, and bread and milk in pewter tumblers. They are Methodists and appeared to live in a comfortable way." Passing by log cabins "of the most wretched description" they met Wilson, the Quaker, who gave them a "nice breakfast." Here and there an old gray-headed woman was spinning at the door of her log house. Apparently what he saw in Illinois was exactly what one sees now in the Kentucky and Tennessee

mountains, spread out thinly on the prairie. Moving north of
the river, and exposed to the beneficent influence of public
schools and cheap lands, these people were in a fair way to
stop being backwoodsmen and to become what they have
been ever since—the folks.

Many of these people remained romantically attached to
the lands across the river. To have come from Kentucky gave
them prestige. They were ready to say with Vachel Lindsay

> I was born in Illinois,
> Have lived there all my days,
> And I have the Northern words,
> And thoughts,
> And ways.

> But my great-grandfathers came
> To the west with Daniel Boone,
> And taught his babes to read
> And heard the redbird's tune;

> And heard the turkey's call,
> And stilled the panther's cry,
> And rolled on the Blue Grass hills,
> And looked God in the eye.

> And feud and Hell were theirs,
> Love, like the moon's desire,
> Love, like a burning mine,
> Love like a rifle fire.

This somewhat absurd and sentimental southernism has been
paraded by Vachel Lindsay. "The inexplicable Mason and
Dixon line, deep dyed and awful ran through our hearts. We
were made conscious of this by all our Lindsay kin. They
were Breckenridge Democrats, remaining for the most part in
Kentucky, but came visiting us in our Ishmaelite loneliness in
this flaming and arrogant G.A.R. state capital." But the Lind-
says, apparently, like a good many of these backwoodsmen,

were not true Virginians but Scotch-Irish who had come to America late in the colonial period, and had been kept moving by landlordism at their backs across the South. Much of the deep-dyed Southern loyalty of these movers across the river was just the ballad imagination of the Scotch-Irish, adding the bonny bluegrass to the banks and braes of old Scotland and the sweet fields of Ireland, and painting in broad acres of plantation and armies of Negroes over the actual memory of an old log cabin very insecure on its underpinnings. The snobbish flaunting of a Kentucky background was one of the things that made Mrs. Abraham Lincoln hard to bear.

Lacking knowledge of books, industrial techniques, and the various arts of good housekeeping, the backwoodsmen brought north with them a wild and simple culture of their own of which Bob Taylor, the declamatory governor of Tennessee, used to say: "The fiddle, the rifle, the axe, and the Bible, the palladium of American liberty, symbolizing music, prowess, labor, and free religion, the four grand forces of our civilization, were the trusty friends and faithful allies of our pioneer ancestry in subduing the wilderness and erecting the great commonwealth of the Republic. Wherever a son of freedom pushed his perilous way into the savage wilds and erected his log cabin, these were the cherished penates of his humble domicile—the rifle on the rack above the door, the axe in the corner, the Bible on the table, and the fiddle, with its streamers of ribbon, hanging on the wall."

To these the frontiersman added two immaterial treasures —his songs and his storytelling. Music, especially song music and a very simple kind of dance music, began to assume a very important place in American life as the Scotch-Irish border became articulate and the Kentucky frontiersmen began moving north into Indiana and Illinois. Somewhere along the Ohio, America started crooning and jigging, and it has been crooning and jigging ever since.

The storytelling in a later generation was to emerge as the Indiana school of literature, tender, sentimental, pretty, and full of quaint folksy humor. But this was while the slender hand of the New England schoolma'am lay gently upon it. A little later Mark Twain, and then O. Henry coming up from the Southern border, began to get courage really to use the frontiersman's narrative technique. For the backwoodsmen had a very definite notion of their own about plot and character, derived from long experience in swapping yarns. Plot had to be clean and clear, and come to a sharp point. A good storyteller, they had learned, was one who begins in a slow, drawling way and lays in the background leisurely, stopping and looking around, and letting every detail sink in, and then, when you are all ready for it, he comes to the point quickly— slap, bang, and the more amazing the point is, the better.

One type of story in which these backwoodsmen were becoming expert was the "tall story" developed out of contests in telling lies—the best liar to get the prize. In these stories the chief character must have had some identifying mark. You had to be able to begin something like this: "Remember the fellow I was telling you about, the fellow with the ugly mug —well, Sir, that fellow was the ugliest man I ever saw. He was so ugly that . . ." and then when you had your audience with their tongues hanging out, you were off on your tale. An example of both plot and character drawing of this type is one of the early traditions about Davy Crockett.

Davy Crockett, it seems, had an awful grin. Talk about his shooting bears, well, sirs, he didn't have to shoot them to kill them. All he had to do was to grin at them. Once he and a friend were going through the woods when they saw a raccoon in a tree. The friend said, "Davy, I dare you to grin that coon down from that limb." So Davy grinned and he grinned and he grinned. But nothing happened. The raccoon was there just the same. (Here the proper thing was for the speaker to look around slowly and let this melancholy fact sink in.) Yes, sirs, the coon was still there. But if you think that proves anything about Davy's grin, you just listen. For when they come close and really looked at that coon, they saw that it wasn't a coon head at all, it was just a knot in the limb of the tree, and sirs, the *bark was all peeled off that knot—just from Davy's grinning!*

One of the storytelling frontiersmen, whose family had been one of the "movers" from Kentucky, grew up in Illinois as young Abe Lincoln. He had all the literary arts of his heritage, including for lofty and solemn moments the language of the Bible. His stories had a quaint, gargoylish sort of humor, and his eloquence a lovely cadence, tender, musical, pathetic. One of his most characteristic "works" was his little epitaph for the dead Indian written when he was a young man.

> Here lies Johnny Kinkapod
> Look kindly on him, gracious God
> As he would do, if he were You,
> And You were Johnny Kinkapod!

3

Until the eighteen-thirties northern Indiana slept serene under its great trees, and the hawthorn bloomed May after May, and no one shattered the white blossoms. Over in Illinois there were beautiful stretches of open prairie, like parks among the woods, into which no plow had sunk. Then the North began to feel the effects of the Erie Canal.

The Erie Canal had been opened on October 26, 1825, when the canal boat "Seneca Chief," bearing a bottle of water from Lake Erie had started off across the whole width of New York and down the Hudson to empty it into the Atlantic Ocean, amidst a salvo of artillery. Across this middle New York State, till then a wilderness, came the advancing line of homes. The city of Buffalo sprang up. The Ohio shores of Lake Erie began to sprout with docks, and in 1832 a steamer moored off the mouth of the Chicago River. Meanwhile, Henry Clay, the great Whig from Kentucky, had made the first great pronouncement on "famine in the midst of plenty." Just as if he were talking in the year 1934, instead of 1824, he had asked why in the richest country in the world starvation

young lady for a dance, and a great deal more helpful as a confidante after the dance was over.

To assist in the social education of the young ladies there was not only *Godey's Lady's Book,* but endless manuals of behavior, all of which my grandfather's family possessed— *How to Be a Lady, The Christian Gentlewoman,* etc.

American tradition which has been so lavish in picturing the life of Southern plantations forgets that there were the opulent big farms owned and run by men who were also "gentlemen" scattered all through the Northwest. In the last decade before the Civil War the standard of living was rising much faster in the North than in the South, for all except a very few wealthy planters near New Orleans and Charleston. Despite the sentimental charm of the plantations in story, members of these more opulent and cultivated Northern agricultural families, visiting Southern friends, were not always impressed. The old Southern farm would seem a little shiftless, and the black servants a nuisance, nothing smart or up to date, just quaint and countrified and somewhat run down.

4

While his farms were developing, my grandfather carried on a most active professional career. As medicine advanced, he often chafed a little because he did not have time to go to the Eastern cities and brush up on the latest scientific knowledge. But he encouraged young men of his family whom he trained to do so, and followed their studies with absorbed interest. There are touching stories of his excitement in his old age when some of these younger physicians in the family performed operations which he had not believed possible. One of the performances that moved him most was the use of chloroform in childbirth. He had seen so much painful childbirth among frontier women! Like many of the more intelligent frontier doctors, he thought freely and boldly on medical questions, and often anticipated modern practice. One thing he was certain of. The most serious troubles among these

queer backwoods people were not physical but psychological.
Many of the persons who had come through the hardships of
pioneering into the beginnings of comfort and culture were
psychic wrecks. There was a good deal of apparent illness
whose source, my grandfather was convinced, was only in the
mind—women suffering from debility; persons with paralyzed
limbs; with queer jerks and spasms; with extreme food phobias,
so that "they could not hold anything on their stomachs." All
these were methods of "escape" for those who spirits had
failed before the hardships of pioneering, enabling them to
rest in bed and be cared for while someone else carried the
burdens. My grandfather and other intelligent frontier physicians had many a discussion of these matters—anticipating, at
least in their observations and their curiosity, the researches
that Charcot and Freud were later to make. They used to
devise tricks to startle their patients into the instinctive use of
a limb which appeared to be paralyzed or to get them to take
in some not easily recognized form the food which they
thought would "poison" them. Many of the circuit-riding
preachers developed a rude psychological skill in handling
these cases, and delivering the "possessed." My grandfather,
disliking the great forest revival meetings, was yet forced to
recognize that the circuit rider had a key to health for these
people which was denied even to the medical profession.

These circuit-riding preachers are enshrined in two American classics—the *Autobiography* of Peter Cartwright, published in 1857, and *The Circuit Rider*, by Edward Eggleston,
published in 1874. Peter Cartwright's home territory was
Kentucky, but he made large swings along the whole frontier,
and in his own story paints broad and long, with rugged realism, the portrait not only of himself but of the more able
circuit rider everywhere. His book is dank and spicy with the
breath of the forest. The endless gloom, the decaying logs on
which Peter often sat talking with a troubled soul, the mossy
cushions on which he knelt down with the sinner and prayed,
his meditations as he rode horseback on the endless bridle

paths, the sudden encounters with strange or violent persons in those somber shades—all these live again in Peter's simple narrative. And withal, before one finishes, one has learned to respect him as a sound, rude man of great common sense. Sprinkled through the narrative are many quaint anecdotes. Once he preached on the text, "Take up thy cross and follow me." At the next meeting he was amazed to see a Dutchman walk into meeting carrying his wife on his back. When Peter asked why the lady was where she was, the Dutchman replied earnestly that Peter had admonished them to take up their crosses, and follow Christ. Since his wife was his great cross in life, he had taken her up and here he was. Perceiving that the Dutchman was quite in earnest, Peter talked to both the wife and the husband, and was proud to record that he brought them both to accept Christ and follow counsels of mutual love, and so they lived happily ever after.

Edward Eggleston called his story *A Tale of an Heroic Age.* "In no other class was the real heroic element so finely displayed. How do I remember the forms and weather-beaten visages of the old preachers, whose constitutions had conquered starvation and exposure, who had survived swamps, alligators, Indians, highway robbers, and bilious fevers. How was my boyish soul tickled with their anecdotes of rude experience! How was my imagination wrought upon by their hairbreadth escapes! How was my heart set afire by their contagious religious enthusiasm so that at eighteen years of age, I bestrode the saddle bags myself, and laid upon a feeble frame the magnificent burden of emulating their toils."

In *The Hoosier Schoolmaster* Eggleston also celebrated another drama of the frontier—often a rude and bloody one, too—the drama of being educated.

The great plan of common schools for all people, made possible by the land provisions of the Ordinance, had an immediate effect on the fertile mind of the Southern backwoodsman. The capable backwoodsman was delighted with education, but he wanted to take it easy, and at the same time to get it in a great hurry, and have something to show when he had it. The two great generations of professional men who educated the Northwest found that Eastern learning had to undergo some modification when brought over the mountains. Teachers, doctors, preachers, lawyers, all learned to improvise principles and techniques. They combined a little of everything from the old culture patterns and translated into intellectual terms the experience of the people themselves. They were dealing with an ignorant but exceedingly shrewd and realistic folk who wanted to snatch a few of the flowers of life now before they died.

Lecture courses flourished. Dancing teachers, elocution teachers, teachers of painting, especially painting on china, could earn a living in any settlement. Out of this great hurry to learn came many characteristics of the American intellectual outlook—the crowding of the colleges with courses in everything; the superficial social snobbishness; the love of the sentimental and the pretty; the demand for results and impatience with the long, slow processes of the older types of learning. Much that had been valuable was too hastily discarded, but much also that was only intellectual junk. And when the new idea finally came to maturity in the great series of land-grant colleges, a new force in higher education was born.

Meanwhile the first generation raised on the common school and free labor tradition in Indiana displayed a cheerful versatility. In 1833 a local poet wrote:

> Blest Indiana, in her soil
> Men seek the sure rewards of toil,
> Men who can legislate or plough,
> Wage politics or milk a cow;
> So plastic are their various parts
> That in the circle of the arts,
> With equal tact the Hoosier loons
> Hunt offices or hunt raccoons.

submissive to their priests, gay, contented, courteous, and apparently retaining the ancestral tastes for dancing, singing, and flowers." But eight years later it is reported that there are 15,000 people in Detroit, and they enjoy "the elegance and luxury of the most polite society. The docks are full of boats. The principal street would be an ornament to any city, and in winter the Detroit River, frozen like marble, presents a scene of carnival gaiety with skaters and sleighers in bright costumes and heavy furs, gliding back and forth to the jingling of bells and the happy bursts of shouting and laughter."

This change was due to the influx of people which the lake business brought, settlers with some capital, persons with the education and the social arts of Eastern cities, coming in the boom years before the great panic of 1837, bright, fashionable, expansive. When the constitutional convention met at Detroit in May 1835 to frame the state government, fifty-two of the eighty-nine members were from New England or the Middle States, and eighteen had grown up in New York. This gave the state its character—enterprising, capitalistic, with very little backwoods background intervening between it and the romance of early French history.

Yet Charles Lanman, who in 1847 made a canoe trip through the Great Lakes, reported that much of Michigan was still virgin solitude. "On the borders of cold and desolate lakes . . . the crane and bittern rear their young. Occasionally on the brow of some jutting crag may be discovered the meagre hut of some poor Indian. Perhaps a barbarous anchorite to whom the voice of his fellow man is a grating sound, and to whom existence is but a mist, a dream, or it may be some disgraced warrior who has been banished from his friends and home, to dwell in this dreary solitude, with no companions but a half-starved dog, rugged pines, and frowning rocks. But this section is said to contain the richest copper mine in the world."

The land, he says, is full of lakes, some "surrounded by comfortable dwellings," but "some little lakes smile in perpetual solitude." And beyond the settlements he finds that the

French-Indian trader is still the "aristocrat of the wilderness."
One of these he describes as living in his log house with his
Indian wife surrounded by a herd of Indian dogs and an Indian brotherhood, and possessing the following pets—one
grizzly bear, two black bears, two fawns, one fox, one coon,
one eagle, two swans, and one owl.

Westward the territory of Wisconsin, cut off from Michigan in 1836, was similar wilderness, with a long and romantic
history of the fur traders and the Jesuit fathers behind it.
While settlers from the South crept northward into it, much
of the state, especially in its northern part, was being exploited
by Eastern capital, working lead mines, financing through the
Northwest Company the American fur trade, and cutting
timber in the "pineries" of the north. This brought a large immigration fresh from Europe, especially the Germans who
established themselves at Milwaukee and made it their own
city. But meanwhile the characteristic folk life of the Middle
West was being created by the streams of Yankee immigration
meeting and marrying with the streams of Scotch-Irish immigration from the Southern border. Such a combination is
described by Hamlin Garland whose epic of his family, beginning with *A Son of the Middle Border* and continuing
through several books, tells the whole social history of the
state.

The capitalistic enterprise of Wisconsin speeded up the
acquisition of land by the settlers, because it gave them a
means of working part of the time for wages. Says Garland,
"Nearly every young man who could get away from the farm
or the village went north in November, into the pine woods
which covered the entire upper part of the state, and my
father, who had been a raftsman and timber cruiser and pilot
ever since his coming west, was deeply skilled with axe and
steering oars. . . . The heroic life he led made him seem very
wonderful in my eyes. . . . As he gathered us all around his
knees at night before the fire, he loved to tell us of riding the
whirlpools of Big Bull Falls or of how he lived for weeks on a

raft with the water up to his knees (sleeping at night in his wet working clothes) sustained by the blood of youth and the spirit of adventure."

Assembling its population rapidly, and from rather miscellaneous sources, Wisconsin came into the Union in 1848, the last of the states created by the great Northwest Ordinance —that great brood raised up by the forethought of Washington, Jefferson, and the New England soldiers, which was to meet and break the power of the "barons of the South." For Wisconsin, coming late on the scene, brought a new and strong force to bear against slavery. Its stout body of industrial workers, investing their wages in homesteads, looking forward to freedom and opportunity for their children, saw in the political theories of the South the greatest menace to better conditions for the working man and his incipient opportunity out here to collect a little capital of his own.

For to the three original great assets of the Old Northwest was now added a fourth, the power of machinery. "Labor is degrading," said the Southerners; "there must be a leisured class." And all over the Northwest wheels and belts on machinery were grinding out the answer. By 1860 it was reported that "farming is comparatively a child's play to what it was twenty years ago, before mowing and reaping and other agricultural machines were invented. The severe manual toil of mowing, raking, patching, and cradling is now performed by machinery operated by horsepower, and man simply oversees the operations and conducts them with intelligence." While the cotton floated down the Mississippi, an increasing burden of corn and wheat and manufactured products went over the 2,000 miles of waterway opened to the Atlantic in the North under the hands of free labor paid by Northern capital, until in 1846 the value of the shipping at Buffalo actually overtopped the value of that at New Orleans!

And all the while the corn and the wheat grew and grew, outshining in yellow gold the silver of the cotton fields. "You can't beat Cotton. Cotton is King!" cried the Southern orators, and from all over Indiana and Illinois and Wisconsin, and Iowa, a million, million tassels of corn and wheat began to answer, like a multitude of tiny bells swinging all together, till they made one deafening clang, "You can't, can't you?"

13

WHAT THEY SAID ABOUT DIXIE

HAT they said about Dixie was most effective not in the pages of the Richmond and Charleston magazines, or even from the lips of the fire-eating senators, but in the simple tales and songs that went up and down the river.

The real word about Dixie had been said when Doctor Deming, a gentleman from Richland County, Ohio, remarked that, on ascending the Ohio River in the steamboat "Fame," he had the opportunity of conversing with a Mr. Dickinson of Pittsburgh, in company with a number of planters and slaveowners from Louisiana, Alabama, and Mississippi. Mr. Dickinson said that though during the boiling season on the Louisiana sugar plantations it was necessary to have twice as much labor as during the raising season, the work could be accomplished by working one set of Negro hands both night and day. Many planters found it most economical to do this, and simply expected to wear out one set of hands every seven years and to replace them. This was corroborated by the various slaveowners on board.

It was said when at Louisville a gentleman took passage having with him a family of blacks, husband, wife, and children. The husband was handcuffed. During the night he jumped into the river, and the master was out $700. The deck hands were saying, next morning, that he had got wind of his master's intention to sell him and two of the children down the river.

It was said by Mr. Tobias Bodinot of Saint Albans, Ohio, "for some years a navigator on the Mississippi River": "The slaves down the Mississippi are half starved. The boats when they stop at night are constantly boarded by slaves, begging for something to eat."

This statement was repeated to a graceful Creole gentleman on board a steamer. "Oh yes," he replied easily, "there are two systems in vogue. One is starve 'em and wear 'em out and replace them." "The other?" "Feed 'em and spoil 'em and keep them, the way I do. But I never make any money. I run into debt."

It was said when a Boston gentleman and a New York gentleman, both apparently in easy circumstances, looking out on the shores of Mississippi sliding by, deplored "Northern fanaticism coming down here and interfering with the customs of the country," and a gentleman from Kentucky who had been standing looking somberly out on these shores turned to them fiercely, and said: "Sir, I am a slaveowner, and I want to tell you that Northern fanaticism is responsible for every decent and humane thing that has been done in the South to improve the lot of the slave for the last twenty years."

It was said when advertisements in the newspapers the boats had brought up from towns farther south began to be read in Illinois and Indiana and Ohio. The *Alabama Banner*, Dadeville, Alabama advertised: "The Undersigned, having an excellent pack of hounds for trailing and catching runaway slaves, informs the public that his prices in future will be as follows." The *Natchez Courier* advertised: "Runaway. Hair curls without showing black blood. Scar on cheek, left hand seriously injured by pistol shot." And thinking of his own family quietly helping slaves that had escaped from Kentucky on their way to Canada, a young Quaker editor in Ohio would read, in the *Nashville Daily Gazette*: "Richard Dillingham

was arrested for having three slaves with him whom he intended to take to a free state. He admitted his crime, and said
he was doing it for the good of the slaves without any ex-
pectation of profit. He belongs to a respectable family and he
is not without the sympathy of those who attended his trial.
It was a foolhardy enterprise in which he embarked and dearly
has he paid for his rashness."

It was said when Abraham Lincoln wrote to his friend
Joshua Speed across the river, with regard to the Fugitive
Slave Act: "I acknowledge your rights and obligations under
the constitution in regard to your slaves. I confess I hate to
see the poor creatures hunted down and caught and carried
back to their stripes and unrequited toil, but I bite my lips and
keep quiet. In 1841, you and I together made a tedious low-
water trip on a steamboat from Louisville to St. Louis. You
may remember as well as I do, that from Louisville to the
mouth of the Ohio, there were on board ten or a dozen slaves
shackled together with irons. That sight was a continued torment to me, and I see something like it whenever I touch the
Ohio or any other slave border. It is not fair for you to assume
that I have no interest in a thing which has, and continually
exercises the power of making me miserable. You ought rather
to appreciate how much the great body of northern people
do crucify their feelings in order to maintain their loyalty to
the constitution and to the Union."

All such voices, the murmurous multitudinous voices of
the river, came together as one voice at the bright town of
Cincinnati, on the upper reaches of the Ohio. And there a
Yankee woman, hearing the voices come and go, come and go,
through years and years, with the lapping of the water, wrote
down what they said in a book, and the book was *Uncle
Tom's Cabin*.

2

But other things more amusing were said about the trip
down the river. There was the dancing of some of those fel-

lows. Gad, if I could only show you! And there was the singing of some of those slaves. "Away back in the beginning, to my mind," said Mark Twain, "their music made all other vocal music cheap; and that early notion is emphasized now. It is utterly beautiful to me, and it moves me as no other music can." Wherever young people were gathered together around the piano, in intelligent households at the head of the great river highway, in Cincinnati or Pittsburgh, they would be experimenting with these strange dances, these wild harmonies. The beautiful young lady would sit dreamily at the piano, picking out a strain here, a strain there—just trying to remember what she had heard the Negroes singing, once on a moonlight night, down in Louisiana. And suddenly, out of these parlor groups a voice was lifted and began to sing, "Weep no more, my lady, Weep no more today" and "Way Down upon the Swanee River, far, far away."

Where did Stephen Foster get his knowledge of the South and the songs of the South? Where Harriet Beecher Stowe got the stories of the South. They came up the river. They came on the tongues of unknown and forgotten journeyers by steam. Foster's father had been in the business of loading flatboats at Pittsburgh for the New Orleans trade and had made a trip down the river twice a year. His brother later had a steamer. Stephen was brought up with the voices of the river in his ears, and his first songs were published from the same town that produced *Uncle Tom's Cabin*—from Cincinnati.

This bright town made one other contribution to the things that people were saying about Dixie. It was the minstrel show. One day a comedian named W. D. Rice was hanging around a stable in Cincinnati and watching the Negroes. Cincinnati was the great gathering place for free Negroes, and there they were rather petted by the inquisitive intelligent Yankee gentry who had made the town their Athens, and encouraged to tell about themselves and display their talents. The Negro was dancing. Rice looked on for a while. And then he went home and practiced that dance. Later he had to put on an act on a stage in Pittsburgh. So he picked up a darky porter named Cuff and took him along to the theater. There he persuaded Cuff to lend him his clothes. Having blacked his own face with cork and put on his head a wig made of blackened moss, Rice went on the stage and danced as he had seen the Negro dancing in the stable at Cincinnati. As he danced he said what he remembered the Negro to have said,

> Old Jim Crow's come to town, as you all must know,
> An' he wheel about, he turn about, he do jus so,
> And every time he wheel about, he jump Jim Crow.

This performance was greeted with tremendous applause, which increased as Rice began to improvise and throw in wisecracks about Pittsburgh—in the midst of which Cuff, getting anxious about his clothes because he had an errand to do for his master, plunged onto the scene and tried to snatch them off Rice. The audience supposed that this, too, was part of the show, and the house rocked while Rice desperately improvised to keep Cuff at bay and the crowd cheering, and poor Cuff, not knowing what it was all about, rushed on, desperate for his pants.

Thus began that great American institution, the minstrel show. In a few years there were a dozen of them going around. The minstrel show was the school of the American theater, the cradle of American song. The first great American actors —Forrest, Booth, Joseph Jefferson—all began as Negro minstrels. Within a few years the most original and skillful of these blackface showmen, E. Byron Christy, had got the rights to introduce to the public an original Ethiopian melody— *Way Down upon the Swanee River*. By this time the thirties had slipped over into the forties, and were gliding along into the fifties. Harriet Beecher Stowe in Cincinnati was still chasing her six children, and listening with tense sympathetic eyes to the tales her free Negro servants told her about their old plantation homes. *Uncle Tom's Cabin* was not yet written, except in the perpetual talk and the lapping of the river.

By this time *The Swanee River* was on everybody's tongue. *Dwight's Journal of Music* for October 2, 1852, reports sourly that this kind of tune is "not musically inspiring. . . . Such a melody breaks out now and then like a morbid irritation on the skin. . . . Pianos and guitars groan with it, night and day; sentimental young ladies sing it; sentimental young gentlemen warble it in midnight serenades; volatile young bucks hum it out stentoriously at all times; all the bands play it; amateur flute players agonize over it at every spare moment; the street organ grinds it out every half hour; the 'sing-stars' carol it on the theatrical boards and at concerts; the chambermaid sweeps and dusts to the measured cadence of *Old Folks at Home*; the butcher boy treats you to a strain or two of it as he hands in the steaks for dinner; the milkman mixes it up strangely with the harsh ding-dong accompaniment of his tireless bell; there is not a 'live darkey,' young or old, but can whistle, sing, dance, and play it, and throw in *Ben Bolt* for good measure."

But visiting European singers and other musicians, of the most impeccable classical training, listened with curiosity to this popular singing, so scorned by the educated American, and the one thing out of that great hurly-burly of a new country that they seemed to remember when they went home was the haunting strains of *Swanee River*. It was not long before all Europe, too, was echoing with it.

The vulgar blackface comedians, whom no educated gentleman in the big cities would stoop to see, but whom all young people stole away to look at, and all below the ranks of gentlemen roared at shamelessly, were no less inexplicably moving to Europeans. The American minstrel shows performed to crowded audiences in London. Thackeray, who by all his habits and prejudices belonged to the class which in America was protesting against the "Ethiopian invasion of our parlors," said of one of these performances: "I heard a humorous balladist not long ago, a humorist with wool on his head and an ultra-Ethiopian complexion, who performed a negro ballad that I confess moistened these spectacles of mine in a most unexpected manner. They have gazed at thousands of tragedy queens dying on the stage and expiring to appropriate blank verse, and I have never wanted to wipe them. They have looked, be it said, at many scores of clergymen without being dimmed, and behold, a vagabond with a corked face and a banjo sings a little song, strikes a wild note, which sets the heart thrilling with happy pity."

So, in one river town, in Cincinnati, was born what, when measured by the number of hearts it has touched all around the globe in its threefold form, in story, theater, and song, is the greatest folk art in the world. Frances P. Gaines, soberly totaling up the sales of *Uncle Tom's Cabin*, estimates that no other story has been read by so many people. As for the plantation shows and the Foster melodies, no one can travel in remote places in the world now without discovering how people of every race, color, and condition love them. I attended a puppet show once in Siam, a clever performance of life-sized puppets which I at first thought must represent early British days in India or Burma, the ladies in Siamese imitations of hooped skirts, the gentlemen in high collars, the blacks whooping and dancing, a white man's mansion in the distance. Then amidst the wild blare of the accompanying Siamese music I began to perceive Southern strains which, though very odd in time and tune, were nevertheless familiar. It was the Siamese idea of an American plantation show, and seated on the ground against a jungle thicket the Siamese were listening with utterly absorbed faces!

I was having lunch once with some American girls at the restaurant in Vipurii in Finland. A note was brought to our table which, when translated, read: "Will the American girls please sing for us the beautiful American folk song, *Swanee River?*" For better or for worse, the black man of the American plantation had become the image of the poor and the lowly of all the world; and his master, the Southern gentleman, and the beautiful Southern young lady, had become the image of all that is gracious and glamorous, beautiful but socially wrong, loved in person but hated in mass, to which the heart and the imagination of the oppressed multitudes are tragically bound while their wills and their minds struggle to be free.

3

And what of Cincinnati, this bright town which holds so unique a place as the creator of the folk art which the multitudes of the modern world have loved best, which has brought more tears to more eyes, and more laughs to more lips, than any other? Probably if we knew as much about the backgrounds of other folk art as about this we should be fortunate.

A generation after its founding Cincinnati was blossoming out as a little Athens. It hummed with printing presses, ran black with ink, reechoed to excited argument. Nor was this Yankee metropolis alone in its cultivation of the higher life. It had a running mate in Pittsburgh up the river, the equally lively town of the Scotch-Irish. Cincinnati exchanged populations with Pittsburgh—going back and forth on the steamers. Apparently people went up to Pittsburgh to sing, and came back to Cincinnati to talk. But in Cincinnati the higher life was not so much interrupted by industry; there was more time to plant gardens; and, besides, it had so many printing presses. So it tended to annex artistic glory that really belonged to Pittsburgh.

Even Charles Dickens admits that the Athens of the wilds was a pretty place. One of his two or three good words for America is for Cincinnati: "Cincinnati is only fifty years old, but it is a beautiful city, I think the prettiest place I have seen here except Boston. It has risen out of the forest like an Arabian Nights city, is well laid out, ornamented in the suburbs with pretty villas, and above all, for this is a very rare feature in America, has smooth turf plots and well kept gardens."

Cincinnati had become the taking-off place for the professional men who civilized the Northwest. And when they had time or money they came back to it gladly. Here were their reserve stores of such culture as had been brought over the mountains. Past its doors went all the world, going or coming, to and from the South. Across the river lay Dixie, and to it as guests came most of cultivated Kentucky and Virginia. When runaway slaves came over the river, the Yankees of responsible professional position would not always hold out a helping hand, but they quietly turned their eyes away while the Quakers did so. When a slaveowner freed his slaves and came, sometimes penniless, across the river, for conscience' sake, how the good Yankees bestirred themselves—to find a house, to help put the children in school, to dig up something, amidst the widespread Yankee enterprise and the shrewdly secreted bits of Yankee capital, which would enable this noble-hearted gentleman to make a suitable living. If they were not successful in this, the Quakers reached out a long, quiet hand from Pennsylvania, and in that hand was opportunity and gold. So there were a good many professional men of Southern origin who made Cincinnati their city.

Education in the Northwest was a booming business. The professional man was flourishing like the cotton and the wheat. But serving the independent and shrewd backwoodsmen required a special attitude. They bought your learning, and your capacity to speak, the way they bought salt and sugar. When a delegation of them came to you and wanted you to write a letter to the paper for them, you seized your pen, and after a preliminary flourish of "Sir:" you wrote not what you thought but what they thought. Any talent you had was at the disposal of everybody. If the boys in Pittsburgh wanted to have a political parade, of course Stephen Foster wrote a song for them. Most cultivated people took pride in this position. It seemed to them the business of those who could speak to talk for those who couldn't, and they developed considerable tact and skill in talking for diverse and often contradictory groups.

The intellectual energy of these people along the Ohio was

amazing. They were met from everywhere. They were going
everywhere. They were starting schools. They were forming
clubs. Every other person seemed to be editing a newspaper.
No time for Eastern formalities. In this world you could tell
a gentleman just by looking at him. And being yourself a
gentleman, you walked up to him, and said, "Pardon me, Sir,
but are you a stranger here. I just came in myself two weeks
ago," and with that the other gentleman took out his creden-
tials, and pretty soon you were saying to your wife, "My
dear, this is Mr. So-and-so, from such a town in Kentucky or
Tennessee. He has very kindly consented to have dinner with
us." The wife was hard put to it, for it was an infallible rule
among Yankee hostesses that linen must at all times be snowy
and beautifully ironed, and there must be that display of fine
china without which a New England woman had sunk low
indeed. This was their way of defying the wilderness. The
first thing Harriet Beecher Stowe did when she had earned a
little money by writing was to spend ten dollars for a tea set.
The hostess was still harder put to it, since she usually had no
one but a free Negro girl in the kitchen, and while she was
running back and forth seeing to her well-set table, she might
miss one or two words of the conversation. Does anyone still
remember the good old Ohio habit of turning around in the
door and saying, "Now don't say a word till I get back!"

Whenever and wherever there was not talk, argument, and
discussion or someone just arrived from somewhere telling a
tremendous story, there was music. Music was not indigenous
among the Yankees. But Pittsburgh was up the river. The
singing, dancing, fiddling Scotch-Irish floated down and inter-
married in Cincinnati, and Cincinnati was a point of dispersion
for the products of their talents. Foster's first songs were com-
posed for a club of young people who met at his house in
Pittsburgh to practice four-part harmonies, and his tunes heard
there seem to have come down the river to Cincinnati on the
next steamboat. Since Cincinnati was trained to speak for
everybody, when the confused voices of the river went

through its channel they came out as everybody's story and everybody's song.

There is just one more feather to put in the cap of this wild half sister of Athens and Florence. Being accustomed to give professional opportunity to intelligent persons from across the river, Cincinnati had acquired as a schoolteacher, a Mrs. Lucy Audubon, wife of a charming but impecunious French painter who went up and down the rivers painting birds. One morning this young woman received on the steamboat from New Orleans a great package which she opened with trembling fingers. There lay the first sixty colored drawings of Audubon's *The Birds of North America!* The birds of Dixie, like the songs of Dixie, sent on their way from Cincinnati, opened to eyes jaded with all other art a new and utterly astonishing world. "Imagine," wrote the well-known French art-critic, Philarète Chasles, when the drawings were later exhibited before enthusiastic crowds in the rooms of the Royal Society of Edinburgh. "Imagine a landscape wholly American, trees, flowers, grass, even the tints of the sky and the waters, quickened with a life that is real, peculiar, trans-Atlantic. On twigs, branches, bits of shore, copied by the brush with the strictest fidelity, sport the feathered races of the New World, in the size of life, each with its particular attitude, its individuality and peculiarities. Their plumages sparkle with nature's own tints; you see them in motion or at rest, in their plays and their combats, in their anger fits and their caresses, singing, running, asleep, just awakened, beating the air, skimming the waves, or rending one another in their battles. It is a real and palpable vision of the New World, with its atmosphere, its imposing vegetation, and its tribes which know not the yoke of man."

4

Withal it was *Uncle Tom's Cabin* that spoke not only to America but to the world in really trumpet tones. The effect of the book was incredible. In Scotland an emancipation fund was raised by penny subscriptions. In Russia and Siam masters moved by the appeal liberated their slaves. Yet Mrs. Stowe never intended to write an abolition document. Her purpose was much more simple—more like Cincinnati. She had moved from Cincinnati to Brunswick, Maine, where her husband was a professor at Bowdoin, and during the winter of 1853, New England was full of excitement over the Fugitive Slave Act. She felt that as a former resident of Cincinnati, she knew all about fugitive slaves, and, like a true high-brow of that city, it was her business to speak for those who could not speak for themselves. Years afterward she wrote to her son, Charles, "I well remember the winter when you were a baby, and I was writing *Uncle Tom's Cabin*. My heart was bursting with anguish excited by the cruelty and injustice our nation was showing to the slave, and praying God to let me do a little, and *raise my cry for them to be heard*." Into her book she poured all that she had seen and known—the sweet plantation life among her friends across the river in Kentucky, the New Orleans life she had heard of from her brother in Louisiana, and from innumerable guests from down the river, the St. Clairs, the Elizas, the George Harrises, whom the citizens of a river town met every day, the stories poured into her ears in her own kitchen by the free black servants, the memory of her Quaker friends and their determined work in helping escaped slaves on their way, which she and her family had honored but in which they had not joined. She was trying to speak for everybody concerned. She was as intent to explain and defend her Southern friends as to blame. Her villain is a Yankee, and the butt of her sharpest satire a Yankee woman. She paints the Southern gentleman, the Southern lady, the Southern plantation home in tenderest colors of remembered friendship. She thought the abolitionists would blame her, and that the Southerners would applaud. "Your book," a friend told her, "will be the great pacificator." She was confounded when a roar of vituperation arose from the South, and the abolitionists—that strange crowd whom she had avoided as queer and unfashionable—took her to their hearts.

Yet, as a matter of fact, the warmest praise of *Uncle Tom* came from the South. It is true that Grayson in Charleston did speak of the "prostituted pen of Mrs. Stowe," that Simms berated her, and that everywhere Southern gentlemen showed how they could speak of a woman whom they had decided not to consider a lady. But the manliest voices were also raised everywhere in her behalf, written into dozens of Southern newspapers, and from Charleston itself there rose one voice, double edged with the Charleston sharpness, double dipped in their own species of literary gall, to say coolly to Mr. Simms and all the other gentlemen that the only trouble with the Yankee woman's book was that she was "far too good to us." This little volume entitled *Uncle Tom at Home: A Review of the Reviewers and Repudiators of Uncle Tom's Cabin,* by F. C. Adams, late of Charleston, South Carolina, is one of the most interesting of the pre-Civil War documents.

"The primrose of a name has done much for the South," says Mr. Adams, "and yet all is not gold that glitters there: the legends of her shaded bowers, noble-hearted planters with human wealth in store, are things that have lived in a name and die in the shadow. . . . The day has passed when men could mount some high-born pinnacle and sound their stentorian voices in behalf of the moral grandeur of an institution when its hideous vices stared them in the face at every turn." To show just what he means by hideous vice, he invites Mr. Simms and the other detractors of the Yankee woman for a ride around Charleston with him, and points out by name and street things which Mrs. Stowe had been too much of a lady to mention. To find Legree, he said, we "didn't have to go into Georgia or Virginia or Tennessee. We found one of the same name close at hand upon James Island, South Carolina, and from there we traced them in a circuit around the judicial circuit of the state. These cases are established beyond mere topics of common conversation."

Why, he asks, when we all know that Mrs. Stowe is not only truthful as far as she goes, but far, far too mild, "has she

called forth these Southern denunciations and epithets . . .
It is because the Yankee woman's little book has disembodied
truths that are sectionally uncomfortable, and no where more
so than in South Carolina."

The critics, as usual, were overwhelmed by the popular
applause, but there was a general impression then, which has
prevailed to this day, that a book so universally loved and
celebrated could not be artistically very good. This impression was intensified when it was turned into a drama, or rather
several different dramas, and began to go the rounds of every
little village and back-alley stage, being performed more times
before more audiences than any other play in English. But
Lowell, the sanest of American critics, reading the book later
in Paris, wrote that he thought the antislavery element had
concealed, at least from Americans, the real greatness of the
book. It was, he said, a story of the order of *Don Quixote*, and
expanded a sectional theme into the cosmopolitanism of genius.

Europe, as usual, rushed to embrace the American popular
art, with George Sand, of all people, at its head. It is amusing to
see George gathering up the good little Yankee woman into
her arms with one hearty literary hug. "Where shall we find
creations more complete?" she asks, "types more vivid, situations more touching, more original than in Uncle Tom's
Cabin—those beautiful relations of the slave with the child of
his master, indicating a state of things unknown among us;
the protest of the master himself against slavery during the
innocent part of his life when his soul belongs to God alone."
She finds St. Clair "fascinating and admirable—this excep-
tional nature, noble, generous, and loving, but too soft and
too nonchalant to be really great." As for Marie St. Clair, she
is a "frightfully truthful portrait. Each of us has seen her and
met her." She finds an exquisite beauty in the scene where
George Harris, "the white slave, embraces for the first time
the shores of a free territory, and presses to his heart wife and
child who are at last *his own*." "The life and death of a little
child and a negro slave—that is the whole book. The child

reading the Bible on the knees of the slave—dying finally in the arms of the slave—all this is so new, so beautiful."

So new, so beautiful—they had said that about Audubon's birds, about Foster's songs, even about the Christy minstrels. So far had we come on our way to a new civilization, a new and better life perhaps for all, that a frontier town receiving and sending on the intellectual and artistic traffic of a still half-savage river could now make London and Paris murmur, "So new! So beautiful!"

14

MEN FROM MISSOURI

AT THE point where the Missouri bursts into the Mississippi, looking like a mammoth mad spring freshet from God knows where, there stood, in pre-Revolutionary times, a cluster of huts to which Indians brought furs to be floated down the river. Marvelous furs they were—deep, rich, and thick, brought over the interior desert from far-off fabulous mountain valleys amidst snow-capped peaks.

By the treaty of Utrecht, in 1763, the western bank of the river came into the possession of the Spaniards. They promptly imposed some formidable stucco architecture on the little fur-trading post, brought in some Spanish priests to take the place of the French fathers, and a Don or two as administrators, and made a Spanish fur-trading city. This was the city of Saint Louis.

But it was lonely for the Spaniards up there on the edge of the great Western vacuum, and not very safe. In front of them were the French, nominally ruled by the British, but hand in glove with the Indians. Behind them was emptiness and the vast unknown. When on the far-off Atlantic coast the Americans began fighting for their freedom from the mother country, all the Mississippi Valley began to seethe and boil.

The Indians were stirring about, for no apparent reason, suspicious, restless. The French were wondering if this was not a good chance to throw off the British yoke and win back the valley for France; and everybody, French, Indians, and British, thought they might as well improve the opportunity to take Saint Louis away from Dons.

So, in 1778 a horde of about 1,500 Indians, led by British officers, attacked Saint Louis from the river. Just at this moment young George Rogers Clark took Kaskaskia for the Americans, and appeared on the east bank of the river, opposite Saint Louis, engaged in recruiting and officering French militia. Seeing this the Indians and British raised the siege and hastily departed. This impressed the Spanish very much. If Americans could keep British off their own frontiers, they might also keep them off the frontiers of Spain. So they generously decided to invite Americans to come across the river, and began with the hero of the backwoodsmen, Daniel Boone.

Boone had been having trouble about his land titles in Kentucky, apparently because of his own failure to register his rights, and with debts there chalked up against him, he was forced again on the trail. There was a good deal of feeling about this along the border, and voices began to run from mouth to mouth till they reached popular writers in the East, telling of Boone's goodness and his wrongs. Thereupon the Spanish offered Boone a grant of approximately 1,000 acres, in what is now Missouri, and land for any friends he might bring across the river. Daniel Boone climbing up over the mountains and looking down into Kentucky had been a symbol of the American people taking possession of the forest. Daniel Boone crossing the river was the symbol of the American people taking possession of the plains.

But though he was becoming a legendary figure in the imagination of the world, dim, prehistoric, wrapped in myth, he was still just a simple man, wise in his own woodcraft, trusted by his own people. The Spanish gave him practically unlimited power over all Americans who came into Missouri.

So he lived, and, in his own fashion, ruled for twenty years, during which so many Americans were granted land by the Spaniards that when the transfer of Louisiana was made in 1804, it was estimated that three-fifths of upper Louisiana was already American.

With the transfer of the territory to the United States Boone again ran into the land speculators. In 1810 his title to the lands granted him by the Spaniards was declared invalid in Washington. But by this time his position, as the symbol of the people, the human form and figure in the vanguard on their onward march upon the wilds, had become invulnerable. A

When Daniel Boone was thus established in his possession of his land by special act. "Your petitioner has spent a long life in exploring the wilds of North America, and has by his own personal exertions, been greatly instrumental in opening the road to civilization in the immense territories now attached to the United States, and in some instances matured into independent states." The Committee of the Senate reported the petition favorably saying: "Daniel Boone, after traversing a length of mountains and uninhabited country discovered, and with a few bold and enterprising fellows, established the first civilized settlement in the present state of Kentucky. . . . Though not officially employed by the United States, he was actually engaged in its behalf. Your petitioner is old, infirm, and though dependent on agriculture, possesses not one acre of that immeasureable territory."

When Daniel Boone was thus established in his possession of about a thousand acres of Missouri, he reserved 181 acres for a farm for himself, and sold the rest. Taking the money he went back to Kentucky and paid every one to whom he owed money. He returned with half a dollar in his pocket but perfectly satisfied. "Now," he said, "when I am gone, no one can say that Boone was not an honest man."

By this time he was an object of great curiosity. But his children and his friends protected him as well as possible in the privacy of his woodland pursuits. He seldom discussed the land titles and speculators which had been his bane. Asked why he had come out to Missouri, he would reply, "Getting too crowded over there. I need elbow room." His stocky form, his ruddy, serene old face, his bright blue eyes, his step light and Indian-like, his soft voice and manner were described again and again, and finally an artist from Boston, Mr. Chester Harding, journeyed out and actually persuaded the old hero to sit for his portrait. The wonder is that a figure which it seems the poets must have invented should actually have lived in the full glare of newspaper publicity, and that, subjected to all this sophisticated scrutiny from artists and littérateurs, he should have seemed to them to be just what the people said he was—in his dignity, his simplicity, and his goodness.

In the year 1845, the state of Kentucky received from the state of Missouri the bones of Daniel Boone, and now he lies honorably entombed in Frankfort.

2

After 1803 Saint Louis, like New Orleans, was an American city. Just before making the Louisiana Purchase Jefferson, with the consent of the Spaniards, had sent two young men named Lewis and Clark from Saint Louis into the interior, to the Pacific Ocean, to inquire into the prospects of the fur trade. Lewis and Clark left Saint Louis a Spanish city; they returned three years later to find it American. But before Lewis could go on to Washington, make his report to President Jefferson, and return as governor of the territory, members of his disbanded troop were being quietly assembled by a Spanish fur trader, Manuel Lisa, to carry on the old trade under the new flag, with more energy and reach than ever.

This Spanish fur trader, whom the United States inherited with the city, was one of our great frontier characters. Character in America knows no race. The peculiar American union of shrewdness, integrity, and apparent simplicity, coming spontaneously to original decisions of momentous racial consequence, courageous beyond belief, yet simple and homely in manner, grows wild on this continent like goldenrod. It is developed by the stringent selection of circumstance from any racial seed.

"When Lewis returns from the Columbia River," says Sydney Greenbie, "Lisa is already so well equipped for an enterprising lunge into the territory that before anyone else has time to realize the import of the relation, he has organized a trading expedition with William Morrison and Pierre Menard, merchants, and corralled John Potts and Peter Wiser out of the disbanded Lewis and Clark troop to go with him. These men, well versed in the lore and skills of the forest, moved far on into what is now Montana, and established a fortified post from which to throw out the usual network of individual trappers and hunters throughout the Crow country. At a distance of 2,000 miles from Saint Louis—a distance Lisa was to cover year after year for nearly two decades, he placated, intimidated, and infuriated the warring tribes by turns. He approached a conclave of 5,000 belligerent Indians with boldness and with skill, traded with them, and passed on against their menacing attempt to bar his advance. He had his men trade in their preserves and bring their pelts to his posts for trade. He discovered the most prolific beaver districts, acquainted himself with innumerable clusters of Indians, mapped streams, by-ways, and trails for his own private purposes, and returned the way he had come, without a serious affray, and with produce rich enough to warrant the support of others in forming the Saint Louis Fur Company during his wintering in Saint Louis in 1818–1819. Despite the ever-increasing risks of the journey, the post at the mouth of the Big Horn River in Montana thereafter became his commuting objective.

"Through channels made safe by his energies, just above the present site of Omaha, Nebraska, Lisa made possible the founding of that city where thousands of immigrants and adventurers were later to flow westward across the lonely prairies into the mountains by the sea. Here in time to come, teams by the hundred, like an endless caravan, were to course past that shelter and pause in the sweltering, treeless dust-bin to give over a day to mending their wheels and harness in perparation for crossing the Great Divide, or to pass a night in drinking, gambling, and carousing.

"Here during the first two decades of the century was Lisa, with only one or two hundred men, looking northward six hundred miles to one fort, and south six hundred miles to another, and counting the distances but as so many stations on a line whose schedule was as punctiliously maintained by mule and on foot as if he had a streamlined zephyr to cover it. A thousand miles or two. It was all one to this Ulysses of our wilds."

Other fur traders were jealous of him, and to them he replied with a touching discourse on success, worthy to stand side by side with some of the exhortations of Benjamin Franklin.

"Cheat the Indians! The respect and friendship they have for me, the security of my possessions in the heart of their country, respond to this charge, and declare with voices louder than the tongues of men that it cannot be true. 'But Manuel gets so much rich fur.' Well, I will explain how I get it. First I put into my operations great activity. I go great distances, while some are considering whether they will start to-day or to-morrow. I impose upon myself great privations; ten months in a year I am buried in the forest, at a vast distance from my own house. I appear as the benefactor not as the pillager of the Indians. I carried them the seed of the large pompion [pumpkin] from which I have seen in their possession the fruit weighing 160 pounds. Also the large bean, the potato, the turnip; and these vegetables now make a comfortable part of their subsistence, and this year I have promised to carry the plough. Besides, my blacksmiths work incessantly for them, charging nothing. I lend them traps, only demanding preference in their trade. My establishments are the refuge of the weak and of the old men no longer able to follow their lodges; and by these means I have acquired the confidence and friendship of these nations, and the consequent choice of their trade."

While Manuel Lisa was organizing the fur trade as a kind of knight-errant, Eastern capital moved in, under the leadership of John Jacob Astor and set up shop in Saint Louis on a grand scale. Astor had a magnificent scheme for tying up the fur trade with the East India and China trade in a vast commercial empire, with a port on the Pacific, at the mouth of the Columbia River, a port on the Atlantic—New York City —and an inland capital at Saint Louis. He intended to connect Saint Louis with the mouth of the Columbia by an overland route, roughly following the trail of Lewis and Clark, and foreshadowing what was later to be the Oregon Trail; and from Astoria, his mart on the Pacific, he expected to send ships westward with furs for China, and eastward with tea for New York, "in a smooth, glittering round." Partly because of the disturbances caused by the War of 1812, this gaudy dream collapsed. But Astor's business organization of the fur trade remained, as the American Fur Company, with principal headquarters at Saint Louis and at Detroit, and a far-flung dominion over the yet unpeopled West.

Thus Saint Louis became the administrative capital of a strange extrapolitical empire, extending two thousand miles into the interior up the Missouri, down the Santa Fe Trail, across the prairies and the buffalo plains, and up and down the mountains; and beyond the utmost limit to which the power of the United States could reach, the fur forts established their wild dominion over hundreds of thousands of square miles of mountain and buffalo range. Parkman, making his way across the plains in the fifties, was relieved to come to the fort of the American Fur Company, at Laramie, Wyoming. "Their officials," he says, "rule with absolute sway. The arm of the United States has little force here, for when we were there, the extreme outposts of her troops were seven hundred miles to the eastward."

3

As the center of the fur trade and administrative capital of the wild West, Saint Louis had a character all its own. Something in it, rough, primitive, smelling of leather and dust, was crossed with influences that seemed "continental" and was brightened with the lavish flinging of gold. E. F. who saw the city of furs in 1838 remarks that there "is an antiquated venerable air about its narrow streets, and the ungainly edifices of one portion of it—the steep-roofed stone cottage of the Frenchman and the tall stuccoed dwelling of the Don." It is full of wild, rough, lounging men. "Most of their days are passed beyond the border of the wild buffalo plains at the base of the Rocky Mountains. Most of them are trappers, hunters, traders to the distant post of Santa Fe, or *engagés* of the American Fur Company."

This new type of Western man was hard to describe; yet everyone felt that he was a new species. One reporter says that he "can scream louder, jump higher, shoot closer, and get more drunk at night and wake more sober in the morning than any other human being this side of the Rocky Mountains." The implication seems to be that, when he got to the Rocky Mountains, he was more so.

One of the men seen about the streets of Saint Louis appears to have been the redoubtable Mike Fink, hero of the Mississippi River, acting as trapper in the company as Ashley's Hundred Men, in 1822. Neihardt sees in him a modern Siegfried or Achilles and the whole story of the fur trade something we should sing as the Greeks sang the fall of Troy or the Germans the Niebelungenlied. Surely, interwoven as it is with the songs of the voyageurs and the wild tom-tom beat of the Indian drums, it is the perfect theme for American opera. In what other land did men singing along the length of a hundred rivers speed such an empire home to civilization?

The first cycle of this epic Neihardt has turned into verse in his story of *The Three Friends*, which is the story of Mike

Fink, and in *The Song of Hugh Glass.* The epic adventures
which he chronicles began with the following advertisement
in the *Missouri Republican* of Saint Louis in 1822.

To Enterprising Young Men

The subscriber wishes to engage one hundred young men to
ascend the Missouri River to its source, there to be employed
for one, two, or three years. For particulars apply to Major
Andrew Henry, near the lead mines, in the County of Washington, who will ascend with and command the party, or of
the subscriber near St. Louis.

WILLIAM H. ASHLEY

When the hundred enterprising young men were assembled, the two parties of Ashley and Henry "contained nearly
all the great names in the history of the West from the time
of Lewis and Clark to the coming of the settlers." "The wanderings of this group during the next ten or fifteen years
cover the entire West. . . . It was the most significant group
of continental explorers ever brought together." Among the
states first explored by them were Wyoming, Idaho, Colorado,
Utah, and Nevada.

Towing their boats and supplies against the muddy current of the Missouri, they started off.

> So, through days of thunder and of sun,
> They pressed to northward. Now the river shrank,
> The grass turned yellow, and the men were lank
> And gnarled with labor. Smooth-lipped lads matured
> 'Twixt moon and moon with all that they endured,
> Their faces leathered by the wind and glare,
> Their eyes grown ageless with the calm, far stare
> Of men who know the prairies or the seas,
> And when they reached the village of the Rees
> One scarce might say, This man is young, this old,
> Except for the beard.

And so the story goes on—the story of rough and simple
men, in a world of dreamlike magnitude and strangeness,

forced to think and act in circumstances which brought out latent powers and latent vice, and gave to their achievements and their failures alike a kind of heroic importance. These folk heroes of all the states of the West are known mostly in oral tradition or in learned histories of the fur trade. Yet one thriving town after another has risen where they pitched their camps, and their names cling to creeks and trails and valleys— though everything else about them is forgotten.

4

The center for outfitting the expeditions of the fur traders was soon moved from Saint Louis up the river to Franklin, and later, as the line of settlements crept up the river, out to Independence, near the present Kansas City. As traders and settlers began to press out into the prairie, Independence and Franklin became outfitting centers for traders going to Santa Fé, emigrant trains setting off for Oregon, and later for gold seekers in California. All these expeditions had mountain men as their guides, and followed the techniques of traveling and camping developed by the fur trade. From Independence, all the great roads to the West were developed, following the paths of the trappers. Southward the trail led down by Santa Fe and across to California, northward to Oregon, branching off to Salt Lake City by the Mormon Trail, and again, when Oregon was reached, branching off to California.

While the center for outfitting the trapping parties was still at Franklin, a lad was growing up there whose slight, coura- geous figure projected against the great scene of the West in times of intense national excitement was to charm the imagina- tion long after the fur trade itself was forgotten. Small, freckled, sandy-haired, Kit Carson rode out of the West into the hearts of the early voyagers to California in prairie wagons. And to this day scarce a hero dashes on to the movie screen in the most hackneyed and commonplace western who does not owe something to him. Though Kit Carson's name, like that of Daniel Boone, was kept going by scribblers back East, like Boone he was subjected to a great deal of sophisticated scrutiny, and stood it just as well. He really was what the taletellers said he was. How wonderful if we could know as much of Achilles or King Arthur!

Kit Carson's folks had come to Missouri as squatters. They were Kentuckians who, like others of the border, had come in the great Scotch-Irish migration to Philadelphia, thence to Virginia, thence westward to Missouri. Kit, an undersized, bandy-legged little towhead, was apprenticed at sixteen to a saddler in Frankfort, Missouri. His principal job was mending saddles for the trappers, or sewing together fur and hide into strange fixin's for the journey westward. As he worked, they told him yarns, of deserts, of Indian forays, but mostly of their favorite town of Taos in New Mexico, where a man could set up in some style with a *señorita* to serve his tamales, and cast something more than an Indian girl's feminine charm upon a bachelor's diggings.

The consequence of this was that, in the fall of 1826, *The Missouri Intelligencer* published the following: "NOTICE: To Whom it May Concern: That Christopher Carson, a boy about sixteen years old, small of his age, but thick set, light hair, ran away from the subscriber living in Franklin, Howard County, Missouri, to whom he was bound to learn the saddler's trade. He is supposed to have made his way to the upper part of the state. All persons are notified not to harbor, support, or subsist said boy under penalty of the law. One cent reward will be given to any person who will bring back said boy."

Thus began the favorite saga of the West, of which other episodes will be found in later chapters.

5

While the fur trade was drawing wild and valiant spirits to Missouri, the Scotch-Irish border had been reaching westward from Kentucky and Virginia. The land along the Mississippi River, and the valleys and banks of streams reaching into the interior, were filling with kindly, simple, hospitable folk for whom the plantation system had made life no longer tenable in the East. Such a family is described by Audubon, in illustration of the regenerative power of the great open spaces.

A family, he says, has been trying to live on the worn-out soil of Virginia consisting of red banks through which the streams have cut, carrying the soil off to their neighbors. Rumors have come to them of new and virgin lands across the Mississippi. So one day they pack and start off. After endless journeying, they come to the Mississippi, cross the river, and squat upon its banks. They plant a garden, and, between nursing the vegetables along, get up some kind of shelter, and acquire the progenitors of future stock. Soon they grow a little surplus, and have some livestock to spare. So they build a raft and send these down to New Orleans, and come home with dollars.

This goes on a while; the planted fields spread farther and farther into the wilderness; the animals reproduce after their kind. The steamboat is now going down the river. So what do we see as progress in Missouri? "And now the vessel approaches their home. See the joyous mothers and daughters as they stand on the bank. A store of vegetables lies around them. A large tub of fresh milk is at their feet, and in their hands are plates filled with rolls of butter. As the steamer stops, three broad hats are waved from the upper decks and soon husband and wife, brothers and sisters, are in each other's arms. The boat carries off the provisions for which value has been left, and, as the captain issues his orders for putting on of steam, the happy family enter their humble dwelling. The husband gives his bag of dollars to his wife, while the brothers present some token of affection to the sisters." So they go on, from comfort to comfort. They marry. A village grows up around them. "The squatters live respected by all who know them, and in due time die regretted."

A much more gaudy description of one of these migrants to Missouri is given by Mark Twain in the first and best chap-

ter of *The Gilded Age*. Squire Hawkins, of Obedstown, East
Tennessee, has decided to seek his fortune in Missouri. The
squire is of good birth, and owns a whole kingdom of Tennessee land which he is holding as a "speculation." Now he
hears from his old crony, Beriah Sellers, that there is a fortune
to be made in Missouri. His wife is skeptical. "I was afraid of
it—was afraid of it! Trying to make our fortune in Virginia,
Beriah Sellers nearly ruined us—and we had to settle in Kentucky and start over again. Trying to make our fortune in
Kentucky, he crippled us again and we had to move here.
Trying to make our fortune here, he brought us clear down to
the ground nearly."

Sure of a mansion in Missouri the family started off. After
about a week of travel they came to "a shabby village which
was caving, house by house, into the hungry Mississippi. The
river astonished the children beyond measure. Its mile breadth
of water seemed an ocean to them, in the shadowy twilight,
and the vague riband of trees on the further shore the verge
of a continent which surely none but they had seen before."

In Missouri, Hawkins bought out a village store for a song,
and with the influx of new settlers slowly prospered a little.
Finally he was even able to build a house full two stories high
and put a lightning rod on it. He fitted out "his house with
'store' furniture from St. Louis, and the fame of its magnificence went abroad in the land. Even the parlor carpet was
from St. Louis—though the other rooms were clothed with
'rag' carpeting of the country. Hawkins put up the first
'paling' fence that had ever adorned the village; and he did
not stop there but whitewashed it. His oilcloth window curtains had noble pictures on them of castles such as had never
been seen anywhere in the world but on window curtains.
Hawkins enjoyed the admiration these prodigies compelled,
but he always smiled to think how poor and cheap they were
compared to what the Hawkins mansion would display in a
future day after the Tennessee land should have borne its
fruit of minted gold. . . . This troubled his wife. It did not

seem wise to her to put one's entire earthly trust in the Tennessee land and never think of doing any work."

As the settlers continued to press up the valley of the Missouri and look out cautiously on the plains, the South made haste to tie Missouri into the Union as a slave state. There were two years of argument in Congress, and back in the country stores of Missouri amidst whistling streams of tobacco juice, before it was finally decided that Missouri should come in freighted forever with slaves. Slaves did not promise to be very profitable in Missouri, and no one there was yet rich enough to embark on the beautiful cycle of buying more and more land to support more and more slaves to till more and more land to support more and more slaves.

But up there the rugged northern coasts of Massachusetts, midst the spitting clams of Old Orchard Beach and Kennebec shore and Penobscot Bay, the string of neat little towns growing comfortable on trade with China and the East, began to clamor that there were enough of them to make a state by themselves. What was the use of hurrying these collections of Western shanties into the Union, when here were real towns, ready-made, snug, complete, with churches and common schools and a means of livelihood lapping at their front doors? What was the Mississippi anyway? Did it think it was the Atlantic Ocean? So finally in 1820 it was settled that Maine and Missouri should come in as a pair, free and slave all ready to cancel each other to zero in Congress. And it was further decreed that the old Mason and Dixon line between the free states and the slave which had run from Pennsylvania along the Ohio River to the Mississippi should continue indefinitely into space at the latitude of 36° 30'. As the debate continued month after month, the last of the great Virginian liberals at Monticello started up out of the peace of old age. It was, said Jefferson, like the "clanging of a fire bell in the night." And what that bell said he knew. It was clanging the knell of the Union. Had not the great slaveowner himself said of the institution from which, like other tragic heroes of Virginia, he could not free himself, "I tremble when I remember that God is just"?

6

Out there on the Missouri frontier the man from Missouri, original of all Western heroes, was in a state of transition from being a Kentuckian whose grandfather came from Virginia.

A certain careless, easy bearing, a devil-may-care *sang-froid*, was already credited to the Virginian border by Cooper. It had been developed by the Kentuckians as a kind of hall-mark, making them recognizable on the river as they came swinging down, marking them in the streets of New Orleans as, not unamiably, they quietly shouldered all other people out of their way. Lincoln's first remark to Emerson, when Sumner took the sage of Concord in to see the great ex-Kentuckian in the White House was "Oh, Mr. Emerson, I once heard you say in a lecture that a Kentuckian seems to say by his air and manners, 'Here I am. If you don't like me, the worse for you.' "

This devil-may-care attitude had, among the ruder spirits on the edge of the plains, its less lovely side. "Indifference to appearance is there a matter of pride," said Anthony Trollope. "A foul shirt is a flag of triumph. A craving for soap and water is as the wail of the weak and the confession of cowardice. . . . No men love money with more eager love than these western men, but they bear the loss of it as an Indian bears his torture at the stake. They are energetic in trade, speculating deeply wherever speculation is possible; but nevertheless they are slow in motion, loving to loaf about. They are slow in speech, preferring to sit in silence, with the tobacco between their teeth. They drink, but are seldom drunk to the eye; they begin it early in the morning and take it in a solemn, sullen, ugly manner, swallowing their spirits and saying nothing as they swallow it. . . . I cannot part with the West [meaning Missouri] without saying in its favor that there is a certain manliness about its men which gives them a dignity of their own. . . . Whatever turns up, the man is still there—still unsophisticated and still unbroken. It has seemed to me that no race of men requires less outward assistance than these pioneers of civilization. They rarely amuse themselves. Food, newspapers, and brandy smashes suffice for life; and while these last, whatever may occur, the man is still there, in his manhood."

If there was in the prairie life, the life of adventure beyond in the uncharted wilds, something which began to invest the rude backwoodsman from across the river with easy, epic dignity, something of that same dignity belonged to the amiable Frenchmen of the villages. The perfect pattern of the man of the West, is given by Parkman in his *Oregon Trail*, and here the hero is a Frenchman.

Henry, he says, was a hunter, born in a French village near Saint Louis, "six feet high, powerfully and gracefully moulded." "The prairies had been his school. He could neither read nor write, but he had a natural refinement and delicacy of mind, such as is very rarely found even in women. His manly face was a perfect mirror of uprightness, simplicity, and kindness of heart. He moreover had a keen perception of character and a tact that would preserve him from flagrant error in any society. Henry had not the restless energy of the Anglo-American. He was content to take things as he found them, and his chief fault rose from an excess of easy generosity impelling him to give away too profusely ever to thrive in the world. Yet it was commonly remarked of him that whatever he might choose to do with what belonged to himself, the property of others was safe in his hands. His bravery was as much celebrated in the mountains as his skill in hunting; but it is characteristic of him that in a country where the rifle is the chief arbiter between man and man, Henry was very seldom involved in quarrels. Once or twice, indeed, his good nature had been mistaken and presumed upon, but the consequences of the error were so formidable that no one was ever known to repeat them. No better evidence of his intrepidity of temper could be asked than the common report that he had killed more than thirty grizzly bears. He was a proof of what unaided nature can do. I have never, in the city or the wilderness, met a better man than my noble and true-hearted friend, Henry Chatillon."

7

To the French-Spanish-Scotch-Irish-Kentucky backwoods mixture of Saint Louis were added the great German migrations. Of these Carl Schurz, one of the great citizens we received from Germany, says in his *Memoirs:* "Two different periods of political upheaval in Germany, that of 1830 and the years following, and that of 1848, had served to drive out of the old Fatherland hosts of men of ability and character, and of both of those immigrations the German element in St. Louis and its neighborhood had its full share."

Of these Germans, said Schurz, "some settled in Illinois opposite St. Louis to raise their corn and wine. Those who, though university men, devoted themselves to agriculture, were called by the Germans, half sportively, half respectfully, the 'Latin farmers.' One of them, Gustav Körner, who practiced law in Belleville, rose to eminence as a judge, as a lieutenant-governor of Illinois, and as a minister of the United States to Spain. Another, Friedrich Münch, the finest type of Latin farmer, lived to a venerable old age in Gasconade County, Missouri, and remained active almost to the day of his death as a writer for newspapers and periodicals under the name of 'Far West.' These men regarded St. Louis as their metropolis and in a large sense belonged to the Germandom of that city."

What Saint Louis looked like after the Germans moved in is told by Edward Dicey, a British Civil War correspondent. "Certainly there is a foreign look about St. Louis. . . . The shops thrown open to the air, the people sitting about the door steps beneath the shade, and the closed lattice shutters are signs of the South. But more than this the actual proportion of foreigners is very large. In the names of the suburbs, such as the Carondelet, there are traces of French settlers; but the German migration has swallowed up every other. In the streets one hears more German spoken than English. . . . Bock bier, lager bier, and Mai wein are advertized for sale at every turning. Americans drink freely, and Germans drink copiously, and when the joint thirstiness of Americans and Germans is developed by the Southern sun it is astonishing the quantity of liquor that can be consumed. . . . German habits, too, have been imported into the city. Even in the lower American theatres the audiences smoke and drink beer handed to them by German waitresses. There are public 'lust gartens' about the town, with German bands."

8

This coming world of the Far West was fittingly represented in the Senate, through all its period of most lusty growth, by the "fantastic" senator, who ranked fourth in power after the great triumvirate, Clay, Webster, and Calhoun, representing the middle border, the North, and the South. Senator Thomas Hart Benton was a true product of the Scotch-Irish border. His father had come to Tennessee with Robertson. He himself, as a fiery young frontier lawyer, in Nashville, in 1813, had put a pistol ball through the shoulder of Andrew Jackson, because Jackson had sworn to horsewhip Benton on sight. But years later he not only became the leader of the Jacksonian Democrats in Congress but carried on a long, stiff-necked, pertinacious fight to expunge Clay's resolution of censure against Jackson from the journals of the Senate.

In him all the native tendencies of the Scotch Irishman were enlarged and intensified to idiosyncrasy by the vast stage of the frontier and the freedom it gave a man of will to do just as he pleased in season and out. He was pigheaded, conceited, combative—and so long winded that the minute he rose to speak, the Senate galleries emptied as if by magic. But he was unflinchingly high principled. His public and personal

life were alike without spot or stain. As Theodore Roosevelt
said, if he was intellectually far inferior to Daniel Webster,
morally he was far superior. And "fantastic" as he seemed to
Harriet Martineau, absurd and pompous to many, his old-
fashioned Scotch-Irish "presence"—the erect bearing, the
elaborate speech, the feeling for the social occasion and its
demands—covered both sense and genuine dignity. Strangers
were greatly impressed by his hospitable, dignified, disciplined
home life, with Mrs. Benton sewing by the hearth, and the
rosy-cheeked, bright-eyed young daughter Jessie, doing the
honors under father's exacting eye. This home in St. Louis he
made the political capital of the West. There he would sit all
day, in the long gallery of the parlor floor looking out on the
inner courtyard "shaded by fine large acacias with their clusters of vanilla scented blooms. Here with his settee, table,
coffee, and fruit, he would hold a morning levee attended by
politicians, prominent St. Louis citizens, army officers, and
old family friends. In the evening others would call."

That expansive imagination of the Scotch-Irish border
which Mark Twain has satirized in *The Gilded Age* was in
Benton a genuine epic sense of the beauty and coming power
of the West. And in his own way he was a great showman—
how great a one will appear later in the chapter on California
in the part he played in painting the large landscape of the
Pacific Coast on the American imagination, making his son-
in-law Frémont and his scout Kit Carson into great American
heroes of the West, and finally "selling" the idea that the railroad was destined to carry on the great work of Columbus
and, blazing across plain and mountain, would forever unite
Europe to the fabled East. In the square in Saint Louis his
statue now stands with his hand pointing west, and under it
his own great words: "There lies *The East*."

15

WHEN IT'S SPRINGTIME
IN THE ROCKIES

WHEN it was springtime in the Rockies, in those early
days before the Civil War, it meant that the winter's
trapping was done, and the long mule train was starting down for civilization. Two thousand miles lay between
them and Saint Louis. It was spring when they started; autumn
when they came in. To a young Frenchman named Charles
Larpenteur, loitering around the narrow streets of the old fur
town one day early in the nineteenth century, they seemed
poetic as a caravan from the desert. He was not a Mississippi
Valley Frenchman, but a moderately polished specimen from
the old country whose parents had come to America to settle
and had bought a small farm near Baltimore. He had been
coming across the continent, making excursions up into the
prairie region, when the wild vision from the Rockies burst
upon his sight. "It is impossible to describe my feelings at the
sight of all that beaver—all those mountain men unloading
their mules, in their strange mountain costume—most of their
garments of buckskin and buffalo hide, but all so well greased
and worn that it took close observation to tell what they were
made of. To see the mules rolling and dusting was most interesting and shocking at the same time; most of them having

carried their burdens of two hundred pounds weight about 2000 miles, return with scarcely any skin on their backs; they are peeled from withers to tail, raw underneath from use of the surcingle, and many are also lame."

That sight determined him. He would go back to the Rockies with the mountain men. But when he applied for a job with a fur establishment, hardened officials cocked their eyes at this mild little youth from France and the Eastern cities. That he was a Frenchman was in his favor. The industry favored the French. That he had some education was not to be disdained. They always needed clerks. But he would take hardening. Probably he would give out. So one after another turned him down. But he was determined. "I will go as common hand," he said. So finally he won. And so, he says, "I said good-bye to civilization for forty years."

Far out there in the mountains, beyond the utmost frontiers of civilization, life was organized for white men along mountain trails and rivers, and in forts or posts—usually at the junction of rivers or trails. The post was a wilderness town, a place for trading with the Indians, organized for defense in a world otherwise without law, and to provide white men with whatever they might need in almost yearlong sojourn in the wilds. During the period between the Louisiana Purchase and the Civil War several states were thus possessed, ruled, crossed with trails, and exclusively inhabited by white men, with no white women, most of them with more or less permanent Indian mates and half-breed families. Some of them were educated men, maintaining at least at the posts some of the observances of gentlemen and keeping books and other cultural resources for the long periods when winter immured them in their fastnesses. Parkman speaks of a fur trader's house, agreeably furnished, where he was amazed to see a pistol lying above a copy of Milton's poems! One traveler reports a long talk with a cultivated gentleman—a man of pure Indian blood, a graduate of Dartmouth, who discoursed on poetry and history and philosophy and proved how much better the wilderness life was than anything in civilization! There were not many such men, most of the trapper heroes being comparatively illiterate. But there were enough to bring into American thought and tradition an interesting vision of life, and to enrich our record with some beautiful descriptions of that grandiose, untouched world of the Rocky Mountains.

There is, for example, Mackenzie's description of southern Idaho, as reported by Ross in *Fur-traders of the Far West*. "Woods and valleys, rock and plains, rivers and ravines alternately met us; but altogether it is a delightful country. There animals of every class rove about undisturbed. Wherever there was a little plain, the red deer were seen grazing in herds about the rivers, and where there was a sapling the industrious and ingenious beaver was at work. Otters sported in the eddies; the wolf and the fox were seen sauntering in quest of prey; on the spreading branches of stunted pines sat the raccoon secure. The badger sat quietly looking from his mound; and in the numberless ravines, among bushes laden with fruit, the black brown and grizzly bear was seen. The mountain sheep and goat as white as snow, browsed on the rocks and ridges, and the bighorn species ran among the lofty cliffs."

To facilitate the assault upon this furry world, a unique and one of the most picturesque of the early institutions of the mountain country was organized—the rendezvous. "In what is now Wyoming," says Sydney Greenbie, "upon the wide expanse of flat land where the sun rises late over the shrill peaks of the Wind River range and sets early under the Wasatch range, looking down upon Salt Lake City; here upon Wind River north of the range or Green River south of the range, the great tryst of the trappers took place, year after year, with Pierre's Hole neath the Grand Teton on the edge of Idaho or Cache Valley just above the great Salt Lake, as other gathering places when agreed upon. . . . Sixteen times in sixteen years they gathered in rendezvous, two hundred white men and a thousand Indians and their families, so ordered by the business man, General William H. Ashley, who saw that the centuries old effort to bring the Indians and the trappers on the plains to converge upon a fort for trading would not work beyond the mountains. And so in 1824 he arranged with his trappers to meet the next year in Green River Valley, and thence in succeeding years Ogden Valley, Cache Valley, Pope Agio River, Wind River, Powder River, or Pierre's Hole. Twenty miles from Henry's Fork on the Snake River, one hundred to two hundred men would gather from all the nooks and crannies of the mountains, plains, and rivers, upon a pre-arranged appointment or after word of mouth had been passed hither and yon from man to man.

"Families for winter months spread in their smoky wigwams begin to talk of packing—packing their skins, their arrows, their garments and their tepees, to move on to the rendezvous. Trappers for months singly or in groups, had set their steel jaws near beaver dams, now pack their pelts and move inward. Day by day the movement toward the distant centre grows, like tiny drops of water from the frozen fastnesses. Drop by drop, man by man, tribe by tribe, reaching for the rendezvous. . . . From the Eastern side of the continent pack trains are pressing to be first across the prairie, fresh with the world's goods—coffee, textiles, hardware, gewgaws, pressing to outstrip their rivals in this furious scramble for furs.

"Like those flowers that blossom for a day upon the desert, so the valleys beneath the Wind River mountains burst into human bloom for five days of rendezvous. Black and troubled seem the lower ranges of hills beside the glittering immensity of the snow-mounds above them. Wild and whirling was the stage on which, circle within circle, the towering tepees of the Indians, floating each its flag, stood within the greater circling of the restless horses and the still more restive natives. Stamping, roaring, running wild, amidst the smoke of camp-fires and the flaming head dress of the feathered chiefs, horses and prideful riders . . . eddies within pools of eddies of men, bargaining, quarreling, drinking, stealing, fighting, swearing, loving, watching, begging, listening, cheating, lying, buying. . . . Five days. The Redmen appear in new blankets, new calicoes, new worsteds, with new guns and new kettles, to remain sheltered within the mountain ranges on the one hand, and on the other hand, pack trains and caravans are moving eastward to the sea, laden with costly furs to be worn by delicate ladies or gentlemen who never made obeisance to the gods upon the ranges. The rendezvous is over once again."

2

The permanent business of the fur trade was, however, administered from the fur posts, or "forts." There were innumerable lesser posts of this sort, here and there along the principal trails, at the confluence of rivers, like wild little villages. In the more important centers there might be several posts or forts near enough for visiting back and forth between the principals and for that mixture of business, warfare, and personal chivalry which made the romance of the fur trade. The most important posts became the first centers for settlement and political administration in the West, and were highly picturesque institutions, with more drama and excitement within their log, stone, or adobe walls than fell even to a medieval castle. These really important posts were four—Bent's Fort on the Arkansas River, which was a center for replenishing the Santa Fe traders, and for furnishing and provisioning soldiers in the Mexican War; Fort Laramie, in Wyoming, on the Oregon Trail, visited by Parkman; Pierre's Fort, in South Dakota, now Pierre, the capital of South Dakota; and, greatest and most dramatic of all, Fort Union on the Yellowstone.

At Bent's Fort Susan Magoffin stopped on her way to Santa Fe, and noted its furnishings with a woman's eye. She said that it looked like an ancient castle, made of burnt brick, very thick, in a generally Mexican style of architecture. "Inside is a large space, some ninety or a hundred feet square. All around this and next to the wall, are rooms, some twenty-five in number. They have dirt floors which are sprinkled with water several times a day to prevent dust. Standing in the center of them is a large wooden post as prop to the ceiling, which is made of logs. Some of these rooms are occupied by boarders as bedchambers. One is a dining room, another a kitchen, a little store, a blacksmith's shop, a barber's ditto, an icehouse which receives perhaps more customers than any other.

"On the south side is an enclosure for stock in dangerous times and often at night. On one side of the top walls are rooms built in the same manner as below. They have a well inside, and fine water it is, especially with ice. At present there are quite a number of boarders. The traders and soldiers, chiefly, with a number of loafers come from the states, come out because they can't live at home. One large room serves as a parlor. There are no sofas, but there are cushions next to the wall on two sides. In the middle is a table with a bucket of water on it."

Fort Laramie, built at the confluence of the Laramie River and the Platte, became a famous center on the Oregon Trail. There was always a stop of some time there, while wagons were mended, cargoes readjusted, and the travelers to Oregon got a rest and put their costumes and belongings in order.

Pierre's Fort in South Dakota was in the heart of the Sioux country and controlled trade and other relations with the Indians of that powerful tribe.

Fort Union, the largest fort of the American Fur Company, was situated at the point where the Yellowstone River joined the Missouri River, just over the border of Montana in what is now North Dakota.

From these forts as centers the trappers pursued the beaver up the three great water systems of the Missouri, the Colorado, and the Columbia rivers, and in the south along the Arkansas and the Rio Grande. "To the individual trapper the innumerable ramifications of these streams were a familiar field of labor," says Chittenden. "It was his duty to seek them out and explore them for beaver. In carrying out this duty during two score years it may be doubted whether there was a rivulet in all the mountains capable of sustaining a beaver family that he did not visit. He was acquainted with all the sources of the trans-Mississippi region, and many a stream which is unknown and unvisited to-day."

3

Of the life of the fur trade, the young Frenchman, Charles Larpenteur, kept a record during forty years. To get safely through an English sentence remained always a problem to him. He was overwhelmed with what he saw, always beating around for a word, getting lost in English verbiage. But he was a natural-born writer. In every event he saw the story; in every person, the character. Always, everywhere, he was endlessly amused; and patiently he recorded it somehow in his crabbed writing. He knew it was a wonderful story. By the light of a guttering candle in the fur forts under the white peaks of the mountains, he was keeping it for posterity, cheering himself with the idea of getting back to the cities and making men's eyes pop with his yarns. "The idea of relating to my Baltimore friends my mountain stories would make me feel, as the Indians say, 'Big Man Me.'"

The manuscript of this record is in the possession of the Minnesota Historical Society, donated to the society by his nephew. Elliott Coues wrote it into grammatical and flowing English and published it as an historical document and it is available here and there in libraries for the specialist. But it is not where it ought to be, side by side on common library shelves, with Dana's *Two Years before the Mast*. For it is the natural twin of that book—the story of the housekeeping of the mountains, as that is the story of the housekeeping of the sea, the simple day-by-day narrative of men who are making themselves comfortable in the wilds, settling every question, in a world without law or established ethics, according to their own notions of sense and justice, establishing the basic pattern of Western character, making it possible in a thousand ways for real homes to set up housekeeping after them. Like Dana's book, it deals largely with food, or with the occasional excitement of getting all one's wardrobe in prime condition. Not so finished as Dana's story, it is in many ways fresher, for there is no precedent in literature for Larpenteur's records and, despite the innumerable narratives of the fur trade, there is a kind of detail which only he thought to put on paper.

Up the Missouri goes the caravan of fur traders with the young Frenchman, starting in the spring, expecting to arrive in the Yellowstone district by fall, and to dig themselves in before the snow buries them. They crawl along, crawl along, crawl along, through minutes, hours, days, mile after mile, 2,000 miles of prairie and summer. A rabid wolf gets among their cattle and bites several and attacks some of the men. Larpenteur's pal, so bitten, runs naked into the wild and cannot be found. When they reach the mountains, the cows get sore feet, and they have to stop and make them shoes of green buffalo hide. They see the mountains rise silvery blue on the horizon. Then, he says, he has to laugh to hear the men all up and down *chattering to the mules,* telling the poor beasts that they are nearly there, hurry along, home and a long rest for the winter, food, no more traveling, no more straining and itching under the burden, travel along, little mules. They reach the site of their winter quarters two and a half miles from Fort Union, the Fort of the American Fur Company, and make their cabins, hurrying to get through before snow. Larpenteur is assigned a broken-down horse and a wagon, and serves as carter. "Here I am," he writes, apparently delighted as usual, "a regular carter of Fort William, in cowskin pants, cowskin coat, buckskin shirt, wolfskin cap, red flannel undershirt, and blue shirt over that, stepping along behind my old horse and cart."

They finish on November 15, and celebrate getting into winter quarters with a feast. The feast consisted of "half a pint of flour to each man, one cup of coffee, one of sugar, and one of molasses to four men. Out of this a becoming feast was made consisting of thick pancakes, the batter containing no other ingredients than pure Missouri water greased with buffalo tallow, but as I had had nothing of the kind for upward of six months I thought I had never tasted anything so good in my life."

For the most part it is a busy, orderly and strictly sober life. When they trade with the Indians, the liquor stores are opened and everybody gets drunk in one glorious, interracial ·spree. But mostly liquor is carefully guarded and limited. There are strict federal laws against selling any liquor to the Indians and every boat is carefully searched as it comes up the river. But their fort got enough through for their own purposes and as for their friends of Fort Union across the way, they have their own still. But just as Dana had reported that a seaman would leave rum any day for hot chocolate, so the trapper would desert a keg of whisky for one pancake. Pancake parties are their dissipation, the perpetual temptation which he who wants to draw any money against the company for his year's wage must strictly avoid, for coffee costs one dollar a pint, sugar one dollar a pound, flour twenty-five cents a pound. It doesn't take many pancakes in a long winter to use up the $250 or $300 cash accruing for wages. Alas, says Larpenteur "many of my poor comrades are in debt."

4

After serving a while at Fort William, Larpenteur prepares to go down with the next caravan and head back to Baltimore. But he receives a very tempting offer to come over to Fort Union as a clerk, on $500 a year salary, which is quite princely in the fur country. And now he is established as a responsible person in one of the great forts. It sounds like nothing so much as a modern college dormitory (though of course Larpenteur does not say this!), Larpenteur as clerk being in a position similar to that of a young instructor on the faculty. The head of the fort, Mr. McKenzie, is a Scotchman whom Larpenteur admires and respects. One of the personages there is an English nobleman, a friend of McKenzie's who is in temporary trouble at home and is rusticating here under the name of Hamilton till it is convenient to return. This individual became a tradition in the Rockies; there were as many stories about his wardrobe, his baths, his perfumes, as about Mike Fink's red hair. From other sources one hears that he actually took a bath and put on a clean shirt every day, that the extent to which he was barbered and shaved was a crime, that he used *perfume*, that he had colored silk handkerchiefs of the finest quality, that when an Indian approached him he shivered and said, "Beasts!" He was "oiled, scented, polished in the highest degree." But Larpenteur, usually so voluble, is kept by his gentlemanly scruples from mentioning this. Perhaps the Englishman's baths seem nothing remarkable. He merely remarks that Hamilton had lived too high abroad and so had brought some gout with him to the Rockies, and that he was "either very pleasant or very crabbed" depending on the state of the gout, but mostly very crabbed. "So he was not liked, though much respected. I must say that I got along with him very well."

As a clerk in Fort Union, he learns that he sits at Mr. McKenzie's table along with the Englishman and must always put on a coat for dinner. This embarrasses him, for, coming as a regular hand from Fort William, he has no coat. However, he is soon outfitted and appears in style, for the fort, among other things, seems to have a haberdashery department.

The college dormitory character of the life now appears in the rules by which every least detail of their life is regulated, and an almost daily crisis for which there is no precedent is settled by something between official fiat and common agreement. As in a college the rules represent laws which the company would have to make and which in any case they would enforce, but so far as possible through discussion and consultation, and sometimes through votes and signatures to petitions and documents they give the illusion that the men are making them themselves. There is always a machinery of law modified by curious and unexpected last-minute decisions, apparently in response to common opinion. But Larpenteur makes no such generalizations. He just reports.

A quaint example of justice in the fort was the case of the Dutchman and the Mexican. A hardened Mexican hand prevailed on a green Dutchman to steal one of the best horses and run off. Faced with pursuit and summary justice the Dutchman lost his nerve and came back and surrendered. Finally the Mexican surrendered too, and both horses came home. But there was a trial of the culprits. They were condemned, and sentenced to thirty-nine lashes each. But when the Dutchman was stripped to the waist, there was his skin, so tender and soft and white. When the executioner laid on the lash, the blood spurted with the first blows. Skin like that, soft tender baby skin, couldn't be hit thirty-nine times! So it was decreed that half as many lashes would do. But when the Mexican was stripped, ah there was a tough brown hide, really worthy of a lash. Everyone saw thirty-nine stripes laid on to it with great satisfaction, and says Larpenteur, the Mexican hardly minded it!

5

The most significant formulation of opinion concerned the question when it was and when it was not legitimate to shoot to kill. In a world where the fort was the only law and the only justice, death was a penalty that had to be kept in reserve. But in view of the general killer tradition of the West, of the quick and ready shooting in the cheap Western romances, of the genuine recklessness with the rifle in many places later, it is very interesting to see how this terrible power of death was handled in the forts. If what Larpenteur reports of Fort Union is typical, it must have been of the greatest value in formulating standards in that wild land.

There was, for example, a Deschamps family there, a half-breed family of free trappers who had a hate for another half-breed family whose patriarch was one Jack Rem. The sympathies of the fort were all with Jack Rem. One night, having obtained some liquor, the half-breeds got into a row, in which the elder Deschamps was killed, apparently by one of the Rems. The storekeeper, not finding Mr. McKenzie, asked Hamilton, the scented Englishman, what to do. "Give them some whisky," said Hamilton, "and put some laudanum in it." The storekeeper did so. "They soon all fell down," says Larpenteur. "On my arrival I saw this amiable family scattered all along the river bank, still fast asleep." The storekeeper was distraught. He thought he had killed them all, and what should he do? "Whereupon," says Larpenteur, "I had to laugh."

But the Deschamps family continued to make trouble, ten of them egged on by the old mother who seems to have been a regular Ma Barker. As free trappers, not under the jurisdiction of the fort but camping there under its general protection, they seem to have had some weapons, but the white men in the fort were unarmed, firearms being kept strictly locked up and distributed only for specified use in an emergency. The disturbances of the Deschamps went along from day to day, Larpenteur cheerfully reporting each incident without comment until one night, about midnight, Mother Deschamps said to her children, "Now, my sons, you are men. You will avenge your father." "This struck them favorably," say Larpenteur, "and being in liquor they immediately killed old Jack Rem, swore that they would also kill all other half-breeds whom they considered his friends, and even threatened the whites in the fort."

Thereupon all the white men went to Mr. McKenzie and demanded weapons. They told him that they had had enough of the Deschamps, and they intended to clean them out now, every one. Mr. McKenzie said he thought they were right. It seemed to be forced on them, and the sooner they made a clean sweep the better. So he distributed weapons and ammunition and said "Go to it."

The white men proceeded slowly, with system. First they

removed all the horses from the Deschamps neighborhood, and then they called on them to send out their women. For a while the Deschamps refused, clinging to the women as a protection, but when after a reasonable time, they saw that the white men intended to shoot anyway, the women were allowed to come out and were removed to safety. Then the best horsemen on the best horses were stationed outside the fort, in order, if they tried to escape, "to run them down like buffaloes." The white men said, "You may defend yourselves, but we don't intend to quit now so long as there is one of you alive." And then, when the Deschamps would not come out to fight, they set fire to their part of the fort and forced them out and killed them every one. All except the last, a young boy. They let him live. But he died of burns and wounds the next day. "After which," says Larpenteur, "we had peace."

Another case of gunplay began as high comedy but ended very near tragedy. Since the fort served as a hotel for anyone who might be abroad in the mountains, a free trapper named Augustin Bourbonnais arrived to spend the winter at Fort Union. He had a pack of beaver, "worth something like $500 which made him feel rich and quite able to pass a pleasant winter. Bourbonnais was only about twenty years of age, a very handsome fellow, and one thing in his favor was his long yellow hair, so much admired by the female sex in this country. This they call *pah-ha-zee-zee*, and one who is so adorned is sure to please them. A few days before his arrival, Mr. McKenzie, who was nearly fifty years old, and perhaps thought it was too cold to sleep alone, had taken to himself a pretty young bedfellow. Mr. Bourbonnais had not been long in the fort before he went shopping, and very soon he was seen strolling about the fort in a fine suit of clothes, as large as life, with his long *pah-ha-zee-zee* hanging down over his shoulders. If he had looked well in buckskins, he certainly looked charming then.

"It happened one evening that Mr. Bourbonnais encouraged by favorable returns of affection went so far as to enter the apartments reserved for Mr. McKenzie. The latter hearing some noises which he ought not to have heard, rushed in upon the lovers and made such a display of his sprig of a shillelah that Mr. Bourbonnais incontinently found his way not only out of the house but out of the fort, with Mr. McKenzie after him. It was amusing to see the genteel Mr. Bourbonnais in his fine suit of broadcloth with the tail of his surtout stretched horizontally to its full extent. But unfortunately for the poor fellow, he would not let the affair end that way, but swore vengeance on Mr. McKenzie. Of course, having been driven out of the fort with a club, he did not think it proper or consistent with his dignity to enter again. So he took board and lodging in an Indian tent, many of which were pitched near the fort, and all his effects were delivered to him. Then it was reported that Mr. McKenzie would be killed, for 'kill him I must,' said Bourbonnais. Next day he was dressed in buckskin, marching up and down calling on Mr. McKenzie to come out."

Mr. McKenzie thought this would wear off, and submitted to staying safe indoors for a day or two. But Mr. Bourbonnais continued his patrol. The thing was becoming absurd. "Mr. McKenzie called a council of his clerks and asked what they were going to do to raise this siege. All agreed that Bourbonnais' life would have to be taken if he did not desist." But they did not feel comfortable about this idea, Mr. McKenzie least of all, and they went so far as to draw up a document stating the reasons for the death, if there should be death, and passing it around for all who wished to sign. Their main object, they said, was not to kill but to scare him away.

Next morning one of Mr. McKenzie's friends was sent out to communicate these resolutions to Bourbonnais and to advise him to leave. But this did no good.

Now the question of procedure arose. None of them would dignify the performance by taking this yellow-haired charmer on in a fair fight. Finally they called Jim Brazo, a mulatto, and asked him if he had the nerve to kill Bourbonnais if he were asked to do so. He said he had. So he was given a rifle and told to get rid of Bourbonnais for them, and he might shoot if necessary.

One morning Brazo came to Larpenteur and said, "I have shot Bourbonnais."

Mr. McKenzie dispatched three or four men with a bookkeeper who had some knowledge of surgery, to see if the man were dead or only wounded, and if he were wounded to bring him in. It seemed he was only wounded. So he was brought into the fort and carefully nursed there till spring, when he departed not very well yet and apparently thoroughly reduced in spirit. Larpenteur even seems to feel some slight compuctions. The man did not look very well when he left. He wondered if he survived.

After forty years in the Indian country, Larpenteur, like all the better type of traders, was very anxious that, in the states fast filling up with white men, the Indians should be handled properly. So he devoted a good deal of anxious thought in his old age to working out plans and advice for prospective Indian agents and left them as his legacy to his adopted country. He advises the appointment of carefully selected Indian governors. "This governor should be provided with all kinds of agricultural implements to be distributed to the Indians. He should furnish them with timber to build and allow each a certain sum in payment for every panel of fence any Indian might put up, besides furnishing him with material to make it, and so much an acre for breaking his land, let it be with plow or hoe. All fences should be horse high, bull strong, and hog tight. Hogs, cattle, and chickens should be distributed, and there should be an agricultural fair annually as in the States. Every three months inspect the Indian houses and give premiums to the first, second, and third best housekeeper. Hold monthly meetings with the chiefs and leading men and as many others as the house can hold."

6

Intermediaries, thus, between the Indians and the white men, between the wilderness and the oncoming settlements, the fur traders lived and labored, tracing for men to come the ways through the mountains, finding out and naming the valleys where someday there would be homes and farms, rearing their rude forts which someday would grow into cities. But only the map in the school geography keeps the memory of them. Who was Pierre, for whom Pierre's Fort was named? Does anyone now know? Yet the name of Pierre Chocteau, the Frenchman, lingers on as the name of the capital city of South Dakota. Who was Laramie?

> From Mississippi to the western Sea,
> From Britain's country to the Rio Grande,
> Their names are written deep across the land
> In pass and trail and river, like a rune.
>
> For a little span,
> Their life-fires flared like torches in the van
> Of westward progress, ere the great wind woke
> To snuff them. Many vanished like a smoke
> The blue air drinks; and e'en of those who burned
> Down to the socket, scarce a tithe returned
> To share at last the ways of quiet men,
> Or see the hearth reek drifting down again
> Across the roofs of old St. Louis town.

16

THE LONE STAR

No accent wounds the reverent air,
No footstep dents the sod,
Lone in the light the prairie lies,
Wrapt in a dream of God.
—JOHN HAY

AR away in the Southwest, some roaming Americans discovered Paradise. "The green grass grew down to the green sea," said Charles Sealsfield, who approached it from Galveston Bay, "and there was only the streak of white foam left by the latter upon the former to serve as a line of demarkation. Before us was a perfectly level plain, a hundred or more miles in extent, covered with long fine grass, rolling in waves before each puff of the sea-breeze, with neither tree nor house nor hill to vary the unbroken monotony of the surface." With kindling eyes the Americans looked in on "forest and meadow, trees and grass, all so fresh and pure, as if just from the hand of the mighty and eternal artificer. No trace of man's sinful hand, but all the beautiful, immaculate work of God."

At night it was even lovelier. "Hurra! There is the house

at last. I can see the lights in the parlor windows. I urged my horse on, but when I came near the house it proved to be an island of trees. What I had taken for candles were fireflies, that now issued in swarms from out the darkness of the islands, and spread themselves over the prairies, darting about in every direction, their small blue flames literally lighting up the plain, and making it appear as if I were surrounded by a sea of Bengal fire. Nothing could be more bewildering than such a ride as mine, on a warm March night, through the interminable, never-varying prairie; overhead the deep blue firmament with its hosts of bright stars; at my feet, and all around, an ocean of magical light, myriads of fireflies floating upon the soft, still air. It was like a scene of enchantment. I could distinguish every blade of grass, every flower, every leaf on the trees, in an unnatural sort of light, and in altered colors. Tuberoses and asters, prairie roses and geraniums, dahlias and vine branches began to wave to range themselves in ranks and rows. The whole vegetable world around me appeared to dance as the swarms of living lights passed over it."

"Who owns it?" asked the first Americans. The answer was uncertain. At first it seemed that this empty garden of the Lord might have been included in the Louisiana Purchase. But with the cession of Florida in 1819, the United States definitely abandoned this claim. Then it must belong to Spain, for Spanish fathers had been here and had built the low blocks of adobe mission buildings at San Antonio. A few priests, a few roving Indians, an official or two—and for the rest the land was empty, and no one seemed to care much about it. There was prairie enough and to spare in that immeasurable southwestern world.

But into the minds of a family in Arkansas there entered the old dream—the dream of Penn, the dream of Oglethorpe. This fresh and virgin world was a chance to reconsecrate a Southern climate to free and self-respecting white labor. No slaves here. No cotton, if cotton meant slaves. Import fine European men, Swiss, Germans, perhaps French, and let them make it a land of wine and oil—another Mediterranean civilization, simple, gay, and gracious. Let some Americans come here, but only some, men of character, no speculators, and not many lawyers. So Oglethorpe had dreamed, landing on the site of Savannah with a plan for a new city of the free in his strong box. So the Austin family began to dream in Arkansas —first Moses Austin, and then his son Stephen, a young circuit judge in that territory.

Moses cautiously communicated his plan to the Mexican government which, in 1821, threw off the rule of Spain, and found officials hospitable. A good idea! The land needed settlers, good workmen, people to exploit its resources, and develop wealth out of which the Mexican aristocracy in time could take its squeeze. Before he could go far with his plan, Moses died, and his son Stephen took up the work.

2

"I entered upon the stage of life with ideas of human nature which had they been true, would have made this earth a paradise," wrote Stephen to his cousin, Mary Austin, ten years later, in a mood of bitter disillusionment. "My temperament was sanguine and confiding, my sensibility acute. The early part of my life was spent happily in the quiet enjoyments of home; and in the dreams of youth unpoisoned by ambition; unruffled by care, unclouded by true knowledge of man. The world was to me what the veiled prophet of Khorassan was to his blind devotees. My angel Mother, and my noble-minded and kind-hearted father were my first standards of human nature. In the ardor of young hope I supposed the rest of the world to be like them. . . . Pecuniary troubles swept away my father's ample fortune, and broke up our family home. Ever ardent and persevering he conceived the idea of a settlement in Texas which I was destined to accomplish.

"I entered this country with my ideas of the perfectibility of human nature but half corrected. . . . For the first time *Ambition* kindled its fires in my breast, but I think I can with truth say that the flame was a mild and gentle one, consisting more of the wish to build up the fortunes and happiness of others, and to realize my dreams of good will to my fellow men, than of the over-bearing spirit of military fame, or domineering power. My ambition was to *redeem this fine country*—our glorious Texas—and convert it into an home for the unfortunate, a refuge from poverty, an asylum for the sufferers from selfish avarice.

"Here the hand of nature had spread her bounties with such profusion that the most indigent, with moderate industry, could make a support. The poor but honest man's cottage would not be looked down upon with contempt from the lofty attics of the lordly palace, for in that particular there would be perfect equality."

He hoped above all to rectify the two great difficulties that were already casting the shadow of desolation on the South—the curse of landlordism and land speculation, and the curse of slavery. "We have some few settlers in Texas," he wrote to Edward Livingston, "now bending under the weight of years, whose youth was spent in building up a home in the wilds of Kentucky or other parts of the west. The Indians, the buffalo, the cane-brakes and the forests gradually disappeared—population and civilization soon changed the face of everything. They rejoiced and looked forward to the enjoyment of quiet old age in their once forest homes, surrounded by their children, and by peace and plenty. It was all a delusion . . . civilization brought with it the *monied mania*. The hostile Indians were replaced by civilized savages of a more brutal and dangerous character, cold-hearted, unprincipled speculators, men who considered that to make a fortune was the great and paramount and only object of human life—lawyers who found in the labyrinths and abstruse sections of the common law, unexhausted and unexhaustible arms for the protection of tergiversation, quibbling, and injustice, and for the ruin of unsuspecting and ignorant honesty.

"The forest homes of the first settlers were converted into

scenes of legal discord and contention—the first emigrants whose enterprise had opened the road for easy entrance of land and law harpies were dragged by them into court and after years of ruinous suspense were finally told that they might go penniless farther west and seek new homes.

"We have a few of another class who have been reared in affluence and were content with their situation—they enjoyed in a prudent manner what they possessed without jeopardizing it by grasping after more—their prudence and systematic way of living availed them nothing—it ruined them, for it gave them credit. Their neighbors and friends needed endorsers. Ruin, beggary, and the total loss of friends was the result."

But, fleeing from the credit system, he says, we find that we have brought some of its evils along with us in the character of many of the settlers in Texas. "We have a number of another class—able bodied men, capable of earning an honest and competent living by labor—but having been raised in a country where the credit system prevails to such an extent that everything is regulated by it, where men of empty pockets and emptier heads with a little credit to begin with, disdain to work, and live by their wits upon the earnings of honest laborers, they have acquired habits of cunning and the art of imposing by appearances and fictions which renders them nuisances to society."

But more troublesome than the credit system, even, was the institution of slavery. "We have some southern men who are longing after negroes to make cotton to buy more negroes. It is vain to tell them of the demoralizing influence of slavery, of its ruinous effect upon the physical energies and enterprise of the community, or to lead forward their imaginations to the period (perhaps not very distant) when the natural increase of the slaves will enable them to massacre their masters and desolate the country."

The fear of land speculation, of exploitation by bankers and other capitalists, and the fear of slavery explain why so good, and so typical an American as Stephen Austin was anxious to leave his own country, and to draw off some of the best citizens from it. The settlement of Texas was one of the first effects of that intolerable situation created by the rapid growth of the cotton kingdom, with its corollary of exploitation by capital and speculation in land and dispossessing of white settlers by slaves. The Mexican government was anxious to get good settlers; it was a new and hopeful state, and Austin hoped that Americans within this new republican confederacy would be able to make better terms for themselves than they could with the political leadership of the Southern plantation states, whence most of his settlers came, or from a federal government dominated by Southern planters and Northern bankers.

3

"When I explored this country in 1821," wrote Stephen to his cousin and confidante, Mary Austin, in 1831, "it was a wild howling, interminable solitude from Sabine to Bexar. The civilized population had not extended beyond the margins of the Sabine in that quarter; and was confined, on the west to the towns of Bexar and La Bahia (the latter is now called Goliad) which were isolated military posts. I found the country so much more valuable than I expected that the idea of contributing to fill it with a civilized and industrious population filled my soul with enthusiasm. . . . I commenced on the solid basis of sound and philanthropic intentions, and of undeviating integrity. I asked the *favor* of the new government of Mexico—that is permission to settle this country, and become one of its citizens. What I asked was granted. I became a Mexican citizen. From that moment honor, and the sanctity of an oath, gratitude—all bound me to Mexico and her interests. Never have I for one moment deviated from the line of duty which those obligations imposed upon me. And I attribute my success (for I may say with pride I have been successful) to this circumstance. Should this government ever attempt to trample upon us, however, honor, duty, justice, the approbation of all good people of all nations will point out the course for us to adopt."

The first difficulty he encountered was the difficulty of Oglethorpe. Skilled artisans and thrifty farmers from Switzerland and Germany shrank from even the smell of black slavery. They had no faith in this enterprise. It was, they thought, only a ruse of the Southern slaveholders, to make them walk into their net. Again and again Austin reports his failure in interesting the Swiss, saying that Ohio is getting them all, as well as desirable German immigrants. He sought Scotch and English yeomen and small English capitalists hoping to reproduce the experience of New England and Pennsylvania in building civilization on the artisan and small shopkeeping class of English. In vain. If they came to America, they either settled on the eastern seaboard or went to Ohio. A Mexican official wrote him that the most desirable population would be the "hardy yeomanry of the New England states." But alas, they also could go to Ohio, or move on into central New York State.

Meanwhile he collected American families. To one of his assistants he wrote: "You will of course not bring nor suffer none to come in company with you who are not good honest citizens, and above all, you will exclude drunkards. I have been heretofore so much troubled with that beastly portion of the human race that my dislike to them has grown into a very strong prejudice."

In the end what he got was dispossessed Southerners—mainly backwoodsmen—with a sprinkling of enterprising and idealistic families from all over the country. He was far from satisfied with this state of affairs. "I do say that North Americans are the most obstinate and difficult people to manage that live on earth . . . I sometimes think that Swiss and German people will promote the prosperity of this country more than North Americans. They will introduce the culture of the vine, olive, etc. They are industrious and moral. They have not in general that horrible mania for speculation which is so prominent a trait in the English and North American character, and above all *they will oppose slavery*. The idea of seeing such a country as this over-run by a slave population almost makes me weep. . . . In the beginning of this settlement I was compelled to hold out the idea that slavery would be tolerated . . . I did this to get a start, for otherwise it would have been next to impossible to have started at all, for I had to draw on Louisiana and Mississippi, slave states, for the first migrants. Slavery is now most positively prohibited by our constitution and by a number of laws, and I hope it may always be so."

While Austin was selecting his immigrants, and making terms with the Mexican government which would allow the Americans to remain practically an autonomous state within the Mexican confederacy, the Mexicans also granted land to other groups of Americans—among them the Galveston Land Company—who hastened to pour into the land which Austin was civilizing, but who were not, like his own colonists, especially selected. The cotton planters began to gloat and see in this land a half-dozen new cotton and slave states, thus securing forever their power in Congress. The Southern talk of annexation alarmed Mexican officials and prejudiced Northern Americans—a prejudice which, more than any other, prevented Austin from getting the very colonists he was seeking.

Still he had a good colony, consisting of strong and natively superior men from among the dispossessed Scotch-Irish backwoodsmen, the same kind of people that, seeping up into Indiana and Illinois, were making the backbone of population for those states. The Jacksonian democracy and economic radicalism native to the border supported both Austin's objection to the "monied mania" and to slavery.

"I am well aware that the total abolition of the credit system as it now exists will to a certain extent cramp the progress of improvement for a time," wrote Austin to Livingston. "It would be impracticable in a country that did not abound in

natural resources or that depended principally on commerce,
but this would not apply to Texas."

He consulted Livingston about the possibility of writing
into the Texas constitution some radical provisions with regard to debt. He proposed that the only security allowed
should be the character for industry and sobriety and honesty
of the debtor, and that it should be forbidden by law to collect
debts coercively. No person should pledge land or property
for debt, and no debt could be collected against property, but
agreements might be made on the basis of the character of
the applicant, alone, for the use of money. Certain exceptions,
he said, should be made—debts to mechanics or laborers for
wages should be collectible against the property of employers.
Debts due the general or local government, he thought, should
also be collectible against appropriate property, and funds in
trust for widows and other defenseless persons should be especially protected. What he was seeking was a means of keeping homesteads out of the hands of harpies who might prey
upon the good nature or conviviality of the head of the family.

Reading these letters of Stephen Austin one cannot but be
touched by the spectacle of these simple, upright families exposed on all sides. At one moment they are concerned because
vagabonds and ruffians of the southwest American border get
in among them; at another there are emissaries of slave interests stirring up trouble; again there are speculators and financial harpies. Pathetically they turn to the Mexican government,
and are met by stupidity and ignorance. Austin, professing to
Americans the greatest faith in the Mexican government, in-
dulges in plain speaking to intelligent Mexican friends. Referring to his own country he said to one of them: "I have
seen a wilderness covered with a dense population in a few
years, and new states erected where at the time of my birth
there was not a single civilized person. I believed that it would
be the same with a free and nascent Mexican nation. I see that
I was mistaken. Before Mexico can develop in that manner, she
must pay the price in a moral revolution in which shall be

overthrown all the customs and the Gothic politico-religious
system set up by Rome and Spain to hold the people in subjection like beasts of burden. Such a revolution she will have
in a century but not in the life-time of one man."

The question is, he says, whether Americans can wait for
the moral revolution. "I was not born in a wilderness, and
have not the patience of the Beraxenos and other inhabitants
of this frontier who are daily enduring the same dangers and
annoyances that their fathers and grandfathers and perhaps
their great-grandfathers suffered, without advancing a single
step or even thinking of advancing. Death is preferable to such
a stagnant existence, such a stupid life."

And back he goes to the old dream. "May we not form a
little world of our own where neither religious, political, or
money-making fanaticism, which are throwing the good people of our native country into all sorts of convulsions shall ever
obtain admission? We will then arrange our cottages—rural,
comfortable, and splendid, the splendor of nature's simplicity.
Gardens and rosy bowers and ever verdant groves and music
and books can all be ours; and that confidence and community
of feeling and tastes which none but congenial minds can ever
know; all these without excessive wealth we can have. Millions could not buy them, but the right disposition can, with
competence, insure them."

America is a land of buried dreams. And no dream was
ever lovelier than that which lies buried deep under the prairie
sod of Texas. The place of its burial shines wan in the light of
a young man's vision which, down there on the wild southwestern frontier, on the black edge of slavery, was indeed as
the light of a lone star.

4

It was not to be. The promise to the Americans of self-
government was not kept. A civil war broke out between the
existing government of Mexico, and a popular general, Santa
Anna. The Texans, taking Santa Anna at his word, believed

him in favor of constitutional government and hopefully supported him. He was successful, but he promptly established a
dictatorship, and set a military governor over the Americans.
George Washington himself could not have done this with
impunity. Austin hotly protested. "It is useless to try to regulate Texas by military force." He pointed out that the reason
the Americans were invited in the first place was that, as riflemen, they were equivalent to a frontier army, and cost Mexico
nothing. If they were antagonized, and Mexican soldiers sent
in, the soldiers would not be half as efficient in keeping off
Indians, and the order and civilization which Texas was creating as a northern bulwark to Mexico would give way to
anarchy.

Going stupidly on, Santa Anna and his government proposed to tie Texas to the state of Coahuila, and govern them
together, Mexican military fashion, as one state. Austin told
them flatly, "It will not do. If you don't make Texas a separate state, she will make herself one." Yet he insisted. "I have
said, and I repeat it—it is not to the interest of Texas to separate herself from Mexico, even if she had the liberty to do it."
"Texas is to-day exposed to separation from Mexico—to
being the sport of ambitious men, of speculators and reckless
money-changers, of seditious and wicked men, of wandering
Indians who are devastating the country, of adventurers, of
revolutionists, of the lack of administration of justice, and of
confidence and moral strength in the government. In short,
for want of government, the country is already on the verge
of anarchy."

To the Americans, however, he spoke in soft and conciliat-
ing tones, even persuading them to accept the combination
with Coahuila, at least for the moment. But the anger of others
in the colony who had not Austin's strong sense of obligation
to Mexico, nor his fear of slavery, was rising. Among others, a
stalwart leader, named Sam Houston, was asserting himself.

Austin now began to dally with the possibility of an
American protectorate over an independent Texas. At first he

would consider it only if there were absolute guarantees that slavery was to be forever prohibited in Texas. Finally, in 1833, he made the last sacrifice. Slavery, he said, must be allowed in Texas. His principles were unchanged but circumstances were too strong for him.

He began to see, also, that revolution might be inevitable. Leaving for Mexico City to make one last plea for his people, he wrote to Captain Henry Austin on April 19, 1833, saying that he had heard that a considerable section of the Mexican army was to be sent into Texas. If we are to be overrun by these disorderly soldiers, he said, "the whole country ought to unite at once and expel or kill the whole of them." "Let us violate no law, nor any just rights of the nation and adhere closely to the principle of seeking a peaceable remedy. That *failing*, I am then ready for war or anything. . . . If there is no other remedy I am for going into it fully, and united, make a business of that at once."

From Mexico City he wrote suggesting that, since there was little hope of a change in the Mexican attitude to Texas, the citizens had better organize a state of their own. This letter fell into the hands of Mexican authorities, who thereupon arrested Austin, at Saltillo, while he was on his way home, and kept him a prisoner for a year. When he was finally released and returned to Texas, he found the whole country in armed revolt. On November 3, 1835, the Texans drew up a Declaration of Independence beginning: "Whereas General Antonio Lopez de Santa Anna and other military chieftains have by force of arms overthrown the federal constitution and dissolved the social compact between the states, therefore the people of Texas, etc. . . ."

Austin was dispatched as a commissioner to the United States to seek aid and supplies for the Texans, which were forthcoming in generous quantities, along with assurances that Americans would look with favor on an independent Texas. A year later he was dead. A brief life, and of a touching and poetic goodness. He was born, as he said, to see life through a "silver veil," and died with the "silver veil but half raised."

5

The mellow old town of San Antonio now lies golden and dusty in the swell of the yellow prairie—streets strung with colored lights and streamers for the ever-recurring fiestas, little chapels where the Virgin smiles wanly amidst tinsel and paper flowers, and, serene under the rainless sky, lie the tan adobe buildings of the old Spanish missions, each with its round hole cut in the roof, "so that the eye of God may look through." Few Americans can stand in the warm palpitant dusk of those buildings, and look out through that hole into the far, blue, prairie sky, without a gratitude to the old Spanish fathers for this consecration of the land. But the blue eye of God has looked down on many cruel and dreadful things in San Antonio, and on none so cruel as the assault on the Alamo, with which the swift, barbaric epic of Texas independence began.

Hearing that the Texans had declared their independence, and had appointed doughty Sam Houston as major general of the armies of Texas to provide for self-defense, Santa Anna himself took to the field, and marched from Laredo to San Antonio where the Americans had garrisoned and fortified an old mission building, the Alamo. This mission Houston had ordered the men to surrender, but they replied that they would rather "die in these ditches" than give them up to the enemy. Penned in the building, the Americans heard the dreadful "fire and death call" of no quarter, used by the Spaniards long ago in the Moorish wars, and knew that they must, indeed, against sheer weight of numbers die in these ditches. But they surrendered hard, forcing the enemy to take the old building room by room, and themselves perished, one by one, a "foolhardy, gallant band."

One of the defenders was Davy Crockett, ending here in a fury of bullets one of the sagas of the frontier. As someone has said, nothing in his life became him more than his manner of going out of it. Another was Captain James Bowie, after whom the bowie knife was named.

Not long after that, at Goliad, a force under Commander James Fanning surrendered to the Mexicans under guarantees of safety. What happened then was described by Walt Whitman.

Retreating they formed in a hollow square with their baggage for breast works.

Nine hundred lives out of the surrounding enemy's, nine times their number, was the price they took in advance.

Their colonel was wounded and their ammunition gone.

They treated for an honorable capitulation, receiv'd writing and seal, gave up their arms, and marched back prisoners of war.

They were the glory of the race of rangers,

Matchless with horse, rifle, song, supper, courtship,

Large, turbulent, generous, handsome, proud, affectionate,

Bearded, sunburnt, drest in the free costume of hunters,

Not a single one over thirty years of age.

The second First Day morning, they were brought out in squads and massacred. It was beautiful early summer.

The work commenced about five o'clock and was over by eight.

None obeyed the command to kneel.

Some made a mad and helpless rush, some stood stark and straight.

A few fell at once, shot in the temple or the heart. The living and dead lay together.

The maim'd and mangled dug in the dirt, the newcomers saw them there.

Some half killed attempted to crawl away.

These were dispatched with bayonets or battered with the blunts of muskets.

A youth not seventeen years old seized his assassin till two more came to release him,

The three were all torn and covered with the boy's blood.

At eleven o'clock began the burning of the bodies;

That is the tale of the murder of the four hundred and twelve young men.

After this Sam Houston and his army were on the warpath in earnest. At San Jacinto, they attacked Santa Anna. The music that led them into battle consisted of one flute which piped away bravely "Will you come to my Bower I have shaded for you?" above which the Americans raised a blood-curdling yell of "Remember the Alamo! Remember Goliad!" When the smoke of battle cleared away, all the Mexican force was wiped out—630 killed, 208 wounded, and 730 prisoners, but only six Texans were killed and twenty-four wounded, among them Sam Houston himself, his leg shattered above the ankle. As Houston sat under a tree, nursing his wounded ankle, some Texans came up with a common soldier whom they had captured. Houston instantly recognized the soldier as the Mexican dictator in disguise, and, as Santa Anna said afterwards, "shook hands and spoke courteously." The story is that at the same time, Santa Anna gave the Masonic distress signal which was recognized by William H. Wharton, who later used his influence to save their captive's life.

The rest of the tale is fantastic. The simple Texans had Santa Anna, the dictator, undisputed sovereign of Mexico, among them, and they proposed to make the most of it. But how? The main thing was to keep him safe till they did some thinking. So they put him on board "The Yellowstone" and set sail for Velasco near Galveston, while things moved fast on shore, and while Santa Anna exerted his considerable capacity to please, entertaining his captors with discourses on the beauty of nature and on the ladies, the "gravy of society."

Sam Houston, elected president of the now free and inde-pendent state of Texas, consulted President Jackson of the United States about the disposition of their captive. Jackson wrote: "His person is still of much consequence to you. He is the pride of the Mexican soldiers and the favorite of the priest-hood. While he is in your power, the difficulties of your enemy in raising another army will continue to be great. The soldiers of Mexico will not willingly march into Texas when they know that their advance may cost their favorite general his life. Let not his blood be shed, unless imperious

necessity demands it as a retaliation for future Mexican mas-
sacres. Both wisdom and humanity enjoin this course in relation to Santa Anna."

Having forced Santa Anna to sign a recognition of the independence of Texas, the Texans then sent him to Washington, by way of Lexington, Kentucky, and Wheeling, Virginia,
to discuss with officials there the whole question of boundaries
between the United States and Mexico. Along the way he was
handsomely entertained and made an agreeable impression, it
being reported that he is "tolerably pleasant of countenance
and speech (which is exclusively Spanish) very polite and
using stately compliments." In the capital city, over which he
had once boasted he would plant the flag of the Republic of
Mexico, he was received with suitable honor, and a complete
ignoring of his rather humiliating position, and after the nego-
tiations were over, was sent home on a United States frigate.

So Texas was now an independent state. It all reads like a
story too good to be history—as if some Homer must have
shaped it and put the dramatic reversal, the *deus ex machina*
ending, all in the right place!

> O bearded, stalwart west-most men
> . . . Your heirs
> Know not your tombs; the great ploughshares
> Cleave softly through the mellow loam
> Where you have made eternal home
> And set no sign. Your epitaphs
> Are writ in furrows. Beauty laughs
> While through the green ways wandering
> Beside her love, slow gathering
> White starry-hearted May-time blooms
> Above your lowly levelled tombs;
> And then below the spotted sky
> She stops, she leans, she wonders why
> The ground is heaved and broken so,
> And why the grasses darker grow
> And droop and trail like wounded wings.

Yea, Time, the grand old harvester,
Has gathered you from wood and plain.
We call to you again, again;
The rush and rumble of the car
Comes back in answer. Deep and wide
The wheels of progress have passed on;
The silent pioneer is gone.
His ghost is moving down the trees,
And now we push the memories
Of bluff bold men who dared and died
In foremost battle quite aside.
                                    —JOAQUIN MILLER

6

Having achieved her independence, Texas applied to the United States for admission to the Union. But this was another question. Restive under the increasing political dominance of the South, which had been greatly enhanced by the personal popularity and genuine ability of President Jackson, the North saw in this whole Texas proceeding just a plot of the cotton kingdom. To the suspicions of the North the Southern orators gave color by rather premature gloating, showing that a lot of cotton could be raised in Texas, figuring that as many as five states could be made out of the territory, and sometimes going on and painting in glowing colors the onward march of Americans and cotton, into Mexico, into Cuba, into Central America.

So for nine years Texas was refused admission to the Union, maintaining itself meanwhile as an independent state. At first its attitude was humble and pleading. Then it tried another tack. Rumors were spread abroad of the influence of Great Britain with the Texans—indeed, there seems to have been some effort among the British to get Texas to abandon slavery. Texas began to look cool to annexation. The Americans were still afraid Great Britain would take over any English-speaking people they themselves failed to look after. The new ruse of Texas worked. In 1845 the question was an

issue in the presidential campaign and President Polk came to
the White House empowered by the apparent will of the people to tie Texas to the United States at any cost. Though
Texas had maintained its freedom for nine years, Mexico still
asserted sovereignty there, and served notice that a bill of
annexation would be tantamount to a declaration of war.

The war was short and in the northern section not even
bloody. General Kearny with an army enlisted mainly in
Missouri came down the Santa Fe trail, picked up 500 stalwart young Mormons, and occupied Santa Fe. Declaring that
New Mexico was now annexed to the United States, he started
off to annex California, but was met by Kit Carson riding
ahead of a little band of dispatch carriers with the news that
California was already ours.

In Mexico American troops, landed at Vera Cruz, hoisted
themselves up onto the great tableland of Mexico, assaulted
and took the fortress of Chapultepec, ran up the Stars and
Stripes above the city, and proceeded to dictate terms. The
terms were mild enough. All the Americans desired was what
they really had anyway, and for that they were ready to pay
cash. The boundary of the Rio Grande which the Texans had
forced Santa Anna to accept was to be continued across the
country, giving California, New Mexico, and Utah to the
United States. In California the Americans and a mixed community of Europeans were tired of Mexico anyway, and
would probably have tied up to Great Britain if the United
States had not presented itself at this moment. In New Mexico
the people could dispense with old Mexico more easily than
with the goods and gadgets, the excitements and joys of life
being imported by American traders. And in the deserts of
Utah the Mormons had already set up. For all this the United
States offered $15,000,000 cash, the price of the Louisiana
territory, and, in addition, assumed the innumerable claims of
American citizens against Mexico for destruction of life and
property during the various revolutionary disturbances. With
the Stars and Stripes waving over the city, Mexico would have

had to take anything she could get. But there was a strong body of sentiment in the United States against anything that savored of blood and conquest and pilfering from the neighbors. Even so the bargain did not satisfy New England. There Lowell's Yankee Hosea Biglow was saying:

"They may talk o' Freedom's airy
    Till they're purple in the face,—
It's a grand great cemetary
    For the barthrights of our race;
They just want this Californy
    So's to lug new slave-states in,
To abuse ye, an' to scorn ye,
    And to plunder you like sin.

. . . .

That air flag's a leetle rotten,
    Hope it aint your Sunday's best;
Fact! it takes a sight o' cotton
    To stuff out a sojer's chest.

. . . .

Ez for war, I call it murder,—
    There you have it plain an' flat;
I don't want to go no furder
    Than my Testyment for that;
God hez said so plump and fairly,
    It's as long as it is broad,
And you got to get up airly
    Ef you want to take in God.

'Taint your eppyletts and feathers
    Make the thing a grain more right;
'Taint afollerin' your bell-wethers
    Will excuse ye in His sight;
If you take a sword and dror it,
    And go stick a feller thru,
Guv'ment aint to answer for it,
    God'll send the bill to you.

17

DOWN THE SANTA FE TRAIL

IAGONALLY beyond Missouri and that "flowery rectangle sloping upward to the Rockies" which was to become the state of Kansas, the round pink hills of New Mexico rise against the sky, and among them, making ribbons of verdure deep down in the fissures of this burnt and empty land, are the streams which, running to the south and southeast, join and at length burst downward to the sea as the Rio Grande. Near the head of the Rio Grande, there was an old city—so old that no one could tell when it had not been. There was a pueblo here in 1539 when Coronado came this way seeking seven golden cities, "very rich, having silversmiths," where the women "wore strings of gold beads and the men girdles of gold." He found nothing except some simple Indians, sitting in the sunshine, on bright-colored blankets, and living in low mud huts, some of them built on shelves against the hill, like beehives.

But the Franciscan missionaries seeking to bring a treasure to the Indians, not to take treasure away, found a path thither up the Rio Grande. In these regions they built seven churches and baptized 14,000 people, with something like forty-eight soldiers and settlers from Spain at their backs. Gradually

Spanish settlers gathered in and around Santa Fe, taught the people to speak their language, and laid a thin veneer of their customs and manners over the pueblo civilization. With some ups and downs—for the Pueblo Indians revolted and at one time massacred 400 of them in Santa Fe and were then able to keep most Spaniards and their priests out for ten years—the Spaniards kept a kind of hold on the city, and made it the northern point of a thin line of settlements leading down through the barren highlands to Mexico City. Santa Fe was the administrative capital for whatever power Spain could exercise in what is now the state of New Mexico.

From Santa Fe a trail eighty miles long led upward to the town of Taos, up among those queer pink hills like baked hams on end, across the stony arroyos, past Santa Clara Pueblo, past Santa Cruz. Going back and forth to Taos, 800 miles across Missouri and Kansas, the mountain men made known in Saint Louis the ways of that sleepy Spanish-Indian world. A lazy people, but fond of gadgets; simple adobe houses, furnished with a string of red peppers, a pile of blankets against the wall for seats by day and beds by night, and a few bowls for water. But themselves—you should see them! They carry everything they own on their backs—men with strings of coin down the sides of their leather breeches, with silk shirts (if they can get them), gaudy handkerchiefs, and hats that should be parasols; girls in laces and ribbons and beads and bright shawls, with rings on their fingers and bracelets and necklaces. So the generous trapper, shopping for his girl in Mexico, went back with anything he could find in the way of Yankee notions —pins, beads, hairpins, shawls, laces, bulging in his saddle bags. Presents for her, and presents for the whole family!

This gave merchants an idea. The Yankee technique of finding what people wanted and taking it to them had already begun to function in the West. Easy enough to set sail with a cargo from Massachusetts to the foreign port of Santa Fe. All you needed was wheels under you instead of keels—and the good old Pennsylvania Dutch wagon, partner to the Yankee schooner in the path of empire, stood ready to do the work.

For fifteen years, while the trappers shopped around for presents for their girls, merchants meditated on the great idea. Zebulon Pike, captured by the Spaniards in 1807 and taken as a prisoner through these regions, reported the picturesque slow-moving society, and the men and girls who loved to dress, and said that there was a market if it could be reached. The first traders who tried to act on his suggestion were captured by the Spaniards and put in jail. But in 1821 Mexico revolted against Spain. Thereupon William Becknell rushed down with packs of whatever he could gather together and came back with his baggage bulging with Spanish dollars. Thereafter a trading caravan to Santa Fe left Missouri every year. At first these caravans left from Saint Louis. Then they moved up the river to Franklin, and outfitted themselves from there. Finally they developed Independence as a center.

When Kit Carson ran away from his master, the saddler, what he did was to join a Santa Fe caravan, and from Santa Fe to make his way to the company of the trappers at Taos. From Saint Louis reports went home to the shoe and textile factories in New England and the Yankee manufacturers of "notions." The Spanish Indian people down Santa Fe way wanted "goods of excellent quality and unfaded colors," and "they do not hesitate to pay the price demanded for an article if it suits their purpose or their fancy." So down the rutted dusty road, through the tall grass of Kansas, went the trail of wagons, with armed escort, carrying "coarse and fine cambrics, calicoes, domestic shawls, handkerchiefs, steam-loom shirtings, and cotton hose," as well as "crapes, bombazettes, silk shawls, and looking glasses."

In February, 1830, the *Missouri Intelligencer* reported: "The inland trade between the United States and Mexico is increasing rapidly. This is perhaps the most curious species of foreign intercourse which the ingenuity and enterprise of American traders ever originated. The extent of country which the caravans traverse, the long journeys they have to make, the rivers and morasses to cross, the prairies, the forests, the all but African deserts to penetrate, require the most steel-formed constitutions and the most energetic minds. The accounts of these inland expeditions remind one of the caravans of the East. The dangers which both encounter—the caravan of the East and that of the West—are equally numerous and equally alarming. Men of high chivalric and somewhat romantic natures are requisite for both."

Down the rutted Santa Fe trail went the wagons, and in time back they came, freighted with three more states for the Union—New Mexico, Utah, and California—and leading by a towrope the state of Texas, which, however, was rolling into the United States of America on its own wheels.

2

The Santa Fe trail has its classical historian—Joseph Gregg, trader in search of health and profit. As Paxon says, "His *Commerce of the Prairies* or *The Journal of a Santa Fe Trader* has no equal in its field except Parkman's *Oregon Trail*." But even Gregg yields before the confidences, first published ten years ago, of the charming Susan Magoffin. When "Mr. Magoffin bore with him a young, rich, and lovely bride of the noblest blood of Kentucky to this mart of commerce," he conferred a great favor on the Muse of History. "She had it not in her nature to know fear. Through all the alarms of camp, toils of the march, and privations of the army, this lady was found cheerful. She was the charm of the social circle of the encampment in hours of ease, and in hours of danger bravest of the brave." All of which does not do justice to Susan. Only her own diary does that.

Susan was the granddaughter of the first governor of Kentucky. As the bride of a young gentleman whose father had come to Kentucky from Ireland, she was setting off in 1845, with eyes "full of longing for a sight of the wide-spreading plains."

Her first night down the trail she sleeps in a tent, and reports blithely, "After a supper at my own table in my own house, I can say what few women in civilized life ever could, that the first house of his own to which my husband took me was a tent, and the first table of my own at which I ever sat was a cedar one, made with only one leg, and that was a tentpole. But as I said, after the first supper at *my own* table, consisting of fried ham, eggs, biscuit, and a cup of shrub—for I preferred it to tea or cafe—I enjoyed a fine night's rest. It was sweet indeed."

Next day they stopped to camp early enough to let Susan plunge delightedly into the prairie and pick bunches of flowers for her house. "Before supper I had a little piece of work to attend to, I mean the feeding of my chickens. It is quite a farm house this:—poultry, dogs, cattles, mules, horses, etc. Altogether my home is not one to be objected to."

Sometimes it is very hot, and Susan, bouncing in her wagon, records: "Now out on the wide prairie. . . . Not a breath of air is stirring and everything is scorching with heat. We have no water and the animals are panting with thirst." Sometimes it rains. "Shut up in a carriage all day with the buffalo robe rolled around you and the rain pouring at ten knots an hour. And at the close of this to be quietly and without any trouble to one's self in to the middle of a bed in a nice dry tent, with writing materials around you . . . sewing, knitting, somebody to talk with, and a house that does not leak . . . I am satisfied, though this is a juicy day *en el campo!*" Next day they drag through the mud at one mile an hour. Susan's nice dry house is washed away, and "the night is spent in fasting and wet clothes."

But the sun comes out again, and Susan is happy. "Oh, this is a life I would not exchange for a good deal. There is such independence, so much free uncontaminated air, which impregnates the mind, the feelings, the every thought with purity. I breathe free without that oppression and uneasiness felt in the gossiping circles of a settled home."

Every stop is a celebration to Susan. There are always flowers to pick. "Of roses there are any quantity. Now at my tent-door there are two bushes, one on either side, and inside nearly all the way from the head of my bed to the door are bushes with full blown roses bursting, and closed buds. It is the life of a wandering princess, mine!" She keeps her tent full of flowers, even when she is not fortunate enough to pitch it in a rose garden. "When I do not wish to get out myself to pick the flowers, the Mexican servants riding mules pick them for me." Sometimes she goes on wild excursions, finds a stream, jumps across it on stones, to "Mi Alma's astonishment." Mi Alma (My Soul) is the husband. One day she picked raspberries and gooseberries and tried to fish. Then after dinner she lay down "with Mi Alma on a buffalo skin with carriage seats for pillows and took what few ladies have done, a siesta in the sun."

Of course there are things in the wilderness that a girl cannot really enjoy. Horrid bugs for example. Susan's special *bête noir* is a most dreadful green bug, "like an alligator in miniature." "I never walk in the grass without holding my dress up high for fear its long arms may chance to grapple with me." And at night there are the wolves. They are a little fearsome, even when one is lying snug in the tent by Mi Alma's dear side. " 'Aakm-ba,-gnaw,-gnow,' they say in quick succession—a mixture of cat, dog, sheep, wolf, and dear knows what else. . . . I lay perfectly still with Mi Alma breathing a sweet sleep by my side. I could not waken him just to keep me company when he was so well engaged."

Sunday comes, and Susan reports with sweet gravity: "The Sabbath on the plains is not altogether without reverence. Everything is perfectly calm. The blustering, swearing teamsters remembering the duty they owe to their Maker have thrown aside their abusive language and are singing the hymns perhaps they were taught by a good pious mother. The little birds are all quiet and reverential in their songs. And nothing is disposed to mar that calm serene silence prevailing over the land. We have not the ringing of church bells nor the privilege of attending public worship, it is true, but we have ample time . . . for thinking on the great wisdom of our Creator, for praising him within ourselves for his excellent greatness in placing before us and entirely at our command so many blessings; in giving us health, minds free from care, the means of knowing and learning his wise designs, etc."

They come to the banks of the Arkansas River and begin to see the buffalo. "They are very ugly ill-shaped things with their long and shaggy hair over their heads, and the great hump on their backs, and they look so droll running." The land gets bleaker and bleaker. No more roses. No more raspberries by running streams. "In some places the country is hilly and covered with large stones, but generally speaking it is a perfectly level plain destitute of everything, even of grass, the great reliever to the eye, and making it painful to the sight."

In this barren world, Susan's spirits flag a little. The bouncing over the rocky road makes her ill. And then the secret is out. Lying by Mi Alma's side, through the long nights, "sweet indeed," picking flowers in the Kansas grass, Susan had been happily nursing her little hope. But the perpetual movement, the rough road—and one day Susan is very ill indeed. Susan, losing the prospect of her own baby, looks with somber envy upon the Indian woman. "She had a fine healthy baby about the same time, and in half an hour after she went to the river and bathed herself and it in it, and this she has continued each day since. Never could I have believed such a thing if I had not been here, and Mi Alma's own eyes had not seen her coming from the river."

Somewhat sobered, Susan thinks of death and God, and what if she had been snatched out of this lovely world and away from Mi Alma? "If I could be sure my idol is not on earth, that loving my dear husband as I do, I am not excluding an Image more precious to the soul of mortals than all things earthly." She hopes God will not judge "either of us" for that "deep devotion felt to each other," and wonders if human love like this is not really the "type of the love of God himself."

They cross the Arkansas, and Susan kisses her own dear native land good-by, "that fair and happy America." Still sober after her experience with the lot of an adventuring bride, Susan thinks: "Maybe I am never to behold its bright and sunny landscape, its happy people, my countrymen, again."

The mountains are heaving on their sight, "large stony hills that run into mountains. It is very hot. . . . So here we have lain in the hot sun with the tent windows raised, eating roast hare and drinking wine for dinner. In brevity we are quite patient under the circumstances." They come to the piñon woods—scrubby trees, she says, from which the Indians gather the piñon nuts. "The scenery here is quite romantic—high rocks covered with cedar trees, shelving and craggy precipices; purling brooks and green groves through which are seen bounding the stately antelope and timid hare, while the ear is greeted by the soft warble of feathered songsters. It is quite the place in which to build a lover's castle and plant his gardens, etc." A dash across more open bare country and "we are surrounded by most magnificent scenery. On all sides are stupendous mountains, forming an entire breastwork to our little camp situated in the valley below." The piñon tree is supplanted by "much taller and more sightly pine."

Mi Alma goes off shooting, and Susan climbs a hill and looks down, thinking, "In that wild glen is he who of all else on earth is most dear to me, wending his way through trees and small undergrowth, leaping ever and anon over the little arroyo (dry creek) that winds through it, in search of game for our fare."

They cross the Red River, and Magoffin must again go hunting. "I am left by Dom Manuel (Sam Magoffin) to superintend the camp," she writes. "Here I am, both Mr. and Mrs. of the whole concern!"

They are coming now to the Mexican village, which, says Susan, is a "fit match for some of the genteel pigsties in the states. The village is made of mud, and surrounded by a fence made of sticks. But the people appear to have peace of mind and contentment." In these villages, the white girl causes great excitement. "Mi Alma would make enough money to buy that village if only he would set me up as a travelling monkey-show and charge for a look at me."

But alas! poor Susan, she has to keep her veil down to protect her blushes, when passing some things "with gentlemen." "The women slap about with their arms and necks bare, perhaps their bosoms, and they are none of the prettiest and whitest. If they cross a creek, they pull their dresses which only cover their calves up to their knees and paddle through the water like ducks, sloshing and spattering everything about them."

When they reach Santa Fe, they find that General Kearny has taken possession of it in the name of the United States, and Susan rides in state as the first white woman to enter under the American flag. "He has not molested the habits, religion, etc., of the people, who are well pleased with their truly republican governor." Susan sets up in a Mexican house, with dirt floor, and nicely whitewashed walls, and goes to market and finds "delicious peaches, grapes, and small melons." She works hard all day getting things in order, trying to direct a Mexican servant, hoping to "gain one bright smile and sweet kiss from my good kind husband when he returns home." She thinks she is a lucky woman to have such a nice house and a "good, attentive, and affectionate husband."

The Spanish ladies call on Susan, and she entertains an Indian chief. She goes to the first Catholic service she has ever attended and to a Spanish ball. The Mexicans are very polite, but two things she has to get used to—the men all seated on one side of the room and the women on the other, and the smoking of cigarettes by ladies. A major came up to her and said, "Madam, will you have a cigarita?" and drew from one pocket a great bunch of corn husks, and from the other a large horn of tobacco, all ready to roll her one. And Susan doesn't really like the American soldiers. "What an everlasting noise these soldiers keep up! From early dawn till late at night they are blowing their trumpets and whooping like Indians."

And so we leave Susan, established at Santa Fe, with the American flag waving over her, and Mi Alma coming home with a bright smile and a sweet kiss—another one of those happy persons who went in the van of the marching Americans everywhere, carrying their little arts and graces, making their homes and nursing their private loves, and, through thick and thin, having apparently a wonderful time.

3

The person in charge of these whooping soldiers from Missouri was a young gentleman of Susan's own north-Irish breed —Colonel William W. Alexander Doniphan—six feet two inches tall, bright hazel eyes, and from Missouri. He had one of the vast poetic family histories of the Scotch-Irish, including the claim of descent from Spanish chivalry in the days of the Moorish wars, which made it quite all right for him to come down the Santa Fe trail under General Kearny's command, together with a bonny brace of lads he had enlisted himself, and take the old Spanish city away from mere Mexicans.

Colonel Doniphan also kept a diary, brief and breezy, a busy soldier's jottings, in purely elementary sentences. Reading it one feels as if one had personally galloped all over New Mexico at breakneck speed. Going down the Rio Grande Valley, Doniphan looks in at a Catholic celebration. "Celebration began at about nine A.M. The Church was crowded with a sea of heads. The house was lighted up with candles. The General and his staff were present. Each one as he entered in went and worshipped the Infant Saviour in the manger, then the Holy Virgin, then the Saviour on the Cross. I was particularly struck with a very aged and decrepit lady who went to the Savior and prayed before him, and wiped her streaming tears on the robes that clothed the image. The firing of the guns and circular rockets was kept up during the ceremonies.

Three or four priests officiated, preaching from the pulpit. Singing and instrumental music. They play the same tunes in serving God as they do in the fandango. They keep good time. Horse-racing after meeting. The whole is a pompous unmeaning show and gross mockery of the pure religion and of the meek and humble Jesus whom they pretend to serve."

Again he records: "Yesterday the old shepherd we had employed took occasion to leave and take a good mule with him. Other Spaniards left us and seventeen government mules left with them."

So he goes on, writing at a gallop, and all that bare, old, venal, sleepy world lives in his hasty words. Local Missouri history makes Doniphan and his men into great heroes. There was as a matter of fact nothing very heroic in what they had to do, riding almost undisputed into that simple land, and saying, "This is mine." Such greatness as there is in the episode is only in a kind of large good nature in the attitude of these lads, and in the romance of the background itself. For here was a continuity of history, strange and foreign, reaching back beyond Plymouth Rock, beyond Jamestown, and, romantic democrats as they were, the Americans were quick to appreciate it all.

The old palace in Santa Fe, now restored as an archaeological museum, still stands as the American forces first saw it. This palace "antedates the settlement of Jamestown, New Amsterdam, and Plymouth, and has stood during three centuries since its erection . . . as the living centre of everything of historic importance in the Southwest. Here . . . the brave Spaniards were massacred in the Revolution of 1680; here . . . was given the order to execute forty-seven Pueblo prisoners; . . . here but a few days later was the war council held which determined on the evacuation of the city; here was the scene of triumph of the Pueblo chieftains as they ordered the destruction of Spanish archives and church ornaments in one grand conflagration; here De Vargas gave thanks to the Virgin Mary to whose aid he attributed his triumphant recapture of the city; here more than a century later, on March 3, 1807,

Lieutenant Pike was brought before Governor Alencaster as an invader of Spanish soil. Here in 1822 the Mexican standard with the eagle and the cactus was raised in token that New Mexico was no longer a dependency of Spain. . . . Here General Kearny formally took possession of the city and slept, after his long and weary march, on the carpeted earthen floor of the palace."

4

After the Americans took possession of New Mexico, life went on there much as before. There was little to attract speculation, and few nooks among the sand hills for settlers to nestle in. From the autumn of 1851 on, its life is chronicled in Willa Cather's *Death Comes for the Archbishop*, which is one of those books that realizes Aristotle's definition of poetry, as fiction more true than history. The book opens with the young Father Latour who had been consecrated Vicar Apostolic of New Mexico and Bishop of Agathonia *in partibus* at Cincinnati the year before, riding among those red conical hills and feeling himself astray in "some geometrical nightmare." "Under his buckskin riding coat he wore a black vest and the cravat and collar of a churchman. . . . There was a singular elegance about the hands below the fringed cuffs of the buckskin jacket. Everything showed him to be a man of gentle birth—brave, sensitive, courteous. His manners, even when he was alone in the desert, were distinguished. He had a kind of courtesy to himself, toward his beasts, toward the juniper tree before which he knelt, and the God whom he was addressing."

The story follows his life in New Mexico—a story without plot or climax, almost without incident; and it makes every pueblo, every ranch, ever American character from Kit Carson and his dark-eyed Mexican señora, to the degenerate murderer Buck Scales, live again as in an untouched photograph. Father Latour had, as he said, come to Santa Fe with the buffalo and he lived to see the railway trains running into Santa Fe. And when he returned to France and to cultivated society

and the luxuries of civilization he used to wake every morning,
so homesick for that bare bright land and the simple hope with
which each day there began that he finally returned to New
Mexico to die. "In New Mexico he always woke as a young
man. Not until he rose and began to shave did he realize that
he was growing older. His first consciousness was a sense of
the light dry wind blowing in through the windows, with the
fragrance of hot sun and sage-brush and sweet clover; a wind
that made one's body feel light and one's heart cry 'Today, to-
day,' like a child's. . . .

"That air would disappear from the whole earth in time,
perhaps; but long after his day. He did not know just when
it had become so necessary to him, but he had come back to
die in exile for the sake of it. Something soft and wild and
free, something that whispered to the ear on the pillow, light-
ened the heart, softly, softly picked the lock, slid the bolts,
and released the prisoned spirit of man into the wind, into the
blue and gold, into the morning, into the morning."

Every civilization needs the desert as it needs the sea. And
it is our blessing that there was so much in New Mexico and
the opening Far West that could be touched by neither the
plow nor the miner's shaft—something large, simple, Biblical in form and spirit, since the Bible is itself a book of the
desert. The first Americans felt it, and the last Americans still
cherish it, making New Mexico the refuge of artists and poets,
a refuge within America itself from the excitement and com-
plexity of being American. All-conquering as the American
spirit is, it has never conquered the old Spanish-Indian Southwest. The land is too great, and its usefulness too little. And so
it remains a refuge, a reminder of values which our own good
fortune makes us elsewhere forget, a place where people weary
of the American drive at high speed learn how little one
needs to live on, if one is content just to live.

So Alice Corbin Henderson in Santa Fe looks wistfully on
at the old Mexican from the mountain peddling firewood.

Pedro Montoya of Arroyo Hondo
   Comes each day with his load of wood,
Piled on two burros' backs, driving them down
   Over the mesa to Santa Fe town.

Pedro Montoya of Arroyo Hondo
   Rides back on one burro and drives the other,
With a sack of blue cornmeal, tobacco, and meat,
   A bit to smoke, and a bit to eat.

Pedro Montoya of Arroyo Hondo—
   If I envied any, I'd envy him.
With a burro to ride, and a burro to drive,
   There is hardly a man so rich alive!

18

ROLL ALONG, PRAIRIE MOON

THE sun had fallen below the crest of the nearest wave of the prairie leaving the usual rich and glowing train in its track. In the centre of this flood of fiery light a form appeared, drawn against the gilded background as distinctly, and seemingly as palpable, as though it would come within the grasp of any extended hand. The figure was colossal; the attitude musing and melancholy."

So Natty Bumpo, the woodsman, hero of Cooper's *Leatherstocking Tales*, is seen in his extreme old age by a wagonful of prairie immigrants, pressing westward into the night, over the sealike swells of the long grass. He is there to end his days on the prairie as a trapper and to do his last service to advancing civilization as guide and protector. This last novel of the series, published in 1826, marks the acceptance into American literary tradition of the heroic world of the West.

Natty Bumpo was now eighty years old, and those eighty years of one man's life symbolized to Cooper the period of the American advance to full possession of the continent. Beginning as a lad in the last French and Indian wars, on the New England frontier, Natty had come west across New York State, following the lakes and rivers. He had been a man in early middle age when, in the novel of *The Pathfinder*, he reached Lake Ontario. A hunter he had been in his early days. Now he was a trapper, a figure already dim and prehistoric, emerging for a minute out of the prairie as out of some large early world, to guide the first steps of the settlers into what seemed to Cooper their last untenanted domain, and then to lie down beside his campfire in the prairie grass, and die.

Speaking as a symbol of the American man on the march, he says: "I was born on the seashore, though most of my life has been passed in the woods. . . . Seventy-five years have I been upon the road, and there are but half that number of leagues in the whole distance after you leave the Hudson on which I have not tasted venison of my own killing. . . . I often think the Lord has placed this barren belt of prairie behind the states, to warn men to what their folly may yet bring the land. Aye, weeks, if not months, may you journey in these open fields, in which there is neither dwelling nor habitation for man or beasts. Even the savage animals travel miles on miles to seek their dens; and yet the wind seldom blows from the East, but I conceit the sound of axes and the crash of falling timber are in my ears." Thus early did men begin to foresee the dilemma of the great dust bowl and the thriftless stripping of the land.

At the time when *The Prairie* was published civilization, advancing along the shores of the Great Lakes, entangled for the time deep in the woods of Wisconsin and eastern Minnesota, was beginning also to look westward to the prairies. The northernmost advance upon the wilds, which was the extension of New England and New York westward to Michigan, Wisconsin, and Minnesota and Iowa, had, of all the belts of settlement, the most orderly, prosperous, cleaned up behind them, brushed up in front of them, and educated as they went along look. That these terms should apply to anything so rudely magnificent as the fur trade seems incredible, but so it is.

For beyond the territory of Wisconsin, the country was

all one magnificent fur dominion. These somber forests, deep
cold lakes, fresh running streams, breaking into the endless
sweep of the open prairie rolling west to infinity, had been the
sacred preserve of the fur trade even before the Americans
took title to them. Zebulon Pike, in 1807, going along day
after day, upstream in canoe, across beautiful lakes, through
deep forests, out into open grass, in a land of brooks and
springs and sky-blue water, reported that British gentlemen of
the Northwest Fur Company were living here alone and with
apparent satisfaction. Pike could not understand this.

"I can only account for the gentlemen of the Northwest
Fur Company contenting themselves in this wilderness for
ten, fifteen, and some for twenty years by the attachment they
contract to the Indian women," wrote Pike. "It appears to me
that the wealth of nations would not induce me to remain
secluded from the society of civilized mankind, surrounded
by a savage and unproductive wilderness without books or
other sources of intellectual enjoyment or being blessed with
the cultivated and feeling mind of a civilized fair one."

2

Yet in the eighteen thirties the wilderness of the Northwest, including all of what is now Minnesota, part of Iowa,
and all land up to the heads of rivers emptying into the Missouri, was being managed by as polished a gentleman as ever
strayed out of a drawing room—H. H. Sibley, a partner in
John Jacob Astor's American Fur Company. When the
time came, he led his kingdom into the Union, as the state of
Minnesota, in the finest kind of shape, remarking that up in
his country the pistol and the bowie knife were not popular,
and that its history was not disgraced by the sanguinary conflicts that marked some other districts of the West.

As territorial delegate to the United States Congress, first
governor of Minnesota, commander of the forces that quelled
the Sioux Indians in 1862–1863, and regent of the university,
Sibley was the most prominent man in Minnesota from 1834

to 1891. His father had been delegate to Congress from Michigan territory and had been afterward United States District Attorney and Judge of the Supreme Court of the state of Michigan. His mother's family had come to Ohio as members of the Society of the Cincinnati, carrying a certificate of membership signed by George Washington himself. She had been educated at the Female Seminary of the Moravians at Bethlehem—then the best American school for girls. So Sibley brought into the fur trade the best professional tradition of the Northwest, and it is almost amusing to see with what an easy grace he managed a business which otherwise seems so rudely heroic, and reported it in polished English.

In the spring of 1829 Sibley began his career by securing a clerkship in John Jacob Astor's American Fur Company at Mackinac, Michigan. "It may seem strange," he says, "that men of education and culture could be induced to endure the hardships, perils, and exposure, incident to the life of an Indian trader. Nevertheless many such could be found among that class. The love of money was not the incentive, for rarely did the trader accumulate or become wealthy. There was a peculiar fascination in such a career, which once entered upon, was seldom abandoned. What constituted that fascination it would be difficult to describe except upon the theory that the tendency of civilized man when under no restraint is toward savagery as the normal condition of the human race. . . . In that wild region . . . one was liberated from all trammels of society, independent and free to act according to his own pleasure. Even the dangers which environed him gave zest to his own pleasure. Moreover, he was regarded by the savages among whom he was thrown as their superior, their counsellor, and their friend. When sickness prevailed in their families, he prescribed for them, when hungry he fed them, and in all things he identified himself with their interests and became virtually their leader. What wonder then that he should exercise so potent an influence on this wild race?"

He admits that he even liked the fights with rival fur companies because they were conducted "with chivalry." It was all right to seduce the Indians from loyalty to the other fur forts, or even to get into a fist fight with them over a valuable package of furs. War was war. But "when the principals met, as they frequently interchanged visits socially, no offensive allusion was made to the existing strife, which was looked upon as purely a matter of business." And if anyone was sick in the fur fort of your worst business enemy, you sent medicine. If you and your enemy were marooned in bad weather, you shared your supplies with him. Sibley deemed this a high and chivalrous way of living and enjoyed the various situations this code of enemy-friend involved him in, as much as if he were knight of a medieval castle, trying to think out his part under a Round Table code.

He also appreciated the basic virtue of the fur trade—the virtue of faithfulness. "It affords me pleasure to bear witness to the fidelity and honesty of the Canadian-French *voyageurs*. In after years, when at the head of a district, as partner of the great American Fur Company of New York, comprising the vast region north of Lake Pepin to the British boundary, and west to the streams tributary to the Missouri River, I had within my jurisdiction hundreds of traders, clerks, and *voyageurs*, almost all of whom were Canadian-French, and I found abundant occasion to prove their honesty and fidelity. In fact, the whole theory of the fur trade was based upon good faith between employers and the employed. Goods, amounting to hundreds of thousands of dollars, nay, millions, were annually entrusted to men, and taken to posts in the Indian country, more or less remote, with no guarantee of any return except the honor of the individual, and it is creditable to human nature that these important trusts were seldom if ever abused."

Once when Sibley was coming to Detroit on business, he learned that there was a serious epidemic of cholera in the city. He immediately told his boatmen that, since they all had families to care for, he would not expose them to the disease.

They were to let him land and proceed overland by carriage alone to the city, sixty miles distant. Immediately they protested that "they had accompanied me thus far, and they did not propose to let me run any risks which they did not share with me, and they hoped I would not insist on separating from them under any circumstances." They did more. They insisted on taking him up to the plague-stricken city in style. "They donned high-crowned hats with an abundance of tinsel cords and black plumes, calico shirts of bright tints exactly alike, and broad worsted belts around their waists. Being all fine athletic fellows, they made quite a striking appearance. The canoe had been gaily painted, and on this occasion two large black plumes and two of bright red of like dimensions adorned the bow and stern of our craft respectively. All things being in readiness, we took our several stations, and in a few moments under the impetus of nine paddles wielded by muscular arms, and the inspiration of a Canadian boat song, in the chorus of which we all joined, we shot down the current of the grand river of the Straits at almost railroad speed."

Is there a prettier scene in opera, than this? And this was no Don Fidelio out of an old legend but just an American capitalist coming back from Minnesota to Michigan on business!

Later, however, when Sibley and his crew were not allowed to land at Mackinac because they had been exposed to cholera, and his men begged to be allowed to take him up to the town anyway and fight their way in, he told them that here chivalry ended. They had been exposed to cholera, and cholera was no laughing matter to anyone. He had medicines and proper precautions all ready and they must obey the law and go into quarantine with him. So they paddled to an island to be quarantined. But the magistrate sent a messenger over to them about sunset, "being convinced by our healthy and vigorous appearance that there was no danger of cholera from contact with us. . . . Our friends were relieved and delighted at our escape from the perils through which we had passed, as nothing had been heard of us since our departure and rumors of disaster were rife." And so the story ends, with medieval French chivalry and modern medicine shaking hands across the wilderness!

3

Over his fur posts dotting the then wild woods and prairies of Minnesota Sibley ruled with amiable serenity. "There being no law," he said, "discipline had to be enforced with a strong hand, though as a general rule, the men were obedient and trustworthy." At a few of the posts, he says, the leaders in charge had a reputation for unusual severity. To these centers of punishment and hard labor men who proved intractable at other posts would be transferred. This was the trapper's equivalent of being "sold down the river."

A thorough gentleman himself, referring to Indian women politely and with respect, tactfully refusing the offer of an Indian girl for himself, he yet looked with indulgent, laughing eyes on the peccadilloes of his trappers. When they traveled, he said, their Indians always required the squaws to carry the baggage across the rivers. "It was the custom for certain lewd fellows of the baser sort," which, said Sibley, included most of the younger men among his trappers, "to gather on the banks and make impertinent allusions to any part of leg or thigh they caught a glimpse of as the waters lifted their skirts. Accordingly the mothers and friends of the young girls would gather and throw stones at the trappers and beat them off with sticks."

Snowed in by the severe Minnesota winter, Sibley says he entertained himself with reading. Among his business letters to New York is a long list of books to be shipped him, comprising most of the standard works of history and literature. When possible, he would visit Fort Snelling, the United States army post near what is now Saint Paul, where he could rest his eye on the fair faces and bright manners and costumes from the East of two or three white ladies. "The game of chess was the

favorite amusement in the garrison, officers and ladies par-
ticipating, and it served as a useful pastime in the evenings."

4

After Wisconsin became a state in 1846, Sibley's principality was detached from it and set up as a territory, and Sibley
went to Congress to represent it. Hearing that a fur trader was
coming down to their halls out of these Northern wilds, everyone was agog to see a great shaggy hero in coonskin cap. They
were amazed when a gentleman strayed in, instead, poised,
erect, serene, impeccably mannered and impeccably costumed,
saying, in effect, "I am Minnesota!"

As the settlers began to pour in, Sibley undertook to protect their interests from land speculators. When the site of
Saint Paul was exposed for sale, and well-dressed crowds
poured in from the East by steamers, ready to set up the city
almost overnight, Sibley, with his trappers at his back, appeared
to bid in lots for the settlers who were already there, breaking
the land and doing the hard work of getting the state ready
for these glossy newcomers. "When the time for business had
arrived, my seat was surrounded by men with huge bludg-
eons." And he adds, suavely, "What was meant I can only
surmise, but I would not have envied the fate of any individual
who would have ventured to bid against me." Reporting the
excellent good order in which the whole question of settlement was managed, Sibley modestly refrained from taking any
credit to himself and his fur posts. The fact was, he said, that
California and Oregon were being opened at the same time,
and all the bad characters were drawn off to those more interesting territories!

Opened to settlement, with Sibley thus graciously playing
host, the great fur principality was rapidly turned into a state
in the same cheerful, prosperous way in which first Michigan
and then Wisconsin, had been taken possession of. On the
sites of the twin cities at the head of navigation on the Mississippi, then called Saint Paul and Saint Anthony, now Saint

Paul and Minneapolis, there was happy excitement. There the housewife coming in could buy mahogany knobs, sleigh bells, and gridirons, gents' cravats, and silk gloves! There was a bakery advertising "cakes, butter crackers, Boston crackers, hard bread and loaf bread, in the latest New York style, and all kinds of candies by wholesale or retail." Already a brewer was demonstrating that "malt liquors of the very best quality can be manufactured in Minnesota." Towns were being tied to each other by stagecoach and sleighs running on regular schedules, "sleighs and carriages are covered and fitted up in a manner to render passengers as comfortable as possible, and no pains will be spared to make the passage as pleasant as can be in a country and on a road so new as this is." In this manner one could go back from Saint Paul to Prairie du Chien, and there connect with stages for Galena, Madison, and Dubuque. And just as the Southerners advanced on new territory with their Negroes ahead of them ready to grow cotton, so the Northwest was advancing on the prairie rolling its farm machinery ahead of it, all ready to grow wheat.

Meanwhile they amused themselves. On July 5, 1849, the Independent Order of Odd Fellows set up a lodge at Saint Paul; the next summer the Saint Paul Methodist Church was holding a fair by candlelight. A splendid bowling saloon had been set up in Saint Paul, and another was opened two years later in Saint Anthony. And on February 27, 1851, it was announced that "At Lott Moffatt's on the evening of February 27, there will be a ball, at which all gentlemen with their ladies, in Minnesota, are invited to be present." A Hunt Club was organized, its objects being "rational amusement, the sports of the chase, and the cultivation of taste for the history of the wild beasts, fowl, birds, and fish of the West."

The Northwest moving on from New England, New York, Ohio, Michigan, and Wisconsin, was carrying its culture with it. Ladies furnishing new houses were advised that they could get excellent copies of the celebrated painting of the Last Supper by da Vinci, and could buy paintings of the

Sioux warrior Wah-ah-cor-dah and the Indian maiden We-nona. They could purchase most standard books, and subscribe for *Punch*, and buy both classical music and the latest popular hits.

Meanwhile prospective farmers were out looking over the virgin domain of the fur traders with an interested eye. What an enthusiast said of it in 1870, men were already saying in 1845. "Wooded prairies, oak openings, hills and vales, watered by lakes and ponds—such is the character of the region lying south of Otter Tail. Over all this section the water is as pure as that gurgling from the hillsides of New Hampshire. Minnesota is one of the best watered states in the Union. The thousands of lakes and ponds dotting its surface are fed by never-failing springs. This one feature adds immeasureably to its value as an agricultural state. In Illinois, Iowa, and Nebraska the farmer is compelled to pump water for his stock and in those states we see wind mills erected for the purpose; but here the ponds are so numerous, and the springs so abundant that far less pumping will be required than in the other states of the Union."

Large and fresh, cool and clean, free from fret and strife, the vision of Minnesota began to shine over the counters of many a drygoods or grocery store back East, and the faint far-off blowing of wind in the pines, and waters murmuring, and birds rising with a whir from the prairie grass would steal like music into the racket of factory and workshop. "If I were a young man, selling corsets and hoop skirts to simpering young ladies in a city store, I would give such a jump over the counter that my feet would touch ground in the centre of a great prairie. I would have a homestead out here. True there would be hard fare at first. The cabin would be of logs. There would be short commons for a year or two. But with my salt pork I would have pickerel, prairie chickens, moose, and deer.

"I should have calloused hands and the backache at times, but my sleep would be sweet. I should have no theatre to visit nightly, no star actors to see, and I should miss the tramp of the great city, the ever-hurrying throng. The first year might be lonely; possibly I should have the blues now and then; but possessing my soul in patience in a twelve-month I should have neighbors. The railroad would come. The little log house would give place to a mansion. Roses would bloom in the garden, morning glories open their blue bells by the doorway. The vast expanse would wave with golden grain. Thrift and plenty and civilization with all its comforts and luxuries would be mine!"

5

South of Minnesota, west of Illinois and Wisconsin, north of Missouri, there was an immense golden prairie that no one knew what to do with. No one even knew to whom it belonged. It had been claimed by the French and ceded to the United States as a part of Louisiana. But the Indians possessed it, and the United States was inclined to leave them there. A Frenchman, Julien Dubuque, had in 1788 set up a fur post in the region of the lead mines and got from the Indians the exclusive right to trade in furs and mine lead at the same time. He had quite a settlement of miners and fur traders. The Indians refused to let other white men, besides Dubuque's colony, mine lead, and the troops of the United States sided with the Indians and undertook to keep this country for them.

The region was tied up first to one state, then to another. For a while it was called Louisiana; then it became part of Indiana Territory; then again Louisiana Territory; then Missouri Territory; then unorganized territory of the United States; then Michigan Territory; then Wisconsin Territory. Finally, in 1838, Wisconsin Territory was divided and the western half of it—this rich and lovely no man's land—was named Iowa.

During the long period when the United States government was trying to keep Iowa for the Indians the settlers were pressing north along the Mississippi, and trappers were going up and down across it, and everywhere government was being organized among the white men in voluntary associations, right in the face of an act of Congress, passed in 1807, forbidding such settlements. Finally a war was precipitated by Black Hawk, an Indian chief, a mimic war which did little except to give the Illinois militia a chance to parade and young Abraham Lincoln his only taste of battle. As a result the Indians ceded the country around the lead mines—9,000 square miles of land —to the United States, and it was formally opened for settlement in 1836.

Immediately the two lines of settlement began to meet and mix—the backwoodsmen coming up the river and the Easterners advancing by the northern route along the Erie Canal and the Lakes. The vehicle of the advance out into the prairie was the Conestoga wagon. Superseded in the East by the railroads and the canals, here were the old wagons—the white domes billowing like clouds upon the prairies, their horses snatching at the prairie grass, loaded with beds and bedding, frying pans and cooking pots, wives and children—homes on wheels, rolling bravely into illimitable space.

This advance on the Iowa prairie has its perfect chronicle in literature. One may read dozens of records by old settlers, dozens of pamphlets locally printed, and then turn to *Vandemark's Folly* by Herbert Quick, and there they are complete —the pure concentrated essence of them distilled in one perfect tale, so clear, so like the original, that one has a feeling, in reading it, that alone and singlehanded, in the person of the Dutch boy from New York, one has settled Iowa one's self. There are all the experiences as told and retold in the early records—the life of the Erie Canal, the trip up the lakes, the rascals and real-estate dealers, the purchase of the prairie wagon, the other line of wagons coming in from Tennessee and Kentucky. There are all the types—the New England grandmother, the sweet Kentucky girl, the young Southern daredevil, the Norwegian peasant, faithful and good. Wherever the Southern backwoodsmen, coming north, met and mingled with the Yankee migration, literature was born. So it was in Indiana, which burst forth with a whole series of tale-tellers and songsters, just as soon as the Yankee schoolteachers had time to teach the backwoodsmen to read and write. So in Wisconsin, Hamlin Garland, combining in himself these two strains, became the chronicler of the settlement. So Iowa became for the states west of the Mississippi what Indiana was to those east of it—the literary spokesman for "The Folks." Iowa has set itself down in American literature complete—its settlement in *Vandemark's Folly*, its slow dreary frontier life on the prairie in Howe's *Story of a Country Town*, its comfortable present in Ruth Suckow's stories—and then has contributed a few romantic exiles like Jig Cook, the founder of the Provincetown Players, to create a literature of discontent with our comfortable, corn-fed civilization.

Back in the East the settling of the prairie states was hailed as America's coming into her own. This was a new world—untouched by Europe, without monument and without precedent, making its own heroic life. Always beyond the settler's cabin were the still unpeopled spaces. Always among quiet homekeeping men, driving behind the plow, coming in with milk pails at night, were strangers, the mountain men from far off, the men with notches on their guns, with strange scars on their faces, with unbelievable skills and fearful histories. And back in the East the literary hacks woke up and, with a gleam in their eyes, seized upon their pens. Here was a theme to make them all Homers! Now they would write epics! And forthwith they began—and wrote westerns.

The poets felt the inspiration, too, and Bryant wrote

> There are the gardens of the Desert, there
> The unshorn fields, boundless and beautiful,
> For which the speech of England has no name—
> The Prairies.

And Walt Whitman, absorbing something everywhere said in his boyhood, wrote later, "Grand the thought that doubtless the child is already born who will see 100,000,000 of people, the most prosperous and advanced in the world, inhabiting the Prairies, the great Plains, and the valley of the Mississippi. It would be grander still to see all these illimitable American areas fused in the alembic of a perfect poem or other aesthetic work, entirely western, fresh and limitless, altogether our own, without a trace of Europe's soil, reminiscence, technical skill or letter."

And out in Nebraska and Iowa school children are reading Neihardt's epic of the fur trappers.

> And now no more the mackinaws come down
> Their gunwales low with costly packs and bales
> A wind of wonder in their shabby sails.
> Their homing oars flung rhythmic to the tide
> And never more the masted keelboats ride
> Missouri's stubborn waters on the lone
> Long zig-zag journey to the Yellowstone.
> Their hulks have found the harbor ways that know
> The ships of all the sagas, long ago,
> The moony haven where no loud gale stirs.
> The trappers and the singing voyageurs
> Are comrades now of Jason and his crew,
> Foregathered in this timeless rendezvous
> Where come at last all seekers of the Fleece.

19

THE OREGON TRAIL

WHILE Congress was wondering what to do with the states which the ambitious South was lugging in on prairie wagons from the Southwest, a Yankee clipper swooped down and deposited another runaway child in the national lap of discord. The Yankee contribution was the Oregon country out of which two states were later made—Oregon and Washington. It was the acquisition of the shipping enterprise of Boston, assisted by those New England missionaries who always went in the wake of the Yankee trade. And there were two other hopeful children in the brood—California, just taken from Mexico, but already colonized by Boston, and the Sandwich Islands, later to be tied into the Union as the Hawaiian Islands.

In our book *Gold of Ophir* we have already told the story of the Northwest coast and the China trade—how young John Ledyard, a runaway from Dartmouth College visiting this coast during the Revolutionary War, with Captain Cook, had first seen the possibility of a three-cornered trade in fur and tea between the Eastern cities, the Indians of the Northwest coast, and China; how he had ultimately "sold" this idea both to Thomas Jefferson in Paris and to a group of

Boston merchants; how this had led to the discovery of the Columbia by a Boston ship under the command of Captain Robert Gray; and how the trade thus inaugurated had been carried on with adventure and profit from the very beginning of our Republic.

This commerce remained the priceless monopoly of Boston. Other cities—Salem, Providence, New York, Philadelphia, even Baltimore—were soon in the East India trade up to their necks, getting rich, having a wonderful time; but they all took the safe and sane European route to the East around the Cape of Good Hope. Only the Boston ships beat their wild way around the Horn. On the Northwest coast the Indians supposed that Boston was the name for all of America and later called any Americans "Boston men." Young aristocrats were seasoned for their future as Boston merchants by being dispatched at seventeen or nineteen on a voyage to the Northwest coast, returning around the world by way of the Sandwich Islands. Most people with Boston relatives knew more about Oregon than they knew about any place west of Amherst. The story of this trade is mainly in the personal reminiscences of the merchants, especially of the most delightful and communicative of them all, William Sturgis. The letters exchanged among the personages in this Northwest-Sandwich Island-Canton trade are bound together in a large manuscript volume in the Harvard Library. On them we drew for choice quotations in our book *Gold of Ophir*, and those who are curious about this interesting adventure are referred to that chronicle.

While Boston was thus annexing Oregon and all outstanding territory, Ledyard's idea was sprouting in the fertile mind of Thomas Jefferson. To connect the Mississippi Valley and the Pacific Coast in the fur trade—what a possibility. Apparently this notion of Ledyard's was in Jefferson's mind when he dispatched Lewis and Clark to find their way through to Oregon and inquire into the prospects of the fur trade. And so the other half of the great trip planned by the Dartmouth boy was achieved—by somebody else.

Lewis and Clark went up the Missouri River and cut through to the sources of the Columbia, and so down that magnificent stream to the sea. What they found is described by Sydney Greenbie in the opening of his book *Frontiers and the Fur Trade*. "In a fast train one may now trace for a day or more the course of that river—the Columbia—which has become the name-sake of America herself. Vast fields of sage and sand and sauntering sand hills, then mountains of basalt and staggering cliffs, unpeopled amphitheatres. A low gray river, bright and full and cheerful, in spite of all the seeming desolation. Clouds of heat against domes of yellow earth, bleak yet heavenly. A stillness that is the compact of all sound. 'The land of Nod on the east of Eden.' Not a tree is to be seen, barely a patch of green turf, and only here and there a clump of sage. Fantastic forms of rock erosion rise like a cluster of men standing back to back as they were wont to do in pioneer days when attacked from all sides—massive promontories, blocked and squared, baked fortresses. . . .

"Thence over into Eden and to Oregon. Here the Columbia lies full and gracious, a river in every inch, down to the bar which separates it from the Pacific. From the summit of Coxcomb Hill at Astoria, one can see it coming down from the northeast, in full possession of itself and all the landscape about. It has business with the sea and concerns itself little with incidental intrusions. To the left lie the Lewis and Clark and Young rivers, pages attending their master."

Lewis and Clark had as a guide a young Indian girl, Sacajawea, who has been adopted as heroine of American tradition, the prototype of all Girl Scouts and Camp Fire Girls. In a book which claims to be her own story as passed down among the Indians, entitled *The Bird Woman*, there is the record not only of this winsome figure but of the white men as remembered by the Indians of the Northwest. Dim, prehistoric, mythological, the white men loom in Indian tradition. "Came now the rest of the white men and made camp, and we watched them, near crazy with wonder at them and the strange and useful things that they had. One of those white men was black. We could not believe that his skin was not covered with shining black paint, until one of us washed his fore-arm, scrubbing and scrubbing it without result. We were struck with the number of different shaped kettles in which the white men cooked their food. We marvelled at the number of fine long guns they carried, and oh, how we wanted to see what was in the many bundles that they carried from the boats to their camp. They had sharp, heavy, wooden handled pieces of shiny hard rock with which they cut wood; with but a few blows of one of them, they cut down good-sized trees. That was great medicine. . . ."

And so they went along, the young Indian girl leading and explaining, the tribes divided between suspicion and curiosity and simple-minded good will. And local verse puts in a claim for her, as tutelary goddess of these regions.

Some day, in the lordly upland where the snow-fed streams divide,
Afoam for the far Atlantic, afoam for Pacific's tide,
There, by the valiant captains whose glory will never dim,
While the sun goes down to the Asian sea, and the stars in ether swim
She will stand in bronze as richly brown as the hue of her girlish cheek,
With broidered robe and braided hair and lips just curved to speak;
And the mountain winds will murmur as they linger along the crest,
"Sho-Sho-ne Sa-ca-ga-we-a, who led the way to the West!"

—Edna Dean Procter

2

The next person to take up the idea of tying the western coast to the eastern by land and sea, was John Jacob Astor, a German-American of expansive ideas, who was engaged both in the fur trade and the East India trade. He conceived the idea of combining them both by running a line of fur posts across the country up the Missouri, through the Rocky Mountains by the trail opened by Lewis and Clark and kept open by the trappers, to Oregon, and establishing there a great fur mart, trading with the Orient and connected with the East by a line of ships. The story of this effort is delightfully told by Washington Irving in *Astoria*, with accounts of the troubles of the two expeditions which started for Astoria, the one across the continent by land, the other by sea, just before the War of 1812. Jefferson wrote Astor: "I considered as a great public acquisition the commencement of a settlement on that western coast of America, and looked forward with gratification to the time when its decendants should have spread themselves throughout the length and breadth of that coast, unconnected with us but by the ties of blood and interest, and enjoying like us the rights of self-government."

When the War of 1812 broke out, Astoria was captured by the British and held till 1818. By its restoration in 1818 the British tacitly recognized that the United States had some claim on the territory based upon the trading operations of the Boston ships for the last thirty years. But all this region had been preempted by the Hudson's Bay Fur Company, who held it effectively, with fortified posts, and who were not ready to welcome rivals or persons who might disturb game preserves with settlement and agriculture. So, when Astoria was returned it was agreed that the territory should not be claimed by either government but be left open for trading by both parties for the next ten years. At the end of this period the time was extended to another decade—until 1838.

3

While the China trade kept looking eastward from the
Sandwich Islands and the fur trade kept looking westward
from Saint Louis, and the trappers opened a zigzag course, up
the rivers, through the mountain defiles, it was the simple Indians, turning into myth the memory of the journey of Lewis
and Clark, who really started an effective movement to take
Oregon. In the fall of 1831 a pathetic little delegation from
the Indian country appeared in Saint Louis, two old chiefs
and two younger Indians, looking for General Clark, who
had come through their country so long ago. "They had
come," says Catlin, the artist, whose portraits of two of them
now hang in the National Gallery in Washington, "to inquire for the truth of a representation which they said some
white men had made amongst them that our religion was better than theirs and that they would all be lost if they did not
embrace it." Various tales about them were soon abroad.
Some said that they were seeking the "Great Book of
Heaven"—the Bible. Others said that they wished "Black
Robes"—that is, Jesuit priests, such as were known to the Indians of the Mississippi Valley, to be sent to them. General
Clark himself apparently understood that they were seeking
Catholic missionaries, for he put them in touch with Catholic
priests in Saint Louis. The good fathers baptized the two old
men, and when they both died that winter in Saint Louis,
held funeral services for them. Catlin, the artist, accompanied
the two younger ones on their way back, 2,000 miles up the
Missouri River, to the mouth of the Yellowstone, and painted
their pictures.

The Indians made quite a stir in the city that winter, and
one whose heart was touched by their plea was William
Walker, an educated Wyandot Indian who had come to
Saint Louis to make arrangements for moving some of his
tribesmen from Sandusky, Ohio, to the present state of Kansas. On March 1, 1833, he published in *The Christian Advo-*

cate and Zion's Herald, the principal publication of the Methodist Church, a moving tale of them, urging that missionaries be sent out to them.

So the original appeal for Catholic missionaries was answered first by Methodists and then by Presbyterians. The Methodists under Jason Lee established a mission among French Canadians and settlers in the Willamette valley, bringing their supplies around from Boston by sea, but themselves going overland. The Presbyterian mission became more famous, partly because it took westward the first white women, and one of them a very charming one, and partly because of the heroic character of its young leader and physician, Doctor Marcus Whitman.

In 1836, with a convoy of trappers of the American Fur Company Marcus Whitman and the Reverend Henry Spaulding set forth on the trail from Saint Louis, with their two brides and a young assistant named Goodyear—a little party of five in which were all the seeds of human drama. For Narcissa Whitman, young, lovely, with golden hair and broad white brow, had been wooed by both missionaries. The rejected suitor, bringing with him the bride he had since married, was a trouble all the way. "The man who came with us," wrote Narcissa to her father, "is one who ought never to have come. My dear husband has suffered more from him in consequence of his wicked jealousy and his great pique toward me than can be known in this world." And apparently there was a fourth sufferer in this tragic quartet, for the girl whom Spaulding had married in "pique" was an invalid all the way, and thereafter in Oregon, though apparently a lady not without courage.

But young and radiant, carrying with her all the glory and trouble of being a woman, Narcissa set forth on the trail and for 2,000 miles was a wonder and an excitement. Indians in families, in companies and tribes gathered above the passes to look at her; hardened trappers saw her go by with wistful eyes. At the rendezvous at Green River, where they

found the trappers and Indians gathered together, in their annual circus, the American Fur Company turned the missionaries over to the Hudson's Bay trappers, who escorted them
through to Oregon.

The principal excitement of the journey was caused by
Doctor Whitman's determination to drive a wagon through.
This wagon meant a great deal to the far-seeing physician. If
a wagon could go through the mountains, then settlers could
follow by this trail bringing their baggage and their wives
and children. If not—but he would not contemplate that
possibility. The wagon was going through. The trappers
naturally thought the wagon a nuisance, and even Narcissa
developed a hate for it. When crossing the present boundary
between Idaho and Wyoming, she wrote: "Husband had a tedious time with the wagon to-day. It got stuck in the creek this
morning when crossing and he was obliged to wade in considerably in getting it out. After that in going between the mountains, on the side of one, so steep that it was difficult for horses
to pass, the wagon upset twice; did not wonder at this at all; it
was a greater wonder that it was not turning somersaults continually. It is not very grateful to my feelings to see him wearing out with such excessive fatigue. . . . He is not as fleshy as
he was last winter. All the most difficult part of the day he has
walked, in laborious attempts to take the wagon." Ten days
later she wrote again: "One of the axle trees of the wagon
broke to-day. I was a little rejoiced; for we were in hopes
they would leave it. Our rejoicing was in vain, for they are
making a cart of the back wheels this afternoon, and lashing
the fore wheels to it—intending to take it through in some
shape or other."

So was the Oregon trail blazed, by one determined man
pushing, pulling, dragging, mending, forcing four wheels to
travel on. Yet even so, Whitman did not get his wagon
through. At Fort Hall, a fur post owned by Nathaniel
Wyeth, a merchant of New England interested in settling
Oregon, they stopped and rested and argued about the

wagon. Goodyear, Whitman's young assistant, said that
either he or the wagon would have to quit. Whitman said he
could spare Goodyear better than the wagon. So leaving
Goodyear behind they went on with their wheels. But at
Fort Boise, the post of the Hudson's Bay Company, now
Boise, Idaho, even Whitman gave up. It was enough to get
themselves through the mountains now. The last part of their
journey was made by boat down the Columbia to Fort Vancouver, the fur post of the Hudson's Bay Company.

Fort Vancouver is a tradition in the early records. In the
eyes of American immigrants, it appears to have been the
next thing to Valhalla, heavenly palace of the Norse gods.
"Fort Vancouver was fortified in grim fashion," says Mrs.
Dye. "There was a stout palisade of fir posts, twenty feet
high, sharpened at both ends and driven into the ground.
There were thick double ribbed and riveted gates in front
and rear, ornamented with brass padlocks and prodigious
keys. A grim old three-storied log-tower formed a bastion at
the northwest corner, bristling with port-holes and cannon.
Some rough hewn stores, magazines, and work shops were
ranged inside the enclosures, with an open court in the middle where the Indians brought their game and peltries. Directly opposite the main entrance stood the governor's residence, a somewhat pretentious two-story structure of heavy
timber morticed Canadian fashion and painted white. Here
Doctor John McLoughlin, Governor of the Hudson's Bay
Company west of the Rocky Mountains, and his chief aide
Douglas, afterwards knighted Sir James, First Governor of
British Columbia, dispensed hospitality after the fashion of
Saxon thanes or lairds of a Highland castle."

As they approached the fort, the *voyageurs*, gathering to
see them come in, raised their voices in a song of welcome,
and Doctor McLoughlin, coming to the gate, offered his arm
to Mrs. Whitman and escorted her in like a visiting queen.

A wonderful man, Doctor McLoughlin. Nothing can
quite bring him down to ordinary size. He pervades the early

record, vast, omniscient, all-powerful. To the several missionary families and other settlers who now began to arrive in
Oregon, by land and sea, he was guardian, instructor, and
friend.

The first thing he usually did was to induct them into the
possibilities of agriculture, by taking them to see his farm. It
covered 3,000 acres "fenced into beautiful fields, sprinkled
with dairy houses, herdsmen and shepherd's cottages," and
provided food for 700 people at the Post. His small private
garden was no less wonderful, with its graveled paths and
strawberry plants trained along the edges of them. Garden-
ing being the favorite avocation of the Yankee ladies, they
usually started in with great energy to emulate Doctor Mc-
Loughlin's horticulture. This entertained him very much.
Every few days an emissary would come to the missionaries
bringing them a huge beet from his garden as a present, or a
specimen of rare fruit, and challenging them to beat that!

Between the Yankee ladies and the example of Doctor
McLoughlin, housekeeping in Oregon was from the first
something to wonder at. No frontier messiness and clumsi-
ness here! They did everything in style. We managed, said
one lady later, to produce a "tidy brown linen cloth, bright
tin plates, knives and forks." And with the table so nicely set,
they had "fried venison, sausages, unbolted bread, butter,
fried cakes, and a bountiful dish of strawberries for dessert."
Next to a well-set table, a trim costume was the gift of the
Yankee woman to the frontier. Even while camping out, the
ladies are proud to record that they "managed to attire themselves neatly and prettily!"

The delightful record of this early Oregon housekeeping
is to be found in a book published in 1850 in Ithaca, New
York, entitled *Ten Years in Oregon, Travels and Adventures
of Doctor E. White and Lady*. It includes copies of various
resolutions drawn up for their own government by the first
settlers before territorial government was established, and a
copy of the petition for territorial government. All the little

details about dinners and wardrobes are in this book. Doctor McLoughlin pervades it, a personage, vast, genial, yet cantankerously and amusingly Scotch. And through it runs always the vision of the mountains. "Towering mountains, solemn forests, and pleasant glades where the beams of the setting sun crept gently and rested lovingly on the greensward."

4

Doctor E. White was Elijah White, one of the missionaries, who returning to the East brought through, in 1841, the first considerable band of settlers, consisting of 112 persons. He also brought to Whitman some very disturbing letters. Rumors of dissension among the missionaries and their dissatisfaction with each other's efforts to convert the Indians had got through to the mission board in Boston. Much of this dissension was due to Spaulding, the unhappy man who had once been Narcissa's suitor and had carried into the wilderness his "pique" against her and jealousy of her husband. He was apparently a good man, devoted and hard working, but he was not happy; his wife was an invalid; he could not work with other people. So the Board sent out word discharging him, recalling some other members of the mission, and ordering the discontinuance of some of the mission stations. To Doctor Whitman this was a great blow. He saw this faraway corner of the continent connected with the East through the Boston ships and with the line of settlements fast moving westward beyond the Mississippi, as a normal part of the great American Union. The work of civilizing the Indians was valuable in itself, for, with missions as a nucleus of training and good will for the natives, the coming settlement might avoid many of the difficulties of other states.

Though winter was coming on, and no one knew better than Whitman what the snow-filled mountain passes were like, he determined to start east to lay before the people there the whole question of Oregon. Amos L. Lovejoy, a lawyer from Massachusetts, who had come out with Doctor White's party, "for his health," agreed to ride back with Whitman. They started on horseback and, riding at breakneck speed to beat the coming winter, made the journey of 500 miles to Fort Hall in eleven days. There they turned southward through the mountain passes to Taos, still trying to beat the snows, but the snows overtook them. The guide lost his way in the storms. Whitman made his way back to Fort Uncompahgre and obtained another guide, while Lovejoy stayed behind alone with the pack animals. Then they fought their way on through passes full of snow; over streams already filling with fantastic towers and spires of ice; over wind-swept mountain heights, freezing, starving, on for thirty days, until they reached Taos. From Taos they got to Bent's Fort. Here, in that old "adobe castle," as Susan Magoffin had called it, there was something like comfort and relaxation. Here poor Lovejoy collapsed, but Doctor Whitman joined a company of Santa Fe traders and went on to civilization.

Whitman, arriving in the East, saw the members of his Board and persuaded them to let him keep the missions at Waiilatpu and Lapwai open, though without helpers to replace those who had left. He visited Washington and there discussed with the Secretary of War the question of establishing a safe and open way across land for emigrants to Oregon. Whitman's suggestion was that along the trail already opened, and partly provisioned by the trappers, there should now be established by the United States government a chain of farming and supply stations. An outline for such a bill was drawn up by Whitman and sent to Secretary Porter, in whose office it was filed and forgotten.

This was Whitman's famous "ride" to save Oregon. A misinterpretation of this episode during the later boundary dispute with Great Britain represented Whitman dashing wildly east on horseback to save Oregon from imminent taking by the British. At the time of the ride, however, the British recognized the right of Americans to settle southward from the Columbia. The question at issue was only how far north the American settlers were entitled to go, but this had nothing to do with Whitman's ride. His problem was to make safe the road to Oregon across territory owned by the United States, and to get both the government and the churches to recognize the actual fact of settlement. The apathy of the government was due largely to the vexatious problem of balancing free state against slave, and to the strong pull of the South on the federal government. Besides, there were many sensible people who thought that we were not half using the territory we already had. Let people stay nearer home and make the most of what the Lord had given them!

5

Meanwhile a thousand settlers had gathered for a march on Oregon, and Doctor Whitman went back with them in the spring, doctoring, advising, guiding all the way, though the actual pathfinding was done by a trapper, Captain John Gantt. The organization and government of this great traveling mass, with their sixty wagons, and thousands of animals on the trail over which Doctor Whitman ten years before had found it almost impossible to push one wagon, was very interesting. It was described with much charm and gusto years later by one of its members, the Honorable Jesse Applegate in *A Day with the Cow Column of* 1843.

"A good marching day, covering, with luck, about twenty miles began at four o'clock in the morning with a discharge of rifles by the sentinels. While the breakfast fires were being lighted in front of the tents, sixty men herded in the great mass of five thousand animals spread in a radius of two miles around the encampment.

"From six to seven breakfast is eaten, the children prepared for the day, and the little items of comfort for mothers with babies were disposed in the wagons. At seven o'clock, the clear notes of the trumpet sound the call to march, and they are off. There are sixty wagons, divided into fifteen platoons. Each platoon is entitled to lead in its turn, the leading platoon to-day being put in the rear to-morrow. But wagons slow to assemble are penalized by being put last. When the line of march forms, there is first the guide, Captain John Gantt, with his aides on horse-back. Then a band of stalwart young men on horses, prepared for a buffalo hunt, and well armed in case of attack by Indians. Then come the wagons, and after that the herders bring up the rear with the animals. The clear notes of a trumpet sound in the front; the pilot and his guards mount their horses; the leading divisions move out of the encampment, and take up the line of march; the rest fall into their places with the precision of clock work, until the spot so lately full of life sinks back into the solitude that seems to reign over the broad plain and rushing river as the caravan draws its lazy length toward the distant El Dorado."

The end of the day, as described by Applegate, is quite idyllic. "It is not yet eight o'clock when the first watch is to be set; the evening meal is just over, and the corral now free from the intrusion of cattle or horses, groups of children are scattered over it. The larger are taking a game of romps; the wee toddling things are being taught that great achievement that distinguishes man from the lower animals. Before a tent near the river a violin makes lively music, and some youths and maidens have improvised a dance upon the green; in another quarter a flute gives its mellow and melancholy notes to the still night air, which, as they float away over the quiet river, seem a lament for the past rather than a hope for the future."

West of Leavenworth there was no means of enforcing law, and no courts. So justice was improvised in the marching columns of immigrants, as at the fur forts. Already there was a strong opposition to the ready shooting in which the wilder sections of the South still took pride. "It was an unwritten law of the plains," says Meeker, that "all grievances, misdemeanors, or accusations of crime must be laid before a jury of elderly men; and no one should take the law into his own hands—in a word, no mob violence." So Doctor Whitman's traveling company of a thousand had its own ruling body. "It was a senate composed of the ablest and most respected fathers of the emigration. It exercised both legislative and judicial powers and its laws and decisions proved it equal and worthy of the high trust reposed in it. Its sessions were usually held on days when the caravan was not moving. It first took the state of the little commonwealth into consideration; revised or repealed rules defective or obsolete, and enacted such others as the exigencies seemed to require. The commonweal being cared for, it next resolved itself into a court to hear and settle private disputes and grievances."

Thus, in marching columns of emigrants was developed a standard of self-government and a personal ethics for the West. The general routine and the basic standards were inherited from the trapping companies, and were communicated to the emigrants by the trappers who served as guides. The grizzled old trapper riding along with the young boys would illustrate at every rock and precipitous turn in their wild course the code of his kind, telling them a story of someone who had, alone and unaided, done what men trusted him to do, and perhaps had died for it there.

The simple routines and ethics of the trappers the educated intelligence of men like Doctor Whitman expanded with all the inherited American ideals of self-government. In physical hardihood and resolution Whitman yielded to no trapper. When they reached the Laramie River and found it flooded, Whitman had the wagons lashed together to make a ferryboat. "No one was willing to risk himself in swimming the river and carrying the line but Doctor Whitman, which he did successfully." When they found the North Platte flooded, Doctor Whitman swam his horse into the boiling current again and again till he had located a ford and then conducted the wagons safely across.

It is hard to be so useful a man in an empty world. Before Doctor Whitman got his emigrants safe to their homes, a mes-

senger met him calling him to attend illness at the Spauldings',
and before he could return and meet his wife who was waiting for him in Oregon, he was called to attend the confinement of one of the ladies of another mission. When he finally
was free to see his wife, he found that an Indian had made an
assault on Mrs. Whitman at midnight in her room, but had
been driven off by a Hawaiian employed at the mission. Mrs.
Whitman had then been taken to Fort Vancouver for protection. Meanwhile, the emigrants came safely through under
the guidance of an old Indian chief named Istikus. Whitman
helped them to settle with whatever facilities the missions
could offer, and Doctor McLoughlin magnificently made up
the deficit.

The first settlements were mainly in the valley of the
Willamette, running southward from Portland to Salem, but
despite Doctor McLoughlin's efforts to discourage any progress north of the river, the settlers pressed in here and there
into what is now the state of Washington. Doctor McLoughlin and the British interests in general thought that the American line should run along the Columbia. A few wished to extend the American country as far north as the fifty-fourth
parallel, which would have included the magnificent country
that is now British Columbia. But in 1846 the matter was settled very reasonably by continuing the boundary of the
United States westward along the forty-ninth parallel, which
gave us what was later the state of Washington.

In the excitement of the 1844 campaign "Fifty-four forty
or fight" became a slogan of the more belligerent American
expansionists. The reason for the belligerency is rather complex. Oregon had been paired with Texas, in the great North-
ern-Southern controversy. So unthinking Democrats squared
off the whole question of the two territories by saying: "If
Mexico objects to taking Texas, fight Mexico; if Great Britain objects to taking Oregon, fight Great Britain." This was
to sweeten Northern opinion with regard to impending bullets on the Southern frontier. But the New Englanders,

whose country Oregon really was, kept protesting that no
one ought to fight anybody. Fortunately the British were of
a like mind. Their claim to land as far south as the Columbia
was entirely reasonable, but this territory had ceased to be of
much use to the Hudson's Bay Company. So the matter was
amicably adjusted, and like many other details in our relations to our great neighbor to the north stands as a precedent
for civilized behavior between nations.

6

The migration of 1843 established Oregon as a place with
real claims to territorial government. For two years the settlers went along governing themselves, under the aegis of
Fort Vancouver. "We are much in want of a currency and
a market," they wrote, "American merchants being as yet a
slender reliance and in view of the large emigrating parties
last year, we should be greatly distressed for necessary articles
of wearing apparel but for the commendable spirit of accommodation on the part of the Hudson's Bay Company."

Previous to the granting of territorial government there
were in 1845 official reports of general "health, cheerfulness,
and prosperity," excellently functioning courts, and good
schools. The missionaries and the cooperation of Fort Vancouver were commonly credited with the ease and good order
with which settlement was achieved. To the Protestants had
now been added some excellent Catholic missions answering
the plea of the Indians for "Black Robes" and meeting the
needs of the many French settlers who had been *voyageurs*
with the fur companies. One of these Catholic missionaries,
Father De Smet, a Belgian who became an American citizen,
was the great mediator all through the Western country between the Indians and the white men. Incessantly traveling
up and down through the whole Western land, voyaging
around the Horn, and nineteen times across the Atlantic, his
travels were said to have covered a mileage equal to nine
times around the earth. He spent years in remote places in the

mountains where there was neither salt, sugar, tea nor coffee, and was sometimes for years out of reach of a letter. A charming person, gracious, humorous, gentle, and resolute, he combined almost fabulous powers of physical endurance with great personal courage, and an ability to act sharply and with decision. Once when threatened by an Indian bully, he knocked the hatchet out of the man's hand, horsewhipped him till he cried for mercy, and then forced him to go back to his tribe and tell just what had happened to him. Yet he was the heroic and indefatigable friend of the Indians, and the blood he kept them from shedding and the white men from shedding in retaliation might fill a considerable sea.

The Catholic missionaries and the Protestants worked co-operatively for the civilization of the Indians, and especially for their training in agriculture; but the Indians themselves grew increasingly restive. The great increase in the number of white settlers aroused their fear and suspicion; and the delay in getting effective government organized because of the disputes in Congress over slavery was making adequate means of self-defense difficult. All the missionaries and priests knew of an approaching storm among the Indians, but they hoped by tact and kindness to placate them.

Then it happened. A Catholic father, the Reverend J. B. A. Brouillet, heard, to his horror, that Indians had surrounded the Whitman mission. Rushing thither, he found the place in ruins, Doctor Whitman and Narcissa dead, amidst the corpses of their helpers, and Stanfield, a Frenchman who had been a helper at the mission, laboring to bring the bodies of the slain to a great grave he had dug for them and to prepare them for burial. Taking the mission sheets for shrouds, the priest helped him to lay out the bodies decently, and to place them in the grave, and then he read the burial service over them—the Indians who had attacked the mission standing at a distance, painted and armed.

Meanwhile, hearing that a number of the missionaries, including most of the women, had been taken captive, a rescue party from Fort Vancouver under Peter Skene Ogden, an intrepid trader, started up the river, and overtaking the captives ransomed them with sixty-three cotton shirts, sixty-two blankets, twelve company guns, 600 loads of ammunition, thirty-seven pounds of tobacco, and twelve flints. The Catholic bishop of the mission at Willamette was using his influence to quiet the Indians and to prevent reprisals by the whites. But as the trouble spread among the Indians, the settlers met and organized defense, the Hudson's Bay Company advancing supplies up to $1,000, and Joseph Meek, a fearless mountain man, was dispatched to Washington to urge the organization of Oregon as a territory and to secure means of defense. The bill for organizing Oregon had long been before Congress, but had been held up by the effort of the Southerners to include even in this Northern state a clause authorizing slavery. Slavery was the last thing the settlers in Oregon wanted or could use. What they needed was soldiers and the right to guard themselves. Their heroic missionary and his wife were dead, and the wolves had dug up and eaten their bodies, so hastily buried by the Catholic priest. The trading company of a foreign power was protecting them, rescuing them, ransoming them, and equipping them. And all a Congress dominated by Southerners could do was to sit in Washington and argue about ways and means of giving them black slaves!

So, amidst the whistling of bullets on that far frontier and the blood-curdling war whoop of the Indians, Oregon was finally accepted into the Union. To the embattled settlers in that far place it seemed that it was high time. Despite the high character of Doctor Whitman's emigrants, and the many men of education and capacity in the territory, the presence of civilized settlements was making it an attractive hangout for bad characters from the mountains and the sea. The Indian subagent, making his report to the United States government wrote: "As sub-agent I have had much to contend with in the midst of lawless Indians of so many different tribes and lawless whites of so many different nations, some bred on the old whale ships, others in the Rocky Mountains, and hundreds on the frontiers of Missouri."

But this is only a shadow in an otherwise high, bright, clean picture. Despite the great splash of blood in which the heroic record of the Whitmans ends and the territorial government begins, the states of Washington and Oregon had a noble history of settlement, politically and socially intelligent, prosperous and orderly from the start, with high standards of housekeeping and agriculture, and all the arts and appurtenances of civilization. Something is due to the Boston ships and Boston tradition which sent people out there properly selected with proper provision; much is due to the missionaries who set the standard of housekeeping and agriculture and did something to mediate between the white men and the Indians; but much is to be credited, too, to the personality of Doctor McLoughlin. It is something unique in the history of nations, the precious heritage of the English-speaking races on this continent, that a man representing another government and a great commercial monopoly whose interests were said not to be served by the settlers' invasion, should have reached across a disputed boundary in such wise and chivalrous daily helpfulness and should have been so wholeheartedly adopted as the culture hero of a people engaged in setting themselves up under a rival flag!

20

THE DESERT STATE OF DESERET

HE strangest and most romantic of the runaway states was the desert state of Deseret—Deseret meaning "The Beehive"—which began knocking at the door and wanting to come in shortly after the territory on which the bees were building their hive had come into the possession of the United States.

This was the community of the Mormons in Utah. Driven out of their city of Nauvoo, which they had made the largest and most beautiful city in Illinois, these determined pioneers had in 1847 made their way over the plains and into the territory still claimed by Mexico. Brigham Young, riding ahead of his pioneers, pointed to the sagebrush and the barren hills, and said, "This is the place," and the hearts of his brave and dusty band answered in the words of the prophet Isaiah, "for in the wilderness shall waters break forth, and streams in the desert."

But they did not wait for God to produce the waters for them. They proceeded to lay out Salt Lake City, and themselves to lead streams from the mountains into it. "For all its bleakness," writes Sydney Greenbie, "its desert, its surrounding chain of naked, snow-spread mountains, Salt Lake City is

390

a romantic, impressive town. Even the simple story of the Mormons is a chapter in courage and conquest not to be forgotten. Scenically, it makes one dream away on the wings of distance—sad-eyed, frugal, stingy, but magnificent. Coming east from California through hundreds of miles of the absurd Joshua trees and the shrivelled humble sage, it was over-powering. The desert had been sprinkled with rain, and the rain had sprinkled the sand with color—vast daubs of lemon colored baby flowers, great splashes of purple flowerets, gray little flowers that seemed forlorn and old at the first flush of being —all against the Nevada after-noon sun and the lonely mountains. Something there is in this negative world that touches the soul, perhaps because of the patience abiding in these decaying hills, patience in decay.

"And to think that here a man could have said with hope and vision, 'This is the promised land. This is the world that appeared as an offering of the Lord. Here we will set up our kingdom.' It seems to me that no such courage could be trifling—no such dream anything short of a miracle. And the miracle came. Their first spring, so the legend goes, the harvest had only just come up when the mountain crickets came in clouds to devour it. Desperate, they turned to prayer. Prayer brought them from the unseen ocean flocks of sea gulls who set to devouring the pests, disgorging as they ate, but destroying the creatures. So the sea gull has become the bird of the state of Utah." A special law protects the sea gulls, and when they are seen against the sky, the reverent Mormon sees in them still the birds of God. In a green park, rising sheer out of a pool of water, stands the sea-gull monument, sculptured by Mahonri Young, grandson of Brigham Young, and inscribed "Sea Gull Monument Erected in Grateful Remembrance of the Mercy of God to the Mormon Pioneers."

2

The Mormon Church was founded in 1830 by Joseph Smith, a young Vermont Yankee in Palmyra, in western New

York, and named the Church of the Latter-day Saints, and incorporated under the laws of the state of New York. Its leader was twenty-five years old, a youth of no local importance, and it had but six charter members. This young man told a strange story. This story as officially related in the present publications of the Mormon Church was that in 1823, when he was still a lad in his teens, "he was directed by a heavenly messenger to a hill not far from the place of his residence, known now as the hill Cumorah, where there was disclosed to him a stone box in which were hidden plates of gold with engravings thereon and instruments for their translation, all of ancient origin. After a time the contents of this box were placed in his possession, and he spent many arduous and eventful months in making a translation of the ancient characters engraved on the plates. He made the translation, as he testifies, with the aid of instruments which were with the plates and with certain spiritual endowments which were given to him. He had assistance in the writing of the translation and a number of other persons saw the plates and handled them. He caused a book to be printed and published in Palmyra, New York, from the translations which he made, which was called *The Book of Mormon*."

Within a year after the founding of the Church of the Latter-day Saints, it had grown from six persons to a membership of 1,500, all of whom believed Smith's story and were ready to abide by his moral and social revelations. "He stood trial on unfounded charges forty times during his life, each time being acquitted. He went into a hostile jurisdiction to face a charge under guarantee of adequate protection on the part of the Governor of the State. The promised protection failed, and he was assassinated in cold blood by a mob, martyr to the cause he espoused." He was thirty-nine at the time of his death. "The story of his life," says the Mormon account, "reads like the history of the Saviour whose representative his followers claim him to be. . . . In more than a hundred years the church has never departed from the organization and principles given to it by the prophet Joseph Smith. All its leaders have built upon the foundations which he laid. Its elaborate social system, its extensive holdings of church and commercial property, its important place in the life and development of communities, its unique and characteristic doctrines, the allegiance and fidelity of its members, and its almost unparalleled history of sacrifice and consecration are all attributable primarily to the inspiration, revelation, devotion, and spiritual power of a humble, faithful, unschooled young man."

This young man was a Yankee. It is not difficult to see in him a family resemblance to Johnny Appleseed—and even to Thoreau and Emerson; to hear occasionally in his sentences an echo of the great Jonathan Edwards. He told a fantastic story and embellished the Christian record with what seems to the modern person an extravagant mythology. But this kind of imaginative thinking was current at the time, partly through the influence of Swedenborg, and visions of a similar type sustained Johnny Appleseed as he tended his blossoming apple trees and breathed from their sweet opening buds the winds of Paradise. Neither the thinking nor the imaginative vision, though strange, is to be despised. "Voyaging strange seas of thought alone," the New England mind had come out on far and fantastic shores. But in Smith's aphorisms: "The glory of God is intelligence"; "It is impossible for man to be saved in ignorance"; "Whatever principle of intelligence we attain unto in this life will rise with us in the resurrection," there spoke, true and ringing, the faith of New England—the faith in intelligence, the will to work hard at learning. When he said, "Adam fell, that man might be," he was making a challenge of the thought that Hawthorne turned over and over in his mind, ruminating on destiny and sin. "This is the work and glory of God; to bring to pass the immortality and eternal life of man," spoke again with the voice of Jonathan Edwards. "And men are that they might have joy" was that smile of confidence and hope which was beginning to light up the face of Puritanism, which shone serene in the gray eyes of Emerson.

There are elements in this complex Mormon theology which have a great appeal to the imagination, and cement anew the ties of human relationship. One is the doctrine of celestial marriage. A man and a woman truly loving each other may be sealed by a priest of the Church to each other in marriage through all eternity, and the children that come to them will come back as their own from age to age, one family going on forever together through all lives, and all probation of experience. Less appealing, but still with a powerful pull at the heartstrings is the idea that one's ancestors—forefathers who were never fortunate enough to hear the Revelation—may be drawn into the Church through the prayers and devotion of their descendants. "The spirit of man not only never dies but lives through stages of eternal progression." Into this progression with one's self may be drawn the spirits of one's own family who have gone before. A genealogical society within the Church fosters the practice of and provides facilities for the accumulation of information about the ancestry of its people. This is to revive the cohesion within the group fostered by the Oriental doctrine of ancestor worship—the vanished fathers and mothers of the race keeping their place by the hearth and receiving the daily honor of the family. But, like the doctrine of celestial marriage, it has a characteristically Occidental and American turn. One's ancestors do not determine one's salvation, but one determines, to some extent, that of the ancestors. The celestial marriage is not made, as marriages are in the East, by the family. It is the consecration of personal choice.

The doctrine which aroused the greatest fear, and which was mainly responsible for the long persecution of the Church, was that of plural marriages. "Plural marriage," says the modern apologist for the Church, "was considered by the Church to be a very sacred principle. Only those who were regarded as being worthy and exemplary in life and conduct and devotion to the Church were permitted to enter into it. It was surrounded by the Church with many limitations and safeguards which were calculated to invest it with lofty, idealistic motives." Like many other among the Mormon arrangements, this plural marriage was practically useful in a frontier world. It gave to women members of the Church home and protection in the hunted wandering life, and brought up many sons and daughters within the family fold. Since 1890 plural marriage has been abandoned by the Church, "and the Church has prosecuted offenders against this injunction."

Of this and the many other Oriental elements in the doctrine of Mormonism, it must be said that New England had for more than a generation been engaged in the great China and India trade. Throughout the great Yankee belt stretching across the Northern country, through New York, Ohio, Michigan, westward, where Mormonism developed, there were probably few families but had some relatives that had gone out to the East, few families to which letters did not come back from Canton, or Bombay, or Singapore. For fifty years New Englanders had been going about in Oriental societies, looking with intelligent, curious eyes on other kinds of civilization, making friends among men who lived in ways quite different from their own. They had learned to see sense and reason in many social arrangements which were outrageous to homekeeping men. They had taken up and woven into the fabric of their thought doctrines by which elsewhere they saw men live nobly—doctrines of preexistence, of family relationships persisting through the ages. Nothing is clearer than that extremely able and intelligent people embraced the doctrines of the Latter-day Saints. They were capable men, highly educated men, some of those first saints, well-read men. There were obviously widespread circles of thinking people to whom Smith's doctrine was truly a revelation. And this must have been because it gathered together in one working unit a number of ideas which were current as the radical thinking of the Yankee belt.

This radical thinking had a strongly socialistic trend. Indeed there was some reason in the complaint of the Southerners that the Yankees in general were socialists. Various schemes for communistic or semicommunistic living were tried in New England, among them the experiment of Brook Farm. Factory owners, as at Lowell, Massachusetts, experimented with communal work and living. A successful community which combined radical doctrines of sex and of labor was founded by another Vermont Yankee at Oneida, New York. This kind of thinking also entered into the substance of Mormonism, making possible a great deal of successful communal enterprise—such as the remarkable irrigation and city water systems in Utah. The eminently prosperous state of Utah, with its high standard of living, is an outgrowth of the same kind of effort that sprinkled the country at the time with short-lived religious and radical "communities."

All the various doctrines which elsewhere seemed "half baked," or more or less crazy, were welded in Mormonism into one consistent whole, making a system of life which was worked out with great social wisdom, and which proved able to sustain a very high standard of living and personal happiness, well rounded, and possessing, both in its visible structures —such as its buildings—and in some of its ideas, a strange and original beauty of its own. The Church drew into itself the best procedures and practical standards of the Yankee belt where it developed and applied them to new conditions of frontier life with imagination and originality and what a Yankee would call "etarnal grit."

3

The Church of the Latter-day Saints began its experiment in community making at Kirtland, Ohio, on Lake Erie, near Cleveland, but was looking out for open territory in the West where it could develop unhampered by the enmity of an already established community. This it seemed to find in Missouri. So to the frontiers of Missouri the Mormons set out. E. F., the jaunty Yankee who was wandering around then in Illinois and along the Mississippi River, met some of the Mormons and reported a long talk with one of them in which this person had told him that "Joe Smith or Joe Smith's father or the devil or some other great personage had somewhere dug up golden plates on which was graven the *Book of Mormon;* that this all mysterious and much-to-be-admired book embraced the chronicles of the lost kings of Israel; that it derived its cognomen from one Mormon, its principal hero, son of Lot's daughter, king of the Moabites; that Christ was crucified on the spot where Adam was interred; that the descendants of Cain were all now under the curse, and no one could possibly designate who they were; that the Saviour was about to descend in Jackson County, Missouri; and that all who were not baptized by Joe Smith or his compeers and forthwith repaired to Mount Zion, Missouri, aforesaid, would assuredly be cut off and that without remedy.

"And yet . . . with all his nonsense, my Mormonite was by no means an ignorant fanatic. He was a native of Virginia, and for fifteen years had been a pedagogue west of the Blue Ridge, from which edifying profession, he had at length been enticed by the eloquence of sundry preachers who had held forth in his schoolhouse. Thereupon, taking to himself a brace of wives, and two or three braces of children by way of stock in trade for the community at Mount Zion, and having likewise taken to himself a one-horse wagon into which were bestowed the moveables, not forgetting a certain big-bellied stone bottle which hung ominously dangling in the rear; I say, having done this, and having moreover pressed into service a certain raw-boned, unhappy looking horse and a certain fat, happy-looking cow which was driven along beside the wagon, away he started, all agog for the promised land."

Established at Independence, Missouri, the Mormons began to build up a community. But the place was on the route to Santa Fe and was frequented by traders and trappers. The Mormons were so much persecuted for their strange opinions and so bothered in working out their plans, that they began to look elsewhere again. After various efforts to work out their

lives in Missouri they found the deserted town of Commerce
in Illinois, built as an experimental community and abandoned.
This they built up into a fine city, which they named Nauvoo,
the largest and best then in Illinois, and its beauty and comfort began to attract some attention. But again they fell afoul
of frontier suspicion and jealousy. Rumors of sexual irregu-
larity were spread. Joseph Smith and his brother were put in
prison and taken from the jail by a mob and shot. There were
dissensions within the Church, mainly over the question of
plural wives. Their life in Illinois was wrecked.

A traveler in this region in 1847 writes with pity and compunction of the ruined city of Nauvoo. He says the Mormon
city had contained 20,000 prosperous persons, but now has no
more than 500 "in mind and body and purse perfectly
wretched. When the city was in its glory, every dwelling
was surrounded by a garden. Now all is ruin, gardens overgrown, doors broken in. In the midst of the ruins stands the
temple of Nauvoo, one of the finest buildings in the country,
built of limestone quarried in the bed of a dry stream. In the
basement there is a baptismal font, supported by twelve oxen
of solid stone, each as large as life."

At the moment when these remarks were written, the main
body of the Mormons of Nauvoo, some 12,000 strong, were
on the march to Mexico. "Go off by yourselves, where you
can live in peace," said Governor Ford of Illinois, chagrined
at being unable to protect them. Reinvigorated with the election of a new leader, Brigham Young, after the death of their
prophet, the Mormons abandoned their beautiful city, and
packing all their household goods which they could carry
away on wagons, crossed the Mississippi. This time they intended to go beyond the boundaries of the United States, fugitives like the Texans from the evils of America, seekers like
them for a Paradise of their own.

Their new leader was one of those men to whom nothing
is impossible. A Vermont Yankee, like Joseph Smith, he was
a thickset, powerful man, fair skinned, blue eyed, blunt and

downright of speech, a living hammer of a man, able to strike
relentlessly at every enemy, physical or social, outside his
ranks, and meanwhile to beat and shape his own people into
an incomparable unity of purpose and social drive. He talked
the Yankee vernacular with frontier plainness. "Don't be so
devilish hoggish as to be afraid to do a day's work without
getting pay for it," he is reported to have said once. "A man
having such a spirit will be damned." Of the more sentimental
kinds of Christian meekness and mildness he made short work.
Patience and devotion in wives was all very well, he said, "but
I never counsel a woman to follow her husband to the devil."
Confession might be good for the soul, but there were limits
to it. "Don't proclaim your sins from the house-tops. Ask forgiveness from those wronged, and, if your sins are unknown,
confess them to God and keep them to yourself."

Taking hold of the Mormon Church he was prepared to
weld it into a prosperous, self-protected, and self-sustaining
society. "Give the people iron and coal, good hard work,
plenty to eat, good schools and good doctrines," he said, "and
it will make them a healthy, wealthy, and happy people."

When the Mormons moved west, seeking a place beyond
the bounds of the United States, Brigham Young carried in
his mind the description Frémont had written of the Great
Salt Lake. In 1843, Frémont had gone up the Oregon trail to the
end of the Wasatch range, and then, with Kit Carson as guide,
had turned southward to explore a region known to the trappers but to no one else. There he saw "the waters of the inland
sea stretching in still and solitary grandeur far beyond the
limits of our vision. . . . Several large islands lifted their high
rocky heads out of the waves; but whether or not they were
timbered was still left to our imagination, as the distance was
too great to determine if the dark hues upon them were woodland or naked rock." Frémont reported that though this was
desert country he believed that the region north of the lake
was suitable for a military post and a civilized settlement. This

apparently led Young to expect more verdure and water there than he found.

The Mormons on the march wintered near Council Bluffs in Iowa during the winter of 1846, while Young talked with trappers and guides about the plains. The appalling barrenness of the region he had dreamed of now began to be clear to him. Jim Bridger, the trapper, told him: "I would give $1000 if I knew an ear of corn could be ripened in mountains." But Young was not a man to flinch. If plants did not grow in this desert, the Mormons would make them! Forthwith he began to study irrigation.

Next summer, in 1847, the army of the Mormons was again on the march. Brigham Young hurried ahead with a selected body of prospectors and seventy-three wagons, traveling rapidly up the Platte on the north bank, and from South Pass striking south for the Great Salt Lake. On July 22, he rode into that baked and blazing land, himself sick, but indomitable, and pointing to the desert said, "This is the place." Instantly he set his party to work to dig an irrigation ditch and plant potatoes, while he himself rode back along the trail to encourage the oncoming parties and tell them they had found their Eden.

Doctor Whitman's marching column of emigrants to Oregon had been a marvel of organization. But Young's was even better. Vigorous organism as he was, he detested some of the kill-joy attitudes to which he had been brought up in a strict New England home, and was determined that, whatever else the Mormons had, they were going to have a little fun and a few of the graces of life even on the dusty road to Deseret. Young's marching columns had sanitary inspectors, musical leaders, women nurses for the sick, comfortable sleeping benches in the wagons for women and children, and overseers to prevent waste, even the waste of a kernel of corn. When they stopped, they had lectures on the geology, geography, and history of the land they were passing through, varied with musical entertainments and sports. Christmas Day,

New Year's Day, Fourth of July, and other holidays they celebrated joyously with booming cannon, pies a foot deep, band music, and dances at night.

During the next few years the march to Utah continued—the march of a determined and hunted people, happy that they had found a new hive so far from civilization that no one could question them, in a place so barren that no one could envy them. Almost immediately the flag of the United States caught up with them; for the United States took title to their land the very year that they arrived. But they made the best of it, and in 1849 joined the Union as a territory calling itself "Deseret" with exactly the government they had, Brigham Young being now called governor and the church elders holding every elective position.

Over the plain between them and the Missouri River the people came pouring, many of them walking every step of the fifteen hundred miles. In the West Hall of the Bureau of Information now, in Salt Lake City, is one of the bravest, most pathetic memorials ever cast into bronze. It is a bronze of the "hand-cart family"—showing father and mother and little child trundling over the plains the little cart which held all their worldly goods, bound for Utah, and the desert city of the busy bees. Four thousand families thus walked fifteen hundred miles over the plains, dragging their possessions in a cart.

4

But once in Utah, settlement went on quickly and with a minimum of discomfort under the almost magically efficient organization of the Church. No backwoods loneliness here, no fighting alone against Indians, sickness, drouth, famine, and the encroachments of richer or more powerful settlers. The weak were within the wall of those whose arms persecution had made strong, and harsh experience had made wise. Utah was colonized in the same prosperous, sociable, efficient way in which Michigan, Wisconsin, and Minnesota were turned

into states, with all the added advantages of cooperative organization and cooperative use of funds. Every family was
allotted an area which it could cultivate and use for private
profit so long as it was thrifty and industrious, but irrigation,
marketing, and the iron, woolen, printing, and mining industries were managed cooperatively, paying fair wages, and
putting all profits into a common fund for fresh undertakings.
In this way the city was laid out, beautiful community buildings planned, the desert settlement provided with pure fresh
water and with an irrigation system, and the Mormons began
to spread up into other valleys. Ogden was founded. Lehi,
American Fork, and Provo became thriving centers. In a few
months colonizers went into Sanpete Colony and made a
treaty with the Indians for the possession of that lovely valley.

From the first all the equipment for the better life as the
Yankee belt understood it was provided for everybody. This
meant clean and comfortable houses, with lawns and flower
beds and a truck garden, and lots of pure water. It meant a
"social hall" and a mutual improvement society, and plays and
music, and schools for everybody from the primary grades to
the University, and newspapers, and a library. While they had
been on the plains Brigham Young had admonished the people to continue even while traveling the education of their
children. From time to time the children were assembled to be
taught the principal facts of geography and history by some
schoolmaster among them. The minute they settled down, the
schools also settled to a regular routine.

Along with their interest in learning, the Mormons toted
books and music across the plains. In the museum in Salt Lake
City is a collection of melodeons and two square pianos
brought thither by ox team. In 1851 the oxen carried the first
extensive collection of books, bought in New York City, for
community reading. The books included the works of Shakespeare, Milton, Byron, Homer, Juvenal, Euripides, Sophocles,
Plato, Herbert Spencer, John Stuart Mill, Emanuel Swedenborg, and John Wesley. Among the scientific works were

Newton's *Principia*, Herschel's *Outlines of Astronomy*, and von Humboldt's *Cosmos*. All the books were read by practically everybody. After a day spent in farming, in hauling in plants and trees from the canyons to make gardens, in building, in working in the communal industries and meeting in the various committees, it was the custom to gather in groups in the various assembly halls to discuss the books.

A theater was started, and became famous in the West. And one very lovely actress saw the light of day in that desert —Maude Adams, born in Salt Lake City when her mother was acting in the stock company there. Similarly music was cultivated. In 1866 the custom of presenting Handel's *Messiah* every year in the tabernacle was started and has continued ever since.

Meanwhile they were making their position in the desert pay economic dividends. When the rush to California began in 1849 the Mormons were already raising fresh vegetables and small fruits, and drove a thriving trade with the caravans. Many, they say, drove hard bargains; but this again is denied. On the whole, Mormons knew the value of a dollar, and saw no reason for dispensing alms to gentiles. Through the remarks of travelers about them runs a curious vexation, as if it were not quite seemly for saints to know how to look after themselves so well.

The strangeness of their doctrines and the reputation for polygamy intensified the fear and even horror with which passers-by looked on the arms the Mormons bore. Parkman speaks of seeing a brigade of these "fanatics" ride by armed to the teeth. Frontier settlers in general expected to be their own military force. A gun was a normal part of the plainsman's costume. But in the eyes of persons rushing to the gold fields from Eastern cities there was something wild, desperate, outlaw-like in these bold, strong, armed men from the mountain defiles. And undoubtedly behind the guns there was a peculiar force. These were men winnowed by misfortune, taught by persecution and hardship. One beautiful city had been destroyed by a mob, and into this beautiful city they were now pulling up by main strength from utter desolation an enemy would come only over all their dead bodies. Brigham Young himself intended now to take no nonsense from anybody. He was in a place where his people had the advantage, and he made it clear that they meant to keep it. And why not? Had they not earned it? Still there are one or two dark legends of frontier brushes with the Mormons, especially the so-called "massacre of Mountain Meadows"—all of which the recording angel may chalk up against the desolation of Nauvoo and the murder of Joseph Smith.

For all this cloud of fear between them and their neighbors, their works speak for them and began to speak early. Mark Twain, going out to Nevada in the early sixties, came with delight and surprise upon this city in the desert. "We strolled about everywhere through the broad, straight, level streets, and enjoyed the strangeness of a city of 15,000 inhabitants with no loafers perceptible in it; and no visible drunkards or noisy people; a limpid stream rippling and dancing through every street in place of a filthy gutter; block after block of trim dwellings, built of 'frame' and sun-burned brick—a great thriving orchard and garden behind every one of them apparently—branches from the street stream winding and sparkling among the garden beds and fruit trees—and a grand general air of neatness, repair, thrift, and comfort, around and about and over the whole. And everywhere were work-shops, factories, and all manner of industries; and intent faces and busy hands were to be seen wherever one looked; and in one's ears was the ceaseless clink of the hammers, the buzz of trade and the contented hum of drums and fly-wheels."

5

Working hard, under rigorous discipline and with matchless enthusiasm, this hive of the bees, in this wild and for the most part idle world, began to prosper, and as it prospered it rolled up collective capital to be administered by the Church.

Every faithful Mormon was expected to give a tenth of all he earned to the Church, and this tithe made a pool of capital which was used with skill to make roads, build bridges, construct railroads, ditches, and canals, and later for the establishment of stores, mines, railroads, insurance companies, developing Utah and reaching out all over the intermountain West. "Through the allegiance, respect, and esteem which the leaders of the Church have been accorded by its people, they have been able to unite and marshal the economic forces in such a manner as to make possible achievements that otherwise would have been impossible. The principle of co-operation has been utilized in almost every line of industrial endeavor."

Under this system—theocratic, socialistic, communistic, call it what you will—the territory of Utah went happily ahead in the years before the Civil War, as the most civilized place between the Mississippi and the Pacific Coast. The people were busy and jubilant. After twenty hunted years they had found their home, and it was blossoming for them in the desert like a rose and the wilderness and the solitary place were indeed glad for them. Long ago the Yankees had discovered that the trouble with things in this world is that they are not in the right place. Just by moving it from one place to another a liability may be turned into an asset—ice, for example. Now these people, inspired and led from Vermont, in their beautiful and prosperous cooperative home, felt that they had improved on the principle. Their policy, says a Mormon apologist, is a place for every man, and every man in his place.

21

SAN FRANCISCO,
OPEN YOUR GOLDEN GATES

BEFORE the gold rush California was a quiet but sociable little suburb of Boston. For half a century or more Boston ships had been stopping there to provide fine raiment for the *señoritas* and *caballeros* and to load up with hides. The hides, as Dana says in *Two Years before the Mast,* would be "tanned, made into shoes, and many of them, very probably, brought back again to California in the shape of shoes and worn out in the pursuit of other bullocks or in curing other hides."

Year after year, men from Boston came back there, and went around and joked with the same fellow keeping the same *pulquería.* They flaunted a bright handkerchief or a bit of ribbon before the same *señorita* or, when the *señorita* grew up, the *señorita's* little sister, and when she admired it, gave it to her. They looked in on the fathers at the mission and asked them if they wanted to buy anything, or had hides to sell, and added, "Ah, Padre, things were better governed in California when the Fathers ruled." This, for a wonder, was not a lie, though agreeable to the poor old padres dispossessed of their temporal power to hear from the lips of some young Yankee rascal. Most of the Yankees were young. They went out to

California and Oregon on their first trips at sixteen, and would have been stupid indeed if they could not retire to the elegant seclusion of Boston at thirty-five or forty.

There was often good society along that long brown California shore. Officers and business executives on the Yankee ships were on visiting terms with several Spanish families of position. A scene from one of these social parties, described by Dana, was lifted bodily and put into the charming technicolor picture—*The Dancing Pirate*. "He was dressed in white pantaloons neatly made, a short jacket of dark silk, gaily figured, white stockings, and thin morocco slippers upon his very small feet. His slight and graceful figure was well adapted to dancing and he moved about with the grace and daintiness of a young fawn. An occasional touch of the toe to the ground seemed to be all that was needed to give him a long interval of motion in the air. . . . After supper the waltzing began which was confined to a very few *gente de razon* and was considered a high accomplishment and mark of aristocracy. Here, too, Don Juan figured greatly, waltzing with the sister of the bride (Dona Augustia, a handsome woman and general favorite) in a variety of beautiful figures which lasted as much as half an hour, no one else taking the floor. They were repeatedly and loudly applauded, the old men and women jumping out of their seats in admiration, and the young people waving their hats and handkerchiefs."

When several ships of different nations were in port, it was great fun. "We roamed about from house to house, listening to all manner of languages. The Spanish was the common ground on which we all met, for every one knows more or less of that. . . . The night before the vessels were ready to sail, all the Europeans united and had an entertainment at the Rosa's hide-house, and we had songs of every nation and tongue. The Germans gave us *Ach, du lieber Augustin*, the three Frenchmen roared the *Marseillaise* hymn. The English and Scotch gave us *Rule Britannia* and *Who'll Be King but Charlie?* and the Spaniards screamed through some national affairs for which I was none the wiser, and we three Yankees made an attempt at *The Star-Spangled Banner*," after which the drinks were poured, "and there followed the mélange which might have been expected."

But even when there were no other European ships, the Yankees usually found some of their friends from the Hawaiian Islands. They were very fond of these Sandwich Islanders. Not being able to remember their names, they christened them again—Pagoda Jack, California Bill, Ban Yan, Foretop, Pelican. "But by whatever names they might be called, they were the most interesting, intelligent, and kind-hearted people I ever fell in with." The Yankees thought it great fun to go up to the Sandwich Island hangout, which they called The Kanaka Coffee House, and tease these jolly islanders. One whom they called "Mr. Bingham" had two teeth missing. They used to tell him that was what he got for eating Captain Cook—which would throw him into agonies of protest.

So this pleasant visiting back and forth between Boston and California around the Horn went on for half a century, during which time only this one Yankee city seemed to know the way thither.

2

The civilization which the first Yankee visitors found in California had been recently established by priests, and had still a certain shine and newness and frontier busyness about it.

Since the Spanish never had enough people to colonize the vast areas to which they laid claim, the enormous Spanish empire rested almost entirely on the work of priests in establishing economically productive, and moderately peaceable communities of native peoples. It was in this way that Spain took possession of the Philippines, of Mexico, and of such parts of Texas and New Mexico as were effectively possessed, and laid the foundation of the present civilization of Cuba and South America. It was a unique form of colonization. No one, not even the French priests, achieved anything like it, mainly because no one else had such success in making the Indians and other native peoples economically productive and self-sufficient. The grand original ideal of the Spanish priesthood had been expressed by the missionary to the West Indies, Las Casas. "All unbelievers have a just right to their possessions, no matter what sins they may have committed in their blindness against national, natural, or divine law. The Apostolic See has given authority over the Indies to the kings of Castile not for the enrichment of the crown, but for the conversion of the natives. Its claim rests on the justice of its laws, and on the fidelity with which it preaches the gospel to the ignorant. He who cannot understand this knows little of Christianity; and he who denies it is no more a Christian than was Mohammed."

That the missions in Latin-American countries constantly fell short of this noble ideal is shown by the bitter and ugly anticlericalism of such countries as Mexico, where the population is largely Indian. But for some reason or other, the Spanish priests, like the French priests, crossing the border into what is now the United States, changed from rascals and oppressors of the poor into holy, unselfish, and most heroic men. Either there were no unworthy priests on the American frontier, or American tradition prefers not to remember them. The American tradition cherishes the fathers of the old California missions as reverently as if they were the Puritan fathers themselves; and Father Junípero Serra, the great priest who founded and administered the missions of California during the late eighteenth century, stands, as he well deserves to do, as one of the great culture heroes of these states.

Father Junípero Serra was born on the island of Majorca, and named Miguel José Serra, but at sixteen, as an ardent young novice in the Franciscan monastery at Palma, he took the name of Junípero, from the favorite disciple of St. Francis. A charming lad, with attractive manners, eager face, and a peculiarly rich, sweet voice, he saw himself as the Francis of the American wilds, carrying the message of his Master to the Indian savages. But not till he was fifty-four did he realize his

dream, and cram passionately into the fifteen years still left
him the hopes and ambitions of a lifetime. For in 1768 he was
appointed to the apparently thankless position of padre presi-
dente of the Franciscan missions to Lower California, whence
the Jesuit missionaries were being expelled, and where his own
order was detailed to take over the work.

While Serra waited to sail for Loreto on the peninsula, the
fifteen Jesuit fathers and one lay brother were assembling
there to say good-by to the arid and God-forsaken land where
they had labored so long, and almost in vain, and which they
had come to love. On February 3, 1768, the fathers had celebrated their last Mass in California, and had knelt in farewell
prayers before our Lady of Loreto, the patroness of the Conquest, now draped in mourning. Then, to the wailing of the
Indians, they had marched down to the shore and set sail.
"By this time the sun had sunk; the twilight changed into
dusk; the sails were run up in the dark; they filled and swelled
with the winds of the night; and before morning . . . they
were far distant on their way. They had left California forever."

The ship that took the Jesuits away carried Serra and the
Franciscans back. The decks and bunks of the ship were still
mournful with the memory of those other fathers, admonish-
ing the Franciscans to be humble and not to grasp at temporal
power. Privately Serra must have wondered how the poor
Indians were to eat, and how they were to be clothed, if
Spanish officials only were to be expected to put their lofty
minds on the material side of mission work. But he took
counsel of the Lord in prayer, and here as on a later occasion,
must have received the answer "Be ye wise as serpents and
harmless as doves." So they landed at Loreto and knelt at the
feet of the Lady of Loreto, patroness of the California peninsula. She had put off her mourning for the Jesuits and was
decked in flowers for the Franciscans, but for Serra kneeling
at her feet there must have been both pity and admonition in
her eyes.

With such a beginning, against the suspicion and interference of the few Spanish officials in California, pretending to administer the province from Monterey, Serra in a quarter of a century built up a mission civilization, whose spiritual achievements may be doubtful, but whose political and economic values were unquestioned. From San Diego to San Francisco, the land was covered with missions, each a productive center reaching out in all directions, making the civil and economic foundation on which first the province, then the Mexican, and finally the American settlement was built. An aging man traveling incessantly from mission to mission, constantly opening new territories, watching the laying of new cornerstones, and the breaking of new fields, consecrating new churches, saying Mass at new altars, laying down laws for new and unprecedented circumstances, taming, teaching, disciplining the savage tribes, Serra kept always a sweet fresh enthusiasm.

On one occasion he recorded in his diary: "Until now we had not seen any women among them [the Indians] and I desired for the present not to see them, fearing that they went naked as the men. When two women appeared talking as rapidly and efficaciously as the sex knows how and is accustomed to do; and when I saw them so honestly covered that we could take it in good part if greater nudities were never seen among the Christian women of the missions, I was not sorry for their arrival." Again, on a fine June day, he set down his admiration of the flowers. "Flowers many, and beautiful . . . and to-day . . . we have met the Queen . . . the Rose of Castile. When I write this I have before me a branch . . . with three roses opened, others in bud, and more than six unpetaled. Blessed be He who created them!"

When fifteen years later, on August 28, 1784, he wrapped his cloak about him and lay down to rest never to wake again in this world, these roses of Castile were brought in great armfuls by the Indians at the mission of Dolores, and laid about his body and over his bier till they completely covered him, and so he was borne to his burial as if in a garden, and interred in the sanctuary before the altar of *Nuestra Señora de Dolores*.

3

Though the Spanish government feared the priests, and constantly curtailed their power and interfered with their operations, the missions made California habitable for white men, and pointed the way to effective use of the land. So here and there, mostly in the neighborhood of the missions, big ranches were set up, with hundreds and thousands of cattle and sheep, managed by Indians trained at the missions. Since, by the end of the eighteenth century the Boston ships were trading with the missions, there were some Americans in California almost from the time of the first actual Spanish settlements.

It was a strange Arcadian world, that of California during the first four decades of the nineteenth century, resting as it did on the quaint cooperation of the Yankees and the priests in putting an economic foundation under the easygoing Spanish and Mexican gentlemen. On the ranches there was a rude abundance—food to spare for man, beast, and every passer-by; flowers, fruits, family *fiestas*. When the Yankee ships were in port, everyone had new clothes. Apart from that, the simple Spanish and Spanish-Indian people seemed never to want anything.

Because of this dreamy contentment, this lack of ambition and desire, pastoral California before 1846 is reported to have been a land virtually without crime. There was no public hangman or executioner; there were no jails, juries, no courts, no sheriffs to serve writs, no lawyers to prosecute or defend. It is recorded that between 1819 and 1846 there were but six murders among the white inhabitants of California. The standard of honesty was so high that houses were without locks, and even the shrewd Yankee captains would give the people what they needed, and return a year and a half later to take their pay in produce. With such money as they had people were extremely generous. It is reported that in one Spanish house, bowls full of silver coins stood in the guest rooms, so that visitors might take what they needed.

These early Californians were no particular models of virtue, apart perhaps from a few priests. But in the later fury and violence of the gold-rush era men looked back to their life as to a golden age. They weren't very good, but they saw no reason for being bad. And so in this tranquil, nonacquisitive society manners blossomed pleasantly, and vanity was enough to make people agreeable, and in small ways even unselfish. Here was the feudal gentleman in his amiable senility—picturesque, idle, hospitable, given to an innocent kind of display, in a world where his large ideas of himself met with no opposition and did no harm, laughed at but tolerated with a certain affection by the hustling Americans. Yankee literature idealized California as Boston men had first known it in the beautiful story *Ramona*, by Helen Hunt Jackson. The whole epic of the early days has since been well told by Stewart Edward White in his series *Gray Dawn, Rose Dawn, Gold.*

4

The lethargic peace of this simple world began to be broken by faint ripples of excitement during the forties, as the oncoming Americans climbed up over the mountains and looked down on this, the last land between them and the other ocean. Some parties, headed for Oregon, turned aside and came down into California. More and more Americans bought land and set up on ranches. Other persons, English, Germans, a few Swiss joined the ranchero society. All were welcome. The country needed people.

Among these settlers was John Augustus Sutter, a Swiss gentleman naturalized as an American citizen, who set up a great feudal barony in the Sacramento Valley, which was a kind of cross between a California mission ranch and a fur fort. On a ranch covering eleven square leagues of land, he had 4,200 cattle, 2,000 horses, and about as many sheep. This

ranch was managed by a whole community of Indians, most
of them, of course, mission trained. Like the missions, he maintained a complete and self-sufficient industrial center, with
blacksmith shop, distillery, flour mill, cannery, etc. His farms
raised wheat, oats, and barley, and excellent fruits and vegetables. But he also carried on a profitable trade in beaver skins
and maintained a force of trappers. His baronial dwelling was
also a fort, which mounted twelve pieces of artillery and
maintained a garrison of forty soldiers in uniform. In short, his
was a little independent state on the borders of Spanish California. The Mexican government recognized his authority by
appointing him a Mexican official, and as such he was able to
give American parties coming over the mountains passes to
permit them to stay in the land.

To the Americans coming into California, Sutter thus became a guardian angel. When they got stuck in the snows in
the passes, he sent up rescue parties after them. To those who
came with money, he sold supplies, and helped them to settle.
To those who arrived penniless or in trouble, he gave largely.
Everybody of importance visited his castle and was entertained handsomely by the ruddy-faced, goodhearted gentleman.

One of the parties he rescued was the remnant of the unfortunate Donner expedition which had started off led by an
excellent and well-to-do man named Donner, with a heroic
wife. When the party was caught in the snows, many of them
perished and, so the horrible tale ran, some of the others ate
their dead companions. When all the rest were brought down,
it was necessary to leave Mr. Donner who was very ill, with
his excellent wife in attendance on him, together with a man
named Marshall and one named Keseberg. When these were
finally reached by a second rescue party, only Keseberg remained. Mr. Donner had died, and it was believed that Kese-
berge had killed and eaten Mrs. Donner. One of the rescuing
party, a man named Fallon, told E. C. Bryant that Keseberg,
when found, "was reclining upon the floor of the cabin smok-

ing his pipe. Near his head a fire was blazing, upon which was a camp kettle full of human flesh. A bucket filled with blood was standing near, and pieces of human flesh, fresh and bloody were standing around."

The story of the cannibalism had by this time been expanded by the newspapers into a hideous myth. *The Daily Californian* published a statement that one of the Donner party had taken a four-year-old boy to bed with him, and had killed and devoured him entirely by morning, and that he had killed another boy of the same age, and eaten him whole before lunch! In the midst of the popular excitement, the kindly Swiss gentleman, Sutter, intervened. After questioning Keseberg he felt that the man was demoralized by his sufferings, but that there was nothing to substantiate the tale of cannibalism. So Keseberg went free, though he lived afterward as a sort of outcast, carrying about him the odor of the charnel house.

Despite this hideous event, California in 1847 was still a pleasant and orderly little community. Americans were coming in more and more rapidly. One of the American additions was Sam Brannan, Mormon elder, leading 200 Mormons from New York around by Cape Horn. His burly, engaging personality, and coarse, direct speech were to play an important part in the community in the gaudy days that were coming. Politically the province was restive. The friars, now almost completely dispossessed of their temporal power, still had control of the economic life of the community, and its social sympathy. Naturally they were antagonistic to Mexico. The residents born in Spain had never reconciled themselves to these revolutionists far away down there in the mountain wilds. The various American, British, and other interests had been represented in California longer than the Mexicans, and saw no particular reason why they should admit the right of Mexicans to own this country, merely because Mexico had revolted from Spain and Spain had claimed this land on the strength of the visits of a few adventurers like themselves. By

1845 people—including rancheros of Spanish birth—were saying that if so many new people were coming to California, they had better tie up to a government better able to guard them and sponsor their business interests abroad than was Mexico. Some thought the British government would be best. Some thought the American government. One of the native California leaders, Vallejo, favored annexation to the United States.

At this juncture the question was dramatically settled by John C. Frémont dashing on the scene with Kit Carson at his side.

5

John C. Frémont is almost forgotten now, but at that moment he was the hero of every red-blooded American boy, the handsome and admired young actor in a popular American "western." This western was being skillfully unfolded to a delighted audience by his father-in-law, Senator Benton of Missouri, in no less a theater than the halls of Congress, and no motion-picture magnate could have marshaled the successive scenes more skillfully.

The players in this great public drama were an amazing quartet. As with so many others in the story of the West, it seems that surely a poet or a dramatist must have invented them. John C. Frémont himself was a young gentleman whose charming Virginian mother, of "good family," had eloped from her husband's house with a French dancing master, and had borne the Frenchman this son John. Without much money and with this skeleton in the family closet, he had nevertheless grown up in the Huguenot American society of Charleston as a gentleman and welcome friend of other young gentlemen, and had obtained a position as topographical engineer in the government service at Washington. There the dashing and romantic young man cast admiring eyes on the young and lovely daughter of Senator Benton, the "Rose of the West," pink cheeked, bright eyed, seventeen, her natural in-

tensity of spirit glowing like a banked fire under the discipline of the Senator's house. Thinking Jessie too young for
marriage, Benton separated the lovers by sending Frémont on
an exploring expedition into the West, which Frémont
promptly executed, finished with talent, and then reappeared
to claim his bride. Finding father still adamant, seventeen-
year-old Jessie determined to marry her lover secretly. But
knowing of her father's opposition, not one Protestant clergyman in Washington would perform the ceremony. Finally an
older woman, a friend of Jessie's, interceded with Father Van
Horseigh of the Catholic Church, and he promised to marry
them. Frémont, when consulted about the propriety of a
Catholic marriage, said he did not care who performed the
ceremony, so long as it was "sure and quick." And so on
October 19, 1841, they were secretly married.

They then undertook to face the redoubtable Senator with
the accomplished fact. The drama of that moment, Jessie later
delighted to picture for her grandchildren. There was the
Senator, in all the thunderous panoply of his famous "presence," blazing with wrath. There was the handsome young
lieutenant, her newly acquired husband, stammering, embarrassed, but determined. "Get out of my house and never cross
my door again," roared Benton. "Jessie shall stay here."

Whereupon Jessie took her husband's arm, and flashing defiance at her father, lifted her eyes to her husband's and in a
clear, solemn voice repeated the words of Ruth: "Whither
thou goest, I will go; and where thou lodgest, I will lodge;
thy people shall be my people, and thy God, my God."

Further the deponent saith not. But Jessie stayed in her
father's house that night, and Frémont left his boarding house
and stayed there with her. Thereafter, in all his discussions of
the great Western question in Congress, Father never let his
audience in Congress forget the charming love story at the
center of it!

Father, Frémont, and Jessie were enough to make any
public event a drama, but the person they attached to finish

the cast outshone them all. He was Kit Carson, the sandy-haired lad we last saw running away to join the trappers at Taos, now a personage on the frontier and married to a Spanish lady in New Mexico whom someone described as "heartbreakingly beautiful." Carson was a very fine fellow, skilled in all the arts of the Western plains, true as steel, swift as an arrow, and all this the great showman in Congress never allowed the public to forget either. Frémont attached Carson as a scout on a series of Western explorations mapped out by his father-in-law. The excellent reports of these written by Frémont himself were printed by the United States government, and extra stories about his adventures with Carson, from Father's remarks in Congress and Jessie's charming letters, were transferred by popular reporters and writers to a public hungry for romance. And now came the climax which brought Kit Carson dashing across the continent with the message that California was ours!

In 1847 Frémont had been dispatched on one of his "scientific" expeditions to the Western coast, attended by sixty soldiers. He asked and obtained permission from the Mexican government to enter California, but when this permission was later withdrawn, he obediently turned northward to Oregon. And now to quote his 1856 biographer who followed Father's statements almost literally. "He had already entered this romantic region, filled with lofty mountains, towering precipices and peaks, placid lakes embosomed in rugged fastnesses, and inhabited by an untamed race of treacherous Indians. It was on the eighth of May that, as he and his bold company rode along, he was astonished by a startling incident. Two horsemen, issuing suddenly from the gorge of the mountains approached him. They proved to be from a guard of six American soldiers, conducting a United States officer who was bearing dispatches from Washington to the United States consul at Monterey, and also some papers and a mysterious introduction for Frémont to the same individual."

The soldiers said that the party they were escorting was

being attacked by Indians. Would Frémont come at once? Frémont and his soldiers wheeled and after riding sixty miles found Lieutenant Gillespie, who by now, it seems, had escaped from the Indians. From him Frémont received not only dispatches but, as Senator Benton afterward touchingly reminded the Congress of the United States, a large packet of letters from his dear young wife.

Happily encamped that evening, reading the letters from his wife, they heard a cry from Carson, and the same instant an Indian arrow pierced the heart of one of their company, a young French *voyageur*. Dropping the letters, Frémont and Carson instantly mustered the soldiers and through the night they fought off the Indians. It was "amid such dangers," said Senator Benton to Congress, "that science was pursued by Mr. Frémont, that the telescope was carried to read the heavens, the barometers to measure the temperature of the air, the pencil to sketch the grandeur of the mountains and to paint the beauty of flowers, the pen to write down whatever was new or useful or strange in the works of nature—it was in the midst of such dangers as these, and in the wildest regions of the furthest west, that Mr. Frémont was pursuing science and shunning war, when the arrival of Lieutenant Gillespie turned him back into California and engaged him in the operations which now claim the attention of the Senate of the United States."

For Lieutenant Gillespie, along with letters from the loved ones, bore a dispatch for Mr. Frémont informing him that California was about to be annexed by Great Britain, and that he was to go there and "use his utmost exertions to conciliate the inhabitants and render them favorable to annexation to the United States." Reaching California, Frémont learned that some of the American settlers were menaced by the Mexicans, and with his sixty soldiers marched to their relief and drove off the enemy, and established himself in control of the area north and west of San Francisco. Then he called a meeting of American settlers and advised them to work for independence from Mexico and the establishment of free government adequate to the needs of California. At this juncture he learned that war had broken out between the United States and Mexico. Now all was simple. Commander Stockton took possession of the country as a conquest of the United States and, in accordance with "a principle recognized under the law of nations" appointed Frémont as governor. That California was thus properly conquered even the official organs of government in Mexico City recognized!

6

And now it seems as if God himself intervened to add the last grand finale to Mr. Benton's western. Gold was discovered on Sutter's lands.

In May, 1848, *The Daily Californian* reported: "The whole country from San Francisco to Los Angeles, from the sea to the base of the sierras, resounds with the cry 'Gold! Gold!' while the field is left half planted, the house half built, and everything is neglected except the manufacture of shovels and pick-axes and means of transportation to the spot where a man obtained $128 of the real stuff in one day's washing, and the average for all is $20 a day."

When the word flashed over the mountains and ran up and down the coast that this land on which Mr. Benton was so busy fixing attention contained gold—gold in unlimited quantities, gold that could be washed out of the sands, picked out of the rocks with the fingernails—the wildest stampede in history began. Into the West they poured, in wagons, on horseback, on foot. Out of the harbors they dashed, in sailing boats, in steamers, in anything that could keep afloat. The news spread to Europe. The ports of the Atlantic were crammed with immigrants seeking transshipment. It ran down the coast of South America and up the other side, and almost all of Chile set sail at once. It flashed across Canada and the trappers dropped their pelts and beat it down the coast. It flashed from ship to ship in the Orient, and across the Pacific they came flying loaded with everybody from maharajas to Chinese. The coursing of the forty-niners across the continent makes a breathless tale, well told from all the old diaries and the innumerable songs of the gold rush in Archer's Hulbert's *The Forty-niners*. The race around the Horn makes a still more breathless one.

"What would have been the fate of the clippers if gold had not been discovered in California," says *Gold of Ophir*, "it is hard to say. Doubtless they would have been slowly supplanted by the steamer without ever having come into their own. But when suddenly a whole growing nation wanted to be lifted bodily from one end of the continent and wafted speedily across to the other, men's imaginations could not permit themselves to be shackled to mere progress. Men wanted speed—the speed of the winds, the speed of lightning. . . . Then it was that a ship became the symbol of happiness. . . . And from the harbors of the Atlantic, bound for Frisco, rose those things of air and sinuous grace—the 'Flying Cloud,' 'Witch of the Waves,' 'Shooting Star,' 'Lightning,' 'Gamecock,' and 'Sovereign of the Seas'. . . in 1850 backed by thousands and thousands of dollars in wagers with the whole of Manhattan and the Atlantic coast mad with excitement, seven clippers slipped out of New York harbor in a race for San Francisco. One of McKay's ships, the 'Sea Witch,' fighting her way sheathed and caked in ice, against darkness and bitter head winds, amidst floes and ice-bergs and a constant drive of snow and sleet, made the passage in ninety-seven days, till then an unimagined record. The next year the 'Sea Witch' raced against two other clippers. Almost side by side they struggled for two weeks through the black weather below the Horn, unwilling to yield an inch of sail to the storm, with the whole world anxious and waiting and fortunes pledged on the result. One captain is reported to have put padlocks on his sails and to have stood on the bridge defying God to make him take in sail. There was no wireless to answer the question of the watchers, day by day. Not a word between New York and San Francisco, and sometimes not another word till the ships had circled the globe themselves outspeeding any news of them that might reach home."

So many people poured in by land and sea that California was organized as a state with no preliminary status as a territory. One day the steamer "Oregon" appeared off the entrance to San Francisco, which Frémont had named "The Golden Gate," decorated with national flags and bearing the banner "California Is a State." News was flashed from Telegraph Hill. All the ships in the harbor struck up any noise they had available. Cannons were fired, guns boomed from the hills, rockets sizzed into the air, bands played on every corner, and the motley population of every race and nation hugged each other and danced wildly on the sand hills.

7

At first the mining was carried on in the easy, generous, honest, noncompetitive way of the country. Hittell tells of a boy who arrived, footsore, hungry, without cash or tools, at a mine where thirty burly fellows were happily digging. When he had told them his tale, one miner said, "Boys, I'll work an hour for that chap if you will." All answered in the affirmative and at the end of an hour $100 worth of gold dust was poured into the boy's handkerchief. The miners then made a list of tools and gave it to the lad. "You go now and buy these tools," they said. "And come back. We'll have a good claim staked out for you; then you've got to paddle for yourself." For a while it was just clean, honest, jolly working under the blue skies, the boys singing as they worked Stephen Foster's ditty which had become the song of the gold rush.

I'll scrape the mountains clean, old girl, I'll drain the rivers dry.
I'm off for California, Susannah, don't you cry.
Oh, Susannah, don't you cry for me.
I'm off for California with my wash bowl on my knee.

Of course most of these first miners were men from near by —trappers, mountain men, recent settlers—men of the West, easy, hardy, good natured, and not very ambitious. They were used to a rough outdoor life, had a sort of code by which they lived it. But when the newcomers began pouring in, the spirit changed rapidly and for the worse. The easy good nature of California was too soft a foundation to sustain the new weight; and the mining societies went rapidly from easily secured peace to carelessly criminal tolerance, and thence to brutally intolerant degeneracy, and finally to "wretched dissolution."

The mining camp on the downgrade is vividly described in the Shirley Letters which appeared from time to time in *Ewer's Pioneer*, published at San Francisco in 1854–1855. Dame Shirley, as she called herself, was a New England woman, and wife of a doctor in a California mining camp. Arriving at the camp she stayed in the hotel, "very awkwardly pieced together by a careless carpenter." The bedrooms had "immense heavy bedsteads, warped and uneven floors, purple calico linings on the walls, and red calico curtains." The six-months-old baby in the hotel was dressed in red, to match the curtains, and "cradled in a champagne basket."

Besides Shirley there were only four other women in the town. When one of these poor souls died, they laid her out on a board supported on butter tubs.

Life in the camp was carelessly jovial. When the Chilean miners celebrated their independence day, the Yankees joined with them, walking fraternally in the procession with them, every one "intensely drunk." But when they were sober, their talk was most amusing. A trapper told bloodcurdling tales of Indian fights. A learned Quaker lectured on literature. The rougher men joked and yarned. The men who had some education and reading carried on endless discussions.

On gala occasions they "fixed up their diggings" in high style, knocking together furniture out of claret cases and coverings of monte tables, hanging everything with fresh red

calico. The revel would consist of dancing—the men, in the
absence of women, dancing with each other—and drinking.
After their Christmas revel they were drunk for days, the
"vigilant committee" rounding up men who were still sober
and condemning them to drink a certain amount. Such parties
beginning gaily would often end in fights and stabbing and
shooting. Many of the men grew ugly under the influence of
liquor. The Spaniards, says Shirley, think it "the grand characteristic of Columbia's children to be prejudiced, opinion-
ated, selfish, avaricious, and unjust."

San Francisco, meanwhile, grew gaudier and gaudier.
Early in 1849 it had been just a string of adobe huts along the
baked brown hills, with a few barrooms and cafés where the
officers and crews of the ships could gather. When the hordes
arrived, there was nowhere to put them. Tents sold at a premium. Shacks were knocked together out of packing boxes.
Old hulls of ships were converted into houses. And large
numbers of people simply camped outdoors. The first real
roofs covered bars and gambling houses, and the first furniture was mostly for houses of ill fame. The population consisted almost exclusively of young men, the majority not being
much over twenty-five. Among the few young women com-
munistically possessed, a baby was now and then born, and by
a miracle even survived, but it was some time before there
were adequate homes. In 1853 Gertrude Atherton's grandfather joined with the ladies of some of the churches to collect in a home the little waifs that were running wild and
naked on the sand hills.

During the rainy season under the wild trampling of innumerable feet the streets of San Francisco became sloughs of
mud. It is stated as a sober fact that teams of horses and mules
actually sank out of sight and were suffocated. Anything at
hand was used to pave them—bags of flour, piles of tobacco,
cookstoves, even pianos. All along these thoroughfares were
such signs as: "Head of Navigation," "Take Sounding," "Stor-
age Room, Inquire Below." By the time the more industrious

and enterprising citizens got a few buildings and houses raised, some brawling crowd would upset a lamp and San Francisco would go up in flames. Within eighteen months San Francisco burned down eight times, being rebuilt each time, more substantially and comfortably than before. The great social institution of the town became the fire companies. The first engine that reached a fire gave its club the place of honor in the community till the next fire blazed.

All resorts in the town were full of miners, or would-be miners, looking often very bizarre. Many of them wore their hair long, and were decorated with bright silk handkerchiefs, squirrel or buck tails in their hats, long chains of gold nuggets swinging on their front, pistols, stilettos, knives, and dirks stuck all over themselves. Many of them actually had "honor" to defend, and shot or stabbed on an instant, if this tender possession was in any way impugned. Homicide was a mere incident in that world. When they really got mad and hanged a man, it was most likely for stealing. But they held their gold lightly for all that, giving it away lavishly, spending wildly for anything that caught their eye, decking popular but not respectable ladies in finery and jewels, and gambling it away. Most of the men who behaved in this way were not bad. They were only young in a world where no one was much older and few wiser.

Among these lads on the loose moved Father Taylor. Rolling a cask of brandy into the center of the plaza, he would stand on it and, as he said, "sing up a thousand or two of them," and then he would pitch in. "Gentlemen, I stand on what I suppose to be a cask of brandy. Keep it tightly bunged and spiled, and it is entirely harmless, and answers some very good purposes. It even makes a very good pulpit." The moral of which was that they needed to be bunged and spiled themselves. Just then some would start a dogfight down the street. Father Taylor would pause and say benignly, "Run along, boys. What an intellectual feast it must be to enlightened, high-minded American gentlemen to see a couple of dogs

fight!" He particularly enjoyed taunting them on the day
after a spree. As they staggered along, blind with a headache,
pockets completely empty of cash, there would be Father
Taylor, standing on a beer barrel in front of a gambling house
describing to an enchanted audience the beautiful party the
boys had been having. Oh, he would tell them, there was just
a grand party last night up there in the American Valley. Did
they hear about it? They had a grizzly bear and a bullfight,
and a magnificent dinner with whisky and then all the gentlemen had the sweet privilege of dancing with each other! Of
course there were one or two difficulties. The bull and the
grizzly wouldn't fight; the food was good but the whisky bad.
But somehow or other, they all kicked around till dawn, and
now every one of the fortunate gentlemen here who went to
that party finds himself minus $100 apiece, bodies worn out,
nerves on edge, stomach nauseated, head aching, blind for want
of sleep. In short, "a more miserable set of fellows can hardly be
imagined on this side perdition."

Every value was askew in that delirious world. The first
wives who ventured out were as tempted as the men. After a
few weeks of reform young husbands would find the society
of a mere wife rather dull, and be drawn back to the solid
masculine company of poker and drink and painting the town
red—upon which some more appreciative soul would immediately enter himself as candidate for the neglected lady's
favor. Even pathetically devoted husbands would see their
wives coolly removed by their best friends and "pardners."

"Of their married felicity but little is known," says Bret
Harte in his story *Tennessee's Partner*, "perhaps for the reason that Tennessee, then living with his partner, one day took
occasion to say something to the bride on his own account, at
which, it is said, she smiled not unkindly and chastely retreated
—this time as far as Marysville, where Tennessee followed her,
and where they went to housekeeping without the aid of a
justice of the peace. Tennessee's partner took the loss of his
wife simply and seriously as was his fashion. But to every-

body's surprise, when Tennessee one day returned from Marysville, without his partner's wife—she having smiled and retreated with somebody else—Tennessee's partner was the first man to shake his hand and greet him with affection.'

In this rough, careless, but goodhearted society, children and pure young girls are credited in tradition with a holy influence. In the *Luck of Roaring Camp* the attempt of the miners to care for the baby which Cherokee Sal, the prostitute, dying left them as a legacy has a most improving effect on their manners and morals. The cabin assigned to Tommy Luck or "The Luck," as he was most frequently called—first showed signs of improvement. "It was kept scrupulously clean and white washed. Then it was boarded, clothed, and painted. The rosewood cradle, packed eighty miles by mule, had, in Stumpy's way of putting it, 'sorter killed the rest of the furniture.' . . . The men who were in the habit of lounging in at Stumpy's to see how The Luck got on, seemed to appreciate the change, and in self defense the rival establishment of 'Tuttle's grocery' bestirred itself and imported a carpet and mirrors. The reflections of the latter on the appearance of Roaring Camp tended to produce stricter habits of personal cleanliness. And Stumpy imposed a kind of quarantine upon those who aspired to the honor and privilege of holding The Luck."

8

Between 1850 and 1855 the gaudy young, masculine population of California began to divide into the Children of Mammon and the Children of Light. The Children of Mammon sank from easy riotousness and irresponsibility to utter degeneracy. The Children of Light, consisting of those early miners who had withdrawn from their rowdy fellows and brought on wives and set up homes with children, now wanted peace, order, and progress, honest business and honest government. In 1851 they roused themselves to clean out the worst gangs of criminals called the Sydney Ducks and The Hounds, and

formed a vigilant committee, the first of these institutions in
the West. Led by determined men, among them William C.
Coleman and Sam Brannan, the burly Mormon, the vigilant
committee proceeded cautiously but with decision, and, when
its work was done, instantly disbanded. "After a few hangings," says the *Annals of San Francisco,* "the social state of the
city was much improved. . . . Crime was now confined to
petty thefts . . . while cases of blood shed—and they were
frightfully many—arose chiefly from the rampant unregulated passions of the people."

During the next few years both the Children of Light and
the Children of Mammon consolidated themselves. Churches
were organized and well attended. Schools were functioning.
In 1853 a public celebration included a parade of school children. Walking along, strange as cherubs in that hitherto wild
male world, their small rosy faces strengthened resolve in
many a quiet heart. Rough men, still without wife or child,
would turn aside and ostentatiously help a mother with her
child. Many a young wife going about her business, clutching
her child by the hand, shone with the ancient glory of the
Madonna on those muddy turbulent streets. Against the gaudy
girls on whom they were throwing away their money, men
began to enshrine in their hearts the angel of the West—the
good woman, the unselfish woman, belonging to her man only,
keeping his house and bearing his children.

Next to the home and the appearance of children, the
strongest force making for righteousness was the secondary
migration of men who came not to mine gold, but simply to
serve a growing community as business or professional men.
Many of the better miners gladly turned from the first weeks
of gold seeking to the pursuit of some former means of livelihood, and, in so doing, began to look for means of respectable
living.

On the other hand, the original gamblers, sharpers, thieves,
ex-convicts of the early rough days had many of them set
up as rich men, forming a gaudy sort of aristocracy of their

own, careless, showy, unscrupulous, giving big parties, patron-izing the ever more gorgeous restaurants, bars, polite gambling halls, and other places of amusement. Among them they had the government safe in their pockets, having developed a most elaborate system of ballot stuffing, and utilizing the political talents of a low-grade type of Southerner. Now and then responsible visitors from the East, shocked by the government, tried to appeal to the federal government in Washington. But it was so occupied with the discussion of slavery and the grow-ing tension between North and South that it could do nothing. Meanwhile the fact that their own political rascals were largely Southern in origin strengthened in California a feel-ing growing up elsewhere in the country that government in the United States, in free as well as slave states, had become a jobbery owned and managed by "nigger traders."

In 1854 there was a determined effort to override the cor-rupt politicians. On September 8, 1854, an editorial in *The Herald* announced. "We say to the ruffians who have en-deavored to take this election out of the hands of the people, who have been striving with bludgeon, dagger, and pistol to ride rough-shod over the people, that there is a feeling abroad that bodes danger to them. They are standing on a volcano that may burst at any moment."

Everywhere men were saying quietly that they had better revive the old vigilance committee. The matter was discussed, ways and means considered, procedures for the future ripened in conversation. But nothing was done. In November, 1855, something happened which made the call more insistent. United States Marshal William H. Richardson was murdered by Charles Cora, a gambler. Instantly the old vigilante, Sam Brannan, sprang to the front warning the people that the cor-rupt courts would never condemn Cora, advising them to punish him themselves. Brannan was arrested for disturbing the peace, but the crowds that followed the sheriff and his prisoner to the station house were so menacing in their sym-pathy with Brannan that he was released. However, the trial followed the course Brannan had prophesied. Cora was elaborately defended with money furnished by Belle Cora, a prostitute who was called by Cora's name because of this great public service to him. Finally the jury disagreed. So Cora was returned to prison and lived there happily surrounded with comforts supplied by Belle and his cronies, while silent rage boiled under the surface of the city.

The rage found a voice in James King of William. James King was a banker of Scotch-Irish origin, who had come to California from Georgetown, in the District of Columbia. To distinguish himself from other persons named James King he quaintly added his father's name to his own, and called himself James King of William. Established as a trusted banker and person of wealth in San Francisco, he had been caught in financial difficulties through other persons' dishonesty, and had promptly stripped himself of all property to meet the obligations of the bank. Living in poverty, with his six children, but in general honor, James King suddenly lifted his voice and began to pour out on the corrupt politicians and moneyed rascals of San Francisco all the vials of a Covenanter's wrath.

His medium was a newspaper *The Evening Daily Bulletin*, which on October 8, 1855, began, evening by evening, to tell the people the exact truth about San Francisco. The disagreement in the Cora trial was announced thus: "Hung be the heavens with black. The money of the gambler and the prostitute has succeeded. . . . Rejoice, ye gamblers and harlots, rejoice with exceeding gladness. . . . Your triumph is great —oh how you have triumphed. Triumphed over everything that is holy and good and virtuous, and triumphed legally— yes, legally."

Naturally people read *The Bulletin*. In no time it overtopped all other papers in circulation and its appearance was the excitement of the day. But the paper was more than a sensation. Rash to madness, courting the assassin's bullet in every word, surely doomed to death by the powers that ruled the city, James King of William was utterly honest, terribly in earnest; and, watching him in horrified admiration, the hearts of the people rose behind him in silent massed loyalty. "The emigration to this state," wrote William H. Rhodes later, in a communication to *The Bulletin*, "from the first discovery of gold, has consisted principally of two classes of men: those who came to work and those who came to steal. . . . These two classes have hitherto been battling against each other in secret. Now an open war has broken out in relentless fury. One or the other must succumb."

Speaking of the situation just before the valiant single voice of King was raised, he says: "Public confidence was shaken, public honor suspected. Many of our best and worthiest citizens sacrificed their property and sent their families to the East. No man felt secure for a moment in the possession of life, property, or reputation. At this juncture Mr. King started *The Bulletin*. At first he was scoffed at as a madman, then pitied as an enthusiast, then respected for his courage, then applauded for his independence, then beloved for his purity, his self-sacrifice, and his noble magnanimity. Finally by a revulsion of public sentiment in his favor, which is without parallel in our history, he stood forth the acknowledged champion of public and private morality, the scourge of villany, the vindicator of the freedom of the press, the friend of every social reform, and the benefactor of his country."

King was doomed to death. One reason for the rising tide of devotion to him was that his readers knew it. "I well remember," wrote W. O. Ayers in an article in *The Overland Monthly*, August, 1886, "meeting him but two days before the curtain rose on the terrible tragedy that was to follow, and looking at him with a sort of reverent wonder, as of a man who carried his life in his hand."

King himself even played with the threats against his life in his editorials in *The Bulletin*. "Bets are now offered, we have been told, that the editor of *The Bulletin* will not be in existence twenty days longer, and the case of Doctor Hogan of the Vicksburg paper who was murdered by the gamblers of that place is cited as a warning. Pah! We went unscathed through worse scenes than the present at Sutter Fort in '48. War, then, is the cry, is it? War between the prostitutes and gamblers on one side, and the virtuous and respectable on the other. War to the knife, and the knife to the hilt. Be it so, then. Gamblers of San Francisco, you have made your election, and we are ready on our side for the issue."

When Selover, a gambler, threatened to kill him, King lost no time in announcing the impending tragedy to his readers. "Mr. Selover it is said, carries a knife. We carry a pistol. We hope neither will be required, but if this rencontre cannot be avoided, why will Mr. Selover persist in perilling the lives of others? We pass every afternoon about half past four to five o'clock along Market Street from Fourth to Fifth Street. The road is wide and not so much frequented as those streets farther in town. If we are to be shot or cut to pieces, for heaven's sake let it be done there."

Imprudent as this was, it is a question whether anything short of it would have brought the situation to a head. As Josiah Royce said later, it was one of those cases in which it was expedient that one man should die for the people. Any one of a hundred men would have killed him sooner or later, but the particular person who did it was a prominent politician and ballot stuffer, James P. Casey, who as inspector of elections was able to throw out all ballots that did not suit him and his associates in government. King announced in *The Bulletin* that Casey was an ex-convict from Sing Sing. When Casey came to King's office to protest this, King said, "It is true, isn't it?" When Casey could not deny it, King refused to listen further and simply put him out the door. As King left his office building that afternoon, Casey was lying in wait for him and shot him.

Bleeding profusely, King was instantly carried to the office of the Express Company. A doctor was called, and for a time it seemed that King might live. Casey meanwhile had been seized and carried to the station house. "In less than five minutes a dense throng had packed the streets; in less than ten minutes it had reached as far as eye could see. . . . 'Hang him! Run him up a lamp post! Hang him! Hang him! . . .' The Monumental bell solemnly sounding its portentous tap, tap . . . tap, tap . . . tap, tap . . . tap, was like a call to arms."

All night the government troops kept order. Meanwhile men were besieging William T. Coleman, begging him to call out the old vigilantes of '51. By next morning, May 15, 1856, the newspapers were printing the following notice: "The members of the Vigilance Committee in good standing will please meet at No. 105 ½ Sacramento Street, this day, Thursday, 15th instant, at nine o'clock, A. M. By order of the Committee of Thirteen," Long before nine the street was thronged. All day long, while King battled feverishly for life, the Committee quietly registered citizens for service with them—men of all professions, Frenchmen and Irishmen, Scotch and Italians, Jews and Gentiles, refusing Negroes and Chinese. By night 1,500 were registered, had formed into companies of a hundred, elected their own officers, and had been provided with muskets. Money poured in as freely as men. Within forty-eight hours after King was shot, the city was in possession of the armed force of its own citizens, and the headquarters of the Committee fortified with sandbags, which caused it to be called "Fort Gunny Bags." Eight thousand citizens were under arms, comprising three-fourths of the adult male population. An insurrectionary government, with practically all important resources and all the responsible citizenry at its back, had overnight quietly supplanted the corrupt established government, and was proceeding to dictate terms.

The terms, for the moment, were surrender of the county jail where Cora and Casey were lodged. Marshal Doane of the Vigilance forces, riding up to the jail presented the following document: "David Scannell, Esquire:—Sir: You are hereby required to surrender forth with the possession of the county jail now under your charge to the citizens who present this demand, and prevent the effusion of blood by instant compliance. By Order of the Committee of Vigilance."

"But," cried Casey to Scannell, "You aren't going to give me up."

"James," said the Sheriff, "There are three thousand armed men coming for you, and I have not thirty supporters about the jail."

So Cora and Casey were quietly removed, and the jail with the other inmates turned back to Scannell with the statement that no other prisoners were needed.

As the prisoners were brought out, a cheer started among the waiting multitudes, but William Coleman, with his genius for raising the expressed sentiments of a mob to another level, and making of them the solemn judgment and inevitable will of the people, removed his hat, as before something sacred and dreadful, and motioned for silence. The silence that fell then, said one spectator, was "something frightful, something un-natural, a silence that could be felt, like the darkness that fell upon the land of Egypt." And in that silence the prisoners were escorted to a carriage and driven away between lines of the citizens.

King meanwhile was fighting death as vigorously as he had fought crime, refusing to give up till he had to, with Father Taylor praying at his side, and the city hanging on each valiant, struggling breath. But on the fifth day after the shooting, the Monumental bell started tolling, and one by one the churches all over the city took up the solemn message, and between the Bulletin Building and Montgomery Block hung the inscription. "The great, the good one, is dead. Who will not mourn." Instantly every office closed and was draped in black; the flags in the harbor stood at half-mast; and members of the Vigilance Committee and other citizens paced the streets with strips of black on their arms.

Two days later 25,000 persons waited to escort his coffin

to its resting place on the bare fog-swept side of Lone Mountain. Just at the moment that the doors of the Unitarian Church opened, and the coffin was borne out, high over the heads of the waiting crowd, in front of the committee rooms, swung the bodies of Casey and Cora, pronounced by a rapid "People's" trial "Guilty. Penalty: Death by Hanging."

At the same moment, bells were set tolling in towns all over California, and messages and subscriptions of money for the family of their dead editor poured in from all over the state. The citizens of Coloma sent a message to the Committee in San Francisco: "If you need help, let the sea speak to the mountains."

9

"Now therefore I, Neely Johnson, Governor of the State of California" . . . read a posted announcement, "do hereby declare the county of San Francisco in a state of insurrection, also all persons subject to military duty within said county to report themselves for duty immediately to William T. Sherman." William T. Sherman, later to be one of the great generals of the Civil War, was a good man, but he was a military person, and thought the elected government of the people should be supported even if it was elected by ballot stuffing. Besides, no one among the regular officers of government had yet taken the measure of this movement.

The answer to Governor Johnson's appeal was not long in coming. The National Guard issued an answering announcement saying that it would "now disband, preferring this course to that of becoming the slaughterers of our fellow citizens. That this corps do now re-organize under the name of the Independent National Guard, holding ourselves subject only to such rules and regulations, in sustaining the cardinal interests of the community, as our best judgments may dictate— hereby repudiating all connection with the present state authorities."

While the regular militia was walking out on the governor,

about seventy-five persons enlisted under General Sherman, and these, reported *The Alta California*, publishing their names and records, were the ruffians of the city. "What does Major General Sherman wish to do? Is it his wish to bring the army of ballot stuffers and rowdies which he may raise in collision with the decent, respectable citizens of San Francisco?" After which General Sherman very sensibly washed his hands of the whole matter.

Governor Johnson then appealed to Franklin Pierce, President of the United States, asking for arms and assistance in putting down the insurrectionists who, he said, "doubtless will proceed with such acts of aggression and disobedience toward the government as will ultimately result in its entire destruction." Instead of ammunition the President sent him a polite letter indicating his grave doubts of "lawful power to proceed in the manner indicated," and transmitting the opinion of the attorney general that there is no evidence that "there has been committed or threatened any act of resistance or obstruction to the constitution, law, or official authority of the United States!"

Thus established, the Vigilance Committee, with minor brushes with the so-called "government," continued to rule San Francisco and to control much of the state until another election day should come around and the people could put in officials to their liking. They occupied themselves meanwhile with public demonstrations of ballot-stuffing devices as applied by the "government," with discussions of government in the newspapers, and with a steady cleaning out of the disreputable persons in the city, putting them on ships and paying their passage to the places they came from. On November 4, they policed the election precincts and had watchers carefully guarding against fraud at the ballot box, as a result of which the People's Party, representing the forces that created and supported the vigilantes, were overwhelmingly elected. "For the next ten years," says Bancroft, "this new reform party did well, purging and purifying, during which time it was a common remark that no city in the world was better governed than San Francisco."

10

The most dramatic of our great cities, San Francisco thereafter was to fall into evil ways and be denounced by her own highly articulate children as one in wickedness with Nineveh and Tyre, and to be purified by a momentary revival of the vigilantes in 1877, and to sin again, and be punished with earthquake and fire, and to retain through all an aspiring spirit of indestructible life. In 1894 the old poet of the Sierras, Joaquin Miller, addressed the Pioneers of '49, now grown old, in the fine Biblical strains which, in California, they like to apply to their city:

> My brave world builders of a world
> That tops the keystone, star of states,
> All hail. Your battle flags are furled
> In fruitful peace. The golden gates
> Are won. The jasper walls be yours.
> Your sun sinks down yon soundless shores.
> Night falls. But lo, your lifted eyes
> Greet gold out-croppings in the skies.

> Companioned with Sierra's peaks
> Our storm-born eagle shrieks his scorn
> Of doubt or death, and upward seeks
> Through unseen worlds the coming morn.
> Or storm or calm or near or far,
> His eye fixed on the morning star,
> He knows as God knows there is dawn,
> And so keeps on, and on, and on.

22

FIVE BLEEDING WOUNDS

T HERE are "five bleeding wounds" to be assuaged, said Henry Clay, when Congress met after the inauguration of President Taylor in 1849.

The five bleeding wounds were: California—should it come in as a free state or a slave state? The territorial organization of Utah and New Mexico—should slavery be allowed there? The boundaries of Texas, already committed to slavery and claiming more of New Mexico than some were disposed to allow; the question of slavery in the District of Columbia— should the federal city, representing the North as well as the South, playing host to the nations of the world, be a town where slaves were led through the avenues in gangs, and slave blocks and slave shambles were visible from the dome of the Capitol itself; and the "underground railway," which under the direction of such prominent Northerners as Theodore Parker and Thurlow Weed, was spiriting slaves away to freedom in Canada, or, as the South said, was deliberately stealing its property. "What is the plan of the President?" cried Clay. "Is it to heal all these wounds?"

As is the custom in America the whole question had been kept in abeyance until after the election. Indeed, because of the wish of the political leaders to avoid a crisis, every question concerning slavery had been carefully soft-pedaled, and the vote for president represented no clear expression of popular opinion on the one matter which was really vital. Now the conditions on the frontiers allowed no further delay. Unless the colonists in Utah, California, Oregon, and even in Texas were given adequate federal backing in defending themselves and establishing law and order, there was every possibility that they would simply vote themselves out of the reach of the American Union into the protection of some government that would look after them—most likely Great Britain. Whether Great Britain would have undertaken the responsibility is another question. But the fur forts of the Northwest, the British ships upon the Pacific, the British business houses in San Francisco and Mexico, stood as a last resort for beleaguered Americans far from home. Here were people who spoke their own language, who shared their standards. And despite the traditional terror of the British in Washington, it must be said that the cooperation of individual Britons with Americans in far places was both generous and intelligent. For the rather hypothetical advantage of sending slaves out to the West, the Americans stood a fair chance of losing not only the land but a portion of their own citizens as well.

2

At the time no one, with the possible exception of Daniel Webster, who was not free to say all that he may have thought, could see where the real difficulty lay. The South was claiming an equal share in the management of the country when the basis for that equality had vanished. The South meant at most 350,000 slaveholders, only a fraction of whom were in a position of genuine leadership, politically, socially, or financially. The rest were simple, uneducated people, dragging along in poverty with one or two slaves. Against this small group there were now 20,000,000 free whites. On the day when those 20,000,000 awoke to their strength and made one cause with free labor, the day of the South was done. It and all its interests would be overwhelmed. But it was not to the interests of Northern capital that this should happen. The great cotton, sugar, and rice industries were largely financed by Northern money. The rich plantations of the South were a valued Northern market. The business of moving all this mighty produce from New Orleans and other Southern ports was in Northern hands. Northern firms managed it, and Northern ships carried it away. And it must be confessed that a good deal of the nefarious business of carrying likely Negroes from Kentucky and Virginia to their death in the deep South was also in Northern tentacles. Not only the capitalists of the South but those of the North were using the old political and social prestige of the South, built on personality and character and genuine beauty of living, to cover a hastily reared, new-rich business and social fabric.

At the beginning the North and the South had started fair and equal—the North to develop a civilization for working-men led and taught by a valued professional class, first by their preachers and later by other educated men; the South to develop a gentleman's civilization, supported like the Greek democracy on slavery, on the theory that fineness of life was not possible for those who worked with their hands, and that scholarship and art and beautiful living could develop only in leisure. In this contest the South had had all the luck. It had the most fertile section of the country. It had a leadership of great personal gifts and splendor of character in the great Virginian dynasty. And for a while it had an incomparable colonial population in the Scotch and Irish migrants who, coming into Pennsylvania and finding good land preempted, had poured southward through the mountain valleys and then westward. To the South they had brought something comparable to the free laboring populations that made the strength of the North—some real sinews of work and war.

These energetic people for a while gave the planter gentry the illusion of great strength and power in the South—pouring westward, setting up new states, opening new lands. They sent their political brains to Congress to fight and talk for the South. They took on the Southern style of living and gave it a certain picturesqueness and dash. But the Scotch-Irish migration had nothing to do with the gentleman ideal of the Southern polity. It was mainly a lucky accident. They just happened to arrive on our shores at a moment when the easiest road to new lands was west by south. And the planter polity never made the most of this inflow of strong and gifted people. They were pushed on and out by land speculators and planters at their back ready to grab up their cleared lands and cabins. After the last of them had been pushed into Texas, there were no more to be pushed anywhere.

Those capable of success under the Southern system had become planters and constituted "the noblest blood" of several states. Many others, especially those with industrial, business, or professional aptitudes, had turned north, to Indiana, Illinois, Iowa. And the rest had taken to the mountains and were living a free but primitive life from which they could not be dislodged.

But after this migration, the South received few other capable groups. The person coming to a new land wanted an opportunity to work for wages, and the chance to acquire a small freehold cheaply and to enjoy a free and honorable neighborhood or group life. This the planter economy did not offer. Unless a man had enough money to set up on a large scale as a planter, there was no place for him. In the North, however, there was lots of work—work for seamen, work in the mills fast developing in New England, in the mines developing in Pennsylvania. And in the West, the great public land domain distributed under the conditions of the Northwest Ordinance had given an opportunity to acquire farms. So the North had gladly received and put to work a handsome increment of Catholic Irish, a large and very intelligent group of Germans, and was sending westward excellent Scandinavian farmers. The free school system of the Northwest made it possible to assimilate these people readily. In the second generation they were all Americans.

Though they had started fair, with all the luck on the side of the South, by the time the nation crossed the Mississippi the huge discrepancy in the real weight and power of the two systems was becoming evident. But the South had the political leadership, and gentlemen bred to politics had a pathetic belief that they could change God and circumstance just by voting. Despite the fast-increasing population of the North, the leadership had hitherto been maintained because of the American system which gives two senators to each state. By keeping the Southern and Northern states balanced, one against the other, and not admitting a Northern state till there was a Southern state to match it, the numbers of senators on each side was exactly even. Beyond that the South trusted to its wits and the cooperation of Northern business to swing the balance in its favor. In the House of Representatives the balance was from the start weighted in favor of the South in another way. The Southerners were allowed some representation for their slaves—one slave being reckoned as equal to three-fifths of a white man. During the earlier years when the South had in the Scotch-Irish the strongest, most pushing, eager group of Western pioneers, the Western interests had been combined with those of the South, as representing agricultural needs in opposition to finance and manufacturing and seafaring. The magic of certain names, such as that of Andrew Jackson, had carried this influence on into the forties.

But with the great panic of 1837, and the long years of depression following it, the character of the West had changed. During hard years, the men who prosper are those who carry no large commitments—and Negro slaves were very large commitments to carry—who are free to move and make the most of anything. So the country emerged from the bad years with the Northwest greatly strengthened. Men had used the time to improve their lands, to build better houses, to set up little local industries. A large new generation had grown up in sobered, ambitious homes and was ready to press on and work new country with its own hands, and develop natural resources in a simple way with its own wits.

Now that the territory west of the river was opening, it was absolutely essential to the interests of the South and the traditional balance of power at least in the Senate that there should be a new slave state for every new free state. But how to achieve this? California could not be made to swallow slavery. Its admission meant that there would be sixteen Northern against fifteen Southern states. To admit California, said Clay, is to heal only one of the five wounds "and to leave the other four to bleed more profusely than ever . . . even if it should produce death itself." "The admission of California," said Calhoun, "will be the test question. If you admit her, it will be notice to us that you propose to use your present strength and to add to it with the intention of destroying irretrievably the equilibrium between the two sections."

What neither capital nor the politicians would see was that the equilibrium had already been irretrievably destroyed. It had been destroyed by every ambitious pioneer family that had left its cleared land and cabin to Negroes and moved over the line into Indiana or Iowa. It had been destroyed by every little businessman of the Northwest who had started a little enterprise to support his family during hard years, and now had half a dozen Germans or Catholic Irish or Scandinavians or other newly arrived people working for him for wages and looking westward for lands of their own. It had been destroyed by a system that had kept the white of the South a "poor white," and left to the South now, in its contest for new states, only men without skills or education or money—even, in many cases without health, listless, demoralized people, ill fed, ill housed, knowing only one thing—that it was disgraceful for white men to work.

3

Faced with its dilemma in the West, the South was at the same time being systematically irritated by the abolitionists. Abolition petitions had long been a sore point in Congress, the great New England leader John Quincy Adams, and some other Northerners, holding that to refuse to hear them was to deny the sacred right of petition. Adams' long battle for the right of petition is one of the great picturesque stories of our history. But unfortunately not all such stories can be included, even in this narrative. During the earlier part of the century few reputable people had had much patience with the abolitionists. In Cincinnati, in Boston even, they were somewhat like the Communists today. Their meetings had been raided. They had been run out of town. In Philadelphia the meetinghouse of the abolitionists was burned. In 1837, in Alton, Illinois, Elijah Lovejoy, the editor of an abolition paper, was brutally murdered, and his murderers acquitted.

But, though many people tried to think that abolitionism was only the idea of a few cranks in Boston, its real strength had been not in New England, but along the Ohio River. The first and strongest moral revulsion against slavery had been in Virginia. All the great Virginians of the Revolutionary period had felt it. The law against slavery had been written by Virginians into the Northwest Ordinance. And the next strongest feeling was in Kentucky where the generous Virginian liberalism was reinforced by the objection of the first pioneers to being dispossessed by plantation owners with slaves. Across the river along the Pennsylvania and Ohio border, people had got the feeling by contagion. As Garrison said, there were a hundred abolition societies outside of New England before there was one in New England. The conversion of New England was due to the strong Yankee opinion flowing backward from Ohio through the North. Yankees in Ohio looking across the river, receiving and helping those who fled across it, white and black, had good reason for objecting and, always communicative, they sent their objections home. So with the Quakers from Pennsylvania and the religious Germans.

Just as the South thought they could settle Western territories by casting votes in Congress, so they thought they could do away with the objection to slavery just by closing the mouths of the abolitionists. But there were things that spoke much louder than abolition lecturers. One was the traffic of the rivers. Slaves were taken down the rivers in gangs, handcuffed together. One such gang on a steamboat was equal to a whole traveling abolition society in making the spectators dislike slavery. One was the slave market in New Orleans. A hundred abolition presses rolling out extras could not have spoken like that. Few casual visitors to the city saw those beautiful plantations with their sheltered kindly life, and their devoted black servants, treated, as Henry Clay said, more like children than slaves. But everybody could visit the slave market. And almost everybody did.

Another kind of speaking against slavery was the letter writing of the Yankee ladies. Yankee women were generally literate and communicative. The Yankee families were large and widespread. Women in a Yankee family in Ohio or Michigan or traveling down the river or in New Orleans on business felt bound to keep in touch with a great variety of relatives, mostly the female relatives. Frank, spicy, completely uncensored, their reports of what they saw and thought went back in crowded mailbags to Aunt Jennie in the village in the New Hampshire hills, and Sister Deborah in the town in Connecticut. And Sister Deborah and Aunt Jennie promptly communicated the same to all the ladies that called, and probably to the sewing circle at the church. These ladies carried it home and talked it all over at the supper table, and then they wrote back, "Henry says that if he . . . etc." The effect of this in forming New England opinion was enormous. The great gifted generation of New England writers who began to lift their voices in the forties, and spoke with increasing poignancy and power up to the Civil War, was brought up on this talk. What, asked the Southerners, did these abolitionists in New England know about slavery? What? Ask Aunt Jennie and Sister Deborah.

Yet the strongest allies of the abolitionists were undoubtedly the Southern apologists themselves. In an evil day for the South, someone had had the bright idea of comparing Northern labor and Southern slavery, saying that Northern labor would be much better off if put in the condition of the Negro of the South. Sometimes the suggestion was couched in idealistic terms. Northern labor, it was said, would never be secure in the North until it could be guaranteed care and food and shelter in old age, and until capital and not labor bore the risks of layoffs and hard times. Sometimes the references were very crude. A Southern capitalist visiting in a Northern resort was sometimes quite capable of speaking airily to a Northern factory owner of "your slaves" and "our black labor." And he never noticed how the thin lips of the Yankee maid waiting on the table set at these words, nor the dagger gleam in the eye of the Yankee boy that held his horse. The Southerners were very proud of this comparison. They made it on all possible occasions. A classic example of it is in Grayson's poem *The Hireling and the Slave* which has been quoted in the chapter "Caciques of the Rice Country." The great classic rejoinder to it is that by Webster, already quoted in the chapter "Go Heave That Cotton." The resentment of this kind of Southern talk runs through *The Biglow Papers:*

> Well, go 'long to help 'em stealin'
>   Bigger pens to cram with slaves;
> Help the men that's always dealin'
>   Insults on your fathers' graves;
> Help the strong to grind the feeble,
>   Help the many against the few;
> Help the men that call your people
>   White-washed slaves and peddlin' crew!

All the abolitionists in the world could never do what the the Southern gentlemen thus casually did for themselves in making the cause of the slaves one with the cause of free labor in the North.

The murder of Lovejoy in Illinois gave a new and dramatic start to the abolition movement. So slaveowners would have a man who spoke against them murdered, would they! Abolitionism thus became a great rallying point for all sorts of things that were threatened—for law against lawlessness, for the independence and security of labor, for the right of free speech and the right of petition. And on this broader basis, the abolition societies began to increase very fast, and many a family restrained from joining them nevertheless gave quiet assent to their principles and helped, at least in confidential conversation among intimates, to spread their propaganda. Pale with anger, lips quivering, eyes blazing, Calhoun appealed again and again to Congress for some means of stopping these dreadful societies, for silencing these "insults to the South." There was no way. As well stop the Mississippi from flowing.

4

But the old Titans in Congress were all ready to go to war against destiny. In the fall of 1849 the three great senators who for thirty years had represented the South, the Middle Border, and the North gathered for their last heroic battle with fate. Old, indomitable, they faced the looming shadow, darkness before them and death at their backs. There came Calhoun, so feeble that he could not speak, but had his speech read for him by Senator Mason of Virginia. There he sat, said Schurz, "the old champion of slavery, himself the picture of his doomed cause—a cause at war with the civilization of the age —vainly struggling against destiny—a cause which neither union or disunion, neither eloquence in council nor skill in diplomacy nor bravery in battle could save."

Almost as feeble, but still dragging his old body up in speech after speech, there was Henry Clay, bringing to the battle once more the beautiful, pathetic courtesy of the old

Virginia border—the feeling that surely, since we are all gentlemen, we can make all go well. "I go," he said, "for honorable compromise wherever it can be made. All legislation, all
government, all society, is formed on the principle of mutual
concession, politeness, comity, courtesy; upon these everything is based. I bow to you to-day because you bow to me.
You are respectful to me because I am respectful to you. Compromises have this recommendation that if you concede anything, you have something conceded to you in return. Let
him who elevates himself above humanity, above its weak-
nesses, its infirmities, its wants, its necessities, say, if he please,
'I will never compromise,' but let no one who is not above
the frailties of our common nature disdain compromise."

And there was Webster, old, too, but rugged as his own
granite New Hampshire hills, carrying even in his bearing the
forewarning of where the real strength in the coming war of
North and South would lie. "That amorphous, craglike face,"
said Carlyle, "the dull black eyes under their precipice of
brows, like dull anthracite furnaces needing only to be blown;
the mastiff mouth accurately closed. I have not traced so much
silent, berserker rage, that I remember of, in any other man."
But in his eyes shone such knowledge of and understanding of
the whole matter as no one else had. His was by far the greatest mind of them all, the widest vision, the most accurate sense
of fact. He stood there with victory behind him—with the
money, the industries, the ships, and even with that intimate
knowledge of the South which the widespread Yankee enterprise put at the command of Northern capital. Above and beyond all this at his back, as he said, stood God himself. He was
the one man in all that strange and futile fighting in Congress
who seems to have clearly grasped the overwhelming fact.
Slavery could not be extended into the Western territories.
Slavery was profitable, possible even, in a moist low country
where agriculture could be pursued by hand labor. If the West
was to be opened, it would have to be by machinery, and by
a type of man corresponding to those whom the land had

already bred—the mountain men, the prairie hunters—in other words, though he did not quite foresee this, by miners and cowboys.

It was all ended, he thought and said. There was no more they could do about it. God had intervened and nature had spoken. Let us leave slavery where it is, and have done. The blow had fallen on the South. The day when its system could compete side by side with the system of the North was past. The one thing necessary was to soften the blow. Concede anything—they would get little enough out of it. Keep them as happy as possible till they themselves awoke to the fatal facts.

John C. Calhoun had never faced facts in all his valiant long career, and with his last breath he was there to deny them. Every time his beloved state of South Carolina was in difficulty, he had a sure remedy. Let's scrap the government of the United States and make one that suits South Carolina better. So here he was now with a plan of government. Let us, he said, restore the balance of power between the North and the South by amending the Constitution to give us two presidents, one for each section and each having a veto! "If you of the North will not do this," he said, "then let our southern states separate and depart in peace."

Depart in peace—there was an echo of this in the North.

> Men had ought to put asunder,
> Them that God has noways joined.

But these echoes were in New England. Out there on the rivers it was another matter. Webster, with his far-off gaze on the map of his country, answered: "Sir, nobody can look over the face of this country at the present moment—nobody can see where its population is the most dense and growing without being ready to admit and compelled to admit that ere long America will be in the valley of the Mississippi. Well now, Sir, I beg to inquire what the wildest enthusiast has to say on the possibility of cutting off that river, and leaving free states

at its source and its branches, and slave states near its mouth.
. . . Here, Sir, are 5,000,000 of free men in the free states
north of the river Ohio; can anybody suppose that this population can be severed by a line that divides them from the
territory of a foreign and alien government down somewhere
—Lord knows where—upon the lower banks of the Mississippi?"

The idea of peaceful secession he scouted. "Peaceable
secession! Sir, your eyes and mine are never destined to see
that miracle. The dismemberment of this vast country without convulsion! The breaking up of the fountains of the deep
without ruffling the surface. . . . Is the great constitution
under which we live here, covering the whole country, is it
to be thawed and melted away as the snows on the mountains
melt under the influence of a vernal sun—disappear almost
unobserved and die off? No, Sir! No, Sir! I will not state
what might produce the disruption of the states, but I see, Sir,
I see it as plainly as I see the sun in heaven—I see that the
disruption must produce such a war as I will not attempt to
describe in its twofold character."

But Clay interposed, still begging them to compromise
amicably all existing questions of slavery upon a "fair, equi-
table, and just basis." He would concede to the North that
California should be admitted with the constitution she had
already formulated, forbidding slavery. He quite understood
the feelings of the North about slave trade in the capital city.
It was painful and unbecoming. He would grant that it should
be abolished there, provided, of course, that the near-by state
of Maryland would agree. He understood the feelings of the
South about the fugitive slaves. These slaves were their property. If you had invested hundreds of dollars in a man, naturally you were entitled to keep him and to have him returned
like any other property if he strayed into some other territory.
He would, therefore, suggest a much more stringent enforcement of the fugitive slave law. As for Utah and New Mexico,
the question was, after all, premature. Why not leave it open

till these territories were ready to come in as states, and see what the people of these localities might then desire?

The debate on these proposals lasted from September to March. It was closed by Webster on March 7, 1850, in a speech which has made the date famous ever since. Up rose the rugged old New Hampshire man, and surveyed the whole question of slavery, historically and geographically. Of the contention of the South that slavery was written into our Constitution, and that to object to it was to be disloyal to the founding fathers, he made short work. As for the founding fathers, there was no doubt that, with a few exceptions from the Far South, they objected to the institution and wished if possible to do away with it. This was as true of the great Virginians as of the New Englanders. The original Constitution, he said, the last work of the Continental Congress and apparently the original germ of the Constitution itself, was the Northwest Ordinance, and there slavery was forbidden. Though out of deference to one section of Southern opinion, such a provision against it was not made in the Constitution itself, it was the prevailing opinion South as well as North that this form of labor was undesirable and would probably die out of itself.

Now, he asked, what had changed this situation? The cotton industry. It had not only made slavery profitable, and therefore desirable and right; it had brought about a condition in which the whole government of the United States throughout the period since the Constitution had been adopted, had been dominated by one single economic interest—the interest of the cotton planters. "The age of cotton became the golden age of our southern brethren. It gratified their desire for improvement and cultivation at the same time that it excited it. The desire grew by what it fed upon, and there soon came to be an eagerness for other territory, a new area or areas, for the cultivation of the cotton crop, and measures leading to this result were brought about rapidly one after another under the lead of southern men at the head of the government, they having a majority in both branches to accomplish their ends. The honorable member from South Carolina observed that there has been a majority all along in favor of the North. If that be true, Sir, the North has acted either very liberally and kindly or very weakly, for they never exercised that majority five times in the history of the government. Never. Whether they were out-generalled, or whether it was owing to other causes, I shall not stop to consider; but no man acquainted with the history of the country can deny that the general lead in politics of the country for three-fourths of the period that has elapsed since the adoption of the constitution has been a southern one."

However, the question of the further extension of slavery in the territory of the United States is now closed, he said, because there is no land into which the institution can now be extended. In no territory not covered by the provisions of the Missouri Compromise is it possible to introduce slavery. Why waste breath discussing slavery in New Mexico, for example? "What is there in New Mexico that could possibly induce anybody to go there with slaves? There are some narrow strips of tillable land on the borders of the rivers; but the rivers themselves dry up before midsummer is gone. All that they can do is to raise some little articles, some little wheat for their tortillas, and that by irrigation. And who expects to see a hundred black men cultivating tobacco, corn, cotton, rice, or anything else on lands in New Mexico made fertile by irrigation?"

As for California, he waved the question aside grandly. "I would not take pains to re-affirm an ordinance of Nature or re-enact the will of God."

What then were we to do about it all? The answer was simple. Protect the slave states in their present property, and cease to annoy them with unnecessary criticism of their domestic institutions. He was for a stringent enforcement of the fugitive slave law. As for the abolition societies—"I do not think them useful. I think their operations for the last twenty years have produced nothing good or valuable." And scathingly he referred to busybodies "who can't think of anything to do for the cause of liberty except to contribute to an abolition press or abolition society or pay an abolition lecturer."

Nevertheless, he felt bound to say that all the offensive talk was not on the side of the North. And here he spoke even more scathingly of those Southerners "who speak of the laboring people of the North as if they were in any way comparable to the slaves of the South . . . or try to prove that the absolute ignorance and abject slavery of the South is more in conformity with the high purposes of immortal rational human beings than the educated, the independent, the free laborers of the North."

5

Webster's speech pleased the business interests of the North, especially those circles in New York, Philadelphia, and Boston which had large investments in the South and were accustomed to do business there. Doctor John T. Metcalfe, for example, wrote to his friend James Colles, a New York merchant with a home in New Orleans, accustomed to travel back and forth between the two cities: "Everybody here is delighted with the great speech of Mr. Webster on the slavery question. As usual with him he has taken the tangled web, and by the wonderful clearness of his logic, unravelled every fibre so that no fair and honest can can fail to understand and be satisfied."

The adjustment of this Colles family to slavery is probably characteristic, too, of the many wealthy families of the North who had connections or property in the South. "When they were in the South, they owned slaves for household purposes," but they gave them their freedom when they moved North for any long period, or took north as free servants the ones to whom they were most attached. "The father of the family disapproved of the idleness encouraged by the multiplicity of slave servants, so that his children were made to wait on themselves. The boys had to brush their own clothes and even their shoes." Families of this sort were endeavoring to hold the balance between the South and the North. Kindly and civilized Northern capitalist families naturally had friends in the South of their own type, planters who treated their slaves humanely, whose people were happy and enjoyed many little comforts, as well as lifelong security—if their masters remained solvent. To such Northerners the representations of the abolitionists seemed grossly exaggerated. And they understood and sympathized with the shadow of fear that hung over the South—the hideous fear of a Negro uprising stimulated by fanatical Northern sympathizers with the slaves. They felt that the South was in a tragic dilemma, and wished, at all costs, to give it time to work out of it. There were a great many discussions about ways and means of simply buying out slavery, raising enough capital in the North to reimburse the whole planter South for changing from slave to free labor. Daniel Webster said he would cooperate to the last limit of his power with any feasible plan of this sort; and Daniel Webster spoke for his masters, the Northern capitalists.

On the other hand, even a sympathetic Northern capitalist had his moments of impatience with the attitude of the South. These fugitive slaves, for example—of course they were their masters' property and should be returned if possible. On the other hand, the hard-boiled employer of Northern workmen could not quite respect the Southerner's attitude. It was a bit softy. After all, what did a slave owner expect? Runaway slaves were just one of the risks of his business. If he treated his slaves well, they probably wouldn't run away. If one of them was still restless and unruly, well, that was his hard luck. He ought to expect accidents of that sort and allow for them in his calculations. No sense in upsetting the whole country and making a lot of bad blood out of just one of the normal troubles of capital in this world! So with the abolitionists. Of course they were cranks. But the mutual calling of names is one of the privileges of a democracy. Suppose these abolitionists did condemn you. Up here in the North we are used to being condemned by somebody. Reformers are always having meetings and passing resolutions and printing pamphlets. Suppose we ran to Congress with it every time somebody called us names!

While Daniel Webster pleased the capitalist circles, and with their cooperation was able to recommend the Compromise of 1850, as outlined by Clay, to the country, his words brought an outcry from the intelligentsia of New England, who had been his friends and admirers. Most of them had embraced the cause of the abolitionists and felt not only that he was unjust to them, but that he knew he was unjust. The explanation of Webster's words was clear enough, said his own friends. He had committed himself to household expenditure which kept him in debt to the bankers. He had sold his integrity—the respect of his only genuine intellectual equals—to a standard of living. Magnificent he had been, but now, wrote Whittier

> Of all we loved and honored, naught
> Save power remains,
> A fallen angel's pride of thought
> Still strong in chains.
> All else is gone; from those great eyes
> The soul is fled.
> When faith is lost, when honor flies,
> The man is dead.
> Then pay the reverence of old days
> To his dead fame;
> Walk backward, with averted eyes,
> And hide the shame.

6

Meanwhile some of the greatest literary talent of the nation had rallied to abolition. When the speech of Daniel Webster began to be discussed in households all over the North, and a flame of indignation ran from home to home and town to town along the border and northward and eastward into New England because of the operations of the fugitive slave raiders, the feeling burst forth, passionate, intense, rich with the buried sentiments of years, in *Uncle Tom's Cabin*. But already the abolitionists had three mighty champions in Lowell, Whittier, and Emerson. Whittier was, perhaps, a natural-born radical. But Lowell and Emerson were not. Men of great moderation and balance, with wide-ranging, rich minds, their stand in this matter was absolutely uncompromising. The generation that was to fight the Civil War was to grow up on their words. And what words they were! It had been one of the fondest dreams of Southern civilization that in the "leisure" made possible by slavery, literature and art would blossom. But when the test came, all the literary talent seemed to be on the wrong side of the Mason and Dixon line.

Lowell had been exercising his talents in collecting typical Yankee opinion and putting it into typical Yankee phraseology. He worked very hard at this task, studying popular speech, writing little discussions of phonetics, noting down turns of phrase as he heard them. The result was the spicy comment of *The Biglow Papers*, one series of which had been written during the Mexican War, and a second series of which began with the Civil War.

> Laboring man and laboring woman
>> Have one glory and one shame,
> Everything that's done inhuman
>> Injures all on 'em the same.
>
> Why, it's just as clear as figgers,
>> Clear as one and one makes two,
> Chaps that make black slaves of niggers
>> Want to make white slaves of you.
>
> Slavery ain't o' nary color,
>> 'Taint the hide that makes it worse
> All it cares for in a feller
>> 'S just to make it fill his purse.

> I'll return ye good for evil
>   Much as we frail mortals can,
> But I won't go help the devil
>   Making man the curse of man;
>
> Call me coward, call me traitor,
>   Just as suits your mean ideas,—
> Here I stand a tyrant-hater
>   And a friend of God and peace.

So Lowell had written. For more than a decade now Whittier had been a spokesman for white labor and the common cause it was ready more and more to make with the black labor of the South.

Tell us not of banks and tariffs—cease your paltry peddler cries.
Shall the good state sink her honor that your gambling stocks may rise?
Would you barter man for cotton, that your gains may sum up higher?
Must we kiss the feet of Moloch, pass our children through the fire?
Is the dollar only real—God and truth and right a dream?
Weighed against your lying ledgers, must our manhood kick the beam?

> Let Virginia

Still shame your gallant ancestry, the cavaliers of old,
By watching round the shambles where the human flesh is sold.

But workmen in Massachusetts, farmers in Pennsylvania, had something else to say.

What asks the Old Dominion? If now her sons have proved
False to their fathers' memory—false to the faith they loved,
If she can scoff at Freedom, and its great charter spurn,
Must we of Massachusetts from truth and duty turn?

We hunt your bondsmen, flying from Slavery's hateful hell—
Our voices at your bidding, take up the bloodhound's yell

We gather, at your summons, above our fathers' graves
From Freedom's holy altar-horns to tear your wretched slaves?

The voice of free broad Middlesex—of thousands as of one,
The shaft of Bunker calling to that of Lexington;
From Norfolk's ancient villages, from Plymouth's rocky bound,
To where Nantucket feels the arms of ocean close her round;
From rich and rural Worcester, where through the calm repose
Of cultured vales and fringing woods, the gentle Nashua flows.

And sandy Barnstable rose up, wet with the salt sea spray,
And Bristol sent her answering shout down Narragansett Bay,
Along the broad Connecticut old Hampden felt the thrill
And the cheer of Hampshire's woodsmen swept down from Hol-
    yoke Hill.
The voice of Massachusetts, of her free sons and daughters,
Deep calling unto deep aloud—the sound of many waters.
Against the burden of that voice what tyrant power shall stand?
No fetters in the Bay State. No slave upon her land.

As for the German farmers of Pennsylvania—

> And that bold hearted yeomanry, honest and true
> Who, haters of fraud, give labor its due;
> Whose fathers of old sang in concert with thine
> On the banks of Swetara the songs of the Rhine,
> The German-born pilgrims who first dared to brave
> The scorn of the proud in the cause of the slave,
> Will the sons of such men yield the lords of the South
> One brow for the brand—for the padlock one mouth?
> They cater to tyrants—they rivet the chain
> Which their fathers smote off on the negro again?

With regard to the attempt to push slavery into the territories
of the West, Whittier had written:

Is this, O countrymen of mine, a day for us to sow
The soil of new-gained empire with slavery's seeds of woe,
To feed with our fresh life-blood the Old World's cast off crime,
Dropped like some monstrous early birth, from the tired lap of
    Time—

To run anew the evil race the lost old nations ran
And die like them of unbelief of God and wrong of man!

If the West is open, let the North colonize it:

So shall the Northern pioneer go joyful on his way
To wed Penobscot's waters to San Francisco's Bay,
And make the rugged places smooth, and sow the vales with grain,
And bear with Liberty and Law the Bible in his train.
The mighty West shall bless the East and sea shall answer sea,
And mountain unto mountain call, "Praise God, for we are free."

When Daniel Webster's great speech burst upon the
North, and all his personal weight, the weight of the greatest
single personality in Congress, was thrown behind the Compromise of 1850 and the more stringent enforcement of the
Fugitive Slave Act, these words of Lowell and Whittier were
in treasured scrapbooks in hundreds of homes. And thousands
of homes, too, had Longfellow's poems on slavery, published
in 1842—not so sharp and searching, rather pretty and sentimental and remote, but very popular. One stanza in these
poems spoke the warning which Lowell and Whittier were
sounding with more ringing blasts:

> There is a poor blind Samson in this land,
> Shorn of his strength, and bound in bonds of steel
> Who may in some grim revel raise his hand
> And shake the pillars of this Commonweal,
> Till the vast Temple of our liberties
> A shapeless mass of wreck and rubbish lies.

As household after household took up the discussion of
Webster's speech, what a getting out of scrapbooks and re-
reading of verses there was, voices choking, tears starting to
their eyes. It was beginning to matter very much to the plain
people of the North. Every liberty their forefathers had
fought and bled for—habeas corpus, trial by jury, the right of
petition, the right of free speech, the dignity and freedom of
labor and its right to rise through thrift and independent enterprise—was threatened in the new slave raid unloosed on the

nation. The new fugitive slave law denied the right of trial by jury to a fugitive slave claiming to be a free man; it imposed fine and imprisonment on any white man who in any way hindered the arrest of a black man whom anyone claimed as a slave; it gave federal commissioners the right to pass on the merits of cases instead of leaving this power with state officials. Nor could one avoid trouble by just keeping quiet. "All good citizens are hereby commanded to aid and assist in the prompt and efficient execution of this law, whenever their services may be required." Mistresses saw maids, who had for years worked happily for them for wages, snatched out of their kitchens. Villages saw quiet and respectable persons with some colored blood, who had been accepted as good neighbors, marched off in manacles. Slavery in its most obnoxious form was now thrust right under the nose of the North, and federal commissioners were there to say, "You have to like it." "The act of Congress of September 18, 1850," said Ralph Waldo Emerson, "is a law which every one of you will break on the earliest occasion—a law which no man can obey, or abet the obeying, without loss of self respect and forfeiture of the name of gentleman."

Thus Calhoun, Clay, and Webster had worked to stanch five bleeding wounds. In stanching the five, they had opened a sixth, and the sixth was mortal. But before the last hope of union ebbed away, all three of the titans were dead. Webster lived to pronounce the funeral oration of his lifelong antagonist in Congress, John C. Calhoun. He lived to know of the death of Clay and of his own defeat as a candidate for the presidential nomination in 1852. And then "he sought the refuge of his lovely home near the resounding surf, there to lie down and die." Not one of them lived to see the coming of the war against whose looming shadow they had battled out their lives.

23

BLEEDING KANSAS

IN THE golden vacuum of the prairies is the sweet little city of Lawrence, Kansas. You come out of the throb of sunshine in the cornfields, and there it is, cool and straight and neat, with double lines of trees on each side of the long, pleasant, homelike streets, and in June roses blooming between the trees. There are memories in the old town, of far away and long ago, of shaded New England towns, memories of places where the tablecloths had to be very starched and very white and of a jewel-like pearly smoothness, achieved by carefully rolling them on rolls of newspaper, with no folds to mar the clear sheen, and, when company came, the table must groan with preserves and best china. There, while all the prairie is going to blazes, one may still find an old New England parlor, dusted and double dusted, arranged with the precision of Euclid, where the curtains at midday are drawn against the sun, and the electric fan sings blessedly, and jessamine flowers in glass bowls drip coolness on every table, and someone comes in every few moments and brings you lemonade in a tall glass.

Now Lawrence is the seat of the University. But this ghost of New England that walks up and down it, so delightfully

chill on a warm day, has one of the most tragic stories to tell
in the history of the prairies—a story tragic enough in itself,
but most tragic in all its implications. For in Lawrence the
Civil War began. No one knew it then. It is obvious enough
now.

It began with talk in capitalistic circles of a railroad from
the Mississippi to California. With the development of the Far
West, there was increasing need of opening and organizing
the great intermediate territory which, almost uninhabited at
the time, was a highway to Utah, Santa Fe, California, and
Oregon—the so-called Nebraska territory. This comprised
the present states of Kansas, Nebraska, North Dakota, South
Dakota, Montana, and parts of Wyoming and Colorado. The
railroad interests and others were anxious to get this immense
region organized—indeed it was necessary to do so for the
adequate protection and servicing of the settled regions beyond. But every attempt to organize was blocked by the
Southern determination that there should be no more free
states, so long as there were no more slave states; and all this
land lay north of the line set by the Missouri Compromise for
the northern bounds of slavery. So Senator Douglas from Illinois, representing railroad interests, enraged Northern labor
and amazed even the Southern leaders by blandly proposing
to repeal the Missouri Compromise and open the whole territory to squatter sovereignty—to be settled by North and
South in competition, and to be voted into the Union, as free
states or slave states, as the future populations might decide.
The act itself declared that its true intent was "not to legislate slavery into any territory or state, nor to exclude it there-
from, but to leave the people thereof perfectly free to form
and regulate their domestic institutions in their own way."

The Senator who thus made this handsome gesture in the
direction of the South was a Vermont Yankee who had moved
in boyhood to southern Illinois. Despite the fond belief of the
South that its Norman blood was peculiarly gifted in politics,
it is strange how dependent the planter interest was on lead-

ers from among the lesser breeds without the law—Scotch-
Irish and Yankee, for example, when it came to get something done in Congress. Now that the great Scotch-Irishman
of humble mountain birth was laid away in his grave, here was
a helpful Yankee all ready to take his place.

Douglas, now the most adroit parliamentarian in Congress,
rallied half of the Northern Democrats to his bill. As for the
South, it "flew to the bill as a moth to a candle."

The bill was passed in the Senate by a vote of thirty-five
to twelve; in the House by a vote of 113 to 100. "The bill
annuls all past compromises with slavery," said Sumner, "and
makes all future compromises impossible. Thus it puts freedom
and slavery face to face and bids them grapple." Here and
there a Yankee looked on shrewdly and thought, "You've
been asking for a fair fight. Now you have it. Go to it, and
may the best man win."

2

The bill brought flaring out of the North a deep-seated and
passionate resentment which no one had foreseen. Douglas
himself said that he was burned so often in effigy that he
might have traveled from Chicago to Boston in the light of
the blazing fires. Several states, feeling that this was a betrayal
of their sincere effort to abide by the obnoxious Compromise
of 1850 expressed their resentment by a renewed opposition
to the Fugitive Slave Act. Michigan, Rhode Island, and Connecticut passed personal liberty laws, virtually annulling the
operation of that act within their boundaries. Meanwhile in a
furious burst of energy the abolition societies, now increased
by a great accession of people hitherto "on the fence," took up
the challenge. Squatter sovereignty indeed! They'd show 'em.
Emigrant aid societies were organized in every state to move
families out into the new territory, to put behind them all the
Northern resources of capital and machinery and social organization. The Yankee belt had by this time a well-developed
technique of settlement. It was not in vain that they had

settled Michigan, Minnesota, and Oregon almost overnight—
smoothly moving a whole civilization, schools, churches, uni-
versities, transportation into place. Now this well-oiled machinery prepared to move on Kansas, propelled by a mighty
force of moral indignation.

The South had no such technique. Southern settlement had
been largely the moving on of individual families, originally
a hardy and able type of woodsmen. There were some families
of this type still available in Missouri and Arkansas, and they
were encouraged to move on and settle Atchison, Leavenworth, and Lecompton. But mostly the old type of Southern
frontiersman was now prosperous and settled, and not to be
moved out from where he was, south or north. What was
available in the way of colonial stock was mainly a shiftless
sort of chronic squatter or a wild roaming population in Missouri brought thither by the trapping interests and the demand
for teamsters in connection with the movement to California,
Oregon, and Utah. Though, being nearer, some Southerners
were the first to reach the disputed territory, when the great
Northern machine of settlement started moving down on
them they were overwhelmed. They could not compete in
numbers, in money, in machinery, in culture, in techniques of
any sort.

Every Northern state east and west had its emigrant
society, and many of the larger cities had units of their own.
Those who volunteered to move to Kansas had behind them
numbers who could not move but who contributed money,
who looked after their affairs at home, who bought out their
business at generous prices, offered to keep the children till
they were settled out there, to send anything after them.

Men were sent ahead to look over the ground and lay out a
capital for the new republic of the free. In the midst of a "very
beautiful prairie" they chose the site of their city and named
it Lawrence after a New England gentleman who was backing
the project, and all was ready. Now from New York and Connecticut, from Ohio and Michigan and Wisconsin, from all

the states of the North, there advanced the determined home-
steaders, proud, valiant, chanting the hymn which Whittier
had written for them:

> We cross the prairies as of old
>   The pilgrims crossed the sea,
> To make the West as they the East
>   The homestead of the Free.
>
> We go to plant her common schools
>   On distant prairie swells,
> And give the Sabbaths of the wild
>   The music of her bells.
>
> Upbearing like the Ark of old
>   The Bible in our van,
> We go to test the truth of God
>   Against the fraud of man.

Into Kansas they poured, the New Haven company, the
New England companies, the New York company, the Ohio
company, the Wisconsin company. The town of Lawrence
appeared almost by magic—a hotel, a printing press, a school,
a church. Everywhere there was the sound of hammers. Everywhere wagons rolled in loaded with bureaus and tables. As
each new company came in there was a rustling around on
the part of those who were already there to greet them. "A
large company from Wisconsin came in," reported Mrs.
Robinson, wife of the Charles Robinson who was later governor of the free staters and commander in chief of their defense. "Two of our ladies arranged to greet them with refreshments of cake, nuts, fruits, and lemonade." The New Haven
company arrived. There was a flurry to have all ready for
them "with neatness and order." Another company came.
Ladies of the Literary Charitable Association gave a social
entertainment at the hotel. There were "refreshments of cakes,
fruits, and ice-cream," and afterwards dancing.

They brought everything along. Doctor Robinson came

home one day to find his wife on the stepladder putting up pictures and engravings. There were big boxes of books. There were dress clothes. There were more pianos than ever emigrated to a wilderness before. And after a harried morning spent in carpentering, digging in the garden, or painting the front fence, everybody seemed to have time to put on nice clothes and go over to someone else's house for tea, or to meet at the hotel for a sociable or literary evening.

Meanwhile they attacked the prairie with machinery. "The music of the hay-cutters with their large mowing machines," says Mrs. Robinson, "has for days chimed in with the noise of hammers, the cheerful voices of teamsters, and the glad carol of singing birds. The appearance of the haymakers is most novel as they ride in among the tall grass, higher than their heads in many places, and bearing now a beautiful tasselled blossom of red with yellow stamens, being seated on their mowers as comfortably as when riding in a buggy." As the Northern machines rode peaceably along, the Yankee ladies looked out the windows and snapped their fingers at the whole South. "Take that for your slaves."

3

As the South began to be aware of this invasion, there was a furious effort to meet it. They, too, organized companies. They, too, tried to collect money. But whom could they send? There was only one thing to do—organize that great floating population of hangers-on which the Far Western enterprise had brought out to the frontiers of Missouri—teamsters out of work, runaway boys hoping to be Western heroes, organize them to move on Kansas to scare these Yankees out—shoot them out if necessary. If they tried to vote a constitution in, send a whole gang of Missouri ruffians in to vote against them, each casting as many votes as possible!

All the while, however, every "poor white" that could be induced to move was sent in. Brewerton, sent out by *The New York Herald* to report the migration, compares the proslavery farm with the free-soiler's claim as follows: "The blessings of slavery," he says, "are more land than the owner can cultivate properly 'at present' or probably ever will; an ill-daubed cabin; a tumble-down chimney; a filthy yard; hogs and poultry running at large where they ought not to be; the fences down; the gate, if there is one, off the hinges; the doors too short for the spaces they are intended to fill; the windows stuffed with old hats and cast off clothing to make up for their deficiencies in glass; timberland half cleared, then left to grow up again; more than a sufficiency of snarling worthless curs. Within—a dirty floor and tobacco stained hearth; furniture broken or half mended; no books; ink hard to find; writing paper laid away since 'the old man writ out a receipt for Sam Harris's nigger about six months ago;' whiskey plenty; a pack of *keards;* the females look sickly, care-worn, over-worked; the children would be better for a little Deown East common schooling."

With this he compares the free-soiler's claim. The timber land, he says, is yielding slowly but steadily to the ax, and everything cleared up as the trees fall. The fields are well cultivated. There is a "rough cabin, but comfortable, with mud plastering and solid logs. The fences are in good order. The gate moves easily. The windows, like the widow's bones, all have panes. The hogs have a pen and the chickens have a coop. There is enough to spare in the store-room and food for the brain on the book shelf. The woman is something more than a domestic drudge. There are fifty things that tell of her feminine taste as well as painstaking neatness in the little adornments of this frontier home. The children get their lessons, and 'say them to Mamma every day.'"

The end of the first summer found the leaders of the movement in Lawrence content in their work, unutterably grateful to God for the gift of this beautiful land, but worried by sporadic attacks from the proslavery men, and "hurrying bands of horsemen, brutal looking and uncouth." Warm, serene, glorious, through Mrs. Robinson's diary of the Free-

Soilers runs like religious music the beauty of the prairie. "In the pillared clouds of morning and evening, when the golden and sapphire mingle, we are reminded of the burnished gates and the streets inlaid with pearl of the New Jerusalem. While watching the changing, flitting shadows, which at one moment make the distant landscape a dead blue, and then of a brown color, with little green spots like oases in the desert, life's changes have been typified in the shadows and the sunny light, and we have grown wiser, treasuring the lesson."

But there were coming now from all directions the "hurrying bands of horsemen, brutal-looking and uncouth."

4

And now we turn to an Englishman, T. H. Gladstone, who has come to New York just to travel and see the country. His attention is fixed by an extraordinary current of discussion about Kansas. There is trouble out there. Oh, just the ordinary troubles of settling a new country, say his friends, and try to pass it off. But Gladstone reads the papers and does not think that these are ordinary troubles. There is something very strange about them. The President makes Kansas the subject of a special message. Gladstone reads the message and is still more amazed. "The papers spoke of a legislative body claiming authority over the residents of Kansas which they had not elected, but which had been forcibly thrust upon them by pistol and bludgeon by a lawless crowd from Missouri. The President said that for all present purposes the legislative body thus constituted and elected was the legitimate assembly of the territory. It was too late to raise the question of legality. They must submit. If they did not, the troops of the United States would be used against them. While the President and pro-slavery persons maintained the authority of the illegally constituted territorial Legislature of Kansas, the opposite party, including most of the Kansas people themselves, asserted the claims of an incipient state legislature which they had elected in prospect of its being admitted as a state."

T. H. Gladstone, as a constitutional Englishman, was now thoroughly interested. So he journeyed to Washington and sat in the galleries of Congress and listened to the discussions. He had not the slightest interest in Kansas as such. He had only the mildest curiosity even about slavery. But he seems to have sized the situation up at a glance. The federal government in this country appeared to him to be sold out and safe in the pockets of a minority gang, who were ready to ride roughshod over every decent principle of human liberty and shoot to kill if one defied them. And all agog, he went down to Charleston and other Southern towns to look at the gang. "I witnessed extraordinary meetings presided over by men of influence, at which addresses of almost incredible violence were delivered on the necessity of 'forcing slavery into Kansas' and spreading the beneficent influence of southern institutions over the new territories, and 'driving back at the point of the bayonet the nigger-stealing scum poured down by northern fanaticism.' " These meetings, he said, closed with an earnest appeal for men and money.

Quite unfamiliar with the character of the nigger-stealing scum, knowing nothing about the books and engravings in Lawrence, the beautiful new farm machinery, the sociables with lemonade and ice-cream, Gladstone now headed for the seat of action, traveling across the South. And the more he saw, the more he wondered. What do they want this institution of slavery for anyway? It keeps them poor. "It is a material and economic as well as a social blight." So he goes along, making just the comparisons Brewerton had made between farms and ordinary homes here and those in the North, until he comes to Saint Louis. There he finds newspapers carrying half-page advertisements of pistols, muskets, and bowie knives, and cuts them out and saves them to show to his own countrymen. By this time he has attended a great many political meetings in the South, designed to arouse the people to protect the constitution of the United States from Kansas fanatics. As a sample of this patriotic ferver, he quotes the *Kickapoo Pioneer*.

After accusing the free-state men of being willing to violate the constitution of their country which explicitly recognizes slavery, the editor asks, "should such men receive any compassion from orderly union-loving people?" No. "Let every man who loves his country and the laws by which it is governed . . . meet in Kansas and *kill off this God-forsaken class of humanity as soon as they place their feet upon our soil.*"

He is speeding on now as fast as he can go to Kansas. Across Missouri armies of "border ruffians" are speeding with him. He hears the street orators shouting as he hurries through; "Ball to the muzzle!" "Knife to the hilt!" "Strike your piercing rifle balls and your glittering steel to their black and poisonous hearts!" He hears a person who says he is a respectable merchant of Kansas City yelling: "I've got to fight for the liberties of my country, and our glorious constitution and rid the place of these cowardly blue-bellied Yankees." A strange country, he thinks. They've got a thing they call a written constitution and they are using it to incite "cold-blooded murder" of the people that to a mere Englishman seem to represent the real Constitution—that is the whole political habit and precedent and tendency of the country.

He reaches the outskirts of Lawrence. The city is on fire. The hotel is in ruins. The printing presses have just been dumped into the river. There is every evidence that the city has been given over to "merciless sack." He meets crowds of the border ruffians armed to the teeth with rifles, cutlasses, and bowie knives," "drunken, bellowing, blood-thirsty demons." "Some displayed a grotesque intermixture in their dress, having crossed their native rough red shirts with the satin vest or narrow dress coat pillaged from the wardrobe of some Lawrence Yankee, or having girded themselves with the cords and tassels which the day before had ornamented the curtains of the Free State Hotel."

So he comes into Lawrence, and writes to *The New York Times* letters describing the whole scene and situation.

5

Mrs. Robinson, meanwhile, the writer of the delightful diary, has gone to prison with her husband, Charles Robinson, whom the people of Kansas had elected as governor and who has been accused of high treason against the government of the United States, for usurping authority and inciting to armed resistance against the Missouri mob. Gladstone, curious as ever, looks into the Robinson matter and pays the governor a very high tribute. He says that the steadfast adherence of the people of Kansas to "peaceful measures" and "their remarkable moderation in the midst of much that might have excited a spirit of resistance was doubtless due chiefly" to the wisdom of their commander in chief and governor, Doctor Robinson. "His arrest was made without legal warrant and his tedious confinement in the goal at Lecompton was equally without sentence or trial."

From the prison his wife sent the pages of her diary burning in the mailbags to her friends in the East, with the plea: "Let it be sounded in the ears of the American people that high treason against the United States consists in arming one's self and friends in defence of homes and property in face of a mob who threaten innocent men with death and timid women with a fate in comparison with which death were infinitely preferable!"

It was sounded. Her diary was shot through the printing press. The remarks of T. H. Gladstone came out in *The New York Times*, were printed as a book in England, and reprinted in America. Brewerton and the other New York correspondents sent back the same tale, Brewerton sharp and acid as Westbrook Pegler reporting Fascism. Before a large audience William Lloyd Garrison had publicly burned a copy of the Constitution of the United States to ashes. Now all over the North simple and plain households were mustering their forces for the next election, determined to take their Constitution back into their own hands or give all remaining copies to Mr. Garrison.

"*It Can't Happen Here,*" they say now. It had happened here. The federal government was possessed by a small band of capitalists representing mainly a single economic interest; and any attempt to dislodge them by ballots they were meeting with bullets. Now that it was actually plain to the North, there was no question. In March, 1854, while the Kansas-Nebraska Bill was still pending, a meeting of citizens of all parties in a schoolhouse in Ripon, Wisconsin, organized the germ of the party which was to carry Abraham Lincoln into the presidency five years later. In Michigan, a large gathering in an oak grove outside the town of Jackson, pledged itself to act faithfully in unison to oppose the extension of slavery and never to stop till the victory was won. As news of the doings in Kansas came back, spontaneously all over the North the new party sprang into being. It did not win the presidential election of 1856, being still so new, but it polled an enormous vote for its candidate, John C. Frémont, the glamorous pathfinder of the West. It began to be clear that with a little more time, and with another candidate, one less of a hero and more of a statesman, the victory was sure.

After that, things moved very fast. A lawyer in Illinois who had been a congressman but had abandoned politics, was aroused to moral indignation by the Kansas question and stumped with Stephen A. Douglas all over the state in the great series of the Lincoln-Douglas debates on Kansas-Nebraska. The Kansas-Nebraska Act, said Lincoln "was conceived in violence, is maintained in violence, and is being executed in violence." Of the party into which he had thrown himself, he said in 1858: "Two years ago the Republicans of the nation mustered over thirteen hundred thousand strong. We did this under the single impulse of resistance to a common danger; with every external circumstance against us. Of strange, discordant, and even hostile elements, we gathered from the four winds, and we formed and fought the battle through, under the constant hot fire of a disciplined, proud, and pampered enemy."

And now the long, homely, awkward, ill-dressed son of the frontier South rose to meet the disciplined, proud, and pampered enemy in the person of the great "Yankee rene-gader"—Senator Douglas himself. On his disadvantages in the contest Lincoln was ruefully humorous. The greatest Senator in Congress—Douglas is bound someday to be President, said Lincoln. To his followers he has everything to offer. "They have seen, in his round, jolly, fruitful face post-offices, land-offices, marshal-ships, and cabinet appointments, chargé-ships and foreign missions bursting and sprouting out in wonderful exuberance, ready to be laid hold of by their greedy hands. . . . On the contrary no one has ever expected me to be presi-dent. In my poor, lean, and lank face, nobody has seen that any cabbages were sprouting out." In less than two years it was Lincoln, not Douglas, who was President!

He began the debates an unknown man, with everything against him. When he finished, his great opponent was re-elected to the Senate, but the startled, speculative eyes of men of the new party all over the country were on him. Let Doug-las go to the Senate. But this honest Abe—this awkward fellow? There was still a higher office.

Meanwhile the people were realizing that not only the Constitution and the Houses of Congress and the weak Presi-dent from Pennsylvania, James Buchanan, were in the hands of the Southern capitalists, but the Supreme Court as well, last bulwark of their liberties. By the Dred Scott decision on March 4, 1857, the Supreme Court was thought to have fore-stalled a Republican victory by declaring that Congress had no power whatever to legislate with regard to slavery in the territories. Hence if they did carry the next elections, they would have to support slavery just the same. Under the Con-stitution, Congress could protect and extend slavery, but not restrict it! Buchanan himself was using every resource of patronage to build up Southern possession of office against a possible Northern victory. The last doubt in the minds of the plain people of the North and most of their intellectual leaders—the schoolteachers, preachers, and popular journalists and most beloved writers—had vanished. It was not a question of North against South. No use in electing tools of Northern capital. They were simply playing into the hands of the South and providing it with voice to speak for it and hands to execute its schemes. But this man out in Illinois—Abraham Lincoln. What of him? A plain man of the people, but more than that—honest. No strings tied to him!

Meanwhile the lawlessness in Kansas on the part of the South had its repercussion in Northern lawlessness. John Brown, an old frontiersman, had rushed with his stalwart sons to the aid of the Free Soilers in Kansas. He was picturesque. He was simple-minded. The Free Soilers appreciated him and his aid, and thought him a hero. Now John Brown, despairing of votes doing anything about this burning wrong, organized a raid in Virginia to free the Negroes and captured the arsenal at Harpers Ferry. His rebellion was promptly put down by a small force of marines under Colonel Robert E. Lee, and John Brown was tried and hanged. He met his end with great dignity. "The cry of the oppressed is my reason and the only thing that prompted me to come here," he said. "I feel just as content to die for God's eternal truth on the scaffold as in any other way."

Conservative Northern opinion repudiated John Brown's action as rash and foolish. But among the abolitionists he became a great hero. Speaking to a great Boston audience, Emerson said that he was a "new saint than whom none purer or more brave was ever led by love of men into conflict and death—the new saint awaiting his martyrdom, and who, if he shall suffer, will make the gallows glorious as the cross." To the Southerners who spoke of "lawlessness," the Yankees, remembering the Missouri border ruffians, were ready to answer, "Lawless Brown was, but who started this business of raids and pistols?" Primitive ruffianism had, they thought, brought out a primitive saint and a hero. But in the South, moderate and thoughtful plantation owners now saw stalking before them in dreadful reality their latent fear—the fear of a slave uprising organized by abolitionists; and they were ready at any cost to vote with the seceding states for self-defense.

6

But a slave uprising was not all the South had to fear. There was every chance of a social war, led probably by Kentucky, Virginia, or Tennessee. Even if secession had succeeded, the planter aristocracy would probably have been shortly borne down by such uprising of the white men of the South who did not own slaves. As it was, the call to arms in such a rebellion was issued by a North Carolinian, Hinton Rowan Helper, in his remarkable book *The Impending Crisis,* which appeared only a few months after John Brown's raid, and which sold a million copies within the next year or two.

Addressing "farmers, mechanics, and working men" Helper pointed out the utter demoralization of the South under the rule of the planters. They have, he said, "reduced our proud cities to niggervilles." Of the city of Charleston he says, "Like all other niggervilles in our disreputable part of the Confederacy [meaning by confederacy the whole United States or what the North called The Union] the commercial emporium of South Carolina is sick and impoverished; her silver cord has been loosed; her golden bowl has been broken; and her unhappy people without proper or profitable employment, poor in pocket and few in number, go mourning and loafing about the streets."

The weakness, inertia, and dilapidation, he says, are to be blamed upon a "usurping minority of the people, and we are determined it shall rest where it belongs." The policy of these slaveowners has been to degrade and starve their own free white mechanics, farmers, and workingmen while making rich, prosperous, and happy the workingmen of the North. We are enslaved to the North. "We want Bibles, brooms, buckets, and books, and we go to the North; we want furniture, glassware, and pianos, and we go to the North. We want fashionable apparel, machinery, medicine, and tombstones, and we go to the North. We are more subservient to the North every day of our lives. In babyhood, we are swaddled in northern muslin; we play with northern toys; we sow our wild oats on northern soil. In old age we put on northern spectacles, take northern medicines, and ultimately are carried in a northern carriage, buried with a northern spade, and covered with a northern tombstone."

The result is that the North grows richer and richer and we grow poorer. In seven slave states—Virginia, North Carolina, Missouri, Arkansas, Tennessee, Florida, and Texas—the combined wealth real and personal, including slaves, is not equal to the combined wealth of the happy freemen of New York State alone. Your farmers, mechanics, workingmen, and others in New York State could buy out these states and the District of Columbia, and all their precious slaves, and still have $133,000,000 in their pockets!

What then are the white men of the South to do? There is no time to lose. Abolitionism is their only safeguard, abolition and unremitting war upon the slaveholding class. "Farmers, mechanics, and working-men, we take this occasion to assure you that the slave-holders whom you have elected to offices of honor and profit have hoodwinked you, trifled with you, and used you as mere tools for the consummation of their wicked designs. They have purposely kept you in ignorance, and have by moulding your passions and prejudices to suit themselves, reduced you to act in direct opposition to your dearest rights and interests."

So he calls on the great majority of the Southern people who do not own slaves to organize for the rebuilding of the South, and to declare among themselves a general strike against the slaveholders. Seven-tenths of the white people of the South have no slaves. In some states like North Carolina two-thirds of the people would vote against slavery if given a chance, the slaveholders of that state, nevertheless, being themselves more moderate, decent, sensible, and honorable than in either of the adjoining states or further South. So with Georgia. It is prosperous and thrifty despite its slaveholders, because it also contains 300,000 free white laborers. If all these people who are suffering from the miserable rule of the slaveholding demagogues will combine to use their political and economic power they may by peaceable means put them out. This is the plan Helper suggests. Let every nonslaveholder agree to the following:

"Never vote for a slave-holder; never co-operate with a slave-holder in politics nor enter into fellowship with him in religion or society; never be a guest in a slave-holding hotel; never employ a physician who owns slaves; encourage the labor of free negroes; put a tax of $60 on every slave-holder, and add to this another $40 afted July 4, 1863; afford no recognition to slave-holders except as ruffians, villains, and criminals."

So far as possible the sale of this volume was stopped in the South but not before it had created, as a member of Congress said, "a situation bordering on violence." But the North took it up and used it as a campaign book, and its circulation was enormous. No other book except *Uncle Tom's Cabin* was of such universal interest.

7

In the midst of all this the old party of the Democrats and the new party of the "Black Republicans" met to nominate their candidates for President. The issue was now clear—capital against labor, the capitalists calling themselves Democrats, the free labor party Republicans. The Southern capitalists were loud in their recriminations against their Northern friends. The trouble, they said, is that you pander to the so-called conscience of your people. If, said Yancey of Alabama, "you had taken the position directly that slavery was right and therefore ought to be, antislavery would be dead in your midst."

This was more than even Northern capital would swallow. "Gentlemen of the South," cried Senator Pugh of Ohio, "you mistake us—you mistake us. We will not do it."

So the Northern Democrats withdrew and nominated Douglas for President, declaring for popular sovereignty in the territories. The Southern democrats met in Baltimore and nominated John C. Breckinridge of Kentucky, declaring outright for slavery in the territories. But the Republicans, in a strong upwelling of popular hope and determination, nominated Honest Abe Lincoln. And it is said that when his name was announced, there went up in the convention hall and along the streets and on and on a cheering and a "roar of voices like the breaking up of the fountains of the great deep."

After ten years of· groping, the awakened democracy had found its purpose, and its man. There he stood, gaunt, worn, plain, "the true type," as Motley said, "of American democracy. There is nothing of the shabby genteel, the would-be-but-couldn't-be fine gentleman. He is the great American demos, honest, shrewd, homely, wise, humorous, cheerful, brave, blundering occasionally, but through blunders struggling onwards toward what he believes the right."

24

UNDER THE ONE, THE BLUE;
UNDER THE OTHER, THE GRAY

THE election of Lincoln was a signal for the barons of the South to act. Four days after the election South Carolina called out 10,000 volunteers. On November tenth and eleventh the two senators from South Carolina resigned. The state intended now to go, but not empty handed. So two days before the convention met to vote secession, she accepted the annual allotment of her share of the United States arms, for 1861. Then, all ready to fight, on the twentieth day of December South Carolina passed the ordinance of secession.

South Carolina had never been comfortable in the Union. Founded as an aristocracy, the colony had found itself unhappily yoked with Pennsylvania and New England, and even with liberal Virginia. "All our troubles," wrote John Adams after a meeting of the Continental Congress, "rise from one source—the reluctance of the southern colonies to a republican form of government. A government for these colonies can be formed only on principles abhorrent to the inclinations of the barons of the South and the proprietary interests of the middle states." Now that the proprietary or capitalist interests of the

North had deserted them, the only tie that linked Charleston and its tributaries to the Union was gone.

Mississippi, Florida, Alabama, Georgia, Louisiana, and Texas followed South Carolina out the door. Forts and arsenals were seized, and the steamer, "The Star of the West," sent to Charleston with reinforcements for the federal Fort Sumter, held by Major Anderson, was driven out of the harbor. Meanwhile a Confederacy of the seceded states was formed, with Jefferson Davis as President.

At first the secessionists, with the connivance of the high officials of Buchanan's administration, had counted on seizing Washington, and, when established in the national capital, with its buildings and archives in their possession, hoped for immediate recognition by foreign governments. But the failure of Maryland to secede and the uncertainty of sentiment in Virginia balked this plan. So the Confederate government established itself at Montgomery, Alabama.

"There before me," said a British reporter, "was Jeff Davis's state department—a large brick building at the corner of a street, with a Confederate flag floating over it. The door stood open and gave on a large hall white washed, with doors plainly painted, belonging to small rooms, in which was transacted much important business, judging by the names written on sheets of paper and applied outside denoting bureaus of the highest functions. . . . I had an opportunity of observing the president very closely. He did not impress me as favorably as I had expected. . . . He is like a gentleman—has a slight figure, little exceeding middle height, and holds himself erect and straight. He was dressed in a rustic suit of slate-colored stuff with a black handkerchief around his neck. . . . Wonderful to relate, he does not chew, and is neat and clean-looking, with hair trimmed and boots brushed. The expression of his face is anxious. He has a very haggard, care-worn, and pain drawn look, though no trace of anything but the utmost confidence and the greatest decision could be detected in his conversation."

The abstention from tobacco was not characteristic of other high officials. Russell reported that Walker, the Secretary of War, was a "ruminator of tobacco and a profuse spitter . . . tall, lean, straight-haired, angular, with fiery impulsive eyes and manner . . . a lawyer, I believe, certainly not a soldier, ardent, devoted to the cause, and confident to the last degree of speedy success."

In this Cabinet there were only two of the great planter gentry, and they soon resigned. It was, like the whole Southern "aristocracy" at this period, a conglomerate. Three of its members were foreign born. Its most gifted member, said, Russell, was the Hebrew, Mr. Judah Benjamin, the attorney general of the Confederate states. "The most brilliant perhaps . . . of the famous southern orators. He is a short, stout man, with a full face, olive colored, and most decidedly Jewish features, with the brightest large black eyes, one of which is somewhat diverse from the other, a brisk, lively, agreeable manner, combined with much vivacity of speech and quickness of speech and quickness of utterance. He is one of the first lawyers or advocates in the United States, and had a large practice at Washington, where his annual receipts from his profession were not less than £8,000 to £10,000 a year. But his love of the card table rendered him a prey to older and cooler hands, who waited till the sponge was full at the end of the session, and then squeezed it to the last drop."

The philosophical basis of the new government was stated by the Vice-President, A. H. Stephens. "The corner stone of our new government rests on the great truth that the negro is not equal to the white man; that slavery—subordination to the superior race—is his natural and normal condition." The organization of government on this brave new principle of the inferiority of somebody else went along, with a flourish, in the period which our Constitution allows between the election of the new president and his taking office. The North was aghast, but helpless—helpless as it had been before other machinery of government, such as the power of a repudiated party to perpetuate its influence on legislation by appointments to the Supreme Court.

But up in Massachusetts Lowell's Yankee cocked his shrewd eye at the new confederacy of states, and issued a report from Southern headquarters.

There are creatures so base that they want it explained
Just what is the total amount that we've gained.
As if we could measure stupendous events
By the low Yankee standard of dollars and cents:
They seem to forget that, since last year revolved,
We've succeeded in getting seceshed and dissolved,
And that no one can't hope to get through dissolution
'Thout some kind of strain on the best constitution.
Who asks for a prospect more flattering and bright
When from here clean to Texas it's all one free fight?

2

The fourth of March, 1861, dawned clear and bright. Every day since he had been elected the friends of Lincoln had counted the days still between them and this day, and wondered if the fourth of March would ever come. Every night they had gone to bed thankful that another day had passed and their man was still alive. A fear of the assassination of Lincoln haunted all the North. No one wished to make a show of soldiers along his passage from Springfield, Illinois, to Washington, lest it should seem a threat to these seceding states of the South. But how to get him through safely? An attempt was made to throw off the track the train that carried him out of Springfield; and at Cincinnati a hand grenade was found concealed in the train. At Philadelphia a detective met Lincoln and warned him that he was to be killed at Baltimore. An Italian refugee, a barber, under the assumed name of Orsini, had reported that on a given signal Lincoln was to be shot by some men who gathered around his carriage in the guise of friends—the murderers then to escape on a vessel waiting to take them to Mobile. Meanwhile General Scott and Senator Seward of New

York, who had been Lincoln's greatest rival for the presidency and was to be his Secretary of State, learned from independent sources that Lincoln's life was in danger, and sent Frederick Seward to Philadelphia to warn him to come into the city of Washington in some quiet way. So, at least, the story was later reported in *The Albany Evening Journal.*

Lincoln agreed to use every precaution, but he made one exception. He had promised to raise the American flag over Independence Hall in Philadelphia. This he said he would do, "if it costs me my life." All his political thinking, he said, derived from the Declaration of Independence; and the reassertion of the truth that "we take to be self-evident," once penned for the American people, by a great Southerner, was his answer to the new doctrine of "inferiority" now discovered by the statesmen down in Montgomery.

Of the Declaration of Independence he had said, in answer to Douglas, in 1858: "We are now a mighty nation, thirty millions, or about thirty, and we own and inhabit about one-fifteenth part of the dry land of the whole earth. . . . We have besides these men descended from the blood of our ancestors among us, half our people who are not descendents at all of these men; they are men who have come from Europe —German, Irish, French, Scandinavian—men that have come from Europe themselves or whose ancestors have come hither, and settled here, finding themselves our equals in all things. If they look back through this history, to trace their connection with those days by blood, they find they have none; they cannot carry themselves back into that glorious epoch and make themselves feel that they are a part of us; but when they look through that old Declaration of Independence, they find that these old men say that we hold these truths to be self-evident, that all men are created equal, and then they feel that that moral sentiment taught in that day evidences their relation to those men; that it is the father of all moral principle in them, and that they have a right to claim it as though they were blood of the blood and flesh of the flesh of the men who wrote that Declaration, and so they are. That is the electric cord in that Declaration that links the hearts of patriotic and liberty-loving men together, that will link those patriotic hearts as long as the love of freedom exists in the minds of men throughout the world."

Now standing in Independence Hall in Philadelphia, disturbed and shaken by the news of the plot to assassinate him, worried about the future, Lincoln was not in his usual fine form. Those who had looked for eloquence here were disappointed, but his words, in their very plainness, have in the circumstances a certain poignancy. Referring to the opening words of the great Declaration, he said: "Now, my friends, can this country be saved on this basis? If it can I will consider myself one of the happiest men in the world if I can help to save it. If it cannot be saved on that principle, it will be truly awful. And if this country cannot be saved without giving up that principle, I was about to say I would rather be assassinated on this spot than surrender it."

But when, by the strength of his "own feeble arm," he saw the flag of his country go shooting up into the "bright glowing sunshine of the morning" and flaunt itself to the wind "without an accident," the tired, worried man felt his spirits lifted. "I could not help hoping that there was in the entire success of that beautiful ceremony at least an omen of what was to come."

So he told the people at Harrisburg, Pennsylvania, where he openly appeared later in the day. The alarm about the attempts on his life had brought out a great show of soldiery. This pleased and troubled him. No man ever went forward to a war more shrinkingly. He was not only a man of peace on principle. His great and vivid imagination refused to react to the pride and panoply of war. Before a display of flags and drums all he could think of was that so many mothers' sons were going to be killed, all broken and bloody, and his mind would instantly leap on to the question, "For what?" and settle there, brooding. Later, in the presence of the vast armies he was called on to review—the largest army hitherto raised in the civilized world—he used to refer jocosely to this shrinking, and say that the truth was he was a physical coward. More than one of his friends felt called upon to explain that "Mr. Lincoln underestimated his own great courage."

So now the display of soldiers in the streets of Harrisburg bothered him. He referred to it with the same awkward dignity which had elsewhere along this painful progress to Washington obliterated his amusing, shrewd, quaint, storytelling style of speech: "While I am exceedingly gratified to see the manifestation of your military force here, and exceedingly gratified at your promise to use it on a proper emergency . . . I do most sincerely hope that it will never become their duty to shed fraternal blood."

After his public appearance in Harrisburg, Mr. Lincoln was taken to the hotel. A special train stood ready to carry him on next day, and the people all looked forward to bidding him farewell and Godspeed, with music and drums and flags. But instead he was quietly spirited away on a special train on the Pennsylvania Railroad, and the telegraph wires out of Harrisburg immediately cut so that no news of this departure could be sent on to waiting assassins. Quietly, as if into an enemy camp, he stole into Washington in the gray of the next morning. And at the time when he should have left Harrisburg, he was safe with Seward in the Willard Hotel.

Some of his adherents were disappointed not to see their hero ride in dashingly, a Lochinvar out of the West, snapping his fingers in the face of the rebels. Democracy in this cautious, unheroic guise lacked charm for the imagination. But Lincoln and his friends thought the future too serious to risk on pageantry and showing off. Leave the parading and the bluster to the statesmen down there in Alabama.

3

When he was safe within the Capitol on that fourth day of March, 1861, a great sigh of relief went up. There he was, the tall, gaunt man on whose drooping shoulders the nation had laid its burden. There he was—still safe. When he stepped forth to deliver his inaugural address, there was only a small polite show of applause. His enemies were too numerous, even in that audience. His friends dared not exasperate them. But there he was, and, breathless, a nation was waiting for him to give the marching orders.

His speech was cautious, but so downright and clear that it reassured even the impatient and nerved them to wait a little longer. With regard to the constitutional position on which the nation was to stand, in opposition to the states' rights doctrines of the South, he spoke with decision: "The Union," he said, "is much older than the Constitution. It was formed by the Articles of Association in 1774. It was matured and continued in the Declaration of Independence in 1776. It was further matured and the faith of all the then thirteen states expressly plighted and engaged that it should be perpetual by the Articles of Confederation in 1778; and finally in 1787 one of the declared objects in ordaining and establishing a Constitution was to form a more perfect union. But if the destruction of the Union by one or a part only of the states is legally possible, the Union is less perfect than before, having lost the vital element of perpetuity. It follows from these views that no state can legally get out of the Union; that resolves and ordinances to that effect are legally void; and that acts of violence within any state or states against the authority of the United States are insurrectionary or revolutionary, according to circumstances."

With regard to the Supreme Court's decisions, he said that such a tribunal was absolutely necessary as a court to which to refer the final arbitrament of cases arising between individuals. But the "candid citizen must confess that if the policy of the government upon vital questions affecting the whole people is to be irrevocably fixed by the decisions of the Supreme Court, the instant they are made . . . the people will have ceased to be their own masters . . . having to that extent practically resigned their government into the hands of that eminent tribunal."

As for the present issue, it was not slavery in the states where it existed nor the right of states to administer, without interference, their own internal economy—for that was granted, and these rights would be upheld. The only issue was the right of a minority to extend an institution in quarters where it was not wanted, or was forbidden by the organic law of the nation, long accepted by both North and South, and furthermore the question was whether a minority, defeated at the polls in its attempt to control the whole nation, has any right to secede.

The immediate policy of the government with regard to the rebellious states was therefore simple. So far as the federal government was concerned, these ordinances and resolutions were just somebody's talk. The federal government had certain property to administer in all the states, and this it would administer as usual. "The power confided to me will be used to hold, occupy, and possess the property and places belonging to the government, and collect the duties and imposts; but beyond what may be necessary for these objects, there will be no invasion, no use of force against or among the people anywhere. . . . The mails unless repelled will continue to be furnished in all parts of the Union."

Then turning to the "president" and the "cabinet" feverishly working down there in Alabama, he said: "In your hands, my dissatisfied fellow-countrymen, and not in mine, is the momentous issue of civil war. You can have no conflict without being yourselves the aggressors. You have no oath registered in Heaven to destroy the government while I have the most solemn one to preserve, protect, and defend it. I am loth to close. We are not enemies but friends. We must not be enemies. Though passion may have strained, it must not break our bonds of affection. The mystic cords of memory, stretching from every battle-field and patriot grave to every living heart and hearth stone all over this broad land, will yet swell the chorus of the Union, when again touched, as they surely will be, by the better angels of our nature."

4

In pursuance of his policy of business as usual, Lincoln sent an unarmed vessel with supplies for Major Anderson's almost starving garrison at Fort Sumter. But the fire-eaters of Charleston had not Mr. Lincoln's scruples about beginning a war. They called on Major Anderson to surrender to them, and when he refused, opened their batteries on the fort. After a gallant but comparatively ineffectual defense by the small and worn-out garrison, it was surrendered on April 13, 1861.

The firing on the flag, the flag which the nation had last thought of as flying fair and free over Independence Hall in Philadelphia, united the North in one passionate call "To arms!" On the fifteenth of April, Lincoln called for 75,000 volunteers from the loyal states to seize and hold forts, places, and property taken from the government by the rebels, and to protect the national capital. Instantly Massachusetts started on the march. From early colonial days Massachusetts and South Carolina had represented opposing principles brought to America from the Cavalier-Puritan conflict in England. Now when the old cavalier city unsheathed its sword, prompt, stout, and furious, its ancient enemy sprang to the cudgel.

The march of Massachusetts heartened the nation as nothing else could have done. Down through the blossoming countryside they swung by train, and at every station the crowds met them cheering, women weeping, bringing them gifts and food and Bibles and mothers' prayers. But through the city they went on foot. When New York saw this sturdy tramp down its streets, it is said that old commercial gentlemen stood at the windows of counting houses and doors of warehouses, with tears in their eyes. But when they reached Baltimore, a mob carrying a secession flag came out to meet them, and in the attack that followed, several of the boys were killed or wounded. Thus the first blood of the war was drawn, on the nineteenth of April, 1861, the anniversary of the Battle of Lexington.

So began a conflict till then unparalleled in the civilized world—a "war which for the number of men involved, the amount of space traversed, the coast line blockaded, of material consumed and results achieved," at that time "surpassed all the wars of history."

The command of the rapidly mobilizing federal forces Lincoln offered to one of the most valued officers of the army of the United States, then known to be loyal to the government—to Robert E. Lee of Virginia. Of his personal dilemma Lee wrote his sister: "The whole South is in a state of revolution, into which Virginia, after a long struggle, has been drawn; and though I recognize no necessity for this state of things, and would have foreborne and pleaded for redress of grievances, real or supposed; yet in my own person I had to meet the question whether I should take part against my native state. With all my devotion to the Union, and the feeling of loyalty and duty of an American citizen, I have not been able to make up my mind to raise my hand against my relatives, my children, and my home. I have therefore resigned my commission in the Army, and save in defense of my native state, with the sincere hope that my services will never be needed, I hope never to draw the sword."

To Lee was given the command of the army of Northern Virginia and the capital of the Confederacy was moved to Richmond. Accepting the high command, Lee kept in his heart certain reservations. He did not fight for the new Southern confederacy. He fought for Virginia—to preserve her sacred soil, to keep safe her life and her institutions. Older than the Union, she had a life and tradition of her own, too glorious to besmirch in political quarrels, too beautiful for any man to let die. If liberty died in all other spots on earth, Lee and many another brave man who fought with him intended that it should live like a vestal fire in the land of him who was called the father of his country.

By what twists and turns a convention of Virginians had ever been brought to vote with the seceding states it is difficult to understand—more difficult to know how far the vote represented the real sentiments of the citizens of the grand old state than whose soil no spot in the whole country was dearer to the imagination of all Americans, except only Plymouth Rock and Independence Hall in Philadelphia. But the die was cast, and every inch of that soil given over to desolation.

North Carolina, of which Helper had said that two-thirds of the people would have voted against slavery, followed Virginia out of the Union. Indeed there was little else the state could do, caught now between Virginia and South Carolina. Tennessee and Arkansas, till then uncertain, followed suit. But the Virginians of the western border refused to go out, and organized a state of their own, West Virginia. And the progeny of the Old Dominion—Kentucky and Missouri—remained loyal, though Kentucky would furnish no troops to fight the South and intended only to maintain an armed neutrality.

After the war was over Lee confessed that not only had he not believed in the original cause of the Confederacy; he had never had any hope that the rebellion would succeed. "I have never believed we could against the gigantic combination for our subjugation make good in the long run our independence unless foreign powers should directly or indirectly assist us. . . . But such considerations really made with me little difference. We had, I was satisfied, sacred principles to maintain and rights to defend, for which we were in duty bound to do our best even if we perished in the endeavor."

So taking the sword in hand, a grand old Galahad, handsome, graceful, gentle, benign, he fought with the pertinacity, the shrewdness, the regardless personal courage of the most desperate outlaw, with the self-abnegation and prayerful piety of a saint, and with the personal manners and sentiments of a most civilized gentleman. And everywhere the hearts of chivalrous lads leaped to his leadership, and brave mothers buckled on their swords and sent them forth after their great leader— to die. For what? It was beneath that high, exultant, poetic courage to ask.

As Lee represented the beautiful personal ideal of the old cavalier South, so Stonewall Jackson represented that other ideal which makes the charm of character in Southern history —the picturesque, intense, stript-for-action integrity and swift and dashing action of the Scotch-Irish border. He was the last of the great ballad characters—a man like his predecessor of that name, who just naturally made legend. Odd, crude, intense, he became the hero of his soldiers. No one could swing an army around as fast as he. No one could call on the god of battles so fervently. His prayers, his severe punishments for breaking the Lord's Day (except of course, when there was a battle to be fought. The Lord in his view did not mind fighting on His day—only work), his tenderness and his justice; even the lemon he was always sucking and his queer mannerisms, became the subject of loving comment. His soldiers believed in him the way they believed in the Lord of Battles. Lee, the polished gentleman of tidewater, greatly appreciated the hero of the mountains, and he appreciated Lee. When they spoke of each other, they did it in the grand manner. When Jackson lost his left arm, Lee said, "You have lost your left arm. I have lost my right." When Jackson lay dying, struck by accident by one of his own soldiers, Lee said that he had rather it had been himself. But Jackson answered, "Better ten Jacksons than one Lee."

Of the army led by Lee and Jackson, the army of Northern Virginia, one can only say what was said of it by Swinton, the historian of the Northern Army of the Potomac. Of our adversary, said Swinton, "who that ever looked on it can ever forget it—that array of tattered uniforms and bright muskets—that body of incomparable infantry—the Army of Northern Virginia, which for four years carried the revolt on its bayonets, opposing a constant front to the mighty concentration of power brought against it; which receiving terrible blows, did not fail to give the like, and which, vital, in all its parts, died only with its annihilation."

5

On both sides the boys were mustering. Never in history had there been such a war, such an outpouring of men on both sides, soldiers of such noble appearance and high character. This was because, as European observers pointed out unceasingly, the whole-citizenry on both sides was involved. Of a thousand men marching to join the colors whom he met in the West, Anthony Trollope wrote: "Taking them altogether they were as fine a set of men as I ever saw collected. No man could doubt on seeing them that they bore on their countenances the signs of a higher breeding and better education than would be seen in a thousand men enlisted in England. I do not mean to argue from this that Americans are better than English. My assertion goes to show that the men generally were taken from a higher level in the community than that which fills our own ranks. . . . Forth they came, fine, stalwart, well grown fellows. . . . Many were fathers of families, many were owners of land, many were educated men capable of high aspirations. . . . As soldiers I could find but one fault with them. Their average age was too high. There men among them with grizzled beards, and many who had counted thirty, thirty-five, and forty years."

Edward Dicey also spoke of the outpouring of men as simply magnificent. From the European point of view they looked unsoldierly. They walked with an easy slouching gait. They glanced to right and left and commented on everything and joked as they went by. They wore their uniforms carelessly. But as men they were collectively most impressive. "Men of high stature and burly frames were rare, except in the Kentucky troops; but on the other hand, small stunted men were almost unknown. I have seen the armies of most European countries, and I have no hesitation in saying that as far as the average raw material of the rank and file is concerned the American is the finest." The Americans, he said, were all unaware of the power which, in the heat of their own internal struggle, they had unconsciously displayed. "The wonder to me is that the Americans are not more intoxicated with the consciousness of their new born strength."

Of the proportion of foreigners in the regiments, he said that about thirty per cent of the inhabitants of the North were born in Europe, and there was a similar proportion of foreign-born in their army. Some Western regiments were almost entirely composed of Germans. Most of the regiments marched to the music of German bands. "The Germans have brought with them into their new fatherland the instinct for instrumental music, and the bands are fine ones, above the average of the French or English line regiment." Except for a few of the more recent immigrants, foreign-born and American represented the same high standard of general citizenry, the result of the generally high level of subsistence in America, combined with free education and opportunity for land owning and economic enterprise.

Observers were equally astonished at the display of material wealth and of education which the nation was making. Of the Northern armies Dicey said: "Their clothing was substantial and fitted easily, their arms were good, and the military arrangements were as perfect as money could buy. . . . The number of papers purchased daily by the common soldiers and the amount of letters sent through the common post was astonishing to a foreigner, though less strange when you considered that every man in the army, with the exception of a few recent immigrants, could read and write. The ministers, too, of the different sects who went out to preach to the troops found no difficulty in obtaining large and attentive audiences." In the 200,000 men collected around the city of Washington, said Edward Dicey, there was less brawling and drunkenness than if "half a dozen English regiments were quartered there." This, of course, was not due to the superiority of Americans to English, per se, but was the difference between a great citizen army and professional soldiery.

The question till then often raised in Europe whether a peaceful citizenry could be safe without a large standing army, whether the citizens themselves could be mobilized and trained quickly enough to be effective in a crisis, Dicey said the American armies had now answered. He had seen mechanics from Philadelphia made into good soldiers in six weeks. Indeed they were much more businesslike than European soldiers. "At the scene of war itself there was no play at soldiering. No gaudy uniforms or crack companies, no distinction of classes. From every part of the North, from the homesteads of New England, from the mines of Pennsylvania and the factories of Pittsburgh, from the shores of the Great Lakes; from the Mississippi valley, and from the far off Texas prairies, these men had come to fight for the Union." Fighting was grim business to them, and they took it seriously.

These soldiers had no patience with the way the political leaders were soft-soaping the slaveholders. They had elected their own leader—and it was the valiant gray ghost of John Brown himself. Their favorite tune was "John Brown's body lies a mouldering in the grave," "that quaint, half grotesque, half passion stirring air." In vain McClellan interdicted the singing of it. They enticed the German bands to play it on all occasions, and defiantly they raised their voices in one shout, "We'll hang Jeff Davis to a sour apple tree." Dicey saw 16,000 of them on their way to Alexandria on their way to embark for the Peninsula. "With colors flying and bands playing regiment after regiment filed past us. In the gray evening light the long endless files bore a phantom aspect. The men were singing, shouting, cheering. Under the cover of darkness they chanted John Brown's hymn in defiance of McClellan's orders, and the heavy tramp of a thousand feet beat time to that strange weird melody. As the New England regiments passed our train, they shouted to us to tell the people at home that we had seen them in Dixie's land and on the way to Richmond. Ah me, how many, I wonder of those who flitted before us in the twilight, came home themselves to tell their own story."

6

In the South there was a similar outpouring. Less numerous than the Northerners and not nearly so well equipped, they, too, were fine men. Russell reported of the mustering of the Southern troops. "The band was playing that excellent quickstep *Dixie*. The men were stout fine fellows, dressed in coarse gray tunics with yellow facings and French caps. They were armed with smooth bored muskets, and their knapsacks were unfit for marching, being waterproof bags swung from the shoulders. The guns had no caissons, and the shoeing of the troops was certainly deficient in soling." In a world given over to masters and slaves, no one had realized what fine free white men there were in the South. Why did they emerge thus from their little slaveless farms to fight for a cause which had kept them, good men as they were, uneducated and poor? Dicey tried to give the answer. They sincerely believed, he said, that the "Lincoln hordes were coming down to destroy their property, burn their houses, and murder their wives and children. Extraordinary as such an illusion was, it could be accounted for partly by the isolation of the South, partly by the extent to which the lower classes receive all their intelligence and all their opinions from their leaders, and still more by the morbid nervousness which the presence of a slave population is sure to be amongst the dominant race."

To them, as to the North, there had come an awakening. They belonged to one land, and that land was Dixie. "For Dixie land I'll take my stand, to live and die for Dixie." Ignorant, each dearly loved his own little neck in the woods, his own Mississippi, Alabama, Georgia; and now these beloved lands had combined and out of the union was rising something new and sweet.

> Something so dim it must be holy,
> A yellow river, a blowing dust,
> Something beyond that you must trust,
> Something so shrouded it must be great,
> The dead men building the living state
> From simmon seed in the sandy bottom.
> The woman South in her rivers laving
> That body whiter than new blown cotton,
> And savage and sweet as a wild orange blossom
> The dark hair streams on the beautiful bosom.
> If there ever has been a land worth saving,
> In Dixie land I'll take my stand
> > To live and die for Dixie.
> > —STEPHEN V. BENÉT

7

But there were larger issues, and on each side the true enemy was capital. Thoughtful Southerners were beginning to see that in the rush and hurry of settling their immense territory, they had lost power over the wealth they themselves were creating. The South was strangled by an intolerable rope of debt, and it was the Northern banker who held the mortgage. Out of his dream of the life beautiful the Southern gentleman was waking, as Lanier wrote later.

> At last
> He woke to find his foolish dreaming past
> And all his best of life an easy prey
> Of wandering scamps and quacks that lined his way
> > With vile array,
> From rascal statesmen down to petty knave;
> Himself, at best, for all his bragging brave,
> A gamester's catspaw, and a banker's slave.

The Southerners wished quite properly that the South and not the North should be enriched by full wealth of their great crops. A separate government seemed to guarantee this. Much of the most foolish, and to the North most irritating, Southern talk was the tentative effort of the South to think out its own problem. But in doing so it was like a Sleeping Beauty waking from a hundred years' nap, and innocently flaunting ideas which the more industrialized and educated North, in the disillusionment of wider and rougher experience, had long since discarded.

The North on its part was fighting capital, too—a new capitalism in the South, mongrel in breed, covering ancient social wrongs with new high-sounding phrases, inciting free men to battle again for causes they had long since thought won. On the two issues involved—the subordination of one race to another, and the freezing of society into capital and labor classes—Lincoln was explicit, and those who elected him agreed with him. "Let us discard this quibbling about this man and the other man, this race and the other race, being inferior," said Lincoln. The proposal that capitalism should be frozen into a stratified society he dealt with in a long and careful message to Congress in December, 1861, which cannot be quoted at length here, as it deserves to be. He intended it as a definition of the real issue of the Civil War, and as such it should be read. Referring to the state papers of the Southern Confederacy, he said that there was one point in their arguments to which he wished to call special attention. "It is the effort to place capital on an equal footing with, if not above labor, in the structure of government. It is assumed that labor is available only in connection with capital; that nobody labors unless somebody else, owning capital, by the use of it induces him to labor. This assumed, it is next considered whether it is best that capital shall hire laborers, and thus induce them to work by their own consent, or buy them, and drive them to work without their consent. Having proceeded thus far, it is assumed that whoever is once a hired laborer is fixed in that condition for life. Now there is no such relation between capital and labor as assumed, nor is there such a thing as a free man being fixed for life in the condition of hired laborer. Both these assumptions are false, and all inferences from them are groundless.

"Labor is prior to and independent of capital. Capital is only the fruit of labor and could never have existed if labor had not first existed. Labor is the superior of capital and deserves much the higher consideration. Capital has rights which are as worthy of protection as any other rights. Nor is it denied that there is and probably always will be a relation between capital and labor producing mutual benefits. The error is in assuming that the whole labor of the community exists within that relation."

In other words the issue of the Civil War was exactly those questions of race and of the stratification of society under dictatorship which have precipitated the conflict between Communism and Fascism in Europe. America as the most economically advanced of the modern states merely reached the state of conflict first. Our war had special characteristics, due to the peculiar nature of our population and to certain pioneer conditions. But it did happen here. We met the issue, and we fought it out, and, once and for all, we sealed our own national purpose with our own hearts' blood.

8

The Southern statesmen had declared that this was a war between capital and labor, capital being the South, and labor the North. But when the real battle came, all the real capital of the country appeared to be in the hands of labor! Everyone had known that, for all the pride and flourish of wealth among the Southern planters, the North was much richer, but no one, not even the Northern bankers, knew how very much richer the North was. Among the laborers and farmers of the North there now appeared to be unlimited resources which no one had counted—a few hundred dollars in Aunt Jemima's stocking, a few thousand tucked away somewhere by Uncle Henry. They had personal property, small freeholds, little shops and industries, and while their sons fought the war they worked. In 1864 the president of the Agricultural Society of Illinois said: "Look over these prairies and observe everywhere the life and activity prevailing. See the railroads pressed beyond their capacity with the freights of our people; the metropolis of the state rearing its blocks with rapidity almost fabulous, and whitening the northern lakes with its commerce; every smaller city, town, village, and hamlet within our borders all astir with improvement; every factory, mill, and machine shop running with its full complement of hands; the hum of industry in every household; more acres of fertile land under culture, fuller granaries, and more prolific crops than ever before; in short observe this state and this people of Illinois are making more rapid progress in population, development, education, and in all the arts of peace than in any former period, and then realize, if you can, that all this has occurred and is occurring in the midst of the most stupendous war ever prosecuted by man."

So despite the gallantry of the Southern troops, and the great skill of their generals, it was from the first a pathetically unequal war. For a while the North fumbled, and McClellan in the East was stalemated by the generalship of Lee, but gradually the North, unprepared for war, began to find its fighting brains, too. First Grant, then Sherman and Sheridan, appeared to oppose to the ballad-like glamour of Stonewall Jackson and Johnston and Lee, the deadly attitude of an aroused peaceful citizenry at last settling down in bitterness to what it could not avoid. To the gay heroes of the South coming forth so boldly to show how grandly they could fight, they said in effect: "You arn't grand, and you arn't glorious. You are fools playing at murder. You are silly show-off boys who have asked for a whipping and whipping is what you are now going to get."

The first evidence of the new spirit was in the Tennessee River campaign which took the Union armies down into the heart of the Confederacy and brought on the stage the dogged personality of Grant. The next was the occupation of the Mississippi Valley, cutting the Confederacy in two, taking Louisiana out of the fighting and making New Orleans, for the time, a Yankee town. When it was known that New Orleans was in the hands of Yankee troops, and that they were coming up the river, the Southerners made haste to burn their cotton.

That precious cotton! How the Confederacy had counted on its one great crop. "Without firing a gun," cried a Southern Senator, "and without drawing a sword, should they make war on us, we could bring the whole world to our feet. What would happen if no cotton were furnished for three years? I will not stop to depict what everyone can imagine; but this is certain, England would topple headlong, and carry the whole civilized world with her. No, you dare not make war on Cotton. No power dares to make war on it. Cotton is King."

But the North shut up the cotton within the Confederacy through its blockade of the Southern ports. British spinning interests were indeed suffering, and the British upper classes were with the Confederacy, going just as far as they could without bringing on war with the North in outfitting ships and assisting the insurgents. But the true sufferers, the British workingmen and women thrown out of employment in the textile factories by lack of Southern cotton, were standing stanch by the North, and it was their influences which kept Great Britain from intervening in behalf of the Confederacy. To President Lincoln, the British trade unions sent a message saying that no matter how they suffered, they knew he was fighting the battle of all laboring men, and they wanted him to know that they were with him. "Impartial history will tell," said John Bright in a speech to the London trade unions, "that when your statesmen were hostile or coldly indifferent, when many of your rich men were corrupt, when your press was mainly written to betray the fate of a continent and its vast population, being in peril, you clung to freedom with an unfaltering trust that God in his infinite mercy will make it the heritage of all his children."

Now up the river, into the heart of the cotton kingdom, the Yankees were coming. And with that gaiety which, in the Southern conduct of the war, seems sometimes supreme courage, and sometimes only a light-minded lack of any real social imagination, the people proceeded not only to burn their cotton but to make a picnic of it. They were burning their hope, their livelihood, the last economic lever of the Confederacy, and this is how they did it. "We went this morning to see the cotton burning," wrote the author of *A Confederate Girl's Diary*, in Baton Rouge. "A sight never before witnessed and probably never again to be seen. Wagons, drays—everything that can be driven or rolled—were loaded with the bales and taken a few squares back to be burned on the commons. Negroes were running around, cutting them open, piling them up, and setting them afire. . . . Up and down the levee as far as we could see, negroes were rolling it down to the brink of the river where they would set them afire and push the bale in to float burning down with the tide. . . . The flat boat was piled with as many bales as it could hold without sinking. Most of them were cut open, while negroes staved in the heads of barrels of alcohol, whiskey, etc., and dashed bucketsful over the cotton. Others built up little chimneys of pine every few feet, lined with pine knots and loose cotton to burn more quickly. There, piled the length of the whole levee or burning in the river, lay the work of thousands of negroes for more than a year past. It had come from every side. Men stood by who owned the cotton that was burning or waiting to burn. They either helped or looked on cheerfully. Charlie owned but sixteen bales—a matter of some fifteen hundred dollars; but he was the head man of the whole affair and burned his own as well as property of the others. A single barrel of whiskey that was thrown on the cotton cost the man who gave it $125. . . . The cotton floated down the Mississippi one sheet of living flame even in the sunlight. It would have been grand at night. But we will have fun watching it this evening anyway; for they cannot get through to-day, though no time is to be lost. Every grog shop has been emptied, and gutters and pavements are floating with liquors of all kinds. So if the Yankees are fond of strong drink, they will fare ill."

The culmination of the effort to open the Mississippi was the siege of Vicksburg. The determination within equaled the determination without. Called upon by Grant to surrender, General Pemberton within the city said: "When the last pound of beef and bacon and flour, the last grain of corn, the last cow and hog and dog shall have been consumed, and the last man shall have perished in the trenches, then, and then only, I will sell Vicksburg." On July 4, 1863, Vicksburg completely starved out, surrendered, and 30,000 Confederate soldiers were taken prisoner. The news of this victory crossed on the wires the news of the Battle of Gettysburg, where Lee, having made a bold dash north into Pennsylvania, was driven back in three days of bitter fighting.

The Mississippi Valley was now in Yankee control from source to mouth. That flexible living spine of the continent, which all agreed could not really be divided, which the Confederacy had hoped to make wholly its own through the power of the port at its mouth—was now in Union hands. It meant much to the North to keep it, more to the South to lose it, for with it went its greatest city. Lincoln announced the news to James C. Conkling on August 26, 1863, in words which his delight made poetic. "The Father of Waters again goes unvexed to the sea. Thanks to the great Northwest for it. Nor yet wholly to them. Three hundred miles up they met New England, Empire, Keystone and Jersey, hewing their way right and left. The sunny South, too, in more colors than one also lent a hand. . . . Nor must Uncle Sam's web feet be forgotten. At all the watery margins they have been present. Not only on the deep sea, the broad bay, and the rapid river, but also up the narrow, muddy bayou, and wherever the ground was a little damp, they have been and made their tracks."

Lincoln had by this time become more than the leader and best current historian of the war. He had become its poet. Few will question that the most beautiful public utterance ever made by any leader on a great public occasion were his solemn, lovely words over the fallen dead at Gettysburg. Out of all those many messages in which he had tried to define the issues in the war he here distilled the essence, in grave and beautiful phrases, half elegy, half prayer: "It is rather for us to be here dedicated to the great task remaining before us, that from these honored dead we take increased measure of devotion; that we here highly resolve that these dead shall not have died in vain; that this nation, under God, shall have a new birth of freedom, and that government of the people, by the people, for the people, shall not perish from the earth."

9

The early months of 1863, culminating in Vicksburg and Gettysburg, marked the crisis of the war. After that the spirit was different on both sides. The North after long fumbling had found itself. The real purpose of the people, the force that set them marching after John Brown's ghost, had at last been admitted in the Proclamation of Emancipation. Despite the great practical difficulties involved in this proclamation, it had the great merit of clearing the atmosphere. The common man knew what he was fighting for now, and no one was going to stop him from saying so.

With the emergence of Grant, the North had settled on its technique of war. Now that the Union forces had got well into the center of the Confederacy in the West, the idea was to push eastward and inward, choking it to death. When the Southern resistance was broken in the center, in the Battle of Chattanooga, all was ready for the last dreadful work. The theory of the Northern leaders, including Lincoln himself and the principal generals, was that, to stop the war, you had to strip this waste of the glamour of gallantry and of all military parade, and you had to show the largest number of citizens just what war was. A German officer once asserted that Germany had learned ruthlessness from the Americans in the Civil War. If so, the Germans and the modern military forces which carry it to such revolting extremes in Spain and China, understood the American lesson very ill indeed.

For the American theory never involved the abuse of people. Of life and fundamental human rights in their occupied territory the Yankee officers were conspicuously tender, and the Southern diaries in general give them full credit for this. What they were utterly ruthless with was property. They had the idea that wholesale and violent destruction of property in war is a way of avoiding the destruction of life. In other words, don't shoot a man. Just destroy his gun. In the later months of the war they carried out this principle in the most dramatic fashion. Sheridan, having defeated the Southern general, Early, went whirling up the Shenandoah Valley, leaving it so bare that it was said that a crow flying over it would have to carry his provisions with him. Even Lincoln, the tender, the merciful, whose heart bled over every mother's son, and who had a physical shrinking from every detail of battle, concurred in the theory that murder might be lessened by using instead every other means of annoyance and destruction. "Hang on like a bull dog," he said in a dispatch to Grant, "and choke and chew as much as possible." The idea was to make the enemy sue for peace without killing him.

The South meanwhile had undergone a great change. Its bluff was called. Its pride was in the dust. It was tired, ragged, and hungry. The high exultant courage of the first years had settled into steady disillusionment. But its resolution was unshaken. "I see no salvation on either side," wrote the intelligent Confederate girl, Sarah Morgan, in her diary, as early as June, 1862. "No glory awaits the southern Confederacy even if it does achieve its independence; it will be a mere speck in the world, without weight or authority. . . . On the other hand, conquered, what hope is there in this world for us? Broken in health and fortune, reviled, contemned . . . without prospect of support for those few of our brothers who return; outcasts without home or honor—would not death or exile be preferable?"

By the end of September of that year she remarks: "Confederate means anything that is rough, unfinished, unfashionable, or poor. You hear of Confederate dresses, which means last year's. Confederate bridle means a rope halter, Confederate silver a tin cup or spoon. Confederate flour is corn-meal, etc." This girl had three brothers in the Confederate army, but one of her brothers was a Union man. The Union brother rescued his sister and his mother from the threatened starvation of all Confederates and got them to the Yankee town of New Orleans. Of her first breakfast outside of the Confederacy, she wrote: "I opened my eyes to behold a tray brought to my bedside with a variety of refreshments. Coffee! Bread! Loaf sugar! Preserves! I opened my mouth to make an exclamation at the unheard of optical illusion, but wisely forebore speaking."

Nevertheless, betweentimes they managed to be astonishingly gay, furbishing up their old dresses, turning molasses, when they could squeeze a little out of the sugar cane, into candy, playing the guitar, and trying never, never, never to flirt with even the best looking and most courteous Federal officer. In Virginia, too, they managed to have parties of some sort to the last. General Lee protested to one of the younger members of his family that the name Lee was appearing too often on social committees. He was delighted to see it in battles, he said, but could dispense with it at balls.

On the other hand there was something very gallant in the way in which the Southern ladies summoned all their little arts of leisure to take them with grace and profit and the maintenance of family morale through days in which the cannon rumbled in the distance. During siege and battle Sarah Morgan gives this as her day's routine. She gets up much earlier than in the old easy days, she says, and for an hour works in her garden. Then she hears the children's lessons, and opening her books works all morning at her own, "reading aloud in French and English, occasionally writing a little in either. . . . Many things I would like to study I am forced to give up, for want of leisure . . . I study only what I absolutely love now."

After her lessons she devotes the few minutes before dinner and all the time after it to sewing, knitting, darning, etc., putting the fast decaying family wardrobe in good order. "I get through with a great deal of sewing. Somewhere in the day, I find half an hour or more to spend at the piano. Before sunset I dress and am free to spend the evening at home or else to walk to Mrs. Brunot's, for it is not safe to go farther than those three squares away from home. From early twilight until supper, Miriam and I sing with the guitar, generally, and after sit comfortably under the chandelier and read until about ten. . . . At ten comes my Bible class for the servants. Lucy, Rose, Nancy, and Dophy assemble in my room and hear me read the Bible. . . . Then one by one they say their prayers —they cannot be persuaded to say them together; Dophy says 'she can't say with Rose cause she aint got no brothers and sisters to pray for, and Lucy has no father and mother,' and so they go." Her day closes with a little court in which she hears the grievances of the servants. For with her father dead, her mother invalided and rendered practically incompetent by worry and grief, her brothers all away, she and her sister must hold their household together, maintain morale, manage the servants, and keep the peace. So she has this nightly court when "all the difficulties and grievances during the day are laid before me, and I sit like Moses judging the children of Israel until I can appease the discord. Sometimes it is not so easy. For instance, that memorable night when I had to work Rose's stubborn heart to a proper pitch of repentance for having stabbed a carving fork into Lucy's arm in a fit of temper." With Federal armies pressing in to free the slaves, and rest-lessness and rebellion running among the weaker of these excitable people, the young daughter of the house, alone with her sister in an enemy world, holding her court among her Negroes, sympathizing, appeasing, praying with them, seems a heroine indeed.

The fair young daughter of the Confederacy buckling her sword on her hero is less in the cynical eye of history than she was in his eyes. But the young daughter of the Confederacy summoning all her arts, all her social tact, her Bible, her prayers, her guitar, her songs, to take her family thus through days in which fighting was within four blocks of her own home—wrapping her mantle of grace around the steel backbone of courage—shames all judgment to reverence. The purely ornamental culture of the Southern lady had its great limitations. But in days of most desperate hardship it proved of most unexpected utility—the very substance of consolation and comfort, a little candle of civilization, kept burning at the window, by whose light men could look out of the howling darkness into what, by some miracle of woman's grace, was still home.

10

The climax of the Yankee war on property was the march of Sherman through Georgia. Through Georgia went the Yankee army, marching in four parallel columns, by four roads, with flags flying, bands playing *John Brown's Body*, and everything they encountered in a sixty-mile swathe they completely destroyed—tore up railroad ties, burned buildings, destroyed crops. Through the soft blue haze of the late fall, over land frosted at night sometimes, tender and springlike in the morning, mild under a blue summer sky at noon, they marched and left the old red soil one gaping wound. And with them rode their commander, General Sherman, thoughtful, tenderhearted, musing as he rode on these stubborn, lovable, foolish people. He had lived in the South, had been a teacher in a Southern school, knew them well and pitied them profoundly. War was Hell. Couldn't he make them see it? He was destroying their property to save their lives. In all that desolation, he said afterward, he knew of no murder or rape committed by his soldiers. On Christmas Day he telegraphed to Lincoln, "I give you the City of Savannah as a Christmas present." The proud city of Charleston, he said, he caused to be evacuated without loss of life. Yet no barbaric conqueror ever did a more systematic job of desolating a land. "This," he said, "may seem a hard species of warfare, but it brings the sad realities of war home to those who have been directly or indirectly instrumental in involving us in its attendant calamities." And again: "If the people raise a howl against my barbarity and cruelty, I will answer that war is war, and not popularity seeking. If they want peace, they and their relatives must stop the war."

Meanwhile Lincoln had been returned to the White House by an overwhelming vote of the people. He had the electoral votes of all states able to vote, except Kentucky, Delaware, and New Jersey, in two of which slaveholders were still powerful. The election showed, as Lincoln said, that "a people's government can sustain a national election in the midst of a great civil war. Until now it has not been known to the world that this was a possibility." It showed, too, that with all the loss of life in the war the man power of the North was as yet undepleted, for there were actually 150,000 more men of voting age than when the war began four years before. "Gold is good in its place," commented Lincoln, "but living, brave, and patriotic men are better than gold."

On March 4, a very different Lincoln faced a very different people, from the worried uncertain man who had seemed to stand up almost alone before a muttering, hostile city just four years before. The three great Southern ports, New Orleans, Savannah, and Charleston, were in Northern hands, while Grant held Lee in Richmond, slowly throttling the life out of his matchless army. Several of the Southern armies had been destroyed. The Shenandoah Valley was a waste and Georgia a desolation. There was triumph in Lincoln's heart and in the hearts of those who heard them, but a bitter and melancholy triumph it was. For was this not their own country they had laid waste, and their own kin dead and dying in that self-made desert?

"Fondly do we hope, fervently do we pray that this mighty scourge of war may soon pass away," said Lincoln in his Second Inaugural Address. "Yet, if God wills that it continue till all the wealth piled by the bondsman's two hundred years and fifty years of unrequited toil shall be sunk, and until every drop of blood drawn with the lash shall be repaid by another drop of blood drawn with the sword; as it was said three thousand years ago, so still it must be said, 'The judgments of the Lord are true and righteous altogether.'

"With malice toward none, with charity for all, with firmness in the right as God gives us to see the right, let us strive on to finish the work we are in, to bind up the nation's wounds, to care for him who shall have borne the battle and for his widow and orphans, to do all which may achieve and cherish a just and lasting peace among ourselves and with all nations."

But down in the desolate South the tired and beaten brothers tightened their belts, clamped their teeth against admission of pain or defeat, and prepared to go on fighting.

> Old folks, young folks, never you care,
> The Yanks are here and the Yanks are there,
> But no Southern gentleman knows despair.
> He just goes on in his usual way,
> Eating a meal every fifteenth day
> And showing such skill in his change of base
> That he never gets time to wash his face,
> While he fights with a fury you'd seldom find
> Except in a Home for the Crippled and Blind
> And can whip five Yanks with a palm-leaf hat,
> Only the Yanks won't fight like that.
>   —STEPHEN V. BENÉT

The end was inevitable. But it was not yet. Once more the Northern leadership hardened its heart and prepared to go forward on a scale which, when compared with what was left to fight with in the South, seems tragic in its magnitude. On March 15, Lincoln drafted 300,000 more men. The army still unconquered was the Army of Northern Virginia. Of it Colonel Archer Anderson, speaking at the unveiling of the statue of Lee in Richmond on May 29, 1890, said: "The Army of Northern Virginia ceased to be recruited; it ceased to be adequately fed. It lived for months on less than one-third rations. It was demoralized not by the enemy in its front, but by the enemy in Georgia and the Carolinas. It dwindled to 35,000 men, holding a front of thirty-five miles, but over the enemy it still cast the shadow of its great name."

General Early, in an address at Lexington, Virginia, in 1872, described the finish. "The retreat from the lines of Richmond and Petersburg began in the early days of April and the remnant of the Army of Northern Virginia fell back more than one hundred miles before its overpowering antagonist, repeatedly presenting front to the latter and giving battle so as to check his progress. Finally from mere exhaustion less than 8,000 men with arms in their hands of the noblest army that ever fought in the tide of time, were surrendered at Appomattox to an army of 150,000 men; the sword of Robert E. Lee without a blemish on it, was sheathed forever, and the flag to which he had added such luster was furled, to be henceforth embalmed in the affectionate remembrance of those who remained faithful during all our trials and will do so to the end."

The respective attitudes of North and South—of the last of the cavaliers before the first of the citizens—was maintained to the end. Lee appeared to make his surrender in a new uniform, tall, handsome, wearing still undimmed the pride and panoply of war. Grant came in, roughly dressed in field uniform, careless, businesslike, refusing by any token to recognize this as a great occasion—just a bit of business to get through—and no fuss about it. He refused to accept Lee's sword, and spoke rather kindly about provisions for Lee's soldiers. At the request of Lee, he agreed to send food to his army for five days, and then of his own accord added that he thought all the soldiers had better keep their horses—they would need them to go home with and to start working on their farms. So it was ended.

Afterward General Long reported that when Lee came away from his meeting with General Grant, "every hat was raised and the faces of thousands of bronzed warriors were bathed in tears. As he rode slowly along the lines, hundreds of his devoted veterans pressed around the noble chief, trying to take his hand, touch his person, or even lay their hands upon his horse, thus exhibiting for him their great affection. The General then with head bare, and tears flowing freely down his manly cheeks, bade adieu to his army."

Richmond had fallen. "When the news was made public on Monday the whole North was thrown into a frenzy of joyous excitement. Every bell in every public building from the Atlantic to the Pacific was rung for hours. Cannon answered to cannon, from mountain to mountain, and from valley to valley." And into the fallen city walked Mr. Lincoln. He was not mounted. He did not ride in a carriage. He had no guard except some soldiers who had rowed him up the James. He just walked along. But, like wind among the grasses, the news spread through the alleys of the city, and soon he was thronged with black people, shouting and singing, "Bless the Lord. Bless the Lord. Glory to God. Glory! Glory!" An old black woman stood in her doorway, weeping, "I thank you, dear Jesus, that I behold President Linkum." A report in *The Atlantic Monthly* said that one old Negro stood in the president's path, and said solemnly, "May de good Lord bless you, President Linkum," and he removed his hat and bowed, the tears streaming down his cheeks. "The president removed his own hat and bowed in silence, but it was a bow which upset the forms, laws, customs, and ceremonies of centuries. It was a death-shock to chivalry, and a mortal wound to caste."

II

"The American people were floating on the high tide of joy," wrote Doctor J. G. Holland, in his life of Lincoln three years later. "All were glad and happy; and, as they returned their thanks to the Giver of all good for victory and peace, they did not forget the instrument He had used in the execution of His plans. Mr. Lincoln's name was on every tongue. The patient man who had suffered the pain of a thousand deaths during the war—who had been misconstrued, maligned, and condemned by personal and party enemies, and questioned and criticized by captious friends—was the man above all others who stood in the sunshine of popular affection. His motives were vindicated, his policy had been sanctioned by success, and his power had been proved. He was the acknowledged savior of his country, and the liberator of a race. He had solved the great problem of popular government; he had settled the one great question of African slavery on the continent. He had won a glorious place in history and his name had been committed to the affectionate safe-keeping of mankind."

The fear of assassination which had haunted the friends of the administration during the earlier years had of late been allayed. "Assassination is not an American practice or habit," said Seward, "and one so vicious and desperate cannot be engrafted on our political system. This conviction of mine has steadily gained strength since the civil war began. Every day's experience confirms it."

Everything seemed as simple as that in those happy days. Chivalry was dead. The play-acting of the South was ended. Reason and common sense would now prevail and bring back brotherhood. But there was still one brief ghastly scene to play before the curtain was rung down.

On the evening of April 14, on the anniversary of the firing on Fort Sumter, as Lincoln sat in his box at Ford's Theatre, a young actor named John Wilkes Booth, brother of the great Edwin, entered the box and shot the President through the brain. "Then the murderer rushed to the front of the box, parted the folds of the flag with which it was draped for the occasion, and leaped to the stage, half falling as he descended, his spurs having caught in the drapery. Then springing to his feet he uttered with theatrical emphasis, the words of the state motto of Virginia *Sic Semper Tyrannis,* and added 'The South is avenged.' "

So Holland described it in his life published almost immediately afterward, representing the contemporary report on all these matters. The President was carried out of the theater across to that simple red brick house now kept as a national monument, carried upstairs and laid in his giant's length diagonally across a bed too short for him. His was a great frame and a strong frame, with all the reserves of his rude frontier boyhood still in it. Though he never recovered consciousness, life would not go out. All night the heart struggled and throbbed against the breast—but in the morning the bells of Washington started tolling, and from city to city all over the land the bells took the story. But otherwise the stillness of death lay upon the capital city. All drinking places were closed; every outlet of the city guarded. For it was learned that the conspirators had intended to murder every chief of the government and the army, and Secretary Seward already lay on the edge of death. The man who stabbed him in three places stabbed four others who tried to interpose.

They did not know till then how much they all loved that simple, homely man. City by city, bells tolling, markets closed, crepe stretched from door to door, the country went into mourning and some of the most earnest voices spoke from the South: "The heaviest blow which has ever fallen on the South has descended," said *The Richmond Whig.* Of all the tributes of the press, that of the British *Punch,* Lincoln's mocking critic throughout the war, was the most unexpected. *Punch* showed a cartoon of Britannia—Britannia who had outfitted Southern ships, supported the Confederate cause, mocked the plebeian of the North—approaching to lay her wreath on the bier, and turning to rebuke *Punch* for all its past gibes at this man.

> You lay a wreath on murdered Lincoln's bier,
> You who with mocking pencil wont to trace
> Broad for the self-complacent British sneer
> His length of shambling limb, his furrowed face,
> His gaunt gnarled hands, his unkempt bristling hair,
> His garb uncouth, his bearing ill at ease,
> His lack of all we prize as debonair,
> Of power to shine or art to please;
> You whose smart pen backed up the pencil's laugh,
> Judging each step as though the way were plain;
> Reckless, so it could point its paragraph,
> Of chief's perplexity or people's pain.
>
> Beside this bier which bears for winding sheet
> The Stars and Stripes he lived to rear anew,
> Between the mourners at the head and feet,
> Say, scurrile jester, is there room for you?

And Punch answered

> Yes, he had lived to shame me from my sneer,
> To lame my pencil and confute my pen,
> To make me own this hind of princes peer,
> The rail-splitter a true-born king of men.
> My shallow judgment I had learned to rue,
> Noting how to occasion's height he rose,
> How his quaint wit made home truth seem more true,
> How ironlike his temper grew by blows—

and so on through a long and earnest eulogy.

The news was announced to the nation on Saturday. On Sunday every church in the Union held services for him. On Tuesday, the body of the President having been embalmed, the White House was thrown open and the people were permitted to take their last farewell of him, "whose kind smile death had forever quenched." "Hundreds of those who pressed around the sacred dust uttered some affectionate word or phrase or sentence." On Wednesday, after the most solemn and elaborate funeral ever held in Washington, the body of the President was sent home through the mourning cities of the land to the West. Slowly the funeral train passed northward through Pennsylvania. As it passed by, bells were tolled in each village, and multitudes gathered at the stations, with offerings of flowers. When the President came to Philadelphia a cannon announced his arrival. A magnificent hearse drawn by eight black horses, carried him to Independence Hall and there in that spot where, four years ago, he had pledged himself in the face of the assassin's bullet to the preservation of the Declaration of Independence, he lay from Saturday to Monday, while a dense unbroken stream of men and women and children went weeping past his bier.

Then the funeral train passed to New York and up the Hudson Valley and then across by the road of the Northern pioneers to his home in the West. "Battling four long years for Liberty and the Right," said a Cleveland paper, "struck down at last when the shouts of victory won rang through the air, he comes back to the Mother West that sent him forth, not with his shield but on it."

So on that spring day in 1865, the greatest of all frontiersmen went home.

Over the breast of the spring, the land, amid cities,
Amid lanes, and through old woods where lately the violets peeped
    through the gray debris,
Amid the grass in the fields each side of the lanes, passing the end-
    less grass,
Passing the yellow-speared wheat, every grain from its shroud in
    the dark brown fields uprisen,
Passing the apple trees' bloom of white and pink in the orchards,

Carrying a corpse to where it shall rest in the grave,
Night and day journeys a coffin.

And standing with bowed heads to see that coffin go on to its last place, there were few Americans then—there are no Americans now—who would not say with Walt Whitman, "This dust was a Man."

This dust was once the Man,
Gentle, plain, just, and resolute, under whose cautious hand
Was saved the Union of These States.

III

SO

CONCEIVED

AND SO

DEDICATED

25

BIND UP THE NATION'S WOUNDS

HE fourteenth of April was the fourth anniversary of the lowering of the flag over Fort Sumter by Major Anderson. There, on that island in the blue harbor, with the empty shell of what was once the proud city of the caciques barren in the distance, stood Major General Anderson, and slowly over that broken and beaten world, he sent the Stars and Stripes up to their old place in the sky. The delegation of famous Americans who had come south by steamer for the ceremony had just heard of the surrender of Richmond. All about them the sunny air was palpitant with the ringing of all the bells of the nation, and joy made them pitiful and generous.

"For the people misled," cried Henry Ward Beecher, "for the multitudes drafted and driven into this civil war, let not a trace of animosity remain. The moment their willing hand drops the musket, and they return to their allegiance, then stretch out your own honest right hand to greet them. Recall to them the old days of kindness. Our hearts wait for their redemption. All the resources of a renovated nation shall be applied to rebuild their prosperity and make smooth the furrows of war."

At that moment there was probably not one honest, decent, kindly household in the whole North which did not say "Amen" to Beecher's words.

That night Abraham Lincoln was assassinated. The news was telegraphed to the party at Fort Sumter next morning. Beecher wrote: "Did ever so many hearts in so brief a time touch such boundless feelings? It was the uttermost of joy; it was the uttermost of sorrow—noon and midnight, without a space between."

In the North the days of mourning for Lincoln were days of renewed bitterness against the South, and renewed and ever-deepened suspicion as more and more of the conspiracy against all the high officials of the federal government came to light. In the South the Confederate Girl wrote in her diary. "This is murder. God have mercy on those who did it." All over Virginia people held meetings, half in terror, half in compunction, and drew up resolutions condemning the act. Mrs. Prior, the wife of a Confederate general in Petersburg, questioned if in any quarter of the country "the virtues of Abraham Lincoln—as exhibited in his spirit of forgiveness and forbearance—are more revered than in the very section which was the battleground of the fight for independence of his rule. It is certainly our conviction that had he lived the South would never have suffered the shame and sorrow of carpetbag rule."

New Orleans and the deep South made haste to drape themselves in black. "To see a whole city draped in mourning is certainly an imposing spectacle," wrote the Confederate Girl in her diary, "and becomes almost grand when it is considered as an expression of universal affliction. So it is, in one sense. For the more violently secesh the inmates, the more thankful they are for Lincoln's death, the more profusely the houses are decked with emblems of woe. They all look to me like 'not sorry for him, but dreadfully sorry to be forced to this demonstration.' "

But as the days wore on, pretended sorrow turned to genuine regret. "If he had lived!" they said, as mild, benign, his memory soared over army officers, carpetbaggers, Yankee schoolteachers, black men representing them in Congress—till all the miseries of Reconstruction, more hopeless to many than the war itself, seemed a long reverberation of that fatal shot.

2

Lincoln's own pronouncements about Reconstruction had been gentle and compassionate. At his last Cabinet meeting he had refused to consider punishment of the Southern leaders as traitors. "I hope," he said, "there will be no persecution, no bloody work after the war is over. No one need expect me to take any part in hanging or killing these men, even the worst of them. Enough lives have been sacrificed. We must extinguish our resentments if we expect harmony and union. There is too much desire on the part of some of our very good friends to be masters, to interfere and dictate to those states, to treat people not as fellow citizens; there is too little respect for their rights. I do not sympathize with these feelings."

His main hope was to feel his way along, knitting into the Union first those states in which there was already some nucleus for renewed loyalty, and some plan for meeting the difficulties. Nevertheless, it is doubtful if any of the main facts which were so bitter to the Southern Bourbons could have been obviated. Military rule would have had to be restored in some places, if only as a police force to put down systematic murder. Probably Lincoln would have been forced reluctantly by circumstance to accept Negro suffrage as he had accepted emancipation and the arming of Negroes to fight for the North. As for the commercial adventurers, the North had been rotten with them throughout the Civil War, and the South had been their happy hunting ground for twenty years before the war. The only difference between the carpetbaggers before the war and the carpetbaggers after was that before the war they set up plantations, faked old family trees, and divided their spoils with the local aristocrats. Now they divided their spoils with the Northern capitalists. That was the real rub.

3

Yet the skies shone peacefully over the tired and battered land that first summer after the war. It was the salvation of the South that the men had the summer to rebuild their devastated farms and lay up something for the winter. And bravely, without a backward look, men who had had 20, 50, 100 slaves turned to the land themselves and raised their first crops unaided, and their ladies scrubbed and cooked and mended the old dresses and trained up the grapevine over the old arbor, and rescued from their hiding places bits of silver or china, and started again to make a home. In Virginia the advice and example of General Lee set a standard for a frank and manly acceptance of the conditions of peace, and a hard-working, unrepining, thrifty farming and housekeeping which should rebuild the wealth of the state and retain, with the altered economic system, the graces of old Southern civilization. He was outspoken in criticizing the genial faults of Virginia, and in recommending that, in the present stringency, they imitate some of the virtues and methods of the North. To a friend who invited him to dinner, and set the table in the old, overflowing style, he said gravely: "Thomas, there was enough dinner to-day for twenty people. All this will have to be changed. You cannot afford it. We shall have to practice economy." He advised scientific farming, such as Washington and Jefferson practiced, and the substitution of white labor for Negroes, leaving the federal government to take care of the latter.

He was anxious that the young people should not neglect the graces of life, but was glad to see the end of some of the former dissipations. To his daughter Mildred, "all life in white and curls," he said rebukingly: "Do not go out to many parties, preserve your simple tastes and manners, and you will enjoy more pleasure. Plainness and simplicity of dress, early hours and rational amusements I wish you to practice." And again: "I hope you will also find time to read and improve your mind. Read history, works of worth, not novels and romances. Get correct views of life, and learn to see the world in its true light. It will enable you to live pleasantly, to do good, and when summoned away to leave without regret." When Mildred received the gift of a piano, he said: "I shall now insist on her resuming her music; she must practice seven hours a day on the piano until she becomes sufficiently proficient to play agreeably to herself and others and promptly and gracefully whenever invited. . . . I think we should enjoy all the amenities of life that are within our reach."

The beauty in Southern character, which is one of the glories of the nation, never shone more brightly than in those dark days after the war. Everywhere brave and quiet people were saying to themselves and to their children: "It was a hard lesson for us, but we needed it. Now please God, we will get rid of our careless southern ways and build out of our calamity a better South." In the training of their children, the better ex-slaveholders were trying to transmute the old pride in aristocracy into a spiritual security—serenity within and poise of bearing without. Mrs. Pryor, in Virginia, speaking of her Northern friends in Washington, admonishes herself thus: "Of course our social life is all over. I have taken my resolution. There are fine ladies in New York whom I used to entertain in Washington. Just so far as they approach me, I will approach them. A card for a card, a visit for a visit. But I imagine I shall not be recognized. I am content. . . . I shall not repine. All the setting, the entourage of a lady is taken from me, but the lady has herself pretty well in hand."

Meanwhile, the brave and honorable willingness of the truly good ex-slaveholders that first summer to go immediately to work, and to rebuild their country on a sounder basis, was matched by kindness and sympathy among families of the same type in the North. At the end of the summer, the National Union Commission, which had aided the families of

Union soldiers during the war, reported on its efforts to extend this same kind of aid to people in the South. "Distress in the track of Sherman's army," they reported, "is great and constantly increasing. Official reports received at this office tell us of women and children who walk from ten to forty miles for bread, and then obtain a morsel, frequently nothing; of naked beings crouching down by the side of their once happy homes, now reduced to nothing except the roots of an old brick chimney, of several counties in northern Georgia in which there is not as much food growing for man or beast as can be found in a respectable northern farm. . . . The Union Commission is answering their appeals for help. It has given assistance to not less than twenty thousand suffering poor in middle Tennessee, and to an incalculable number in Eastern Tennessee through the New England branch." Through the Baltimore branch, the Commission reports that it has sent food and clothing to 15,000 in Richmond, and distributed nearly 2,000 schoolbooks and Bibles and over $3,000 of supplies chiefly in the valley of the Shenandoah, and has sent in less quantities to various points from Little Rock in the West to San Fernandino in the South.

In the well-meant effort of the North to help the South, there was no end of difficulties. Supplies bought with money poured out generously from even lean Northern purses would go through the hands of profiteers and arrive in worse than useless condition. The humiliation of proud Southern families in receiving aid was matched by the embarrassment of Northern officers and officials in giving it.

Mrs. Pryor, wife of the Confederate general, rather than see her family starve, applied to the army for rations. To get her card she understood she would have to take the oath of allegiance, but in the circumstances she was prepared to do this.

"Have you taken the oath?" asked the young officer.

"No," she said.

He looked at her gently and began making out her card. "I don't require it of you," he said.

Receiving her rations, she found the meat spoiled, the cereal worm-eaten. She thereupon wrapped it up and sent it to Major General Hartsuff, with this message: "Is the commanding general aware of the nature of the ration issued this day to the destitute women of Petersburg?"

She received in answer this note: "Major General Hartsuff is sorry he cannot make right all that seems so wrong. He sends the enclosed. Some day General Pryor will repay."

The enclosed was the following: "The Quartermaster and Commissary of the Army of the Potomac are hereby ordered to furnish Mrs. Roger A. Pryor with all she may demand or require, charging the same to the private account of George L. Hartsuff." To this Mrs. Pryor replied: "Mrs. Roger A. Pryor is not insensible to the generous offer of Major General Hartsuff, but he *ought to have known* that the ration allowed for the destitute women of Petersburg must be enough for Mrs. Roger A. Pryor."

In every Southern city and county there were Southern ladies like Mrs. Pryor and Yankee officers and even carpetbaggers like Major General Hartsuff, and between them they ultimately made such reconstruction as there was.

4

During the first summer, the busy farming and rebuilding in the South, and the genuine good will of Northern people in contributions of money and goods, served to conceal still active centers of trouble, North and South. By the time Congress met, in December, 1865, constitutional conventions had been held in practically all the states, governors had been elected, legislatures assembled, and representatives chosen to the Congress of the United States, and Johnson reported that "sectional animosity was surely and rapidly merging itself into a spirit of nationality."

But there was a group in Congress that looked on all this

with a cynical eye. "Can the leopard change his spots like
this?" they asked. "The victory we have won with arms we
will lose at the ballot box." And events promptly justified
them. The various legislatures enacted Black Codes, designed,
in some cases perhaps in good faith, to stop Negro vagrancy
and disorder. In Mississippi the freedman was not allowed to
hold land; in Louisiana every Negro was required to be in the
regular service of some white person or former owner. From
the Southern point of view this was justified by the undeveloped state of the Negro. From the radical Northern point of
view it was just slavery again under another name.

When April, 1866, came around Lowell reported in the
words of Mr. Biglow what was fast becoming a prevailing
opinion in the North:

> April's come back; the swellin' buds of oak
> Dim the far hillsides with a purplish smoke;
>
> But that white dove Carolina scared away,
> Five years ago, just such an April day;
> Peace, that we hoped would come and build last year
> And coo by every housedoor, isn't here,—
> Nor won't never be, for all our jaw,
> Till we're as brave in politics as war!
>
> My friends, you never gathered from my mouth,
> No, not one word agin the South as South,
> Nor there ain't a living man, white, brown, nor black,
> Gladder'n what I should be to take 'em back;
> But all I ask of Uncle Sam is fust
> To write up on his door, "No goods on trust."
> Give us cash down in equal laws for all,
> And they'll be snug inside afore next fall.
> Give what they ask, and we shall have Jamaica
> Worth minus some considerable an acre;
> Give what they need, and we shall get 'fore long
> A nation all one piece, rich, peaceful, strong;
> Make them American, and they'll begin

> To love their country as they loved their sin;
> Let 'em stay southern, and you've kept a sore
> Ready to fester as it done before.

As for the South objecting to Northern insistence on equality for the Negroes,

> Folks you've just licked, far as I ever see,
> Are about as mad as they know how to be;
> It's better than the Rebs themselves expected
> 'Fore they see Uncle Sam wilt down henpected;
> Be kind's you please, but firstly make things fast,
> For plain Truth's all the kindness that will last.

So, whether they like it or not, tell them they must treat their Negroes as we treat our poor immigrant Irish in Boston:

> You take the Darkies as we took the Paddies;
> Ignorant and poor we took them by the hand,
> And they're the bones and sinews of the land.

This is better for the Negroes, and it will be better for the masters:

> But I know this: our money's safest trusted
> In something, come what will, that can't be busted,
> And that's the old American idea,
> To make a man a Man and let him be.

What was all the war for, he asks, if we are to let these Southerners begin to insert their stupid snobberies, their ways of keeping themselves and their country poor and making a row for their neighbors, into the laws of the land:

> Oh my patience! must we wriggle back
> Into the old crooked pettifogging track,
> When our artillery-wheels a road have cut
> Straight to our purpose if we keep the rut?
> War's dead waste except to wipe the slate
> Clean for the ciphering of some nobler fate.
>
> I seem to hear a whispering in the air,
> A sighing like, of unconsoled despair,

That comes from nowhere and from everywhere,
And seems to say, "Why died we? Warn't it, then,
To settle, once for all, that men was men?
Oh, earth's sweet cup snatched from us barely tasted,
The grave's real chill is feeling life was wasted!
Oh, you we left, long-lingerin' at the door,
Loving you best, cause we loved Her the more,
That Death, not we, had conquered, we should feel
If she upon our memory turned her heel,
And unregretful throwed us all away
To flaunt it in a Blind Man's Holiday!"

While the sober sentiment of the North was rallying to the cry from Massachusetts and Pennsylvania, "Men are men," there was an outbreak of violence here and there in the South which made the radicals say, "I told you so." One of these, in New Orleans, was particularly outrageous. The constitutional convention which had met in 1864 to frame a constitution for Louisiana, when the state was occupied by Union troops as conquered territory, reassembled in New Orleans in 1866 to consider some amendments to the former constitution. They had no official power, it seems. They were just meeting.

These men were set upon and massacred. A committee reporting to Congress, on the basis of the testimony of seventy-five persons, said that "men were shot while waving handkerchiefs in token of surrender and submission. White men and black with arms uplifted praying for life were answered by shot and blow from knife and club; the bodies of some were pounded to a jelly; a colored man was dragged from under a street crossing and killed at a blow; men concealed in outhouses and among piles of lumber were eagerly sought for and slaughtered or maimed without remorse; the dead bodies on the street were violated by shot, kick, or stabbed; the face of a man just breathing his last was gashed by a knife or razor in the hands of a woman; an old gray-headed man who was peacefully walking the streets at a distance from the Institute was shot through the head, etc."

Meanwhile Northerners who had gone south with the best intentions in the world—businessmen with a little capital to start industries, Yankee philanthropists and schoolteachers, government officers and officials—were finding that the problem of popular government or even of everyday peace and order down here was very different from that of some Massachusetts or Ohio town. There was not only sullenness and resentment and open disloyalty among a "conquered" people. There was an essential confusion which no good will on either side could obviate.

The South was not a nation honorably defeated in a war. It was a section which had undergone a social revolution. The old slaveholders were a dispossessed class as surely as the aristocrats in France after the French Revolution. Nor could the North, if it wished, give them back their property and their power. The sentiment of the majority of the poorer white people, quite apart from the Negroes, would never have permitted it. This social revolution was not created by the North. It was due the South anyway, and even if the secession had succeeded would probably have been the first problem a victorious Southern government would have to deal with. The basis of this white man's revolution of the South was not only hatred of the slaveowner, but intense resentment and fear of the Negro. The ignorant, dispossessed white man of the South, comparing his poverty and his daily humiliation with the prosperous, happy, and self-respecting condition of Northern carpenters, plasterers, draymen, and so forth, looked on the Negro with a sullen eye. This black skin was the source of all his trouble, and he hated it accordingly. Race prejudice in the South is not the prejudice of the master class.

On the other hand, the Negroes who had been house servants despised and looked down on the "poor white trash." At the end of the war such Negroes as were in a position to have any leadership among their own people possessed half and three-quarters white blood, and that, in many cases, the "best" blood of the South. Their manners, their notions of gentility, their whole standard of life had been set by the ruling class, in whose households they had been petted or trusted dependents. The Negro of some advancement had an unerring eye for what he called "quality" in white men. He honored it among Southern gentlemen, and as the Northerners came down, he began to pick and choose among them, classing some of them as Northern quality, folks who at home must be like Colonel So-and-so, and many as just more "po' white trash."

This attitude is expressed in an interesting book *Facts of Reconstruction*, by John R. Lynch, a colored man of Mississippi who was a Representative of that state in Congress during the later Reconstruction period. The portrait of John R. Lynch shows a fine-looking brown gentleman with all the bearing, grooming, and, presumably manners of a Southern gentleman. His simple and modest report of Reconstruction in Mississippi reflects the amiable snobbery of the master class as unconsciously adopted by colored men who shared the blood and the social manners of that class. He says that the poor whites hated the Negroes because on the large Southern estates many Negroes had been trained as artisans, carpenters, ironworkers, and foremen of gangs. In many places there were more Negroes trained for industrial work and skillful in it than white men. In the coming industrialization of the South, which all groups looked for, the poorer white men were afraid that the Negroes might have an advantage over them. Of the poor white men in Mississippi he says: "At that time, they were, with few exceptions, less efficient, less capable, and knew less about matters of state and governmental administration than many of the ex-slaves. . . . Colored men did not look with favor on political alliance with the poor whites and it must be confessed that, with very few exceptions, the poor whites did not desire such an alliance."

This strong force of instinctive but by no means faulty Negro judgment, selecting leaders among white men, naturally aroused intense fear in the "poor whites." And it was this fear which was written into many of the so-called "Black Codes." In South Carolina, for example, it was enacted that the Negro should not engage in any occupation outside of farming or domestic service except under special license. This was probably to prevent competition in the industrial jobs which all hoped were now coming to the South.

Andrew Johnson, as President, represented the more ambitious and forceful declassed white men of the Northern and mountain regions. His whole interest was in a government for the Southern states which would put all white men on the same level, but leave the Negro in that subordination which his backward condition seemed to call for. What the more ambitious of the laboring and small yeoman class wanted now was a white man's country, with white labor, and with many industries and business ventures offering a variety of employment—another Connecticut or Massachusetts or Pennsylvania.

But at this point a strong voice was raised in Congress from the very states which the "New South" most desired to imitate. It said in effect: "If you want our results, you must use our methods. No discrimination against any labor on any grounds. A free chance for all." The industrial North was building its prosperity by admitting every people of every sort, as immigrants and laborers, and educating and Americanizing them and giving them a free road upward. It feared that discrimination against the Negro was an opening wedge for other discrimination on other grounds—against Catholics, against Jews, against non-Nordics, or Slavs. This would dam up the sources of the now prosperous and useful immigration, make for trouble in the industrial centers, and completely spoil a victorious system, which was making not only for more widespread comfort for the workers, but actually for more wealth for the capitalists than any that had ever been tried.

Thaddeus Stevens of Pennsylvania and Charles Sumner of Massachusetts who represented this point of view, were, of course, idealists. But idealists of the old original Pennsylvania and Massachusetts type had always been worth their weight in gold to the industry and banking of their states. Led by Stevens and Sumner, the opposition in Congress to Johnson's policy and to the Black Codes was expressed in the Fourteenth Amendment to the Constitution.

This guarantee of civil liberties to the Negro was, said Sumner, a right that "was to belong to every person that drew breath upon American soil. He might be poor, weak, humble, or black; he might be of Caucasian, Jewish, Indian, or Ethiopian race; he might be of French, German, English, or Irish extraction; but before the Constitution amended as proposed all these distinctions would disappear. He would not be poor, weak, humble, or black; nor would he be French, German, English, or Irish. He would be a man, the equal of all his fellowmen."

Meanwhile the disturbances in the South reinforced the opinion of the radicals—that the section was not ready for self-government. Between ignorant and disorderly Negroes, ignorant and rascally poor whites, Northern profiteers, and proud and violent ex-Bourbons there was an amount of disturbance which no civil government could cope with. There were good people of all these classes, patient Negroes, pathetically ready to work their way up; intelligent white artisans and farmers, eager to write into the state laws some of the advantages of the North, such as free education. There were honest and helpful carpetbaggers and wise and generous ex-slaveholders. But for the time they were overwhelmed by the general disorder and could not work together.

The objection of even very reasonable Northern people to the state of affairs in the South was expressed by Lowell in *The Biglow Papers*. He said that Columbia was acting like a widow with a stiff-necked boy

> Who stamps and says he won't come in for supper;
> She must sit up for him, as weak as Tupper,
> Keepin' the Constitution on to warm,
> Till he'll accept her 'pologies in form;

The neighbors tell her he's a cross-grained cuss
That needs a hidin' eye 'fore he comes to wuss;
"No," says Ma Seward, "he's as good as the best,
All he wants now is sugar plums and rest."
"He sarsed my Pa," says one; "He stoned my son,"
Another adds. "Oh, well, 'twas just for fun."
"He tried to shoot our Uncle Samwell dead."
" 'Twas only trying a new gun he hed."
"Wal, all we ask's to hev it understood
You'll take his gun away from him for good."

In order to take the gun away for good, Congress in March,
1867, reorganized the South into five military districts which
were put under the administration of the army till the people
there could be trained, disciplined, and persuaded to organize
peaceful and stable state governments, including the Negroes
on whom it was now decided the suffrage must be conferred.
The five districts were: Virginia; the Carolinas; Georgia,
Florida, and Alabama; Mississippi and Arkansas; Louisiana and
Texas. The generals who were to preside over these districts
were chosen by Grant and Stanton, Lincoln's secretary of
war. Grant and other generals had gone to all lengths to keep
Southern commanders from being prosecuted after the war
and had represented their interests with determination and
kindness. But they were now convinced that the army must
police the South. The registering of the Negro vote was now
considered absolutely necessary. "You need the votes of the
negroes as you once needed their bayonets," said Sumner. To
the objection that the Negroes were ignorant and politically inexperienced, it could be answered that this was true of many of
the white men also. When Southern aristocrats said they
wouldn't be ruled by Northern carpetbaggers, some Yankees
said: "You used to be ruled by northern negro traders and mort-
gaged to northern profiteers. We are an improvement on them."

This whole program of the radicals was disapproved by
President Johnson, but Congress, reinforced by the people's
vote in 1866, was strong enough to pass laws over his veto. To

protect members of his Cabinet, like Stanton, from dismissal because they were working with the radicals, Congress passed a Tenure of Office Act providing that no civil officer of the government should be removed except with the consent of the Senate. When Johnson, disregarding this, dismissed Stanton, Congress impeached him. The trial opened March 5, 1868, with Chief Justice Chase presiding. Though Northern sentiment was against Johnson, it soon appeared that there was no real misdemeanor to charge him with except a radical disagreement on public policy between him and a two-thirds majority in Congress. Lyman Trumbull, one of the senators who voted for his acquittal, expressed the sentiments of all reasonable men when he said: "I cannot vote to convict and depose the chief magistrate of a great nation when his guilt was not made palpable by the record. Once set the example of impeaching a president for what, when the sentiment of the hour shall have subsided, will be regarded as insufficient causes, and no future president will be safe who happens to differ with a majority of the House and two-thirds of the Senate on any measure deemed by them important. Blinded by partisan zeal, with such an example before them, they will not scruple to remove out of their way any obstacle to the accomplishment of their purposes, and what then becomes of the checks and balances of the constitution so carefully devised and so vital to its perpetuity? They are all gone. In view of the consequences likely to flow from this day's proceedings should they result in conviction on what my judgment tells me are insufficient charges and proofs, I tremble for the future of my country. I cannot be an instrument to produce such a result."

Thus by the integrity and independence of some senators voting against their party in this issue did our government again weather one of the dangerous crises of this period.

Nevertheless, the sentiment of reasonable men which did not sustain the impeachment of the President, refused to sustain the President's policy. Just as serious as impeaching the chief executive for unpopular opinions was the proposal to allow in the basic law of the land any discrimination against any class, race, or color whatsoever, on any pretext. This, too, would set a precedent which might threaten at some future time the security and citizenship of the majority of Americans. Implicit in Southern social theory was the poison of Nordicism. There was an effort not only to separate white from black, but to distinguish in the white race, and even in the English race itself, certain pure and holy strains called Nordic. Even the New Englanders, than whom no Americans were on the whole more Nordic, were, according to one Southern race theory, the descendants of Saxon serfs as distinguished from the master race of England, the Normans. It was the Northern horror of this whole way of thinking that had rallied many different kinds of people to the support of the abolitionists. It was the same horror that brought them now to the support of the radical program in the South. The Negro must be put on the same footing before the laws as any other group and be given an opportunity for free education and free labor contracts under proper protection.

That this was the opinion of a majority of the voters was registered in the presidential election of 1868, which put Grant in the White House with a mandate to carry out the radical Congressional policy in the South. We had not fought the Civil War to kill off in Southern slaveowners a certain style of thinking which we regarded as a threat to the social peace and comfort of Americans as a whole and then to have the same set of opinions reappear in the depressed white classes which the fall of the slaveholders had released.

5

The regime imposed on the South by the Reconstruction Act was obnoxious to white men of the South of all classes, but the more ambitious or less squeamish of the "scalawags" made the best of it; and some thoughtful and independent ex-slaveowners actually cooperated with it. During this period one of the governors of Mississippi under Northern rule was Governor Alcorn, a former slaveowner and man of wealth.

Under military supervision, conventions were called to make a constitution ensuring equal rights for Negroes, including the right to vote. In many of these conventions there were Negro representatives—"black and tan conventions," they were called. Meanwhile the Negro was to be prepared for citizenship and for economic independence by several means. Schools were started everywhere for him, though in some places school buildings were burned down by mobs as fast as they were put up. In every state there was a Freedmen's Bureau which took charge of the Negro, trying to settle him in independence on land, overseeing his labor contracts, protecting him in the courts. The most potent means of controlling and training the Negro both to be a good Republican and to look after his own rights were the Union League Clubs. With fashionable headquarters in New York and most of the Northern cities, these clubs sent out organizers through the South who drew the Negros together in clubs under the leadership of white men. Great secrecy surrounded the operations of these clubs, lest Negroes should be intimidated from joining them, and skillful paraphernalia was devised to bring home their doctrines to the imagination of the colored man. For example, meetings began in darkness, and out of the darkness there came the sounds of clanking chains and groans under the lash. This was to represent to the Negro his former state. Then the candles were brought in, and the kind white persons from the North appeared. This was to represent to the Negro his release. Then the Negroes were told by these white deliverers what they should do to ensure their freedom. Detractors said that the sum and substance of this lesson was "Vote for the Republican Party." But undoubtedly there were idealists and persons of genuine sense and good will who gave the Negro some good advice and otherwise protected him.

The Northerners who were honestly trying to train the Negro were anathema in some Southern communities. They were often represented as unscrupulous betrayers of their own race, preying upon Negro credulity for selfish ends, and the Negroes were represented as incapable of education. Yet no one can read such a work as Booker T. Washington's *Up from Slavery* or can follow the social history of the Negro race since the Civil War without the greatest appreciation of the grit and ambition of the Negroes and the character of white men and women who braved social ostracism to help them.

Of Hampton Institute during these early years, Booker T. Washington says: "Most of the students were men and women —some as old as forty years of age. As I now recall the scene of my first year, I do not believe that one often has the opportunity of coming into contact with three or four hundred men and women who were so tremendously in earnest as these men and women were. Nearly every hour was occupied in study or work. Nearly all had had enough actual contact with the world to teach them the need of education. Many of the older ones were, of course, too old to master the textbooks very thoroughly, and it was often sad to watch their struggles. But they made up in earnestness what they lacked in books. Many of them were as poor as I was, and besides having to wrestle with their books, they had to struggle with a poverty which prevented their having the necessities of life. Many of them had aged parents who were dependent upon them, and some of them were men who had wives whose support they had in some way to provide for.

"The great and prevailing idea that seemed to take possession of every one was to prepare himself to lift up the people at his home. No one seemed to think of himself. And the officers and teachers, what a rare set of human beings they were! They worked for the students night and day, in season and out of season. They seemed happy only when they were helping the students in some manner. Whenever it is written—and I hope it will be—the part the Yankee teachers played in the education of the negroes immediately after the war will make one of the most thrilling parts of the history of this country.

The time is not far distant when the whole South will appreciate this service in a way that it has not yet been able to do."

On the other hand, most Negro writers express great objection to any attempt to stir them up against the white people or to commiserate with them too much on their former sufferings. Many Negroes were actually sorry for their former masters and quick to resent reflection upon them. In 1872 *The Clarion,* a Democratic paper in Mississippi said, "While they (the colored people) have been naturally tenacious of their newly acquired privileges, their general conduct will bear them witness that they have shown consideration for the feelings of the whites."

Booker T. Washington says of Negroes in Virginia; "Deep down in their hearts was a strange and peculiar attachment to old Marster and old Missus, and to their children, which they found it hard to think of breaking off. With these they had spent in some cases nearly half a century, and it was no light thing to think of parting. Gradually one by one, stealthily at first, the older slaves began to wander . . . back to the 'big house' to have a whispered conversation with their former owners as to the future."

Booker T. Washington thought it both untrue and unwise to overemphasize the evils of slavery for the black people. "When we rid ourselves of prejudice or racial feeling and look facts in the face," he says, "we must acknowledge that, notwithstanding the cruelty and moral wrong of slavery, the ten million negroes inhabitating this country who themselves or their ancestors went through the school of American slavery are in a stronger and more hopeful condition, materially, intellectually, morally, and religiously, than is true of an equal number of black people in any other portion of the globe." The permanent and serious injury of slavery was, he thought, the injury to the white people of the South. "The slave system on our place, in large measure, took the spirit of self-reliance and self-help out of the white people. My old master had many boys and girls, but not one, so far as I know, ever mastered a single trade or special line of productive industry. . . . When freedom came, the slaves were almost as well fitted to begin life anew as the master, except in the matter of book-learning and ownership of property. The slave-owner and his sons had mastered no special industry. They unconsciously had imbibed the feeling that manual labor was not the proper thing for them. On the other hand, the slaves, in many cases, had mastered some handicraft, and none were ashamed, and few unwilling, to work."

During those early years when the most intense pressure was forcing the Negro upward, the more intelligent ones were casting an interested eye on the superior Yankee housekeeping and workmanship. Booker T. Washington gratefully learned from the Yankee lady the art of really dusting a room. He appreciated the bath and made haste to adopt it. He became a connoisseur in the matter of clean sheets on beds and the art of lying comfortably between them. And whisperings went among the Negro that this, too, was "quality."

6

The period of military Reconstruction beginning in 1868 and ending in 1875 was one of intense humiliation to the ex-slaveowners. Much of the humiliation was inevitable. Their South, their sweet and pleasant land which they so idealized, lay open now and all its seamy sides were subjected to pitiless inspection. The kindest Yankee could not prevent them from realizing how run down their properties were, how slovenly their general management, how frequent was homicide in the gentleman's code. The miseries of Reconstruction were in exact proportion to the inherent weakness of the state's habitual self-government and general economics. Three states, Tennessee, Virginia, and North Carolina, came off with comparatively little trouble because there was already a wholesome senti-ment of self-government, and a moderately just social system, with no large proportion either of Negroes or white people in a depressed condition. The two states that suffered most were

South Carolina and Louisiana, which had never had nor wished for any real democracy. South Carolina had been founded as an aristocracy and had been proud to remain so. Louisiana had been bought and added to the American Union without even the consent of its citizens. In a third group of states, Texas and Arkansas, the conditions were an aggravated form of incomplete Western settlement—lawless bands, bad men, ready shooting, undeveloped resources. Reconstruction there was mainly a matter of hastening normal civilization as in any lawless Western territory.

The whole problem was aggravated both for the Southerners and for honest Northern administrators and settlers by the general political and economic corruption. This was not a local matter. How much corruption there was in the administration of any given Southern state it is difficult to tell. But it is probably safe to say that in no Southern state was government more corrupt at this period than in the good old wealthy state of New York. Of the government of New York City in 1868, Horace Greeley wrote in *The New York Tribune* on November 2: "The Republicans of this city are, as they have always been, a minority. They would not be if the city were not governed so as to make her vast array of thieves, emigrant swindlers, sailor pluckers, blacklegs, pocketbook clippers, baggage smashers, and brothel keepers a unit against them. . . . There is no vice, no outlook of human depravity, that is not made to bring grist to the Democratic mill."

One of the perpetual economic scandals in the South at this period was that of the railroad building, in such states as Alabama. The South wished and needed the railroads, and practically all classes invited them. But railroad building in the Far West at this period, as well as in the South, has a history which, in the current records, smells to heaven. Yet one must not be deceived by the universal outcry against corruption. There had been corruption for a good many years before the Civil War and no one had noticed it. The outcry was at least a wholesome sign of an awakening public conscience.

Some carpetbaggers were corrupt and some workers among the Negroes fanatic. On the other hand perhaps the majority of ex-slaveholders, good people as they were, were also unreasonable. They were people awakened from a dream, and the pain of dawning self-knowledge was something no one could save them from. Yet there remains what is always the redeeming feature of the South—something of sheer loveliness in manner and feeling. Most of the letters of Sidney Lanier at this period reflect this lovely nature—sweet, affectionate, ready to throw an idealizing glamour even over distress, and bearing hardship with a bravery the more heartbreaking because it makes the utmost of heroism look like unpremeditated grace. In a letter to Hayne he wrote: "We have—let me see—yes, we have eaten two silver pitchers, one or two dozen silver forks, several sofas, innumerable chairs, and a huge—bedstead." To Bayard Taylor, who tried to help him with literary introductions, Lanier wrote in 1875: "I could never describe to you what a mere drought and famine my life has been as regards that multitude of matters which I fancy one absorbs when one is in an atmosphere of art, or when one is in conversational relation with men of letters, with travelers, with persons who have either seen or written or done large things. Perhaps you know that, with us of the younger generation in the South since the war, pretty much the whole of life has been merely not dying."

Yet when one compares the poetry of Lanier, his sweet singing through these dark and starving days, with the poetry of the South before the war—the melodious melancholy of Poe, the pretty artifices of Hayne and Pinckney—one cannot but feel that here, for the first time, is the beauty of the South released. Physical suffering there might be, and social humiliation, but something was open now that through all the period of slavery had been shut. The voices of singers and storytellers that were to rise all over the South among this "younger generation since the war" was evidence of the same release. Lanier, like many other Southerners of that period, found what little

opportunity there was in New York City. New York, originally the capital of the only landed aristocracy of the North,
had always been looked on by the South as its own Northern
metropolis. Thither Southerners with professional training or
a little salvaged capital flocked after the war, and here they
sometimes happily reconstructed their lives. General Pryor,
husband of one of the most attractive of the Confederate
diarists, was one who did so. The devotion of Southerners to
New York was later expressed by O. Henry, to whom the
Bagdad-on-the-Hudson always remained the very queen of
cities. In New York City, Lanier met "some cultivated people," was introduced with indefatigable kindness by Bayard
Taylor, played his own charming musical compositions *Black-
birds* and *Swamp Robins*, and was hailed as the founder of
American music. "These compositions are at once American,
un-German, classic, passionate, poetic, beautiful." There he
also played the flute in the orchestra for a brief period, and
lost himself "in the stormy glories of the orchestra."

But New York was large and miscellaneous, and everybody pleaded for notice there. A better center for the released
intellectual life of the South fast developd at Baltimore. Baltimore combined the social traditions of the South with an almost Philadelphian solidity of character and finance. As the
southernmost of the cities which remained true to the Union,
it was in a position to reach out and gather in the talent and
ambition of the South after the war. Ultimately Lanier obtained a position there as professor of poetry at Johns Hop-
kins University, and his too short life ended there in the
sunshine of a belated spring.

For all this dreary postwar period in the South the most
truthful record is in literature and fiction rather than in official
history. Official records and reports are contradictory and
frequently vituperative, on one side or the other, and books
which reflect them, like Bowers' *Tragic Era*, are still murky
with the passions of the period. A very elaborate survey of
conditions in the South was made by investigators for Con-

gress in 1875, and this, with innumerable memorials, speeches, records of hearings, and so forth at the time, makes extremely good reading, full of vivid concrete details, and intelligent generalizations by intelligent people. But reading it, one finds it almost impossible to decide, amidst so many conflicting statements, just what was the truth of any given situation. But the sons and daughters, grandsons and granddaughters of the South, growing up and hearing in the uncensored intimacy of family life stories of the period and judgments softened by time, seem to have arrived at something like a truthful picture. This picture is in several notable works of fiction. One of the first was by Thomas Nelson Page, of an old tidewater Virginia family, whose grandfather had been the youthful friend of Jefferson and recipient of his confidences about the girls of their acquaintance. His story of *Red Rock* deals with the postwar military rule in Virginia. While it has an air of being idealized, this is mainly because all characters and issues are so simplified, and does not alter its essential justice. His noble Virginians have some quaint little Southern ways, like addressing anyone they look down on as "dog," and sweeping by with heads held high and flashing eyes. On the other hand, he is entirely just to the average of Yankee officers and well-intentioned Northern settlers. Virginians, as he shows them, are compact of all virtues, but it is impossible to make a Virginian in fiction as noble as some Virginians have been in life. The simplest family letter of Robert E. Lee puts the most idealizing pen to shame. With all its amiable old-fashioned fiction mannerisms, *Red Rock* is both an excellent story and probably as fair a record of Reconstruction as there is.

Another record which betters the histories is the picture of Reconstruction in Georgia by Margaret Mitchell in *Gone With the Wind*. This is a remarkably fair picture of the life of various kinds of Southern people after the war. Its types are much less hackneyed than those of the older fiction, and it is written with an awareness of certain nuances in current tradition, certain kinds of knowledge which only grandmother passes on to granddaughter in the privacy of the family, that no official history can hope to equal.

A story popular at the time, which has much less background but is readable in its shallow way, is *The Carpet Bagger*, by Opie Read and Frank Pixley, based on a stage play of that name. It is the story of Melville Crance, carpetbag governor of Mississippi, a "tall rather gaunt man of fifty with a serious face and the Yankee light of humor in his eye. In Chicago he had been an auctioneer, and at the beginning of the war had joined a cavalry regiment. It was said that he had served with distinction. No one could doubt his courage. No one had cause to suspect that he ever entertained an honest thought. He was not well educated but he was far from ignorant. On one occasion he was heard to remark, 'Oh, whenever I find that a man has more education than I have I skip his learning and hit his common sense.'" This, the authors believe, was the typical carpetbagger.

A Southern lady says to Crance, "I shall be pleased to give you full credit for every creditable thing you do."

"Thank you," exclaimed the Carpetbagger ironically, "but I am not certain that I ever do anything of that sort."

In the end he is converted to an honest interest in the affairs of the state and shows courage in fighting politicians of his own party. As a reformed character he receives his reward in the arms of the sweet Southern lady. That Reconstruction must thus end in the sound of wedding bells was the favorite idea of fiction. Almost every diary from that region shows that the young Yankees and the young Southerners had through this hard period always glamour in each other's eyes. They were just different enough to pique each other's interest, just enough alike to make for ready sympathy and understanding. Everywhere, in that soft, open, simple rural world of the South, where there is so much time to dream and to flirt amidst the magnolias, and in the gray shadows of the live oaks, in boats on sleepy rivers, on bridle paths through the rank undergrowth, meeting eyes and touching hands were effectually making peace.

7

Most stories of this period have much to say of the Ku-Klux Klan and similar organizations. (The word Ku-Klux is derived from the Greek *kyklos*, a circle.) The Klan was started as a secret society among some college students in Pulaski, Tennessee, who dressed themselves up in white robes and masks as a lark—just a version of the game of "hanting" which youngsters still play. But Nathan B. Forrest, a Confederate general, saw in the society a means of intimidating the Negroes and scaring into silence or driving from the country other persons obnoxious to the former slaveowners.

In a short time the Ku-Klux was a widespread and powerful organization, perfected in a full play of the fairy-tale imagination of the South. Its riders, hooded in white and masked, rode on horses with muffled hoofs, and had their disguises so arranged that they could be shot up from two to four feet in height, swelling into vast white emanations in the darkness. The entire South was in the "Empire" under the rule of General Forrest, the Grand Wizard. Each state was a Realm. Counties were Provinces; Senatorial districts, Dominions; and communities, Dens. The officers were Grand Dragons, Grand Titans, Grand Cyclops, Hydras, Furies, Goblins, Genii, and Night Hawks. The Hooded Riders made believe that they were the ghosts of Confederate soldiers returned to make order and frighten the wicked. They usually operated in small groups studiously ignorant of each other's movements so that, under oath, they could disclaim knowledge of another group.

The excuse for the existence of this hooded order was, said Mrs. Jarvis of North Carolina, the "gross insults to women by negroes and degenerate whites. Old men were abused. Our sisters were safe nowhere. Harrowing anxiety and sleepless fear hung over the community like a threatened tornado. The unbridled propensities of a newly liberated race, the grudge of people who were the off-scourings of civilization among the whites, made life one unceasing dread. Those who held the offices were the creation of the mongrel combination of political influence whose life-blood was the foulest bilge water in the cesspools of the vicious and depraved." This last sentence is in the best style of the Southern Daughter of the Confederacy at that period. Actually local government was not much different from what it had always been, except that interests other than those of slaveholders were represented, sometimes honestly, sometimes otherwise.

Yet the best evidence that some such intimidation was necessary is not only that reasonable Southern gentlemen cooperated with the Klan, but that they left it openly and publicly when the emergency was past. One gentleman said: "I belonged to the order and I have never regretted it. I was so located that they needed my services though I was only eighteen years of age. I had intimated a desire to join, but I did not know that I had been ballotted on or accepted when an intimate friend of our family some ten years older than myself called to me from the veranda one morning and asked me if I would take a drive with him. We were soon speeding down a public highway in lighthearted conversation when suddenly he hurried into the woods. He would not explain the cause of this unexpected movement. When far away from the road, we were suddenly surrounded by a weird and mysterious sight of ghostly beings. They would run and leap but there was no sound. Some would extend themselves into wonderful proportions and shrink as suddenly into insignificant pigmies. I never knew just how it happened, but I soon found myself kneeling by a stump. Around me were strangely wrought but terribly stern faces masking I knew not what. In uncomfortable proximity to my head I discovered a perfect shower of glittering daggers and grinning pistols."

A human skull was then presented to the young man and

he was required to place his hand upon it and vow himself to secrecy.

"My allegiance," he says, "was to the Caucasian race, and our mothers and sisters were our patron saints. Swift punishment was to be inflicted upon those who would seek to destroy the honor of women dependent on us for protection. . . . We were to assist in a kind of secret policing of the entire community for the general good, and the mutual protection of each other in cases of necessity. We were to assist in providing for those who might suffer in the performance of duty. We were to help provide for the needy."

The dissolution of the Klan by General Forrest in 1869, and public withdrawal from it of the better men ended such usefulness as it had as an emergency measure. Its continuance or revival since then has had no excuse.

In addition to the Ku-Klux Klan there were a number of other organizations—Knights of the White Camelia, the White League, the Pale Faces, the Order of the White Rose. Gentlemen of the South always had fancied themselves in the role of knights. And now they were faring forth in a holy crusade for the protection of the pure white flower of a lady's virtue. But nothing was said of the dusky rose of virtue in many a dark-eyed, dark-skinned girl bearing a child to some knight of this pure white race. After all, the sociological fact remains that most of the people in whom the blood of the races is mixed have dark-skinned mothers. A great furor was being raised at this time in the South about miscegenation— as if that was what the freedom of the Negro would surely lead to. Yet it would be hard to discover any system of life in which the temptations to mixture of the blood are so great as in the inevitable intimacies of domestic servitude. Free colored men, earning their own living, building their own homes, and wishing to possess their own women, are probably as safe a guard against miscegenation as a whole botanical garden full of white flowers.

In 1871 Congress passed the Ku-Klux Act, empowering

the President to intervene with military force in any district dangerously overrun by the hooded knights. Only once was the act invoked in any locality, and that was when martial law was declared in 1871 in nine counties of South Carolina. By this time reasonable Southern gentlemen were already out of the Klan, and order and some comfort were reestablished in all but the most recalcitrant states.

Apart from the disorder, which began to disappear after two or three years, as the better type of Southerner rebuilt his home and reasserted authority in his own community, the most vexatious problems the Northern administration had to deal with were the labor contracts, both for Negroes and for unskilled white labor. This was not solved then, and remains in some sections virtually unsolved to this day. We still have to do something about the share-cropper system of raising cotton, which is a legacy from that time. After the war, large owners of land had no money with which to hire labor. But they were in some cases able to get credit for food at wholesale prices with a large interest charge added thereto, the bill to be paid when the cotton was sold. These supplies they could then let workers on their land have at retail price, which was to be deducted at the end of the year from their wages. To compound for the high interest rates which they paid, they marked the price of these goods up 50 or 100 per cent over the retail price elsewhere. The laborer, having no money, had to buy from the planter's store. The result of this beautiful system was that, at the end of the year, when the cotton was sold, the planter often found himself still in debt and the share-cropper or worker on his place found that his share did not cover what he had consumed.

In mortgaging his land for the supplies to keep men working, the planter usually had to agree to plant every available acre to cotton. This meant sometimes not even a truck garden for the laborer, nor a place for cow or pig which might have reduced his high bill for food. By various expedients, including the "ploughing under of cotton" in order both to raise the price and to release land for raising food for consumption so as to reduce the bill for bought goods, the New Deal is trying to deal with the system seventy years after the end of the war. One of the difficulties with it in many places was that states passed laws decreeing that no laborer should be allowed to leave the land till he had paid the debt to the planter. This was reasonable enough, from one point of view. But since the share-cropper, in the nature of things, could not catch up with his debt, it made him virtually a serf, bound to the land. A report to Congress in 1875 says that some Negroes by extraordinary effort have got free from the system by forming cooperative groups and renting the land themselves for cash. By this means, says the report, they can afford to pay as much as $10 an acre and still get ahead.

Many honest Yankees, with their long-accumulated knowledge of ways and means of saving capital themselves and keeping out of the hands of large debt-creating organizations, were ready to help the South build up business. With reasonable shrewdness and industry on the part of Southerners, they did very well. Despite the depression of 1873, there were parts of the South which were beginning to feel more comfortable and prosperous than they had ever been. But the Reconstruction program in its more ideal aspects was wrecked less by political corruption or even the innate cussedness of a certain die-hard type of Southern Bourbon than by the enormous overhead charge on capital, and the squeeze which all sorts of people had to take, by their own showing legitimately, out of any money that came into the South. The South desperately needed money and materials of all sorts and of necessity must pay any interest charges that were asked.

The depression of 1873 shifted the attention of the public from the Bourbon rule in the South to the iniquities of Northern capital and its tools, the politicians. Hard times in the North brought an outbreak of strikes among industrial workers, and, confronted with their own troubles, Northern idealists were ready to stop worrying about the South and let the leading citizens there rule as best they might. This resulted in the restoration of a kind of oligarchic control by such ex-slaveowners as were still men of position and substance, reinforced by ambitious white men who had risen from the lowlier levels, and by Northern carpetbaggers who had cast in their lot permanently with the South, and, in most cases, had married there. This control was under the aegis of the Democratic party and resulted in what has ever since been called "the Solid South." Many of the civil rights of the Negro were quietly nullified and no questions asked, and no particular effort made to raise or educate poorer white citizens.

Though the long Reconstruction effort was but half a victory for the North, it was a victory nonetheless. The point that the majority of the American people had really struggled for was gained. They had refused, under any stress of temporary need, to write into the basic law of the land any principle of discrimination against any class, creed, or race whatsoever. They had met the grandfather of present European Fascism, as displayed in such countries as Germany, and they had with uncompromising determination laid him low.

Meanwhile, with what seems at long distance remarkable speed, the South emerged into comfort and peace. On December 21, 1867, Robert E. Lee, visiting Petersburg, said: "When our armies were in front of Petersburg, I suffered so much in body and mind on account of the good townspeople, especially on that gloomy night when I was forced to abandon them, that I have always reverted to them in sadness and sorrow. My old feelings returned to me as I passed well remembered spots and recalled the ravages of hostile shells. But when I saw the cheerfulness with which the people were working to restore their condition and witnessed the comforts with which they were surrounded, a load of sorrow which has been pressing on me for years was lifted from my heart."

South Carolina was a state in which civil disturbance lasted longest and both the preponderance of Negroes and the great gulf between the upper and lower ranks of white people made the social condition unhealthy. Yet even there the grace of the old life was restored by 1875. Lanier, in 1876, reported that Charleston was "full of affable decorum, and no visitor with the least perception of the fitness of things can stay in this pleasant old city for a day or two without imbibing this sense of genial old-time dignity, to the extent of wishing that Charleston might always be as it is, at once sober-suited and queer and delightful." It never does to despair even if one has lost one's slaves. For the discovery of phosphate rocks near by was again bringing wealth to Charleston.

As for the state government of South Carolina *The York-ville Inquirer* reported that "for the first time since Reconstruction our state government is honorably recognized abroad and commanding respectful mention."

The general comfort and congratulation and good will even to Yankees were shown by an outbreak of patriotic celebrations. It began to be remembered that North and South had fought the Revolutionary War together and had one Fourth of July. Such a celebration was held at Charlotte, North Carolina, in May, 1875, to celebrate the Declaration of Mecklenburg. The governor of South Carolina, representative of the government that was at last commanding respect, addressed North Carolina and the South at that time. And who was this good governor they were so proud of? He was a Yankee from Massachusetts and a carpetbagger!

Looking back to the raising of the flag over Charleston just ten years ago and all that they had suffered and survived since that day, he said: "Look back just ten years and contrast the scene. The ashes of your houses and barns were then warm. Your stock was utterly gone. Your implements of labor were destroyed. The condition of the mass of laborers had suddenly been changed from slavery to freedom. Every feature of the farmer's situation seemed to be in a sad and hopeless confusion or prostration. Now look on this scene. Here is cotton more than rivalling in quantity and quality the best days before the war. Here is stock, blooded and native, horses and neat stock worthy of the reputation of any agricultural community. Here is contentment and peace between laborer and employer. Here are your wives and children, grace and beauty of the best type, all giving evidence of that unparalleled recuperation which Barnwell has witnessed. And yet men are heard sometimes to despair of South Carolina. Some there are who dwell gloomily on the past, and think the proper attitude for our state is as a modern Niobe, in the dust and sackcloth of defeat and despair."

Most of the well-known Confederate diaries of this period end on a note of reconciliation and self-congratulation.

In 1912 James Gouper, as an old man, wrote: "Whilst belonging to the class of slaveowners and a Confederate soldier, I say, without hesitation, that no greater benefit ever befell any country than the emancipation of the negroes of the South. The Anglo-Saxon then found that, with his own brains and hands, he could make the lands of the South the garden spot of the earth. . . . Thank God, it is over, and I share the privilege of seeing my people emerge from the dark days of Reconstruction to the present with its glorious promise."

26

THE LAST FRONTIER

HOT dusty day in July, 1864. The Reverend Mr. Blanchard, president of Wheaton College, was far from home, and farther still from that furious marching of the Union troops, southward and eastward, on to Atlanta, on to the sea. He was traveling in the Wild West, and had stopped at Council Bluffs, Iowa. And this was what he saw:

"When you approach this town the ravines and gorges are white with covered wagons at rest. . . . Myriads of horses and mules, the largest and finest I ever saw, drag on the moving mass of humanity toward the setting sun, while the oxen and cows equal them in number. A large ferry, plying rapidly all the day long, makes no diminution in the crowd, though twenty and thirty animals are carried over at once, and trips take but little time. As my inquiries run, not one half are for Idaho. California, Denver, Arizona, Oregon are receiving multitudes, and most of them have families and settle there."

During the years between 1858 and 1878, while the South, comprising eleven states, was locked in a death grip with the rest, the still unorganized area of the West was marked out into as many states, peopled and provided with railroads; and by the time the South was reconstructed and knit back into the Union, an area larger than the South had been added to the pattern of the states, and the territorial outline of our country completed. Busy, passionate, rushing years they were in the West. The wildest, most grandiose portion of all our domain, the vast mountain upheavel running north from Mexico to Canada, sinking into alkali wastes, thundering with streams, shot through with gold and silver—this, the ancient dominion of the trappers and the last stand of the Indian tribes, was conquered league by league. All the drama of American settlement, from Plymouth Rock to the Golden Gate, was but a prelude to this, the last melodramatic act.

2

The last big rush to the West began with the discovery of gold in Colorado, the news being flashed up and down the East on the new telegraph wires, as a Christmas gift to the nation, in the winter of 1858. Prospectors had been among the hills west of Kansas that summer, and had even started a little town called Denver, and had begun to talk about being a territory all by themselves. Finally they had located gold on Pike's Peak. Instantly the rush started. They used to career across Kansas in prairie schooners sporting on their canvas dome the words "Pike's Peak or bust." Before the season was over more than one wagon was left stranded by the way. The owner of one carefully painted under his original inscription the words, "Busted, by gosh!"

In the mountains of Colorado half a dozen mining camps turned swiftly into towns—Golden, Boulder, Black Hawk, Central City, Idaho Springs, and a former colleague of Horace Greeley was publishing at Denver *The Rocky Mountain News*. By the end of the summer the rocky backyard of Kansas was already a territory and looking forward to being a state. "Here we go," said *The Rocky Mountain News*, "a regular triple-headed government machine; south of forty degrees we hang on to the skirts of Kansas, north of forty degrees to those of Nebraska; straddling the line we have just elected a delegate to the United States Congress from the 'Territory of Jefferson,' and ere long we will have in full blast a provisional government of Rocky Mountain growth and manufacture."

Cheerful, breezy, washing gold down from the creeks, buying civilization like prefabricated houses from farther east, Colorado started off. But a turn was soon given to the rush. Gold there was, but it could not be got out by individual miners. It was mining company business. So off started the prospectors for Nevada and Arizona, and meanwhile capitalism moved in, solid, well organized, and laid over the Wild West immediately a thin veneer of sophistication and even of elegance.

A rather charming account of going to Colorado appears in *Argonaut Tales* by Edmund Wells. There is the long progress in the emigrant train through the Indian country. At one point the two old scouts, Kit Carson and Jim Bridger, ride down to meet the train and are embarrassed by being invited by an Eastern lady to a dinner set on a white tablecloth. Stealing surreptitious glances at the lovely daughter of the hostess, Bridger whispers to Kit: "They are a sight likelier looking than the squaw ladies, ain't they?" Kit Carson and Bridger explain that they had been trapping up in this region and consorting with some of the Indians, and they heard that Sittin' Bull was thinking of coming down and attacking an emigrant train coming in from the Missouri River. From this he had been dissuaded by Red Cloud who told him this would bring all the soldiers down on the Indians. "But me and Jim knowed Sittin' Bull to be a treacherous and heathen old liar, though he ain't scared to go on the war-path any time, and with his cut-throat Indians put something over onto the whites that ain't humane nor invitin' . . . and me and Jim come over here intendin' that if Bull would change his mind we would flank him and put him out of bizness." All of which is set down as simple history and not as a movie scenario!

With much trepidation and a few scares they got through

the Indian country and arrived in Denver. "We found Denver an active and stirring young city, situated on the east side of the South Platte River . . . filled to overflowing with anxious and enthused people of all classes and grades."

In Denver they located their claim, and set out for the higher regions. "The absolute charm of the whole trip was now around and about us: the steep, rocky mountain slopes, sky-scraping cliffs, and dizzy benches, covered with dense growths of ever-green pines and silver-frosted firs, sending through the air on the electrical currents of the altitudes, the pungent ozone." Passing through Black Hawk terraced a mile long on the mountain side, they met a determined orderly crowd engaged in hanging a man. This man, Van Horn by name, had been a member of the notorious gang of Quantrell in Missouri and had run off to Colorado with his "chief's favorite, beautiful paramour." Setting up in style in Central City as wealthy persons contemplating extensive mining engagements, they had been hospitably entertained by everybody, largely through the efforts of the popular clerk of the hotel, Ralph Coleman. But unfortunately the lady had cast her eyes on Coleman, and, ladies being scarce in that gallant world, had lured him to an assignation with her, during which Van Horn had shot him, and, recovering the charmer, had hurried out of town. They were overtaken. Van Horn was given one of the swift and orderly but not completely unfair trials which the vigilantes in California had established a technique for, and had then been hanged. The jury recommended that the lady in question be returned to Quantrell in Kansas with a letter from the People's Tribunal offering him the dead body of his rival!

Having seen Van Horn hanged, our reporter went on with the quiet, returning crowd to Central City, the mushroom social capital of the mountains. "Central City with her gilded and mirrored halls, chains of alluringly brilliant lamp-lights, ravishing music and the voluptuous dance, peals of mirth and hilarity, beautiful forms and décolleté gowns, tempting smiles and flirtation, with prudence flung to the winds as round and round they go in the dizzy waltz."

3

West of Utah, miners wandering among the mountains had found silver on Mount Davidson. This was enough to start a state. Something to pay taxes with—what more did they need? So at Carson City, named for our good friend Kit, the miners collected, seceded from Brigham Young's kingdom, and set up as a state on their own. In 1862, after considerable negotiation with headquarters in Washington, this became the territory of Nevada, with a government whose most interesting member was Mark Twain, secretary to his brother who had been appointed territorial secretary. The history of this adventure in state making is in *Roughing It*.

"Secretary of Nevada Territory," says Mark Twain, was "an office of such imposing grandeur that it concentrated in itself the duties and dignities of Treasurer, Comptroller, Secretary of State, and Acting Governor in the Governor's absence. A salary of $1800.00 a year and the title of Mr. Secretary gave to the great position an air of wild and imposing grandeur."

They set off on a long and exciting stagecoach journey during which Mark Twain met Slade, a noted villain who had been so successful in making away with other villains that the Overland Stage Company had hired him and transferred him to the Rocky Ridge division in the Rocky Mountains, to see if he could perform a like miracle there. "It was the very paradise of outlaws and desperadoes. There was absolutely no semblance of law there. . . . The commonest misunderstanding was settled on the spot with the revolver or the knife. Murders were done in open day and with sparkling frequency, and nobody thought of inquiring into them. It was considered that the parties who did the killing had their private reasons for it; for the other people to have meddled would have been looked upon as indelicate. After a murder all that Rocky Mountain etiquette required of a spectator was that he should help the gentleman bury his game—otherwise his churlishness would surely be remembered against him the first time he killed a man himself and needed a neighborly turn in interring him.

"Slade took up his residence sweetly and peacefully in the midst of this hive of horse-thieves and assassins, and the very first time one of them aired his insolent swaggerings in his presence, he shot him dead. He began a raid on the outlaws and in a singularly short space of time he had completely stopped their depredations on the stage stock, recovered a large number of stolen horses, killed several of the worst desperadoes of the district, and gained such dread ascendency over the rest that they respected him, admired him, feared him, obeyed him."

All this Mark Twain had heard. They rolled up to the stage station, and "sat down to breakfast with a half savage, half civilized company of armed and bearded mountaineers, ranchmen, and station employees. The most gentlemanly appearing, quiet, and affable officer we had yet found along the road in the Overland Company's service was the person who sat at the head of the table at my elbow. Never youth stared and shivered as I did when I heard him called Slade."

After which Mark Twain appends the account of Slade's later end from the history of the *Vigilantes of Montana*, who ultimately found it best for the peace of the Rockies to hang him! "From Fort Kearny West," says Professor Dimsdale, author of this history, "he was feared a great deal more than the Almighty."

In the end Mark Twain comes to love the stage and his "snuggery among the mail bags." He loved to "contemplate the majestic panorama of mountains and valleys spread out below us and eat ham and hard boiled eggs while our spiritual natures revelled alternately in rainbows, thunderstorms, and peerless sunsets."

After twenty days they reached Carson City, having "fed fat with wonders all the way." "Visibly our new home was a desert, walled in by barren snow-clad mountains. There was not a tree in sight. There was no vegetation except the endless sagebrush and greasewood. . . . Long trains of freight wagons in the distance enveloped in masses of dust suggested pictures of prairies on fire. . . . Every step we passed the skeleton of some dead beast of burden, with its dust-colored skin stretched tightly over its empty ribs. Frequently a solemn raven sat upon the skull or the hips and contemplated the passing coach with meditative serenity." The main street of Carson City consisted of "four or five blocks of little frame stores which were too high to sit down on but not high enough for various other purposes." That was all they saw the first day (besides seeing a man shot!) because the daily Washoe zephyr set in. "A soaring dust drift about the size of the United States set edgewise came with it, and the capital of Nevada Territory disappeared from view."

Like many other hopeful persons without capital, Mark Twain began looking around for places where the gold or silver could be picked up with a shovel. "We traded some of our 'feet' for 'feet' in other people's claims. In a little while we owned largely in the Gray Eagle, the Columbiana, the Branch Mint, the Maria Jane, the Universe, the Root Hog or Die, the Samson and Delilah, the Treasure Trove, the Golconda, the Sultana, the Boomerang, the Great Republic, the Grand Mogul, and fifty other mines that had never been molested with a pick. . . . We were stark mad with excitement, drunk with happiness, smothered under mountains of prospective wealth, arrogantly compassionate toward the plodding millions who knew not our marvelous canyon—but our credit was not good at the grocer's."

As it was in Nevada, so it was in Idaho, Colorado, Montana, Arizona. Scarcely a mountain solitude but bears mute testimony, in the bare bones of a skeleton, in a rude tombstone, in a deserted cabin or an abandoned town, to the brief hope that had flared here and had gone out. On a piece of lumber half buried in the earth one traveler found this epitaph rudely cut, as if with a jackknife:

> Here lays the bones of old A. C. Oakes
> The feller that started this dam big hox.

It is in the nature of miners not to stay put. A local ditty celebrates the fate and the undiminished hope of many of these Rocky Mountain seekers.

For forty years I've hammered, dug, and tried to make a strike;
I've buried twice the powder Custer ever saw.
I've made just coin enough to keep poorer than a snake.
My jack's ate all my works on mining law.
I've worn gunny sacks for overalls, and California socks,
I've burnt candles that would reach from here to Maine;
I've lived on powder, smoke, and bacon—
That's no lie, boy, I'm not fakin'—
But I still believe we'll strike it just the same.

So, still believing, those who did not get rich in Colorado or Nevada turned up among the grand gray hills of Idaho, reinforced by lads from Oregon and Washington territory. In the summer of 1861, 5,000 hopefuls were camping there, and, meeting in an angle between the Clearwater and Snake rivers, cheerfully indifferent to the fact that this was a reserve of the Nez Percé Indians, they set up the town of Lewiston. Scattering through the mountains, finding gold here and gold there, they built camps and gave them names. But before they could assemble from their several valleys and mountain sides and decide what slice of territory to claim, and how to organize it, a number of them began to rush north, following old trails of the trappers, into what is now Montana. Virginia City was formed there with an overflow from Boise City, Idaho, and had at one time 15,000 inhabitants, but many of these walked away and reappeared on the road to Fort Benton at the spot where the present city of Helena began to take shape in 1864. However, by 1862 enough miners had decided to stay in Idaho to make it a territory.

Along with Idaho, Arizona was organized as a territory in 1862. This stamping ground of the Apache Indians had been bought from Mexico in 1854, in a transaction known as the Gadsden Purchase, with a view to acquiring a suitable way through for a railroad across the South to the Pacific. "At the time of the transfer of the territory from Mexican to American ownership, there were two towns or villages therein inhabited chiefly by Mexicans and Indians from the neighboring mountains who, when off the trail of warfare and pillage, recruited their wasted strength and enjoyed their plunder as congenial citizens. These towns were Tuquelson [Tucson] where the Franciscan friar Marco de Niza in 1538, when on his way in search of the magic seven cities of Cibola, stopped and rested before entering the great desert lying before him. He found Tuquelson (map of Pedro Font 1777) a pleasant village of semi-civilized Indians—Montezuma Mexicans. . . . The second town was Tubac. There were a few outlying ranches nearby." So says the author of the *Argonaut Tales*.

All this region was the pleasant domain of one American trapper from Tennessee, Pauline Weaver. "The excellent judgment and wisdom used and displayed in his mingling and dealing with the Indians was recognized by them and he grew to have great influence and favor among the Apaches. He was bold, fearless, and resourceful according to Apache measurement of producing chivalric results, and because of his frank, open, and fair intercourse with them was often selected as arbiter of disputes and quarrels, not only between individual Indians but between the different bands and tribes. . . . He had acquired the quick eye and ear of the Indian and could read perfectly the Apache code of mountain and desert signals. Among them he was known as 'Quah-a-ha-na,' peacemaker or good talker."

At Tucson the Spanish had had some silver mines. Following the Gadsden Purchase Colonel Charles D. Poston went to Tucson and acquired mining rights and began to think that his prospective mines were a good reason for having a state of his own. "The hatching of the babe was effected at an oyster supper and smoker given by the Colonel in Washington City to which were invited a sufficient number of the members of Congress who would pass the bill creating the territory of Arizona, and thereby provide against their expiring terms of office by some financial venture in a new and rich mining country. The supper finished, the guests relaxed into a coma of black coffee and columns of smoke arising from the fragrant Havana cigars furnished by the host. Whilst in this lavish haze the official slate was made up, and the territory of Arizona was virtually created and organized. The only thing left to be done was to count the votes of the senators and congressmen, induce President Lincoln to sign the bill, and appoint and commission a batch of territorial officers, when all bells would be rung with merry chimes.

"On the reading of the list mine host discovered that he was not on the official slate. He heatedly inquired of his honored guests where he was to get off or on the job he had so successfully incubated; the offices were all irrevocably parceled out and from the royal division no appeal had been provided.

"Finally it was discovered that the new territory was domiciled by a horde of incorrigible, hostile Indians, and properly the office of Indian Agent should be created, and the Colonel was taken care of." He consoled himself by remembering that almost no one besides Indians lived in Arizona, anyway. So he was the ruler of all the people there were! He marked off a considerable section of Arizona as an Indian reservation and settled himself there in security and comfort as the big white chief of the Apaches, while "his official colleagues off the Reserve were borrowing trouble because of the war-whoop fringing every trail; and taking caution of themselves for the safety of their scalps."

Meanwhile an oddly assorted collection of white men had been settling here and there in Arizona. In 1857 a company of lumbermen from Maine had established a camp in the Santa

Rita Mountains to whipsaw pine lumber. Miners were coming in from all directions, and with them such bad characters as the vigilante societies had run out of other states. In 1862 a company of Union soldiers from California, having marched east to aid the Union forces in New Mexico, were disbanded and began to look for gold and silver and ranches in Arizona. So Arizona fast acquired some population besides Apaches. The center of this new life was the town of Prescott, which was a commercial center for the mining country of northern Arizona. The layout of Prescott was typical. "Whiskey Row extended from Gurley Street along the west side of Montezuma Street for two blocks south, well to the brow of the hill overlooking old Fort Misery, and farther on to Happy Valley." The aristocratic male resort of the town was Cob Web Hall, "the upper ten and most strictly high grade saloon in the block," run by an old China sea captain. "He was an exceptionally interesting and engaging character. His many years of roving the seas and mingling with the subjects of all nations so standardized his own nationality that his pronounced Americanism and mental-poised personality was an inspiration for good citizenship throughout the town, and drew to his business the best of the saloon-going element."

A rival of the sea captain in the respect of this wild town was old Rudolph, the wandering Jew, who claimed that he had been in every city, town, and mining camp of the United States. He "looked back and lived in the past, proudly claiming direct descent from the Mosaic Israelite of Biblical record. . . . Rudolph was a fountain of practical information. He was good-natured, agreeable, and untiring in his cleverness to do personal favors."

Though women were as scare as they were valuable in a mining town, Prescott boasted a genuine glamour girl. She was Pauline Markham, a charming and competent actress who coming there with a theatrical troupe found the place so profitable that her company stayed on, Pauline "waging a coquettish war of powerful poundings on the frontierized ribs and heart-strings of the amorous competing territorial and army officials. She was an open sesame to the well-filled gold dust and nugget pouches of the thrifty, bewhiskered miners. Consequently the opera season was a protracted and profitable one in the frontier town."

But alas, one snowy night, after the show was over, two masked men stole into Pauline's room, wrapped her in buffalo and bear robes, thrust her into a closed hack and drove rapidly away, her stifled cries for help ringing on the night air. When her manager heard it, "with an oath of revenge he started in search of her in the direction of the Pacific Coast City [San Francisco] and was never heard of afterwards." Nor was Pauline, at least by the genial old Homer of the *Argonaut Tales*.

Edmund Wells says that his tales are true. He was right there, and wrote it all down in his diary. Just one more of his prize preliminary sketches for a movie continuity, before we leave Arizona! One cold night, when all the most select society of Prescott was gathered at the China sea captain's palace, Cob Web Hall, someone happened to notice a bundle of cloth lying on the bar. "The Captain rolled the bundle along the bar and opened it up, where, cuddled away in a fancy wicker basket, swaddled in a soft downy robe, lay a chubby black-eyed baby girl, wide awake and ravenously swallowing her dimpled little fists. Beside it was a quart nursing bottle filled to its neck and ready for action. The Captain tenderly and cautiously held the little stranger aloft to the view of his friends, when there went up from them a round of hearty and welcome cheers for the tiny waif." When it appeared that no one knew where the baby came from, nor how it got there, "Each of the miners present put in a claim for its adoption, for who better than he could make fit provisions for its maintenance in some good family home or safe foundling institution, and finally ending with the most select lady's seminary. To end the contention, Captain Fisher proposed that the matter be settled by everyone present taking a throw of

dice at ten dollars a chance, the pool to go with the baby. It
was unanimously agreed to.

"As the game progressed, cheers went up when high
numbers were made by the different throws. Colonel Bob
Groom, bachelor, civil-engineer by profession . . . threw
four fives and was by acclamation declared the winner. His
broad-brimmed sombrero tilted back on the crown of his
proudly poised gray head, amidst the echoing cheers, he
stroked his long gray beard, and, smiling with the air of a
winning Olympic athlete, pompously straightened up to his
six feet three and from under his heavy grizzled eyebrows
triumphantly looked his defeated contestants over.

" 'Hold on,' loudly called out Judge Charley Hall. 'I have
the last throw,' and, squaring himself in front of the bar, the
crowd gradually edging back to give him plenty of elbow
room, shaking the box vigorously, with a dash he twirled the
dice upon the bar, rolling up four sixes. Excessive shouts of
joy went up from all but Colonel Bob, and an outpouring of
congratulations flooded the Judge, although he was subject to
the suspicion of having dice-loaded the game.

"Colonel Bob, however, yielded gracefully and admitted
his defeat, but claimed the right to name the baby, to which
the Judge without hesitancy consented.

" 'Boys,' commanded the Colonel, 'gather around for the
christening. Fill the bumpers to the brim with champagne.'
While Captain Fisher held the baby in full view far above
their heads, the Colonel spoke: 'As the bead of this sparkling
wine ascends to the surface, so may the destiny of this little
waif rise from obscurity and sparkle amongst the stars of
heaven on earth, uplifting humanity, making us better men
and better women. And in memory of this presence I now
christen thee, little miss, and name thee, Chance Cobweb Hall.'
'Amen,' soberly responded the crowd."

An all too brief sketch of the after career of this young
lady is in *Argonaut Tales*, waiting for a motion picture to fill
it out and make it all live again.

4

At first these mining states kept in communication with the East by the Pony Express, which, says Mark Twain, was "the fleet messenger who sped across the continent from St. Joe [Missouri] to Sacramento, carrying letters nineteen hundred miles in eight days."

From the stagecoach Mark Twain saw the pony rider go by. "Away across the endless dead level of the prairie a black speck appears against the sky, and it is plain that it moves. . . . In a second or two it becomes a horse and rider, rising and falling, rising and falling—sweeping toward us, nearer and nearer, growing more and more distinct, more and more sharply defined, nearer and still nearer, and the flutter of the hoofs comes faintly to our ear—another instant a whoop and a hurrah from our upper deck, a wave of the rider's hand but no reply, and man and horse burst past our excited faces, and go winging away like the belated fragment of a storm."

All the while the railroads were pressing westward. Illinois and Indiana were a network of roads, and the railroad was now puffing just ahead of agricultural settlement into the prairie. To encourage the building of roads, the federal government gave away great blocks of land, which the road was to sell to settlers, using the proceeds to finance the railroad building. But when it came to bridging hundreds of miles of land too barren to plow, too bleak even to give away, the roads naturally hesitated. As early as 1844, Asa Whitney, a China trader, offered to build a railroad from Lake Michigan to the Pacific, provided that Congress would give him a strip sixty miles wide straight across the country at a nominal price. This was an enlargement of Whitman's idea of a chain of farms and supply stations, running from the Mississippi to Oregon along the trails of the trappers. Whitney went about the country lecturing on his great idea, but, like many other hopeful plans, it was lost in the growing dissensions between North and South. If there was to be a railroad, the South wanted it, and to that end encouraged the Gadsden Purchase in 1854 which put Arizona on our map.

But the dream of the China traders was taken up by Senator Benton in Congress, and his impassioned plea on the subject marks one of those many moments when our political history leaped to the starry height of epic poetry. "In 1849," says *Gold of Ophir*, "he brought a convention of hard-headed railroad men to their feet when he cried: 'Let us make the iron road, and make it from sea to sea, states and individuals making it east of the Mississippi and the nation making it west. . . . Let us rise above everything sectional, personal, local. Let . . . it be adorned with . . . the colossal statue of the great Columbus—whose design it accomplishes, hewn from a granite mass of a peak of the Rocky Mountains overlooking the road . . . pointing with outstretched arm to the western horizon, and saying to the flying passengers, 'There is the East.'"

With the development of the mining territories all these embryo Rocky Mountain states began to call for railroads. Mark Twain reports that Governor Nye, of Nevada, being embarrassed by "camp followers" from the East, who were called "The Irish Brigade," suggested that they survey a railroad westward from Carson City. "When the legislature meets, I will have the necessary bill passed and the remuneration arranged.

"What, a railroad over the Sierra Nevada Mountains!"

"Well, then, survey it eastward to a certain point."

So he turned them loose on the desert. "They surveyed very slowly, very deliberately, very carefully. They returned every night during the first week, dusty, footsore, tired and hungry, but very jolly. They brought in a great store of prodigious hairy spiders—tarantulas—and imprisoned them in covered tumblers upstairs in the 'ranch.' After the first week they had to camp on the field, for they were getting well eastward. They made a good many inquiries as to the location of that 'certain point,' but got no information. At last to a peculiarly urgent inquiry of 'How far eastward?' Governor Nye telegraphed back: 'To the Atlantic Ocean, blast you! And then bridge it and go on.' "

In 1862 Congress passed the Union Pacific Act, subsidizing a railroad to the Pacific with ten sections of public lands and the loan of $16,000 of United States bonds per mile. The Central Pacific Corporation of California was to start from the Pacific, and meet the Union Pacific coming on from the East at the borders of the state. But the Central Pacific got busy first and drove so far eastward that it was allowed to go first into Nevada, and then into Utah. Meanwhile the Union Pacific was racing westward, great companies of workmen pushing along at the rate of two and a half miles a day, dragging their supplies, their beds, and their saloons, dance halls, and gambling dens after them. "Hell on Wheels," Samuel Bowles of *The Springfield Republican* called the gaudy train that went in the wake of the railroad men. "Hell would have to be raked in order to furnish them." But the Central Pacific had Chinese workmen, humble, thrifty, usually obedient, and the gauds they carried with them were picturesque with curly Chinese inscriptions and fluttering streamers and quaint tin-pan music, but quieter, even though laden with the sickish sweet atmosphere of opium. From the point of view of the capitalists and the lovers of at least moderate peace, the honors were all with the Chinese workmen.

On May 10, 1869, the two lines met at Ogden, Utah, where two men with silver hammers drove the last spikes, two of gold and two of silver, into the last tie. The last spike was driven by Sidney Dillon, president of the Union Pacific, before a gathering of notable people who had come on from both coasts. All over the United States bells were rung and the event duly interpreted by orators. Bret Harte produced the poem of the day:

> What was it the Engines said,
> Pilots touching, head to head,

Facing on a single track,
Half a world behind each back?

After the engine from the East had told of the wonders of
civilization it was bringing out to this wild empty West, the
engine from the West retorted:

You brag of the East! *You* do?
Why I bring the East to *you!*
All the Orient, all Cathay
Find through me the shortest way;
And the sun you follow here
Rises in my hemisphere.

5

The last spike driven into the last tie of the Union Pacific
was the last deadly spike also in the Indian sovereignty over
the last free Indian domain. For two centuries the Indians had
been pushed westward. For a century a not ungenerous, and
occasionally conscience-stricken federal government had consoled itself with the thought that if the Indians would hunt and
fish and roam about instead of settling down like other good
Americans, at least God had provided a place for them. The
Western plains would never be habitable by white men. Let
the Indians have them. Even today there are voices reminding
us that the late dust storms of the West were due to plowing
land which should never have been plowed. One strip
should have been left as hunting ground for the Indians, a vast
forest reserve, protecting the headwaters of the Western
rivers.

But circumstance, rather than the deliberate will of the
American government, had broken faith with the Indians. The
country through which for a generation the Indians had allowed emigrant trains to pass with only occasional molesta-
tions could be made into ranches after all. Kansas was already
a state. The golden wheat was sweeping over the prairies of
Nebraska. Dakota, land of the Sioux Indians, was organized in

1861 into a territory between Nebraska and Minnesota, with farmers ready to push in from both sides.

Meanwhile the Indian prophet Smoholla, in Nevada, was spreading over the plains a new Indian religion, beautiful and pathetic as it was impossible.

"You ask me to plough the ground," he said. "Shall I take a knife and tear my mother's bosom? Then when I die she will not take me to her bosom to rest.

"You ask me to dig for stones! Shall I dig under the skin for her bones? Then when I die I cannot enter her body to be born again.

"You ask me to cut grass and make hay and sell it, and be rich like white men, but how dare I cut my mother's hair."

And he announced with finality: "My young men will never work. Men who work cannot dream, and wisdom comes to us in dreams."

Bewildered, worried, tribe after tribe adopted the new religion. In vain Smoholla included in his teaching a doctrine of only passive resistance, saying that the Great Spirit "told us not to quarrel or fight or strike or shoot one another; that the Whites and the Indians were to be all one people." Poor gentle soul! As if Indians who must not work, but only dream dreams, could ever be one people with the mercilessly industrious white man!

Up in the North the individualistic Sioux welcomed the new idea, and found in it only a strengthening of their determination to stand their ground and have no plows and railroads in their lands. Had not the kindly and honest Nez Percés seen the town of Lewiston, Idaho, planted square in the middle of the reservation guaranteed to them? All these Plains Indians were a very different people from the red men who had first grappled with the whites in the woods of New England and Virginia. For three centuries they had been in constant touch with the white men. Practically all Indian chiefs for a century had had family alliances with white men, and white men of no mean quality. Often high-bred Scotchmen or Frenchmen had been domiciled among them, and had taken part in their tribal conclaves, directing them, thinking with them, trying to be their friends. All the while, too, there had been the fathers—the French fathers, the Spanish fathers.

⟨At the moment when the railroad was going through, there were several Indian chiefs—Red Cloud, Sitting Bull, Black Kettle, Red Sleeves—trying to think out the Indian problem, with more or less disinterestedness, more or less capacity for leadership. Of these Black Kettle seems an especially tragic figure. "The Chief . . . showed much natural intelligence and judgment," said Edmund Wells, who saw him in 1862. "In manner he was dignified, positive, and grave, as are all leading men among the plains Indians. A study of his prominent features, magnificent physique, and self-poised figure impressed one with the marvels of wild nature, a master type of the spirited North American Indian—a heroic model for the sculptor's chisel." He discussed the past of the Cheyenne Indians of whom he was ranking chief, and all their mistakes in dealing with the white men. "White chiefs talked that the Great Spirit of the white man was better and stronger and Cheyenne must believe in him and give up the Great Spirit of the Cheyennes for he was no good. He told the Indian to go on the war-path." He drew circles in the ground, one within another, showing how the circle allowed to the Indian was getting smaller and smaller. "His pensive and care-worn face expressed sorrow and doubt. Slowly shaking his head and swinging his extended arm as he pointed to the horizon on all sides, Black Kettle said: 'Now, white men and soldiers are more than the antelope and the buffalo; more trouble is coming. Cheyennes must again heap fight um.'" Two years later he showed how his warriors could fight by wiping out the Holladay stage line.

In 1866, while the railroads were approaching each other across the West, a special committee on the Condition of the Indian Tribes went out through the Indian country, and published an illuminating report in January, 1867. As a result all the tribes were called in peace conferences. In one way or another bargains were patched up with most of them, including the abandonment of a proposed railroad across Sioux territory to which Red Cloud objected. So secure did the Indian agents feel that they afterward issued rations of rifles and ammunition for hunting—the rifles of the very best quality. Almost immediately the young braves broke out of bounds, and turned the rifles on settlers in sporadic attacks all over the West. Thereupon all peaceful Indians were ordered to congregate at Fort Cobb for supplies and protection, under General Hazen, and a warning issued that the army intended to go after the rest. Black Kettle came to the camp claiming to be at peace, but his record by this time was so black that Hazen ordered him off. Late in the autumn, several detachments of soldiers started off on punitive expeditions, the most famous being that under Major General Custer. Custer surprised and completely annihilated Black Kettle's village, killing men, women, and children. He then went on the war path, up and down the West, wherever there were Indian disturbances, as a kind of military police force. In 1874 when gold was discovered in the Black Hills in Dakota Territory, and the usual rush began thither, Custer was sent to see that the Sioux kept the peace. The young braves were wandering about, menacing and restless. Custer ordered them back into the reservation on pain of shooting, and, when they did not obey, himself went after them and was slain by an Indian ambush, June 25, 1876.

However, this policing of the West by the army, miserable and mistaken as many of the individual encounters were, unjust to the better spirits among the Indians, whose tragedy was that they lacked not good will but organization, throttled the last resistance out of them. They were content to be gathered on reservations—at least they had no spirit left to be less than content. In 1867 Wyoming was organized as a territory, and the last Indian country definitely fixed in what is now the state of Oklahoma. Since then the effort has been to educate the Indians for full citizenship, and to protect them from unwise

alienation of their lands. There have been good Indian agents
—and some very bad ones. It is a long story, and tragic with
the most hopeless tragedy of all—the tragedy that inheres not
only in human ill will but in circumstance and the very nature
of things.

Yet one great wrong the Indians have been spared. The
white man has accepted the inheritance of Indian blood without social reluctance, with even a kind of pride. They were
the first Americans, and so American sentiment has always accepted them, according to them in marriage and inheritance a
fellowship granted to no other race beyond the line of white.
A man whose grandmother was a full-blooded Kaw Indian
was but recently Vice-President of the United States, and
might, by a chance turn of the wheel of fortune, have been
president. And the most beloved American of recent times,
Will Rogers, used to say that his ancestors didn't come over on
"The Mayflower." They were here on the dock waiting to
greet the ship when it came in.

At the moment when the last annihilating conflict of the
whites with the Indians was beginning, and the railroads pressing to their meeting place were vanquishing for ever the trapper and the hunter, a group of officers and soldiers stopped at
the tent of old Pauline Weaver, the Arizona trapper. "Everything within was in apparent order as the old scout was in the
habit of keeping it. His rifle was standing in the corner of the
tent within easy reach. Beside it his powder horn and bullet
pouch were hanging at the head of his bunk, his belt, revolver,
and hunting knife just above it. His hat, coat, and hunting
shirt were hanging on a nail driven in the tent center post, his
knapsack underneath. Covering the dirt floor in front of his
bed lay a large rug of soft hair lobo or mountain wolf skins.
Stretched at full length on his back, Pauline's lifeless body was
lying on his bunk. A blanket was tucked closely about the
body, and the face covered with a towel which had been taken
from a nail in the tent ridge-pole overhead. On the table by

his bunk a candle-stick stood. The candle had died in the socket.

"The surroundings, the moccasin tracks, the careful folding of the dead body in its blanket shroud, the towel over the face, the undisturbed personal effects, no evidence of violence, the tying and fastening of the tent door flaps on the outside, all looked mysterious and uncanny to the silent officers and soldiers who flocked to the dead hero's tent. And they marveled."

The marvel was only a commonplace in that trapper's life of the early West, of which the dead body of Pauline, there at the feet of the soldiers, on that October morning in 1867, was the dramatic, symbolic end. He had been nursed through his last hours by the Indian woman who loved him. And local verse, written or quoted by Wells, says farewell not only to the trapper but to his humble Indian wife, in verses which soar true and beautiful on the wings of poetry, above the halting feet of mere grammar.

She nursed him quietly through the silent night
As the candle to its socket was burning;
Then fled to the high cliffs, in the morning gray light,
To escape the pale-face's coming.

She wrapped him snugly in his blanket shroud
When the candle was burnt to the socket;
Then dropped the flap door as she passed the tent out
With the outside tent strings she did latch it.

The whippoorwill mourning in the willows o'er head
Started the lion's fierce roar on the mountain;
Where the whispering pines soughed requiems to the dead,
For the pitcher was broke at the fountain.

Bright twinkling stars in their tread through the sky
Pointed the trail for his wandering spirit;
As it winged its flight home bound on high,
In a lodge where she hoped for to meet it.

White man. Oh! White man, you sure let me go,
To my people far beyond the wide river;
Waving a long, long good-bye to her dead friend there below,
She dropped down the sky-line for ever.

6

With the coming of the railroads, there began the greatest
battle of the West, the stark and bloody conflict with the Bad
Man. Always this fellow had been ahead of the settlements;
and what he could do to God-fearing and law-abiding persons
had been shown in the Border Ruffian warfare of Kansas. But
agricultural communities cannot support many bad men.
There is not enough there that is easy to steal. You can't put
agricultural machinery into your saddle bags and ride off with
it, or surreptitiously pocket an acre of wheat. Now the mining
enterprise gave the bad man what he had needed all along—
some ready capital. And it filled the local citizen's pockets and
the channels of local trade with something all too easy to make
away with—actual gold and silver. Above all, it enabled him
to buy up the local courts and the government.

Of Nevada in 1860, Bancroft says, in that high-colored style
of his which in his *History of Popular Tribunals* gives his vast
collection of newspaper facts an epic gorgeousness: "Bloated
dissipation sunned itself upon the street corners, and lust and
lewdness flaunted their gay attire along the thoroughfares.
Mingling with the whiskey-stained visages of the dominant
race were the black and yellow-skinned element found in
every important town along the Pacific coast; and seasoning
the mass with infernal relish was woman of every shade of influence, from distraught wives seeking release from unwelcome bonds, and grass-widows panting for new alliances to
the openly profane and gaudily decked professional."

Above these murky scenes there shone for Colorado, Idaho,
Montana, Nevada, and Arizona two stars of hope. One was
Utah and the other was California. Bad men did not flourish
in Utah. They smelled the Mormon odor of sanctity afar off

and hastened on to Nevada instead. "Were any disposed to praise the Mormons," says Bancroft, "or in any wise to do them justice, then might the lovers of law and order, the opposers of the vigilance principle, give them credit for living without mobs, without any popular, or legal, or other tribunal save those simple forms which lead with the least possible time and cost to justice."

But the average early citizen of the West felt that the Lord had not called him to be a Mormon, and confessed with shame that in the still embryonic government of the Western territories he could not yet master Brigham Young's method of making judges and officials keep their hands clean of gambler's gold. So he turned to California. One of the contemporary reporters on conditions in Nevada expressed the general feeling. "Washoe is now to California what the latter was at one time to all the world beside—a receptacle for the vagrant, the vicious, and the unfortunate. . . . This country, this coming state of Washoe, when it shall have had the age of her sister California, will be able to boast as much public intelligence and virtue, and to make as fair an historic record as she."

When any one of the mining territories got to the point of wanting to be like California, it generally organized a vigilance committee and started on a career of hanging. But as Bancroft says, the average peaceful citizen does not fancy himself in the role of public hangman. So extraordinary efforts were made to distinguish the true People's Tribunal from a mere lynching mob. In the first place before the committee could act effectively, it was necessary to enlist practically every responsible and sober householder, along with persons of known integrity representing the law, education, and even the church. In the second place, great stress was placed on quiet and order and obedience to the control of chosen leaders. Often it was forbidden to cheer, even when the most notorious rascal was dangled from the rope, or to stay around a gibbet after a victim was hanged. People must disperse quietly and immediately go to their own homes. Sometimes the committee had enough power to put a ban on the sale of all intoxicating liquors during its deliberations. Generally it would throw out any person who was drunk. In the third place, it was usually insisted that the accused person, however well known he and his crimes might be, must be put through the form of an orderly trial. The speed with which a court could be organized, lawyers for prosecution and defense appointed, and judgment given was sometimes breathtaking.

The vigilance committee usually could not get the absolutely essential cooperation of the responsible persons of the community till it was clear that the courts and the political officers were powerless. Always the committee acted in direct defiance of them, though sometimes with the secret connivance of some officials. In a drawn battle between it and the local government, it depended on a general appeal to "The People" elsewhere—the People, in the American understanding of the word, being the persons in any community who have founded or expect to found secure and permanent homes and to support and if necessary to protect them by their own efforts.

If the People's Tribunal began to get out of hand, an anti-vigilance committee could be formed to check up on the committee.

In Montana, after a long and worthy career of public hangings on the part of the vigilance committee, the following notice was served on the self-constituted protectors of public safety: "We now, as a sworn band of law-abiding citizens, do hereby solemnly swear that the first man that is hanged by the vigilants of this place, we will retaliate five for one, unless it is done in broad daylight so that every one may know what it is for. We are all well satisfied that in times past you did some glorious work, but the time has come when law should be enforced. Old fellow-members, the time is not like what it was. We had good men with us; but now there is a change. There is not a thief that comes to this country but rings himself into the present committee. We know you all.

You must not think you can do as you please. We are American citizens and you shall not drive and hang whom you please." (Signed) FIVE FOR ONE

In the People's Tribunal the communities of the mountain West found an almost invincible weapon against political corruption and that judicial circumambulation and delay which has been the curse of every American community in which crime has the means of subsidizing itself with ready money. Crime flourishes and punishment lags when something like the gold and silver of the West, or the enormous receipts of the bootleg industry during the Prohibition era, gives the criminal the means of buying himself off. In this sense money is undoubtedly the root of all evil. In the Rocky Mountain West the connection was so open and so elementary that it serves as a laboratory demonstration of crime in America for all time.

Against this the People's Tribunal opposed something invincible because it could not be reached by gold or crime. It was character. For effectiveness the Tribunal must enlist and hold the men whom everybody knew to be above reproach, unbought and unbuyable. In the committee was pooled the community's secret knowledge of men's character. The silent assent of some men was a weapon with which the people could oppose courts, governors, and even organized militia, and, having it, they could appeal straight over the heads of their own territory, and even of the whole Rocky Mountain West, and know that they would be vindicated. Few situations ever put such a premium on character—on that reputation which a man lays up in the bosom of the community, moment by moment, encounter by encounter in the humble course of the day's business.

The character of the community valued was well defined. It was perfect integrity combined with great caution—a tendency to go slow, a readiness to reverse action instantly, at the first sign of anything shady, and a capacity to stand like a rock against mob incitement, and be shot down without flinching where you stood. In all the numerous communities where genuine Popular Tribunals were organized, such characters emerged. They were chosen for leadership by almost wordless agreement. They carried the whole group with them. So long as such men stayed with the committee it was invincible. It defied governor, courts, and militia alike, and was vindicated by outside or federal investigators. The day they walked out on the committee, however—and they often did this quite publicly—that day it became only a lynching mob, and government and militia were able to run it down.

With the People's Tribunals, so led and so organized, modern persons calling themselves vigilants, and sometimes used to intimidate laborers, have, of course, nothing to do. The great vigilance battles of the early West were never with laboring groups and seldom with "foreigners." They were with the large racketeers, usually established as men of wealth, or with public officials elected by ballot stuffing, and owned body and soul by criminal financial interests. Generally the person punished was as natively American as the sagebrush. The Tribunal set a dangerous precedent, but under the circumstances, what else could the people do, for the protection of their property and their homes?

The value of the People's Tribunal, as opposed to the courts, was that its action was swift, and it was dramatic. An example of its method is the series of hangings in Boise, Idaho, in 1866. At that time both the sheriff, who was named Dave Updyke, and the local courts were dishonest. At a public trial, an honest man, named Raymond, gave some testimony unwelcome to the rascals who had the local government in their pockets. After the trial a man named Clark swaggered up to Raymond and told him his testimony was a lie. Raymond replied that he told only the truth. Clark then rushed on Raymond, who dodged and drew his pistol. Clark also drew. To bystanders who tried to interfere, Raymond said, "Don't worry. I won't shoot."

"Shoot," said Clark. "I'm going to fire."

"I don't want to shoot," said Raymond. "I'll give you the first shot."

Thereupon Clark shot, but the cap snapped without exploding the charge. Raymond stood still without lifting his hand to shoot. Clark then took a second deliberate aim, and this time murdered him.

This happened on April 2. On April 7, Clark was hanging dead just outside the town of Boise, and pinned to the gibbet was the following announcement:

Justice has now commenced her righteous work. This suffering community which has already lain too long under the ban of ruffianism shall now be renovated of its thieves and assassins. Forbearance has at last ceased to be a virtue, and an outraged community has most solemnly resolved on self-protection. Let this man's fate be a terrible warning to all of his kind, for the argus eye of justice is no more sure to see than her arm will be certain to strike. The soil of this beautiful valley shall no longer be desecrated by the presence of thieves and assassins. This fatal example has no terror for the innocent, but let the guilty beware, and not delay too long, and take warning.

[*Signed*] XXX

A week later, the body of the sheriff was hanging in a shed between two houses, with this inscription pinned to it:

DAVE UPDYKE

Accessory after the fact to the Port Neuf stage robbery.

Accessory and accomplice to the robbery of the stage near Boise City in 1864.

Chief conspirator in burning property on the overland stage line.

Guilty of aiding and assisting West Jenkins, the murderer, and other criminals to escape while you were sheriff of Ada County.

Accessory and accomplice to the murder of Raymond.

Threatening the lives and property of an already outraged and suffering community.

[*Signed*] XXX

Next day the body of James Dixon was hanging to a tree. On it was posted the notice

JAKE DIXON

Horse-thief, counterfeiter, and road agent generally.
A dupe and tool of Dave Updyke.

[*Signed*] XXX

with this addition below:

All the living accomplices in the above crimes are known through Updyke's confession, and will surely be attended to. The roll is being called.

[*Signed*] XXX

A full explanation of this exhibit was then given in *The Idaho Statesman*. "Space forbids us to mention the numerous atrocities that make up the long list committed here in Boise City. The last one was the deliberate murder of Raymond because he testified to the truth in a court of law. Before his almost lifeless body was removed from the place where he fell, D. C. Updyke stepped up to a prominent citizen of this place and significantly said, 'That affair grew out of the law-suit yesterday, and there will be many more like it.' The whole tenor of the preliminary examination of Clark gave the assurance that the same means that had defeated justice so often before were to be used to the utmost in this case. That Clark was committed to await trial, and was seized and executed is well known. Updyke was most ferocious in his threats against several citizens whom he charged with having a hand in the execution, and finally, as he left town, announced his intention of returning to pay Boise City one more visit to get even, or to that effect. He has been executed, as has also the confederate who went away with him. As to the terror that has reigned for the last two years, it has come to an end. Good citizens and peaceable men walk the streets and go about their business in comparative safety. The grand jury that is now in session when their labors are done may disperse without danger of being assassinated for the discharge of their duty. There is no alarm in the community and no terror except for those who prey upon society and their fellow men. Such is the exact condition of affairs to-day."

H. H. Bancroft's mammoth volumes about the popular tribunals, and Professor Dimsdale's philosophical account of the vigilantes of Montana are epics in the raw. Here is the great elemental theme, of the war of good and evil; here is behavior in the grand style; and here is that which makes life desperately important—always and forever Death in the background. Mostly these villains of the West are just rats and sneaks. It is the good men who stand out in monumental grandeur. But now and then a bad man has some redeeming dignity or charm. Of Slade, the notorious agent of the Overland Stage, whom Mark Twain met, and whom the vigilantes of Montana ultimately hanged, Professor Dimsdale remarks: "Captain Slade was the idol of his followers, the terror of his enemies and of all that were not within the charmed circle of his dependents. In him generosity and destructiveness, brutal lawlessness and courteous kindness, firm friendship and volcanic outbreaks of fury were so mingled that he seemed like one born out of date. He should have lived in feudal times."

So should they all, no doubt. But then, as Bancroft philosophically remarks: "Nothing was created in vain. Even desperadoes serve a good purpose sometimes. Along the American border during the past century they have done far more toward the execution of justice in killing each other than was done by all the law courts of the land. What a godsend it is to a community for five or six of their ruffians to kill each other, leaving only one survivor for the people to hang!"

7

From the bad man of the West it is a relief to turn to the gracious pastoral figure of the cowboy crooning to his herds under midnight stars.

In the seventies there developed in the Southwest, especially in Texas, an enormous cattle business, the cattle feeding on the luxuriant grass of the open range in Texas all winter, and being then rounded up by their several owners and their cowboys, branded, and driven north to market to Fort Dodge in Kansas. Large herds were also taken north to Montana where the young cattle were developed for market. Among these cowboys that art of song, which had been the consolation of the Scotch-Irish border and the amusement of the back-woodsmen, had a new birth, in simple lays recording their experiences, and intended to entertain themselves in their long hours watching their herds, and to win a little applause from the boys when they were all gathered together. Simple lads, the cowboys were masters of a few extraordinary skills with lariat and horseflesh, but otherwise innocent and sentimental —just boys from families all over the country, but mainly from the South and the middle border, living a rather simple outdoor life, with a limited number of important and, to the observer, picturesque responsibilities. Their principal crime was getting drunk and sometimes falling in with gamblers on payday, and many were the efforts of cowboy preachers to keep them from the saloons and recall to them the prayers of the good mother at home. Many of the cowboy songs, com-posed perhaps when the poet was recovering from a spree, solemnly warn other boys against drink and bad men.

Perfect democracy existed within the cowboy ranks. In one outfit there might be a Negro, a British younger son of good family, and an assorted collection of all-American types. But they were all cowboys together, and honor among them was distributed in accordance with the personal gifts and qualities suitable to their own environment and not in accord-ance with the rules of that great far-off world, which seemed dim and unreal now to these boys on the plains.

Most of the cowboy's dreams and hopes are written into his songs, which have a place in American love not second even to the minstrelsy of the South. There is, for example, the ever-recurring song of homesickness, of which *Bury Me Not on the Lone Prairie* is best known.

Oh, bury me not on the lone prairie
Where the wild coyotes will howl over me
In a narrow grave just six by three—
Oh, bury me not on the lone prairie.

Where the buzzard beats, and the wind goes free—
Oh, bury me not on the lone prairie.

There are endless picturesque complaints of the hard life.

The cowboy's life is a dreary, dreary life,
All out in the midnight rain;
I'm almost froze, with water on my clothes,
Way up on the Kansas line.

Before you try cow-punching, kiss your wife,
Take a heavy insurance on your life,
Then cut your throat with a Barlow knife,
   For it's easier done that way.

But when the cowboy later indulged in reminiscences, his troubles were softened by time.

There were hard old times on Bitter Creek
   That never can be beat.
   It was root hog or die
Under every wagon sheet.
We cleaned up all the Indians,
Drank all the alkali,
And it's whack the cattle on, boys,
   Root hog or die.

There was good old times in Salt Lake
   That never can pass by.
It was there I first spied
   My China girl called Wi.
She could smile, she could chuckle,
   She could roll her hog eye.
Then it's whack the cattle on, boys.
   Root hog or die.

But the cowboy had his moments of exhilaration, especially on payday.

> Goin' back to draw my money,
> Goin' back home to see my honey,
> With my knees in the saddle and my seat in the sky,
> I'll quit punching cows in the sweet bye and bye.

One thing the cowboy liked to do was to call the roll of all the Western states and territories and express his poor opinion of them all—somewhat as follows:

> TEXAS:
> The rattlesnake bites you, the scorpion stings,
> The mosquito delights you with buzzing wings,
> The sand burrs prevail and so do the ants,
> And those who sit down need half soles on their pants.

> The red pepper grows on the banks of the brook.
> The Mexicans use it in all that they cook.
> Just dine with a Greaser and then you will shout
> "I've hell on the inside as well as the out."

> ARKANSAS:
> Farewell to swamp angels, canebrakes, and chills,
> Farewell to sage and sassafras and corn-dodger pills;
> For if ever I see this land again, I'll give to you my paw,
> It will be through a telescope from here to Arkansaw.

But a cowboy following his herds could console himself with the memory of worse jobs in the West—such as buffalo skinning, for example:

> Our meat it was buffalo hump and iron-wedge bread,
> And all we had to sleep on was buffalo robe for bed.
> The fleas and the gray-backs worked on us.
> Oh, boys, it was not slow.
> I'll tell you there's no worse hell on earth
> Than the range of the buffalo.

The tragedy of the cowboy was "going wrong"—getting involved with gamblers while drunk or being caught by saloon logic in a net of lawless gunplay—one of those wretched Western situations in which if you shoot you are done for, and if you don't you are done for just the same. Many songs bemoan this tragedy and warn cowboys against it.

> It was once in the saddle I used to go dashing,
> It was once in the saddle I used to go gay.
> First to the dram-house, then to the card-house.
> Got shot in the breast. I am dying to-day.

Against the temptations of his life, the cowboy set his hopes, his dreams, and his simple religion. His hope was generally for a ranch of his own. His dream was of the girl who would make the ranch a home. His religion was picked up from cowboy circuit riders, and naïvely fitted to his own simple hopes and fears, and his own musings under the great night sky.

> Still I wish that some kind hearted girl would pity on me take
> And relieve me from the mess that I am in.
> That angel, how I'd bless her if this her home she'd make
> In the little old sod shanty on my claim.

The cowboy with a herd of his own, riding behind all his worldly wealth, looks up to the sky and ventures on a prayer that will be all his own.

> Bless the round-up year by year
> And don't forget the growing steer,
> Water this land with brooks and rills
> For my cattle that roam on a thousand hills.
>
> One thing more, and then I'm through,
> Instead of one calf give me two.
> I may pray different from other men
> But I've had my say and now Amen.

It was when riding as night watch behind the great moving mass of cattle going north that the cowboy's meditations soared the highest. He thought of heaven, and scraps of hymns, and the hereafter, and God, and the Judgment Day. Looking at the stars he asks

> Are they worlds with their ranges and ranches?
> Do they ring with rough rider refrains?
> Do the cowboys scrap there with Comanches
> And other red men of the plains?

And when he felt very good, or very repentant for the last spree, or very tender, remembering mother at home or the girl he was going to marry, he vowed that he'd keep clear of drink, and gambling games and save his money, and altogether conduct himself so that he might be "Rounded up in glory bye and bye."

When I was a very young woman looking for adventure in the stifling, distance-enpurpled dust of Wyoming, I met an old man who was universally hailed as the last of the great cowboy preachers—a sturdy, strong old man with broad, benign brow, and patriarchal long white hair and beard (the beard stained with tobacco juice), wearing a black sombrero, and a quaint cross between a cowboy's riding costume and a preacher's shirt and vest and coat. "They liked me," he said serenely, "I could ride in anywhere, even into a saloon, and get 'em all listening, sometimes tears rolling down their faces. I could make 'em throw away their whisky and shake hands with the man they was going to kill."

"And how did you do it?" I asked.

"Oh, I'd been a cowboy myself," he said, "and I knew there was three things that would always get 'em. It was either mother, or home, or heaven, and in bad cases I talked about all three!"

A charming figure—the cowboy! A simple workingman, he emerges in his own songs as the gallant, innocent, foolish image of all the dear mothers' boys and girls' sweethearts of the world, and in the van of the oncoming homes of which he dreams so wistfully, he rides away over the rim of our last frontier.

> Hail to barbed wire.
> It broke the free range, sent the cowman west—
> Cowboys in dimmer distance, riding, riding,
> Into rich sunset light, whence lingering notes
> Drift over dusky distances of trail.
>
> —CARL SANDBURG

27

EMPTY SADDLES
IN THE OLD CORRAL

THE gray and elderly among the present living Americans opened their eyes in the late seventies or early eighties on an America which seemed to have come to the end of all roads. Everything that till then had made the drama and excitement of American life—the battle with the Indians, the conflict over slavery, the settling of new territories—was ended. They seemed to have ended suddenly and at almost the same time. And with them, in each section of the country, ended also the dominant way of life, which time and collective adventure had made beautiful. The Old South was dead. Maritime New England, the New England of the clipper and the whaler, of the China and India trade and the adventures of the far South Seas, was dying. And the Wild West was breathing its last gasp. The clipper was gone from the sea, and the covered wagon from the prairie, and the rider on horseback from the old forest trail. Our glad, highhearted, beautiful youth was ended, and what faced us seemed, for the moment, only a humdrum, though prosperous maturity.

With all trails to the Promised Land fenced across with barbed wire, with no dramatic hopes and faiths on which to mount and ride away, the Americans began to take stock of themselves.

The first sign of the new spirit was a great outburst of political and economic "muckraking." From 1873 to 1878 there was a long and bitter depression brought on by over-speculation in Western railroad bonds and exceedingly shady financing of railroad building. For several years the financial interests had been running wild. In 1869 Jay Gould and Jim Fisk set out to corner the gold supply of the United States and actually secured $120,000,000. When the price of gold reached 162 the Secretary of the Treasury placed $4,000,000 on the market and the crazy attempt crashed in ruin. An investigation implicated a brother-in-law of President Grant in the conspiracy but it proved the old hero himself guiltless. In 1872 it was rumored that the Crédit Mobilier, a construction company which had built a large part of the Union Pacific Railroad, was buying up the votes of Congress. The investigation that followed was stupendous. Several senators and congressmen were found guilty and their expulsion from Senate and House was voted. Swiftly on this shock to the nation followed the general collapse.

The lesson of it all and its connection with our whole pioneering theory of life was driven home by Mark Twain in *The Gilded Age,* which he wrote in collaboration with Charles Dudley Warner. His idea for the book was excellent, but the execution is so poor, except in rare spots, that its effect for the present reader is spoiled. He carries a family which has the misfortune to own vast undeveloped acres of Tennessee land westward to Missouri and then back into the whirlpool of Washington politics, in a wild career of hope, poverty, dupery, and only half-conscious rascality all founded in the speculative hope that the increasing value of their lands would make them rich without work. As he said, this poison of speculation is not in the great financiers alone. Who made possible their nefarious manipulations? It was the thousands upon thousands of schoolteachers and clergymen and other good respectable

people who were ready to invest in the offerings of the speculators because they were willing their bit of money should
make more for them than money can honestly make.

Relentlessly, in his more effective moments, Mark Twain
satirized all the idle, dreaming inhabitants of little prairie villages who intrigued for the passage of the railroad through
their towns. "Hawkeye [the city which lay in the normal
course of the railroad] had always declined to subscribe anything toward the railway, imagining that her large business
would be a sufficient compulsory influence; but now Hawkeye was frightened; and before Colonel Sellers knew what he
was about, Hawkeye in a panic, had rushed to the front and
subscribed such a sum that Napoleon's attractions suddenly
sank into insignificance, and the railroad concluded to follow
a comparatively straight course instead of going miles out
its way to build up a metropolis in the muddy desert of Stone's
Landing.

"The thunderbolt fell. . . . Hawkeye rose from her
fright, triumphant and rejoicing, and down went Stone's
Landing. One by one, its meager parcel of inhabitants packed
up and moved away, as the summer waned and the fall approached. Town lots were no longer saleable, traffic ceased, a
deadly lethargy fell upon the place once more, the *Weekly
Telegraph* faded into an early grave, the wary tadpole returned
from exile, the bull frog resumed its ancient song, the tranquil turtle sunned his back upon bank and log and drowsed
his grateful life away as in the sweet old days of yore."

Another one of the thousands of real estate booms in the
van of the railroads had collapsed. And who collapsed us?
asks Mark Twain. Not the big rascals alone, but all the fond
and foolish leading citizens like Colonel Sellers, and the men
and women who hoped to get rich without working for it,
and the innumerable small persons who were seduced from
honest retailing of coffee and sugar and dry goods into selling
their fellow citizens gold bricks.

Meanwhile he dealt with a high hand with the Senate

scandals. "Yes, the nation was excited, but Senator Dillworthy was calm—what was left of him after the explosion of the shell. Calm and up and doing. What did he do first? What would you do first if you had tomahawked your mother at the breakfast table for putting too much sugar in your coffee? You would ask for a 'Suspension of public opinion.' That is what Senator Dillworthy did. It is the custom. He got the usual amount of suspension. Far and wide he was called a thief, a briber, a promoter of steamship subsidies, railroad swindles, robberies of the government in all possible forms and fashions. Newspapers and everybody else called him a pious hypocrite, a sleek oily fraud, a reptile who manipulated temperance movements, prayer meetings, Sunday schools, public charities, missionary enterprises, all for his private benefit. And as these charges were backed up with what seemed to be good and sufficient evidence, they were believed with national unanimity."

The attack on shady politics, financial manipulators, unjust monopolies, and wasters of the national resources has continued from that day to this, with increasing energy, and gave us first the doughty personality of Theodore Roosevelt, and now another Roosevelt too near to us for present appraisal. In the Rooseveltian leadership of this battle there was the old cheerful, picturesque knight-errantry of the American attack on the wicked world. Riding along, with face shining with hope and faith, dealing blow for blow and word for word, and having a wonderful time, not very subtle, never bothering to be consistent, but carrying life easily in the grand manner and finding that time and tide work with him who does so, this leadership some future historian may also find richly, uniquely American. But we are still too close to it to know that.

2

Along with the cheerful energy, and native sharp-tongued wit with which the leaders began to go after the enemy in their midst, there was, however, a new and somber spirit. Multitudes till now inarticulate were getting their heads sufficiently above the struggle for mere existence to know how miserable they were and had got enough education in the common schools to be able to say so. So all over the country, from the sons and daughters of pioneers, there went up a cry of protest. The cry began in the Middle West and the sharpest social criticism, the most devastating "realism," and the most continuous effort to do something about everything has come from there. Here "the folks" of America had finally settled down—the people who wanted good farms and steady incomes, and healthy families of children with a chance to be better than their fathers. And now, while they never denied that in the rich prairies they had found their Promised Land, there were two fatal difficulties about it. One was that the rent and taxes and mortgage on the land were too high, which was an old pioneering objection in America. The other difficulty was a new one, and utterly devastating—they themselves weren't fit to live in a Promised Land. "We are dull; we are mediocre," they began to cry. "We have no eye for beauty, no sense for the finer things of life, no grace, no depth, no polish, no joy of living." It was as if in those many mirroring waters of their own great valley they had suddenly seen their own faces, and they did not like them.

The first great book to set forth the new point of view was *The Story of a Country Town*, published by E. W. Howe in 1882. E. W. Howe was the editor of *The Atchison Globe* in Kansas and wrote his novel on the kitchen table at night after his noisy children had gone to bed. After trying it in vain on several publishers, he finally printed it himself, and sent a copy to Mark Twain. Mark Twain answered in a long letter written in pencil, full of notes and comments on the book, saying that it was the first time he had ever been willing to furnish an author an opinion of his book. "But I like *The Story of a Country Town* so much that I am glad to say so. Your style is so simple, sincere, direct, and at the same time so clear and strong that I think it must have been born in you.

Your picture of the arid village life is vivid and what is more, true. I know, for I have seen and lived it all." All over the country other readers felt as Mark Twain did, and the demand for the book was so great that publishers who had refused the manuscript now begged for the privilege of reprinting it. "Our records," wrote one, "show that we rejected the story in manuscript, but alas, we are all liable to err." Both Henry Holt and Wagnalls discharged readers for refusing the story instead of sending it higher up. Others who refused it and then asked to reprint it or did actually reprint it were Harpers, Houghton Mifflin, and Scribner's.

The Story of a Country Town is a plain, stark tale written in an unpretentious, slightly stiff style, level and monotonous as a prairie in March, the kind of generally mediocre English which the average reporter on a Western paper writes. It reports a simple story of humble domestic life and marital jealousy. The people all talk to each other in a stiff, plain style, like people moving uneasily on the high heels of grammar. There is none of the grace and humor of some of the earlier Middle Western writing in dialect. This is the Middle West, not in its original cheerful and amusing ignorance, but adolescent and awkward and just graduating from grammar school. But as one reads on, one is lost in a great story, so plain, so painful, so monotonously, levelly true that it seems to make any other kind of writing trivial and unimportant. Here is the prairie West, dull, gaunt, bleak, looking out on the world with devastating candor, meeting it with unassailable dignity. The tragedy of the story is as new in American literature as the tone; for the self-made hero's manly and devoted efforts to make a home, successful on the material side to the point of moderate prosperity, are crushed by something he and his bride had never reckoned on—their lack of emotional training and guidance. Here is the first agonized note of a cry that was to echo and reecho through the literature of the Middle West. "What shall it profit a man, if he shall gain the whole world, and lose his own soul?" What are houses and barns and lands and money in the bank if our culture is insufficient to the enjoyment of them?

The heroine of Howe's story is the heroine of all Western tradition—the young schoolma'am, the dear and beautiful young lady, usually from parts east, who came to a prairie village and brought it culture. Few of the heroines that men have worshiped have had such a genuine outpouring of love and gratitude at their feet as this good, hard-working girl, and few have deserved it more. Howe's tribute is touching in its studious understatement. "I am certain that her dress was inexpensive, and that she spent little of her money in this way, for most of it was sent to her family; but her taste and skill were such that she was always neatly and becomingly attired, being able to work over an old garment on Saturday and appear on Sunday the best dressed woman in the county. I have thought that she was familiar with all the fashions in women's dress without ever having seen them, for she was always in advance of the plates in the *Lady's Book* taken by my mother. With more fortunate surroundings she might have been a remarkable woman. But while there were many others less good and pretty who were better off, and while she may have had at one time bright hopes for the future, her good sense taught her that there really was no reason why she should expect anything better now. And so it came to pass that she was simply mistress of the Fairview school and mistress of all our hearts, and did what good was possible without vain regrets for that which might have come to pass but did not."

3

During these years a boy was growing up first in Wisconsin, then in Minnesota, then on the Dakota prairies, who took up the task of telling the savage truth about the America we were building. This was Hamlin Garland. Touched by the grace of New England, more sweetly articulate than Howe, his protest was divided between the old protest of the pioneer against debt and land speculation, and the new protest that life is sour till we have culture equal to material opportunity. And in the foreground of all his studies stands always the pathetic worn figure of the pioneer woman; in the background the remembered charm of New England. All this is in his earlier stories, especially in the collection *Main-Travelled Roads*. But the full tale of it is in the autobiography of his youth, published in 1917, and entitled *A Son of the Middle Border*, which belongs to this earlier period in all its materials. "The farther west I went," says Garland, telling of his return from the East in his young manhood, "the lonelier became the box-like habitations of the plain. Here were the lands over which we had hurried in 1881, lured by government land of the farther west. The free lands were gone and so at last the price demanded by the speculators must be paid.

"This wasteful method of pioneering, this desolate business of lonely settlement, took on a new and tragic significance as I studied it. Instructed by my new philosophy, I now perceived that these plowmen, these wives and daughters, had been pushed out into these lonely ugly shacks by the force of landlordism behind. These plodding Swedes and Danes, these thrifty Germans, these hairy Russians, had all fled from the feudalism of their native lands and were here because they had no share in the soil from which they sprung, and because in the settled communities of the eastern states, the speculative demand for land had hindered them from acquiring even a leasing right to the surface of the earth.

"I clearly perceived that our Song of Emigration had been in effect the hymn of fugitives."

The protest against the farm thus set going swelled, too, in our literature and was crystallized in one poem very widely quoted, "The Man with the Hoe," by Edwin Markham.

> Bowed by the weight of centuries he leans
> Upon his hoe and gazes on the ground,
> The emptiness of ages in his face,
> And on his back the burden of the world.
> Who made him dead to rapture and despair,

A thing that grieves not and that never hopes,
Stolid and stunned, a brother to the ox?
Who loosened and let down this brutal jaw?
Whose was the hand that slanted back this brow?
Whose breath blew out the light within this brain?

4

Hungry for culture, famished for grace and leisure, the West turned to New England. What New England meant to that empty world, a splendid vital young Indian girl from a reservation told me, told me with her voice thrilling, with tears in her eyes. She had come to visit friends of her own race in an Indian school near a Western university, and had been invited by some good New England ladies connected with the university faculty to come to their rooms for tea. Later when she told me this story, it just happened that I had known these ladies. In the plenitude of my own Eastern background, I had thought them a little prim and quaint and their cultural interests thin and faded and dreadfully prophylactic. Nothing but the gentle, mild, sweet, and thoroughly sterilized in music or literature or art was admitted into their maiden sanctum. But of this there was plenty—Longfellow and books of essays, and reproductions of old masters on the wall, and sweet pieces like *Narcissus*, and Mendelssohn's *Spring Song* on the piano. But when the Indian girl spoke of them, I saw them with quite other eyes. There she sat, bold and brown, ripe with the golden vitality of the prairies, and they served her weak tea in thin little gold-banded china cups, and slices of lemon, and thin soft white sandwiches. They showed her the old masters on the wall, and described old European cities where they had gone on a vacation tour. They asked her about Indian songs, and sweetly tinkled on the piano MacDowell's *To a Water Lily* and told her it was a song about a flower. She went back to the reservation in a dream. Oh, the beautiful, beautiful life that some people knew how to live; oh, the lovely things with which one could fill one's hours if one knew how—never a blank moment, never the sick, dull ennui of having nothing to do! She looked out on all the Indians sitting apathetically in the sunshine, heavy with boredom, and it seemed like bliss beyond hope that there was a way out of this. She could go away and learn the beautiful things to fill the hours with, and come back and teach them all. And so she did, and with furious young energy propelled herself straight into a New England college, and left it to go back to the Indians, still blazing with gospel light!

Strong and vital, ravenous as if with the hunger of all the ages, young America began to turn to New England, to Europe, lapping up the most unlikely little cake crumbs of knowledge, loving best what seemed most completely unsuitable. Children of the prairies deserted in shoals and plunged into the intellectual and artistic stew of New York or Paris. A passion for Greek appeared in the prairies, and took the sons of pioneers, like Jig Cook, restlessly wandering back to die, as an imitation Greek, in Delphi, and the daughters of self-made rich men, like Eva Potter Palmer, and set them up as mistresses of homes in Athens, with Greek maidens spinning under marble columns. It sent Isadora Duncan dancing all over Europe, a wild, gentle emanation of a strange new world, borrowing from the Greek vases and rituals and turning it to something wild and new and free. Later, having imitated the Greeks to her heart's content, Isadora confessed that her dancing was the spiritual offspring of Walt Whitman: "And this dancing that has been called Greek—it has sprung from America. It is the dance of the America of the future. All these movements—where have they come from? They have sprung from the great Nature of America, from the Sierra Nevada, from the Pacific Ocean as it washes the coast of California, from the great spaces of the Rocky Mountains, from the Yosemite Valley, from the Niagara Falls." But you had to go a long way round by Athens and Paris to know that.

Back in New England, the wise old Brahmins were a bit amused by the way the West and the South were rushing to sit at their feet. Oliver Wendell Holmes said: "They are doing us up in spices like so many dead Pharaohs." Emerson in an ironic public speech referred to the great fame of Concord as a manufacturing center. It is true, he said, that Concord has no seaport, no water power, no cotton, oil, or marble. The granite is better in Fitchburg, and even the Concord ice has bubbles in it. "The town then is reduced to manufacturing school teachers for the southern and western market."

5

But once the habit of looking at the neighbors with a slightly jaundiced eye was established, the older sections of the country came under review, too, and did not fare very well. The general opinion was that they were beautiful but dead, and even their own aspiring authors made haste to say so. So Mary E. Wilkins wrote stories of neat, placid, New England villages, largely inhabited by women living on tiny incomes. The men who appear rudely in this maiden world are not the traditional Yankee type at all—shrewd, lean. They are mostly stout, simple-minded, big fellows whose uncouthness contrasts painfully with the ladylike fineness of the women, making great havoc in their spotless kitchens, getting tangled in the embroidery cotton, and quite upsetting the cat! Edith Wharton, as a wealthy summer visitor on the New England mountain frontier, went further in *Ethan Frome* and delineated a kind of cruel, bare life which one may live all one's days in a dozen New England towns and countrysides and never see at all. It is a beautiful piece of craftsmanship, but tells of a life not distinctive of New England, running counter, indeed, to the general tendency of New England life from the beginning to sociability and devious self-amusement. It is characteristic rather of any low level of culture west or east, where the social arts have been crowded out by bare poverty.

Edith Wharton was more in her element when she attacked the watertight social compartments of old New York. She found her native city mean and mediocre, with rows of houses of a deadly chocolate color, quite lacking in the architectural beauty of European cities. "Out of doors in the mean, monotonous street, without architecture, without great churches or palaces, or any visible memorials of an historic past, what could New York offer to a child whose eyes had been filled with shapes of immortal beauty and immemorial significance? One of the most depressing impressions of my childhood is my recollections of the intolerable ugliness of New York, of its untended streets and the narrow houses so lacking in external dignity, so crammed with smug and suffocating upholstery. How could I understand that people who had seen Rome and Seville, Paris and London, could come back to live contentedly between Washington Square and Central Park?"

To such a thin snobbish cry from uptown, a great burly figure striding along, with coat flapping, long locks waving under his broad-brimmed hat, luminous eyes looking out like lamps over "Manhattoes, my city," answered roughly. "What has New York to offer?" asked Walt Whitman. "Look and listen!"

The blab of the pave, tires of carts, sluff of boot-soles, talk of the promenaders,
The heavy omnibus, the driver with his interrogating thumb, the clank of the shod horses on the granite floor,
The snow-sleighs, clinking, shouting, pelts of snow-balls,
The hurrah for popular favorites, the fury of rous'd mobs,
The flap of the curtained litter, a sick man inside borne to the hospital,

What living and buried speech is always vibrating here, what howls restrained by decorum,
Arrests of criminals, slights, adulterous offers made, acceptance, rejections with convex lips,
I mind them or the show or resonance of them—I come and I depart.

Everywhere a newly emerging mass of the people were beginning to talk back to the select circles of the old cities. Everywhere the established circles of the "best people" were growing absurd under the frank eye of the new commoner. Only in the South a tenderly reminiscent sentiment clung round the society that had been. Thomas Nelson Page was writing beautifully of life *In Ole Virginia*, and, as the century drew to its end, one scribbler after another discovered, behind the crowded levees and dim steaming waters, and trolley cars clanging merrily down between rows of palm trees, and rose-embowered homes of new millionaires rising overnight, the dim, delicate ghost of what had been New Orleans. Of these George W. Cable made New Orleans his literary business, spreading a faint wash of sugary sentiment over the lovable but feeble gentry of the old Creole city. What he saw behind the modern city was another Cranford—a world of little delicacies, little considerations, mild pleasures enjoyed with the innocent abandon of children, small precisions of conduct and manners, delicate exactitude of conscience, gentle dignity, and an anxious consideration for each other's habits and prejudices—a sheltered life, innocently sociable.

All these, said Hamlin Garland to William D. Howells, are but the various efforts of America to find her own soul. "In my judgment the men and women of the South, the West, and the East are working (without knowing it) in accordance with a great principle, which is this: American literature in order to be great, must be national, and in order to be national must deal with conditions peculiar to our own land and climate. Every genuinely American writer must deal with the life he knows best and for which he cares the most. Thus Joel Chandler Harris, George W. Cable, Joseph Kirkland, Sarah Orne Jewett, and Mary Wilkins, like Bret Harte, are but varying phases of the same movement, a movement which is to give us at last a really vital and original literature."

6

"Then presently everything began to revolve around, to center in a single lonely figure, that of a silently stepping man, who slipped to the door any hour of the day, and begged for one thing and only one, a cup of coffee." So Lisette Woodworth Reese, in her reminiscences of her childhood on the edge of Baltimore, remembers the coming on the American scene of the tramp. "The tramp became not only a legend but a legion. Every gap in a hedge, every hollow in a road, belched forth a tramp. Of course this man or these men were only out-runners of that great army of their unemployed comrades which was beginning to alarm publicists at this time, or else the congenital beggars and wanderers well known from year to year, but grown bolder because of the confused attitude of the community during a dwindling prosperity."

The tramp, like other of the modern problems, appeared in the great depression of 1874–1878. As the century drew on, he became even a picturesque figure, and many writers, scribblers, even future politicians, were in his ranks in his youth. Joining the hoboes became the substitute for running away to sea or going west.

The tramp as a congenital wanderer or youth in search of adventure was just an old American friend in a new guise. But as the outrunner of the great army of unemployed, he was a sinister figure, and so the public felt him to be. For one of the trails on which America had come suddenly against the barbed wire fence was the old rocky, hopeful upward trail of labor. So long as the free land lasted, American thought had dealt easily and cheerfully with labor. Only in the South had it seemed a problem at all, and that, said Northern capitalists and workmen, was because the South was stupid about it. The dominant civilization of America, originating in New England and Pennsylvania, annexing all the Atlantic colonies southward into Virginia, and proceeding westward as the "Yankee" theory of life, had been a civilization created for workingmen by workingmen. Skilled artisans and professional man were the preferred immigrants in early New England— the workers with hand and brain; and to these Pennsylvania had added, with pride, the skilled farmer. The social theory of these colonies approved the merchant and gave him a higher social standing than was customary, especially in the case of the retail trader. But landlords, persons who lived on incomes, "gentlemen" and idlers, were theoretically anathema.

By the time capital and labor was made a great public issue by the economic theorists of the South, just before the Civil War, the ultimately dominant Yankee theory was that in America there should be no opposition of capital and labor and no crystallizing of men into capitalist and labor castes. Again and again, Northern leaders, from Webster to Lincoln, explained that, in the American view, the laborer is always potentially a capitalist, and the chance to save his wages and become a capitalist in his later years and set some man to working in turn for him is the reward which America holds out to every worthy laborer. In his great message to Congress on the subject, answering the Southern theory of capital and labor, in December, 1861, Lincoln pointed out that in the majority of cases labor and capital were one, the capitalists who employed some labor laboring with their workmen; the owners of farms and shops virtually hiring themselves and the members of their own families to work for themselves. Webster, drawing his information, perhaps, from his friends and sponsors, the Biddles, bankers of Philadelphia, asserted that five-sixths of the property of the North was owned by the laborers of the North. To this body of theory Henry Clay of Kentucky had added his picture of "The American System," by which he meant such a balance between the manufacturing industries of the East and the agricultural activities of the West, that ever more prosperous and well-paid Eastern laborers would be able increasingly to absorb the products of ever-developing Western farms, and send back to them in ever more glittering streams the product of loom and factory to beautify their homes and adorn their ladies. This idea, first expressed by Henry Clay in 1824, has always had an influence on Henry Ford; and it has been expanded and brought up to date in the theory of the New Deal. It is undoubtedly an idea of sound American vintage and of a most respectable antiquity.

Over and above the issue of Negro slavery, the Civil War had been a stupendous victory for the section which espoused this whole "American" theory against the section which would crystallize capital and labor into permanent opposing castes. The victory, as all liberals made haste to point out, was due to the immensely greater wealth made possible by one theory as against the other.

Now in the late seventies and early eighties the enormous development of corporate wealth, and the growth of vast enterprises covering the whole continent, such as the railroads, brought the whole problem to life again in a new and sinister form. Since most of the earlier American laboring men were already accommodated with farms, or had accumulated capital under the American system and had enterprises of their own, the enormous new demand for labor on the railroads and in the mines was met by importing laborers en bloc, the more ignorant and alien the better. In the West great companies of Chinese were brought in. In the East, where the earlier Irish, German, and Scandinavian migrations had been happily absorbed in the population, capitalists scoured the earth for docile, alien persons who could be induced to work for any wages they set—Italians, Greeks, Croats, Czechs, Slovaks, Poles, Hungarians, Russians. At first these laborers got no sympathy in any quarter. The native laborers resented them as foreigners brought in to beat down wages and standards of living. The communities felt that they were too different to be comfortable neighbors. The capitalists were prepared to browbeat them as something not even human.

So there was created a condition in which the capitalists and a press owned and dominated by rich men were able to divert the American mind from its normal belief in and honor for the toiler to a fear of and antagonism to "labor" as a foreign, dangerous, and anarchistic abstraction here to overthrow our free institutions.

For decades the battle raged furiously. In 1877 there were railroad strikes in many parts of the country, involving pitched battles between striking workmen and militia. At Chicago in 1886 there was an anarchist outbreak in Haymarket Square, in which the original throwing of a bomb was not so violent and undemocratic as the trial and execution of "suspects" which followed. A few years later a young anarchist named Alexander Berkman tried to kill Henry Clay Frick, an executive of the Carnegie plants. Two years later there was the Pullman strike in Chicago, as a result of which a Federal District Court sent Eugene V. Debs, head of the American Railway Union, to jail for disobeying a sweeping injunction which forbade any kind of activity on the part of unions involved in the contest.

These and other similar affairs left sores which rankled for years, some of which are rankling yet. There was widespread belief that the courts were being manipulated by sinister capitalistic interests—that in a much more subtle form the situation was that of the early mining days in the West, when gamblers' gold owned the agencies of justice. The intelligentsia in general thought that, whenever the issue of "anarchism" was imported into a case involving labor, it was a bogey to divert public attention from the nefarious manipulations of interests backstage in the trial. This opinion has persisted down to recent times, when it flared anew in the Sacco-Vanzetti case.

Into the social confusion caused by unregulated capitalism and the constant throwing into industrial communities of great undigested masses of new workmen, cut off by barriers of language and of custom from immediate association with native labor, Samuel Gompers succeeded in introducing a measure of order in the organization in 1886 of the American Federation of Labor. The American Federation of Labor accepted the old American idea that the laborer formed no independent caste, and that his aim like that of every other sensible man was to accumulate out of his wages some capital which would give him greater freedom of life and enterprise. It therefore avoided all talk of the class struggle, and concentrated, like the capitalists themselves, on using its collective strength to make the best possible bargains—for increasingly high wages, shorter hours, and good working conditions. On this simple plan it went ahead with great success. It succeeded in stopping the importation of Chinese labor, and of other aliens to work under contract, and ultimately in limiting all immigration. It kept up a constant fire against "unfair" practices, and gradually drew to itself the sympathy and trust of the more liberal intelligentsia and even of some of the capitalists themselves. Lillian Wald reports that once at a conference of employers of needleworkers on strike, Jacob Schiff was shocked to hear one of the employers say: "This meeting will take us nowhere. The whole problem comes down to a question of supply and demand. I may be forced to pay so little for the work out of one pocket that I shall have to help with relief from my charity pocket." Leaving the meeting in protest, he asked some social workers what he could do personally to help the union with their strike. Without contributing directly to the union, he made funds available which were used for the families of strikers, and when the union finally won, he said proudly, "*We* won that strike." If traditional American sentiment was against a fixed caste of laborers, it was just as set against a fixed caste of capitalists. In the more thoughtful capitalist groups individuals began to demonstrate their objection to living and thinking in the established groove of "exploiters" by walking over to the side of labor.

From the early years of the gay nineties on there was another long and bitter depression during which every kind of protest against things as they were and plan for making them better took root and blossomed. In 1892 a million voters approved the Populist platform which declared that America was ruled by a plutocracy, that impoverished labor was laid low under the tyranny of a hireling army, that homes were covered with mortgages, that the press was the tool of wealth, that corruption dominated the ballot box, and that "the fruits of toil of millions are boldly stolen to build up colossal fortunes for a few unprecedented in the history of mankind; and the possessors of these in turn despise the republic and endanger liberty." And a few years later Bryan sprang into the center of the limelight as the white hope of America with his fiery protest to the plutocrats that they were not to be allowed to crucify democracy "upon a cross of gold."

7

During these years when our present "New Deal" hung like a seed packet at the heart of the decaying flower of the older life of America, the dominating question was the ever-recurring cycle of industrial depression. Without wars or great foreign expansion to break the rhythm, depression followed depression in regular order from the Civil War to the end of the century. Every depression brought out a whole series of panaceas, and some very useful permanent reforms. If it had not been for the fact that a number of different circumstances, including the World War, broke the regular series of depressions between the beginning of the century and our last great debacle, the great radical and reforming force of this recurring general hardship would by this time surely have propelled us straight into the millennium.

Among the various books inspired by the search for an antidepression serum, there were three of wide influence at the time and of great permanent interest. They were *Progress and Poverty* by Henry George, *Looking Backward* by Edward Bellamy, and *The Theory of the Leisure Class* by Thorstein Veblen.

Progress and Poverty, published in 1880, was a long and thoughtful treatise on economics, flatly denying most of the old assumptions of the political economists, and richly illustrated with references to American experience. George especially objected to the law of Malthus that population tends to press upon the limits of possible food, and therefore that the more people there are, the less there is to go around. This, said George, is not true in America. We have not and probably never will have enough people to eat all the food or use all the other goods that the American continent can and does produce. The only thing that can keep us poor is an arbitrary and artificial limitation on the capacity of our continent to produce wealth, and an equally artificial check on the distibution of wealth that is produced. So, looking for the cause of poverty in America, he found it just where every shrewd pioneer, from Daniel Boone down, had found it, in speculation in the land and natural resources. Land was held out of proper use by people who bought it and waited for the rise in its value which would come about through the collective effort of the community.

His remedy is to turn all increased value on land over and above an original ground price back to the community which has created the value, in the form of taxes, and to use it in enterprises for the general enhancement of the common life. There need be no other tax, for this would furnish all that was necessary, and the money spent by the community would return in increased well-being and activity for all. "Give labor a free field and full earnings; take for the benefit of the whole community the fund which the growth of the community creates, and want and fear of want will be gone. The springs of production would be set free, and the enormous increase of wealth would give the poorest ample comfort." This plan was called the Single Tax. George has many followers to this day who believe he has the solution for our economic ills; and during the last depression the numbers of believers increased by leaps and bounds.

Vividly written, illustrated by many observations of the American scene, *Progress and Poverty* is one of the books of the century, a book on which a thoughtful man can still cut his intellectual eyeteeth. Particularly interesting is George's solemn warning that a democratic form of government, co-existing with an increasing tendency to the unequal distribution of wealth, is the most dangerous of the political forms. "When the disparity of condition increases, so does universal suffrage make it easy to seize the source of power, for the greater is the proportion of power in the hands of those who feel no direct interest in the conduct of the government; who, tortured by want and embruted by poverty, are ready to sell their votes to the highest bidder or follow the lead of the most blatant demagogue; or who, made bitter by hardships, may even look upon profligate and tyrannous government with the satisfaction we may imagine the proletarians and slaves of Rome to have felt, as they saw a Caligula or Nero raging among the rich patricians."

A few years later the battle was taken up by Edward Bellamy whose *Looking Backward* was the literary sensation of the year 1887. The book was good reading then, and remains good reading to this day, and even grows more interesting, as we progress down the century to that year 2000 in which Bellamy expected all his dreams of the perfect society to be realized. Bellamy tells the story of a man who went to sleep in the year 1887 and woke in the year 2000, in a vastly improved world. From this world he looks back and criticizes the generally barbarous condition of society in the year 1887. In the year 1887, he said, "It was no doubt the common opinion of thoughtful men that society was approaching a critical period which might result in great changes. The labor troubles, their causes, course, and cure, took the lead of all other topics in the public prints, and in serious conversation."

The cause of the labor troubles, and of the general insecurity and tension of life, was the unorganized scramble for the means of subsistence, which meant that a great deal of material and the labor of a great many people was wasted, under the leadership of a few who stole and lied and destroyed actual wealth, and deceived and enslaved their fellows, all to get what they did not need and could not use. "It is not hard to understand the desperation with which men and women who, under other conditions, would have been full of gentleness and ruth, fought and tore each other in the scramble for gold, when we realize what it meant to miss it, what poverty was in that day. For the body it was hunger and thirst, torment by heat and frost, in sickness neglect, in health unremitting toil; for the moral nature it meant oppression, contempt, and the patient endurance of indignity, brutish associations from infancy, the loss of all the innocence of childhood, the grace of womanhood, the dignity of manhood; for the mind it meant the death of ignorance, the torpor of all those faculties which distinguish us from the brutes, the reduction of life to a round of bodily function."

"Ah, my friends," says the happy citizen of the year 2000, "if such a fate as this were offered you and your children as the only alternative of success in the accumulation of wealth, how long do you fancy would you be in sinking to the moral level of your ancestors?"

One of the great gains of the year 2000 is the release of women from those chains of enforced idleness, coquetry, and that dependence on men in marriage against which they were chafing in 1887. "It seems to me that women were more than any other class the victims of your civilization. There is something which, even at this distance of time, penetrates one with pathos in the spectacle of their ennuied, undeveloped lives, stunted at marriage, their narrow horizon, bounded so often, physically, by the four walls of home, and morally by a petty circle of personal interests. . . . Marriage when it comes does not mean incarceration for them, nor does it separate them in any way from the larger interests of society, the bustling life of the world. Only when maternity fills a woman's mind with new interests does she withdraw from the world for a time. Afterwards, and at any time, she may return to her place among her comrades, nor need she ever lose touch with them. Women are a very happy race now-a-days, as compared with what they ever were before in the world's history, and their power of giving happiness to men has of course been increased in proportion."

One of his most exciting experiences in this wonderful age of A.D. 2000 was finding music in every home. " 'It appears to me, Miss Leete,' I said, 'that if we could have devised an arrangement for providing everybody with music in their homes, perfect in quality, unlimited in quantity, suited to every mood, and beginning and ceasing at will, we should have considered the limit of felicity already attained, and ceased to strive for further improvements.'

"Whereupon the obliging young lady made me sit down comfortably and, crossing the room, merely touched one or two screws, and at once the room was filled with the music of a grand organ anthem—filled, not flooded, for by some means the volume of the melody had been perfectly graduated to the size of the apartment. I listened scarce breathing to the close.

" 'Grand,' I cried, as the last great wave of sound broke and ebbed away in silence . . . 'but where is the organ?'

" 'Wait a moment, please,' said Edith. 'I want to have you listen to this waltz before you ask any questions. I think it is perfectly charming,' and as she spoke the sound of violins filled the room with the witchery of a summer night."

And had these happy persons in the year 2000 thus invented the radio? No, they were only bringing music into their homes from a central hall by telephone! From all of which it may be seen that already, in the year 1938, we have overpassed the greatest dreams of 1887, so far as some of the mechanics and personal relations in our lives are concerned, but economically we are still stuck fast in the same old ditch.

The attempt to educate American economic and social thinking up to the level of our grand new continent and magnificent new age of machinery was made in a quite different way by Thorstein Veblen in *The Theory of the Leisure Class*, published in 1899. Like Henry George's *Progress and Poverty*, this expressed an idea latent in radical American thinking from the very beginning. Born of a Norwegian family in the Northwest, Veblen cast a sardonic eye upon the struggle of the emerging masses, not only of the earlier American strains, but of the many whose fathers and mothers had recently come from Europe. And so he drags out that good old bête noire of Pennsylvania and New England, the feudal gentleman, and gives him a final trouncing. What we are all reaching for in social life is the useless, show-off life of a childish and barbarous era, whose aristocrats were merely predacious beasts. The heraldic devices of aristocrats, he says, quite properly show a "predilection for the more rapacious birds and beasts of prey. . . ." In barbaric society the most honorable activity is killing somebody, he says, "And this high office of slaughter, as an expression of the slayer's prepotence, casts a glamour of worth over every act of slaughter and over all the tools and accessories of the act. . . . At the same time employment in industry becomes correspondingly odious and . . . the handling of the tools and implements of industry falls beneath the dignity of able-bodied men."

This was no new idea in America. It was what the Civil War was all about. Probably in no country in the world had a dominant group made such a head-on attack on the old feudal theories of barbaric leisure as the "Yankees." But in this new society of the end of the century, filled with people but one generation away from Europe, with all sorts of newly rich persons grasping for culture without having gone through the discipline of settling the wilderness, social snobbery was parading in the rags and tags of aristocracy. Pitilessly Veblen analyzes the everlasting struggle to keep up with the Joneses. The most honorable thing in our predatory society, he says, is waste. Predacious business exploits our determination to pay more for an article than it is worth. "While men may have set out with disapproving an inexpensive manner of living because it indicated inability to spend much, and so indicated a lack of pecuniary success, they ended by falling into the habit of disapproving cheap things as intrinsically dishonorable and unworthy because they are cheap."

Against the idle, adolescent, show-off tendency of the predacious male, the labor movement and the woman's movement are natural protests. The workingman's self-assertion against his exploiters is the assertion of a more mature social outlook, since he who can really earn his keep by productive labor is necessarily a more grown-up person than he who lives, like a child, on somebody else. So with women. They are more grown up than men because nature at least gave them one real job in life; and naturally they object to being dominated by the immature male notion of living. So our present social struggles, says Veblen, are hopeful signs. Some part of the population at least is growing out of adolescence.

This was sound American doctrine. The Puritans brought it to New England and the Quakers to Pennsylvania. The Civil War was again and again envisaged as the trouncing of the spoiled-boy part of the population by the part that had begun to grow the sinews of manhood. Veblen, himself, being of the first generation of Americans, remarks that the childish, show-off, fine-lady and -gentleman attitude to wealth is strongest among those to whom wealth is new and is already dying out among groups of the population who have been longer exposed to the pride of possessions.

Veblen is particularly acrid with regard to the agitation for the classics which was strong in the land-grant colleges of the period. "The enjoyment and the bent derived from the habitual contemplation of the life, ideals, speculations and methods of consuming time and goods in vogue among the leisure class of classical antiquity, for instance, is felt to be higher, nobler, worthier than what results from like familiarity with the everyday life and knowledge and aspirations of a commonplace humanity in a modern community. . . . The gratification and the culture or the spiritual attitude and habit of mind resulting from habitual contemplation of the anthropomorphism, clannishness, and leisurely self-complacency of the gentlemen of an early day, or from familiarity with the animistic superstitions and the exuberant truculence of the Homeric heroes, for instance, is, aesthetically considered, more legitimate than the corresponding results derived from a matter of fact knowledge of things and contemplation of latter-day civic or workmanlike efficiency."

The Theory of the Leisure Class is a great book. Nothing more alive and interesting to a mature intelligence was written in English on either side of the water in the late nineteenth century. Some readers have complained that the style is difficult. Yet like other great books, it lives by its style. Behind these acid, roundabout, anthropological and economic reflections lies the whole landscape of emerging middle-class America at the end of the century, etched in with a master hand.

8

During the first decade of the new century, the center of the new, tumultuous struggle for the better life was Chicago. "The great grey city," said Frank Norris, "brooking no rival, imposed its dominion upon a reach of country larger than many a kingdom of the Old World. . . . Out, far out, far away in the snow and shadow of northern Wisconsin forests, axes and saws bit the bark of century old trees, stimulated by this city's energy. Just as far to the southward pick and drill leaped to the assault of veins of anthracite, moved by her central power. Her force turned the wheels of harvester and seeder a thousand miles distant in Iowa and Kansas. Her force spun the screws and propellers of innumerable squadrons of lake steamers crowding the Sault Sainte Marie. For her and because of her all the central states, all the great Northwest roared with traffic and industry; saw-mills screamed; factories, their smoke blackening the sky, clashed and flamed; wheels turned; pistons leaped in their cylinders; cog gripped cog; beltings clasped the drums of mammoth wheels; and converters of forgers belched into the clouded air their tempest of molten steel.

. . . "Here of all her cities, throbbed the true life—the true power and spirit of America; gigantic, crude, with the crudity of youth, disdaining rivalry; sane and healthy and vigorous; brutal in its ambition, arrogant in the new-found knowledge of its giant strength, prodigal in its wealth, infinite in its desires. In its capacity boundless, in its courage indomitable; subduing the wilderness in a single generation, defying calamity, and through the flame and debris of a commonwealth in ashes rising suddenly renewed, formidable and titanic."

Here in Chicago centered the financial control of the food, not only of America but of a large part of the world. To the public this grip of money upon their very vitals was symbolized in the wheat pit and in the stockyards, which became the subject of the two most epochal books of the day.

Frank Norris tells the epic of the wheat in a powerful tumultuous story of speculation in the Chicago wheat pit, with wheat as the great deity with which mortals battle. Jadwin, the great speculator, tries to do with wheat what Jim Fisk tried with gold and corner all the food of the world. At the moment of success, with all the available wheat in his control, all over the country, the new wheat was swinging gold in the sun, on the new acreage which his own high prices had caused to be planted.

"For an instant came clear vision. What were these shouting, gesticulating men of the Board of Trade, these brokers, traders, and speculators? It was not these he fought. It was that fatal New Harvest. It was the Wheat. It was, as Gretry had said, the very Earth itself. What were those scattered hundreds of farmers of the Middle West, who because he had put the price so high had planted the grain as never before? What had they to do with it? Why, the Wheat had grown itself. Demand and supply—these were the two great laws the Wheat obeyed. Almost blasphemous in his effrontery, he had tampered with those laws and had aroused a Titan. He had laid his puny human grasp upon Creation, and the very earth herself, the great mother, feeling the touch of the cobweb that the human insect had spun, had stirred at last in her sleep and sent her omnipotence moving through the grooves of the world, to find and crush the disturber of her appointed courses."

In the great financier, playing with the sustenance of millions, Frank Norris thought he had found another epic hero, grander than Achilles, more terrible than Siegfried; and in the great elemental forces of our mass civilization, the food by which we live, the enormous corporate machinery moving that food, the financial machinery determining the exchange of toil for bread, he thought he had found forces more gigantic than the Titans of old, dangers more horrible than any dragon. As he had told the story of wheat and its financial machinery in *The Pit*, so he told the story of wheat and the railroads in *The Octopus*, whose scene is laid in California. To him there was nothing commonplace or banal in this modern world we were building. It was stupendous, terrible, and our very cities, our very architecture revealed in the forms they were taking the dangerous powers within. He sees the Chicago Stock Exchange Building at night as "black, grave, monolithic, crouching on its foundations like a monstrous Sphinx with blind eyes, silent, grave." Within the Board of Trade Building is "some great, some resistless force . . . that held the tide of the streets within its grip, alternately drawing it in and throwing it forth." This is the new world, said Norris. If we are to rise above helplessness in it and trembling fear before these gods and demons of our own creation, we must throw off economic superstition as men in the past have had to throw off religious superstition, and face our idols bravely and smash them when we have to.

Another book about Chicago, of epic reach and power, and of great influence, was Upton Sinclair's *The Jungle*. The jungle was the Chicago stockyards, which are surveyed from the point of view of a Lithuanian family of workmen in the yards. To Jurgis, the Lithuanian, the stockyards were marvelous. "He had dressed hogs himself in the forest of Lithuania; but he had never expected to live to see one hog dressed by several hundred workmen. . . . To Jurgis it seemed almost profanity to speak about the place as did Jokubas, skeptically; it was a thing as tremendous as the universe—the laws and ways of working no more than the universe to be questioned or understood. All that a mere man could do, it seemed to Jurgis, was to take a thing like this as he found it, and do as he was told; to be given a place in it and a share in its wonderful activities was a blessing to be grateful for, as one was grateful for sunshine and rain." The story goes on, a dense, powerful story of labor in the shambles, a story reeking with raw meat. "Then suddenly the big butcher president leaped upon a pile of stones and yelled: 'It's off, boys. We'll all of us quit again.' And so the cattle-butchers declared a new strike on the spot; and gathering their members from the other plants where the same trick had been played, they marched down Packer's Avenue, which was thronged with a dense mass of workers, cheering wildly. Men who had got to work on the killing beds dropped their tools and joined them; some galloped here and there on horseback, shouting the tidings, and within half an hour the whole of Packingtown was on strike again and beside itself with fury." Thereupon the packers brought in hordes of Negro strikebreakers. "The ancestors of these black people had been savages in Africa; and since then they had been chattel slaves or had been held down by a community ruled by the traditions of slavery. Now for the first time they were free—free to gratify every passion, free to wreck themselves. They were wanted to break a strike, and when it was broken they would be shipped away, and their present masters would never see them again; and so whiskey and women were brought in by the car-load and sold to them, and hell was let loose in the yards. Every night there were stabbings and shootings; it was said that the packers had blank permits which enabled them to ship dead bodies from the city without troubling the authorities. They lodged men and women on the same floor; and with the night there began a saturnalia of debauchery scenes such as had never been witnessed in America. And as the women were the dregs from the

brothels of Chicago, and the men were for the most part ignorant country negroes, the nameless diseases of vice were
soon rife, and this where food was being handled and sent out
to every corner of the civilized world."

When the people of America read the last sentence and
others like it, a shudder went up from every dinner table in
the land. Hardly a reader of the book but was a vegetarian
for at least a day or two after finishing it! Upton Sinclair had
intended to show the criminal unscrupulousness of the meat
corporations in dealing with their workers. What he more
successfully showed was their unscrupulousness in dealing
with the consumer. Forthwith there was an immense agitation for stricter federal control of food products. As he said,
he had aimed at the heart of the public and had hit its stomach
instead!

9

From that time in the seventies when America came to
the end of all old roads and turned down the broad highway we now are on, the great army of the seekers for the
good life have marched in two parallel armies. One army
comes down, drums beating, flags flying, against the great invisible, dastardly enemy of industrial and financial exploitation, which spreads a poison gas of poverty and fear of poverty. The other goes with white banners gleaming and uplifted
faces and eyes full of vision to the building of a physical,
spiritual culture which shall equal the material opportunity of
our continent and our great new technical control of nature.
Our material world may not be all we desire, they say, but it
is already better than we are. The true enemies are not without but within.

An immediate, naïve expression of this idea was the universal concern for better health, diet, physical culture, and
personal good looks, which has continued to this day, and has
vastly improved the physical well-being of children, and has
even begun to hold off the former physical demoralization of

middle age. Here it was observed that many physical ills are really mental and emotional in origin. In earlier times, there had been a refuge from these ills in the church. But the church was failing. Its language was archaic; its symbolism had lost its meaning. Everywhere people were groping for a restatement of the meaning of life in terms of modern knowledge and modern forms of thought. They wanted not Christian theology but Christian Science. The great hunger for a modern restatement of Christian faith, one which dealt directly with sickness and poverty, and called them by name, and showed you what to do about them, was met by a remarkable book published in 1875, entitled *Science and Health with a Key to the Scriptures* by Mary Baker Eddy.

Mary Baker Eddy was born at Bow, New Hampshire, and spent all her life within the currents of that strange New England thinking, at once so shrewd and practical, and yet so completely without the bounds and limits set to most Western ideas by our European philosophical and religious inheritance. Launched in his own tight little craft on the boundless sea of speculation, the New Englander was ready to go anywhere. In particular he liked the East. If he adopted an Oriental idea he shrewdly twisted it to his own uses, out of all semblance to the original. But always there was on his far, marine horizon the dreaming outline of pagodas and the enshrined Buddha. But however the various currents of thoughts might sway his fancy hither and thither, the New Englander had one great instrument of navigation—his Bible. He read the Bible carefully and steadily; but he thought about it like no one on earth but himself.

What New England speculation, charting its course by the Bible, was able to do in the way of creating an American religion had already been demonstrated in the Book of Mormon and the remarkable society based on it. Now a gentle middle-aged New England woman, looking around for help in her ever-increasing invalidism, one day climbed the stairs of a building in Portland, Maine, to consult with one P. P. Quimby, a "mental healer." She entered Quimby's office "a frail shadow of a woman. Three weeks later, in her forty-second year, she found herself for the first time well in mind and body, her soul flooded with the light of a great idea."

Carefully, with constant, reverent study of the Bible, she set herself to the almost insuperable task of getting her revelation into words. Without genuine literary gifts, with in some respects an untrained mind, she was driven by an overmastering conviction. What she wished to say, what she felt that God was saying through her, constantly eluded her. It remains obscure and even clumsy to the end. There is, for example, her constant reference to "Our Father-Mother God." The idea of God as both father and mother is not only more appealing to the modern imagination; it is sounder philosophically than the original naïve ascription of male sex alone to the Creator. Still the phrase does not slip so sweetly off the tongue as "Our Father who art in Heaven." At times, however, her paraphrases of Biblical sentences are both simple and felicitous, as when she turns the petition "Give us this day our daily bread" into "Give us grace for to-day; feed the famished affections."

Like Joseph Smith, she reiterates the old New England faith in the use of the mind. "The time for thinkers has come. Truth, independent of doctrines and time-honored systems knocks at the portal of humanity. Contentment with the past and the cold conventionality of materialism are crumbling away. Ignorance of God is no longer the stepping stone to faith."

Having herself, in the moment of her revelation, passed out of the long invalidism of her youth and early maturity into perfect health and a great sense of physical well-being that lasted to the end of her long life, Mrs. Eddy believed that the illumination which would come to others from sharing her faith would heal all physical ills. "Christian Science exterminates the drug, and rests on Mind alone as the curative principle, acknowledging that the Divine Mind has all power."

Christian Science was able to induce that conversion which is the test of all religion. Accepting it, men and women were healed. They were released into a larger, happier, and more serene life. And as a result of their new attitudes they found all things going better with them. They made more money; they stood in a happier relation to their fellows. They were free from a nightmare of fears and inhibitions, and apart from a persistent stubbornness on two or three points affecting physical health, they have taken an enlightened and courageous stand on most social issues. Of all criticisms of Christian Science the least valid is that it is materialistic. It offers health and prosperity to its members. The idea that religion should do anything else is archaic asceticism rooted in conditions which never obtained on the American continent. All genuine American religion from the days of the Quakers and Puritans till now has expected the true believer to be well and happy and comfortably prosperous in this world.

A number of other groups—the Theosophists, the Bahai group with its center in Chicago, and the professors of New Thought—had ideals of living colored with the dreams of the Orient, but Christian Science is interesting to the social historian because it so plainly represents to our day an old and time-honored mode of American religious thinking.

While the New England capacity to combine practical usefulness and science with what in any other hands would be the cloudiest mysticism found a voice in Mrs. Eddy, another voice spoke up in our other American center of light—the Region of Brotherly Love, reiterating for modern men the Pennsylvania faith in fraternity.

Across the river from the old city of Brotherly Love, in Camden, New Jersey, the good gray poet, Walt Whitman, was singing a new gospel—the gospel of adhesiveness. He loved everybody, provided they came in crowds, everybody but a certain kind of gentleman, "smartly attired, countenance smiling, form upright, death under the breast bones, hell under the skull bones,"

From the press of my foot to earth spring a hundred affections.

I am enamored of growing outdoors,
Of men that live among cattle or taste of the ocean or the woods,
Of the builders and steerers of ships and the wielders of axes and
    mauls, and the drivers of horses.
I can eat and sleep with them, week in and week out.
What is commonest, cheapest, nearest, easiest is Me,
Me going in for my chance, spending for vast returns,
Adorning myself to bestow myself on the first that will take me,
Not asking the sky to come down to my good will,
Scattering it freely for ever.

I will scatter myself among men and women as I go
I will toss new gladness and roughness among them.
Whoever denies me, it will not trouble me.
Whoever accepts me, he or she shall be blessed and shall bless me.

"Do you know," he asked, "what it is to be loved by strangers?" "The efflux of the soul is happiness." "By love we are
rightly charged," and have life henceforth "a poem of new
joys." "The fluid and attaching character is the freshness and
sweetness of man and woman."

    In this great, surging, crowded America he saw man de-
livered at last from the swaddling clothes of its earlier skulk-
ing affections, coming forth in new bravery and health, "forth
stepping from the unrealized baby-days," finding his neighbor
and comrade on all the streets of the world,

Allons, after the great Companions, and to belong to them,
They, too, are on the road—they are the swift and majestic men—
    they are the greatest women.

28

AN ASYLUM FOR THE WORLD

I AM sure that if the immigrant to America were ever to dream of the things that await him at his journey's end," says the candid Rumanian immigrant, M. E. Ravage in his book, *An American in the Making,* "there would be no need of any laws to keep him out. . . . One may be willing to submit with a kind of grim cheerfulness to train robbers and steerage pirates, to sea-sickness and home-sickness, to customs officials, and even, though this really too much even to Ellis Island inspectors, and count the whole thing— with heart-ringing farewells thrown in—as a tolerably fair exchange for the right to live and the means of living. But no one, I would insist, would for a moment consider the whole transaction if he suspected that he must, before he is through, become an American into the bargain. Mortal man is ready for everything except spiritual experience.

"For I need hardly tell you that becoming an American is a spiritual adventure of the most volcanic variety. . . . To be born in one world and to grow to manhood there, to be thrust then into the midst of another with all one's racial heritage, with one's likes and dislikes, aspirations and prejudices, and to be abandoned to the task of adjusting within one's own being

623

the clash of opposed systems of culture, tradition, and social convention—if this is not heroic tragedy, I should like to be told what is."

During the later decades of the nineteenth century this heroic tragedy was being lightly wished on innocent souls from the most out-of-the-way corners of Europe, by American capitalism, at the rate of half a million, and finally of a million, a year. Rapid technical development had made possible great corporate enterprises—railroad building, laying of telegraph wires, enormous agricultural yields, and rapidly increasing manufacturing; and, for all this, great armies of new workmen were necessary. The current economic theory—at least the one congenial to capitalists—was that taught to young business men at Yale by Professor William G. Sumner. "Wages of employees and the price of products have nothing to do with each other; wages have nothing to do with the profits of the employer; they have nothing to do with the cost of living or the prosperity of business. They are really governed by the supply and demand of labor, as every strike shows, and by nothing else." During the telegraph strike of 1883, Sumner said: "The only question was whether the current wages for telegraphing were sufficient to bring out an adequate supply of telegraphers." From this theory it followed that, if you wanted to get your labor cheap, you had to provide for an oversupply of it. The more laborers there were per job, the less the laborer would have to work for. If he couldn't make enough to keep him alive, help him out with charity.

So every kind of person was encouraged to come to America to work. As Professor Beard says: "Not since the patricians and capitalists of Rome scoured the known world for slaves— Celts, Iberians, Angles, Gauls, Saxons, Jews, Egyptians, and Assyrians—to serve them and then disappeared under a deluge of strange colors had the world witnessed such a deliberate over-turn of a social order by the masters of ceremonies."

This dastardly idea of beating down the price of labor by keeping an oversupply of it, and pouring into industrial com-

munities people too different in language and custom to combine easily with more experienced workmen in fighting for
their personal rights, was "sold" to the American public under
an old and honorable label. According to this label, America
was the asylum for the poor and persecuted of the world. So it
was and had been. But in the days when it was a genuine asylum,
there were great tracts of unappropriated land; the civilization of America was still in the making and could profit readily
by new customs and ideas; and people seeking America as an
asylum were already convinced of the worth of the concep-
tions of life and liberty dominant there, and came prepared to
adopt them, half converted before they left their own shores.
All earlier comers to this true asylum went together through
the discipline of breaking the land, making new communities,
building up their life, in equality.

But in the late nineteenth century none of the earlier conditions of asylum obtained. And the people who would respond most readily to the new lure, and who were desired
because, being alien, they could more easily be "controlled,"
were not the wary inhabitants of northern Europe, long acquainted with America; but isolated groups in Russia, in
central and eastern Europe. Some promise of freedom and
opportunity was held out to them. But the main lure was that
in America everybody is rich. Usually the immigration from
a given center would be started by some compatriot returned
from abroad, flashily dressed, with money in his pockets, telling wonderful tales of wealth in America. Many of them were
no doubt unconscious dupes. Everywhere some immigrants to
America had actually succeeded, and did return prosperous
and happy with genuine tales of satisfaction.

Probably very few capitalists who thought immigration a
good thing, and whose wives and daughters and sons in college
worked devotedly to Americanize the newcomers, were conscious of being part of a deep-laid plot against everything
America had stood for. They, too, accepted the notion of

asylum. It made them feel virtuous while doing something profitable.

This being the condition of the last great immigration to America, there are no more heartening books in American literature than the personal narratives by immigrants which began to be published early in the twentieth century—among them *The Making of an American*, by Jacob Riis, a Dane; *An American in the Making*, by M. E. Ravage, a Rumanian; *The Promised Land*, by Mary Antin, a Russian Jewess; and *From Immigrant to Inventor*, by Michael Pupin, the Serbian scientist. Candid and generous, accepting their final Americanization as a great spiritual experience, adopting the principles of our nation with the enthusiasm of converts, they speak a reassurance that had gone from the native literature. Kinder books were never written. Americans of the older vintage, quite properly disturbed by the common dilemma into which unregulated capitalism had plunged both the newcomers and themselves, could only read them with gratitude, and hasten to clasp in fellowship the hands so frankly and generously held out. If anything were needed to substantiate the American faith in "the people"—the average mass of householding citizens of any nation or color—the last great story of Americanization would do it.

2

All the stories of Americanization follow the same general outline. There is the snug little provincial village in Denmark, in Russia, in Rumania, in Serbia, in Poland, where everybody moves in the groove cut by his ancestors, living simple, decent, peaceable lives, often with very little opportunity for education, and with almost no money. But there are traditional observances, feasts, music, stories—right and proper ways of doing things. There comes a sudden disturbance—the renewed persecution of the Jews in Russia, threats to the nationality of villages in disputed territory, or a food shortage. As they look hither and thither, not knowing where to turn, a glamorous ex-compatriot returns from America, jingling coin, and tells them of the Land of Promise. Usually they start with very little money, often with the help of an emigrant aid society. Generally they are rather young—boys looking for a place in life, ambitious parents of young children. A considerable proportion of them are above the laboring or peasant class, small shopkeepers and businessmen who have met reverses, university graduates or professional men who are misfits in a small provincial society. The appeal of the new opportunity is naturally not to the clod of a man, but to the lively, articulate, ambitious, dissatisfied, adventurous, imaginative type. In countries where the mass of the people is illiterate, the propaganda of emigration spreads most easily among those with some education, persons who have at least heard of America, who have some notions about freedom and opportunity, and possess what the early Americans used to speak of with pride as "general ideas."

Arriving in America full of golden dreams, the immigrant was plunged direct into the slums. Resentment and horror of the slums runs through all the books by immigrants. "I know," said Ravage, "that the idea prevalent among Americans is that the alien imports his slums with him to the detriment of his adopted country, that the squalor and the misery and the filth of the foreign quarters in the large cities of the United States are characteristic of the native life of the peoples who live in those quarters. But that is an error and a slander. The slums are emphatically not of our making. So far is the immigrant from being accustomed to such living conditions that the first thing that repels him on his arrival in New York is the realization of the dreadful level of life to which his fellows have sunk. And when by sheer use he comes to accept these conditions himself, it is with something of a fatalistic resignation to the idea that such is America."

Ravage saw with horror respectable citizens selling cabbages from hideous carts and massed in shrill, gesticulating crowds in those monstrous dirty caves that were the streets of lower New York. It grieved him to see Jonah Gershon, who had been chairman of the hospital committee in his home town in Rumania, and a prominent grain merchant, dispensing soda water and selling lollipops. And there was Shoma Lobel, descendant of rabbis and himself a learned scholar, peddling matches and shoestrings and candles in a basket!

Mary Antin found her home in Dover Street, Boston, heavy with the airs of degradation. Dover Street was the heart of the South End ghetto, impinging at its northern end on Chinatown. It was crowded and it was filthy. Day and night its population seemed to burst through the doors and crowd the streets. Some people tried to scrub their poor tenements, but nobody cleaned the streets. Yet there, miraculously, she found what her parents had come to America to seek. "In Dover Street I was shackled with a hundred chains of disadvantage, but with one free hand I planted little seeds, right there in the mud of shame, that blossomed into the honied rose of wildest freedom."

3

The road out of the slums led first to the labor office. Generally, whatever his background, the only opening for a new immigrant was unskilled work with his hands. Many who had been of the white-collar class abroad later spoke with great appreciation of the American discipline of manual labor. Their first transforming experience was the breaking down of their class-conscious attitude to working with their hands. Michael Pupin said that he soon perceived that the American adaptability which he observed on every occasion was due to the general manual training. "Lack of manual training was a handicap which I felt on every step during my early progress in America. My whole experience confirms me in the belief that manual training of the youth gives them a discipline which school books alone can never give." He learned to appreciate the fact that Benjamin Franklin, and Lincoln, and other American heroes were men who had worked with their hands.

Ravage, looking down on the students at the University of Missouri as ignoramuses because they cared nothing for European history and less for the class struggle, got his first real intellectual shock when they showed up his appalling ignorance. He could not drive a nail into a plank without hurting his fingers. He did not know what a persimmon was, nor how cider was made, nor where the molasses on the table came from. He could not swim, nor skate, nor harness a horse, nor milk a cow. He did not know that gales, tornadoes, cyclones, and sandstorms were as distinguishable from one another as hexameters from alexandrines. Gradually, he says, it dawned on him that there were more kinds of knowledge than were discussed in Warschauer's Russian teahouse, or in the works of insurgent literati, and he had to revise his notion of the heathen of Missouri.

They got their education everywhere, these eager children of the slums. Ravage even confesses that the sweatshop was for him the cradle of liberty and his first university. There he discovered that there were other kinds of people than his own countrymen. He learned about Chekhov and de Maupassant and Herbert Spencer from a little black-eyed Russian girl. He learned to read newspapers. He dipped into the books somebody obligingly lent him, and was finally led off by his fellow workers to lectures. He heard about Darwin, and the principles of air pressure, and Hamlet versus Don Quixote, in the various workers' classes and discussion groups. Perhaps, he said, they did not understand it all, but they drank it in with intoxicating joy. These lectures and classes were echoes from a higher world.

The immigrant was fortunate, however, if the employment office sent him out of the slums and the sweatshops to a job in the country. To be sure some of these jobs were dreary enough. To men from the snug little villages of Europe open American country often looked like the howling wilderness. Riis found the Allegheny Mountains appalling. He would climb a hill, only to find that there were bigger hills beyond, an endless swelling sea of green without a clearing anywhere. He tried coal mining, and emerged into the sunset like one who had been dead and had come to life. The world had never seemed so wondrous fair. He and his companion stood and watched light slowly fade on the mountaintops, and the last gleam die out of the window of the stone church. Then they went straight to the company's store and gave up their picks. He would never, he said, go down into a mine again. And he never did.

But Pupin, more fortunate, found in his first job on a Delaware farm a pastoral idyll. "He who has never seen the Delaware peach-orchards of those days in full bloom, when in the month of May the ground is a deep velvety green, and when the southern sky seen through the golden atmosphere of a sunny May day reminds one of those mysterious landscapes which form the background of some of Raphael's Madonna pictures—he who has never seen that glorious sight does not know the heavenly beauty of this little earth. No painter would dare to put on canvas the cloth of flaming gold which on that balmy Sunday afternoon covered the ripples of the sun-kissed Delaware River."

Riding from the barnyard to the fields, on a cart, behind a team of mules, the Serbian lad, jaunty in his red fez, observed with excitement that a golden-haired Vila was cautiously watching him. A Vila, he explains, is the Serbian word for good fairy. No Serbian hero ever perished through misfortune if he had the good luck to win the friendship of a Vila. So he watched carefully for his fairy, and when he saw her he gave her his best Balkan salute.

Of course the Vila was only a fair-haired American girl. But she brought him good fortune like any fairy. For ultimately they struck up a friendship, and after supper he would sit with her and her kind mother, while they listened absorbed to his tales of Serbia, and, in turn, corrected his English speech and told him stories of American history—a social interchange delightful and romantic to both sides. And so the great American scientist, to whom we owe so much in the development of radio and other modern techniques, was received by the people into their native fold.

Touchingly imaginative, looking out with dazzled eyes on the wonders of this new world, the gifted immigrant children discovered some of our great public buildings. So Mary Antin found the Boston Public Library, and joyously appropriated it. "It was my habit to go slowly up the low broad steps to the palace entrance, pleasing my eyes with the majestic lines of the building, and lingering to read again the carved inscriptions: Public Library. . . . Built by the People. . . . Free to All. Did I not say that it was my palace? Mine, because I was a citizen; mine, though I was born an alien; mine, though I lived on Dover Street. My palace—mine."

So she would lean against the pillar in the entrance hall, and watch the spectacled scholars come down the steps, and the fine-browed women enter and walk quietly past her, and she would feel that they and she had this one glorious thing in common, this noble treasure house of learning.

So Pupin, a field hand off a Delaware farm, wandered into the campus of Princeton University. It seemed to him a noble and sacred place, like the pictures he had seen of Hilendar, the famous monastery on Mount Athos, on the Aegean Sea, founded by St. Sava in the twelfth century, where men lived a dedicated life of learning. As he was walking about in awe, a friendly student caught up with him, was curious about the foreign land he had come from, and said pleasantly that he hoped Pupin would someday be a student at Princeton. The immigrant boy went on in a daze, illimitable vision opening before him. "A student at Princeton! With fellow students and friends like this divinely handsome and gentle youth who accompanied me to the railroad station. Impossible."

Everywhere in the immigrant's stories emerge these lovely figures of the boys and girls of the American people—just ordinary boys and girls, like your son and daughter, or mine. But to the bewildered foreign child from the slums they looked like angels of beauty, and were dressed like nobles, and when they spoke naturally and kindly to him, as if he were one of themselves, welcoming him to all they possessed, as a matter of course, every chain of disadvantage seemed to fall away. "I said to myself, exultingly," reports Ravage, "that however America might have broken faith with me in other respects, her promise of democratic equality she had scrupulously fulfilled." And he adds generously, in another place, that the equality offered was always equality with the best. "These capitalists and oppressors were making me into a gentleman!"

4

In the chaos of the immigrant's first years in America, two institutions stood out like lighthouses over a dark and stormy sea. One was the public school, and the other was the settlement house. Mary Antin records that her poor father, disappointed in all else, still thought that the agony of transplantation to America was worth it because here he could send his children to school. "I think Miss Nixon guessed what my father's best English could not convey. I think she divined that by the simple process of delivering our school certificates to her, he took possession of America."

The high priestess who received Mary Antin from her father's hand at the door to the temple of learning was a young and pretty woman. So are they all, in the record. Daughters often of Irish or Germans who had come to this country but a generation before, almost colossally ignorant of the vast and complicated book learning which some of the more educated foreigners like Antin had been exposed to abroad, they yet held in their kind and pretty hands the gift of knowledge for which the immigrant so humbly sued—the instinctive knowledge of the American way of life. The public school teacher, the young woman "teaching a few years till she gets married," like the young Yankee schoolma'am in the West, is one of the heroines of American culture. Memory enshrines her, and gratitude canonizes her. She was kind; she was lovely to look at; she wore a nice dress; she explained with infinite patience, and met all races and social classes alike with graceful good humor. To persons just arrived she looked like the fairest flower in the gardens of privilege. But she only smiled sweetly and gave them one and all the great American welcome. "This is yours, too. Come in and let's enjoy it together." There have been complaints that the American school system has been too much dominated by women, especially by young women; that what young children need is more of the influence of mature men and real scholars. Perhaps! Yet in the past it is questionable whether any number of bearded scholars could have achieved the work of this graceful young hostess at the door to the higher life for all.

"Miss Nixon," says Mary Antin, "aided the little foreigners so skilfully and earnestly in our endeavors to 'see a cat' and 'hear a dog bark,' and 'look at the hen' that we turned over page after page of the ravishing history, eager to find out how the common world looked, smelled, and tasted in the strange speech. . . . Miss Nixon was pretty, and she must have looked well with her white teeth showing in the act [of pronouncing difficult sounds over and over] but I was too solemnly occupied to admire her looks. I did take great pleasure in her smile of approval, whenever I pronounced well; and her patience and perseverance in struggling with us over that thick little word [the definite article] are becoming to her even now, after fifteen years.

"Whenever the teachers did anything special to help me over my private difficulties, my gratitude went out to them, silently. It meant so much to me that they halted the lesson to give me a lift, that I needs must love them for it. Dear Miss Carroll, of the second grade, would be amazed to hear what small things I remember, all because I was so impressed at the time with her readiness and sweetness in taking notice of my difficulties."

One of these young heroines of learning, Myra Kelley, wrote a charming book about her various young charges from the immigrant quarters. But hundreds and thousands have done what she did, with the same simplicity, kindness, and humor, and never thought they were making culture history. And Mary Antin, at least, makes haste to record her love for the speech which a series of charming and patient young teachers taught her, a great girl of fifteen, fresh from Russia, sitting with babies in the first, second, third, and fourth grades. "I shall never have a better opportunity to make public declaration of my love for the English language. I am glad that American history runs, chapter for chapter, the way it does; for thus America came to be the country I love so dearly. I am glad, most of all, that the Americans began by being Englishmen, for thus did I come to inherit this beautiful language in which I think. It seems to me that in any other language happiness is not so sweet, logic is not so clear. I am not sure that I could believe in my neighbors as I do if I thought of them in un-English words. I could almost say that my conviction of immortality is bound up with the English of its promise." She loves English because through all its vowels and consonants sound the voices of girl teachers who were kind and patient and lovely, and who in utmost sincerity held out to her, awkward, foreign, poor, ill-clad, and living on Dover Street, the hope that she could be just like them. Could Aristotle have accomplished more?

In the last decade of the century there appeared another institution now enshrined in the immigrant's reminiscences—the settlement house. The first settlement house in America was opened in September, 1889, when Miss Jane Addams and Miss Ellen Gates Starr, who had been her best friend at college, moved quietly into the fine old house, in one of the slums of Chicago, which they had rescued from its use as a tenement house, and restored to its original homelike dignity. They had not come to establish a city mission or to reform the inhabitants of the neighborhood. They were just going to live there, and draw other intelligent people thither, and be hospitable and neighborly as occasion arose. What Miss Addams and her friends were seeking was not the salvation of the slums, but their own personal salvation. They were rebels against the isolation of well-to-do people, against the jejune idealism of their college training, against their personal ignorance of all these matters so tumultuously discussed in the papers—the conditions of labor, the dangers of the foreign invasion, the increasing spread between wealth for the few and poverty for the masses. They came to live in the slums in search of a richer and fuller life, and to get acquainted with the people there in a simple and friendly way as neighbors.

So, establishing themselves at Hull House, Miss Addams and Miss Starr proceeded exactly as if they were moving into one of the more aristocratic portions of town. They furnished a house as they would have furnished it in another part of the city, with photographs and other ornaments from Europe, with family mahogany and books. And then they proceeded to make friends with their neighbors, to take an interest in local affairs, and to offer hospitality exactly as if they were ladies in their own social set uptown.

Out of this simple procedure grew all the famous settlement houses in the big cities, with their multifarious activities, their mingling of races and classes and interests. The stories of two of the most famous ones are written in Jane Addams' *Twenty Years at Hull House* and Lillian Wald's *Windows on Henry Street*. To our civilization they are what the salons were to eighteenth century France, the meeting places for art and literature and social idealism; but, in taking into their midst the lowliest economic orders, they have given intellectual and artistic richness to their social fabric which was unknown to the purely aristocratic drawing rooms. It was in the settlement houses that the various artistic and intellectual gifts of the latest increment of Americans began to be observed. It was here that cultivated people of the earlier strains, feeling a cultural barrenness and general anemia in American life, were quickened to a new romance of outlook by something that till then had throbbed and sung, and beaten in vain against the walls of the new immigrant's isolation. The excitement of social interchange in the settlement houses was quite mutual.

So Lillian Wald remembers that Irving Berlin's haunting music was born but a block from her settlement house, and that George Gershwin admits that he was of the neighborhood, but he cannot remember in which house he lived because he moved so often. Sophie Braslau's father was friend and ally to the settlement, and she often came back to give her beautiful voice and her art for its entertainment. Settlement house children grew up to be artists and journalists, and public officials, and quite as much of an honor to their alma mater as any Harvard graduate.

So Mary Antin records with fervor the manifold charms of Hale House in Boston, and how it molded the children of the slums into "noble men and women." So at the opening of the Kings' Daughters' Settlement House, Jacob Riis wrote: "It stands, that house, within a stone's throw of many a door in which I sat friendless and forlorn, trying to hide from the policeman who would not let me sleep; within hail of the Bend of the wicked past, atoned for at last; of the Bowery boarding house where I lay senseless on the stairs after my first day's work in the newspaper office, starved nigh to death. But the memory of the old days has no sting. Its message is one of hope; the house itself is the key-note. It is the pledge of a better day, of the defeat of the slum with the helpless heredity of despair. That shall damn no longer lives as yet unborn. Children of God are we. That is our challenge to the slum, and on earth we shall yet claim our heritage of light."

5

With all the help of school and settlement house, the immigrant stories are eloquent of the moral ruin of this plunge of uprooted people into the festering, crawling junk pile of industry. The selfish intention of industry was to get labor so poor and alien, and so bowed down by necessity and ignorance that it would work for any wages. The slums and immigrant centers were not American. They were a shrieking offense to everything America had ever stood for.

Most immigrants had lived decent and regular lives in the small communities at home, but their moral traditions were tied up with customs so special, often so formal and so fixed in the patterns of ages long past, that they were bound to collapse in the large and fluid life of the New World. Anxious that their children should be Americans, old immigrants meekly saw the religion of their forefathers flouted, and every law of good behavior thrown to the wind. If they undertook to control the children, the children deserted them. Jane Addams said that boys of ten would refuse to sleep at home, preferring the freedom of an old brewery or warehouse. For days these boys would live on milk or bread they stole from the back porches after the early morning delivery. They said they had no fun at home. Dissipated young men would pride themselves on living without working and despise the sober and thrifty ways of immigrant parents. Yet the old parents, unable to speak English, were dependent on their Americanized children for understanding of this strange new land, and received from the young and foolish new doctrines that they dared not subscribe to—because they seemed so wrong—and yet dared not reject, on pain of being left out forever from the light and promise, the plenty and the freedom which obviously were spread out before them.

Mary Antin, always kind and generous in her faith in America, says: "This sad process of disintegration of home life may be observed in almost any immigrant family of our class and with our traditions and aspirations. It is part of the process of Americanization, an upheaval preceding the state of repose. It is the cross that the first and second generations must bear, an involuntary sacrifice for the sake of future generations. These are the pains of adjustment, as racking as the pains of birth. And as the mother forgets her agonies in the bliss of clasping her babe to her breast, so the bent and

heart sore immigrant forgets exile and homesickness and ridi-
cule and loss and estrangement when he beholds his sons and
daughters moving as Americans among Americans."

For something there was about being an American that
was like salvation to the immigrant. Even intelligent immigrants from superior backgrounds, like Jacob Riis, felt it. He
had come from a neat, snug, happy Danish town, representing the most advanced European culture, from a family of
education and rank in the town. Here he was at first only an
immigrant boy. When he returned to Denmark he returned
to a higher social status than he had yet attained in America.
Yet the day came when going back was a deadly disappointment. One day, at Elsinore, he lay sick, looking out to sea
and across to the blue mountains of Sweden, feeling deeply
depressed, missing something. Suddenly a ship went by, flying
from its mast the Stars and Stripes. "That moment I knew.
Gone were illness, discouragement, gloom . . . I sat up in
bed and shouted and laughed and cried by turns, waving my
handkerchief to the flag out there . . . I had found it, and
my heart, too, at last. I knew that it was my flag, that my
children's home was mine; indeed that I also had become an
American in truth."

Ravage, returning after a homesick year at the University
of Missouri, longing to be back in the dear Rumanian home
fold again, was shocked to see a Rumanian funeral. It seemed
to him ludicrous, frightful, barbarous. "I had been part of
such a performance myself, and the grief of it still lingered
somewhere in my motley soul. But now I could only think of
the affecting simplicity, the quiet unobtrusive solemnity of
a burial I had witnessed the previous spring in the West."
Going about uneasily, seeing his Rumanian friends and kin,
he suddenly understood how he must have looked to the
heathen of Missouri, and at that moment, he says, he was
threatened with a new faculty, strange to the East Side—a
sense of humor. Trying to explain how he felt about things
to his former friends and to his relatives, he met only blank

looks and hurt feelings. So down he sat and poured out his heart in a letter to the American lad who had been his college roommate in the West. "That barbarian in Missouri was the only human being, strangely enough, in whom I could now confide with the hope of being understood."

In the fall he went back, and was delighted to find his college friend at the railroad station waiting to meet him, as he had seen various rural-looking youth met by friends the year before. Boys came up and slapped him on the shoulder; joked and laughed with him in their hearty, boisterous manner. He was asked to join boarding clubs, to become a member of debating societies, to come and see this or that fellow. He had not realized till then that during the previous year when he was so lonely and so foreign and different, the barriers between him and these lads had been steadily breaking down. His sensitiveness, his intellectual pride, his superciliousness were suddenly dissolved in one rich glow of feeling. "I felt my heart going out to my new friends. I had become one of them. I was not a man without a country. I was an American."

But it is Mary Antin, as usual, who lifts the whole experience of being an American into the most beautiful universality, and setting it in its place in space and time, brings to its end, in the soul of one little ex-Russian-Jewish girl, sitting outside the Boston Public Library, this story of our America.

Mary had gone with the Natural History Club from the settlement house to look for specimens on the beach at Nahant. She had been happy, and had felt joyously one with the other girls, during the merry luncheon on the rocks, with talk and laughter between sandwiches, and "strange jokes intelligible only to the practicing naturalist." At the Public Library she parted with her friends, and stood for a moment outside this, her favorite *palace*. She was thinking of what the naturalist had been telling them about *Evolution*. "My hair was damp with sea-spray; the roar of the tide was in my ears. Mighty thoughts surged through my dreams, and I trembled with understanding.

"I sank down on the granite ledge beside the entrance to the Library, and for a moment I covered my eyes with my hand. In that moment I had a vision of myself, the human creature, emerging from the dim places where the torch of history has never been, creeping slowly into the light of civilized existence, pushing more steadily forward to the broad plateau of modern life, and leaping at last, strong and glad, to the intellectual summit of the latest century. . . .

"But hark to the clamor of the city all about. This is my latest home, and it invites me to a glad new life. The endless ages have indeed throbbed through my blood, but a new rhythm dances in my veins. My spirit is not tied to the monumental past, any more than my feet were bound to my grandfather's house below the hill. The past was only my cradle, and now it cannot hold me, because I am grown too big; just as the little house in Polotzk, once my home, has now become a toy of memory, as I move about in the wide spaces of this splendid palace, whose shadow covers acres. No, it is not that I belong to the past, but the past that belongs to me. America is the youngest of the nations and inherits all that went before in history. And I am the youngest of America's children, and into my hands is given all her priceless heritage, to the last white star espied through the telescope, to the last great thought of the philosopher. Mine is the whole majestic past, and mine the shining future!"

SOURCES

THE following represent a rather small selection out of the much larger number of books consulted in writing *American Saga*. Familiar general histories and collected works of well-known authors are, in general, omitted. Only a few of the many interesting books by such an author as Simms are mentioned. The editions chosen for mention are frequently those which have particularly interesting illustrations or are remarkable for some other obvious reason. State historical collections, which are always informing and have been freely consulted, are barely mentioned, as are many of the pamphlets and locally printed materials to tbe found in the local history section of the Library of Congress. I can only hope that anyone following up the books here listed will come upon the rest.

ABBOTT, JOHN S. C. *The History of the Civil War in America*. New York, 1866.

ADAMS, CHARLES FRANCIS. *The Life of John Adams*, begun by John Quincy Adams, completed by Charles Francis Adams. Philadelphia, 1871.

ADAMS, FRANCIS COLBURN. *Uncle Tom at Home. A Review of the Reviewers and Repudiators of Uncle Tom's Cabin*. Philadelphia, 1853.

ADAMS, JOHN. *Letters of John Adams Addressed to His Wife*. Edited by his grandson, Charles Francis Adams. Boston, 1841.

ADAMS, JOHN. *Twenty-six Letters upon Interesting Subjects Respecting the Revolution in America. Written in Holland in the Year 1780 by His Excellency John Adams.* New York, printed by John Fenno at his office, No. 9 Maiden Lane, 1789.

ADAMS, JOHN QUINCY. *Diary.* Ed. by Allan Nevins. New York, 1929.

ADDAMS, JANE. *Twenty Years at Hull House.* New York, 1911.

ALEXANDER, WILLIAM T. *History of the Colored Race in America.* Kansas City, Missouri, 1887.

ALLAN, WILLIAM. *History of the Campaign of General T. J. (Stonewall) Jackson in the Shenandoah Valley of Virginia.* Philadelphia, 1880.

ALLEN, A. T., compiler. *Ten Years in Oregon. Travels and Adventures of Doctor E. White and Lady.* Ithaca, 1850.

ALLEN, ETHAN. *A Brief Narrative of the Proceedings of the Government of New York Relative to Their Obtaining the Jurisdiction of Land to the Westward from the Connecticut River.* Bennington, 1774.

ALLISON, JOHN. *Dropped Stitches in Tennessee History.* Nashville, 1897.

ALTROCCHI, JULIA COOLY. *Snow Covered Wagons. Donner Party Expedition.* New York, 1936.

ALVORD, CLARENCE W. *The Mississippi Valley in British Politics.* Cleveland, 1917.

ANONYMOUS. *Belle of Baltimore. Collection of Nigger Melodies.* New York, 1850.

ANONYMOUS. *Charleston, S. C. A satiric poem showing that slavery still exists in a country which boasts above all others of being the seat of liberty.* London, 1851.

ANONYMOUS. *My Ride to the Barbecue, or Revolutionary Reminiscences of the Old Dominion, by an Ex-member of Congress.* New York, 1860.

ANONYMOUS. *The Far West, or a Tour beyond the Mountains. By E. F.* New York, 1838.

ANONYMOUS. *The Old Pine Farm, or the Southern Side. Comprising Loose Sketches from the Experience of a Southern Country Minister in South Carolina.* Nashville and New York, 1860.

ANONYMOUS. *Pencillings about Ephrata, Pa. By a Visitor.* Philadelphia, 1856.

ANONYMOUS. *Princeton College. Glimpses of Colonial Society and the Life at Princeton College, 1766–1773. By one of the class of 1763.* Philadelphia, 1803.

ANONYMOUS. *The Reign of Terror in Kansas. By an eye-witness.* Boston, 1856.

ANONYMOUS. *The Traveller's Directory, and Emigrant's Guide, Containing Several Descriptions of Different Routes through the State of New York, Ohio, Indiana, Illinois, and the Territory of Michigan.* Buffalo, 1832.

ANBURY, THOMAS. *Travels through the Interior Parts of North America.* London, 1789.

ANDERSON, CHARLES CARTER. *Fighting by Southern Federals.* New York, 1912. (Record of 634,255 Southern soldiers who fought for the preservation of the Union in the Civil War.)

ANDREWS, JOHN. *History of the War with America, France, Spain, and Holland.* 4 vols. London, 1785.

ANTIN, MARY. *The Promised Land.* Boston, 1911.

APPLEGATE, JESSE. *A Day with the Cow-column in 1843.* Ed. with introduction and notes. Chicago, 1934.

ARCHDALE, JOHN. *A New Description of That Fertile and Pleasant Province of Carolina.* London, 1707.

ATWATER, CALEB. *Remarks Made on a Tour to Prairie du Chien,* 1829. Columbus, Ohio, 1831.

AUSTIN, STEPHEN. *The Austin Papers.* Ed. by Eugene C. Barker. 2 vols., printed by Government Printing Office, Washington, D. C., 1924–1928. Vol. 3 printed at Austin by University of Texas, 1927.

BANCROFT, HUBERT HOWE. *Works.* 30 vols. San Francisco, 1882–1890.

BARBER, JOHN WARNER. *The History and Antiquities of New England, New York, New Jersey, and Pennsylvania.* Hartford, 1856.

BARROWS, WILLIAM. *The General, or Twelve Nights in the Hunter's Camp.* Boston, 1869.

BARTRAM, WILLIAM. *Travels.* Philadelphia, 1791. Ed. by Mark Van Doren. New York, 1928.

BATES, DAVID HOMER. *Lincoln in the Telegraph Office.* New York, 1907.

BELLAMY, EDWARD. *Looking Backward.* Boston, 1889.

BELLOWS, HENRY W. *Historical Sketch of the Union League Club.* New York, 1879.

BENÉT, STEPHEN VINCENT. *John Brown's Body.* New York, 1928.

BENTON, ELBERT J. *The Wabash Trade Route.* Baltimore, 1903.

BENTON, THOMAS HART. *Speech on Highway to the Pacific in the Senate.* Dec. 16, 1850, a pamphlet.

———. *Thirty Years.* 2 vols. New York, 1854–1856.

BIGGS, STEPHEN. *Pages from the Early History of the West . . . with Special Reference to the History of Methodism.* Cincinnati, 1868.

BISHOP, HARRIET E. *Floral Home, or First Years of Minnesota.* New York, 1857.

BLAIR, WALTER, and FRANKLIN J. MEINE. *Mike Fink.* New York, 1933.

BLANCHARD, CLAUDE. *Journal,* 1780–1783. Albany, 1876.

BOND, BEVERLEY W. *The Civilization of the Old Northwest.* New York, 1934.

BONNEY, EDWARD. *The Banditti of the Prairies.* Chicago, 1856.

Boston Port and Seaman's Aid Society. *Life of Father Taylor.* Boston, 1904.

BOUCICAULT, DION. *The Octaroon, or Life in Louisiana.* New York, 1861.

BOWERS, CLAUDE. *The Tragic Era.* Cambridge, 1929.

BOWLES, SAMUEL. *Across the Continent.* Springfield, 1865.

BOYD, BELLE. *Belle Boyd in Camp and Prison, Written by herself.* New York, 1865.

BOYD, MINNIE C. *Alabama in the Fifties.* New York, 1931.

BRACKINRIDGE, HENRY M. *Views of Louisiana.* Pittsburgh, 1814.

BRADBURY, JOHN. *Travels in North America.* Liverpool, 1817.

BRADFORD, JOHN. *Historical Notes on Kentucky from the Western Miscellany.* Compiled by G. W. Stipp, 1827. San Francisco, 1932.

BREWERTON, GEORGE D. *Wars of the Western Border*. New York, 1859.

BRICKELL, JOHN. *Natural History of North Carolina*. Dublin, 1737.

BRYAN, MARY NORCUTT. *A Grandmother's Recollection of Dixie*. New Bern, North Carolina, 1912.

BRYAN, WILLIAM S., and ROBERT ROSE. *History of the Pioneer Families of Missouri*. St. Louis, 1856. (Contains excellent record of Daniel Boone.)

BUCKINGHAM, JAMES S. *The Slave States of America*. London, 1842.

BULLOCK, WILLIAM. *Virginia Impartially Examined*. London, 1649.

BURR, AARON. *Reports of the Trials of Col. Aaron Burr . . . for Treason.* Philadelphia, 1808.

BURTON, RICHARD F. *The City of the Saints*. (Salt Lake City.) London, 1861.

BUTLER, FRANCES ANNE KEMBLE. *Journal of a Residence on a Georgia Plantation*. New York, 1863.

BYRD, WILLIAM. *The Westover Manuscripts*, Petersburg, Virginia, 1841. (Several later editions.)

CAIRD, SIR JAMES. *Prairie Farming in America*. London, 1859.

CALDWELL, MARY F. *General Jackson's Lady; A Story of the Life and Times of Rachel Donelson*. Nashville, 1936.

CALHOUN, JOHN C. *Works*. New York, 1851-1856.

CAMPANIUS HOLM, THOMAS. *A Short Description of the Province of New Sweden*. Trans. by Peter S. Du Ponceau. Philadelphia, 1834.

CANNON, MILES. *Waiilatpu, Its Rise and Fall, Featuring the Journey of Narcissa Prentiss Whitman*. Boise, Idaho, 1915.

CARRUTHERS, WILLIAM A. *The Knights of the Horse-shoe*. New York, 1882.

CARTER, CLARENCE E. *The Territorial Papers of the United States*. 5 vols. Government Printing Office, 1934-1937.

CARTWRIGHT, PETER. *Autobiography*. Ed. by W. P. Strickland. New York, 1857.

CHAMBERS, GEORGE. *A Tribute to the Principles, Virtues, Habits, and Public Usefulness of the Irish and Scotch Early Settlers of Pennsylvania*. Chambersburg, Pennsylvania, 1871.

CHAPMAN, THOMAS JEFFERSON. *Old Pittsburg Days*. Pittsburgh, 1900.

Charleston Mercury. Essays on the origin of the federal government, tending to show that it emanates not from the people collectively but from the people of the respective states, acting as confederate sovereignties. Charleston, 1830.

CHASE, SALMON P. *A Sketch of the History of Ohio*. Cincinnati, 1833.

CHASTELLUX, FRANÇOIS JEAN, MARQUIS DE. *Travels in North America*. London, 1787.

CHAUVENET, WILLIAM M. The lure of the great Northwest, fifty years ago. *Journal of American History*, vol. II No. IV pp. 633-642.

CHITTENDEN, HIRAM M. *The American Fur Trade of the Far West*. New York, 1936.

CHITTENDEN, L. E. *Abraham Lincoln's Speeches*. New York, 1895.

CHRESTIAN, BOLIVAR. *The Scotch-Irish Settlers in the Valley of Virginia*. Richmond, 1860.

CHURCHILL, WINSTON. *The Crossing*. New York, 1904. And other works.

CLAIBORNE, JOHN H. *William Claiborne of Virginia*. New York, 1917.

CLARK, GEORGE ROGERS. *The Capture of Old Vincennes*. Original narrative of Clark and of his opponent, Governor Henry Hamilton. Ed. by Milo M. Quaife. Indianapolis, 1927.

CLAY-CLOPTON, VIRGINIA. *A Belle of the Fifties*, 1853–1866. New York, 1905.

CLEMENS, JEREMIAH. *Bernard Lile, an Historical Romance, Embracing the Periods of the Texas Revolution and the Mexican War*. Philadelphia, 1856.

COALE, CHARLES B. *Life and Adventures of Wilburn Waters*. Richmond, 1878. (Virginia frontier life.)

COBBETT, WILLIAM. *A Year's Residence in the United States*. London, 1819.

COBLENTZ, STANTON A. *Villains and Vigilantes, the Story of James King of William*. New York, 1936.

COFFIN, CHARLES C. *The Boys of '61*. Boston, 1866.

———. *The Seat of Empire*. (Minnesota.) Boston, 1870.

COLLES, JAMES. *Life and Letters*. Ed. by Emily J. DeForest. New York, 1926. (New York business family in New Orleans.)

COLTON, C. *Tour of the American Lakes and Northwest Territory*. London, 1933.

COLTON, CALVIN. *The Works of Henry Clay*. 10 vols. New York, 1904.

CONNELLY, WILLIAM E. *Doniphan's Expedition and the Conquest of New Mexico*. Kansas City, 1907.

———. *Quantrill and the Border Wars*. Cedar Rapids, Iowa, 1910.

Confederate States of America. Official Reports of battles. Richmond, 1864.

COOK, JAMES H. *Fifty Years on the Old Frontier*. New Haven, 1923.

COOKE, JOHN ESTEN. *Hammer and Rapier*. New York, 1870.

———. *My Lady Pokahontas*. Boston, 1885. And other works.

COUES, ELLIOTT. *Audubon and His Journals*. New York, 1897.

CRAIG, HUGH. *Grand Army Picture Book*. New York, London, 1890.

CRAWFORD, MEDOREM. *Journal . . . of His Trip across the Plains with the Oregon Pioneers of 1842*. Eugene, Oregon, 1897.

CRÈVECOEUR, HECTOR ST. JEAN DE. *Letters from an American Farmer*. London, 1782. Reprinted in Everyman's ed., 1912.

CROCKETT, DAVID. *Crockett's Exploits and Adventures in Texas*. Philadelphia, 1836.

———. *Autobiography*. Philadelphia, 1834. Ed. with introduction by Hamlin Garland, New York, 1923.

CUMMINS, JIM. *Jim Cummins Book, Written by Himself* (The life story of the James gang and their comrades, etc.) Denver, 1903.

CURTIS, NEWTON M. *The Hunted Chief, or the Female Ranchers. A Tale of the Mexican War*. New York, 1847.

DALE, HARRISON C. *The Ashley-Smith Explorers and the Discovery of a Central Route to the Pacific, 1822–1829*. Cleveland, 1918.

DANA, C. W. *The Great West, or the Garden of the World, with Statistics and Facts from the Hon. Thomas H. Benton, Sam Houston, and Col. John C. Frémont*. Boston, 1853.

DANA, RICHARD H. *Two Years before the Mast*. New York, 1840.

DAVIES, BENJAMIN. *Some Account of the City of Philadelphia*. Philadelphia, 1794.

DAVIS, JEFFERSON. *A Short History of the Confederate States of America*. New York, 1890.

DAWSON, SARAH MORGAN. *A Confederate Girl's Diary*. Boston, 1913.

DAY, SAMUEL P. *Down South, or an Englishman's Experiences at the Seat of the American War by the Special Correspondent of the Morning Herald*. London, 1862.

DELANO, AMASA. *A Narrative of Voyages and Travels in the Northern and Southern Hemispheres*. Boston, 1818. (Typical East India trader's record by one of President Roosevelt's family.)

DENIS, ALBERTA J. *Spanish Alta California*. New York, 1927.

DE SAUSSURE, NANCY. *Old Plantation Days*. New York, 1907.

DESHIELDS, JAMES T. *Border Wars of Texas*. Tioga, Texas, 1912.

DEVEREUX, MARGARET. *Plantation Sketches*. Cambridge, 1906.

DE VRIES, DAVID PETERSON. *Voyages from Holland to America, 1632–1644*. New York, 1857.

DICEY, EDWARD. Contributions to the *London Spectator* on American Civil War, in 1862.

DONDORE, DOROTHY A. *The Prairie and the Making of Middle America*. Cedar Rapids, Iowa, 1926.

DOUGLAS, THOMAS. *Autobiography of Thomas Douglas, Late Judge of the Supreme Court of Florida*. New York, 1856.

DRAKE, BENJAMIN. *Life of Tecumseh and His Brother, the Prophet*. Cincinnati, 1841.

DRAKE, DANIEL. *Natural and Statistical View of Cincinnati*. Cincinnati, 1815.

———. *Pioneer Life in Kentucky*. Cincinnati, 1870.

DRAKE, SAMUEL G. *The History and Antiquities of Boston*. Boston, 1856.

DRESSLER, ALBERT, ed. *Letters of a Pioneer Senator*. Original extracts from the mail-bag of a California statesman of the fifties. San Francisco, 1925.

DYE, EVA EMERY. *McLoughlin and Old Oregon*. Chicago, 1900.

EARLY, JUBAL À. *A Memoir*. Lynchburg, 1867.

EATON, JOHN H. *Life of Andrew Jackson, Commenced by John Reid*. Philadelphia, 1817.

———. *Complete Memoirs*. Philadelphia, 1878.

EGGLESTON, EDWARD. *The Circuit Rider*. New York, 1878.

———. *The Hoosier Schoolmaster*, 1883.

———. *Brant and Red Jacket*. New York, 1879.

EGGLESTON, GEORGE C. *American War Ballads*. New York, 1889.

———. *The Bale Marked X, a Tale of Blockade Running*. Boston, 1902.

———. *Evelyn Byrd*, Boston, 1904.

ELZAS, BARNETT ABRAHAM, *The Jews of South Carolina*. Charleston, 1903.

FAUST, ALBERT B. *Charles Sealsfield (Karl Postl); Materials for a Biography . . . His Influence upon American Literature*. Baltimore, 1892,

———. *The German Element in the United States*. 2 vols. New York, 1927.

FEATHERSTONHAUGH, GEORGE. *Excursion through the Slave States*. London, 1844.

FILSON, JOHN. *The Discovery and Settlement and Present State of Kentucke*. Wilmington, 1784. Facsimile of this edition, Filson Club, Louisville, 1929.

FINLEY, JOHN H. *The French in the Heart of America*. New York, 1915.

FITCH, WILLIAM E. *Some Neglected History of North Carolina, Being an Account of the Regulators and the Battle of Almanance*. New York, 1905.

FITE, EMERSON D. *Social and Industrial Conditions in the North during the Civil War*. New York, 1910.

FLEMING, WALTER L. *Documentary History of Reconstruction*. Cleveland, 1906.

———. *The Ku Klux Testimony Relating to Alabama*. Montgomery, 1903.

FLINT, THOMAS. *The First White Man of the West*. (Daniel Boone.) Cincinnati, 1856.

FLOWER, RICHARD. *Letters from Lexington and the Illinois*. London, 1819.

FORBES, THOMAS S. *John Murray Forbes' Horseback Ride to Alabama, 1831*. Montgomery, 1904.

FOULKE, W. D. *Life of Oliver P. Morton*. Indianapolis, 1899.

———. *A Hoosier Autobiography*. New York, 1922.

FOWLER, JACOB. *The Journal of Jacob Fowler, Narrating an Adventure from Arkansas through the Indian territory*. New York, 1898.

FRANKLIN, BENJAMIN. *Works*. Philadelphia, 1808–1818.

FREEMAN, NATHANIEL C. *Parnassus in Philadelphia. A Satire*. Philadelphia, 1854.

FRÉMONT, JOHN C. *The Life of John Charles Frémont and His Narrative of Explorations and Adventures*. Memoir by Samuel M. Schmucker, A.M. New York and Auburn, 1856.

FRIES, ADELAIDE L. *The Moravians in Georgia*. Raleigh, N. C., 1905.

FULKERSON, HORACE S. *Random Recollections of Early Days in Mississippi*. Vicksburg, 1885.

GARCES, FRANCISCO T. H. *Diary*. Ed. by Elliott Coues. New York, 1900. (Spanish Southwest.)

GARLAND, HAMLIN. *A Son of the Middle Border*. New York, 1917. Also other works.

GARLAND, ROBERT. *The Scotch-Irish in Western Pennsylvania*. Pittsburgh, 1923.

GARNER, JAMES W. *Reconstruction in Mississippi*. New York, 1901.

GARRETT, PAT F. *Authentic Life of Billy the Kid*. Ed. Maurice G. Fulton, New York, 1927.

GATES, CHARLES M., ed. *Five Fur Traders of the Northwest*. Minneapolis, 1933.

GEORGE, HENRY. *Progress and Poverty*. New York, 1879.

GIFFORD, RUTH, compiler. *Early California—1544–1848*. Los Angeles, 1935.

GIST, CHRISTOPHER. *Journals*. Ed. by William M. Darlington. Pittsburgh, 1893.

GLADSTONE, T. H. *An Englishman in Kansas*. New York, 1857.

GRANT, ULYSSES S. *Personal Memoirs*. New York, 1909.

GREEN, ASHBEL. *Life of Ashbel Green, V.D.M. Begun to be Written by Himself in His Eighty-second Year and Continued to his Eighty-fourth.* New York, 1849. (Concerns Revolutionary War in Philadelphia and Princeton University.)

GREENE, JOHN P. *Facts Relative to the Expulsion of the Mormons . . . from the State of Missouri.* Cincinnati, 1839.

GREENWOOD, ANNIE PIKE. *We Sage-brush Folks.* New York, 1934.

GREGG, JOSIAH. *Commerce of the Prairies, Journal of a Santa Fe Trader, 1831–1839.* New York, 1845.

GRAYSON, PORTE. Virginia illustrated. *Harpers' Monthly Magazine.* 1885–1856.

GRAYSON, WILLIAM J. *The Hireling and the Slave.* Charleston, 1856.

GUITERMAN, ARTHUR. *Ballads of Old New York.* New York, 1920.

——. *I Sing the Pioneer.* New York, 1926. (Ballads of the making of the nation.)

HALE, EDWARD EVERETT. *Stories of the War Told by Soldiers.* Boston, 1879.

HALL, JAMES. *Sketches of the History, Life, and Manners in the West.* Cincinnati, 1834.

HAMMOND, JOHN. *Leah and Rachel, or the Two Fruitful Sisters, Virginia and Maryland.* London, 1656.

HANIGHAN, FRANK. *Santa Anna, the Napoleon of the West.* New York, 1934.

HART, ALBERT BUSHNELL. *American History Told by Contemporaries.* 4 vols. New York, 1897–1901.

HARTE, BRET. *Poems.* Boston, 1871.

——. *Tales of the Argonauts.* Boston, 1882.

HAY, JOHN. *The Breadwinners, a Social Study.* New York, 1884.

——. *Democracy, an American Novel.* New York, 1908. (Also attributed to Henry Adams and Clarence King.)

——. *Poems.* Boston, 1899.

HAYNE, PAUL HAMILTON. *Poems.* Complete ed. Boston, 1882.

HAYWARD, MARSHALL DE LANCEY. *Ballads of Courageous Carolinians.* Raleigh, 1914.

HELPER, HINTON R. *The Impending Crisis in the South and How to Meet It.* New York, 1857.

HENDERSON, ALICE CORBIN. *Red Earth, Poems of New Mexico.* Chicago, 1920.

——. *The Turquoise Trail, an Anthology of New Mexico Poetry.* New York, 1928.

——. *Brothers of Light, the Penitentes of the Southwest.* New York, 1937.

HENDERSON, ARCHIBALD. *Richard Henderson, and the Occupation of Kentucky, 1775.* Cedar Rapids, Iowa, 1914.

——. *The Transylvania Company and the Founding of Henderson, Ky.* Henderson, Kentucky, 1929.

HERNDON, WILLIAM H. *The True Story of a Great Life. The History and Personal Recollections of Abraham Lincoln by . . . His Friend and Law Partner.* Springfield, Illinois, 1888.

HERRICK, FRANCIS HOBART, ed. *Delineations of American Scenery and Character by John James Audubon.* New York, 1926.

HEWATT, ALEXANDER. *An Historical Account of the Rise and Progress of the Colonies of South Carolina and Georgia.* London, 1779.

HEYWARD, DuBOSE. *Carolina Chansons, Legends of the Low Country.* New York, 1922.

HIGGINSON, THOMAS WENTWORTH. *A Ride through Kansas.* New York, 1856.

HIGHES, ELIZABETH. *The California of the Padres or Footprints of Ancient Communism.* San Francisco, 1875.

HILTZENHEIMER, JACOB. *Extracts from the Diary of Jacob Hiltzenheimer of Philadelphia, 1765–1798.* Ed. by his great-grandson, Jacob Cox Parsons. Philadelphia, 1893.

HIMROD, JAMES L. *Johnny Appleseed. The True Story of Jonathan Chapman.* Chicago, 1926.

HIRSH, ARTHUR H. *The Huguenots of Colonial South Carolina.* Durham, North Carolina, 1928.

HOBART-HAMPDEN. CHARLES AUGUSTUS. *Never Caught. Personal Adventures in Blockade Running during the American Civil War, 1863–4.* London, 1867.

HOLLAND, J. G. *The Life of Abraham Lincoln, Late President of the United States.* Springfield, 1866.

HOUCK, LOUIS, ed. *The Spanish Regime in Missouri, a Collection of Papers and Documents Relating to Upper Louisiana.* Chicago, 1909.

House of Representatives. *Report Dealing with the Situation in Louisiana, 1874–75.* Government Printing Office, Washington, D. C. 1875.

HOWE, E. W. *The Story of a Country Town.* Atchison, Kansas, 1882.

HOWE, GEORGE. *The Scotch-Irish and Their First Settlements on the Tiger River and Other Neighboring Precincts in South Carolina.* Columbia, South Carolina, 1861.

HOWE, HENRY. *Historical Collections of the Great West.* Cincinnati, 1873.

HUBBARD, WILLIAM L. *American History and Encyclopedia of Music.* 10 vols. Toledo, 1908–1910.

HUHNER, LEON. *The Jews in Georgia in Colonial Times.* Baltimore, 1902.
———. *Some Jewish Associates of John Brown.* New York, 1908.

HULBERT, ARCHER BUTLER, ed. and compiler. *The Forty Niners.* Boston, 1931.
———. *The Call of the Columbia.* Denver, 1934.
———. *Marcus Whitman, Crusader.* Denver, 1936.

IMLAY, GILBERT. *A Description of the Western Territory of North America.* London, 1793.

ISE, JOHN. *Sod and Stubble, the Story of a Kansas Homestead.* New York, 1936.

ISELEY, ELISE D. *Sunbonnet Days. As Told to Her Son, Bliss Iseley.* Caldwell, Idaho, 1935.

JACKSON, HELEN HUNT. *Ramona.* Boston, 1884.

JAMESON, ANNA B. *Winter Studies and Summer Rambles in Canada.* London, 1838.

JEFFERSON, JOSEPH. *Autobiography.* New York, 1890.

JOHNSON, GERALD W. *Andrew Jackson. An Epic in Homespun.* New York, 1927.

JOHNSTON, MARY. *To Have and To Hold*. New York, 1900.

——. *The Great Valley*. Boston, 1926.

JUDAH, SAMUEL B. H. *The Buccaneers, a Romance of Our Own Country in Its Ancient Day*. New York, 1827. (Stories of pirates down to Captain Kidd.)

KARSNER, DAVID. *Debs: His Authorized Life and Letters*. New York, 1919.

KENDALL, GEORGE W. *The War between the United States and Mexico*. Illustrated, embracing pictorial drawings of all the principal conflicts by Carl Nebel. New York, 1851.

KENNEDY, JOHN. *Swallow Barn*. Philadelphia, 1832.

——. *Horse-shoe Robinson*. Philadelphia, 1835.

——. *Life and Character of George Calvert, First Lord Baltimore*. Baltimore, 1845.

——. *Slavery the Mere Pretext of the Rebellion, Not Its Cause*. Philadelphia, 1863.

KENTON, EDNA C. *The Indians of North America . . . from the Jesuit Relations*. New York, 1927.

KINZIE, JULIETTE A. *Waubun, the Early Days of the Northwest. Narrative of Travel in Wisconsin and Illinois*. New York and Cincinnati, 1856.

KOCH, FREDERICK H. *Carolina Folk Plays*. New York, 1922.

KOHN, ADELBERT. *Olde Philadelphia; Historical Landmarks; Reproductions in Color of the Most Noted Prints and Original Sketches of the Best Known Artists of Early Philadelphia—Bird, Mumford, Etc.* Philadelphia, 1908.

LA BREE, BENJAMIN. *The Pictorial Battles of the Civil War*, Illustrated by upwards of 1000 Engravings. 2 vols. New York, 1885.

LANIER, SIDNEY. *Florida, Its Scenery, Climate and History*. Philadelphia, 1876.

——. *Poems, Edited by His Wife*. New York, 1891.

——. *Letters, 1866–1881*. New York, 1899.

LANMAN, CHARLES. *A Summer in the Wilderness. A Trip up the Mississippi and around Lake Superior*. Philadelphia, 1847.

LAPPIN, SAMUEL S. *Where the Long Trail Begins*. Cincinnati, 1913. (Narrative of a wagon journey from Illinois to Missouri in 1870.)

LARPENTEUR, CHARLES. *Diary*. Ed. by Elliott Coues. New York, 1898.

LAUDONNIÈRE, RENÉ. Narrative of Ribaut's Whole and True Discovery of Florida, in *The Genesis of South Carolina*, 1562–1670. Ed. by William A. Courtney. Columbia, South Carolina, 1907.

LAUGHLIN, HENRY H. *American History in Terms of Human Migration*. Extracts from the hearings before the Committee on Immigration and Naturalization, House of Representatives, March 7, 1928. Government Printing Office, Washington, D. C., 1928.

LEE, HENRY. *Memoirs of the War in the Southern Department of the United States*. Washington, 1827.

LEE, ROBERT E. *Recollections and Letters of General Robert E. Lee*. New York, 1924.

LELAND, JOHN A. *A Voice from South Carolina . . . with a Journal of a Reputed Ku Klux and an Appendix.* Charleston, 1879.

LEWIS, MERIWETHER. *History of the Expedition under Lewis and Clark, a New Edition, Faithfully Reprinted from the Authorized Edition of 1814.* New York, 1893.

LINCOLN, ABRAHAM. *Complete Works.* Ed. by John G. Nicolay and John Hay with introduction by Richard Watson Gilder. New York, 1905.

LOGAN, MARY S. (Mrs. John A.). *Reminiscences of a Soldier's Wife.* New York, 1913.

LONGSTREET, AUGUSTUS R. *Georgia Scenes, Characters, and Incidents.* Augusta, 1835. An American classic many times reprinted but too little known.

LOVEJOY, JOSEPH C. *Memoir with Introduction by John Quincy Adams.* New York, 1938.

LOWTHER, MINNIE KENDALL. *Blennerhasset Island in Romance and Tragedy.* Rutland, Vermont, 1936.

MAGOFFIN, SUSAN S. *Down the Sante Fe Trail.* Diary ed. by Stella M. Drum. New Haven, 1927.

MARRYAT, FRANK. *Mountains and Mole-hills.* New York, 1855. (California through English eyes.)

MARTIN, ASA EARL. *The Anti-slavery Movement in Kentucky, Prior to 1850.* Louisville, Filson Club publication, No. 29.

MARTINEAU, HARRIET. *Society in America.* 3 vols. New York, 1837.

MARTYN, BENJAMIN. *Reasons for Establishing the Colony of Georgia.* London, 1733.

MASEFIELD, JOHN. *Chronicles of the Pilgrim Fathers.* Everyman's ed. New York, 1910.

MASON, HARRISON D. *Old Economy As I Knew It.* Crafton, Penna., 1926.

Massachusetts Emigrant Aid Company. *Organization, Objects, and Plan of Operations of the Emigrant Aid Company, also a Description of Kansas for the Information of Emigrants.* Boston, 1854.

MATIN, JOHN HILL. *Historical Sketch of Bethlehem in Pennsylvania, with Some Account of the Moravian Church.* Philadelphia, 1872.

McCARTY, WILLIAM. *Songs, Odes, and Other Poems on National Subjects.* Philadelphia, 1842.

McGUFFEY, W. J. *Old Favorites from the McGuffey Readers.* New York, 1836.

McKAY, RICHARD C. *South Street, a Maritime History of New York.* New York, 1934.

MEAD, CHARLES. *Mississippi Scenery, a Poem Descriptive of the Interior of North America.* Philadelphia, 1819.

MEIGS, WILLIAM M. *Life of John C. Calhoun.* 2 vols. New York, 1917.

MELISH, JOHN. *Travels in the United States, 1806–11.* 2 vols. Philadelphia, 1812.

MELYN, CORNELIS. *Broad Advice to the United Netherlands Provinces.* Trans. from the Dutch for the New York Historical Society. New York, 1857.

MERCHANT OF PHILADELPHIA (pseud.). *Memoirs and Autobiography of Some of the Wealthy Citizens of Philadelphia with a Fair Estimate of Their Estates, Founded upon Facts.* Philadelphia, 1846. Includes Stephen Girard.

MERRILL, O. *The True History of the Kansas Wars, Illustrated with Colored Engravings.* Cincinnati, 1856.

MIDDLETON, ALICIA H. ed. *Life in Carolina and New England during the 19th Century, As Illustrated by Letters of the Middleton Family.* Bristol, Rhode Island, 1929.

MILBURN, WILLIAM H. *The Pioneers, Preachers, and People of the Mississippi Valley.* New York, 1860.

MILLER, JOAQUIN. *Paquita, the Indian Heroine,* Hartford, 1881.

———. *My Own Story.* Chicago, 1890.

———. *Poetical Works.* New York, 1923.

———. *California Diary, 1855–1857.* Seattle, 1936.

MILLER, MARION MILLS. *Great Debates in American History.* 14 vols. New York, 1913.

MILLS, W. J. *Historic Houses of New Jersey.* Philadelphia, 1902.

MINNICH, HARVEY C. *William H. McGuffey and His Readers.* New York, 1936.

MONETTE, JOHN WESLEY. *History of the Discovery and Settlement of the Valley of the Mississippi by the Three Great European Powers, Spain, France, and Great Britain.* New York, 1846.

MONTGOMERY, ELIZ. *Reminiscences of Wilmington, Delaware.* Philadelphia, 1851.

MONTGOMERY, SIR ROBERT. *A Discourse Concerning the Designed Establishment of a New Colony to the South of Carolina, in the Most Delightful Colony of the Universe.* London, 1717.

———. *Azalia, a Historical Legend of Georgia.* Savannah, 1870.

MORRISON, SAMUEL E. *Maritime History of Massachusetts.* Boston, 1921.

MORROW, HONORÉ WILLSIE. *We Must March.* New York, 1925. Novel about Marcus Whitman.

MORSE, JEDIDIAH. *A Compendious History of New England.* Charlestown, Massachusetts, 1820.

NEIHARDT, JOHN G. *The Splendid Wayfaring,* New York, 1920.

———. *Song of Hugh Glass.* New York, 1924.

———. *Song of the Three Friends.* New York, 1924. And other works.

NEILL, EDWARD D. *Dahkotah Land and the Dahkotah Life.* Philadelphia, 1859.

NEVINS, ALLAN, ed. *American Social History as Recorded by British Travelers.* New York, 1931.

NORRIS, FRANK. *The Pit.* New York, 1903.

———. *The Octopus.* New York, 1931.

NORRIS, JOHN. *Profitable Advice for Rich and Poor . . . but Especially the Laborious Poor in That Fruitful, Pleasant, and Profitable Country* (of Carolina). London, 1712.

OGG, FREDERICK A. *The Old Northwest.* New Haven, 1919.

OGLETHORPE, JAMES E. *A New and Accurate Account of the Provinces of South Carolina and Georgia.* London, 1733.

——. *Letters.* Collections of Georgia Historical Society. Savannah, 1873.

O'HANLON, JOHN. *Life and Scenery in Missouri.* Dublin, 1890. (Reminiscences of a missionary priest.)

PAGE, THOMAS N. *In Ole Virginia.* New York, 1887.

——. *Red Rock.* New York, 1898.

——. *The Old Dominion.* New York, 1908.

PALOU, FRANCESCO. *The Expedition into California of the Venerable Padre Fray Junipero Serra.* From unpublished letters and Catholic records. San Francisco, 1934.

PARKMAN, FRANCIS. *Pioneers of France in the New World.* First copyrighted, 1865. Boston, 1924. And other works.

PARSON, C. G., M.D. *Inside View of Slavery.* Boston, 1855.

PATE, HENRY CLAY. *John Brown.* New York, 1859.

PARTON, JAMES. *Life of Andrew Jackson.* New York, 1860.

——. *General Butler in New Orleans.* New York, 1864.

PAXSON, FREDERIC L. *History of the American Frontier.* Cambridge, 1924.

PEPPER, GEORGE W. *Personal Recollections of Sherman's Campaigns in Georgia and the Carolinas.* Zanesville, Ohio, 1866.

PERKINS, JAMES H. *Annals of the West.* Pittsburgh, 1857.

PETIGRU, JAMES L. *Life, Letters, and Speeches of James L. Petigru, the Union Man of South Carolina.* Washington, 1920.

PHILLIPS, WILLIAM A. *The Conquest of Kansas by Missouri and Her Allies.* Boston, 1856.

PIDGIN, CHARLES F. *Blennerhasset, a Dramatic Romance in a Prologue and Four Acts.* Boston, 1901.

PIKE, ALBERT. *Hymns to the Gods and Other Poems.* 1873–1882. Reprinted Little Rock, Arkansas, 1916.

PIKE, JAMES S. *The Prostrate State. South Carolina under Negro Rule.* New York, 1874.

PIKE, JOHN. *Journal of Reverend John Pike of Dover, N. H.* Cambridge, 1876.

PIKE, ZEBULON. *Expeditions.* Ed. by Elliott Coues. New York, 1895.

PILLMAN, PHILLIP. *The Present State of the European Settlements on the Mississippi.* London, 1770.

PINCKNEY, ELIZA L. *Journals and Letters.* 1723–1793. Wormsloe, Georgia, 1850.

POE, EDGAR ALLAN. *Doings of Gotham.* First published, Pottsville, Pennsylvania, 1929.

POWERS, FRED P. *Tales of Old Taverns.* Germantown, Pennsylvania, 1912.

POYAS, ELIZABETH A. *The Olden Time of Carolina.* Charleston, 1855.

——. *Our Forefathers, Their Homes and Churches.* Charleston, 1860.

PRICE, SAMUEL W. *The Old Masters of the Blue Grass.* Louisville, 1902.

PRYOR, SARA A. *Reminiscences of Peace and War.* New York, 1905.

PUPIN, MICHAEL. *From Immigrant to Inventor.* New York, 1923.

RADCLIFFE, WILLIAM. *Fishing from Earliest Times.* London, 1921.

RADIN, PAUL. *The Story of the American Indian.* New York, 1927.

RAMSDELL, CHARLES W. *Reconstruction in Texas.* Columbia studies in history. New York, 1910.

RANCK, GEORGE W. *Boonesborough; Its Founding, Pioneer Struggles.* Louisville, 1901.

RANDOLPH, THOMAS JEFFERSON. *Memoir, Correspondence, and Miscellanies from Thomas Jefferson.* Boston, 1830.

RAPER, CHARLES L. *Social Life in Colonial North Carolina.* Raleigh, 1903.

RAVAGE, M. E. *An American in the Making.* New York, 1917.

RAYNAL, the ABBÉ. *The Revolution in America.* Trans. from the French. Dublin, 1781.

Reports of the Trial of Aaron Burr for Treason. Philadelphia, 1808.

RICHARDS, STEPHEN L. (of the Council of the Twelve Apostles.) *About Mormonism, Sociological, Economic, Doctrinal, Historical.* Salt Lake City. Official contemporary explanation of the Mormon Church.

RICHARDSON, JAMES D. *Messages and Papers of the Confederacy.* 2 vols. Nashville, 1905.

RIDDING, ISABELLA R. *Life and Times of Jonathan Bryan, 1708–1788.* Savannah, 1901.

RIIS, JACOB A. *The Making of an American.* New York, 1901.

RILEY, SUSAN B. *Life and Works of Albert Pike to 1860—"Fine Arkansas Gentleman and Poet."* Nashville, 1934.

ROBINSON, SARA T. *Kansas, Its Interior and Exterior Life.* Boston, 1856.

RODNEY, THOMAS. *Diary of Thomas Rodney, 1776–1777.* Ed. by Caesar Rodney. Wilmington, 1888.

ROSSITER, W. S. *A Century of Population Growth, 1790–1900.* Bureau of Census, 1909.

ROTHERT, OTHO A. *The Filson Club, Including Lists of Publications.* Louisville, 1922.

ROYCE, JOSIAH. *California, a Study in American Character.* Boston, 1886.

RUSH, BENJAMIN. *Manners of the German Inhabitants of Pennsylvania, Written in 1789.* Ed. with notes by I. Daniel Rupp. Philadelphia, 1875.

RUSSELL, W. H. *My Diary, North and South.* Boston, 1863.

SABIN, EDWIN L. *Kit Carson Days,* 2 vols. New York, 1935.

SAFFORD, WILLIAM A. *The Blennerhasset Papers.* Cincinnati, 1864.

SAXON, LYLE. *Father Mississippi.* New York, 1927.

———. *Fabulous New Orleans.* New York, 1928.

———. *Old Louisiana.* New York, 1929.

———. *Lafitte, the Pirate.* New York, 1930.

SCHENCK, DAVID. *North Carolina, 1780–81.* (Cornwallis campaign.) Raleigh, 1889.

SCHOOLCRAFT, HENRY R. *Journals of Western Travels.* London, 1821. Albany, 1821.

SCHUCKERS, J. W. *Life and Public Services of Salmon P. Chase.* New York, 1874.

SCHULTZ, JAMES W. *The Bird-woman (Sacajawea); Her Own Story Now First Given to the World.* New York, 1918.

SCHURZ, CARL. *Reminiscences.* 3 vols. New York, 1907–1908.

SCOTT, WINFIELD. *Memories.* New York, 1864.

SEALSFIELD, CHARLES (Karl Postl). *Life in the New World.* New York, 1842.

————. *The Cabin Book.* New York, 1844.

————. *The Frontier Life.* New York, 1856.

SENIOR, NASSAU W. *American Slavery.* London, 1856.

SEYMOUR, E. *Sketches of Minnesota, the New England of the West.* New York, 1850.

SHEA, JOHN D. G. *Discovery and Exploration of the Mississippi Valley with the Original Narratives of Marquette, Allouez, Membre, Hennepin, and Anastase Douay.* New York, 1852.

SHERIDAN, PHILIP H. *Personal Memoirs,* New York, 1902.

SHERMAN, WILLIAM T. *Official Account of His . . . March . . . through Georgia.* New York, 1865.

SIBLEY, H. H. *Reminiscences of the Early Days of Minnesota.* Saint Paul, 1880.

SIGOURNEY, LYDIA H. *Letters to Young Ladies.* New York, 1837.

SIMMS, WILLIAM G. *Border Beagles.* Philadelphia, 1840.

————. *Beauchampe.* Philadelphia, 1842.

————. *The Lily and the Totem.* New York, 1850.

————. *Charlemont.* New York, 1856. And other works.

SINCLAIR, UPTON. *The Jungle.* New York, 1906.

SMALL, WILLIAM F. *Guadeloupe, A Tale of Love and War.* Philadelphia, 1860. Mexican War.

SMET, FATHER PIERRE JEAN DE. *Oregon Missions and Travels.* New York, 1847.

SMITH, ALICE R. HUGER. *A Carolina Rice Plantation in the Fifties.* New York, 1936.

SMITH, JOHN. *Travels and Works.* Ed. by Edward Arber. 2 vols. Edinburgh 1910.

SMITH, JOSEPH. *General Joseph Smith's Appeal to the Green Mountain Boys.* Nauvoo, Illinois, 1843.

SMITH, WILLIAM H. *The St. Clair Papers.* Cincinnati, 1882.

SMITH, ZACHARIAH F. *The Battle of New Orleans.* Louisville, 1904.

SOULE, FRANK. *Annals of California.* New York, 1855.

SPARKS, JARED. *Life of John Ledyard.* Cambridge, 1829.

SPEED, THOMAS. *The Wilderness Road.* Louisville, 1886.

STAPLETON, AMMON. *Memorials of the Huguenots in America.* Carlisle, Pennsylvania, 1901.

STEDMAN, EDMUND C. *A Library of American Literature.* 11 vols. New York, 1889–1890.

STELLE, CHARLES J. *Major General Anthony Wayne and the Pennsylvania Line in the Continental Army.* Philadelphia, 1893.

STENHOUSE, FANNY (Mrs. Thomas B. H.). *The Tyranny of Mormonism.* London, 1888.

STENHOUSE, THOMAS B. H. *The Rocky Mountain Saints.* New York, 1873.

STERNDAM, JACOB. *Memoir of the First Poet in New Netherland, with His Poems Descriptive of the Colony.* The Hague, 1861.

STEVENSON, BURTON E. *American History in Verse for Boys and Girls.* Boston, 1932.

STEWART, CATHERINE. *New Homes in the West*. Nashville, 1843.

STEWART, ELEANOR P. *Letters of a Woman Home-steader*. Boston, 1914.

STONE, WILLIAM LEETE. *The Poetry and History of Wyoming Valley (Pa.) Containing Campbell's Gertrude with a Biographical Sketch of the Author by Washington Irving, and the History of Wyoming*. New York and London, 1841.

———. *Border Wars of the American Revolution*. New York, 1845.

STOWE, CHARLES E. *Life of Harriet Beecher Stowe, Compiled from Her Letters and Journals*. Boston, 1891.

STOWE, HARRIET B. *La case du père Tom . . . augmentée d'une notice de George Sand*. Paris, 1853.

———. *A Key to Uncle Tom's Cabin*. Boston and Cleveland, 1853.

———. *Dred, a Tale of the Dismal Swamp*. Boston, 1856.

———. *The Minister's Wooing*. New York, 1859.

———. *Oldtown Folks*. Boston, 1869.

SUTTER, JOHN AUGUSTUS. *Diary*. San Francisco, 1932.

SWINTON, WILLIAM. *The Twelve Decisive Battles of the War*. New York, 1867.

Texas, Republic of. *Journal of the Fourth Congress of the Republic of Texas, 1839–1840*. Edited by Harriet Smithers, Austin, Texas, 1931.

THOMPSON, EVEN F. *A Brief Chronicle of Rufus Putnam and His Rutland Home*. Worcester, 1930.

TROLLOPE, ANTHONY. *North America*. London, 1862.

WALD, LILLIAN. *Windows on Henry Street*. Boston, 1934.

WALKER, CHARLES M. *History of Athens County, Ohio . . . and First Settlement of the State*. Cincinnati, 1869.

WALKER, THOMAS. *Journal of an Exploration of Kentucky, 1750*. Louisville, 1898.

WALLINGTON, NELLIE U. *American History told by American Poets*. 2 vols. New York, 1911.

WARNER, CHARLES DUDLEY. *On Horse-back (through the South)*. Boston, 1888.

WARREN, HENRY W. *Reminiscences of a Mississippi Carpet-bagger*. Holden, Massachusetts, 1914.

WASHINGTON, BOOKER T. *Up from Slavery*. New York, 1901.

WASHINGTON, GEORGE. *Washington's Political Legacies, to Which is Annexed an Appendix containing an Account of His Illness, Death, and National Tributes . . . .to His Memory, with a Biographical Outline of His Life and Character*. Boston, 1800.

———. *Writings of George Washington*. Ed. by Worthington C. Ford. 14 vols. New York, 1889–1893.

———. *Washington and the West; Being George Washington's Diary of 1784 Kept during His Journey into the Ohio Basin . . . and a Commentary on the Same*. New York, 1905.

WAY, WILLIAM. *History of the New England Society of Charleston*. Charleston, 1920.

WEBSTER, HOMER J. William Henry Harrison's administration of Indian territory. *Indiana Historical Society Publications,* vol. 4.

WELLS, EDMUND. *Argonaut Tales.* New York, 1927.

WERTENBAKER, THOMAS J. *Patrician and Plebeian in Virginia.* Charlottesville, 1910.

WHITE, STEWART EDWARD. *The Story of California Including Three Novels: Gold; Gray Dawn; and Rose Dawn.* New York, 1927. And other works.

WHITMAN, NARCISSA. *Letters, 1843–47.* Portland, Oregon, 1894.

WILEY, C. H. *Utopia, a Picture of Life at the South.* Philadelphia, 1852.

WILLARD, MARGARET W. ed. *Letters on the American Revolution.* Cambridge, 1925.

WILLIAM, FATHER (pseud.). *Recollections of Rambles at the South.* New York, 1854.

WILLIAMS, GEORGE W. *History of the Negro Race in America.* 2 vols. New York, 1883.

WILLIAMS, R. H. *With the Border Ruffians, 1852–68.* New York, 1907.

WINTHROP, JOHN. *Journal—History of New England.* 2 vols. New York, 1908.

WOODBURN, JAMES A. *Life of Thaddeus Stevens.* Indianapolis, 1913.

———. *The Ulster Scot; His History and Religion.* London, 1915.

———, ed. *The New Purchase by Robert Carlton,* edited. Princeton, 1916.

WOODS, JOHN. *Two Years Residence in the Illinois Country.* London, 1882.

WYETH, JOHN B. *Oregon.* Cambridge, 1833.

Utah. *Tourist's Guide.* Salt Lake City, 1935.

VAN RENSSELAER, SARAH R. *Ancestral Sketches.* New York, 1882.

VESTAL, STANLEY. *Kit Carson.* Cambridge, 1928.

VICKERS, GEORGE M. *Under Both Flags . . . Written by Celebrities of Both Sides.* Philadelphia, 1896.

ZINKE, F. B. *Last Winter in the United States.* London, 1868.

INDEX

G